The Visual Culture Reader

The Visual Culture Reader brings together the key writings in the exciting new interdisciplinary field of visual culture.

The *Reader* covers a wealth of visual forms including photography, painting, sculpture, fashion, advertising, virtual reality and other electronic imaging systems. The extracts are grouped into thematic sections, each with an introduction by Nicholas Mirzoeff. The opening section traces the pioneering work in visual culture over the last fifteen years, and includes two specially written articles by Irit Rogoff and Ella Shohat and Robert Stam. Subsequent sections address: A Genealogy of Visual Culture; Visual Culture and Everyday Life; Virtuality: Virtual Bodies, Virtual Spaces; Race and Identity in Colonial and Postcolonial Culture; Gender and Sexuality; Pornography.

Taken as a whole, the essays provide a comprehensive response to the diversity of contemporary visual culture, and address the need of our modern and postmodern culture to render experience in visual form.

Contributors: Malek Alloula, Oriana Baddeley, Anne Balsamo, Roland Barthes, Geoffrey Batchen, Suzanne Preston Blier, Susan Bordo, Sandra Buckley, Judith Butler, Anthea Callen, Néstor García Canclini, Lisa Cartwright, James Clifford, Jonathan Crary, Michel de Certeau, René Descartes, Carol Duncan, Richard Dyer, John Fiske, Michel Foucault, Anne Friedberg, Coco Fusco, Tamar Garb, Paul Gilroy, Donna Haraway, bell hooks, Martin Jay, Reina Lewis, Anne McClintock, Marshall McLuhan, Nicholas Mirzoeff, Timothy Mitchell, Lynda Nead, Adrian Piper, Griselda Pollock, Mary-Louise Pratt, Ann Reynolds, Irit Rogoff, Andrew Ross, Ella Shohat, Robert Stam, Marita Sturken, Paul Virilio, Thomas Waugh.

Editor: Nicholas Mirzoeff is Associate Professor of Art at the State University of New York, Stony Brook. He is the author of *Bodyscape: Art, Modernity and the Ideal Figure* (1995).

The Visual Culture Reader

Edited, with introductions by

Nicholas Mirzoeff

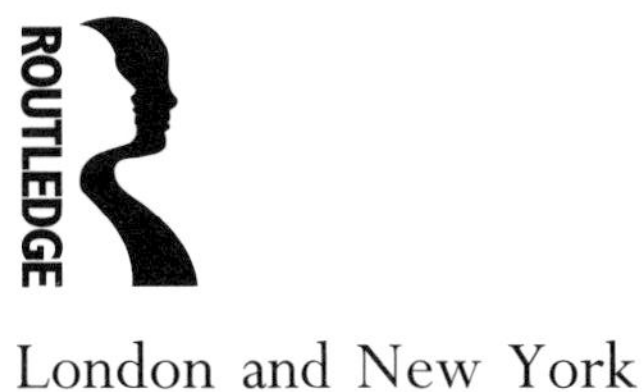

London and New York

First published 1998
by Routledge
11 New Fetter Lane, London EC4P 4EE

Simultaneously published in the USA and Canada
by Routledge
29 West 35th Street, New York, NY 10001

Typeset in Perpetua by
The Florence Group, Stoodleigh, Devon

Printed and bound in Great Britain by
Butler and Tanner Ltd, Frome and London

British Library Cataloguing in Publication Data
A catalogue record for this book is available from the British Library

Library of Congress Cataloguing in Publication Data
A catalogue record for this book has been requested

ISBN 0-415-14133-8 (hbk)
0-415-14134-6 (pbk)

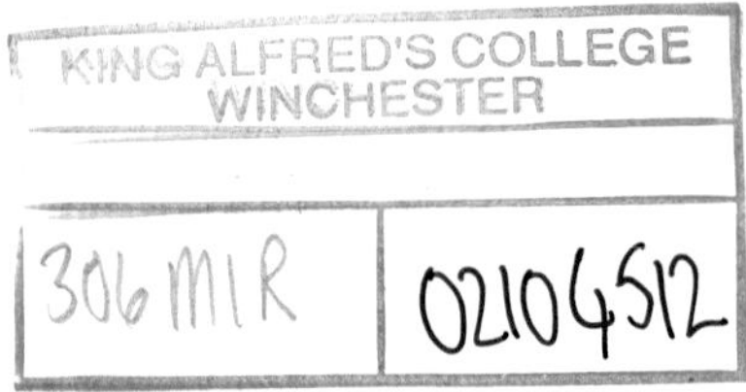

Contents

PART THREE
VIRTUALITY: VIRTUAL BODIES, VIRTUAL SPACES

PART FOUR
RACE AND IDENTITY IN COLONIAL AND POSTCOLONIAL CULTURE

PART FIVE GENDER AND SEXUALITY

PART SIX
PORNOGRAPHY

Illustrations

Acknowledgements

Even more than most, this book is a compilation of the thoughts and suggestions of a group rather than the product of one individual. Rebecca Barden at Routledge first suggested the idea for this book and it would never have happened without her energy, as well as that of Katherine Hodkinson, Julia Reid and Chris Cudmore, who undertook much of the drudgery associated with compilation volumes. The various readers for Routledge provided very useful suggestions in agreement and dissent with the project. My understanding of this subject is what it is because of conversations I have had with Ann Bermingham, Anthea Callen, Hank Drewal, John Fiske, E. Ann Kaplan, Moyo Okediji, Ann Reynolds, Irit Rogoff, Mary Sheriff and many others.

As ever, my greatest debt is to Kathleen Wilson, the most acute of critics and the best of partners. This book was put together in two years either side of the birth of our daughter Hannah. They have both tolerated my scurrying around on and off the computer to get this project completed: I owe them more than I can say and this book is for them.

Permissions

We gratefully acknowledge permission to reproduce the following essays:

Malek Alloula, from *The Colonial Harem*, Minneapolis, Minnesota University Press, 1986, pp. 3–15.

Oriana Baddeley, 'Engendering New Worlds: Allegories of Rape and Reconciliation', in Oriana Baddeley (ed.), *New Art from Latin America: Expanding the Continent*, Art and Design Profile no. 37, *Art and Design*, 1994, pp 10–18.

Anne Balsamo, 'On the Cutting Edge: Cosmetic Surgery and the Technological Production of the Gendered Body', *Camera Obscura* 22, Jan. 1992, pp. 207–14, 217–21, 225–26.

Roland Barthes, 'The Rhetoric of the Image,' in *Image-Music-Text*, New York, Noonday, 1977, pp. 32–37.

Geoffrey Batchen, 'Spectres of Cyberspace', *Afterimage* 23(3) Nov.–Dec. 1995), pp. 6–7.

Suzanne Preston Blier, 'Vodun Art, Social History and the Slave Trade', *in African Vodun: Art, Psychology and Power*, Chicago, Chicago University Press, 1995, pp. 23–31.

Susan Bordo, 'Reading the Slender Body', in Mary Jacobus, Evelyn Fox Keller and Sally Shuttleworth (eds), *Body/Politics: Women and the Discourses of Science*, London and New York, Routledge, pp. 83–96; 109–110.

Sandra Buckley, ' "Penguin in Bondage": A Graphic Tale of Japanese Comic Books', in Constance Penley and Andrew Ross (eds), *Technoculture*, Minneapolis, Minnesota University Press, 1991, pp. 165–68, 170–81.

Judith Butler, 'Gender Is Burning: Questions of Appropriation and Subversion', in *Bodies That Matter*, London and New York, Routledge, 1993, pp. 121–40.

—— 'Prohibition, Psychoanalysis, and the Heterosexual Matrix,' in *Gender Trouble: Feminism and the Subversion of Identity*, London and New York, Routledge, 1990, pp. 50–54.

Néstor García Canclini, 'Remaking Passports: Visual Thought in the Debate on Multiculturalism', *Third Text* 28/29 (Autumn/Winter 1994), pp. 139–46.

Lisa Cartwright, 'Science and the Cinema', in *Screening the Body: Tracing Medicine's Visual Culture*, Minneapolis, Minnesota University Press, 1995, pp. 1–16.

James Clifford, 'On Collecting Art and Culture,' in *The Predicament of Culture: Twentieth-Century Ethnography, Literature, and Art*, Cambridge, Mass., Harvard University Press, 1988, pp. 215–29.

Jonathan Crary, 'The Camera Obscura and Its Subject', in *Techniques of the Observer: On Vision and Modernity in the Nineteenth Century*, Cambridge, Mass., MIT Press, 1990, pp. 38–50.

Michel de Certeau, from *The Practice of Everyday Life*, Berkeley, University of California Press, 1984, pp. 24–30.

René Descartes, 'Optics', in *Selected Philosophical Writings*, trans. John Cottingham, Robert Stoothoff and Dugald Murdoch, Cambridge, Cambridge University Press, 1988, pp. 57–63.

Carol Duncan, 'The Modern Art Museum', in *Civilizing Rituals: Inside Public Art Museums*, London and New York, Routledge, 1995, pp. 115–28.

Richard Dyer, 'Idol Thoughts: Orgasm and Self-reflexivity in Gay Pornography', *Critical Quarterly* 36 (Spring 1994), pp. 49–62.

John Fiske, 'Videotech', in *Media Matters: Race and Gender in US Politics*, Minneapolis, Minnesota University Press, 1996, pp. 208–17.

Michel Foucault, 'Of Other Spaces', *Diacritics*, Spring 1986, pp. 22–27.

Anne Friedberg, 'The Mobilized and Virtual Gaze in Modernity: Flâneur/Flâneuse', in *Window Shopping: Cinema and the Postmodern*, Berkeley, University of California Press, 1993, pp. 15–32.

Coco Fusco, from 'The Other History of Intercultural Performance', in *English Is Broken Here*, New York, New Press, 1995, pp. 37–41, 47–50.

Tamar Garb, 'The Forbidden Gaze: Women Artists and the Male Nude in Late Nineteenth-Century France', in Kathleen Adler and Marcia Pointon (eds), *The Body Imaged: The Human Form and Visual Culture since the Renaissance*, Cambridge, Cambridge University Press, 1993, pp. 33–42.

Paul Gilroy, 'Art of Darkness: Black Art and the Problem of Belonging to England', in *Small Acts: Thoughts on the Politics of Black Cultures*, London, Serpent's Tail, 1993, 74–85.

Donna Haraway, 'The Persistence of Vision', in *Simians, Cyborgs, and Women: The Reinvention of Nature*, London and New York, Routledge, 1991, pp. 188–96.

bell hooks, 'Representing Whiteness: Seeing *Wings of Desire*', in *Yearning: Race, Gender and Cultural Politics*, Boston, South End Press, 1990, pp. 65–71.

Martin Jay, 'The Scopic Regimes of Modernity', in Hal Foster (ed.), *Vision and Visuality*, Seattle, Bay Press, 1988, pp. 3–7, n. 1–13.

Reina Lewis, 'Looking Good: The Lesbian Gaze and the Fashion Industry', *Feminist Review* 55, Spring 1997, pp. 92–109.

Anne McClintock, from 'Soft-Soaping Empire: Commodity Racism and Imperial Advertising', in *Imperial Leather: Race, Gender and Sexuality in the Colonial Contest*, London and New York, Routledge, 1995, pp. 209–19.

Marshall McLuhan, 'Woman in a Mirror', in *The Mechanical Bride: Folklore of Industrial Man*, Boston, Beacon Press, 1967 [1951], pp. 80–82.

Timothy Mitchell, 'Orientalism and the Exhibitionary Order', in Nicholas Dirks (ed.), *Colonialism and Culture*, Ann Arbor, University of Michigan Press, 1992, pp. 289–300: n. 1–29.

Lynda Nead, from *The Female Nude: Art, Obscenity and Sexuality*, London, Routledge, 1992, pp. 87–96.

Adrian Piper, 'Passing for White, Passing for Black', in Joanna Frueh, Cassandra L. Langer and Arlene Raven (eds), *New Feminist Criticism: Art, Identity, Action*, New York, Icon Editions, 1992, pp. 216–17, 223–33.

Griselda Pollock, 'Modernity and the Spaces of Femininity', in *Vision and Difference: Femininity, Feminism, and the Histories of Art*, London and New York, Routledge, 1988, pp. 50–55, 70–79, 205, 207–8.

Mary-Louise Pratt, 'From the Victoria Nyanza to the Sheraton San Salvador', in *Imperial Eyes: Travel-Writing and Transculturation*, London and New York, Routledge, 1992, pp. 200–13.

Ann Reynolds, 'Visual Stories' first appeared in different form in Lynne Cooke and Peter Wollen (eds), *Visual Display: Culture beyond Appearances*, Seattle, Bay Press, 1995.

Andrew Ross, 'The Gangsta and the Diva,' first published in Thelma Golden (ed.), *Black Male: Representations of Masculinity in Contemporary American Art*, New York, Abrams, 1994, pp. 159–66; revised and updated.

Marita Sturken, from 'The Wall, the Screen and the Image: The Vietnam Veterans Memorial,' *Representations* 35 (Summer 1991), revised and updated.

Paul Virilio, from *The Vision Machine*, Bloomington, Indiana University Press/BFI, 1994, pp. 1–19.

Thomas Waugh, 'The Third Body: Patterns in the Construction of the Subject in the Gay Male Narrative Film,' in Martha Gever, Pratibha Parmar and John Greyson (eds), *Queer Looks: Perspectives on Lesbian and Gay Film and Video*, London and New York, Routledge, 1993, pp. 141–61.

Introductions/Provocations

Chapter 1

Nicholas Mirzoeff

WHAT IS VISUAL CULTURE?[1]

SEEING IS A GREAT DEAL MORE than believing these days. You can buy a photograph of your house taken from an orbiting satellite or have your internal organs magnetically imaged. If that special moment didn't come out quite right in your photography, you can digitally manipulate it on your computer. At New York's Empire State Building, the queues are longer for the virtual reality New York Ride than for the lifts to the observation platforms. Alternatively, you could save yourself the trouble by catching the entire New York skyline, rendered in attractive pastel colours, at the New York, New York resort in Las Vegas. This virtual city will be joined shortly by Paris Las Vegas, imitating the already carefully manipulated image of the city of light. Life in this alter-reality is sometimes more pleasant than the real thing, sometimes worse. In 1997 same-sex marriage was outlawed by the United States Congress but when the sitcom character Ellen came out on television, 42 million people watched. On the other hand, virtual reality has long been favoured by the military as a training arena, put into practice in the Gulf War at great cost of human life. This is visual culture. It is not just a part of your everyday life, it *is* your everyday life.

Understandably, this newly visual existence can be confusing. For observing the new visuality of culture is not the same as understanding it. Indeed, the gap between the wealth of visual experience in contemporary culture and the ability to analyse that observation marks both the opportunity and the need for visual culture as a field of study. Visual culture is concerned with visual events in which information, meaning or pleasure is sought by the consumer in an interface with visual technology. By visual technology, I mean any form of apparatus designed either to be looked at or to enhance natural vision, from oil painting to television and the Internet. Such criticism takes account of the importance of image making, the formal components of a given image, and the crucial completion of that work by its cultural reception.

This volume offers a selection of the best critical and historical work in the past decade that has both created and developed the new field. It is a little different to some other Readers currently in circulation. As the field is still so fluid and subject to debate, it is as much an attempt to define the subject as to present a commonly agreed array of topics. As a result, it does not simply offer latest 'cutting-edge' (i.e. most recent) material, but a mixture of new writing and a reprise of the best pioneering work that has given rise to this field, an understanding of which is often assumed by current literature. After digesting this Reader, you will be ready to plunge into the critical maelstrom and equipped to deal with the unceasing flow of images from the swirl of the global village.

Postmodernism is visual culture

Postmodernism has often been defined as the crisis of modernism, that is to say, the wide-ranging complex of ideas and modes of representation ranging from overarching beliefs in progress to theories of the rise of abstract painting or the modern novel. Now these means of representation no longer seem convincing without any alternative having emerged. As a result, the dominant postmodern style is ironic: a knowing pastiche that finds comment and critique to be the only means of innovation. The postmodern reprise of modernism involves everything from the rash of classical motifs on shopping malls to the crisis of modern painting and the popularity of Nickelodeon repeats. In the context of this book, the postmodern is the crisis caused by modernism and modern culture confronting the failure of its own strategy of visualizing. In other words, it is the visual crisis of culture that creates postmodernity, not its textuality. While print culture is certainly not going to disappear, the fascination with the visual and its effects that was a key feature of modernism has engendered a postmodern culture that is at its most postmodern when it is visual.

During this volume's compilation, visual culture has gone from being a useful phrase for people working in art history, film and media studies, sociology and other aspects of the visual to a fashionable, if controversial, new means of doing interdisciplinary work, following in the footsteps of such fields as cultural studies, queer theory and African-American studies. The reason most often advanced for this heightened visibility is that human experience is now more visual and visualized than ever before. In many ways, people in industrialized and post-industrial societies now live in visual cultures to an extent that seems to divide the present from the past. Popular journalism constantly remarks on digital imagery in cinema, the advent of post-photography and developments in medical imaging, not to mention the endless tide of comment devoted to the Internet. This globalization of the visual, taken collectively, demands new means of interpretation. At the same time, this transformation of the postmodern present also requires a rewriting of historical explanations of modernism and modernity in order to account for 'the visual turn'.

Postmodernism is not, of course, simply a visual experience. In what Arjun Appadurai has called the 'complex, overlapping, disjunctive order' of postmodernism, such tidiness is not to be expected (Appadurai 1990). Nor can it be found in past epochs, whether one looks at the eighteenth-century coffee-house public culture celebrated by Jürgen Habermas, or the nineteenth-century print capitalism of newspapers and publishing described by Benedict Anderson. In the same way that these authors highlighted one particular characteristic of a period as a means to analyse it, despite the vast range of alternatives, visual culture is a tactic with which to study the genealogy, definition and functions of postmodern everyday life. The disjunctured and fragmented culture that we call postmodernism is best imagined and understood visually, just as the nineteenth century was classically represented in the newspaper and the novel.

Western culture has consistently privileged the spoken word as the highest form of intellectual practice and seen visual representations as second-rate illustrations of ideas. Now, however, the emergence of visual culture as a subject has contested this hegemony, developing what W.J.T. Mitchell has called 'picture theory'. In this view, Western philosophy and science now use a pictorial, rather than textual, model of the world, marking a significant challenge to the notion of the world as a written text that dominated so much intellectual discussion in the wake of such linguistics-based movements as structuralism and poststructuralism. In Mitchell's view, picture theory stems from

> the realization that *spectatorship* (the look, the gaze, the glance, the practices of observation, surveillance and visual pleasure) may be as deep a problem as various forms of *reading* (decipherment, decoding, interpretation, etc.) and that 'visual experience' or 'visual literacy' might not be fully explicable in the model of textuality.
>
> (Mitchell 1994: 16)

While those already working on or with visual media might find such remarks rather patronizing, they are a measure of the extent to which even literary studies have been forced to conclude that the world-as-a-text has been challenged by the world-as-a-picture. Such world pictures cannot be purely visual, but by the same token, the visual disrupts and challenges any attempt to define culture in purely linguistic terms.

That is not to suggest, however, that a simple dividing line can be drawn between the past (modern) and the present (postmodern). As Geoffrey Batchen has argued, 'the threatened dissolution of boundaries and oppositions [the postmodern] is presumed to represent is not something peculiar to a particular technology or to postmodern discourse but is rather one of the fundamental conditions of modernity itself' (Batchen 1996: 28). Understood in this fashion, visual culture has a history that needs exploring and defining in the modern as well as postmodern period. However, many current uses of the term have suffered from a vagueness that makes it little more than a buzzword. For some critics, visual culture is simply 'the history of images' handled with a semiotic notion of representation (Bryson, Holly and Moxey 1994: xvi). This definition creates a body of material so vast that no one person or even department could ever cover the field. For others it is a means of creating a sociology of visual culture that will establish a 'social theory of visuality' (Jenks 1995: 1). This approach seems open to the charge that the visual is given an artificial independence from the other senses that has little bearing on real experience. In this volume, visual culture is used in a far more interactive sense, concentrating on the determining role of visual culture in the wider culture to which it belongs. Such a history of visual culture would highlight those moments where the visual is contested, debated and transformed as a constantly challenging place of social interaction and definition in terms of class, gender, sexual and racialized identities. It is a resolutely interdisciplinary subject, in the sense given to the term by Roland Barthes: 'In order to do interdisciplinary work, it is not enough to take a "subject" (a theme) and to arrange two or three sciences around it. Interdisciplinary study consists in creating a new object, which belongs to no one.' As one critic in communications studies has recently argued, this work entails 'greater levels of uncertainty, risk and arbitrariness' than have often been used until now (McNair 1995: xi). As visual culture is still an idea in the making, rather than a well-defined existing field, this Reader aims to help in its definition of visual culture rather than present it as a given.

Visualizing

One of the most striking features of the new visual culture is the visualization of things that are not in themselves visual. Rather than myopically focusing on the visual to the exclusion of all other senses, as is often alleged, visual culture examines why modern and postmodern culture place such a premium on rendering experience in visual form. Among the first to call attention to this development was the German philosopher Martin Heidegger, who called it the rise of the world picture. He pointed out that

> a world picture . . . does not mean a picture of the world but the world conceived and grasped as a picture. . . . The world picture does not change from an earlier medieval one into a modern one, but rather the fact that the world becomes picture at all is what distinguishes the essence of the modern age.
>
> (Heidegger 1977: 130)

Visual culture does not depend on pictures but on this modern tendency to picture or visualize existence. This visualizing makes the modern period radically different from the ancient and medieval world in which the world was understood as a book. More importantly, pictures were seen not as representations, artificial constructs seeking to imitate an object, but as being closely related, or even identical, to that object. For the Byzantine Church an icon *was* the saint it represented, and many medieval relics and reliquaries took their power from being a part of a saintly or divine body. The power of such icons was recently demonstrated when Italian firefighters risked their lives to save the Turin Shroud, which is held to bear the imprint of Christ's face.

By contrast, the modern period makes countless reproductions of its imagery that have become indistinguishable from one another in what Walter Benjamin famously called the 'age of mechanical reproduction'. Such visualizing, always common, has now become all but compulsory. This history has many origins ranging from the visualizing of the economy in the eighteenth century to the development of the diagnostic medieval gaze and the rise of photography as the principal means of defining reality in the early nineteenth century. It has had some of its most dramatic effects in medicine, where everything from the activity of the brain to the heartbeat is now transformed into a visual pattern by complex technology. As this example shows, visualizing does not replace linguistic discourse but makes it more comprehensible, quicker and more effective.

One of the key tasks of visual culture is to understand how these complex pictures come together. They are not created from one medium or in one place as the overly precise divisions of academia would have it. Visual culture directs our attention away from structured, formal viewing settings like the cinema and art gallery to the centrality of visual experience in everyday life. At present, different notions of viewing and spectatorship are current both within and between all the various visual subdisciplines. It does, of course, make sense to differentiate. Our attitudes vary according to whether we are going to see a movie, watch television, or attend an art exhibition. However, most of our visual experience takes place aside from these formally structured moments of looking. As Irit Rogoff points out in her essay in this volume, a painting may be noticed on a book jacket or in an advert; television is consumed as a part of domestic life rather than as the sole activity of the viewer; and films are as likely to be seen on video, in an aeroplane or on cable as in a traditional cinema. Just as cultural studies has sought to understand the ways in which people create meaning from the consumption of mass culture, so does visual culture prioritize the everyday experience of the visual from the snapshot to the VCR and even the blockbuster art exhibition.

Visual culture is a necessarily historical subject, based on the recognition that the visual image is not stable but changes its relationship to exterior reality at particular moments of modernity. As philosopher Jean-François Lyotard has argued: 'Modernity, wherever it appears, does not occur without a shattering of belief, without a discovery of the *lack of reality* in reality – a discovery linked to the intervention of other realities' (Lyotard 1993: 9). As one mode of representing reality loses ground, another takes its place without the first disappearing. The formal logic of the *ancien régime* image (1650–1820) first gave way to the dialectical logic of the photograph in the modern period (1820–1975). The traditional image obeyed its own rules that were independent of exterior reality. The perspective system, for example, depends upon the viewer examining the image from one point only, using just one eye. No one actually does this, but the image is internally coherent and thus credible. As perspective's claim to be the most accurate representation of reality lost ground, film and photography created a new, direct relationship to reality, to the extent that we accept the 'actuality' of what we see in the image. A photograph necessarily shows us something that was at a certain point actually before the camera's lens. This image is dialectical because it sets up a relationship between the viewer in the present and the past moment of space or time that it represents.

However, the photograph was not dialectical in the Hegelian sense of the term – that the thesis of the formal image was countered by the antithesis of photography and resolved into a synthesis. On the contrary, postmodernism marks the era in which visual images and the visualizing of things that are not inherently visual have accelerated dramatically without there being any clear goal in mind. Perspective images sought to make the world comprehensible to the powerful figure who stood at the single point from which they were drawn. Photographs offered a potentially more democratic visual map of the world. Now the filmed or photographic image no longer indexes reality because everyone knows it can be undetectably manipulated by computers. The paradoxical virtual image 'emerges when the real-time image dominates the thing represented, real time subsequently prevailing over real space, virtuality dominating actuality and turning the concept of reality on its head' (Virilio 1994: 63). Think of the film produced by 'smart' bombs used in the Gulf War, which showed targets being destroyed, only for it later to emerge that they missed as often as any other bomb: what then were we actually seeing in those films? These virtualities of the postmodern image constantly seem to elude our grasp, creating a crisis of the visual that is more than a specialized problem for the traditional visual disciplines.

Everyday life

The notion of the world picture is no longer adequate to analyse this changed and changing situation. The extraordinary proliferation of images cannot cohere into one single picture for the contemplation of the intellectual. Visual culture seeks to find ways to work within this new (virtual) reality to find the points of resistance in the crisis of information and visual overload in everyday life. To adapt Michel de Certeau's phrase, visual culture is thus a tactic, rather than a strategy, for 'the place of the tactic belongs to the other' (de Certeau 1984: xix). A tactic is carried out in full view of the enemy, the society of control in which we live (ibid.: 37). Although some may find the military overtones of tactics off-putting, it can also be argued that in the ongoing culture wars, tactics are necessary to avoid defeat. Just as earlier enquiries into everyday life sought to prioritize the ways in which consumers created different meanings for themselves from mass culture, so will visual culture explore the ambivalences, interstices and places of resistance in postmodern everyday life from the consumer's point of view.

The (post)modern destruction of reality is accomplished in everyday life, not in the studios of the avant-garde. Just as the situationists collected examples of the bizarre happenings that pass as normality from the newspapers, so can we now see the collapse of reality in everyday life from the mass visual media. In the early 1980s, postmodern photographers like Sherrie Levine and Richard Prince sought to question the authenticity of photography by appropriating photographs taken by other people. This dismissal of photography's claim to represent the truth is now a staple of popular culture in tabloid magazines like the *Weekly World News* as well as more respected publications. Photography operates in such a climate of suspicion that O.J. Simpson's lawyer could plausibly dismiss a photograph showing his client wearing the rare shoes worn by the killer as fakes, only to be outdone when thirty more pictures were discovered. One photograph alone no longer shows the truth. Similarly, some of the most avidly followed television series bear no resemblance to reality at all. Soap operas construct a parallel universe in which the return of a long-lost twin brother is scarcely cause for comment and the death of a character is not to be taken as any indication that he or she will not return the following week. Soap opera is pure television, to adapt Alfred Hitchcock's phrase, *because* of its unrealistic staging, not despite it. Soap is also perhaps the most international visual format, commanding national attention in countries as disparate as Russia, Mexico, Australia and Brazil. Reality is destroyed daily in hour-long slots across the globe.

Yet the visual is not simply the medium of information and mass culture. It offers a sensual immediacy that cannot be rivalled by print media: the very element that makes visual imagery of all kinds distinct from texts. This is not at all the same thing as simplicity but there is an undeniable impact on first sight that a written text cannot replicate. It is the feeling created by the opening sight of the spaceship filling the screen in *2001: A Space Odyssey*; by seeing the Berlin Wall come down on live television; or by encountering the shimmering blues and greens of Cézanne's landscapes. It is that edge, that buzz that separates the remarkable from the humdrum. It is this surplus of experience that moves the different components of the visual sign or semiotic circuit into a relation with one another. Such moments of intense and surprising visual power evoke, in David Freedberg's phrase, 'admiration, awe, terror and desire' (Freedberg 1989: 433). This dimension to visual culture is at the heart of all visual events.

Let us give this feeling a name: the sublime. The sublime is the pleasurable experience in representation of that which would be painful or terrifying in reality, leading to a realization of the limits of the human and of the powers of nature. The sublime was first theorized in antiquity by Longinus, who famously described how 'our soul is uplifted by the true sublime; it takes a proud flight and is filled with joy and vaunting, as though it has itself produced what it had heard'. The classical statue known as *Laocoon* is typical of the sublime work of art. It shows the Trojan warrior and his children fighting a serpent that will soon kill them. Their futile struggle has evoked the sublime for generations of viewers. The sublime was given renewed importance by Enlightenment philosopher Immanuel Kant, who called it 'a satisfaction mixed with horror'. Kant contrasted the sublime with the beautiful, seeing the former as a more complex and profound emotion leading a person with a taste for the sublime to 'detest all chains, from the gilded variety worn at court to the irons weighing down the galley slave'. This preference for the ethical over the simply aesthetic has led Lyotard to revive the sublime as a key term for postmodern criticism. He sees it as 'a combination of pleasure and pain: pleasure in reason exceeding all presentation, pain in the imagination or sensibility proving inadequate to the concept' (Lyotard 1993: 15). The task of the sublime is then to 'present the unpresentable', an appropriate role for the relentless visualizing of the postmodern era. Furthermore, because the sublime is generated by an attempt to present ideas that have no correlative in the natural world – for example, peace, equality, or freedom – 'the experience of the sublime feeling demands a sensitivity to Ideas that is not natural but acquired through culture' (Lyotard 1993: 71). Unlike the beautiful, which can be experienced in nature or culture, the sublime is the creature of culture and is therefore central to visual culture.

However, there is no question of a blanket endorsement of Lyotard's reworking of Kant. On the one hand, Kant dismissed all African art and religion as 'trifling', as far removed from the sublime as he could imagine. To less prejudiced eyes, African sculptures like nail-laden *nkisi* power figures are remarkable instances of the combination of pleasure and pain that creates the sublime, as well as being motivated by the desire to show the unseeable. This example highlights the fundamental challenge for visual studies of learning ways to describe what Martin J. Powers has called 'a fractal network, permeated with patterns from all over the globe'. However, Powers does not simply argue for an all-inclusive worldwide web of the visual image, but emphasizes the power differentials across the network. At present, it must be recognized that visual culture remains a discourse of the West about the West, but in that framework 'the issue', as David Morley reminds us, 'is how to think of modernity, not so much as specifically or *necessarily* European . . . but only contingently so' (Morley 1996: 350). Seen in the long span of history, Euramericans – to use the Japanese term – have dominated modernity for a relatively brief period of time that may well now be drawing to a close. In short, the success or failure of visual culture may well depend on its ability to think transculturally, oriented to the future, rather than take the rear-mirror anthropological approach to culture as tradition.

What's next?

What is the future for visual culture? In everyday life, the development of the Internet II, Digital Video Discs and High-Definition TV make it clear that visualizing is here to stay. Within the cloistered world of the academy, on the other hand, there are those who have dedicated themselves to ensuring that visual culture is eradicated as a field of study. While splendidly defiant, such attitudes recall King Canute's orders to the tide rather than being likely to succeed. Behind this dismissal lies a pattern of one part of the intellectual elite siding with the avant-garde theories of modernism in alliance with the privileges of the wealthy. For it is noticeable that much of the Marxist and modernist rhetoric often used to critique the idea of visual culture is in fact emerging from the art history departments of Ivy League universities. In a tradition that stretches back to Adorno's dismissal of popular culture in the 1940s, Marxism and conservatism find themselves in a curious alliance, using different languages and strategies to attain the same goal.

Casting visual culture in this light places it in the role of the underdog, which can of course be a very privileged position in academia. So the parallel example of the institutionalization of cultural studies in the United States is perhaps the best place to look for lessons for the fledgling interdiscipline. After a flurry of excitement in the early 1990s, cultural studies has lost its way, disrupted on the one hand by intellectual crises like the Sokal affair (in which a deliberately fake article on science and cultural studies was successfully published in the journal *Social Text*) and on the other by the energies of many practitioners being consumed by creating syllabuses, exams and reading lists for new degrees in cultural studies. There is unquestionably a crisis of contemporary visuality. The answer to that crisis is unlikely to be found in a reading list. Rather than simply create new degrees in the old structures of the liberal arts canon, let us try to create ways of doing postdisciplinary work.

Visual culture ought not to sit comfortably in already existing university structures. It should rather form part of an emerging body of postdisciplinary academic endeavours from cultural studies, gay and lesbian studies, to African-American studies, and so on, whose focus crosses the borders of traditional academic disciplines at will. The viability of such approaches relies on their continued ability to challenge their host institutions, not in their easy absorption within them. This is why I think of visual culture as a tactic, rather than an academic discipline. It is a fluid interpretive structure, centred on understanding the response to visual media of both individuals and groups in everyday life. Its definition comes from the questions it asks and the issues it seeks to raise. Like the other approaches mentioned above, it hopes to reach beyond the traditional confines of the university to interact with people's everyday lives.

How to use this book

This Reader may well be used as an assigned text in a variety of classes. It is not, however, conceived as a textbook. For the very definition of visual culture as a field is what is currently at stake. If this book were somehow to act as a fusion of Janson's *History of Art* (1995), Bordwell's *Classical Hollywood Cinema* (1985) and Fiske's *Understanding Popular Culture* (1989) it would have failed. It seeks rather, in the expressive term used by Robert Stam and Ella Shohat in their introductory essay, to be a provocation – to cause new questions to be asked and to force a re-examination of long-accepted procedures. The two essays that follow in this introductory section take this task further in two complementary ways. Irit Rogoff has done much to spread discussion of visual culture both within the Universities of California and London and beyond. In her essay 'Studying Visual Culture', especially written for this volume, she examines the present state of the field and considers how it might progress. Taking issue with the 1996 special issue of the journal *October*, which was highly critical of the very notion of visual culture, Rogoff argues that

> at stake therefore are political questions concerning who is allowed to speak about what, which clash with intellectual positions that wish for us all the possibility of engaging with all the texts and images and other stimuli and frameworks we encounter, of breaking down the barriers of permissible and territorialized knowledge rather than redrawing them along another set of lines.

In their intervention, Robert Stam from film studies and Ella Shohat from cultural studies, take a look at visual culture from the outside. Here they offer one means of reconceptualizing visual culture that moves away from the Euramerican progression of realism/modernism/postmodernism to a polycentric, globalized field of study. The need to abandon this Eurocentric modernist version of history is perhaps the greatest single challenge for the emerging practice of visual culture. As Stam and Shohat conclude, the goal should be a 'mutual and reciprocal relativization', offering the chance of 'coming not only to "see" other groups, but also, through a salutary estrangement, to see how [each] is itself seen'.

The subsequent sections carry introductions of their own. Where I have edited selections, material omitted within a paragraph is indicated by ellipses (. . .). The omission of one or more paragraphs is indicated by ellipses within square brackets [. . .] in the middle of the page. My own summary of omitted material is enclosed by square brackets []. I would like to end this chapter by calling attention to the realities that have shaped this book. Once there was a perfect Visual Culture Reader that existed in my mind. Then the need to obtain permissions, combined with the limits of space and budgets, intruded and the result is what you see before you – necessarily imperfect. I have selected material that would spark as many correspondences and points of debate as possible within the frame of the volume. None the less, I think it likely that everyone currently working in one of the visual disciplines will think that there is not enough from their field and too much from the others. While I have tried to make its geographical and temporal coverage as wide as possible, universality was impossible, resulting in some difficult choices having to be made. Let me point to some of the obvious gaps for which there are no intellectual justifications beyond the need to create artificial limits. Although visual culture seems to me to be an aspect of modernity in the widest sense, there is little coverage of seventeenth- and eighteenth-century subjects. In selecting twentieth-century material I have tended to opt for work on post-1945 subjects, while the geographical coverage is weakest in terms of Asia and Oceania. No doubt many other criticisms can and will be made but I hope readers will prefer to enjoy what is included rather than carp over what has been omitted. In each section, the essays and extracts offer a sense of the developing understanding of a particular topic in recent years, interacting both within and without that section. My introductory essays will show how I connect the different contributions without pretending to exhaust their richness. If the book succeeds in provoking passionate argument and dissent, I shall judge it to have been a success.

Note

1 The material in this introduction is taken from the first chapter of my companion volume, *Visual Culture: An Introduction* (Routledge, forthcoming).

References

Appadurai, Arjun (1990) 'Disjuncture and Difference in the Global Cultural Economy', *Public Culture*, vol. 2, no. 2, Spring.

Anderson, Benedict (1989) *Imagined Communities*, London: Verso.

Batchen, Geoffrey (1996) 'Spectres of Cyberspace', *Artlink*, vol. 16, no. 2 & 3, Winter, pp. 25–28.

Bordwell, David, Staiger, Janet and Thompson, Kristin (1985) *The Classical Hollywood Cinema*, New York: Columbia University Press.

Bryson, Norman, Holly, Michael Ann, and Moxey, Keith (1994) *Visual Culture: Images and Interpretations*, Hanover and London: Wesleyan University Press.

De Certeau, Michel (1984) *The Practice of Everyday Life*, trans. Stephen F. Rendall, Berkeley and Los Angeles: University of California Press.

Fiske, John (1989) *Understanding Popular Culture*, London, Routledge.
Freedberg, David (1989) *The Power of Images: Studies in the History and Theory of Response*, Chicago: Chicago University Press.
Heidegger, Martin (1977) 'The Age of the World Picture', in William Lovitt (trans.), *The Question Concerning Technology and Other Essays*, New York and London: Garland.
Janson (1995) *Janson's History of Art*, New York: Prentice Hall.
Jenks, Christopher (1995) *Visual Culture*, London: Routledge.
Lyotard, Jean-François (1993) *The Postmodern Explained*, Minneapolis: Minnesota University Press.
McNair, Brian (1995) *An Introduction to Political Communication*, London: Routledge.
Mitchell, W.J.T. (1994) *Picture Theory*, Chicago: University of Chicago Press.
Morley, David (1996) 'EurAm, Modernity, Reason or Alterity: or Postmodernism, the Highest Stage of Cultural Imperialism?', in D. Morley and Kuan-Hsing Chen (eds) *Stuart Hall: Critical Dialogues in Cultural Studies*, London: Routledge.
Virilio, Paul (1994) *The Vision Machine*, London: British Film Institute.

Further reading

Bender, Gretchen, and Druckrey, Timothy (1994) *Cultures on the Brink: Ideologies of Technology*, Seattle: Bay Press.
Bryson, Norman *et al.* (1991) *Visual Theory: Painting and Interpretation*, New York: HarperCollins.
Burgin, Victor (1996) *In/Different Spaces: Place and Memory in Visual Culture*, Berkeley: University of California Press.
Cooke, Lynne, and Wollen, Peter (1995) *Visual Display: Culture Beyond Appearances*, Seattle: Bay Press.
Debord, Guy (1994) *The Society of the Spectacle*, New York: Zone.
Marcus, George E, (1996) *Connected: Engagements with Media*, Chicago: Chicago University Press.
Nochlin, Linda (1989) *The Politics of Vision: Essays on Nineteenth-Century Art and Society*, New York, HarperCollins.
Solomon-Godeau, Abigail (1991) *Photography at the Dock*, Minneapolis, Minnesota University Press.
Williams, Linda (1989) *Viewing Positions: Ways of Seeing Film*, New Brunswick, Rutgers University Press.

Chapter 2

Irit Rogoff

STUDYING VISUAL CULTURE

I raise my eyes and I see America.
(Newt Gingrich, *New York Times*, 19 April 1995)

'And please remember, just a hint of starch in Mr. Everett's shirts.' For one brief moment their eyes actually met, Blanche was the first to look away. 'Yes ma'am.' After Grace left the kitchen, Blanche sat down at the table. Was it just the old race thing that had thrown her off when her eyes met Grace's? Her neighbor Wilma's father said he'd never in his adult life looked a white person in the eye.
(Barbara Neely, *Blanche on the Lam*, 1992)

His smoldering eyes saw right through my tremulous heart.
(Barbara Cartland, *The Pirate's Return*, 1987)

HOW CAN WE CHARACTERIZE the emergent field 'visual culture'? To begin with, we must insist that this encompasses a great deal more than the study of images, of even the most open-ended and cross-disciplinary study of images. At one level we certainly focus on the centrality of vision and the visual world in producing meanings, establishing and maintaining aesthetic values, gender stereotypes and power relations within culture. At another level we recognize that opening up the field of vision as an arena in which cultural meanings get constituted, also simultaneously anchors to it an entire range of analyses and interpretations of the audio, the spatial, and of the psychic dynamics of spectatorship. Thus visual culture opens up an entire world of intertextuality in which images, sounds and spatial delineations are read on to and through one another, lending ever-accruing layers of meanings and of subjective responses to each encounter we might have with film, TV, advertising, art works, buildings or urban environments. In a sense we have produced a field of vision version of Derrida's concept of *différance* and its achievement has had a twofold effect both on the structures of meaning and interpretation and on the epistemic and institutional frameworks that attempt to organize them. Derrida's conceptualization of *différance* takes the form of a critique of the binary logic in which every element of meaning constitution is locked into signification in relation to the other (a legacy of Saussurian linguistics' insistence on language as a system of negative differentiation). Instead what we have begun to uncover is the free play of the signifier, a freedom to understand meaning in relation to images, sounds or spaces not necessarily perceived to operate in a direct, causal or epistemic relation to either their context or to one another. If feminist deconstructive writing has long held the place of writing as the endless displacement of meaning, then visual culture provides the visual articulation of the continuous displacement of meaning in the field of vision and the visible.

This insistence on the contingent, the subjective and the constantly reproduced state of meanings in the visual field is equally significant for the institutional or disciplinary location of this work. If we do not revert exclusively to ascribing meaning exclusively to an author, nor to the conditions and historical specificities of its making, nor to the politics of an authorizing community, then we simultaneously evacuate the object of study from the disciplinary and other forms of knowledge territorialization. Perhaps then we are at long last approaching Roland Barthes's description of interdisciplinarity not as surrounding a chosen object with numerous modes of scientific inquiry, but rather as the constitution of a new object of knowledge. The following brief attempt to engage with the arena of visual culture will touch on some of these themes as well as on the thorny politics of historical specificity: its advantages, its limitations, and the dangers and freedoms inherent in attempting to move out of a traditional and internally coherent and unexamined model of what it means to be historically specific.

Vision as critique

In today's world meanings circulate visually, in addition to orally and textually. Images convey information, afford pleasure and displeasure, influence style, determine consumption and mediate power relations. Who we see and who we do not see; who is privileged within the regime of specularity; which aspects of the historical past actually have circulating visual representations and which do not; whose fantasies of what are fed by which visual images? Those are some of the questions which we pose regarding images and their circulation. Much of the practice of intellectual work within the framework of cultural problematics has to do with being able to ask new and alternative questions, rather than reproducing old knowledge by asking the old questions. (*Often in class the students complain that the language of theoretical inquiry is difficult, that 'it is not English'. They need considerable persuasion that one cannot ask the new questions in the old language, that language is meaning. In the end almost always their inherent excitement at any notion of 'the new' wins the day and by the end of the trimester someone invariably produces a perfectly formulated remark about discourse, representation and meaning usually followed by a wonder-filled pause at the recognition that they have just uttered something entirely 'different'.*)

By focusing on a field of vision and of visual culture operating within it, we create the space for the articulation of (but not necessarily the response to) such questions as: What are the visual codes by which some are allowed to look, others to hazard a peek, and still others are forbidden to look altogether? In what political discourses can we understand looking and returning the gaze as an act of political resistance? Can we actually participate in the pleasure and identify with the images produced by culturally specific groups to which we do not belong? These are the questions which we must address to the vast body of images that surrounds us daily. Furthermore we need to understand how we actively interact with images from all arenas to remake the world in the shape of our fantasies and desires or to narrate the stories which we carry within us. In the arena of visual culture the scrap of an image connects with a sequence of a film and with the corner of a billboard or the window display of a shop we have passed by, to produce a new narrative formed out of both our experienced journey and our unconscious. Images do not stay within discrete disciplinary fields such as 'documentary film' or 'Renaissance painting', since neither the eye nor the psyche operates along or recognizes such divisions. Instead they provide the opportunity for a mode of new cultural writing existing at the intersections of both objectivities and subjectivities. In a critical culture in which we have been trying to wrest representation away from the dominance of patriarchal, Eurocentric and heterosexist normativization, visual culture provides immense opportunities for rewriting culture through our concerns and our journeys.

The emergence of visual culture as a transdisciplinary and cross-methodological field of inquiry means nothing less and nothing more than an opportunity to reconsider some of the present culture's thorniest problems from yet another angle. In its formulation of both the objects of its inquiry and of its methodological processes, it reflects the present moment in the arena of cultural studies in all of its complexities. How would I categorize this present moment? From the perspective I inhabit it seems to reflect a shift from a phase of intensely analytical activity we went through during the late 1970s and the 1980s, when we gathered a wide assortment of tools of analysis to a moment in which new cultural objects are actually being produced. While deeply rooted in an understanding of the epistemological denaturalization of inherited categories and subjects revealed through the analytical models of structuralist and poststructuralist thought and the specific introduction of theories of sexual and cultural difference, these new objects of inquiry go beyond analysis towards figuring out new and alternative languages which reflect the contemporary awareness by which we live out our lives. All around us fictions such as Toni Morrison's *Beloved*, autobiographies such as Sara Suleri's *Meatless Days*, films such as Terry Zwygoff's *Crumb* and complex multimedia art installations such as Vera Frenkel's *Transit Bar*, live out precarious and immensely creative relations between analysis, fiction and the uneasy conditions of our critically informed lives.

One of the most important issues cultural studies has taken on is to provide a 'hands-on' application of the epistemological shift which Gayatri Spivak has characterized thus: 'It is the questions that we ask that produce the field of inquiry and not some body of materials which determines what questions need to be posed to it.' In doing so we have affected a shift from the old logical-positivist world of cognition to a more contemporary arena of representation and of situated knowledges. The emergence of a relatively new arena such as visual culture provides the possibility of unframing some of the discussions we have been engaged in regarding presences and absences, invisibility and stereotypes, desires, reifications and objectifications from the disciplinary fields – art history, film studies, mass media and communications, theoretical articulations of vision, spectatorship and the power relations that animate the arena we call the field of vision – which first articulated their status as texts and objects. Thereby unframing them from a set of conventional values as *either* highly valued *or* highly marginalized *or* outside of the scope of sanctioned vision altogether. Equally they are unframed from the specific histories of their making and the methodological models of analyses which have more recently served for their unmaking. The field that I work in, which labors heavy-handedly under the title of the critical theorization of visual culture (or visual culture for short) does not function as a form of art history or film studies or mass media, but is clearly informed by all of them and intersects with all of them. It does not historicize the art object or any other visual image, nor does it provide for it either a narrow history within art nor a broader genealogy within the world of social and cultural developments. It does not assume that if we overpopulate the field of vision with ever more complementary information, we shall actually gain any greater insight into it.

(*When I was training as an art historian, we were instructed in staring at pictures. The assumption was that the harder we looked, the more would be revealed to us; that a rigorous, precise and historically informed looking would reveal a wealth of hidden meanings. This belief produced a new anatomical formation called 'the good eye'. Later, in teaching in art history departments, whenever I would complain about some student's lack of intellectual curiosity, about their overly literal perception of the field of study or of their narrow understanding of culture as a series of radiant objects, someone else on the faculty would always respond by saying 'Oh, but they have a good eye.'*)

Nor does this field function as a form of art (or any other visual artefact) criticism. It does not serve the purpose of evaluating a project, of complementing or condemning it, of assuming some notion of universal quality that can be applied to all and sundry. Furthermore it does not aim at cataloguing the offenses and redressing the balances, nor of enumerating who is in and who is out, of what was chosen and what was discarded. These were an important part of an earlier project in which the glaring exclusions, erasures and distortions of every form of otherness – women, homosexuals and non-European peoples to mention a few categories – had to be located and named and a judgment had to be passed on the conditions of their initial exclusion. All of this, however, would constitute a 'speaking about': an objectification of a moment in culture such as an exhibition or a film or a literary text, into a solid and immutable entity which does not afford us as the viewing audience, the possibilities of play, the possibilities of rewriting the exhibition (or the site of any other artefact) as an arena for our many and different concerns. It would assume that the moment in culture known as the exhibition should ideally dictate a set of fixed meanings rather than serve as the site for the continuous (re)production of meanings.

In fact the perspectives that I would like to try and represent, the critical analysis of visual culture, would want to do everything to avoid a discourse which perceives of itself as 'speaking about' and shift towards one of 'speaking to'. In the words of Trinh T. Min-ha, 'Tale, told, to be told/Are you truthful?', acknowledging the complexities inherent in any speech act does not necessarily mean taking away or compromising the qualities of a fine story.

> Who speaks? What speaks? The question is implied and the function named, but the individual never reigns, and the subject slips away without naturalizing its voice. S/he who speaks, speaks to the tale as S/he begins telling and retelling it. S/he does not speak about it. For without a certain work of displacement, 'speaking about' only partakes in the conservation of systems of binary opposition (subject/object I/it, we/they) on which territorialized knowledge depends.

Trinh suggests here not merely that in reading/looking we rewrite ('speak about') the text. More importantly, she recognizes that in claiming and retelling the narratives ('speaking to'), we alter the very structures by which we organize and inhabit culture.

It is this questioning of the ways in which we inhabit and thereby constantly make and remake our own culture that informs the arena of visual culture. It is an understanding that the field is made up of at least three different components. First, there are the images that come into being and are claimed by various, and often contested histories. Second, there are the viewing apparatuses that we have at our disposal that are guided by cultural models such as narrative or technology. Third, there are the subjectivities of identification or desire or abjection from which we view and by which we inform what we view. While I am obviously focusing here on the reception rather than the production of images and objects or environments, it is clearly one of the most interesting aspects of visual culture that the boundary lines between making, theorizing and historicizing have been greatly eroded and no longer exist in exclusive distinction from one another.

For some years I have been wondering about the formation of a counter viewing position to that old art historical chestnut '*the good eye*'. Are we developing 'the mean eye, the jaundiced, skeptical eye'? Is the critical eye one that guards jealously against pleasure? Hardly so, if we are to engage with the fantasy formations that inform viewing subjectivities. For the moment, and following some of Laura Mulvey's later work within feminist film theory, I have settled on the notion of '*the curious eye*' to counter the 'good eye' of connoisseurship. Curiosity implies a certain unsettling; a notion of things outside the realm of the known, of things not yet quite understood or articulated; the pleasures of the forbidden or the hidden or the unthought; the optimism of finding out something one had not known or been able to conceive of before. It is in the spirit of such a 'curious eye' that I want to open up some dimension of this field of activity.

Perhaps one of the best indications of just how destabilizing this form of 'curiosity' for the not-yet-known can be, is the alarm which seems to be caused by the clearly emerging institutional formations of this new field of 'visual culture'. A recent issue of the journal *October* contained a questionnaire on the subject of this emergent arena of inquiry. All of the statements to which correspondents were asked to reply indicated some profound sense of loss – the loss of historical specificities and of material groundings and of fixed notions of quality and excellence, etc., which the editors who had set them seem to view as the loss of the grounding navigational principles for their activities. Apparently the most alarming of all has been the infiltration of the field of art history by something termed the 'anthropological model'. I puzzled long and hard over both this analysis and the dread it seemed to provoke. I spoke to all my sophisticated cultural anthropologist acquaintances to try and understand what they may have foisted on us unawares. I read all the predictable responses to the questionnaire set by the *October* editors, and still not the slightest glimmer of comprehension emerged. Finally, reading through Tom Conley's very refreshing and extremely well-judged response 'Laughter and Alarm', it seemed that all this fuss was being provoked by the growing presence or preference for a 'relativist' model of cultural analysis. As far as I could make out, the so-called 'relativism' of this assumed anthropological model involves a nontransferable specificity for the context of any cultural production. Thus the ability to establish a set of inherent values or criteria of excellence for images or cultural objects which would transcend the conditions of their making and constitute a metacultural relationality (as for example in the traditional modernist model for the historical avant-garde of Europe and the United States as a set of international, interlinked, innovative art movements sharing a particular confrontational spirit and a commitment to formal experimentation) is seemingly negated or sacrificed through this more current relational model.

Now, the editors of *October* who have articulated all of these anxieties about the erosion of good old art history through the encroaching dangers of so-called anthropological relativism are hardly an intellectually naïve lot; indeed they were in part responsible for acquainting my generation of art historians and critics with important analytical models and with important cultural criticism from both France and Germany as well as debates carried on in the US. Nor are they in any way provincial intellectuals, locked up within the confining frameworks of one single, national, cultural discussion. They are clearly more than aware that the notion of 'relativist' carries within it all kinds of intimations of cultural conservatism. One of the most publicized cases of polemics for and against historical relativism was the case of the 1980s German *Historikerstreit*, in which a group of conservative German historians such as Nolte and Broszat began making claims for a study of German fascism in the 1930s and 1940s as relational to all the other fascisms and totalitarian regimes around at that same historical moment. The German neo-conservative historians' project was underpinned by a politics that aimed at lessening guilt through undermining historical specificity both at the level of cause and of effect. The accusations of 'relativism' with which this writing project was greeted by more left-liberal historians in the West were due largely to the fact that much of this writing was aimed at a *re-evaluation*, in moralizing terms, of the events and policies of the period. Thus nationalist-socialist fascism was graded in relation to other Western fascisms and to Soviet totalitarian regimes and was found either to have been a response to them or to have similarities with them, or to compare not quite so horrifically with these other models. What it did not attempt was to reframe understandings of a very notion of fascism or to think it away from a national history, or to understand it in relation to certain values and aesthetics within the modern period, or any of the other possibilities available for unframing a discussion of fascism and gaining an alternative set of understandings into it, of actually questioning the certainty that we *know* what fascism, the object of inquiry, is. Cultural specificity in this particular historical discussion takes the form of two fixities: (a) a discrete, stable and clearly known object of study and (b) discrete, stable and fixed contexts (in this case of national cultures with clear lines of division between them) which contain and separate their histories. It presumes to know, in no uncertain terms, what a political movement is, where a national culture begins and ends, and it assumes that endlessly complex social, cultural, racial and sexual differences might actually coalesce around such a dramatic articulation of a subject known as 'fascism'. In contrast the cultural studies project which *October* characterizes as having been infiltrated by a so-called 'anthropological model' aims at establishing internal cultural specificities which can in turn attempt intercultural conversations while maintaining the necessary regard for the value and serious significance of *anyone*'s cultural production. There is a world of acute political difference between the politics of these two cultural/analytical projects which seem to be conflated here. So how to explain what is clearly a most confusing political slippage?

I could adopt a mean-spirited and pragmatic attitude and say that all this is simply about the loss of territories of knowledge and reputations established in given disciplinary fields which are being called into question (the fields, not the reputations) by the emergence of other, newer fields. But that would be disrespectful to a publication that contributed much to my own intellectual development and it would only serve the purpose of personalizing a serious political issue and thereby devaluing its importance. To address the argument as presented in *October* both in its stated terms and with attention to the alarm underlying it is to take issue with the cautioning against undifferentiated relativism and unsituated knowledges being put forward by its editors. Clearly, notions of 'relativism' cannot be dragged around from one discussion to another with complete disregard to the politics that inform each of these. To unframe hierarchies of excellence and of universal value that privilege one strand of cultural production while committing every other mode to cultural oblivion, as claims the not fully articulated accusation in *October*, does not mean that one is launching an undifferentiated universalism in which everything is equal to everything else. Rather it opens up the possibilities for analyzing the politics that stand behind each particular relativist model and of differentiating between those rather than between the supposed value of objects and images. The history whose loss the editors of *October* seem to be lamenting has not disappeared, it has simply shifted ground. In visual culture the history becomes that of the viewer or that of the authorizing discourse rather than that of the object. By necessity this shift in turn determines a change in the very subject of the discussion or analysis, a shift in which the necessity for having the discussion in the first place and for having it in a particular methodological mode and at a particular time become part of this very discussion. This conjunction of situated knowledge and self-reflexive discourse analysis accompanied by a conscious history for the viewing subject hardly seems grounds for such a pessimistic lament, simply an opportunity for a bit of self-consciousness and a serious examination of the politics inherent in each project of cultural assessment. (*The whole discussion reminds me of a dreadful sociology conference I attended a few years ago at Berkeley in which a very authoritative and very senior woman sociologist complained that without standards of excellence how would she be able to hire and fire people or accept or dismiss students? A fellow attendee at the conference who happened to be sitting next to me kept muttering under his breath in a very heavy Swedish accent 'Why don't you already stop hiring and firing?' (Enough said.)*

Spectatorship in the field of vision

The space this investigation inhabits is the field of vision, which is a much wider arena than a sphere for the circulation of images or questions regarding the nature of representation. This space, the field of vision, is to begin with a vastly overdetermined one. In the West, it bears the heavy burden of post-Enlightenment scientific and philosophical discourses regarding the centrality of vision for an empirical determination of the world as perceivable. In these analyses we find the gaze described as an apparatus of investigation, verification, surveillance and cognition, which has served to sustain the traditions of Western post-Enlightenment scientificity and early modern technologies. The limitations of such historical accounts of the field of vision as central to the continuing Western Enlightenment project (such as Martin Jay's exceptionally scholarly and informative recent book *Downcast Eyes*) is that it is vacated of any political dynamics or models of subjectivity. It becomes a neutral field in which some innocent objective 'eye' is deployed by an unsituated viewer. Therefore the kind of looking that was sanctioned and legitimated by scientific imperatives or the kind of surveillance which claimed its necessity through the establishment of civility through a rooting out of criminality, can now be understood through questions about who is allowed to look, to what purposes, and by what academic and state discourses it is legitimated. The recent spate of literature regarding 'vision' as it appears in numerous learned discourses does precisely the opposite of what 'visual culture' sets out to do. It reproduces a tedious and traditional corpus of knowledge and tells us how each great philosopher and thinker saw the concept of vision within an undisputed philosophical or other paradigm. Most ignominiously, feminist theorists such as Luce Irigaray (who in their writing undid territorialities of hierarchized, linear knowledge), get written into this trajectory in some misguided form of tribute to feminism via its inclusion within the annals of Western thought. By contrast, a parallel discussion in visual culture might venture to ask how bodies of thought produced a notion of vision in the service of a particular politics or ideology and populated it with a select set of images, viewed through specific apparatuses and serving the needs of distinct subjectivities.

The discussion of spectatorship *in* (rather than *and*) sexual and cultural difference, begun within feminist film theory and continued by the critical discourses of minority and emergent cultures, concerns itself with the gaze as desire, which splits spectatorship into the arena of desiring subjects and desired objects. Currently such binary separations have been increasingly tempered by the slippages between the ever-eroding boundaries of exclusive objecthood or coherent subjecthood. At present we have arrived at an understanding that much of initial sexual and racial identity in the field of vision is formed through processes of negative differentiation: that whiteness needs blackness to constitute itself as whiteness; that masculinity needs femininity or feminized masculinity to constitute its masculinity in agreed upon normative modes; that civility and bourgeois respectability need the stereotypical unruly 'others' – be they drunks or cultural minorities or anyone else positioned outside phantasmatic norms – to define the nonexistent codes of what constitutes 'acceptable' behavior. However, at the same time we have understood that all of these are socially constructed, 'performative' rather than essentially attributed, and therefore highly unstable entities. Thus the field of vision becomes a ground for contestation in which unstable normativity constantly and vehemently attempts to shore itself up. Films such as *The Crying Game* or *The Last Seduction* played precisely with the erosion of assumptions that something – gender identity in both cases – 'looks like' that which names it and the cataclysmic results which such processes of destabilization produce. Spectatorship as an investigative field understands that what the eye purportedly 'sees' is dictated to it by an entire set of beliefs and desires and by a set of coded languages and generic apparatuses.

Finally the field of vision is sustained through an illusion of transparent space. This is the illusion of transparency which is claimed in the quote from Newt Gingrich with which I began this essay: 'I raise my eyes and I see America.' In this scenario, he has the ability to see. America – in all its supposed unity and homogeneity – is there available to his vision; it can be seen by him and the space between them is a transparent entity in which no obstacles obscure the directness and clarity of (his) vision. Politically and philosophically this condition has been best theorized by Henri Lefebvre in *The Production of Space* (1991) when he says:

> Here space appears as luminous, as intelligible, as giving action free rein. What happens in space lends a miraculous quality to thought, which becomes incarnate by means of a *design* (in both senses of the word). The design serves as a mediator – itself of great fidelity – between mental activity (invention) and social activity (realization); and it is deployed in space. The illusion of transparency goes hand in hand with a view of space as innocent, as free of traps or secret places. Anything hidden or dissimulated – and hence dangerous – is antagonistic to transparency, under whose reign everything can be taken in by a single glance from the mental eye which illuminates whatever it contemplates.

To some extent the project of visual culture has been to try and repopulate space with all the obstacles and all the unknown images, which the illusion of transparency evacuated from it. Space, as we have understood, is always differentiated: it is always sexual or racial; it is always constituted out of circulating capital; and it is always subject to the invisible boundary lines that determine inclusions and exclusions. Most importantly it is always populated with the unrecognized obstacles which never allow us to actually 'see' what is out there beyond what we expect to find. To repopulate space with all of its constitutive obstacles as we learn to recognize them and name them, is to understand how hard we have to strain to see, and how complex is the work of visual culture.

The visual conditions of historicizing

I have attempted to map out some constitutive components of the arena of visual culture. Most importantly I need to try to articulate the importance of its operations as a field of knowledge. In the first instance I would argue that the unframing operations I have described above might lead towards a new object of study which would be determined around issues. Those issues in turn are determined by the various urgent cultural conditions and cultural problematics with which we are faced every day. To be able to assemble a group of materials and a variety of methodological analyses around an issue that is determined out of cultural and political realities rather than out of traditions of learned arguments, seems an important step forward in the project of reformulating knowledge to deal responsibly with the lived conditions of highly contested realities, such as we face at the turn of this century in the West.

This is however also a cautionary moment: as we divest ourselves of historical periods, schools of stylistic or aesthetic affiliation, national cultural locations, or the limitations of reading objects through modes and conditions of production, we run the danger of divesting ourselves of self location. It is at this point that we enter perhaps the thorniest and most contentious aspect of this entire project, for it has become clear to each and every one of us – though we may belong to radically different collectives and cultural mobilizations within the arena of contemporary feminist, multicultural and critically/theoretically informed culture – that historic specificity is a critically important part of coming into cultural recognition and articulation. Every movement that has attempted to liberate marginalized groups from the oppressions of elision and invisibility has, to all intents and purposes, insisted on having something to say, on having a language to say it in, and on having a position from which to speak.

My own coming into critical consciousness took place within the feminist theory of the 1980s in Europe and the United States. Without doubt, the historical uncovering and location of earlier female subjects and their numerous histories and the insistence on speaking as women were a very important part of feminist critique, just as emergent cultural minority discourses are presently important in the rewriting of culture by previously colonized peoples. Having established these as both intellectually important and institutionally legitimate, the next phase moved to using gender as a category for the analysis of such categories as style or periodicity or such overall categories as 'modernism', which enfold both. (*And this was not at all simple – I will never forget the comments of a Vassar art history professor after a lecture I gave there on the visual construction of masculinity and masculine artistic privilege through self-portraiture. He announced uncategorically that my few comments on the subsidiary female figures within these paintings were far more interesting than my efforts at theorizing the visual constructions of masculinity and that as a feminist art historian I should stick with those.*)

At stake therefore are political questions concerning who is allowed to speak about what. These can set up limitations to our intellectual capacity to engage with all the texts, images and other stimuli and frameworks we encounter; to break down the barriers of permissible and territorialized knowledge rather than simply redraw them along another formalized set of lines. The answer lies, to my mind at least, in substituting the historical specificity of that being studied with the historical specificity of he/she/they doing the studying. In order to effect such a shift without falling prey to endless anecdotal and autobiographical ruminating which stipulates experience as a basis for knowledge, we attempt to read each culture through other, often hostile and competitive, cultural narratives. This process of continuous translation and negotiation is often exhausting in its denial of a fixed and firm position, but it does allow us to shift the burden of specificity from the material to the reader and prevents us from the dangers of complete dislocation. Perhaps it might even help us to understand that at the very moment in which historical specificity can provide liberation and political strength to some of the dispossessed, it also imprisons others within an old binary structure that no longer reflects the conditions and realities of their current existence.

I should like to demonstrate this process by presenting a condensed version of a long project in which I have been involved over the past three years. The project is in several parts and involves different types of activity, both historical and critical, often involving a certain amount of fiction writing. The starting point for me has been my need to think through some issues regarding projects of public commemoration and the political uses they serve in different cultures at different times. My need to think through these problems, in relation to one another and against their official articulation by the commemorating culture, has to do with my location as a native of Israel, as someone who has for many years spent long periods of time in Germany and has been very involved with political culture on the German left, and most recently as a teacher and cultural organizer in the US where I have become acquainted with, and shaped by, discussions of multiculturalism and cultural difference. As a native of Israel I grew up in the shadow of a trauma, the genocide of European Jews during the Second World War and of its consequences in the establishment of the modern state of Israel. Simultaneously this history served in covert and unacknowledged ways to legitimate numerous acts of violence; against the indigenous population of Palestine and for the marginalization of Arab Jews, who were not perceived as part of this European horror, which perversely came to define rights of inclusion and participation within the Jewish state of Israel. Perhaps even more importantly, the plethora of commemoration practices of this horror within Israel became extremely important in maintaining a culture of constant and high anxiety within the population of the country, a kind of manifest haunting which could not be shaken despite all evidence of military and technological supremacy in the eastern Mediterranean. No matter how many battles were won and how many enemies vanquished, no matter how often the US assured the population of its undying support and loyalty, not to mention huge and constant influxes of cash and privileged markets, people in Israel have continued to live out their days driven by a fear of annihilation which the ever-present Holocaust monuments have sustained and maintained. So that has been one part of the political urgency of my project, to question the contemporary political uses of commemoration practices.

At the same time I have had to face the recent spate of commemoration activities in Germany and to contend with German discourses of guilt and of compulsory public memory. Operating in this other context, I understood that discourses of guilt and monumental public commemoration affect a form of historical closure. To begin with they assume that one can replace an absence (many millions of murdered subjects) with a presence (a column or a statue or a complex conceptual set of public space interrogations). Second, the protagonists are frozen into binary, occupying positions of victim and perpetrator, both of whom have seemingly come to a miserable end. The newly hybridized and continuing cultural development of not only Jewish and German but also many other lives affected by the cataclysmic events of fascism and war, elsewhere around the globe and in relation to other geographies and cultures, is denied in its entirety. Finally the historic trauma of the Holocaust linked to the specter of European fascism becomes the index of all political horror and its consequence, imposing once again a Eurocentric index of measure and political identity on the very concept of political horror.

Viewed from the perspective of the US I have watched with dismay the emergence of more and more Holocaust museums across the country over the past four years. Situated within the contexts of the current culture wars exemplified by the multicultural contestation of the traditional and ongoing supremacy of European American cultural legacies, these museums have begun to take on an extremely disturbing dimension: a form of rewriting of the recent past in which a European account of horror would vie with the locally generated horror of slavery and the annihilation of native peoples. It also assumes the form of a 're-whitening' of the migrant heritage of the United States at a moment in which immigration is constantly discussed through non-European and racially marked bodies. This is disturbing in more ways that I can recount in this quick summary of a problematic, but primarily I have been thinking of the ways in which this account writes all of the Jewish world as European, which of course it never has been, and the ways in which it sets up contestations of horror within US histories, between Jewish, African-American and Native American populations.

As a culturally displaced person I move between all of these cultures and languages and inhabit positions within all of their political discourses. My displacement being neither tragic nor disadvantaged but rather the product of restless curiosity, I have an obligation to write all these problematics across one another and to see whether they yield insights beyond their specific cultural and political location. As anyone who inhabits an intercultural or cross-cultural position (which increasingly, with ever-growing self-consciousness, is most of us) knows, this constant translation and mediation process is a deeply exhausting business and one would like to put it to some productive use so that the permanent unease might unravel some other possible perspective on problems viewed almost exclusively from within each of the cultures involved. While I have had the opportunity to write each one within its own context, that was merely the reproduction of an analysis situated within a culture. What then are the possibilities of unframing these problematics and seeing how they interlink and inform one another? Perhaps even more importantly I would like to see if I can find a model of opening up a uniquely European horror to a relationality with all the political horror experienced by migrating populations elsewhere around the globe around the same time. I think that the loss of historical specificity in this instance will be compensated for by the undoing of an indexical hierarchy of horrors, in which one is culturally privileged over others. I hope that in the process some understanding of the degree to which 'Trauma' informs all of our originary myths, means that some patterns and symptoms are shared by the culture at large, even if its populations have radically different specific histories. It might even help me to think through the constant state of cultural haunting, the underlying conditions of unease emanating from shared but denied histories between the West and non-West, that silently ruffle the surfaces of our daily lives.

That, in a nutshell, constitutes the political urgency of the specific project I am describing, and in writing projects published elsewhere, I hope to demonstrate a possible model for its exploration within the arena of visual culture. These have taken the form of long-term collaborations with conceptual artist Jochen Gerz, with video and multimedia artist Vera Frenkel, and with computer and electronic artist George Legrady. These are collaborations in which I approach the work with my specific issues at hand and invariably find in it a set of thoughts and images that allow me to formulate the next stage of my investigation. In turn my theoretical articulations locate the artists' work within a set of cultural debates in which the visual arts rarely find representation. It assumes the form of a practice, of a 'writing with' an artist's work rather than about it, a dehierarchization of the question of whether the artist, the critic or the historian, the advertising copywriter or the commercial sponsor, the studio or the director, has the final word in determining the meaning of a work in visual culture. (*Oddly this lesson was learned far from the field of dealing with contemporary objects, through Derek Jarman's extraordinary film* Caravaggio *which, more than anything I had encountered in the early 1980s, produced a model for 'contemporizing history' and reading historical artefacts through current preoccupations such as the instability of the sexual nature of gender categories. After seeing this film I experienced the very necessary delights of uncertainty, of never being quite sure of what I was looking at.*)

One of the many advantages of encountering and analyzing issues of commemoration across a broad range of visual representations that function in public and in private spaces, that tease the viewer with their reluctant visible presence or with their entire physical absence, that broadcast on monitors or lie within the bowels of the computer waiting to be unfolded in real time, is that they straddle the spatial trajectory between memory and commemoration: a trajectory that seems parallel to our dilemma within the intellectual work of the academy. In the unframed field of vision there exist possibilities for simultaneously remembering as we structure solid commemorative arguments, amass facts and juggle analytical models.

Chapter 3

Ella Shohat and Robert Stam

NARRATIVIZING VISUAL CULTURE

Towards a polycentric aesthetics

QUESTIONS OF MODERNISM and postmodernism are usually 'centered' within the limited and ultimately provincial frame of European art. The emerging field of 'visual culture', for us, potentially represents a break with the Eurocentrism not only of conservative 'good eye' art history but also with presumably radical, high-modernist avant-gardism, which perhaps explains the apoplectic reactions that 'visual culture' has sometimes provoked. In our view, 'visual culture' as a field interrogates the ways both art history and visual culture have been narrativized so as to privilege certain locations and geographies of art over others, often within a stagist and 'progressive' history where realism, modernism and postmodernism are thought to supersede one another in a neat and orderly linear succession. Such a narrative, we would suggest, provides an impoverished framework even for European art, and it collapses completely if we take non-European art into account.

Our purpose here is to recast these questions not only by stressing the aesthetic contributions of non-European cultures but also by insisting on the longstanding interconnectedness between the arts of Europe and those outside it. We want to address visual culture in a way that does not always assume Europe – taken here in the broad sense to include the neo-Europes that colonialism installed around the world – as the normative culture of reference. Traditional art history, in this sense, exists on a continuum with official history in general, which figures Europe as a unique source of meaning, as the world's center of gravity, as ontological 'reality' to the world's shadow. Endowing a mythical 'West' with an almost providential sense of historical destiny, Eurocentric history sees Europe, alone and unaided, as the motor, the *primum mobile*, for progressive historical change, including progressive change in the arts. An arrogant monologism exalts only one legitimate culture, one narrative, one trajectory, one path to aesthetic creation.[1]

Most writing on modernism, for example, restricts its attention to movements in European and North American capitals like Paris, London, New York and Zurich, while consigning to oblivion similar modernist movements in such places as São Paolo, Havana, Mexico City and Buenos Aires (to speak only of Latin America). Periodization and theoretical formulations too have been relentlessly monochromatic. A single, local perspective has been presented as 'central' and 'universal,' while the productions of what is patronizingly called 'the rest of the world,' when discussed at all, are assumed to be pale copies of European originals, aesthetically inferior and chronologically posterior, mere latter-day echoes of pioneering European gestures. The dominant literature on modernism often regards Europe as simply absorbing 'primitive art' and anonymous 'folklore' as raw materials to be refined and reshaped by European artists. This view prolongs the colonial trope which projected colonized people as body rather than mind, much as the colonized world was seen as a source of raw material rather than of mental activity or manufacture. Europe thus appropriated the material and cultural production of non-Europeans while denying both their achievements and its own appropriation, thus consolidating its sense of self and glorifying its own cultural anthropophagy.

The notion of non-European cultural practices as untouched by avant-gardist modernism or mass-mediated postmodernism, we would argue, is often subliminally imbricated with a view of Africa, Latin America and Asia as 'underdeveloped' or 'developing,' as if it lived in another time zone apart from the global system of the late capitalist world. Such a view bears the traces of the infantilizing trope, which projects colonized people as embodying an earlier stage of individual human or broad cultural development, a trope which posits the cultural immaturity of colonized or formerly colonized peoples. As diplomatic synonyms for 'childlike,' terms like 'underdevelopment' project the infantilizing trope on a global scale. The Third World toddler, even when the product of a millennial civilization, is not yet in control of his body/psyche and therefore needs the help of the more 'adult' and 'advanced' societies.[2] Like the sociology of 'modernization' and the economics of 'development,' the aesthetics of modernism (and of postmodernism) often covertly assume a telos toward which Third World cultural practices are presumed to be evolving. Even such a generally acute cultural theorist as Fredric Jameson, in his writings on Third World literature and film, tends to underestimate the radical revisioning of aesthetics performed by Third World and diasporic artists. Although he is (thankfully) inconsistent on this point, Jameson in his unguarded moments seems to conflate the terms of political economy (where he projects the Third World into a less developed, less modern frame), and those of aesthetic and cultural periodization (where he projects it into a 'pre-modernist' or 'pre-postmodernist' past). A residual economism or 'stagism' here leads to the equation of late capitalist/postmodernist and precapitalist/pre-modernist, as when Jameson speaks of the 'belated emergence of a kind of modernism in the modernizing Third World, at a moment when the so-called advanced countries are themselves sinking into full postmodernity.'[3] Thus the Third World always seems to lag behind, not only economically but also culturally, condemned to a perpetual game of catch-up, in which it can only repeat on another register the history of the 'advanced' world. This perspective ignores the 'systems theory' that sees all the 'worlds' as coeval, interlinked, living the *same* historical moment (but under diverse modalities of subordination or domination). It also ignores the view that posits the neologistic cultures of Latin America, for example – products of uneven development and of multifaceted transactions with other cultures, as the privileged scenes of copy and pastiche – as themselves the proleptic site of postmodernist practices.

A more adequate formulation, in our view, would see temporarily as scrambled and palimpsestic in all the worlds, with the pre-modern, the modern, the postmodern coexisting globally, although the 'dominant' might vary from region to region. Thus the Pennsylvanian Dutch, who eschew all modern technology, and the cybernetic technocrats of Silicon Valley, both live in 'postmodern' America, while the 'stone-Age' Kayapo and sophisticated urban Euro-Brazilians both live in Brazil, yet the Kayapo use camcorders while the sophisticates adhere to supposedly 'archaic' Afro-Brazilian religions. Thus all cultures, and the texts generated by these cultures, we assume, are multiple, hybrid, heteroglossic, unevenly developed, characterized by multiple historical trajectories, rhythms and temporalities.

As seen through this grid, visual culture manifests what Canclini calls 'multitemporal heterogeneity,' i.e. the simultaneous, superimposed spatio-temporalities which characterize the contemporary social text. The widely disseminated trope of the palimpsest, the parchment on which are inscribed the layered traces of diverse moments of past writing, contains within it this idea of multiple temporalities. The postmodern moment, similarly, is seen as chaotically plural and contradictory, while its aesthetic is seen as an aggregate of historically dated styles randomly reassembled in the present. For Bakhtin, all artistic texts of any complexity 'embed' semantic treasures drawn from multiple epochs. All artistic texts, within this perspective, are palimpsestic, analyzable within a millennial, *longue durée*. Nor is this aesthetic the special preserve of canonical writers, since dialogism operates within all cultural production, whether literate or non-literate, high-brow or lowbrow. European or non-European. Rap music's cut'n'mix aesthetic of sampling, for example, can be seen as a street-smart embodiment of this temporally embedded intertextuality, in that rap bears the stamp and rhythm of multiple times and meters. As in artistic collage or literary quotation, the sampled texts carry with them the time-connoted memory of their previous existences.

The palimpsestic multi-trace nature of art operates both within and across cultures. The multicultural dialogue between Europe and its others, for example, is not of recent date. Although a Eurocentric narrative constructs an artificial wall of separation between European and non-European culture, in fact Europe itself is a synthesis of many cultures, Western and non-Western. The notion of a 'pure' Europe originating in classical Greece is premised on crucial exclusions, from the African and Asiatic influences that shaped classical Greece itself, to the osmotic Sephardi-Judaic-Islamic culture that played such a crucial role during the so-called Dark Ages (an ethnocentric label for a period of oriental ascendancy), the Middle Ages, and the Renaissance. All the celebrated milestones of European progress – Greece, Rome, Christianity, Renaissance, Enlightenment – are moments of cultural mixing. The 'West' then is itself a collective heritage, an omnivorous *mélange* of cultures; it did not simply absorb non-European influences, as Jon Pietersie points out, 'it was constituted by them.'[4] Western art, then, has always been indebted to and transformed by non-Western art. The movement of aesthetic ideas has been (at least) two-way, hence the Moorish influence on the poetry of courtly love, the African influence on modernist painting, the impact of Asian forms (Kabuki, Noh drama, Balinese theater, ideographic writing) on European theater and film, and the influence of Africanized forms on such choreographers as Martha Graham and George Ballanchine.

The debt of the European avant-gardes to the arts of Africa, Asia, and indigenous America has been extensively documented. Leger, Cendrars, and Milhaud based their staging of *La Création du Monde* on African cosmology. Bataille wrote about pre-Columbian art and Aztec sacrifices. Artaud fled France for the Mexico of the Tarahumara Indians; and the avant-garde generally cultivated the mystique of Vodun and of African art. The British sculptor Henry Moore, in this same vein, modeled his recumbent statues on the Chac Mool stone figures of ancient Mexico. Although it may be true that it was the 'impact of surrealism,' as Roy Armes suggests, 'that liberated the Caribbean and African poets of Negritude from the constraints of a borrowed language,' it was also African and Asian and American indigenous art that liberated the European modernists by provoking them to question their own culture-bound aesthetic of realism.[5]

While a Euro-diffusionist narrative makes Europe a perpetual fountain of artistic innovation, we would argue for a multidirectional flow of aesthetic ideas, with intersecting, criss-crossing ripples and eddies. Indeed, it could be argued that many of the highpoints of Western creativity – the Renaissance, modernism – have been those moments when Europe loses its sealed-off and self-sufficient character; moments when its art was most hybridized, most traversed by currents from elsewhere. European modernism, in this sense, constituted a moment in which non-European cultures became the catalysts for the supersession, within Europe, of a retrograde culture-bound verism, in which Africa, Asia, and the Americas stimulated alternative forms and attitudes.

Nor can one assume that 'avant-garde' always means 'white' and 'European,' nor that non-European art is always realist or pre-modernist.[6] Even the equation of 'reflexivity' with European modernism is questionable. Within the Western tradition reflexivity goes at least as far back as Cervantes and Shakespeare, not to mention Aristophanes. And outside Europe, the Mesoamerican *teoamoxtli* or cosmic books feature *mise-en-abîme* images of deerskin drawn upon the deerskins of which they are made, just as the Mayan *Popol Vuh* 'creates itself in analogy with the world-making it describes or narrates.'[7] African scholars, meanwhile, have discerned common elements in deconstruction and Yoruba *oriki* praise poetry, specifically indeterminacy, intertextuality and constant variability.[8] And for Henry Louis Gates, the Yoruba trickster-figure Eshu-Elegbara emblematizes the deconstructive 'signifying' of African-derived art forms.

Third World cinema too has been rich in avant-garde, modernist, and postmodernist movements. Quite apart from the confluence of Brechtian modernism and Marxist modernization in the 'new cinemas' of Cuba (Alea), Brazil (Guerra), Egypt (Chahine), Senegal (Sembene), and India (Sen), there have been many modernist and avant-garde films in the Third World, going all the way back to films *like São Paulo: Sinfonia de una Cidade* (São Paulo: Symphony of a City, 1928) and *Limite* (1930), both from Brazil, and forward through the Senegalese director Djibril Diop Mambete's *Touki-Bouki* (1973) and, from Mauritania, Med

Hondo's *Soleil O* (1970) and *West Indies* (1975) to the underground movements of Argentina and Brazil, through Kidlat Tahimik's anti-colonialist experiments in the Philippines. The point is not to brandish terms like 'reflexive' or 'deconstructive' or 'postmodern' as honorifics – you see, the Third World is postmodern too! – but rather to set the debates within a relational framework in terms of both space and time.

Our specific goal here is to interrogate the conventional sequencing of realism/modernism/postmodernism by looking at some of the alternative aesthetics offered by Third World, postcolonial, and minoritarian cultural practices: practices that dialogue with Western art movements but which also critique them and in some ways go beyond them. While much recent writing has been devoted to exposing the exclusions and blindnesses of Eurocentric representations and discourses, the actual cultural productions of non-Europeans have been ignored, a neglect which reinscribes the exclusion even while denouncing it, shifting it to another register. Part of the burden of this essay is to reframe the debates about modernism and postmodernism in visual culture by foregrounding certain alternative aesthetics associated with non-European and minoritarian locations. These aesthetics bypass the formal conventions of dramatic realism in favor of such modes and strategies as the carnivalesque, the anthropophagic, the magical realist, the reflexive modernist, and the resistant postmodernist. These aesthetics are often rooted in non-realist, often non-Western or para-Western cultural traditions featuring other historical rhythms, other narrative structures, other views of the body, sexuality, spirituality, and the collective life. Many incorporate non-modern traditions into clearly modernizing or postmodernizing aesthetics, and thus problematize facile dichotomies such as traditional/modern, realist/modernist, and modernist/postmodernist.

These movements have also been fecund in neologistic aesthetics, literary, painterly and cinematic: '*lo real maravilloso americano*' (Carpentier), 'anthropophagy' (the Brazilian Modernists), the 'aesthetics of hunger' (Glauber Rocha), '*Cine imperfecto*' (Julio García Espinosa), 'cigarette-butt aesthetics' (Ousmane Sembene), the 'aesthetics of garbage' (Rogerio Sganzerla), 'Tropicalia' (Gilberto Gil and Caetano Veloso), the 'salamander' (as opposed to the Hollywood dinosaur) aesthetic (Paul Leduc), 'termite terrorism' (Gilhermo del Toro), 'hoodoo aesthetics' (Ishmael Reed), the 'signifying-monkey aesthetic' (Henry Louis Gates), 'nomadic aesthetics' (Teshome Gabriel), 'diaspora aesthetics' (Kobena Mercer), '*rasquachismo*' (Tomas-Ibarra Frausto), and '*santeria* aesthetics' (Arturo Lindsay). Most of these alternative aesthetics revalorize by inversion what had formerly been seen as negative, especially within colonialist discourse. Thus ritual cannibalism, for centuries the very name of the savage, abject other, becomes with the Brazilian modernists an anti-colonialist trope and a term of value. (Even 'magic realism' inverts the colonial view of magic as irrational superstition.) At the same time, these aesthetics share the ju-jitsu trait of turning strategic weakness into tactical strength. By appropriating an existing discourse for their own ends, they deploy the force of the dominant against domination. Here we shall explore just a few of these aesthetics. In each case, we are dealing simultaneously with a trope – cannibalism, carnival, garbage – with an aesthetic movement, and implicitly with a methodological proposal for an alternative model for analyzing visual (multi) culture.

The archaic postmodern

Artistic modernism was traditionally defined in contradistinction to realism as the dominant norm in representation. But outside of the West, realism was rarely the dominant; hence modernist reflexivity as a reaction against realism, could scarcely wield the same power of scandal and provocation. Modernism, in this sense, can be seen as in some ways a rather provincial, local rebellion. Vast regions of the world, and long periods of artistic history, have shown little allegiance to or even interest in realism. Kapila Malik Vatsayan speaks of a very different aesthetic that held sway in much of the world:

> A common aesthetic theory governed all the arts, both performing and plastic, in South and South East Asia. Roughly speaking, the common trends may be identified as the negation of the principle of realistic imitation in art, the establishment of a hierarchy of realities where the principle of suggestion through abstraction is followed and the manifestation in the arts of the belief that time is cyclic rather than linear . . . This tradition of the arts appears to have been pervasive from Afghanistan and India to Japan and Indonesia over two thousand years of history.[9]

In India, a two-thousand year tradition of theater circles back to the classical Sanskrit drama, which tells the myths of Hindu culture through an aesthetic based less on coherent character and linear plot than on the subtle modulations of mood and feeling (*rasa*). Chinese painting, in the same vein, has often ignored both perspective and realism. Much African art, similarly, has cultivated what Robert Farris Thompson calls 'mid-point mimesis,' i.e. a style that avoids both illusionistic realism and hyperabstraction.[10] The censure of 'graven images' in Judeo-Islamic art, finally, cast theological suspicion on directly figurative representation and thus on the very ontology of the mimetic arts. Indeed, it was only thanks to imperialism that mimetic traditions penetrated the Islamic world. As appendages to imperial culture, art schools were founded in places like Istanbul, Alexandria, and Beirut, where the artists of the 'Orient' learned to 'disorient' their art by mimicking Mimesis itself in the form of the veristic procedures of Western art.

Just as the European avant-garde became 'advanced' by drawing on the 'archaic' and 'primitive,' so non-European artists, in an aesthetic version of 'revolutionary nostalgia,' have drawn on the most traditional elements of their cultures, elements less 'pre-modern' (a term that embeds modernity as telos) than 'para-modern.' In the arts, we would argue, the distinction archaic/modernist is often non-pertinent, in the sense that both share a refusal of the conventions of mimetic realism. It is thus less a question of juxtaposing the archaic and the modern than deploying the archaic in order, paradoxically, to modernize, in a dissonant temporality which combines a past imaginary communitas with an equally imaginary future utopia. In their attempts to forge a liberatory language, for example, alternative film traditions draw on para-modern phenomena such as popular religion and ritual magic. In Nigeria, filmmaker Ola Balogun explains, it is less appropriate to speak of 'performing arts' than to speak of 'ritual or folk performances or of communicative arts . . . ceremonies of a social or religious nature into which dramatic elements are incorporated.'[11] In some recent African films such as *Yeelen* (1987), *Jitt* (1992), and *Kasarmu Ce* (This Land Is Ours, 1991), magical spirits become an aesthetic resource, a means for breaking away, often in comical ways, from the linear, cause-and-effect conventions of Aristotelian narrative poetics, a way of defying the 'gravity,' in both senses of that word, of chronological time and literal space.

The values of African religious culture inform not only African cinema but also a good deal of Afro-diasporic cinema, for example Brazilian films like Rocha's *Barravento* (1962) and Cavalcanti's *A Forca de Xango* (The Force of Xango, 1977), *Ogum* (Ogum's Amulet, 1975), Cuban films like *Patakin* and *Ogum*, and African-American films like Julie Dash's *Daughters of the Dust*, all of which inscribe African (usually Yoruba) religious symbolism and practice. Indeed, the preference for Yoruba symbolism is itself significant, since the performing arts are at the very kernel of the Yoruba religions themselves, unlike other religions where the performing arts are grafted on to a theological/textual core. The arts inform the religions in multifaceted ways. The arts – costume, dance, poetry, music – create the appropriate atmosphere for worship. The arts also inform cosmogony and theology. The figure of Olodumare, as creator of the universe, can be seen as the greatest artist, and many of the spirits (*orixás*) are not only artists (Ogum is the patron-deity of all those who work with metals, for example) but they also have artistic tastes. The notion that the classical Greek pantheon is noble and beautiful and at the very roots of Western civilization, while the gods of Africa are merely the vestigal superstitions of a backward people, also belongs in the trashcan of Eurocentric hierarchies. As poetic figures, the *orixás* now play an artistic role in Africa and the diaspora akin to the role of the classical deities of the Greek pantheon within literature, painting and sculpture. We are not here speaking of a discourse of the 'authentic,' but rather of a sophisticated deployment of cultural knowledges. The *orixás* permeate the sculpture of 'Mestre Didi,' the photography of Pierre Verger; the painting of Carybe, the plays of Wole Soyinka, and the music of Olodum, Ile Aiyé, and Timbalada, and recently of Paul Simon and David Byrne. Indeed, Arturo Lindsay speaks of a 'neo-Yoruba' genre of contemporary art.[12]

The question of the contemporary aesthetic implications of ancient African religions illustrates the pitfalls of imposing a linear narrative of cultural 'progress' in the manner of 'development' theory, which sees cultures as mired in an inert, pre-literate 'tradition,' seen as the polar antithesis of a vibrant modernity. Some recent African films scramble this binarism by creating a kind of village or extended family aesthetic which fosters a collective traditional space, but now within an overarching modernist or postmodernist frame. Jean-Pierre Bekolo's *Quartier Mozart* (1992), which portrays a Cameroon neighbourhood (the 'Mozart Quarter' of the title), never sutures us via point-of-view editing into the individual desires of single characters of either gender; sexuality, as in carnival, becomes a quasi-public affair. In the film's 'magical' format, a sorceress (Maman Thekla) helps a schoolgirl, 'Queen of the Hood,' enter the body of a man ('My Guy') in order to explore gendered boundaries. The sorceress takes the shape of 'Panka,' familiar from Cameroonian folklore, who can make a man's penis disappear with a handshake. While the magical devices of *Quartier Mozart* are on one level 'archaic' – in that they translocate traditional folktale motifs into a contemporary setting – the style is allusively postmodern (referring especially to Spike Lee and his witty direct-address techniques), media-conscious (the neighborhood girls prefer Denzel Washington to Michael Jackson) and music-video slick.

Carnivalesque subversions

Another alternative aesthetic, and one that further problematizes the canonical narrativizing of art history, is the tradition of the 'carnivalesque.' Within the standard modernist narrative, the historical avant-gardes represent a radical break with the past, a decisive rupture with the mimetic tradition. In another perspective, however, the historical avant-gardes can be seen as a return to earlier traditions such as the Menippeia and the carnivalesque. As the transposition into art of the spirit of popular festivities, the carnivalesque forms a counter-hegemonic tradition with a history that runs (to speak only of Europe) from Greek Dionysian festivals (and classical Greece, we recall, was an amalgam of African, Asian, and Greek elements) and the Roman saturnalia through the grotesque realism of the medieval 'carnivalesque' (Rabelasian blasphemies, for example) and baroque theater, to Jarry, surrealism, and on to the counter-cultural art of recent decades.

Given the decline of the carnival ethos and the emergence of an individualist society, carnival could no longer be a collective cleansing ritual open to all the people; it became a merely artistic practice, the instrument of a marginalized caste. Carnival shares with the avant-garde its impulse toward social, formal, and libidinal rebellion, but the modernist rebellion could no longer be allied with popular adversary culture. The elimination of carnival as a real social practice led to the development of salon carnivals, compensatory bohemias offering what Allon White calls 'liminoid positions' on the margins of polite society. Thus movements such as expressionism and surrealism took over in displaced form much of the grotesque bodily symbolism and playful dislocations – exiled fragments of the 'carnivalesque diaspora' (White) – which had once formed part of European carnival. Carnival, in this modified form, is present in the provocations of Dada, the dislocations of surrealism, in the hermaphrodytic torsos of Magritte, in the violations of social and cinematic decorum in Buñuel's *L'Âge d'Or*, in the travesty-revolts of Genet's *The Maids* or *The Blacks*, and indeed in the avant-garde generally. In fact, it is in its formal transgressions, and not only in its violations of social decorum, that the avant-garde betrays its link to the perennial rituals of carnival. (And carnival itself, as a counter-institutional mode of cultural production, can be seen as proleptic of the avant-garde.) Thus it is possible to see the more democratizing of the avant-garde movements – we are not speaking here of high-toned autotelic modernism – not so much as decisive breaks with tradition but rather as one of the perennial rediscoveries of the corporeal outrageousness and anti-grammaticality of the upside-down world of the carnivalesque.[13]

Although European real-life carnivals have generally degenerated into the ossified repetition of perennial rituals, it would be Eurocentric to speak of the 'end of carnival' as a resource for artistic renovation. First, nearly all cultures have carnival-like traditions. Among the Navajos (Dineh), special rituals exist for overturning good order and respectable aesthetics. The concept of *rasquachismo* (from Nahuatl) similarly evokes deliberate bad taste and the ludic undermining of norms.[14] For the Hopi, ritual clowns are those who violate conventional expectations in a spirit of gay relativity.[15] Wherever one finds inequities of power, wealth, and status, one also finds a culture of the 'world upside down.' Thus the saturnalia of ancient Rome, carnival in the Caribbean, and the Feast of Krishna in India all translate popular rebelliousness through images of millenarian reversals. Second, in contemporary Latin America and the Caribbean, carnival remains a living, vibrant tradition, where a profoundly mestizo culture builds on indigenous and African traditional festivals to forge an immensely creative cultural phenomenon. It is not surprising, in this sense, that many Latin American theorists have seen the carnivalesque as a key to Latin American artistic production. What was remote and merely metaphoric for European modernism – magic, carnival, anthropophagy – was familiar and quasi-literal for Latin Americans. Indeed, many of the talismanic phrases associated with Latin American art and literature – 'magical realism,' 'quotidian surreality' – not only assert an alternative culture but also suggest the inadequacy of the high mimetic European tradition for the expressive needs of an oppressed but polyphonic culture. It was partly his contact with such festivals, and with Haitian *Vodun*, that led the Cuban writer Alejo Carpentier to contrast the quotidian magic of Latin American life with Europe's labored attempts to resuscitate the marvelous.[16] If the best that Europe can come up with is 'the intersection on a dissecting table of an umbrella and a sewing machine,' Carpentier suggests, the Americas could offer the explosive counterpoints of indigenous, African, and European cultures thrown up daily by Latin American life and art: counterpoints where the tensions are never completely resolved or harmonized, where the cultural dialogue is tense, transgressive, and endlessly surprising. Rather than merely reflect a pre-existing hybridity, the Brazilian cinema (of a Glauber Rocha for example) actively hybridizes, it stages and performs hybridity, counterpointing cultural forces through surprising, even disconcerting juxtapositions. At its best, it orchestrates not a bland pluralism but rather a strong counterpoint between in some ways incommensurable yet nevertheless thoroughly co-implicated cultures.

What Bakhtin calls 'carnivalization' is not an 'external and immobile schema which is imposed upon ready-made content' but 'an extraordinary flexible form of artistic visualization, a peculiar sort of heuristic principle making possible the discovery of new and as yet unseen things.'[17] As theorized by Bakhtin, carnival as an artistic practice transforms into art the spirit of popular festivities, embracing an anticlassical aesthetic that rejects formal harmony and unity in favor of the asymmetrical, the heterogeneous, the oxymoronic, the miscegenated. Carnival's 'grotesque realism' turns conventional aesthetics on its head in order to locate a new kind of popular, convulsive, rebellious beauty: one that dares to reveal the grotesquery of the powerful and the latent beauty of the 'vulgar.' In the carnival aesthetic, everything is pregnant with its opposite, within an alternative logic of permanent contradiction and nonexclusive opposites that transgresses the monologic true-or-false thinking typical of a certain kind of positivist rationalism. Carnival also proposes a very different concept of the body. Instead of an abstract rage against figuration – which Nicholas Mirzoeff sees as encoding hostility to the body itself – carnival proposes a gleefully distorted body of outlandish proportions.[18]

The carnival body is unfinished, elastic, malleable; it outgrows itself, transgresses its own limits and conceives new bodies. Against the static, classic, finished beauty of antique sculpture, carnival counterposes the mutable body, the 'passing of one form into another,' reflecting the 'ever incompleted character of being.'[19] By calling attention to the paradoxical attractiveness of the grotesque body, carnival rejects what might be called the 'fascism of beauty,' the construction of an ideal type or language of beauty in relation to which other types are seen as inferior, 'dialectical' variations.

This is hardly the place to survey the vast repertoire of the cinematic carnivalesque.[20] Suffice it to say that carnival has taken very diverse forms. There are films that literally thematize carnival (*Black Orpheus*, *A Propos de Nice*, *Xica da Silva*); films that anarchize institutional hierarchies (*Born in Flames*); films that foreground the 'lower bodily stratum' (George Kuchar, John Waters); films that favor grotesque realism (*Macunaima*) and anti-grammaticality (Bruce Conner, Rogerio Sganzerla); films that celebrate social and racial inversions (Alea's *The Last Supper*). Brazilian cinema especially has always been deeply impregnated by the cultural values associated with carnival. The '*chanchadas*' or *filmes carnavalescos* (carnivalesque films), the musical comedies popular from the 1930s through the 1950s, were not only released at carnival time but were intended to promote the annual repertory of carnival songs.[21] One *chanchada*, namely *Carnaval Atlantida* (1952) proposes a model of cinema based on sublime debauchery and carnivalesque irony. (Modernist reflexivity is not the special preserve of elite culture; it can also characterize popular and mass-mediated culture.) The film revolves around a Euro-Brazilian film director, Cecilio B. De Milho (Cecil B. De Corn), who finally abandons his plan for an epic production of the story of Helen of Troy. Hollywood-dictated standards, he discovers, with their ostentatious sets and the proverbial cast of thousands, are simply not feasible in a poor, Third World country. Against the overreaching De Milho, other characters argue for a more popular, less lofty adaptation, recommending that the director discard the proposed epic in favor of a carnival film. In one sequence, De Milho explains his conception of *Helen of Troy*. His elitist, grandiose vision is contrasted with the point of view of two Afro-Brazilian studio janitors and aspiring scriptwriters (Cole and Grande Otelo), through whose eyes we move from De Milho's 'scene' to the scene as they imagine it: the black singer Blecaute appears dressed in Greek costume, singing *Dona Cegonha*, a carnival samba written for that year's celebration, accompanied by Grande Otelo tripping over his toga. European themes, then, had to be parodically relocated within the context of Brazilian carnival. '*Helen of Troy* won't work,' De Milho is told, 'the people want to dance and move.' The Hollywood/Greek model is dropped in favor of an Africanized popular culture.

Carnival favors an aesthetic of mistakes, what Rabelais called a *gramatica jocosa* ('laughing grammar') in which artistic language is liberated from the stifling norms of correctedness. Carnivalesque art is thus 'anti-canonical,' it deconstructs not only the canon, but also the generating matrix that makes canons and grammaticality. The concept of 'laughing grammar' reminds one of how black musicians have historically turned 'lowly' materials (washboards, tubs, oil drums) into vibrant musicality, or how jazz artists have stretched the 'normal' capacities of European instruments by playing the trumpet 'higher' than it was supposed to go, by 'hitting two keys, mis-hitting keys (like Monk did), flubbing notes to fight the equipment.'[22] In such cases, the violation of aesthetic etiquette and decorum goes hand in hand with an implicit critique of conventional social and political hierarchies. Arthur Jafa (director of photography for *Daughters of the Dust*) speaks of the cinematic possibilities of 'black visual intonation,' whereby 'irregular, nontempered (nonmetronomic) camera rates and frame replication . . . prompt filmic movement to function in a manner that approximates black vocal intonation,' forging the filmic equivalent of the tendency in black music to 'treat notes as indeterminate, inherently unstable sonic frequencies rather than . . . fixed phenomena.'[23] The possibilities of an 'aesthetic of mistakes' are suggestively evoked in the work of pioneering African-American filmmaker William Greaves. In his reflexive *SymbioPsychoTaxiPlasm – Take One* (filmed in 1967 but still to be commercially released), the filmmaker-in-the-film becomes the catalyst whose very refusal to direct instigates a revolt (devoutly desired by the director) on the part of actors and crew. With the filming of 'Over the Cliff' in Central Park – consisting of endless reshooting of the same scene of marital breakup – as a decoy, the director provokes the crew and cast to film themselves arguing about the director's manipulative refusal to direct. With Miles Davis's *In a Silent Way* on the soundtrack, the film is built, like jazz itself, on signifying 'mistakes': the film runs out, the camera jams, the actors become restless and irritable. The film analogizes jazz's relation to the European mainstream by performing a filmic critique of dominant cinema conventions and subtly evoking, in a *tour de force* of improvisation, multiple resistances and insurgent energies against diverse authoritarianisms and oppressions.

Modernist anthropophagy

Another important aesthetic movement from a non-European location, and one that casts further doubt on linear stagist narratives of artistic progress, is the 'anthropophagic' movement from Brazil, a movement which was self-designated as 'modernist' yet which anticipated aspects of both postmodernity and postcoloniality. The currently fashionable talk of 'hybridity' and 'syncretism,' usually associated with 'postcolonial' theory, elides the fact that artists/intellectuals in Brazil (and the Caribbean) were theorizing hybridity over half a century earlier. The fact that the achievements of Brazilian artists like Oswald de Andrade and Mario de Andrade are not as well known as those of a James Joyce or an Alfred Jarry, has less to do with the originality of their intervention than with the inequitable distribution of artistic laurels around the world, where cultural prestige partially depends on the power of a country and the dissemination of its language. The Brazilian modernists of the 1920s wrote from the 'wrong' location and in the 'wrong' language.

The 'Modern Art Week' held in São Paulo in February 1922 was an attempt by Brazilian poets, musicians, and visual artists to break with the Europhile academicism of the time. The 'Anthropophagy' movement mingled homages to indigenous culture with aesthetic modernism. On one level, artists like Oswald de Andrade and Mario de Andrade qualify as early examples of James Clifford's 'ethnographic surrealism,' with its fascination with the primitive, with the difference that the Brazilian modernists were more 'inside' of the cultures they were investigating. Mario de Andrade's anthropological and musical researches, for example, became a way of probing, with mingled distance and identification, his own roots as an artist of indigenous, African, and European ancestry. The Brazilian movement not only called itself modernism (*modernismo*) but saw itself as allied and conceptually parallel to European avant-garde movements like futurism, Dada and surrealism. In two manifestos – 'Manifesto of Brazilwood Poetry' (1924) and 'Cannibalist Manifesto' (1928) – Oswald de Andrade pointed the way to an artistic practice at once nationalist and cosmopolitan, nativist and modern. In the earlier text, de Andrade called for an 'export-quality' poetry that would not borrow imported 'canned' European models but would find its roots in everyday life and popular culture. Where colonialist discourse had posited the Carib as a ferocious cannibal, as diacritical token of Europe's moral superiority, Oswald called in the 'Cannibalist Manifesto' for a revolution infinitely 'greater than the French revolution,' namely the 'Carib revolution,' without which 'Europe wouldn't even have its meager declaration of the rights of man.'[24] The cannibalist metaphor was also circulated among European avant-gardists; but cannibalism in Europe, as Augusto de Campos points out, never constituted a cultural movement, never defined an ideology, and never enjoyed the profound resonances within the culture that it did in Brazil. Although Alfred Jarry in his *Anthropophagie* (1902) spoke of that '*branche trop negligée de l'anthropophagie*' and in '*L'Almanach du Père Ubu*' addressed himself to '*amateurs cannibals*,' and although the Dadaists entitled one of their organs *Cannibale* and in 1920 Francis Picabia issued the '*Manifeste Cannibale Dada*,' the nihilism of Dada had little to do with what Campos called the 'generous ideological utopia' of Brazilian anthropophagy.[25] Only in Brazil did anthropophagy become a key trope in a longstanding cultural movement, ranging from the first 'Cannibalistic Review' in the 1920s, with its various 'dentitions,' through Oswald de Andrade's speculations in the 1950s on anthropophagy as 'the philosophy of the technicized primitive,' to the pop-recyclings of the metaphor in the tropicalist movement of the late 1960s.

There was, of course, a good deal of concrete interanimation between the Brazilian and European avant-gardes. Blaise Cendrars, Le Corbusier, Marinetti, and Benjamin Peret all went to Brazil, just as Oswald de Andrade, Sergio Millet, Paulo Prado, and other key figures in the Brazilian modernist movement made frequent trips to Europe. The Brazilian modernist painter Tarsila do Amaral studied with Fernand Leger, and she and her husband Oswald numbered Leger, Brancusi, Satie, Cocteau, Breton, Stravinsky, and Milhaud among their close friends. Oswald de Andrade saluted surrealism, in a self-mockingly patronizing and 'stagist' manner, as one of the richest 'pre-anthropophagic' movements. Although anthropophagy 'set its face against the Occident,' according to Andrade, it warmly 'embraces the discontented European, the European nauseated by the farce of Europe.'[26] The exoticizing metaphors of the European avant-garde had a strange way of 'taking flesh' in the Latin American context, resulting in a kind of ironic echo effect between the European and Latin American modernism. When reinvoiced in Brazil, all this became quite concrete and literal. Thus Jarry's 'neglected branch of anthropophagy' came to refer in Brazil to the putatively real cannibalism of the Tupinamba, and surrealist 'trance writing' metamorphosed into the collective trance of Afro-Brazilian religions like *candomble*. Brazilian familiarity with the 'madness' of carnival, with African-derived trance religions, thus made it easy for Brazilian artists to assimilate and transform artistic procedures that in Europe had represented a more dramatic rupture with ambient values and spiritual traditions.

The Brazilian modernists made the trope of cannibalism the basis of an insurgent aesthetic, calling for a creative synthesis of European avant-gardism and Brazilian 'cannibalism,' and invoking an 'anthropophagic' devouring of the techniques and information of the super-developed countries in order the better to struggle against domination. Just as the aboriginal Tupinamba Indians devoured their enemies to appropriate their force, the modernists argued, Brazilian artists and intellectuals should digest imported cultural products and exploit them as raw material for a new synthesis, thus turning the imposed culture back, transformed, against the colonizer. The modernists also called for the 'de-Vespucciazation' of the Americas (the reference is to Amerigo Vespucci) and the 'de-Cabralization' of Brazil (referring to Pedro Cabral, Brazil's Portuguese 'discoverer'). The *Revista de Antropofagia* (Cannibalist Review) laments that Brazilians continue to be 'slaves' to a 'rotting European culture' and to a 'colonial mentality.'[27] At the same time, the notion of 'anthropophagy' assumes the inevitability of cultural interchange between 'center' and 'periphery,' and the consequent impossibility of any nostalgic return to an originary purity. Since there can be no unproblematic recovery of national origins undefiled by alien influences, the artist in the dominated culture should not ignore the foreign presence but must swallow it, carnivalize it, recycle it for national ends, always from a position of cultural self-confidence. (Anthropophagy in this sense is just another name for transcultural intertextuality, this time in the context of asymmetrical power relations.)

As exploited by the Brazilian modernists, the cannibalist metaphor had a negative and a positive pole. The negative pole deployed cannibalism to expose the exploitative social Darwinism of class society. But the positive pole was ultimately more suggestive: radicalizing the Enlightenment valorization of indigenous Amerindian freedom, it highlighted aboriginal matriarchy and communalism as a utopian model. De Andrade wanted to liberate culture from religious mortification and capitalist utilitarianism. Synthesizing insights from Montaigne, Nietzsche, Marx, and Freud, along with what he knew of native Brazilian societies, he portrayed indigenous culture as offering a more adequate social model than the European one, a model based on the full enjoyment of leisure. Playing on the Portuguese word '*negocio*' – 'business,' but literally 'neg-ocio,' or the negation of leisure, de Andrade offered a proto-Marcusean encomium to '*sacer-docio*' or 'sacred leisure.'[28] Here again we find a literalization of the metaphors of the European avant-garde. The Dadaists too had called for 'progressive unemployment' and Breton's surrealist 'rules' had forbidden regular work. Brazilian artist-intellectuals, however, had the advantage of being able to point to existing indigenous societies quite free both from work, in the occidental sense of salaried labor, and from coercive power. And these societies lived not in poverty but in material abundance.

Much later, the modernist movement came to inflect Brazilian cinema through the cultural movement called tropicalism, which emerged in Brazil in the late 1960s. Indeed, a São Paulo art historian recycles cannibalist tropes to suggest that anthropophagy continues to empower artists: 'Brazilian art of the twentieth century is a totemic banquet in which Father-Europe is being devoured.'[29] Like Brazilian modernism (and unlike European modernism), tropicalism fused political nationalism with aesthetic internationalism. Here we will briefly cite just three of the many films influenced by both modernism and tropicalism. Joaquim Pedro de Andrade's *Macunaima* (1969), based on Mario de Andrade's modernist classic, turns the theme of cannibalism into a springboard for a critique of repressive military rule and of the predatory capitalist model of the short-lived Brazilian 'economic miracle.' Nelson Pereira dos Santos *How Tasty Was My Frenchman* (1971) subverts the conventional identification with the European protagonists of captivity narratives by maintaining a neutral and ironic attitude toward the titular Frenchman's deglutition by the Tupinamba. Artur Omar's *Triste Tropico* (1974), finally, also draws on the taproot of anthropophagy. Best defined as a fictive anthropological documentary, the film's title, transparently alluding to Lévi-Strauss's ethnographic memoir about Brazil, triggers an evocative chain of cultural associations. While Lévi-Strauss went from Europe to Brazil only to discover the ethnocentric prejudices of Europe, the protagonist of *Triste Tropico* goes to Europe – and here his trajectory parallels that of innumerable Brazilian intellectuals – only to discover Brazil. Thus the film inserts itself into the ongoing discussion of Brazil's problematic cultural relationship to Europe, a discussion undergoing frequent changes of etiquette: 'indianism,' 'nationalism,' 'modernism,' 'tropicalism.'

Triste Tropico's opening shots – traffic in São Paulo, old family album photographs – lead us to expect a fairly conventional documentary. The off-screen narrator, speaking in the stilted delivery to which canonical documentaries have accustomed us, tells us about a certain Arthur Alvaro de Noronha, known as Dr Artur, who returned from studies in Paris to practice medicine in Brazil. Home-movie footage shows a man with his family; we infer that the man is Dr Artur. In Paris, we are told, the doctor became friendly with André Breton, Paul Eluard, and Max Ernst. This is our first clue that a truly surreal biography awaits us. As the film continues, the narration becomes progressively more improbable and hallucinatory. The doctor becomes involved with Indians, compiles an almanac of herbal panaceas, becomes an indigenous Messiah, and finally degenerates into sodomy (an exclamatory intertitle underlines the horror!) and cannibalism, thus recapitulating the trajectory of a certain body of colonialist literature. The descent of the story into this Brazilian *Heart of Darkness* coincides with our own descent into a tangled jungle of cinematic confusion. For the images gradually detach themselves from the narration, becoming less and less illustrative and more and more disjunctively chaotic. We begin to suspect that we have been the dupes of an immense joke, as if Borges had slyly rewritten Conrad and that the illustrious Dr Artur is merely the figment of the imagination of the director, whose name, we may remember, is also Artur.

The central procedure of *Triste Tropico* is to superimpose an impeccably linear (albeit absurd) narration on extremely discontinuous sounds and images. While the off-screen narration is coherent (within the limits of its implausibility), all the other tracks – image, music, noise, titles – form a serial chaos, an organized delirium of wildly heterogeneous materials: amateur movies, European travel footage, shots of Rio's carnival, staged scenes, archival material, clips from other films, engravings, book covers, almanac illustrations. Within this audio-visual bricolage we encounter certain structured oppositions: some specifically cinematic (black/white versus color; old footage versus new) and some broadly cultural: coast and interior, 'raw' Brazil and 'cooked' Europe; Apollonian order and Dionysian frenzy; *la pensée sauvage* and *la pensée civilisée*, but presented in such a way as to offer what would now be called a postmodern take on structuralism.

The aesthetics of garbage

Another feature of alternative bricolage aesthetics is their common leitmotif of the strategic redemption of the low, the despised, the imperfect, and the 'trashy' as part of a social overturning. This strategic redemption of the marginal also has echoes in the realms of high theory and cultural studies. One thinks, for example, of Derrida's recuperation of the marginalia of the classical philosophical text; of Bakhtin's exaltation of 'redeeming filth' and of low 'carnivalized' genres; of Benjamin's 'trash of history' and his view of the work of art as constituting itself out of apparently insignificant fragments; of Camp's ironic reappropriation of kitsch; of cultural studies' recuperation of subliterary forms and 'subcultural styles'; and of visual culture's democratization of the field of art. In the plastic arts in the US, the 'garbage girls' (Mierle Laderman Ukeles, Christy Rupp, Betty Beaumont) deploy waste disposal as a trampoline for art. Ukeles, for example, choreographed a 'street ballet' of garbage trucks.[30] Joseph Cornell, similarly, turned the flotsam of daily life – broken dolls, paper cutouts, wine glasses, medicine bottles – into luminous, childlike collages. In the cinema, an 'aesthetics of garbage' performs a kind of ju-jitsu by recuperating cinematic waste materials. For filmmakers without great resources, raw-footage minimalism reflects practical necessity as well as artistic strategy. In a film like *Hour of the Furnaces*, unpromising raw footage is transmogrified into art, as the alchemy of sound-image montage transforms the base metals of titles, blank frames, and wild sound into the gold and silver of rhythmic virtuosity. Compilation filmmakers like Bruce Conner, Mark Rappaport, and Sherry Millner/Ernest Larsen rearrange and re-edit pre-existing filmic materials, while trying to fly below the radar of bourgeois legalities. Craig Baldwin, a San Francisco film programmer, reshapes outtakes and public domain materials into witty compilation films. In *Sonic Outlaws*, he and his collaborators argue for a media *détournement* which deploys the charismatic power of dominant media against itself, all the time displaying a royal disregard for the niceties of copyright. Baldwin's anti-Columbus quincentennial film *O No Coronado!* (1992), for example, demystifies the conquistador whose desperate search for the mythical Seven Cities of Cibola led him into a fruitless, murderous journey across what is now the American southwest. To relate this calamitous epic, Baldwin deploys not only his own staged dramatizations but also the detritus of the filmic archive: stock footage, pedagogical films, industrial documentaries, swashbucklers, and tacky historical epics.

In an Afro-diasporic context, the 'redemption of detritus' evokes another, historically fraught strategy, specifically the ways that dispossessed New World blacks have managed to transmogrify waste products into art. The Afro-diaspora, coming from artistically developed African culture but now of freedom, education, and material possibilities, managed to tease beauty out of the very guts of deprivation, whether through the musical use of discarded oil barrels (the steel drums of Trinidad), the culinary use of throwaway parts of animals (soul food, *feijoada*), or the use in weaving of throwaway fabrics (quilting). This 'negation of the negation' also has to do with a special relationship to official history. As those whose history has been destroyed and misrepresented, as those whose very history has been dispersed and diasporized rather than lovingly memorialized, and as those whose history has often been told, danced, and sung rather than written, oppressed people have been obliged to recreate history out of scraps and remnants and debris. In aesthetic terms, these hand-me-down aesthetics and history-making embody an art of discontinuity – the heterogeneous scraps making up a quilt, for example, incorporate diverse styles, time periods and materials – whence their alignment with artistic modernism as an art of jazzy 'breaking' and discontinuity, and with postmodernism as an art of recycling and pastiche.[31]

Eduardo Coutinho's documentary *O Fio da Memoria* (The Thread of Memory, 1991), reflects on the sequels of slavery in Brazil. Instead of history as a coherent, linear narrative, the film offers a history based on disjunctive scraps and fragments. Here the interwoven strands or fragments taken together become emblematic of the fragmentary interwovenness of black life in Brazil. One strand consists of the diary of Gabriel Joaquim dos Saints, an elderly black man who had constructed his own dream house as a work of art made completely out of garbage and detritus: cracked tiles, broken plates, empty cans. For Gabriel, the city of Rio represents the 'power of wealth,' while his house, constructed from the 'city's leftovers,' represents the 'power of poverty.' Garbage thus becomes an ideal medium for those who themselves have been cast off and broken down; who have been 'down in the dumps'; who feel, as the blues line had it, 'like a tin can on that old dumping ground.' A transformative impulse takes an object considered worthless and turns it into something of value. Here the restoration of the buried worth of a cast-off object analogizes the process of revealing the hidden worth of the despised, devalued artist himself.[32] This recuperation of fragments also has a spiritual dimension in terms of African culture. Throughout West and Central Africa, 'the rubbish heap is a metaphor for the grave, a point of contact with the world of the dead.'[33] The broken vessels displayed on Kongo graves, Robert Farris Thompson informs us, serve as reminders that broken objects become whole again in the other world.[34]

At the same time, we witness an example of a strategy of resourcefulness in a situation of scarcity. The trash of the haves becomes the treasure of the have-nots; the dark and unsanitary is transmogrified into the sublime and the beautiful. What had been an eyesore is transformed into a sight for sore eyes. The burned-out light bulb, wasted icon of modern inventiveness, becomes an emblem of beauty. With great improvisational flair, the poor, tentatively literate Gabriel appropriates the discarded products of industrial society for his own recreational purposes, in procedures that inadvertently evoke those of modernism and the avant-garde: the formalists' 'defamiliarization,' the cubists' 'found objects,' Brecht's 'refunctioning,' the situationists' '*détournement*.'

As a diasporized, heterotropic site, the point of promiscuous mingling of rich and poor, center and periphery, the industrial and the artisanal, the organic and the inorganic, the national and the international, the local and the global; as a mixed, syncretic, radically decentered social text, garbage provides an ideal postmodern and postcolonial metaphor. As a place of buried memories and traces, meanwhile, garbage exemplifies what David Harvey calls the 'time–space compression' typical of the acceleration produced by contemporary technologies. In Foucault's terms, garbage is 'heterochronic'; it concentrates time in a circumscribed space. (Archeology, it has been suggested, is simply a sophisticated form of garbology.) As time materialized in space, it is coagulated sociality, a gooey distillation of society's contradictions.

As the quintessence of the negative, garbage can also be an object of artistic ju-jitsu and ironic reappropriation. In aesthetic terms, garbage can be seen as an aleatory collage or surrealist enumeration, a case of the definitive by chance, a random pile of *objets trouvés* and *papiers collés*, a place of violent, surprising juxtapositions.[35] Garbage, like death and excrement, is also a great social leveler; the trysting point of the funky and the chi-chi, the terminus for what Mary Douglas calls 'matter out of place.' As the lower stratum of the socius, the symbolic 'bottom' of the body politic, garbage signals the return of the repressed. It is the place where used condoms, bloody tampons, infected needles, and unwanted babies are left: the ultimate resting place of all that society both produces and represses, secretes and makes secret. The final shot of Buñuel's *Los Olvidados*, we may recall, shows the corpse of the film's lumpen protagonist being unceremoniously dumped on a Mexico City garbage pile. Grossly material, garbage is society's id; it steams and smells below the threshold of ideological rationalization and sublimation. At the same time, garbage is reflective of social prestige; wealth and status are correlated with the capacity of a person (or a society) to discard commodities, i.e. to generate garbage. (The average American discards 5 pounds of garbage per day.) Like hybridity, garbage too is power-laden. The power elite can gentrify a slum, make landfill a ground for luxury apartments, or dump toxic wastes in a poor neighborhood.[36] They can even recycle their own fat from rump to cheek in the form of plastic surgery.

It is one of the utopian, recombinant functions of art to work over dystopian, disagreeable, and malodorous materials. Brazil's *udigrudi* (underground) filmmakers of the late 1960s were the first, to our knowledge, to speak of the 'aesthetics of garbage' (*estetica do lixo*). The valorization of 'sleaze, punk, trash, and garbage' that Jameson posits as characteristic of First World postmodernism, was already present in the palpably grubby 'dirty screens' of the Brazilian movement. (This historical priority confirms the Latin American conviction that Latin America, as a marginalized society caught in a peculiar realm of irony imposed by its neocolonial position, was postmodern *avant la lettre*.) The garbage movement's film manifesto, Sganzerla's *Red Light Bandit* (1968), began with a shot of young *favelados* dancing on burning garbage piles. The films were made in the São Paulo neighborhood called '*boca de lixo*' (mouth of garbage) a red-light district named in diacritical contrast with the high-class, red-light district called '*boca de luxo*' (mouth of luxury). For the underground filmmakers, the garbage metaphor captured the sense of marginality, of being condemned to survive within scarcity, of being the dumping ground for transnational capitalism, of being obliged to recycle the materials of the dominant culture.[37] The title of Eduardo Coutinho's (much later) 'garbage' documentary *Boca de Lixo* (literally 'mouth of garbage', but translated as 'The Scavengers,' 1992) directly links it to the 'aesthetics of garbage,' since its Portuguese title refers to the São Paulo district where the 'garbage' films were produced. The film centers on impoverished Brazilians who survive thanks to a garbage dump outside of Rio, where they toil against the backdrop of the outstretched, ever-merciful arms of the Christ of Corcovado.

Jorge Furtado's *Isle of Flowers* (1989), meanwhile, brings the 'garbage aesthetic' into the postmodern era, while also demonstrating the cinema's capacity as a vehicle for political/aesthetic reflection. Rather than an aestheticization of garbage, here garbage is both theme and formal strategy. Described by its author as a 'letter to a Martian who knows nothing of the earth and its social systems,' Furtado's short uses Monty Python-style animation, archival footage, and parodic/reflexive documentary techniques to indict the distribution of wealth and food around the world. The 'isle of flowers' of the title is a Brazilian garbage dump where famished women and children, in groups of ten, are given five minutes to scrounge for food. But before we get to the garbage dump, we are given the itinerary of a tomato from farm to supermarket to bourgeois kitchen to garbage can to the 'Isle of Flowers.' Furtado's edited collage is structured as a social lexicon or glossary, or better surrealist enumeration of key words such as 'pigs,' 'money,' and 'human beings.' The definitions are interconnected and multi-chronotopic; they lead out into multiple historical frames and historical situations. In order to follow the trajectory of the tomato, we need to know the origin of money: 'Money was created in the seventh century before Christ. Christ was a Jew, and Jews are human beings.' As the audience is still laughing from this abrupt transition, the film cuts directly to the photographic residue of the Holocaust, where Jews, garbage-like, are thrown into death camp piles. (The Nazis, we are reminded, were no strangers to recycling.)

But this summary gives little sense of the experience of the film, of its play with documentary art form and expectations. First, the film's visuals – old TV commercials, newspaper advertisements, healthcare manuals – themselves constitute a kind of throwaway, visual garbage. (In the silent period of cinema, we are reminded, films were seen as transient entertainments rather than artistic durables and therefore as not worth saving; during the First World War they were even recycled for their lead content.) Second, the film mocks the positivist mania for factual detail by offering useless, gratuitous precision: 'We are in Belem Novo, city of Porto Alegre, state of Rio Grande do Sul. More precisely, at 30 degrees, 12 minutes and 30 seconds latitude south, and 51 degrees 11 minutes and 23 seconds longitude west.' Third, the film mocks the protocols of rationalist science, through absurd classificatory schemes ('Dona Anete is a Roman Catholic female biped mammal') and tautological syllogisms ('Mr' Suzuzki is Japanese, and therefore a human being'). Fourth, the film parodies the conventions of the educational film, with its authoritative voice-over and quiz-like questions ('What is a history quiz?'). Humor becomes a kind of trap; the spectator who begins by laughing ends up, if not crying, at least reflecting very seriously. Opposable thumbs and highly developed telencephalon, we are told, have given 'human beings the possibility of making many improvements in their planet', a shot of a nuclear explosion serves as illustration. Thanks to the universality of money, we are told, we are now

'Free!' – a snippet of the 'Hallelujah Chorus' celebrates the thought. Furtado invokes the old carnival motif of pigs and sausage, but with a political twist; here the pigs, given equitable distribution down the food chain, eat better than people.[38] The tomato links the urban bourgeois family to the rural poor via the sausage and the tomato within a web of global relationality. In this culinary recycling, we are given a social examination of garbage; the truth of a society is in its detritus. The socially peripheral points to the symbolically central.

In all these films, the garbage dump becomes a critical vantage point from which to view society as a whole. The garbage dump shows the endpoint of an all-permeating logic of commodification, logical telos of the consumer society, and its ethos of planned obsolescence. Garbage becomes the morning after of the romance of the new. In the dump's squalid phantasmagoria, the same commodities that had been fetishized by advertising, dynamized by montage, and haloed through backlighting, are now stripped of their aura of charismatic power. We are confronted with the seamy underside of globalization and its facile discourse of one world under a consumerist groove. Garbage reveals the social formation as seen 'from below.' As the overdetermined depot of social meanings, garbage is the place where hybrid, multi-chronotopic relations are reinvoiced and reinscribed. Polysemic and multivocal, garbage is seen literally (garbage as a source of food for poor people, garbage as the site of ecological disaster), but it is also read symptomatically, as a metaphorical figure for social indictment (poor people treated like garbage; garbage as the 'dumping' of pharmaceutical products or of 'canned' TV programs; slums (and jails) as human garbage dumps). These films reveal the 'hidden transcripts' of garbage, reading it as an allegorical text to be deciphered, a form of social colonics where the truth of a society can be 'read' in its waste products.

Towards a polycentric visual culture

The visual, in our view, never comes 'pure,' it is always 'contaminated' by the work of other senses (hearing, touch, smell), touched by other texts and discourses, and imbricated in a whole series of apparatuses – the museum, the academy, the art world, the publishing industry, even the nation state – which govern the production, dissemination, and legitimation of artistic productions. It is not now a question of replacing the blindnesses of the 'linguistic turn' with the 'new' blindnesses of the 'visual turn.' To hypostasize the visual risks of reinstalling the hegemony of the 'noble' sense of sight (etymologically linked to wisdom in many languages) over hearing and the more 'vulgar' senses of smell and taste. The visual, we would argue, is 'languaged,' just as language itself has a visual dimension. Methodological grids, or 'new objects of knowledge,' furthermore, do not supersede one another in a neat, clear-cut progression. They do not become extinct within a Darwinian competition. They do not die; they transform themselves, leaving traces and reminiscences. The visual is also an integral part of a culture and of history, not in the sense of a static backdrop (rather like second unit background footage in a Hollywood matte shot), but rather as a complexly activating principle. The visual is simply one point of entry, and a very strategic one at this historical moment, into a multidimensional world of intertextual dialogism.

We have called here for a polycentric, dialogical, and relational analysis of visual cultures existing in relation to one another. We have tried to project one set of histories across another set of histories, in such a way as to make diverse cultural experiences concurrent and relatable within a logic of co-implication. Within a polycentric approach, the world of visual culture has many dynamic locations, many possible vantage points. The emphasis in 'polycentrism' is not on spatial or primary points of origins or on a finite list of centers but rather on a systematic principle of differentiation, relationality, and linkage. No single community or part of the world, whatever its economic or political power, should be epistemologically privileged.

We do not see polycentrism as a matter of first defining modernism as a set of attributes or procedures, and then 'finding' these attributes in the cultural productions from other locations. It is not a matter of 'extending the corpus' or 'opening up the canon' in an additive approach, but rather of rethinking the global relationalities of artistic production and reception. For us, art is born *between* individuals and communities and cultures in the process of dialogic interaction. Creation takes place not within the suffocating confines of Cartesian egos or even between discrete bounded cultures but rather between permeable, changing communities. Nor is it a question of a mindless 'anthropological' leveling which denies all criteria of aesthetic evaluation but rather of historically grounded analyses of multicultural relationality, where one history is read contrapuntally across another in a gesture of mutual 'haunting' and reciprocal relativization.

Our larger concern has been not to establish priority – who did what first – but rather to analyze what mobilizes change and innovation in art. It has become a commonplace to speak of the exhaustion (and sometimes of the co-optation) of the avant-garde in a world where all the great works have already been made. But in our view aesthetic innovation arises, not exclusively but importantly, from multicultural knowledges. It emerges from the encounter of a Picasso with African sculpture for example; from the comings and goings between Europe and Latin America of an Alejo Carpentier; from the encounter of a Rushdie with the West; from the encounter of a Mario de Andrade simultaneously with surrealism, on the one hand, and Amazonian legend on the other. Innovation occurs on the borders of cultures, communities, and disciplines. 'Newness enters the world,' according to Salman Rushdie, through 'hybridity, impurity, intermingling, the transformation that comes of new and unexpected combinations of human beings, ideas, politics, movies, songs [from] . . . Melange, hotchpotch, a bit of this and a bit of that.'[39]

Central to a truly polycentric vision is the notion of the mutual and reciprocal relativization, the 'reversibility of perspectives' (Merleau-Ponty); the idea that the diverse cultures should come to perceive the limitations of their own social and cultural perspective. Each group offers its own exotopy (Bakhtin), its own 'excess seeing,' hopefully coming not only to 'see' other groups, but also, through a salutary estrangement, to see how it is itself seen. The point is not to embrace completely the other perspective but at least to recognize it, acknowledge it, take it into account, be ready to be transformed by it. By counterpointing embodied cultural perspectives, we cut across the monocular and monocultural field of what Donna Haraway has characterized as 'the standpoint of the master, the Man, the One God, whose Eye produces, appropriates and orders all difference.'[40] At the same time, historical configurations of power and knowledge generate a clear asymmetry within this relativization. The culturally empowered are not accustomed to being relativized; the world's institutions and representations are tailored to the measure of their narcissism. Thus a sudden relativization by a less flattering perspective is experienced as a shock, an outrage, giving rise to a hysterical discourse of besieged standards and desecrated icons. A polycentric approach, in our view, is a long-overdue gesture toward historical equity and lucidity, a way of re-envisioning the global politics of visual culture.

Notes

1 We do not equate 'European' with 'Eurocentric,' any more than feminism equates 'masculine' with 'phallocentric.' The term 'Eurocentric' does not have to do with origins but with epistemologies. See Robert Stam and Ella Shohat, *Unthinking Eurocentrism: Multiculturalism and the Media*, London: Routledge, 1994.

2 See Carl Pletsch, 'The Three Worlds, or the Division of Social Scientific Labor, circa 1950–1970,' *Comparative Studies in Society and History*, vol. XXIII, no. 4 (1981), pp. 565–90.

3 Fredric Jameson, *The Geopolitical Aesthetic: Cinema and Space in the World System*, Bloomington and London: Indiana University Press and British Film Institute, 1992, p. 1.

4 Jan Pietersie, 'Unpacking the West: How European is Europe?' Unpublished paper given to us by the author.

5 See Roy Armes, *Third World Filmmaking and the West*, Berkeley: University of California Press, 1987.

6 We have in mind both the 'Third World allegory' essay and *The Geopolitical Aesthetic*.

7 See Brotherston, *Book of the Fourth World*, p. 48.

8 See Karin Barber, 'Yoruba Oriki and Deconstructive Criticism,' *Research in African Literature*, vol. 15, no. 4 (Winter 1984).

9 Quoted in Armes, op. cit., p. 135.

10 See Robert Farris Thompson, *African Art in Motion: Icon and Act*, Berkeley: University of California Press, 1973.

11 Ola Balogun, 'Traditional Arts and Cultural Development in Africa,' *Cultures*, no. 2, 1975, p. 159.

12 See Arturo Lindsay, *Santería Aesthetics in Contemporary Latin American Art*, Washington and London: Smithsonian, 1996, Preface, p. xx. For more on representations of Afro-Brazilian religions in Brazilian art, see Robert Stam, *Tropical Multiculturalism: A Comparative History of Race in Brazilian Cinema and Culture*, Durham: Duke University Press, 1997.

13 For more on carnival, see Mikhail Bakhtin, *Rabelais and His World*, trans. Helene Iswolsky, Cambridge, Mass.: MIT Press, 1968. See Robert Stam, *Subversive Pleasures: Bakhtin, Cultural Criticism, and Film*, Baltimore: Johns Hopkins University Press, 1989.

14 Lucy Lippard, *Mixed Blessings: New Art in a Multicultural Age*, New York: Pantheon, 1990, p. 201.

15 Ibid., p. 202.

16 See Alejo Carpentier, 'De lo Real Maravilloso Americano,' *Cine Cubano*, no. 102, (1982), pp. 12–14.
17 Mikhail Bakhtin, *Problems of Dostoevsky's Poetics*, trans. Caryl Emerson, Minneapolis: University of Minnesota Press, 1984, p. 166.
18 See Nicholas Mirzoeff, *Bodyscape: Art, Modernity, and the Ideal Figure*, London: Routledge, 1995.
19 Bakhtin, *Rabelais*, p. 32.
20 See Robert Stam, *Subversive Pleasures: Bakhtin, Cultural Criticism and Film*, Baltimore: Johns Hopkins University Press, 1989.
21 See Joao Luiz Vieira, *Hegemony and Resistance: Parody and Carnival in Brazilian Cinema*, PhD dissertation, New York University, 1984. See also Joao Luiz Vieira and Robert Stam, 'Parody and Marginality,' in Manuel Alvarado and John O. Thompson (eds) *The Media Reader*, London: British Film Institute, 1989.
22 Arthur Jaffa, in Gina Dent (ed.) *Black Popular Culture*, p. 266.
23 Ibid., pp. 249–54.
24 For an English version of the 'Cannibalist Manifesto,' see Leslie Bary's excellent introduction to and translation of the poem in *Latin American Literary Review*, vol. XIX, no. 38 (July–December 1991).
25 Augusto de Campos, *Poesia, Antipoesia, Antropofagia*, São Paulo: Cortez e Moraes, 1978, p. 121.
26 See Maria Eugenia Boaventura, *A Vanguarda Antropofagica*, São Paulo: Attica, 1985, p. 114.
27 For more on modernist 'anthropophagy,' see Robert Stam, 'Of Cannibals and Carnivals,' in R. Stam, *Subversive Pleasures*, op. cit.
28 See Pierre Clastres, *Society Against the State*, New York: Zone Books, 1987.
29 See Paulo Herkenhoff, 'Having Europe for Lunch: A Recipe for Brazilian Art,' *Polyester*, vol. II, no. 8 (Spring) 1984.
30 See Lucy Lippard, 'The Garbage Girls,' *in The Pink Glass Swan: Selected Feminist Essays on Art*, New York: The New Press, 1995.
31 The African-American environmental artist known as 'Mr Imagination' has created 'bottle-cap thrones, paintbrush people, cast-off totems, and other pieces salvaged from his life as a performing street artist.' See Charlene Cerny and Suzanne Seriff (eds) *Recycled Reseen: Folk Art from the Global Scrap Heap*, New York: Harry N. Abams, 1996.
32 My formulation obviously both echoes and Africanizes the language of Fredric Jameson's well-known essay 'Third World Literature in the Era of Multinational Capitalism,' *Social Text*, no. 15 (Fall) 1986.
33 See Wyatt MacGaffey, 'The Black Loincloth and the Son of Nzambi Mpungu,' in *Forms of Folklore in Africa: Narrative, Poetic, Gnomic, Dramatic*, Austin: University of Texas Press, 1977, p. 78.
34 See Robert Farris Thompson and Joseph Cornet, *The Four Moments of the Sun: Kongo Art in Two Worlds*, Washington: National Gallery, 1981, p. 179.
35 For a survey of recycled art from around the world, see Charlene Cerny and Suzanne Seriff, *Recycled, Reseen: Folk Art from the Global Scrap Heap*, New York: Abrams, 1996.
36 For more on the discourse of garbage, see Michael Thompson, *Rubbish Theory: The Creation and Destruction of Value*, Oxford: Oxford University Press, 1979; Judd H. Alexander, *In Defense of Garbage*, Westport, Conn.: Praeger, 1993; William Rathje and Cullen Murphy, *Rubbish! The Archeology of Garbage*, New

York: Harper Collins, 1992; and Katie Kelly, *Garbage: The History and Future of Garbage in America*, New York: Saturday Review Press, 1973.

37 Ismail Xavier, *Allegories of Underdevelopment: From the 'Aesthetics of Hunger' to the 'Aesthetics of Garbage'*, PhD dissertation, New York University, 1982.

38 The pig, as Peter Stallybrass and Allon White point out, was despised for its specific habits: 'its ability to digest its own and human faeces as well as other "garbage", its resistance to full domestication; its need to protect its tender skin from sunburn by wallowing in the mud.' See *The Politics and Poetics of Transgression*, Ithaca: Cornell University Press, 1986.

39 See Salman Rushdie, 'In Good Faith: A Pen against the Sword,' *Newsweek*, 12 Feb. 1990, p. 52. Interestingly, Europe itself has begun to recognize the artistic value of these hybrid cultures. It is no accident, in this sense, that Nobel Prizes in literature are now going to postcolonial and minority writers, or that the most recent Cannes Film Festival accorded special honors to the Egyptian Chahine and the Iranian Kiorostami.

40 See Donna Haraway, 'Situated Knowledges: The Science Question in Feminism and the Privilege of Partial Perspective,' in Andrew Feenberg and Alastair Hannay (eds), *Technology and the Politics of Knowledge*, Bloomington: Indiana University Press, 1995, p. 184.

PART ONE

A genealogy of visual culture: from art to culture

Introduction to part one

■ Nicholas Mirzoeff

THIS PART PRESENTS a selection of the best pioneering work over the last fifteen years that has led to the emergence of a field of intellectual enquiry known as visual culture. There are of course many possible ways to tell this story. (This section could well be read in conjunction with part five, section (a) on the gaze and sexuality, which concentrates on film and medical imaging.) Here I have chosen to show how a critical examination of vision itself and its representation in art history has led to a significant shift in methodology in the past decade. For even this conservative visual discipline has moved beyond the standard disciplinary boundaries to the consideration of art in relation to culture and as culture. The rethinking of vision has led different art historians and critics to a gradually expanding range of interdisciplinary contacts from philosophy to feminist and gender studies and anthropology. For while the biology of vision has no doubt remained more or less constant, different cultures and societies have given greatly different emphasis to the resulting perception. There is a risk that such study simply ends up reiterating what past generations have mistakenly thought about the operations of the eye, which, while amusing and conducive to an appropriate realization of the fallibility of that named as science, is not necessarily very productive. At some point in this process it became apparent that what was in fact needed was a new interdisciplinary subject based on vision and its representations, in other words visual culture.

The first excerpt is from the founding text of modern Western visual studies. René Descartes' *Discourse on the Method* (1637). It is common in continental Europe to see Descartes' work as marking the beginning of modernity. It was certainly the inception of a modern notion of vision and its central place in modern society. For Descartes turned a very sceptical eye to the received truths of medieval and early modern philosophy and found himself unable to go further than his famous principle: 'I think therefore I am.' Even this formula depended upon two unprovable assertions: that the thinker was not insane and that God, who created humanity, did not lie. As a demonstration of his method, Descartes turned to optics, or the study of vision, a key area of medieval scholastic theology. For light was held to be the means by which God revealed himself to humanity and was thus in itself divine. Western thinkers had made little progress in understanding the operations of light and vision because they did not consider the question to be important. They were even uncertain as to whether vision occurred from the entry of something into the eye or as a result of the eye itself emitting rays. The favoured notion was that objects emitted 'intentional essences': copies of themselves that decreased in size until they entered the eye. How then, philosophers wondered, was it possible to see very large, distant or close-up objects? On a more everyday level, artisans had discovered as early as the twelfth century that lenses could aid eyesight but no one knew why they worked and so there was no possibility of refining this knowledge.

Descartes simply brought light down to earth by considering it to be a material element, rather than a manifestation of the divine. In a few elegant pages he demonstrated that the rays of light were refracted by the lens of the eye to form an inverted image on the retina, and stated the inverse sine law that allows refraction to be calculated from the angle of incidence with the lens. It now became clear that the tiny upside-down image created by the eye had nothing to do with the object seen and that it was the mind – or the soul, as Descartes put it – that interprets the retinal image. In opening up a gap between the observer and the observed, Descartes made possible modern observational science, which seeks to produce results that can be recreated by a separate observer.

Until recently it was also assumed that Descartes' philosophy, combined with the Renaissance geometry of one-point perspective, formed the fundamental basis for all modern visual representation and interpretations of vision. However, this 'Cartesian perspectivalism' as Martin Jay calls it, was at best a mixed marriage. For Renaissance perspective used exactly those medieval theories of vision that Descartes had just proved wrong, creating a visual pyramid in order that the 'intentional essences' could enter the eye. The point of this pyramid was thus to be located at the eye of the spectator, giving one-point perspective its name. Descartes himself contributed to this confusion of models, for he noted that the retinal image was formed in accordance with the rules of perspective, suggesting that these were in fact natural laws. At the same time, he showed that in order to represent an object in an engraving using perspective, it was necessary to distort its real appearance:

> In accordance with the rules of perspective [engravings] often represent circles by ovals better than by other circles, squares by rhombuses better than other squares, and similarly for other shapes. Thus it often happens that in order to be more perfect as an image and to represent an object better, an engraving ought not to resemble it.

Descartes was aware that perspective was a representational code that Erwin Panofsky later called a 'symbolic form', but also saw that code as having a place in the natural world.

It is this awareness of the conventional nature of representation that has attracted modern commentators on Descartes, while previous generations placed greater emphasis on his founding of mathematical descriptions of the natural world. In his ground-breaking essay excerpted in this volume, Martin Jay took these arguments a stage further to suggest that there was no single modern mode of vision, which he calls 'scopic regimes', but several: 'the scopic regime of modernity may best be understood as a contested terrain, rather than as a harmoniously integrated complex of visual theories and practices' (Jay 1988). He emphasizes that Cartesian perspectivalism did not produce the definitive truth about sight and its representation but one highly influential mode of representing vision, the visual grid: 'This new concept of space was geometrically isotropic, rectilinear, abstract and uniform. The *velo* or veil of threads Alberti used to depict it conventionalized space in a way that anticipated the grids so characteristic of twentieth-century art'. The difference is that Renaissance artists believed that the triangular receding space produced by perspective was a representation of how the eye actually saw, whereas modern artists who made use of the grid, like Piet Mondrian, did so because they knew it was abstract.

In his analysis of the rhetoric of the image reprinted here, the French literary critic Roland Barthes had added a third term to the debate over representation (Barthes 1977). In his earlier structuralist work, Barthes had concentrated on dividing signs into two halves – the signifier, that which is seen, and the signified, that which is meant. In this essay he refined his analysis to look at the different ways in which meaning can be derived from a sign. Looking at an advertisement for pasta sauce, Barthes shows that the name of the sauce '*Panzani* gives not simply the name of the firm but also, but its assonance, an additional signified, that of "Italianicity"'. The first meaning is referential, the second more allusive. Barthes called them 'denotational' and 'connotational' respectively. Beyond these linguistic messages that the advertiser hopes to convey, Barthes notes that there is still the element that he called 'pure image' in the scene. This element is neither connotational nor denotational but is in fact a 'message without a code', that is to say, at one level the objects simply are what they are and cannot be reduced any further. Barthes's semiology – the science of signs – offered a practical means to analyse the complex ways in which visual representation both creates meaning and has emotional impact.

In her classic book *Vision and Difference*, art historian Griselda Pollock put sign analysis within the perspective of gender (Pollock 1988). She calls our attention to the ways in which the modern grid of visual representation claims to be an abstraction but is in fact fundamentally structured by gender. While the imagined viewer of one-point perspective had usually been depicted as a man, such gendered distinctions became far more rigid in the nineteenth century. Looking at the famous depictions of women by impressionist painters like Edouard Manet, which so often deal with sexuality and its commercial exchange, Pollock asks:

'How can a woman relate to the viewing positions proposed [by] these paintings?' In order to find an historically accurate answer, she analyses the viewpoint of the nineteenth-century poet Charles Baudelaire, who exalted the dandy or *flâneur* as, in his words, 'as prince [who] everywhere rejoices in his incognito'. The ideal viewer of the perspectival pyramid was now the anonymous male figure passing unrecognized through the crowds of the modern city. The primary object of his gaze was modern women, divided into two categories, the 'lady' and the 'fallen woman'. The 'lady' was seen at the theatre and in parks, whereas the 'fallen woman' could be seen backstage, in bars and cafés and of course in brothels. Women and women artists were supposed to look only within those sections designated ladylike. In theory, then, 'the gaze of the *flâneur* articulates and produces a masculine sexuality, which in the modern sexual economy, enjoys the freedom to look, appraise and possess'. Since Pollock's work was first published both she and other writers have come to describe ways in which women were able to enjoy the pleasures of looking and representing. Like the psychoanalytic theorizing of film spectatorship that was so influential in the 1970s and 1980s (see part five), however, Pollock introduced important ways of thinking of the visual grid or pyramid as gendered.

Carol Duncan continued this line of analysis in looking at the display of modern art in the museum, specifically New York's Museum of Modern Art (Duncan 1995). Due to its iconic status in the modern art world, MoMA is more than just another museum – it has become part of the definition of modern art itself. Duncan analyses how MoMA's displays facilitate the male viewpoint described by Griselda Pollock. She shows how two depictions of women by male artists – Picasso's *Les Demoiselles d'Avignon* and Willem de Kooning's *Woman I* – 'masculinize museum space with great efficiency'. Drawing iconographic comparisons between *Woman I* and sculptures of the Gorgon, as well as the stereotyped poses of pornography, Duncan shows how modern art seeks to experience the 'dangerous realm of woman–matter–nature and symbolically to escape it into male–culture–enlightenment'. Partly as a result of such criticism the display at MoMA has been drastically altered since her essay first appeared, now even finding room for contemporary women artists like Cindy Sherman. Duncan's landmark essay was part of a movement towards institutional critique that has had considerable impact on artists, critics and curators alike. It is now sufficiently well accepted that some museums, like the National Museum of the American Indian, incorporate it into their display techniques. The visitor to NMAI is offered the comments of a museum professional, an anthropologist and a member of the people who made the object under discussion without any attempt to resolve the differing points of view. That decision is up to the spectator.

It is no coincidence that a discussion of the gendering of modernism leads to that of non-Western art. For Baudelaire, the fallen woman was 'the perfect image of the savagery that lurks at the heart of civilization'. Picasso tried to visualize this heart of darkness in his *Les Demoiselles d'Avignon* by giving the women faces drawn from Egyptian art and African masks. As Duncan remarks, 'in this context, the use of African art constitutes not an homage to "the primitive" but a means of framing woman as "other"'. It was also a crucial part of modern Western culture that it collected and displayed objects from 'primitive' cultures in ethnographic museums. In this excerpt from his acclaimed book, *The Predicament of Culture*, James Clifford argues that this fascination with collecting the objects of other peoples was never motivated by respect for such work but was always about defining the Western self as acquisitive and possessive (Clifford 1988). He points out many contradictions within the classifying systems used to distinguish 'art' from 'souvenirs' and 'ethnographic artefacts': 'Cultural or artistic "authenticity" has as much to do with an inventive present as with a past, its objectification, preservation or revival'.

Clifford refuses to separate 'Western' and 'non-Western' visual culture and instead arranges them into a symbiotic grid of his own that cuts a slice across the Western visual pyramid. In what he calls the art-culture system, the meaning of Western art is dependent on its being distinguished from non-Western culture. Both are also distinguished from their negatives, such as commercial reproductions in the case of art. If non-Western objects are sufficiently admired, like Benin bronzes or Ming vases, they can be transferred to the 'art' side without disturbing the system. Further, Clifford suggests that it is possible for art to move towards the culture side, as has happened at the Paris Musée d'Orsay, where the Impressionist art discussed by Griselda Pollock has been arranged 'in the panorama of a historical-cultural "period"'. Clifford's analysis suggests that the often-repeated need to contextualize museum objects with what Duncan calls 'different, more complex, and possibly even multiple scenarios that could build on a broader range of human experience' is a possibility already envisaged by the art-culture system. His insight can be applied to other aspects of visual culture. Many critics disparage the mass culture of Hollywood films, while praising the independent film sector. Likewise television is widely condemned by intellectuals with appropriate exceptions being made for documentaries and programmes on the arts. In Clifford's view, these seeming alternatives are really interdependent; they are two sides of the same visual system of representation. By trying to exclude certain objects as mere culture while exalting others as art, traditional criticism finds itself endlessly repeating the terms of this binary opposition, so characteristic of modernism.

Visual culture has developed as a means of trying to move beyond this impasse. The earlier elements of analysis are still important – analysis of the visual, sign analysis, gender, class and race – but they now need to be put into a different framework. One critic who has offered such a framework is Paul Virilio (Virilio 1989; 1994). Whereas the essays cited above have their point of departure in one of the traditional disciplines, such as art history or anthropology, Virilio looks at the visual in and of itself. In this extract from his unique book, *The Vision Machine*, the key elements are not objects – whether artistic or cultural – but attributes, especially light, movement and speed. He is as likely to discuss the seventeenth-century police lieutenant La Reynie, whose invention of lighting inspectors known as impressionists made Paris into the 'city of light', as the more familiar figures like Edgar Degas associated with that name. Leaving aside the static forms of the grid and the sign, Virilio sees modernity as a constant 'acceleration in the transmission of messages'. For him, the key engine of change is war. He argues that the trauma of the First World War was

> the moment of panic when the mass of Americans and Europeans could no longer believe their eyes, when their *faith in perception* became slave to the faith in the technical sightline: in other words, the visual field was reduced to the line of fire.
>
> (Virilio 1994: 16–17)

The famous film of the 'smart' weapons descending on their targets during the Gulf War represents the highest stage of this substitution of targeting for perception. Much excitement has surrounded the invention of virtual reality but in this context, it should be remembered that it was first developed to simulate battlefield conditions. Virilio thus argues that the crisis that has been called postmodernism is not 'the death of God, of man, of art, and so on . . . What has in fact happened was simply the progressive disintegration of a faith in perception'. His aphoristic style and wide-ranging scope may not convince everyone and it would be hard to agree with all his assertions. None the less Virilio's work offers one possible way out of the art–culture maze towards a new understanding of the visual culture in which we live. More importantly, his dazzling work shows how productive it can be to step outside the disciplinary frameworks that prescribe what objects should be looked at and how in order to simply ask: what am I looking at and why?

References and further reading

Barthes, Roland (1977) *Image-Music-Text*, New York: Noonday.

—— (1981) *Camera Lucida*, New York: Noonday.

Bordo, Susan (1987) *The Flight to Objectivity: Essays on Cartesianism and Culture*, Albany: SUNY Press.

Clifford, James (1988) *The Predicament of Culture: Twentieth-Century Literature, Ethnography and Art*, Cambridge, Mass.: Harvard University Press.

Damisch, Hubert (1994) *The Origins of Perspective*, Cambridge, Mass.: MIT Press.

Duncan, Carol (1995) *Civilizing Rituals: Inside Public Art Museums*, London: Routledge.

Foster, Hal (ed.) (1988) *Vision and Visuality*, Seattle: Bay Press.

Jay, Martin (1988) 'The Scopic Regimes of Modernity', in H. Foster (ed.) *Vision and Visuality*, Seattle: Bay Press.

—— (1993) *Downcast Eyes: The Denigration of Vision in Twentieth-Century French Thought*, Berkeley: University of California.

Kemp, Martin (1990) *The Science of Art: Optical Themes in Western Art from Brunelleschi to Seurat*, New Haven: Yale University Press.

Lindberg, David C. (1976) *Theories of Vision from al-Kindi to Kepler*, Chicago: University of Chicago Press.

Pollock, Griselda (1988) *Vision and Difference: Femininity, Feminism and Histories of Art*, London: Routledge.

Virilio, Paul (1989) *War and Cinema: the Logistics of Perception*, Bloomington: Indiana University Press.

—— (1994) *The Vision Machine*, Bloomington: Indiana University Press.

Wallis, Brian (ed.) (1984) *Art after Modernism: Rethinking Representation*, New York: New Museum of Contemporary Art.

Chapter 4

René Descartes

OPTICS

Discourse One: Light

THE CONDUCT OF our life depends entirely on our senses, and since sight is the noblest and most comprehensive of the senses, inventions which serve to increase its power are undoubtedly among the most useful there can be. And it is difficult to find any such inventions which do more to increase the power of sight than those wonderful telescopes which, though in use for only a short time, have already revealed a greater number of new stars and other new objects above the earth than we had seen there before. Carrying our vision much further than our forebears could normally extend their imagination, these telescopes seem to have opened the way for us to attain a knowledge of nature much greater and more perfect than they possessed . . . But inventions of any complexity do not reach their highest degree of perfection right away, and this one is still sufficiently problematical to give me cause to write about it. And since the construction of the things of which I shall speak must depend on the skill of craftsmen, who usually have little formal education, I shall try to make myself intelligible to everyone; and I shall try not to omit anything, or to assume anything that requires knowledge of other sciences. This is why I shall begin by explaining light and light-rays; then, having briefly described the parts of the eye, I shall give a detailed account of how vision comes about; and, after noting all the things which are capable of making vision more perfect, I shall show how they can be aided by the inventions which I shall describe.

Now since my only reason for speaking of light here is to explain how its rays enter into the eye, and how they may be deflected by the various bodies they encounter, I need not attempt to say what is its true nature. It will, I think, suffice if I use two or three comparisons in order to facilitate that conception of light which seems most suitable for explaining all those of its properties that we know through experience and for then deducing all the other properties that we cannot observe so easily. In this I am imitating the astronomers, whose suppositions are almost all false or uncertain, but who nevertheless draw many very true and certain consequences from them because they are related to various observations they have made.

No doubt you have had the experience of walking at night over rough ground without a light, and finding it necessary to use a stick in order to guide yourself. You may then have been able to notice that by means of this stick you could feel the various objects situated around you, and that you could even tell whether they were trees or stones or sand or water or grass or mud or any other such thing. It is true that this kind of sensation is somewhat confused and obscure in those who do not have long practice with it. But consider it in those born blind, who have made use of it all their lives: with them, you will find, it is so perfect and so exact that one might almost say that they see with their hands, or that their stick is the organ of some sixth sense given to them in place of sight. In order to draw a comparison from this, I would have you consider the light in bodies we call 'luminous' to be nothing other than a certain movement, or very rapid and lively action, which passes to our eyes through the medium of the air and other transparent bodies, just as the movement or resistance of the bodies encountered by a blind man passes to his hand by means of his stick. In the first place this will prevent you from finding it strange that this light can extend its rays instantaneously from the sun to us. For you know that the action by which we move one end of a stick must pass instantaneously to the other end, and that the action of light would have to pass from the heavens to the earth in the same way, even though the distance in this case is much greater than that between the ends of a stick. Nor will you find it strange that by means of this action we can see all sorts of colours. You may perhaps even be prepared to believe that in the bodies we call 'coloured' the colours are nothing other than the various ways in which the bodies receive light and reflect it against our eyes. You have only to consider that the differences a blind man notices between trees, rocks, water and similar things by means of his stick do not seem any less to him than the differences between red, yellow, green and all the other colours seem to us. And yet in all those bodies the differences are nothing other than the various ways of moving the stick or of resisting its movements. Hence you will have reason to conclude that there is no need to suppose that something material passes from objects to our eyes to make us see colours and light, or even that there is something in the objects which resembles the ideas or sensations that we have of them. In just the same way, when a blind man feels bodies, nothing has to issue from the bodies and pass along his stick to his hand; and the resistance or movement of the bodies, which is the sole cause of the sensations he has of them, is nothing like the ideas he forms of them. By this means, your mind will be delivered from all those little images flitting through the air, called 'intentional forms',[1] which so exercise the imagination of the philosophers. You will even find it easy to settle the current philosophical debate concerning the origin of the action which causes visual perception. For, just as our blind man can feel the bodies around him not only through the action of these bodies when they move against his stick, but also through the action of his hand when they do nothing but resist the stick, so we must acknowledge that the objects of sight can be perceived not only by means of the action in them which is directed towards our eyes, but also by the action in our eyes which is directed towards them. Nevertheless, because the latter action is nothing other than light, we must note that it is found only in the eyes of those creatures which can see in the dark, such as cats, whereas a man normally sees only through the action which comes from the objects. For experience shows us that these objects must be luminous or illuminated in order to be seen, and not that our eyes must be luminous or illuminated in order to see them. But because our blind man's stick differs greatly from the air and the other transparent bodies through the medium of which we see, I must make use of yet another comparison.

Consider a wine-vat at harvest time, full to the brim with half-pressed grapes, in the bottom of which we have made one or two holes through which the unfermented wine can flow. Now observe that, since there is no vacuum in nature (as nearly all philosophers acknowledge), and yet there are many pores in all the bodies we perceive around us (as experience can show quite clearly), it is necessary that these pores be filled with some very subtle and very fluid matter, which extends without interruption from the heavenly bodies to us. Now, if you compare this subtle matter with the wine in the vat, and compare the less fluid or coarser parts of the air and the other transparent bodies with the bunches of grapes which are mixed in with the wine, you will readily understand the following. The parts of wine at one place tend to go down in a straight line through one hole at the very instant it is opened, and at the same time through the other hole, while the parts at other places also tend at the same time to go down through these two holes, without these actions being impeded by each other or by the resistance of the bunches of grapes in the vat. This happens even though the bunches support each other and so do not tend in the least to go down through the holes, as does the wine, and at the same time they can even be moved in many other ways by the bunches which press upon them. In the same way, all the parts of the subtle matter in contact with the side of the sun facing us tend in a straight line towards our eyes at the very instant they are opened, without these parts impeding each other, and even without their being impeded by the coarser parts of the transparent bodies which lie between them. This happens whether these bodies move in other ways – like the air which is almost always agitated by some wind – or are motionless – say, like glass or crystal. And note here that it is necessary to distinguish between the movement and the action or tendency to move. For we may very easily conceive that the parts of wine at one place should tend towards one hole and at the same time towards the other, even though they cannot actually move towards both holes at the same time, and that they should tend exactly in a straight line towards one and towards the other, even though they cannot move exactly in a straight line because of the bunches of grapes which are between them. In the same way, considering that the light of a luminous body must be regarded as being not so much its movement as its action, you must think of the rays of light as nothing other than the lines along which this action tends. Thus there is an infinity of such rays which come from all the points of a luminous body towards all the points of the bodies it illuminates, just as you can imagine an infinity of straight lines along which the actions coming from all the points of the surface of the wine tend towards one hole, and an infinity of others along which the actions coming from the same points tend also towards the other hole, without either impeding the other.

Moreover, these rays must always be imagined to be exactly straight when they pass through a single transparent body which is uniform throughout. But when they meet certain other bodies, they are liable to be deflected by them, or weakened, in the same way that the movement of a ball or stone thrown into the air is deflected by the bodies it encounters. For it is very easy to believe that the action or tendency to move (which, I have said, should be taken for light) must in this respect obey the same laws as the movement itself. In order that I may give a complete account of this third comparison, consider that a ball passing through the air may encounter bodies that are soft or hard or fluid. If the bodies are soft, they completely stop the ball and check its movement, as when it strikes linen sheets or sand or mud. But if they are hard, they send the ball in another direction without stopping it, and they do so in many different ways. For their surface may be quite even and smooth, or rough and uneven; if even, either flat or curved; if uneven, its unevenness may consist merely in its being composed of many variously curved parts, each quite smooth in itself, or also in its having many different angles or points, or some parts harder than others, or parts which are moving (their movements being varied in a thousand imaginable ways). And it must be noted that the ball, besides moving in the simple and ordinary way which takes it from one place to another, may move in yet a second way, turning on its axis, and that the speed of the latter movement may have many different relations with that of the former. Thus, when many balls coming from the same direction meet a body whose surface is completely smooth and even, they are reflected uniformly and in the same order, so that if this surface is completely flat they keep the same distance between them after having met it as they had beforehand; and if it is curved inward or outward they come towards each other or go away from each other in the same order, more or less, on account of this curvature . . . It is necessary to consider, in the same manner, that there are bodies which break up the light-rays that meet them and take away all their force (namely bodies called 'black', which have no colour other than that of shadows); and there are others which cause the rays to be reflected, some in the same order as they receive them (namely bodies with highly polished surfaces, which can serve as mirrors, both flat and curved), and others in many directions in complete disarray. Among the latter, again, some bodies cause the rays to be reflected without bringing about any other change in their action (namely bodies we call 'white'), and others bring about an additional change similar to that which the movement of a ball undergoes when we graze it (namely bodies which are red, or yellow, or blue or some other such colour). For I believe I can determine the nature of each of these colours, and reveal it experimentally; but this goes beyond the limits of my subject. All I need to do here is to point out that the light-rays falling on bodies which are coloured and not polished are usually reflected in every direction even if they come from only a single direction . . . Finally, consider that the rays are also deflected, in the same way as the ball just described, when they fall obliquely on the surface of a transparent body and penetrate this body more or less easily than the body from which they come. This mode of deflection is called 'refraction'.[2]

[. . .]

Discourse four: The senses in general

Now I must tell you something about the nature of the senses in general, the more easily to explain that of sight in particular. We know for certain that it is the soul which has sensory awareness, and not the body. For when the soul is distracted by an ecstasy or deep contemplation, we see that the whole body remains without sensation, even though it has various objects touching it. And we know that it is not, properly speaking, because of its presence in the parts of the body which function as organs of the external senses that the soul has sensory awareness, but because of its presence in the brain, where it exercises the faculty called the 'common' sense. For we observe injuries and diseases which attack the brain alone and impede all the senses generally, even though the rest of the body continues to be animated. We know, lastly, that it is through the nerves that the impressions formed by objects in the external parts of the body reach the soul in the brain. For we observe various accidents which cause injury only to a nerve, and destroy sensation in all the parts of the body to which this nerve sends its branches, without causing it to diminish elsewhere. . . .[3] We must take care not to assume – as our philosophers commonly do – that in order to have sensory awareness the soul must contemplate certain images[4] transmitted by objects to the brain; or at any rate we must conceive the nature of these images in an entirely different manner from that of the philosophers. For since their conception of the images is confined to the requirement that they should resemble the objects they represent, the philosophers cannot possibly show us how the images can be formed by the objects, or how they can be received by the external sense organs and transmitted by the nerves to the brain. Their sole reason for positing such images was that they saw how easily a picture can stimulate our mind to conceive the objects depicted in it, and so it seemed to them that the mind must be stimulated to conceive the objects that affect our senses in the same way – that is, by little pictures formed in our head. We should, however, recall that our mind can be stimulated by many things other than images – by signs and words, for example, which in no way resemble the things they signify. And if, in order to depart as little as possible from accepted views, we prefer to maintain that the objects which we perceive by our senses really send images of themselves to the inside of our brain, we must at least observe that in no case does an image have to resemble the object it represents in all respects, for otherwise there would be no distinction between the object and its image. It is enough that the image resembles its object in a few respects. Indeed the perfection of an image often depends on its not resembling its object as much as it might. You can see this in the case of engravings: consisting simply of a little ink placed here and there on a piece of paper, they represent to us forests, towns, people, and even battles and storms; and although they make us think of countless different qualities in these objects, it is only in respect of shape that there is any real resemblance. And even this resemblance is very imperfect, since engravings represent to us bodies of varying relief and depth on a surface which is entirely flat. Moreover, in accordance with the rules of perspective they often represent circles by ovals better than by other circles, squares by rhombuses better than by other squares, and similarly for other shapes. Thus it often happens that in order to be more perfect as an image and to represent an object better, an engraving ought not to resemble it. Now we must think of the images formed in our brain in just the same way, and note that the problem is to know simply how they can enable the soul to have sensory awareness of all the various qualities of the objects to which they correspond – not to know how they can resemble these objects. For instance, when our blind man touches bodies with his stick, they certainly do not transmit anything to him except in so far as they cause his stick to move in different ways according to the different qualities in them, thus likewise setting in motion the nerves in his hand, and then the regions of his brain where these nerves originate. This is what occasions his soul to have sensory awareness of just as many different qualities in these bodies as there are differences in the movements caused by them in his brain.

[. . .]

Notes

1 A reference to the scholastic doctrine that material objects transmit to the soul 'forms' or 'images' (Fr. *espèces*, Lat. *species*) resembling them.

2 Discourses Two and Three are omitted here.

3 There follows an account of the function of the nerves and animal spirits in producing sensation and movement. Cf. *Treatise on Man*, AT XI 132 ff and *Passions*.

4 See note 1 above.

Chapter 5

Martin Jay

SCOPIC REGIMES OF MODERNITY

THE MODERN ERA, it is often alleged,[1] has been dominated by the sense of sight in a way that set it apart from its premodern predecessors and possibly its postmodern successor. Beginning with the Renaissance and the scientific revolution, modernity has been normally considered resolutely ocularcentric. The invention of printing, according to the familiar argument of McLuhan and Ong,[2] reinforced the privileging of the visual abetted by such inventions as the telescope and the microscope. 'The perceptual field thus constituted,' concludes a typical account, 'was fundamentally nonreflexive, visual and quantitative.'[3]

Although the implied characterization of different eras in this generalization as more favorably inclined to other senses should not be taken at face value,[4] it is difficult to deny that the visual has been dominant in modern Western culture in a wide variety of ways. Whether we focus on 'the mirror of nature' metaphor in philosophy with Richard Rorty of emphasize the prevalence of surveillance with Michel Foucault or bemoan the society of the spectacle with Guy Debord,[5] we confront again and again the ubiquity of vision as the master sense of the modern era.

But what precisely constitutes the visual culture of this era is not so readily apparent. Indeed, we might well ask, borrowing Christian Metz's term, is there one unified 'scopic regime'[6] of the modern or are there several, perhaps competing ones? For, as Jacqueline Rose has recently reminded us, 'our previous history is not the petrified block of a single visual space since, looked at obliquely, it can always be seen to contain its moment of unease.'[7] In fact, may there possibly be several such moments, which can be discerned, if often in repressed form, in the modern era? If so, the scopic regime of modernity may best be understood as a contested terrain, rather than a harmoniously integrated complex of visual theories and practices. It may, in fact, be characterized by a differentiation of visual subcultures, whose separation has allowed us to understand the multiple implications of sight in ways that are now only beginning to be appreciated. That new understanding, I want to suggest, may well be the product of a radical reversal in the hierarchy of visual subcultures in the modern scopic regime.

Before spelling out the competing ocular fields in the modern era as I understand them, I want to make clear that I am presenting only very crude ideal typical characterizations, which can easily be faulted for their obvious distance from the complex realities they seek to approximate. I am also not suggesting that the three main visual subcultures I single out for special attention exhaust all those that might be discerned in the lengthy and loosely defined epoch we call modernity. But, as will soon become apparent, it will be challenging enough to try to do justice in the limited space I have to those I do want to highlight as most significant.

Let me begin by turning to what is normally claimed to be the dominant, even totally hegemonic, visual model of the modern era, that which we can identify with Renaissance notions of perspective in the visual arts and Cartesian ideas of subjective rationality in philosophy. For convenience, it can be called Cartesian perspectivalism. That it is often assumed to be equivalent to the modern scopic regime *per se* is illustrated by two remarks from prominent commentators. The first is the claim made by the art historian William Ivins, Jr, in his *Art and Geometry* of 1946 that 'the history of art during the five hundred years that have elapsed since Alberti wrote has been little more than the story of the slow diffusion of his ideas through the artists and peoples of Europe.'[8] The second is from Richard Rorty's widely discussed *Philosophy and the Mirror of Nature*, published in 1979: 'in the Cartesian model the intellect inspects entities modeled on retinal images. . . . In Descartes' conception – the one that became the basis for "modern" epistemology – it is *representations* which are in the "mind." '[9] The assumption expressed in these citations that Cartesian perspectivalism is *the* reigning visual model of modernity is often tied to the further contention that it succeeded in becoming so because it best expressed the 'natural' experience of sight valorized by the scientific world view. When the assumed equivalence between scientific observation and the natural world was disputed, so too was the domination of this visual subculture, a salient instance being Erwin Panofsky's celebrated critique of perspective as merely a conventional symbolic form.[10]

But for a very long time Cartesian perspectivalism was identified with the modern scopic regime *tout court*. With full awareness of the schematic nature of what follows, let me try to establish its most important characteristics. There is, of course, an immense literature on the discovery, rediscovery, or invention of perspective – all three terms are used depending on the writer's interpretation of ancient visual knowledge – in the Italian Quattrocento. Brunelleschi is traditionally accorded the honor of being its practical inventor or discoverer, while Alberti is almost universally acknowledged as its first theoretical interpreter. From Ivins, Panofsky, and Krautheimer to Edgerton, White, and Kubovy,[11] scholars have investigated virtually every aspect of the perspectivalist revolution, technical, aesthetic, psychological, religious, even economic and political.

Despite many still disputed issues, a rough consensus seems to have emerged around the following points. Growing out of the late medieval fascination with the metaphysical implications of light – light as divine *lux* rather than perceived *lumen* – linear perspective came to symbolize a harmony between the mathematical regularities in optics and God's will. Even after the religious underpinnings of this equation were eroded, the favorable connotations surrounding the allegedly objective optical order remained powerfully in place. These positive associations had been displaced from the objects, often religious in content, depicted in earlier painting to the spatial relations of the perspectival canvas itself. This new concept of space was geometrically isotropic, rectilinear, abstract, and uniform. The *velo* or veil of threads Alberti used to depict it conventionalized that space in a way that anticipated the grids so characteristic of twentieth-century art, although, as Rosalind Krauss has reminded us, Alberti's veil was assumed to correspond to external reality in a way that its modernist successor did not.[12]

The three-dimensional, rationalized space of perspectival vision could be rendered on a two-dimensional surface by following all of the transformational rules spelled out in Alberti's *De Pittura* and later treatises by Viator, Dürer, and others. The basic device was the idea of symmetrical visual pyramids or cones with one of their apexes the receding vanishing or centric point in the painting, the other the eye of the painter or the beholder. The transparent window that was the canvas, in Alberti's famous metaphor, could also be understood as a flat mirror reflecting the geometricalized space radiating out from the viewing eye.

Significantly, that eye was singular, rather than the two eyes of normal binocular vision. It was conceived in the manner of a lone eye looking through a peephole at the scene in front of it. Such an eye was, moreover, understood to be static, unblinking, and fixated, rather than dynamic, moving with what later scientists would call 'saccadic' jumps from one focal point to another. In Norman Bryson's terms, it followed the logic of the Gaze rather than the Glance, thus producing a visual take that was eternalized, reduced to one 'point of view,' and disembodied. In what Bryson calls the 'Founding Perception' of the Cartesian perspectivalist tradition:

> the gaze of the painter arrests the flux of phenomena, contemplates the visual field from a vantage-point outside the mobility of duration, in an eternal moment of disclosed presence; while in the moment of viewing, the viewing subject unites his gaze with the Founding Perception, in a moment of perfect recreation of that first epiphany.[13]

[. . .]

Notes

1 See, for example, Lucien Febvre, *The Problem of Unbelief in the Sixteenth Century: The Religion of Rabelais*, trans. Beatrice Gottlieb (Cambridge, Mass.: Harvard University Press, 1982) and Robert Mandrou, *Introduction to Modern France, 1500–1640: An Essay in Historical Psychology*, trans. R.E. Hallmark (New York: Holmes & Meier, 1975).

2 Marshall McLuhan, *Understanding Media: The Extensions of Man* (New York: McGraw-Hill, 1964); Walter J. Ong, *The Presence of the Word: Some Prolegomena for Cultural and Religious History* (New Haven: Yale University Press, 1967); see also Elizabeth L. Eisenstein, *The Printing Press as an Agent of Change: Communications*

and Cultural Transformations in Early Modern Europe, 2 vols (Cambridge: Cambridge University Press, 1979).

3 Donald M. Lowe, *History of Bourgeois Perception* (Chicago: University of Chicago Press, 1982), p. 26.

4 For an account of the positive attitude towards vision in the medieval church, see Margaret R. Miles, *Image as Insight: Visual Understanding in Western Christianity and Secular Culture* (Boston: Beacon Press, 1985). Contrary to the argument of Febvre and Mandrou, which has been very influential, she shows the extent to which sight was by no means widely demeaned in the Middle Ages.

5 Richard Rorty, *Philosophy and the Mirror of Nature* (Princeton: Princeton University Press, 1979); Michel Foucault, *Discipline and Punish: The Birth of the Prison*, trans. Alan Sheridan (New York: Vintage Books, 1979); Guy Debord, *Society of the Spectacle*, rev. edn (Detroit: Black and Red, 1977).

6 Christian Metz, *The Imaginary Signifier: Psychoanalysis and the Cinema*, trans. Celia Britton *et al.* (Bloomington: Indiana University Press, 1982), p. 61.

7 Jacqueline Rose, *Sexuality in the Field of Vision* (London: Verso, 1986), pp. 232–33.

8 William M. Ivins, Jr, *Art and Geometry: A Study in Space Intuitions* (Cambridge, Mass.: Harvard University Press, 1946), p. 81.

9 Rorty, op. cit., p. 45.

10 Erwin Panofsky, 'Die Perspektive als "symbolischen Form" ', *Vorträge der Bibliothek Warburg* 4 (1924–1925), pp. 258–331.

11 William M. Ivins, Jr, *On the Rationalization of Sight* (New York: Metropolitan Museum of Art, 1938); Panofsky, 'Die Perspektive als "symbolischen Form" '; Richard Krautheimer, 'Brunelleschi and Linear Perspective,' in *Brunelleschi in Perspective*, comp. Isabelle Hyman (Englewood Cliffs, N.J.: Prentice-Hall, 1974); Samuel Y. Edgerton, Jr, *The Renaissance Discovery of Linear Perspective* (New York: Basic Books, 1975); John White, *The Birth and Rebirth of Pictorial Space*, 3rd edn (Cambridge, Mass.: Belknap Press, 1987); Michael Kubovy, *The Psychology of Perspective and Renaissance Art* (Cambridge: Cambridge University Press, 1986).

12 Rosalind E. Krauss, *The Originality of the Avant-Garde and Other Modernist Myths* (Cambridge, Mass.: The MIT Press, 1985), p. 10.

13 Norman Bryson, *Vision and Painting: The Logic of the Gaze* (New Haven: Yale University Press, 1983), p. 94.

Chapter 6

Roland Barthes

RHETORIC OF THE IMAGE

ACCORDING TO AN ANCIENT etymology, the word *image* should be linked to the root *imitari*. Thus we find ourselves immediately at the heart of the most important problem facing the semiology of images: can analogical representation (the 'copy') produce true systems of signs and not merely simple agglutinations of symbols? Is it possible to conceive of an analogical 'code' (as opposed to a digital one)? We know that linguists refuse the status of language to all communication by analogy – from the 'language' of bees to the 'language' of gesture – the moment such communications are not doubly articulated, are not founded on a combinatory system of digital units as phonemes are. Nor are linguists the only ones to be suspicious as to the linguistic nature of the image; general opinion too has a vague conception of the image as an area of resistance to meaning – this in the name of a certain mythical idea of Life: the image is re-presentation, which is to say ultimately resurrection, and, as we know, the intelligible is reputed antipathetic to lived experience. Thus from both sides the image is felt to be weak in respect of meaning: there are those who think that the image is an extremely rudimentary system in comparison with language and those who think that signification cannot exhaust the image's ineffable richness. Now even – and above all if – the image is in a certain manner the *limit* of meaning, it permits the consideration of a veritable ontology of the process of signification. How does meaning get into the image? Where does it end? And if it ends, what is there *beyond*? Such are the questions that I wish to raise by submitting the image to a spectral analysis of the messages it may contain. We will start by making it considerably easier for ourselves: we will only study the advertising image. Why? Because in advertising the signification of the image is undoubtedly intentional; the signifieds of the advertising message are formed *a priori* by certain attributes of the products and these signifieds have to be transmitted as clearly as possible. If the image contains signs, we can be sure that in advertising these signs are full, formed with a view to the optimum reading: the advertising image is *frank*, or at least emphatic.

The three messages

Here we have a Panzani advertisement: some packets of pasta, a tin, a sachet, some tomatoes, onions, peppers, a mushroom, all emerging from a half-open string bag, in yellows and greens on a red background.[1] Let us try to 'skim off' the different messages it contains.

The image immediately yields a first message whose substance is linguistic; its supports are the caption, which is marginal, and the labels, these being inserted into the natural disposition of the scene, '*en abyme*'. The code from which this message has been taken is none other than that of the French language; the only knowledge required to decipher it is a knowledge of writing and French. In fact, this message can itself be further broken down, for the sign *Panzani* gives not simply the name of the firm but also, by its assonance, an additional signified, that of 'Italianicity'. The linguistic message is thus twofold (at least in this particular image): denotational and connotational. Since, however, we have here only a single typical sign,[2] namely that of articulated (written) language, it will be counted as one message.

Putting aside the linguistic message, we are left with the pure image (even if the labels are part of it, anecdotally). This image straightaway provides a series of discontinuous signs. First (the order is unimportant as these signs are not linear), the idea that what we have in the scene represented is a return from the market. A signified which itself implies two euphoric values: that of the freshness of the products and that of the essentially domestic preparation for which they are destined. Its signifier is the half-open bag which lets the provisions spill out over the table, 'unpacked'. To read this first sign requires only a knowledge which is in some sort implanted as part of the habits of a very widespread culture where 'shopping around for oneself' is opposed to the hasty stocking up (preserves, refrigerators) of a more 'mechanical' civilization. A second sign is more or less equally evident; its signifier is the bringing together of the tomato, the pepper and the tricoloured hues (yellow, green, red) of the poster; its signified is Italy or rather *Italianicity*. This sign stands in a relation of redundancy with the connoted sign of the linguistic message (the Italian assonance of the name *Panzani*) and the knowledge it draws upon is already more particular; it is a specifically 'French' knowledge (an Italian would barely perceive the connotation of the name, no more probably than he would the Italianicity of tomato and pepper), based on a familiarity with certain tourist stereotypes. Continuing to explore the image (which is not to say that it is not entirely clear at the first glance), there is no difficulty in discovering at least two other signs: in the first, the serried collection of different objects transmits the idea of a total culinary service, on the one hand as though Panzani furnished everything necessary for a carefully balanced dish and on the other as though the concentrate in the tin were equivalent to the natural produce surrounding it; in the other sign, the composition of the image, evoking the memory of innumerable alimentary paintings, sends us to an aesthetic signified: the '*nature morte*' or; as it is better expressed in other languages, the 'still life';[3] the knowledge on which this sign depends is heavily cultural. It might be suggested that, in addition to these four signs, there is a further information pointer, that which tells us that this is an advertisement and which arises both from the place of the image in the magazine and from the emphasis of the labels (not to mention the caption). This last information, however, is co-extensive with the scene; it eludes signification in so far as the advertising nature of the image is essentially functional; to utter something is not necessarily to declare *I am speaking*, except in a deliberately reflexive system such as literature.

Thus there are four signs for this image and we will assume that they form a coherent whole (for they are all discontinuous), require a generally cultural knowledge, and refer back to signifieds each of which is global (for example, *Italianicity*), imbued with euphoric values. After the linguistic message, then, we can see a second, iconic message. Is that the end? If all these signs are removed from the image, we are still left with a certain informational matter; deprived of all knowledge, I continue to 'read' the image, to 'understand' that it assembles in a common space a number of identifiable (nameable) objects, not merely shapes and colours. The signifieds of this third message are constituted by the real objects in the scene, the signifiers by these same objects photographed, for, given that the relation between thing signified and image signifying in analogical representation is not 'arbitrary' (as it is in language), it is no longer necessary to dose the relay with a third term in the guise of the psychic image of the object. What defines the third message is precisely that the relation between signified and signifier is quasi-tautological; no doubt the photograph involves a certain arrangement of the scene (framing, reduction, flattening) but this transition is not a *transformation* (in the way a coding can be); we have here a loss of the equivalence characteristic of true sign systems and a statement of quasi-identity. In other words, the sign of this message is not drawn from an institutional stock, is not coded, and we are brought up against the paradox (to which we will return) of a *message without a code*. This peculiarity can be seen again at the level of the knowledge invested in the reading of the message; in order to 'read' this last (or first) level of the image, all that is needed is the knowledge bound up with our perception. That knowledge is not nil, for we need to know what an image is (children only learn this at about the age of four) and what a tomato, a string-bag, a packet of pasta are, but it is a matter of an almost anthropological knowledge. This message corresponds, as it were, to the letter of the image and we can agree to call it the literal message, as opposed to the previous symbolic message.

If our reading is satisfactory, the photograph analysed offers us three messages: a linguistic message, a coded iconic message, and a non-coded iconic message. The linguistic message can be readily separated from the other two, but since the latter share the same (iconic) substance, to what extent have we the right to separate them? It is certain that the distinction between the two iconic messages is not made spontaneously in ordinary reading: the viewer of the image *receives at one and the same time* the perceptual message and the cultural message, and it will be seen later that this confusion in reading corresponds to the function of the mass image (our concern here). The distinction, however, has an operational validity, analogous to that which allows the distinction in the linguistic sign of a signifier and a signified (even though in reality no one is able to separate the 'word' from its meaning except by recourse to the metalanguage of a definition). If the distinction permits us to describe the structure of the image in a simple and coherent fashion and if this description paves the way for an explanation of the role of the image in society, we will take it to be justified. The task now is thus to reconsider each type of message so as to explore it in its generality, without losing sight of our aim of understanding the overall structure of the image, the final interrelationship of the three messages. Given that what is in question is not a 'naive' analysis but a structural description,[4] the order of the messages will be modified a little by the inversion of the cultural message and the literal message; of the two iconic messages, the first is in some sort imprinted on the second: the literal message appears as the *support* of the 'symbolic' message. Hence, knowing that a system which takes over the signs of another system in order to make them its signifiers is a system of connotation,[5] we may say immediately that the literal image is *denoted* and the symbolic image *connoted*.

Notes

1 The *description* of the photograph is given here with prudence, for it already constitutes a metalanguage.

2 By *typical sign* is meant the sign of a system in so far as it is adequately defined by its substance: the verbal sign, the iconic sign, the gestural sign are so many typical signs.

3 In French, the expression *nature morte* refers to the original presence of funereal objects, such as a skull, in certain pictures.

4 'Naive' analysis is an enumeration of elements, structural description aims to grasp the relation of these elements by virtue of the principle of the solidarity holding between the terms of a structure: if one term changes, so also do the others.

5 Cf. R. Barthes, *Eléments de sémiologie, Communications* 4, 1964, p. 130 [trans. *Elements of Semiology*, London 1967 & New York 1968, pp. 89–92].

Chapter 7

Griselda Pollock

MODERNITY AND THE SPACES OF FEMININITY

Investment in the look is not as privileged in women as in men. More than other senses, the eye objectifies and masters. It sets at a distance, and maintains a distance. In our culture the predominance of the look over smell, taste, touch and hearing has brought about an improvement of bodily relations. The moment the look dominates, the body loses its materiality.

(Luce Irigaray (1978). Interview in M.-F. Hans and G. Lapouge (eds) *Les Femmes, la pornographie et l'érotisme*, Paris, p. 50)

Introduction

The schema which decorated the cover of Alfred H. Barr's catalogue for the exhibition 'Cubism and Abstract Art' at the Museum of Modern Art, New York, in 1936 is paradigmatic of the way modern art has been mapped by modernist art history. Artistic practices from the late nineteenth century are placed on a chronological flow chart where movement follows movement connected by one-way arrows which indicate influence and reaction. Over each movement a named artist presides. All those canonized as the initiators of modern art are men. Is this because there were no women involved in early modern movements? No.[1] Is it because those who were, were without significance in determining the shape and character of modern art? No. Or is it rather because what modernist art history celebrates is a selective tradition which normalizes, as the *only* modernism, a particular and gendered set of practices? I would argue for this explanation. As a result any attempt to deal with artists in the early history of modernism who are women necessitates a deconstruction of the masculinist myths of modernism.[2]

These are, however, widespread and structure the discourse of many counter-modernists, for instance in the social history of art. The publication *The Painting of Modern Life: Paris in the Art of Manet and his Followers*, by T.J. Clark,[3] offers a searching account of the social relations between the emergence of new protocols and criteria for painting – modernism – and the myths of modernity shaped in and by the new city of Paris remade by capitalism during the Second Empire. Going beyond the commonplaces about a desire to be contemporary in art, 'il faut être de son temps',[4] Clark puzzles at what structured the notions of modernity which became the territory for Manet and his followers. He thus indexes the Impressionist painting practices to a complex set of negotiations of the ambiguous and baffling class formations and class identities which emerged in Parisian society. Modernity is presented as far more than a sense of being 'up to date' – modernity is a matter of representations and major myths – of a new Paris for recreation, leisure and pleasure; of nature to be enjoyed at weekends in suburbia; of the prostitute taking over and of fluidity of class in the popular spaces of entertainment. The key markers in this mythic territory are leisure, consumption, the spectacle and money. And we can reconstruct from Clark a map of Impressionist territory which stretches from the new boulevards via Gare St Lazare out on the suburban train to La Grenouillère, Bougival or Argenteuil. In these sites, the artists lived, worked and pictured themselves.[5] But in two of the four chapters of Clark's book, he deals with the problematic of sexuality in bourgeois Paris and the canonical paintings are *Olympia* (1863, Paris, Musée du Louvre) and *A Bar at the Folies-Bergère* (1881–82, London, Courtauld Institute of Art) (Figure 7.1).

It is a mighty but flawed argument on many levels but here I wish to attend to its peculiar closures on the issue of sexuality. For Clark the founding fact is

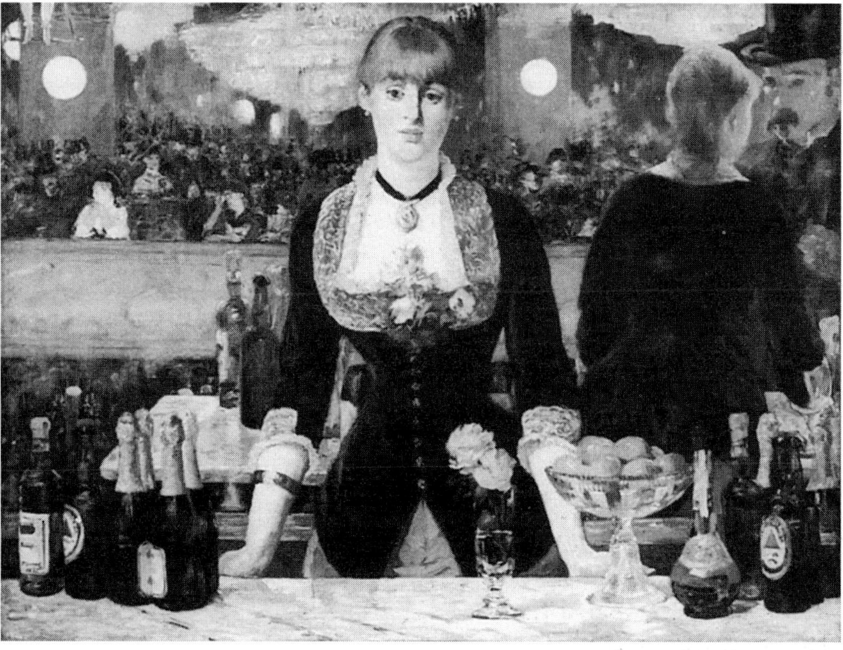

Figure 7.1 Edouard Manet, *A Bar at the Folies-Bergère*, 1881–2 (Courtesy of the Courtauld Gallery, London)

class. Olympia's nakedness inscribes her class and thus debunks the mythic classlessness of sex epitomized in the image of the courtesan.[6] The fashionably blasé barmaid at the Folies evades a fixed identity as either bourgeois or proletarian but none the less participates in the play around class that constituted the myth and appeal of the popular.[7]

Although Clark nods in the direction of feminism by acknowledging that these paintings imply a masculine viewer/consumer, the manner in which this is done ensures the normalcy of that position, leaving it below the threshold of historical investigation and theoretical analysis. To recognize the gender-specific conditions of these paintings' existence one need only imagine a female spectator and a female producer of the works. How can a woman relate to the viewing positions proposed by either of these paintings? Can a woman be offered, in order to be denied, imaginary possession of Olympia or the barmaid? Would a woman of Manet's class have a familiarity with either of these spaces and its exchanges which could be evoked so that the painting's modernist job of negation and disruption could be effective? Could Berthe Morisot have gone to such a location to canvass the subject? Would it enter her head as a site of modernity as she experienced it? Could she as a woman experience modernity as Clark defines it at all?[8]

For it is a striking fact that many of the canonical works held up as the founding monuments of modern art treat precisely with this area, sexuality, and this form of it, commercial exchange. I am thinking of innumerable brothel scenes through to Picasso's *Demoiselles d'Avignon* or that other form, the artist's couch. The encounters pictured and imagined are those between men who have the freedom to take their pleasures in many urban spaces and women from a class subject to them who have to work in those spaces often selling their bodies to clients, or to artists. Undoubtedly these exchanges are structured by relations of class but these are thoroughly captured within gender and its power relations. Neither can be separated or ordered in a hierarchy. They are historical simultaneities and mutually inflecting.

So we must enquire why the territory of modernism so often is a way of dealing with masculine sexuality and its sign, the bodies of women – why the nude, the brothel, the bar? What relation is there between sexuality, modernity and modernism? If it is normal to see paintings of women's bodies as the territory across which men artists claim their modernity and compete for leadership of the avant-garde, can we expect to rediscover paintings by women in which they battled with their sexuality in the representation of the male nude? Of course not; the very suggestion seems ludicrous. But why? Because there is a historical asymmetry – a difference socially, economically, subjectively between being a woman and being a man in Paris in the late nineteenth century. This difference – the product of the social structuration of sexual difference and not any imaginary biological distinction – determined both what and how men and women painted.

[. . .]

The painter of modern life

One text above all charts this interaction of class and gender. In 1863 Charles Baudelaire published in *Le Figaro* an essay entitled 'The painter of modern life'. In this text the figure of the flâneur is modified to become the modern artist while at the same time the text provides a mapping of Paris marking out the sites/sights for the flâneur/artist. The essay is ostensibly about the work of a minor illustrator Constantin Guys but he is only a pretext for Baudelaire to weave an elaborate and impossible image of his ideal artist, who is a passionate lover of crowds, and incognito, a man of the world.

> The crowd is his element as the air is that of birds and water of fishes. His passion and profession are to become one flesh with the crowd. For the perfect flâneur, for the passionate spectator, it is an immense joy to set up house in the heart of the multitude, amid the ebb and flow of movement, in the midst of the fugitive and the infinite. To be away from home and yet feel oneself everywhere at home; to see the world and to be the centre of the world and yet remain hidden from the world – such are a few of the slightest pleasures of those independent, passionate, impartial natures which the tongue can but clumsily define. The spectator is a *prince* and everywhere rejoices in his incognito. The lover of life makes the whole world his family.[9]

The text is structured by an opposition between home, the inside domain of the known and constrained personality and the outside, the space of freedom, where there is liberty to look without being watched or even recognized in the act of looking. It is the imagined freedom of the voyeur. In the crowd the flâneur/artist sets up home. Thus the flâneur/artist is articulated across the twin ideological formations of modern bourgeois society – the splitting of private and public with its double freedom for men in the public space, and the pre-eminence of a detached observing gaze, whose possession and power is never questioned as its basis in the hierarchy of the sexes is never acknowledged. For as Janet Wolff has argued, there is no female equivalent of the quintessential masculine figure, the flâneur; there is not and could not be a female flâneuse.

Women did not enjoy the freedom of incognito in the crowd. They were never positioned as the normal occupants of the public realm. They did not have the right to look, to stare, scrutinize or watch. As the Baudelairean text goes on to show, women do not look. They are positioned as the *object* of the flâneur's gaze.

> Woman is for the artist in general . . . far more than just the female of man. Rather she is divinity, a star . . . a glittering conglomeration of all the graces of nature, condensed into a single being; an object of keenest admiration and curiosity that the picture of life can offer to its contemplator. She is an idol, stupid perhaps, but dazzling and bewitching. . . . Everything that adorns women that serves to show off her beauty is part of herself . . .
>
> No doubt woman is sometimes a light, a glance, an invitation to happiness, sometimes she is just a word.[10]

Indeed woman is just a sign, a fiction, a confection of meanings and fantasies. Femininity is not the natural condition of female persons. It is an historically variable ideological construction of meanings for a sign W*O*M*A*N which is produced by and for another social group which derives its identity and imagined superiority by manufacturing the spectre of this fantastic Other. *WOMAN* is both an idol and nothing but a word. Thus when we come to read the chapter of Baudelaire's essay entitled 'Women and Prostitutes', in which the author charts a journey across Paris for the flâneur/artist, where women appear merely to be there as spontaneously visible objects, it is necessary to recognize that the text is itself constructing a notion of WOMAN across a fictive map of urban spaces – the spaces of modernity.

The flâneur/artist starts his journey in the auditorium where young women of the most fashionable society sit in snowy white in their boxes at the theatre. Next he watches elegant families strolling at leisure in the walks of a public garden, wives leaning complacently on the arms of husbands while skinny little girls play at making social class calls in mimicry of their elders. Then he moves on to the lowlier theatrical world where frail and slender dancers appear in a blaze of limelight admired by fat bourgeois men. At the café door, we meet a swell while indoors is his mistress, called in the text 'a fat baggage', who lacks practically nothing to make her a great lady except that practically nothing is practically everything for it is distinction (class). Then we enter the doors of Valentino's, the Prado or Casino, where against a background of hellish light, we encounter the protean image of wanton beauty, the courtesan, 'the perfect image of savagery that lurks in the heart of civilization'. Finally by degrees of destitution, he charts women, from the patrician airs of young and successful prostitutes to the poor slaves of the filthy stews.

Attempting to match the drawings by Guys to this extraordinary spectacle will disappoint. In no way are the drawings as vivid, for their project is less ideological and altogether more mundane as in the manner of the fashion plate. None the less they provide some interest in revealing how differently the figures of females are actually represented according to location. The respectable women chaperoned or accompanied by husbands in the park pass by fused almost with their clothing so that, decorporealized, their dress defines their class position and meaning. In spaces marked out for visual and notional sexual consumption, the bodies are in evidence, laid out, opened up and offered to view while drapery functions to reveal a sexualized anatomy.

Baudelaire's essay maps a representation of Paris as the city of women. It constructs a sexualized journey which can be correlated with impressionist practice. Clark has offered one map of impressionist painting following the trajectories of leisure from city centre by suburban railway to the suburbs. I want to propose another dimension of that map which links impressionist practice to the erotic territories of modernity. I have drawn up a grid using Baudelaire's categories and mapped the works of Manet, Degas and others on to this schema.[11]

From the loge pieces by Renoir (admittedly not women of the highest society) to the *Musique aux Tuileries* of Manet, Monet's park scenes and others easily cover this terrain where bourgeois men and women take their leisure. But then when we move backstage at the theatre we enter different worlds, still of men and women but differently placed by class. Degas's pictures of the dancers on stage and rehearsing are well known. Perhaps less familiar are his scenes illustrating the backstage at the Opéra, where members of the Jockey Club bargain for their

GRID I

LADIES	THEATRE (LOGE)	debutantes; young women of fashionable society	RENOIR	CASSATT
	PARK	matrons, mothers, children, elegant families	MANET	CASSATT MORISOT
FALLEN WOMEN	THEATRE (BACKSTAGE)	DANCERS	DEGAS	
	CAFÉS	mistresses and kept women	MANET RENOIR DEGAS	
	FOLIES	THE COURTESAN 'protean image of wanton beauty'	MANET DEGAS GUYS	
	BROTHELS	'poor slaves of filthy stews'	MANET GUYS	

evening's entertainment with the little performers. Both Degas and Manet represented the women who haunted cafés, and as Theresa Ann Gronberg has shown, these were working-class women often suspected of touting for custom as clandestine prostitutes.[12]

Thence we can find examples sited in the Folies and cafés-concerts as well as the boudoirs of the courtesan. Even if *Olympia* cannot be situated in a recognizable locality, reference was made in the reviews to the café Paul Niquet's, the haunt of the women who serviced the porters of Les Halles and a sign for the reviewer of total degradation and depravity.[13]

Women and the public modern

The artists who were women in this cultural group of necessity occupied this map but partially. They can be located all right but in spaces above a decisive line. *Lydia at the Theatre*, 1879 and *The Loge*, 1882 situate us in the theatre with the young and fashionable but there could hardly be a greater difference between these paintings and the work by Renoir on this theme, *The First Outing*, 1876 (London, National Gallery of Art), for example.

The stiff and formal poses of the two young women in the painting by Cassatt were precisely calculated as the drawings for the work reveal. Their erect posture, one carefully grasping an unwrapped bouquet, the other sheltering behind a large fan, create a telling effect of suppressed excitement and extreme constraint, of unease in this public place, exposed and dressed up, on display. They are set at an oblique angle to the frame so that they are not contained by its edges, not framed and made a pretty picture for us as in *The Loge* by Renoir, where the spectacle at which the scene is set and the spectacle the woman herself is made to offer, merge for the unacknowledged but presumed masculine spectator. In Renoir's *The First Outing* the choice of a profile opens out the spectator's gaze into the auditorium and invites her/him to imagine that she/he is sharing in the main figure's excitement while she seems totally unaware of offering such a delightful spectacle. The lack of self-consciousness is, of course, purely contrived so that the viewer can enjoy the sight of the young girl.

The mark of difference between the paintings by Renoir and Cassatt is the refusal in the latter of that complicity in the way the female protagonist is depicted. In a later painting, *At the Opera*, 1879 (Figure 7.2), a woman is represented dressed in daytime or mourning black in a box at the theatre. She looks from the spectator into the distance in a direction which cuts across the plane of the picture but as the viewer follows her gaze another look is revealed steadfastly fixed on

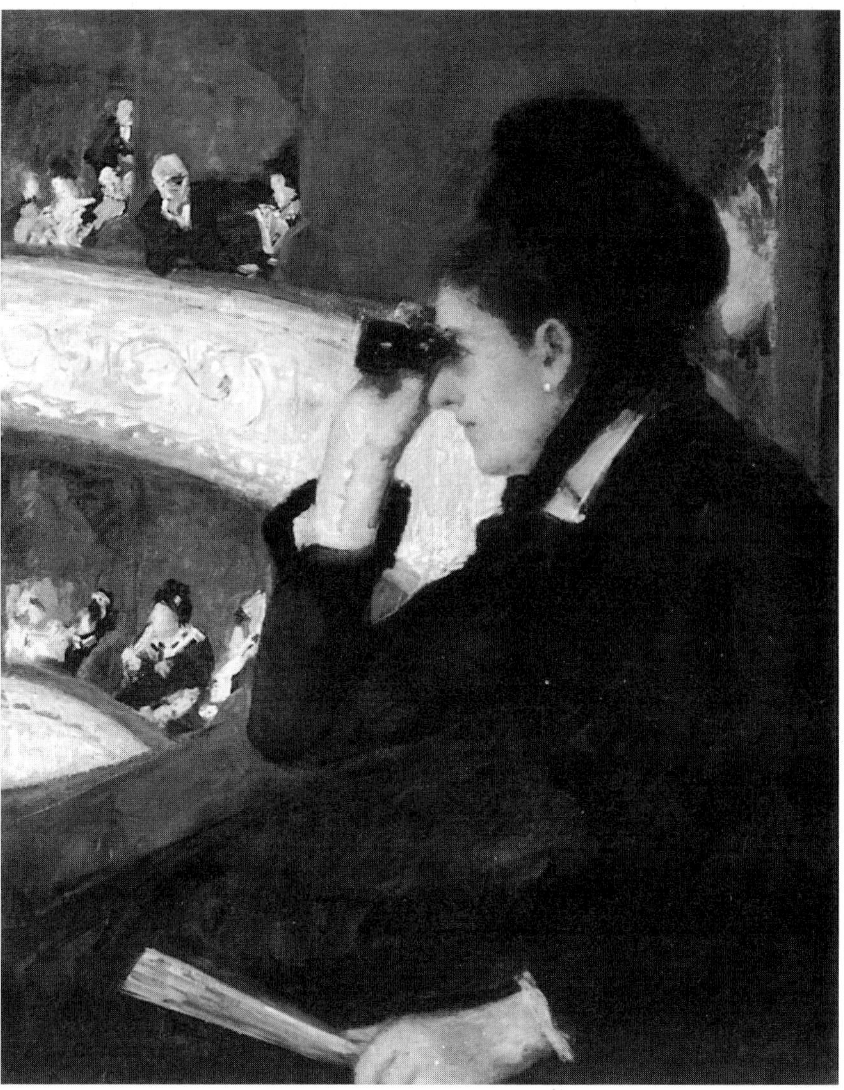

Figure 7.2 Mary Cassatt, *At the Opera*, 1879
(Hayden Collection: courtesy of the Museum of Fine Arts, Boston)

the woman in the foreground. The picture thus juxtaposes two looks, giving priority to that of the woman who is, remarkably, pictured actively looking. She does not return the viewer's gaze, a convention which confirms the viewer's right to look and appraise. Instead we find that the viewer outside the picture is evoked by being as it were the mirror image of the man looking in the picture.

This is, in a sense, the subject of the painting – the problematic of women out in public being vulnerable to a compromising gaze. The witty pun on the spectator outside the painting being matched by that within should not disguise the serious meaning of the fact that social spaces are policed by men's watching women and the positioning of the spectator outside the painting in relation to the man within it serves to indicate that the spectator participates in that game as well. The fact that the woman is pictured so actively looking, signified above all by the fact that her eyes are masked by opera glasses, prevents her being objectified and she figures as the subject of her own look.

Cassatt and Morisot painted pictures of women in public spaces but these all lie above a certain line on the grid I devised from Baudelaire's text. The other world of women was inaccessible to them while it was freely available to the men of the group and constantly entering representation as the very territory of their engagement with modernity. There is evidence that bourgeois women did go to the cafés-concerts but this is reported as a fact to regret and a symptom of modern decline.[14] As Clark points out, guides for foreigners to Paris such as Murray's clearly wish to prevent such slumming by commenting that respectable people do not visit such venues. In the journals Marie Bashkirtseff records a visit she and some friends made to a masked ball where behind the disguise daughters of the aristocracy could live dangerously, playing with sexual freedom their classed gender denied them. But given both Bashkirtseff's dubious social position, and her condemnation of the standard morality and regulation of women's sexuality, her escapade merely reconfirms the norm.[15]

To enter such spaces as the masked ball or the café-concert constituted a serious threat to a bourgeois woman's reputation and therefore her femininity. The guarded respectability of the lady could be soiled by mere visual contact, for seeing was bound up with knowing. This other world of encounter between bourgeois men and women of another class was a no-go area for bourgeois women. It is the place where female sexuality or rather female bodies are bought and sold, where woman becomes both an exchangeable commodity and a seller of flesh, entering the economic domain through her direct exchanges with men. Here the division of the public and private mapped as a separation of the masculine and feminine is ruptured by money, the ruler of the public domain, and precisely what is banished from the home.

Femininity in its class-specific forms is maintained by the polarity virgin/whore which is mystifying representation of the economic exchanges in the patriarchal kinship system. In bourgeois ideologies of femininity the fact of the money and property relations which legally and economically constitute bourgeois marriage is conjured out of sight by the mystification of a one-off purchase of the rights to a body and its products as an effect of love to be sustained by duty and devotion.

Femininity should be understood therefore not as a condition of women but as the ideological form of the regulation of female sexuality within a familial, heterosexual domesticity which is ultimately organized by the law. The spaces of femininity – ideologically, pictorially – hardly articulate female sexualities. That is not to accept nineteenth-century notions of women's asexuality but to stress the difference between what was actually lived or how it was experienced and what was officially spoken or represented as female sexuality.[16]

In the ideological and social spaces of femininity, female sexuality could not be directly registered. This has a crucial effect with regard to the use artists who were women could make of the positionality represented by the gaze of the flâneur – and therefore with regard to modernity. The gaze of the flâneur articulates and produces a masculine sexuality which in the modern sexual economy enjoys the freedom to look, appraise and possess, in deed or in fantasy. Walter Benjamin draws special attention to a poem by Baudelaire, 'A une passante' ('To a passer-by'). The poem is written from the point of view of a man who sees in the crowd a beautiful widow; he falls in love as she vanishes from sight. Benjamin's comment is apt: 'One may say that the poem deals with the function of the crowd not in the life of a citizen but in the life of an erotic person.'[17]

It is not the public realm simply equated with the masculine which defines the flâneur/artist but access to a sexual realm which is marked by those interstitial spaces, the spaces of ambiguity, defined as such not only by the relatively unfixed or fantasizable class boundaries Clark makes so much of but because of cross-class sexual exchange. Women could enter and represent selected locations in the public sphere – those of entertainment and display. But a line demarcates not the end of the public/private divide but the frontier of the spaces of femininity. Below this line lies the realm of the sexualized and commodified bodies of woman, where nature is ended, where class, capital and masculine power invade and interlock. It is a line that marks off a class boundary but it reveals where new class formations of the bourgeois world restructured gender relations not only between men and women but between women of different classes.[18]

[. . .]

Notes

1 For substantive evidence see Lea Vergine, *L'Autre moitié de l'avant-garde, 1910–1940*, translated by Mireille Zanuttin, (Italian edn 1980), Paris, Des Femmes, 1982.

2 See Nicole Dubreuil-Blondin, 'Modernism and Feminism: Some Paradoxes' in Benjamin H.D. Buchloh (ed.), *Modernism and Modernity*, Halifax, Nova Scotia, Press of Nova Scotia College of Art and Design, 1983. Also Lillian Robinson and Lisa Vogel, 'Modernism and History', *New Literary History*, 1971–72, iii (1), 177–99.

3 T.J. Clark, *The Painting of Modern Life: Paris in the Art of Manet and his Followers*, New York, Knopf, and London, Thames & Hudson, 1984.

4 George Boas, 'Il faut être de son temps', *Journal of Aesthetics and Art Criticism*, 1940, 1, pp. 52–65; reprinted in *Wingless Pegasus: A Handbook for Critics*, Baltimore, Johns Hopkins University Press, 1950.

5 The itinerary can be fictively reconstructed as follows: a stroll on the *Boulevard des Capucines* (C. Monet, 1873, Kansas City, Nelson Atkins Museum of Art),

across the *Pont de l'Europe* (G. Caillebotte, 1876, Geneva, Petit Palais), up to the *Gare St Lazare* (Monet, 1877, Paris, Musée d'Orsay), to catch a suburban train for the 12-minute ride out to walk along the *Seine at Argenteuil* (Monet, 1875, San Francisco, Museum of Modern Art) or to stroll and swim at the bathing-place on the Seine, *La Grenouillère* (A. Renoir, 1869, Moscow, Pushkin Museum), or to *Dance at Bougival* (A. Renoir, 1883, Boston, Museum of Fine Arts). I was privileged to read early drafts of Tim Clark's book now titled *The Painting of Modern Life* and it was here that this Impressionist territory was first lucidly mapped as a field of leisure and pleasure on the metropolitan/suburban axis. Another study to undertake this work is Theodore Reff, *Manet and Modern Paris*, Chicago, University of Chicago Press, 1982.

6 Clark, op. cit., p. 146.

7 Ibid., p. 253.

8 While accepting that paintings such as *Olympia* and *A Bar at the Folies-Bergère* come from a tradition that invokes the spectator as masculine, it is necessary to acknowledge the way in which a feminine spectator is actually implied by these paintings. Surely one part of the shock, of the transgression effected by the painting *Olympia* for its first viewers at the Paris Salon, was the presence of that 'brazen' but cool look from the white woman on a bed attended by a black maid in a space in which women, or to be historically precise bourgeois ladies, would be presumed to be present. That look, so overtly passing between a seller of woman's body and a client/viewer, signified the commercial and sexual exchanges specific to a part of the public realm which should be invisible to ladies. Furthermore its absence from their consciousness structured their identities as ladies. In some of his writings T.J. Clark correctly discusses the meanings of the sign woman in the nineteenth century as oscillating between two poles of the *fille publique* (woman of the streets) and the *femme honnête* (the respectable married woman). But it would seem that the exhibition of *Olympia* precisely confounds that social and ideological distance between two imaginary poles and forces the one to confront the other in that part of the public realm where ladies do go – still within the frontiers of femininity. The presence of this painting in the Salon – not because it is a nude but because it displaces the mythological costume or anecdote through which prostitution was represented mythically through the courtesan – transgresses the line on my grid derived from Baudelaire's text, introducing not just modernity as a manner of painting a pressing contemporary theme, but the spaces of modernity into a social territory of the bourgeoisie, the Salon, where viewing such an image is quite shocking because of the presence of wives, sisters and daughters. The understanding of the shock depends upon our restoration of the female spectator to her historical and social place.

9 Charles Baudelaire, 'The Painter of Modern Life', in *The Painter of Modern Life and Other Essays*, translated and edited by Jonathan Mayne, Oxford, Phaidon Press, 1964, p. 9.

10 Ibid., p. 30.

11 The pictures to fit the schema would include the following examples:

A. Renoir, *La Loge*, 1874 (London, Courtauld Institute Galleries).
E. Manet, *Music in the Tuileries Gardens*, 1862 (London, National Gallery).
E. Degas, *Dancers Backstage*, c. 1872 (Washington, National Gallery of Art).

E. Degas, *The Cardinal Family*, *c*. 1880, a series of monotypes planned as illustrations to Ludovic Halévy's books on the backstage life of the dancers and their 'admirers' from the Jockey Club.
E. Degas, *A Café in Montmartre*, 1877 (Paris, Musée d'Orsay).
E. Manet, *Café, Place du Théâtre Français*, 1881 (Glasgow, City Art Museum).
E. Manet, *Nana*, 1877 (Hamburg, Kunsthalle).
E. Manet, *Olympia*, 1863 (Paris, Musée du Louvre).

12 Theresa Ann Gronberg, 'Les Femmes de brasserie', *Art History*, 1984, 7 (3).

13 See Clark, op. cit., 296, n. 144. The critic was Jean Ravenal writing in *L'Epoque*, 7 June 1865.

14 See Clark, op. cit., p. 209.

15 The escapade in 1878 was erased from the bowdlerized version of the journals published in 1890. For discussion of the event see the publication of excised sections in Colette Cosnier, *Marie Bashkirtseff: un portrait sans retouches*, Paris, Pierre Horay, 1985, pp. 164–65. See also Linda Nochlin, 'A Thoroughly Modern Masked Ball', *Art in America*, November 1983, 71 (10). In Karl Baedecker, *Guide to Paris*, 1888, the masked balls are described but it is advised that 'visitors with ladies had better take a box' (p. 34) and of the more mundane *salles de danse* (dance halls) Baedecker comments, 'It need hardly be said that ladies cannot attend these balls.'

16 Carl Degler, 'What Ought to Be and What Was; women's sexuality in the nineteenth century', *American Historical Review*, 1974, 79, pp. 1467–91.

17 Benjamin, op. cit., p. 45.

18 I may have overstated the case that bourgeois women's sexuality could not be articulated within these spaces. In the light of recent feminist study of the psychosexual psychology of motherhood, it would be possible to read mother–child paintings by women in a far more complex way as a site for the articulation of female sexualities. Moreover in paintings by Morisot, for instance of her adolescent daughter, we may discern the inscription of yet another moment at which female sexuality is referred to by circling around the emergence from latency into an adult sexuality prior to its strict regulation within marital domestic forms. More generally it would be wise to pay heed to the writings of historian Carroll Smith-Rosenberg on the importance of female friendships. She stresses that from our post-Freudian vantage point it is very difficult to read the intimacies of nineteenth-century women, to understand the valencies of the terms of endearment, often very physical, to comprehend the forms of sexuality and love as they were lived, experienced and represented. A great deal more research needs to be done before any statements can be made without the danger of feminists merely rehearsing and confirming the official discourse of masculine ideologues on female sexualities. (C. Smith-Rosenberg 'Hearing Women's Words: a Feminist Reconstruction of History', in her book *Disorderly Conduct: Visions of Gender in Victorian America*, New York, Knopf, 1985.)

Chapter 8

Carol Duncan

THE MODERN ART MUSEUM

[LET US EXAMINE how two of art history's most important female images masculinize museum space. The images I will discuss, both key objects in the MoMA, are Picasso's *Demoiselles d'Avignon* and de Kooning's *Woman I*.

Picasso's *Demoiselles d'Avignon*, 1906–7 (Figure 8.1) was conceived as an extraordinarily ambitious statement – it aspires to revelation – about the meaning of Woman. In it, all women belong to a universal category of being existing across time and place. Picasso used ancient and tribal art to reveal her universal mystery: Egyptian and Iberian sculpture on the left and African art on the right. The figure on the lower right looks as if it was directly inspired by some primitive or archaic Gorgon-like deity. Picasso would have known such figures from his visits to the ethnographic art collections in the Trocadero in Paris. A study for the work closely follows the type's symmetrical, self-displaying pose. Significantly, Picasso wanted her to be prominent – she is the nearest and largest of all the figures. At this stage, Picasso also planned to include a male figure on the left and, in the axial center of the composition, a sailor – an image of horniness incarnate. The self-displaying woman was to have faced him, her display of genitals turned away from the viewer.

In the finished work, the male presence has been removed from the image and relocated in the viewing space before it. What began as a depicted male–female confrontation thus turned into a confrontation between viewer and image. The relocation has pulled the lower right-hand figure completely around so that her stare and her sexually inciting act – an explicit invitation to penile penetration and the mainstay of pornographic imagery – are now directed outward. Other figures also directly address the viewer as a male brothel patron. Indeed, everything in the work insists on a classic men-only situation. To say it more bluntly – but in language more in the spirit of the work – the image is designed to threaten, tease, invite, and play with the viewer's cock. Thus did Picasso monumentalize as

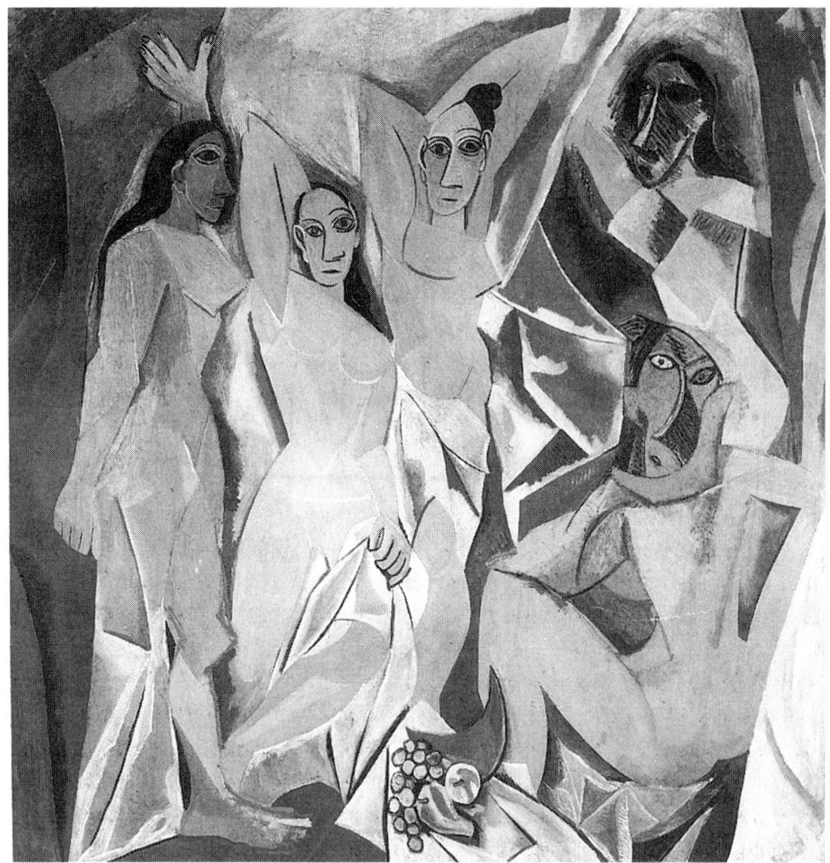

Figure 8.1 Pablo Picasso, *Les Demoiselles d'Avignon*, 1906–7
(Courtesy of the Museum of Modern Art, New York. Acquired through the Lillie P. Bliss Bequest. Photograph © 1994 The Museum of Modern Art, New York)

the ultimate truth of art a phallic moment *par excellence*. As restructured, the work forcefully asserts to both men and women the privileged status of male viewers – the only acknowledged invitees to this most revelatory moment. In so doing, it consigns women to a place where they may watch but not enter the central arena of public high culture – at least not as visible, self-aware subjects. The alternative role – that of the whore – was and still is for most women untenable.

Finally, the mystery that Picasso unveils about women is also an historical lesson. In the finished work, the women have become stylistically differentiated so that one looks not only at present-tense whores but also back down into the ancient and primitive past, with the art of 'darkest Africa' and works representing the beginnings of Western culture (Egyptian and Iberian idols) placed on a single spectrum. Thus does Picasso use art history to argue his thesis: that the awesome goddess, the terrible witch, and the lewd whore are all but facets of the same eternal creature, in turn threatening and seductive, imposing and self-abasing, dominating and powerless. In this context, the use of African art constitutes not a homage to 'the primitive' but a means of framing women as 'other,' one whose savage, animalistic inner self stands opposed to the civilized, reflective male's.

De Kooning's *Woman I* is the *descendant* of Picasso's *Demoiselles*. For many years, it hung at the threshold to the gallery containing the New York School's biggest 'breakthroughs' into pure abstraction: Pollock's flings into artistic and psychic freedom, Rothko's sojourns in the luminous depths of a universal self. Newman's heroic confrontations with the sublime, Still's lonely journeys into the back beyond of culture and consciousness, Reinhardt's solemn and sardonic negations of all that is not Art. And always seated at the doorway to these moments of ultimate freedom and purity, and literally helping to frame them was *Woman I*. So necessary was her presence just there, that when she had to go on loan, *Woman II* came out of storage to take her place. With good reason, De Kooning's *Women*, like Picasso's *Demoiselles*, are exceptionally potent ritual artifacts. They, too, masculinize museum space with great efficiency. (In the present installation, *Woman I* has been moved into the very center of the gallery in which the New York School's largest and most serene abstract works hang. Although her placement there is dramatic, it also disrupts the room's transcendent quietude).

The woman figure had emerged gradually in de Kooning's work in the course of the 1940s. By 1951–52, it fully revealed itself in *Woman I* as a big, bad mama – vulgar, sexual, and dangerous (Figure 8.2). De Kooning imagines her facing us with iconic frontality, large, bulging eyes, an open, toothy mouth, and massive breasts. The suggestive pose is just a knee movement away from open-thighed display of the vagina, the self-exposing gesture of mainstream pornography. These features are not unique in the history of art. They appear in ancient and primitive contexts as well as modern pornography and graffiti. Together, they constitute a well-known figure type. The Gorgon of ancient Greek art is an instance of that type and bears a striking resemblance to de Kooning's *Woman I*. Like *Woman I*, she both suggests and avoids the explicit act of sexual self-display; at other times, she spreads her thighs wide open. Often flanked by animals, she appears in many cultures, archaic and tribal, and is sometimes identified as a fertility or mother goddess.

As a type, with or without animals, the configuration clearly carries complex and probably contradictory symbolic possibilities. Specified as the Gorgon witch, the image emphasizes the terrible and demonic aspects of the mother goddess – her lust for blood and her deadly gaze. Especially today, when the myths and rituals that may have once suggested other meanings have been lost – and when modern psychoanalytic ideas are likely to color any interpretation – the figure appears intended to conjure up infantile feelings of powerlessness before the mother and the dread of castration: in the open jaw can be read the *vagina dentata* – the idea of a dangerous, devouring vagina, too horrible to depict, and hence transposed to the toothy mouth. Feelings of inadequacy and vulnerability before mature women are common (if not always salient) phenomena in male psychic development. Myths like the story of Perseus and visual images like the Gorgon can play a role in mediating that development by extending and recreating on the cultural plane its core psychic experience and accompanying defenses. Publicly objectified and communally shared in imagery, myth, and ritual, these individual fears and desires may achieve the status of authoritative truth. In this sense, the presence of Gorgons on

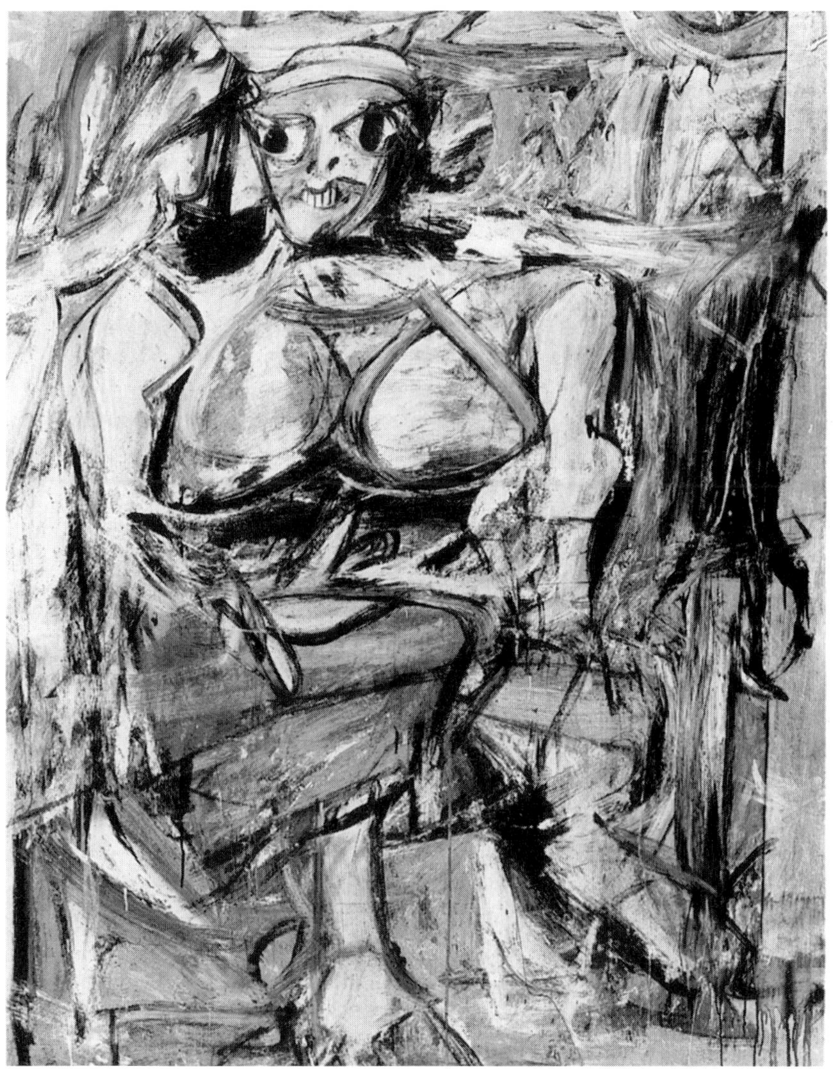

Figure 8.2 Willem De Kooning, *Woman I*, 1952
(Courtesy of the Museum of Modern Art, New York. Photograph © 1994 The Museum of Modern Art, New York)

Greek temples – important houses of cult worship – is paralleled by *Woman I*'s presence in a high-cultural house of the modern world.

The head of de Kooning's *Woman I* is so like the archaic Gorgon that the reference could well be intentional, especially since the artist and his friends put great store in ancient myths and primitive images and likened themselves to archaic and tribal shamans. The critic Thomas Hess evokes these ideas in an essay about de Kooning's 'women.' According to Hess, de Kooning painting a 'woman' was an artistic ordeal comparable to Perseus slaying the Gorgon, for to accomplish his end, de Kooning had to grasp an elusive, dangerous truth 'by the throat' without looking at it directly.

> And truth can be touched only by complications, ambiguities and paradox, so, like the hero who looked for Medusa in the mirroring shield, he must study her flat, reflected image every inch of the way.[1]

But then again, the image type is so ubiquitous, we needn't try to assign de Kooning's *Woman I* to any particular source in ancient or primitive art. *Woman I* can call up the Medusa as easily as the other way around. Whatever he knew or sensed about the Gorgon's meanings, and however much or little he took from it, the image type is decidedly present in his work. Suffice it to say that de Kooning was aware, indeed, explicitly claimed, that his 'women' could be assimilated to the long history of goddess imagery. By placing such figures at the center of his most ambitious artistic efforts, he secured for his work an aura of ancient mystery and authority.

Woman I is not only monumental and iconic. In high-heeled shoes and brassiere, she is also lewd, her pose indecently teasing. De Kooning acknowledged her oscillating character, claiming for her a likeness not only to serious art – ancient icons and high-art nudes – but also to pinups and girlie pictures of the vulgar present. He saw her as simultaneously frightening and ludicrous. The ambiguity of the figure, its power to resemble an awesome mother goddess as well as a modern burlesque queen, provides a superbly designed cultural, psychological, and artistic artifact with which to enact the mythic ordeal of the modern artist-hero – the hero whose spiritual adventures become the stuff of ritual in the public space of the museum. It is the *Woman*, powerful and threatening, who must be confronted and transcended on the way to enlightenment (or, in the present MoMA, in the very midst of it). At the same time, her vulgarity, her 'girlie' side – de Kooning called it her 'silliness' – renders her harmless (and contemptible) and denies the terror and dread of her Medusa features. The ambiguity of the image thus gives the artist (and the viewer who has learned to identify with him) both the experience of danger and a feeling of overcoming (or perhaps simply denying) it. Meanwhile, the suggestion of pornographic self-display – it will be more explicit in his later works – specifically addresses itself to the male viewer. With it, de Kooning exercises his patriarchal privilege of celebrating male sexual fantasy as public high culture.

Thomas Hess understood exactly the way in which de Kooning's 'women' enabled one both to experience the dangerous realm of woman–matter–nature and symbolically escape it into male–culture–enlightenment. The following passage is a kind of brief user's manual for any of de Kooning's 'women' (and his other, more abstract paintings as well, since they, too, usually began as female figures). It also articulates the core of the ritual ordeal I have been describing. Hess begins with characterizing de Kooning's materials. They are clearly female, engulfing, and slimy, and must be controlled by the skilled, instrument-wielding hands of a male:

> There are the materials themselves, fluid, viscous, wet or moist, slippery, fleshy and organic in feel; spreading, thickening or thinning under the artist's hands. Could they be compared to the primal ooze, the soft underlying mud, from which all life has sprung? To nature?

Now comes the artist, brandishing his phallus-tool, to pierce, cut, and penetrate the female flesh:

> And the instruments of the artist are, by contrast, sharp, like the needle-point of a pencil; or slicing, like the whiplash motion of the long brush.

And finally, the symbolic act of the mind that the viewer witnesses and re-lives:

> Could not the artist at work, forcing his materials to take shape and become form [be a] paradigm? The artist becomes the tragicomic hero who must go to war against the elements of nature in the hope of making contact with them.[2]

De Kooning is hardly alone in embodying the artist-hero who takes on the fearsome and alluring woman. The type is common enough in high culture. To cite a striking example: an interesting drawing/photomontage by the California artist Robert Heinecken, *Invitation to Metamorphosis*, similarly explores the ambiguities of a Gorgon-girlie image. Here the effect of ambiguity is achieved by the use of masks and by combining and superimposing separate negatives. Heinecken's version of the self-displaying woman is a composite consisting of a conventional pornographic nude and a Hollywood movie-type monster. As a well-equipped Gorgon, her attributes include an open, toothy mouth, carnivorous animal jaws, huge bulging eyes, large breasts, exposed female genitals, and one nasty-looking claw. Her body is simultaneously naked and draped, enticing and repulsive, and the second head, to the left of the Gorgon head – the one with the seductive smile – also wears a mask. Like the de Kooning, Heinecken's *Invitation* sets up a psychologically unstable atmosphere fraught with deception, allure, danger, and wit. The image's various components continually disappear into and reappear out of each other. Behaving something like de Kooning's layered paint surfaces, they invite ever-shifting, multiple readings. In both works, what is covered becomes exposed, what is opaque becomes transparent, and what is revealed conceals something else. Both works fuse the terrible killer-witch with the willing and exhibitionist whore. Both fear and seek danger in desire, and both kid the danger.

In all of these works, a confrontation is staged between a Perseus-like artist-hero and a lewd, uncivil, and uncontrollable female. And in every case, the danger is forced back behind the divide of art. Like Picasso in the *Demoiselles*, de Kooning summons support from the most ancient artistic cultures. But he also draws on modern pornography. Indeed, it is de Kooning's achievement to have opened museum culture to the potential powers of pornography. By way of exploring how the pornographic element works in the museum context, let us look first at how it works outside the museum.

A few years ago, an advertisement for *Penthouse* magazine appeared on New York City bus shelters. New York City bus shelters are often decorated with near-naked women and sometimes men advertising everything from underwear to real estate. But this was an ad for pornographic images as such, that is, images designed not to sell perfume or bathing suits, but to stimulate erotic desire, primarily in men. Given its provocative intent, the image generates very different and – I think for almost everyone – more charged meanings than the ads for underwear. At least one passer-by had already recorded in red spray-paint a terse, but coherent response: 'For Pigs.'

Having a camera with me, I decided to take a shot of it. But as I set about focusing, I began to feel uncomfortable and self-conscious. As I realized only later, I was experiencing some prohibition in my own conditioning, activated not simply by the nature of the ad, but by the act of photographing such an ad in public. Even though the anonymous inscription had made it socially safer to photograph – it placed it in a conscious and critical discourse about gender – to photograph it was still to appropriate openly a kind of image that middle-class morality says I'm not supposed to look at or have. But before I could sort that out, a group of boys jumped into the frame. Plainly, they intended to intervene. Did I know what I was doing?, one asked me with an air I can only call stern, while another admonished me that I was photographing a *Penthouse* ad – as if I would not knowingly do such a thing.

Apparently the same culture that had conditioned me to feel uneasy about what I was doing also made *them* uneasy about it. Boys this age know very well what's in *Penthouse*. Knowing what's in *Penthouse* is knowing something meant for men to know; therefore, knowing *Penthouse* is a way of knowing oneself to be a man, or at least a man-to-be, at precisely an age when one needs all the help one can get. I think these boys were trying to protect the capacity of the ad to empower them as men by preventing me from appropriating an image of it. For them, as for many men, the chief (if not the only) value of pornography is this power to confirm gender identity and, with that, gender superiority. Pornography affirms their manliness to themselves and to others and proclaims the greater social power of men. Like some ancient and primitive objects forbidden to the female gaze, the ability of pornography to give its users a feeling of superior male status depends on its being owned or controlled by men and forbidden to, shunned by, or hidden from women. In other words, in certain situations a female gaze can *pollute* pornography. These boys, already imprinted with the rudimentary gender codes of the culture, knew an infringement when they saw one. (Perhaps they suspected me of defacing the ad.) Their harassment of me constituted an attempt at gender policing, something adult men routinely do to women on city streets.

Not so long ago, such magazines were sold only in sleazy porn shops. Today ads for them can decorate mid-town thoroughfares. Of course, the ad as well as the magazine cover, cannot itself be pornography and still be legal (in practice, that tends to mean it can't show genitals), but to work as advertising, it must *suggest* pornography. For different reasons, works of art like de Kooning's *Woman I* or Heinecken's *Invitation* also refer to without actually being pornography – they depend upon the viewer 'getting' the reference without being mistakable for pornography. Given those requirements, it is not surprising that these artists' visual strategies have parallels in the ad. Indeed, *Woman I* shares a number of features with it. Both present frontal, iconic, monumental figures that fill and even overflow their picture surfaces, dwarfing viewers and focusing attention on head, breasts, and torso. Both figures appear powerful and powerless at the same time, with massive bodies made to rest on weakly rendered, tentatively placed legs, while arms are cropped, undersized, or feeble. And with both, the viewer is positioned to see it all should the thighs open. And of course, on *Penthouse* pages, thighs do little else but open. However, de Kooning's hot mama has a very different purpose and cultural status from a *Penthouse* 'pet.'

De Kooning's *Woman I* conveys much more complex and emotionally ambivalent meanings. The work acknowledges more openly the fear of and flight from as well as a quest for the woman. Moreover de Kooning's *Woman I* is always upstaged by the artist's self-display as an artist. The manifest purpose of a *Penthouse* photo is, presumably, to arouse desire. If the de Kooning awakens desire in relation to the female body, it does so in order to deflate or conquer its power of attraction and escape its danger. The viewer is invited to relive a struggle in which the realm of art provides escape from the female's degraded allure. As mediated by art criticism, de Kooning's work speaks ultimately not of male fear but of the triumph of art and a self-creating spirit. In the critical and art-historical literature, the 'women' themselves are treated as catalysts or structural supports for the work's more significant meanings: the artist's heroic self-searching, his existentialist courage, his pursuit of new pictorial structures or some other artistic or transcendent end – in short, the mythic stuff of art-museum ritual.

I wish to be especially clear at this point that I have no quarrel either with the production or the public display of these or other works like them. My concern rather is with the ritual scenarios of art museums and the way they do and do not address women and other visitors. If I am protesting anything in museums, it is not the presence of *Woman I* or the *Demoiselles* but the exclusion of so much *else* from museum space. What I would like to see is a truly revisionist museum, with different, more complex, and possibly even multiple scenarios that could build on a broader range of human experience – sexual, racial, and cultural – than the present pathetically narrow program that structures most modern art museums today. Indeed, such a program might well promote a deeper understanding even of the museum's modernist old masters by recognizing their flights and fears as historically specific responses to a changing world. A more open museum culture could illuminate rather than perpetuate the profound and on-going crisis of masculinity that marks so much museum art.

I have been arguing, from the example of the MoMA and other collections, that the history of modern art is a built structure that privileges men in ways that are both obvious and subtle. Certainly more women artists could be integrated into museum programs even as things now stand – figures like Joan Mitchell, Louise Nevelson, Agnes Martin, or Eva Hesse have already been fitted into the story of progressive abstraction without disrupting it. But the problem involves more than numbers and is not merely a question of adding women to the familiar narrative. What has kept women artists out of art history is not merely biased curators (who, in any case, are not more biased than anyone else). It is no small thing for women artists to face an overwhelmingly authoritative tradition that has made it highly problematic for them to occupy public art space as women. For many, the entire art world – its art schools, critics, dealers, and especially its summit museum spaces – has seemed organized to maintain a universe precisely structured to negate the very existence of all but white males (and a few token 'exceptions').

And yet, for the last twenty-five years or so, as repercussions of the civil rights and women's movements – and, more recently, the lesbian and gay movement – have reached the art world, museum space has begun to open up. Women artists are often still confined to marginal spaces or temporary exhibitions, but it is no longer possible to ignore their presence in the art world. While older artists such as Marisol, Louise Bourgeois, and Alice Neel have become more visible, younger artists such as Barbara Kruger, Cindy Sherman, and Kiki Smith – to name only a few – have begun to de-masculinize the museum and rescript its ritual, bringing with them new concerns and often, a critical outlook that cannot easily be assimilated to the museum's normal ritual ordeal.

[. . .]

Notes

1 Thomas B. Hess (1959) *Willem de Kooning*, New York: George Braziller, p. 7.
2 Thomas B. Hess (1972) *Willem de Kooning: Drawings*, New York and Greenwich, CN: New York Graphic Society, p. 18 (note 24).

Chapter 9

James Clifford

ON COLLECTING ART AND CULTURE

There is a Third World in every First World, and vice-versa.
(Trinh T. Minh-Ha, 'Difference,' *Discourse* 8)

THIS CHAPTER IS composed of four loosely connected parts, each concerned with the fate of tribal artifacts and cultural practices once they are relocated in Western museums, exchange systems, disciplinary archives, and discursive traditions. The first part proposes a critical, historical approach to collecting, focusing on subjective, taxonomic, and political processes. It sketches the 'art-culture system' through which in the last century exotic objects have been contextualized and given value in the West. This ideological and institutional system is further explored in the second part, where cultural description is presented as a form of collecting. The 'authenticity' accorded to both human groups and their artistic work is shown to proceed from specific assumptions about temporality, wholeness, and continuity. The third part focuses on a revealing moment in the modern appropriation of non-Western works of 'art' and 'culture,' a moment portrayed in several memoirs by Claude Lévi-Strauss of his wartime years in New York. A critical reading makes explicit the redemptive metahistorical narrative these memoirs presuppose. The general art-culture system supported by such a narrative is contested throughout the chapter and particularly in the fourth part, where alternative 'tribal' histories and contexts are suggested.

Collecting ourselves

Entering
You will find yourself in a climate of nut castanets,
A musical whip

From the Torres Straits, from Mirzapur a sistrum
Called Jumka, 'used by Aboriginal
Tribes to attract small game
On dark nights,' coolie cigarettes
And mask of Saagga, the Devil Doctor,
The eyelids worked by strings.

James Fenton's poem 'The Pitt Rivers Museum, Oxford' (1984: 81–84), from which this stanza is taken, rediscovers a place of fascination in the ethnographic collection. For this visitor even the museum's descriptive labels seem to increase the wonder ('. . . attract small game/on dark nights') and the fear. Fenton is an adult-child exploring territories of danger and desire, for to be a child in this collection ('Please sir, where's the withered/Hand?') is to ignore the serious admonitions about human evolution and cultural diversity posted in the entrance hall. It is to be interested instead by the claw of a condor, the jaw of a dolphin, the hair of a witch, or 'a jay's feather worn as a charm/in Buckinghamshire.' Fenton's ethnographic museum is a world of intimate encounters with inexplicably fascinating objects: personal fetishes. Here collecting is inescapably tied to obsession, to recollection. Visitors 'find the landscape of their childhood marked out/Here in the chaotic piles of souvenirs . . . boxroom of the forgotten or hardly possible.'

Go
As a historian of ideas or a sex-offender,
For the primitive art,
As a dusty semiologist, equipped to unravel
The seven components of that witch's curse
Or the syntax of the mutilated teeth. Go
In groups to giggle at curious finds.
But do not step into the kingdom of your promises
To yourself, like a child entering the forbidden
Woods of his lonely playtime.

Do not step in this tabooed zone 'laid with the snares of privacy and fiction/And the dangerous third wish.' Do not encounter these objects except as curiosities to giggle at, art to be admired, or evidence to be understood scientifically. The tabooed way, followed by Fenton, is a path of too-intimate fantasy, recalling the dreams of the solitary child 'who wrestled with eagles for their feathers' or the fearful vision of a young girl, her turbulent lover seen as a hound with 'strange pretercanine eyes.' This path through the Pitt Rivers Museum ends with what seems to be a scrap of autobiography, the vision of a personal 'forbidden woods' – exotic, desired, savage, and governed by the (paternal) law:

He had known what tortures the savages had prepared
For him there, as he calmly pushed open the gate
And entered the wood near the placard: 'TAKE NOTICE
MEN-TRAPS AND SPRING-GUNS ARE SET ON THESE PREMISES.'
For his father had protected his good estate.

Fenton's journey into otherness leads to a forbidden area of the self. His intimate way of engaging the exotic collection finds an area of desire, marked off and policed. The law is preoccupied with *property*.

C.B. Macpherson's classic analysis of Western 'possessive individualism' (1962) traces the seventeenth-century emergence of an ideal self as owner: the individual surrounded by accumulated property and goods. The same ideal can hold true for collectivities making and remaking their cultural 'selves.' For example, Richard Handler (1985) analyzes the making of a Québécois cultural 'patrimoine,' drawing on Macpherson to unravel the assumptions and paradoxes involved in 'having a culture,' selecting and cherishing an authentic collective 'property.' His analysis suggests that this identity, whether cultural or personal, presupposes acts of collection, gathering up possessions in arbitrary systems of value and meaning. Such systems, always powerful and rule governed, change historically. One cannot escape them. At best, Fenton suggests, one can transgress ('poach' in their tabooed zones) or make their self-evident orders seem strange. In Handler's subtly perverse analysis a system of retrospection – revealed by a Historic Monuments Commission's selection of ten sorts of 'cultural property' – appears as a taxonomy worthy of Borges' 'Chinese encyclopedia': '(1) commemorative monuments; (2) churches and chapels; (3) forts of the French Regime; (4) windmills; (5) roadside crosses; (6) commemorative inscriptions and plaques; (7) devotional monuments; (8) old houses and manors; (9) old furniture; (10) "les choses disparues" ' (1985: 199). In Handler's discussion the collection and preservation of an authentic domain of identity cannot be natural or innocent. It is tied up with nationalist politics, with restrictive law, and with contested encodings of past and future.

Some sort of 'gathering' around the self and the group – the assemblage of a material 'world,' the marking-off of a subjective domain that is not 'other' – is probably universal. All such collections embody hierarchies of value, exclusions, rule-governed territories of the self. But the notion that this gathering involves the accumulation of possessions, the idea that identity is a kind of wealth (of objects, knowledge, memories, experience), is surely not universal. The individualistic accumulation of Melanesian 'big men' is not possessive in Macpherson's sense, for in Melanesia one accumulates not to hold objects as private goods but to give them away, to redistribute. In the West, however, collecting has long been a strategy for the deployment of a possessive self, culture, and authenticity.

Children's collections are revealing in this light: a boy's accumulation of miniature cars, a girl's dolls, a summer-vacation 'nature museum' (with labeled stones and shells, a hummingbird in a bottle), a treasured bowl filled with the bright shavings of crayons. In these small rituals we observe the channelings of obsession, an exercise in how to make the world one's own, to gather things around oneself tastefully, appropriately. The inclusions in all collections reflect wider cultural rules – of rational taxonomy, of gender, of aesthetics. An excessive, sometimes even rapacious need to *have* is transformed into rule-governed, meaningful desire. Thus the self that must possess but cannot have it all learns to select, order, classify in hierarchies – to make good collections.[1]

Whether a child collects model dinosaurs or dolls, sooner or later she or he will be encouraged to keep the possessions on a shelf or in a special box or to set up a doll house. Personal treasures will be made public. If the passion is for Egyptian figurines, the collector will be expected to label them, to know their dynasty (it is not enough that they simply exude power or mystery), to tell 'interesting' things about them, to distinguish copies from originals. The good collector (as opposed to the obsessive, the miser) is tasteful and reflective.[2] Accumulation unfolds in a pedagogical, edifying manner. The collection itself – its taxonomic, aesthetic structure – is valued, and any private fixation on single objects is negatively marked as fetishism. Indeed a 'proper' relation with objects (rule-governed possession) presupposes a 'savage' or deviant relation (idolatry or erotic fixation).[3] In Susan Stewart's gloss, 'The boundary between collection and fetishism is mediated by classification and display in tension with accumulation and secrecy' (1984: 163).

Stewart's wide-ranging study *On Longing* traces a 'structure of desire' whose task is the repetitious and impossible one of closing the gap that separates language from the experience it encodes. She explores certain recurrent strategies pursued by Westerners since the sixteenth century. In her analysis the miniature, whether a portrait or doll's house, enacts a bourgeois longing for 'inner' experience. She also explores the strategy of gigantism (from Rabelais and Gulliver to earthworks and the billboard), the souvenir, and the collection. She shows how collections, most notably museums – create the illusion of adequate representation of a world by first cutting objects out of specific contexts (whether cultural, historical, or intersubjective) and making them 'stand for' abstract wholes – a 'Bambara mask,' for example, becoming an ethnographic metonym for Bambara culture. Next a scheme of classification is elaborated for storing or displaying the object so that the reality of the collection itself, its coherent order, overrides specific histories of the object's production and appropriation (pp. 162–65). Paralleling Marx's account of the fantastic objectification of commodities, Stewart argues that in the modern Western museum 'an illusion of a relation between things takes the place of a social relation' (p. 165). The collector discovers, acquires, salvages objects. The objective world is given, not produced, and thus historical relations of power in the work of acquisition are occulted. The *making* of meaning in museum classification and display is mystified as adequate *representation*. The time and order of the collection erase the concrete social labour of its making.

Stewart's work, along with that of Phillip Fisher (1975), Krzystof Pomian (1978), James Bunn (1980), Daniel Defert (1982), Johannes Fabian (1983), and Rémy Saisselin (1984), among others, brings collecting and display sharply into view as crucial processes of Western identity formation. Gathered artifacts – whether they find their way into curio cabinets, private living rooms, museums of ethnography, folklore, or fine art – function within a developing capitalist 'system of objects' (Baudrillard 1968). By virtue of this system a world of *value* is created and a meaningful deployment and circulation of artifacts maintained. For Baudrillard, collected objects create a structured environment that substitutes its own temporality for the 'real time' of historical and productive processes: 'The environment of private objects and their possession – of which collections are an extreme manifestation – is a dimension of our life that is both essential and imaginary. As essential as dreams' (ibid.: 135).

A history of anthropology and modern art needs to see in collecting both a form of Western subjectivity and a changing set of powerful institutional practices. The history of collections (not limited to museums) is central to an understanding of how those social groups that invented anthropology and modern art have *appropriated* exotic things, facts, and meanings. (*Appropriate*: 'to make one's own,' from the Latin *proprius*, 'proper,' 'property.') It is important to analyze how powerful discriminations made at particular moments constitute the general system of objects within which valued artifacts circulate and make sense. Far-reaching questions are thereby raised.

What criteria validate an authentic cultural or artistic product? What are the differential values placed on old and new creations? What moral and political criteria justify 'good,' responsible, systematic collecting practices? Why, for example, do Leo Frobenius' wholesale acquisitions of African objects around the turn of the century now seem excessive? (See also Cole 1985 and Pye 1987.) How is a 'complete' collection defined? What is the proper balance between scientific analysis and public display? (In Santa Fe a superb collection of Native American art is housed at the School of American Research in a building constructed, literally, as a vault, with access carefully restricted. The Musée de l'Homme exhibits less than a tenth of its collections: the rest is stored in steel cabinets or heaped in corners of the vast basement.) Why has it seemed obvious until recently that non-Western objects should be preserved in European museums, even when this means that no fine specimens are visible in their country of origin? How are 'antiquities,' 'curiosities,' 'art,' 'souvenirs,' 'monuments,' and 'ethnographic artifacts' distinguished – at different historical moments and in specific market conditions? Why have many anthropological museums in recent years begun to display certain of their objects as 'masterpieces'? Why has tourist art only recently come to the serious attention of anthropologists? (See Graburn 1976; Jules-Rosette 1984.) What has been the changing interplay between natural-history collecting and the selection of anthropological artifacts for display and analysis? The list could be extended.

The critical history of collecting is concerned with what from the material world specific groups and individuals choose to preserve, value, and exchange. Although this complex history, from at least the Age of Discovery, remains to be written, Baudrillard provides an initial framework for the deployment of objects in the recent capitalist West. In his account it is axiomatic that all categories of meaningful objects – including those marked off as scientific evidence and as great art – function within a ramified system of symbols and values.

To take just one example the *New York Times* of December 8, 1984, reported the widespread illegal looting of Anasazi archeological sites in the American southwest. Painted pots and urns thus excavated in good condition could fetch as much as \$30,000 on the market. Another article in the same issue contained a photograph of Bronze Age pots and jugs salvaged by archeologists from a Phoenician shipwreck off the coast of Turkey. One account featured clandestine collecting for profit, the other scientific collecting for knowledge. The moral evaluations of the two acts of salvage were sharply opposed, but the pots recovered were all meaningful, beautiful, and old. Commercial, aesthetic, and scientific worth in both cases presupposed a given system of value. This system finds intrinsic interest and beauty in objects from a past time, and it assumes that collecting everyday objects from ancient (preferably vanished) civilizations will be more *rewarding* than collecting, for example, decorated thermoses from modern China or customized T-shirts from Oceania. Old objects are endowed with a sense of 'depth' by their historically minded collectors. Temporality is reified and salvaged as origin, beauty, and knowledge.

This archaizing system has not always dominated Western collecting. The curiosities of the New World gathered and appreciated in the sixteenth century were not necessarily valued as antiquities, the products of primitive or 'past' civilizations. They frequently occupied a category of the marvelous, of a present 'Golden Age' (Honour 1975; Mullaney 1983; Rabassa 1985). More recently the retrospective bias of Western appropriations of the world's cultures has come under scrutiny (Fabian 1983; Clifford 1986). Cultural or artistic 'authenticity' has as much to do with an inventive present as with a past, its objectification, preservation, or revival.

Since the turn of the century, objects collected from non-Western sources have been classified in two major categories: as (scientific) cultural artifacts or as (aesthetic) works of art.[4] Other collectibles – mass-produced commodities, 'tourist art,' curios, and so on – have been less systematically valued; at best they find a place in exhibits of 'technology' or 'folklore.' These and other locations within what may be called the 'modern art-culture system' can be visualized with the help of a (somewhat procrustian) diagram.

A.J. Greimas' 'semiotic square' (Greimas and Rastier 1968) shows us 'that any initial binary opposition can, by the operation of negations and the appropriate syntheses, generate a much larger field of terms which, however, all necessarily remain locked in the closure of the initial system' (Jameson 1981: 62). Adapting Greimas for the purposes of cultural criticism, Fredric Jameson uses the semiotic square to reveal 'the limits of a specific ideological consciousness, [marking] the conceptual points beyond which that consciousness cannot go, and between which it is condemned to oscillate' (ibid.: 47). Following his example, I offer the following map (see Figure 9.1) of a historically specific, contestable field of meanings and institutions.

Beginning with an initial opposition, by a process of negation four terms are generated. This establishes horizontal and vertical axes and between them four semantic zones: (1) the zone of authentic masterpieces, (2) the zone of authentic artifacts, (3) the zone of inauthentic masterpieces, (4) the zone of inauthentic artifacts. Most objects – old and new, rare and common, familiar and exotic – can be located in one of these zones or, ambiguously, in traffic, between two zones.

The system classifies objects and assigns them relative value. It establishes the 'contexts' in which they properly belong and between which they circulate. Regular movements toward positive value proceed from bottom to top and from right to left. These movements select artifacts of enduring worth or rarity, their value normally guaranteed by a 'vanishing' cultural status or by the selection and pricing mechanisms of the art market. The value of Shaker crafts reflects the fact that Shaker society no longer exists: the stock is limited. In the art world work is recognized as 'important' by connoisseurs and collectors according to criteria that are more than simply aesthetic (see Becker 1982). Indeed, prevailing definitions of what is 'beautiful' or 'interesting' sometimes change quite rapidly.

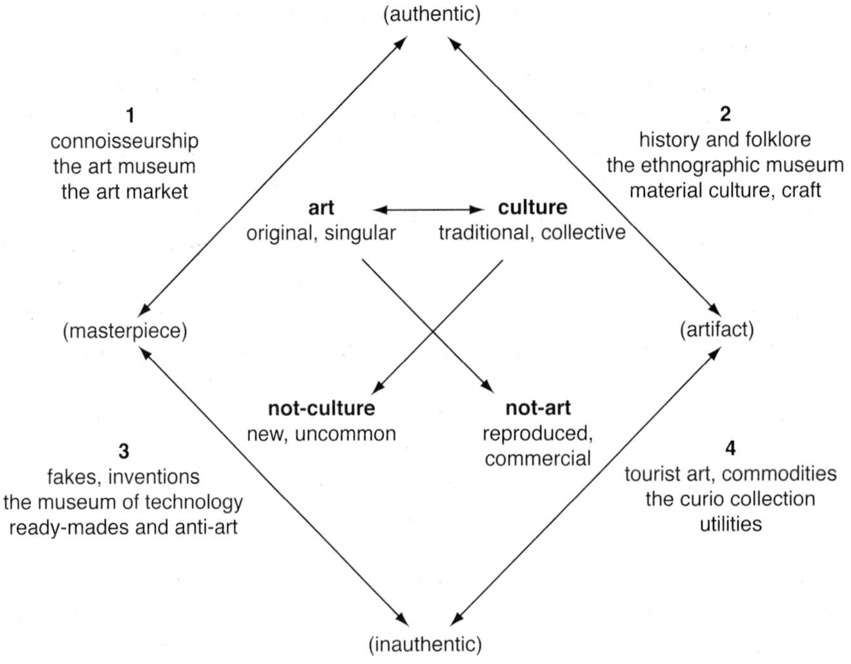

Figure 9.1 'The Art–Culture System': a machine for making authenticity (Diagram: James Clifford)

An area of frequent traffic in the system is that linking zones 1 and 2. Objects move in two directions along this path. Things of cultural or historical value may be promoted to the status of fine art. Examples of movement in this direction, from ethnographic 'culture' to fine 'art,' are plentiful. Tribal objects located in art galleries (the Rockefeller Wing at the Metropolitan Museum in New York) or displayed anywhere according to 'formalist' rather than 'contextualist' protocols (Ames 1986: 39–42) move in this way. Crafts (Shaker work collected at the Whitney Museum in 1986), 'folk art,' certain antiques, 'naive' art are all subject to periodic promotions. Movement in the inverse direction occurs whenever art masterworks are culturally and historically 'contextualized,' something that has been occurring more and more explicitly. Perhaps the most dramatic case has been the relocation of France's great impressionist collection, formerly at the Jeu de Paume, to the new Museum of the Nineteenth Century at the Gare d'Orsay. Here art masterpieces take their place in the panorama of an historical-cultural 'period.' The panorama includes an emerging industrial urbanism and its triumphant technology, 'bad' as well as 'good' art. A less dramatic movement from zone 1 to zone 2 can be seen in the routine process within art galleries whereby objects become 'dated,' of interest less as immediately powerful works of genius than as fine examples of a period style.

Movement also occurs between the lower and upper halves of the system, usually in an upward direction. Commodities in zone 4 regularly enter zone 2, becoming rare period pieces and thus collectibles (old green glass Coke bottles).

Much current non-Western work migrates between the status of 'tourist art' and creative cultural-artistic strategy. Some current productions of Third World peoples have entirely shed the stigma of modern commercial inauthenticity. For example, Haitian 'primitive' painting – commercial and of relatively recent, impure origin – has moved fully into the art-culture circuit. Significantly this work entered the art market by association with zone 2, becoming valued as the work not simply of individual artists but of *Haitians*. Haitian painting is surrounded by special associations with the land of voodoo, magic, and negritude. Though specific artists have come to be known and prized, the aura of 'cultural' production attaches to them much more than, say, to Picasso, who is not in any essential way valued as a 'Spanish artist.' The same is true, as we shall see, of many recent works of tribal art, whether from the Sepik or the American Northwest Coast. Such works have largely freed themselves from the tourist or commodity category to which, because of their modernity, purists had often relegated them; but they cannot move directly into zone 1, the art market, without trailing clouds of authentic (traditional) culture. There can be no direct movement from zone 4 to zone 1.

Occasional travel occurs between zones 4 and 3, for example when a commodity or technological artifact is perceived to be a case of special inventive creation. The object is selected out of commercial or mass culture, perhaps to be featured in a museum of technology. Sometimes such objects fully enter the realm of art: 'technological' innovations or commodities may be contextualized as modern 'design,' thus passing through zone 3 into zone 1 (for example, the furniture, household machines, cars, and so on displayed at the Museum of Modern Art in New York).

There is also regular traffic between zones 1 and 3. Exposed art forgeries are demoted (while none the less preserving something of their original aura). Conversely, various forms of 'anti-art' and art parading its unoriginality or 'inauthenticity' are collected and valued (Warhol's soup can, Sherrie Levine's photo of a photo by Walker Evans, Duchamp's urinal, bottle rack, or shovel). Objects in zone 3 are all potentially collectible within the general domain of art: they are uncommon, sharply distinct from or blatantly cut out of culture. Once appropriated by the art world, like Duchamp's ready-mades, they circulate within zone 1.

The art-culture system I have diagramed excludes and marginalizes various residual and emergent contexts. To mention only one: the categories of art and culture, technology and commodity are strongly secular. 'Religious' objects can be valued as great art (an altarpiece by Giotto), as folk art (the decorations on a Latin American popular saint's shrine), or as cultural artifact (an Indian rattle). Such objects have no individual 'power' or mystery – qualities once possessed by 'fetishes' before they were reclassified in the modern system as primitive art or cultural artifact. What 'value,' however, is stripped from an altarpiece when it is moved out of a functioning church (or when its church begins to function as a museum)? Its specific power or sacredness is relocated to a general aesthetic realm.

It is important to stress the historicity of this art-culture system. It has not reached its final form: the positions and values assigned to collectible artifacts have changed and will continue to do so. Moreover a synchronic diagram cannot represent zones of contest and transgression except as movements or ambiguities among fixed poles.

Indeed, much current 'tribal art' participates in the regular art-culture traffic *and* in traditional spiritual contexts not accounted for by the system (Coe 1986). Whatever its contested domains, though, generally speaking the system still confronts any collected exotic object with a stark alternative between a second home in an ethnographic or an aesthetic milieu. The modern ethnographic museum and the art museum or private art collection have developed separate, complementary modes of classification. In the former a work of 'sculpture' is displayed along with other objects of similar function or in proximity to objects from the same cultural group, including utilitarian artifacts such as spoons, bowls, or spears. A mask or statue may be grouped with formally dissimilar objects and explained as part of a ritual or institutional complex. The names of individual sculptors are unknown or suppressed. In art museums a sculpture is identified as the creation of an individual: Rodin, Giacometti, Barbara Hepworth. Its place in everyday cultural practices (including the market) is irrelevant to its essential meaning. Whereas in the ethnographic museum the object is culturally or humanly 'interesting,' in the art museum it is primarily 'beautiful' or 'original.' It was not always thus.

Elizabeth Williams (1985) has traced a revealing chapter in the shifting history of these discriminations. In nineteenth-century Paris it was difficult to conceive of pre-Columbian artifacts as fully 'beautiful.' A prevailing naturalist aesthetic saw *ars Americana* as grotesque or crude. At best, pre-Columbian work could be assimilated into the category of the antiquity and appreciated through the filter of Viollet-le-Duc's medievalism. Williams shows how Mayan and Incan artifacts, their status uncertain, migrated between the Louvre, the Bibliothèque Nationale, the Musée Guimet, and (after 1878) the Trocadéro, where they seemed at last to find an ethnographic home in an institution that treated them as scientific evidence. The Trocadéro's first directors, Ernest-Théodore Hamy and Rémy Verneau, showed scant interest in their aesthetic qualities.

The 'beauty' of much non-Western 'art' is a recent discovery. Before the twentieth-century many of the same objects were collected and valued, but for different reasons. In the early modern period their rarity and strangeness were prized. The 'cabinet of curiosities' jumbled everything together, with each individual object standing metonymically for a whole region or population. The collection was a microcosm, a 'summary of the universe' (Pomian 1978). The eighteenth century introduced a more serious concern for taxonomy and for the elaboration of complete series. Collecting was increasingly the concern of scientific naturalists (Feest 1984: 90), and objects were valued because they exemplified an array of systematic categories: food, clothing, building materials, agricultural tools, weapons (of war, of the hunt), and so forth. E.F. Jomard's ethnographic classifications and A.H.L.F. Pitt Rivers' typological displays were mid-nineteenth-century culminations of this taxonomic vision (Chapman 1985: 24–25). Pitt Rivers' typologies featured developmental sequences. By the end of the century evolutionism had come to dominate arrangements of exotic artifacts.' Whether objects were presented as antiquities, arranged geographically or by society, spread in panoplies, or arranged in realistic 'life groups' and dioramas, a story of human development was told. The object had ceased to be primarily an exotic 'curiosity' and was now a source of information entirely integrated in the universe of Western

Man (Dias 1985: 378–79). The value of exotic objects was their ability to testify to the concrete reality of an earlier stage of human Culture, a common past confirming Europe's triumphant present.

With Franz Boas and the emergence of relativist anthropology, an emphasis on placing objects in specific lived contexts was consolidated. The 'cultures' thus represented could either be arranged in a modified evolutionary series or dispersed in synchronous 'ethnographic presents.' The latter were times neither of antiquity nor of the twentieth century but rather representing the 'authentic' context of the collected objects, often just prior to their collection or display. Both collector and salvage ethnographer could claim to be the last to rescue 'the real thing.' Authenticity, as we shall see, is produced by removing objects and customs from their current historical situation – a present-becoming-future.

With the consolidation of twentieth-century anthropology, artifacts contextualized ethnographically were valued because they served as objective 'witnesses' to the total multidimensional life of a culture (Jamin 1982: 89–95; 1985). Simultaneously with new developments in art and literature, as Picasso and others began to visit the 'Troca' and to accord its tribal objects a non-ethnographic admiration, the proper place of non-Western objects was again thrown in question. In the eyes of a triumphant modernism some of these artifacts at least could be seen as universal masterpieces. The category of 'primitive art' emerged.

This development introduced new ambiguities and possibilities in a changing taxonomic system. In the mid-nineteenth century pre-Columbian or tribal objects were grotesques or antiquities. By 1920 they were cultural witnesses and aesthetic masterpieces. Since then a controlled migration has occurred between these two institutionalized domains. The boundaries of art and science, the aesthetic and the anthropological, are not permanently fixed. Indeed, anthropology and fine arts museums have recently shown signs of interpenetration. For example, the Hall of Asian Peoples at the New York Museum of Natural History reflects the 'boutique' style of display, whose objects could never seem out of place as 'art' on the walls or coffee tables of middle-class living rooms. In a complementary development downtown, the Museum of Modern Art has expanded its permanent exhibit of cultural artifacts: furniture, automobiles, home appliances, and utensils – even hanging from the ceiling, like a Northwest Coast war canoe, a much-admired bright green helicopter.

While the object systems of art and anthropology are institutionalized and powerful, they are not immutable. The categories of the beautiful, the cultural, and the authentic have changed and are changing. Thus it is important to resist the tendency of collections to be self-sufficient, to suppress their own historical, economic, and political processes of production (see Haacke 1975; Hiller 1979). Ideally the history of its own collection and display should be a visible aspect of any exhibition. It has been rumored that the Boas Room of Northwest Coast artifacts in the American Museum of Natural History was to be refurbished, its style of display modernized. Apparently (or so one hopes) the plan has been abandoned, for this atmospheric, dated hall exhibits not merely a superb collection but a moment in the history of collecting. The widely publicized Museum of Modern Art show of 1984, ' "Primitivism" in Twentieth-Century Art', made apparent (as it celebrated) the precise circumstance in which certain ethnographic objects suddenly became works of universal art. More historical self-consciousness in the display and viewing of non-Western objects can at least jostle and set in motion the ways in which anthropologists, artists, and their publics collect themselves and the world.

At a more intimate level, rather than grasping objects only as cultural signs and artistic icons (Guidieri and Pellizzi 1981), we can return to them, as James Fenton does, their lost status as fetishes – not specimens of a deviant or exotic 'fetishism' but *our own* fetishes.[5] This tactic, necessarily personal, would accord to things in collections the power to fixate rather than simply the capacity to edify or inform. African and Oceanian artifacts could once again be *objets sauvages*, sources of fascination with the power to disconcert. Seen in their resistance to classification, they could remind us of our *lack* of self-possession, of the artifices we employ to gather a world around us.

Notes

1 On collecting as a strategy of desire see the highly suggestive catalogue (Hainard and Kaehr 1982) of an exhibition entitled 'Collections Passion' at the Musée d'Ethnographie, Neuchâtel, June to December 1981. This analytic collection of collections was a *tour de force* of reflexive museology. On collecting and desire see also Donna Haraway's brilliant analysis (1985) of the American Museum of Natural History, American manhood, and the threat of decadence between 1908 and 1936. Her work suggests that the passion to collect, preserve, and display is articulated in gendered ways that are historically specific. Beaucage, Gomila, and Vallée (1976) offer critical meditations on the ethnographer's complex experience of objects.

2 Walter Benjamin's essay 'Unpacking My Library' (1969: 59–68) provides the view of a reflective devotee. Collecting appears as an art of living intimately allied with memory, with obsession, with the salvaging of order from disorder. Benjamin sees (and takes a certain pleasure in) the precariousness of the subjective space attained by the collection.

> Every passion borders on the chaotic, but the collector's passion borders on the chaos of memories. More than that: the chance, the fate, that suffuse the past before my eyes are conspicuously present in the accustomed confusion of these books. For what else is this collection but a disorder to which habit has accommodated itself to such an extent that it can appear as order? You have all heard of people whom the loss of their books has turned into invalids, of those who in order to acquire them became criminals. These are the very areas in which any order is a balancing act of extreme precariousness.
>
> (Benjamin 1969: 60)

3 My understanding of the role of the fetish as a mark of otherness in Western intellectual history – from DeBrosses to Marx, Freud, and Deleuze – owes a great deal to the largely unpublished work of William Pietz; see 'The Problem of the Fetish, I' (1985).

4 For 'hard' articulations of ethnographic culturalism and aesthetic formalism see Sieber 1971, Price and Price 1980, Vogel 1985, and Rubin 1984. The first two works argue that art can be understood (as opposed to merely appreciated) only in its original context. Vogel and Rubin assert that aesthetic qualities transcend their original local articulation, that 'masterpieces' appeal to universal or at least transcultural human sensibilities. For a glimpse of how the often incompatible categories of 'aesthetic excellence,' 'use,' 'rarity,' 'age,' and so on are debated in the exercise of assigning authentic value to tribal works, see the richly inconclusive symposium on 'Authenticity in African Art' organized by the journal *African Arts* (Willett *et al.* 1986).

5 For a post-Freudian positive sense of the fetish see Leiris 1929, 1946; for fetish theory's radical possibilities see Pietz 1985, which draws on Deleuze; and for a repentant semiologist's perverse sense of the fetish (the 'punctum') as a place of strictly personal meaning unformed by cultural codes (the 'studium') see Barthes 1980. Gomila (1976) rethinks ethnographic material culture from some of these surrealist-psychoanalytic perspectives.

References

Ames, Michael (1986) *Museums, the Public, and Anthropology: A Study in the Anthropology of Anthropology*, Vancouver: University of British Columbia Press.

Barthes, Roland (1980) *La chambre claire*, translated by Richard Howard as *Camera Lucida*, New York: Hill and Wang (1981).

Baudrillard, Jean (1968) *Le système des objets*, Paris: Gallimard.

Beaucage, Pierre, Jacques Gomila and Lionel Vallée (1976) *L'experience anthropologique*, Montreal: Presses de l'Université de Montréal, pp. 71–133.

Becker, Howard (1982) *Art Worlds*, Berkeley: University of California Press.

Benjamin, Walter (1969) *Illuminations*, Hannah Arendt (ed.), New York: Schocken Books.

Bunn, James (1980) 'The Aesthetics of British Mercantilism', *New Literary History* 11: 303–21.

Chapman, William (1985) 'Arranging Ethnology: A.H.L.F. Pitt Rivers and the Typological Tradition', *History of Anthropology*, Volume 3, *Objects and Others*, George Stocking (ed.), pp. 15–48, Madison: University of Wisconsin Press.

Clifford, James (1986) 'On Ethnographic Allegory' in *Writing Culture*, James Clifford and George Marcus (eds), Berkeley: University of California Press, pp. 98–121.

Coe, Ralph (1986) *Lost and Found Traditions: Native American Art: 1965–1985*, Seattle: University of Washington Press.

Cole, Douglas (1985) *Captured Heritage: The Scramble for Northwest Coast Artifacts*, Seattle: University of Washington Press.

Defert, Daniel (1982) 'The Collection of the World: Accounts of Voyages from the Sixteenth to the Eighteenth Centuries', *Dialectical Anthropology* 7: 11–20.

Dias, Nelia (1985) 'La fondation de Musée d'Ethnographie du Trocadéro (1879–1990): Un aspect de l'histoire institutionelle de l'anthropologie française'. Thesis, troisième cycle, Ecole des Hautes Etudes en Sciences Sociales, Paris.

Fabian, Johannes (1983) *Time and the Other: How Anthropology Makes Its Object*, New York: Columbia University Press.

Feest, Christian (1984) 'From North America', in *'Primitivism' in Twentieth-Century Art*, William Rubin (ed.), New York: Museum of Modern Art, pp. 85–95.

Fenton, James (1984) *Children in Exile: Poems 1968–1984*, New York: Random House.

Fisher, Philip (1975) 'The Future's Past', *New Literary History* 6 (3): 587–606.

Gomila, Jacques (1976) 'Objectif, objectal, objecteur, objecte', in Pierre Beaucage, Jacques Gomila, and Lionel Vallée, *L'expérience anthropologique*, Montreal: Presses de l'Université de Montréal, pp. 71–133.

Graburn, Nelson (ed.) (1976) *Ethnic and Tourist Arts*, Berkeley: University of California Press.

Greimas, A.J. and François Rastier (1968) 'The Interaction of Semiotic Constraints', *Yale French Studies* no. 41: 86–105.

Guidieri, Rémo and Francesco Pellizzi (1981) Editorial, *Res* 1: 3–6.

Haacke, Hans (1975) *Framing and Being Framed*, Halifax: The Press of the Nova Scotia College of Art and Design.

Hainard, Jacques and Rolland Kaehr (eds) (1982) *Collections passion*, Neuchâtel: Musée d'Ethnographie.

Handler, Richard (1985) 'On Having a Culture: Nationalism and the Preservation of Quebec's *Patrimoine*', *History of Anthropology*, Volume 3, *Objects and Others*, George Stocking (ed.), Madison: University of Wisconsin Press, pp. 192–217.

Haraway, Donna (1985) 'Teddy Bear Patriarchy: Taxidermy in the Garden of Eden, New York City, 1908–1936', *Social Text*, Winter: 20–63.

Hiller, Susan (1979) Review of 'Sacred Circles: 2,000 Years of North American Art', *Studio International*, December: 8–15.

Honour, Hugh (1975) *The New Golden Land*, New York: Pantheon.

Jameson, Fredric (1981) *The Political Unconscious: Narrative as a Socially Symbolic Act*, Ithaca: Cornell University Press.

Jamin, Jean (1982) 'Objets trouvés des paradis perdus: A propos de la Mission Dakar-Dijibouti', in *Collections passion*, J. Hainard and R. Kaehr (eds), Neuchâtel: Musée d'Ethnographie, pp. 69–100.

Jamin, Jean (1985) 'Les objets ethnographiques sont-ils des choses perdues?', in *Temps perdu, temps retrouvé: Voir les choses du passé au présent*, J. Hainard and R. Kaehr (eds), Neuchâtel: Musée d'Ethnographie, pp. 51–74.

Jules-Rosette, Benetta (1984) *The Messages of Tourist Art*, New York: Plenum.

Leiris, Michel (1929) 'Alberto Giacometti', *Documents* 1 (4): 209–11. Translated by J. Clifford in *Sulfur* 15 (1986): 38–41.

Leiris, Michel (1946) *L'age d'homme*, Paris: Gallimard. Translated by Richard Howard (1985) as *Manhood*, Berkeley: North Point Press.

Macpherson, C.B. (1962) *The Political Theory of Possessive Individualism*, Oxford: Oxford University Press.

Mullaney, Steven (1983) 'Strange Things, Gross Terms, Curious Customs: The Rehearsal of Cultures in the Late Renaissance', *Representations*, 3: 40–67.

Pietz, William (1985) 'The Problem of the Fetish, 1', *Res* 9 (Spring): 5–17.

Pomian, Kryzsztof (1978) 'Entre l'invisible et le visible: La collection', *Libre* 78 (3): 3–56.

Price, Sally and Richard Price (1980) *Afro-American Arts of the Suriname Rain Forest*, Berkeley: University of California Press.

Pye, Michael (1987) 'Whose Art Is It Anyway?', *Connoisseur*, March: 78–85.

Rabassa, José (1985) 'Fantasy, Errancy, and Symbolism in New World Motifs: An Essay on Sixteenth-Century Spanish Historiography', Ph.D. diss., University of California, Santa Cruz.

Rubin, William (ed.) (1984) *'Primitivism' in Modern Art: Affinity of the Tribal and the Modern*, 2 volumes, New York: Museum of Modern Art.

Saisselin, Rémy (1984) *The Bourgeois and the Bibelot*, New Brunswick, NJ: Rutgers University Press.

Sieber, Roy (1971) 'The Aesthetics of Traditional African Art', in *Art and Aesthetics in Primitive Societies*, Carol F. Jopling (ed.), New York: Dutton, pp. 127–45.

Stewart, Susan (1984) *On Longing: Narratives of the Miniature, the Gigantic, the Souvenir, the Collection*, Baltimore: Johns Hopkins University Press.

Vogel, Susan (1985) 'Introduction', in *African Masterpieces from the Musée de l'Homme*, New York: Harry Abrams, pp. 10–11.

Willett, Frank *et al.* (1976) 'Authenticity in African Art', *African Arts* 9 (3): 6–74 (special section).

Williams, Elizabeth (1985) 'Art and Artifact at the Trocadéro', in *History of Anthropology*, Volume 3, *Objects and Others*, George Stocking (ed.), Madison: University of Wisconsin Press, pp. 145–66.

Chapter 10

Paul Virilio

A TOPOGRAPHICAL AMNESIA

'THE ARTS REQUIRE WITNESSES,' Marmontel once said. A century later Auguste Rodin asserted that it is the visible world that demands to be revealed by means other than the latent images of the phototype.

In the course of his famous conversations with the sculptor, Paul Gsell remarked, apropos Rodin's *The Age of Bronze* and *St John the Baptist*,[1] 'I am still left wondering how those great lumps of bronze or stone actually seem to move, how obviously immobile figures appear to act and even to be making pretty strenuous efforts. . . .'

Rodin retorts, 'Have you ever looked closely at instantaneous photographs of men in motion? . . . Well then, what have you noticed?'

'That they never seem to be making headway. Generally, they seem to be standing still on one leg, or hopping.'

'Exactly! Take my "St John", for example. I've shown him with both feet on the ground, whereas an instantaneous photograph taken of a model performing the same movement would most likely show the back foot already raised and moving forward. Or else the reverse – the front foot would not yet be on the ground if the back leg in the photograph were in the same position as in my statue. That is precisely why the model in the photograph would have the bizarre look of a man suddenly *struck with paralysis*. Which confirms what I was just saying about movement in art. People in photographs suddenly seem frozen in mid-air, despite being caught in full swing: this is because every part of their body is reproduced at exactly the same twentieth or fortieth of a second, so there is no gradual unfolding of a gesture, as there is in art.'

Gsell objects, 'So, when art interprets movement and finds itself completely at loggerheads with photography, which is an *unimpeachable mechanical witness*, art obviously distorts the truth.'

'No', Rodin replies, 'It is art that tells the truth and photography that lies. For *in reality time does not stand still*, and if the artist manages to give the impression that a gesture is being executed over several seconds, their work is certainly much less conventional than the scientific image in which time is abruptly suspended. . . .'

Rodin then goes on to discuss Géricault's horses, going flat out in the painting *Race at Epsom*, and the critics who claim that the photographic plate never gives the same impression. Rodin counters that the artist condenses several successive movements into a single image, so *if the representation as a whole is false in showing these movements as simultaneous, it is true when the parts are observed in sequence, and it is only this truth that counts since it is what we see and what impresses us.*

Prompted by the artist to follow the progress of a character's action, the spectator, scanning it, has the illusion of seeing the movement performed. This illusion is thus not produced *mechanically* as it would later be with the snapshots of the chronophotographic apparatus, through retinal retention – photosensitivity to light stimuli – but *naturally*, through eye movement.

The *veracity* of the work therefore depends, in part, on this solicitation of eye (and possibly body) movement in the witness who, in order to *sense* an object with maximum clarity, must accomplish an enormous number of tiny, rapid movements from one part of the object to another. Conversely, if the eye's mobility is transformed into fixity

> *by artificial lenses or bad habits*, the sensory apparatus undergoes distortion and vision degenerates. . . . In his greedy anxiety to achieve his end, which is to do the greatest possible amount of good seeing in the shortest possible time, the starer neglects the only means whereby this end can be achieved.[2]

Besides, Rodin insists, the *veracity* of the whole is only made possible through the lack of precision of details conceived merely as so many material props enabling either a falling short of or a going beyond immediate vision. The work of art requires witnesses because it sallies forth with its image into the depths of a material time which is also our own. This sharing of duration is automatically defeated by the innovation of photographic instantaneity, for if the instantaneous image pretends to scientific accuracy in its details; the snapshot's image-freeze or rather *image-time-freeze* invariably distorts the witness's felt temporality, *that time that is the movement of something created.*[3]

The plaster studies on show in Rodin's atelier at Meudon reveal a state of evident anatomical breakdown – huge, unruly hands and feet, dislocated, distended limbs, bodies in suspension – the representation of movement pushed to the limits of collapse or take-off. From here it is only a step to Clément Ader and the first aeroplane flight, the conquest of the air through mobilisation of something heavier than air which is followed, in 1895, by cinematography's mobilisation of the snapshot, *retinal take-off*, that moment when, with the achievement of metabolic speeds, '*all that we called art seems to have become paralytic*, while the film-maker lights up the thousand candles of his projectors'.[4]

When Bergson asserts that *mind is a thing that endures*, one might add that it is our duration that thinks, feels, sees. The first creation of consciousness would then be its own speed in its time-distance, speed thereby becoming causal idea, idea before the idea.[5] It is thus now common to think of our memories as multidimensional, of thought as transfer, transport (*metaphora*) in the literal sense.

Already Cicero and the ancient memory-theorists believed you could consolidate natural memory with the right training. They invented a *topographical system*, the Method of Loci, an imagery-mnemonics which consisted of selecting a sequence of places, locations, that could easily be ordered in time and space. For example, you might imagine wandering through the house, choosing as loci various tables, a chair seen through a doorway, a windowsill, a mark on a wall. Next, the material to be remembered is coded into discrete images and each of the images is inserted in the appropriate order into the various loci. To memorise a speech, you transform the main points into concrete images and mentally 'place' each of the points in order at each successive locus. When it is time to deliver the speech, all you have to do is recall the parts of the house in order.

The same kind of training is still used today by stage actors and barristers at court. It was members of the theatre industry like *Kammerspiel* theorists Lupu Pick and the scenarist Carl Mayer who, at the beginning of the 1920s, took the whole thing to ludicrous lengths as a film technique, offering the audience a kind of cinematic *huis clos* occurring in a unique place and at the exact moment of projection. Their film sets were not expressionist but realist so that familiar objects, the minutiae of daily life, assume an obsessive symbolic importance. According to its creators, this was supposed to render all dialogue, all subtitles superfluous.

The silent screen was to make the surroundings speak the same way practitioners of *artificial memory* made the room they lived in, the theatre boards they trod speak, *in retrospect*. Following Dreyer and a host of others, Alfred Hitchcock employed a somewhat similar coding system, bearing in mind that viewers do not manufacture mental images on the basis of what they are immediately given to see, but on the basis of their memories, *by themselves filling in the blanks and their minds with images created retrospectively, as in childhood*.

For a traumatised population, in the aftermath of the First World War, the *Kammerspiel* cinema altered the conditions of invention of artificial memory, which was itself also born of the catastrophic disappearance of the scenery. The story goes that the lyrical poet Simonides of Chios, in the middle of reciting a poem at a banquet, was suddenly called away to another part of the house. As soon as he left the room, the roof caved in on the other guests and, as it was a particularly heavy roof, they were all crushed to a pulp.

But with his sharpened memory, Simonides could recall the exact place occupied by each of the unfortunate guests and the bodies could thus be identified. It then really dawned on Simonides what an advantage this method of picking places and filling them in with images could be in practising the art of poetry.[6]

In May 1646 Descartes wrote to Elizabeth, 'There is such a strong connection between body and soul that thoughts that accompanied certain movements of our body at the beginning of our lives, so on accompanying them later.' Elsewhere he tells how he once as a child loved a little girl with a slight squint, and how *the impression his brain received through sight whenever he looked at her wandering eyes* remained so vividly present that he continued to be drawn to people with the same defect for the rest of his life.

The moment they appeared on the scene, the first optical devices (Al-Hasan ibn al-Haitam aka Alhazen's camera obscura in the tenth century, Roger Bacon's instruments in the thirteenth, the increasing number of visual prostheses, lenses, astronomic telescopes and so on from the Renaissance on) profoundly altered the contexts in which mental images were topographically stored and retrieved, the *imperative to re-present oneself*, the imaging of the imagination which was such a great help in mathematics according to Descartes and which he considered a veritable part of the body, *veram partem corporis*.[7] Just when we were apparently procuring the means to see further and better the unseen of the universe, we were about to lose what little power we had of imagining it. The telescope, that epitome of the visual prosthesis, projected an image of a world beyond our reach and thus another way of moving about in the world, the *logistics of perception* inaugurating an unknown conveyance of sight that produced a telescoping of near and far, a *phenomenon of acceleration* obliterating our experience of distances and dimensions.[8]

More than a return to Antiquity, the Renaissance appears today as the advent of a period when all intervals were cleared; a sort of morphological 'breaking and entering' that immediately impacted on the reality-effect: once astronomic and chronometric apparatuses went commercial, geographical perception became dependent on anamorphic processes. Painters such as Holbein, who were contemporaries of Copernicus, practised a kind of iconography in which technology's first stab at leading the senses astray occupied centre stage thanks to singularly mechanistic optical devices. Apart from the displacement of the observer's point of view, complete perception of the painted work could only happen with the aid of instruments such as glass cylinders and tubes, the play of conical or spherical mirrors, magnifying glasses and other kinds of lenses. The reality-effect had become a dissociated system, a puzzle the observer was unable to solve without some traffic in light or the appropriate prostheses. Jurgis Baltrusaïtis reports that the Jesuits of Beijing used anamorphic equipment as instruments of religious propaganda to impress the Chinese and to demonstrate to them 'mechanically' that man should experience the world as an illusion of the world.[9]

In a celebrated passage of *I Saggiatore* (1623), Galileo exposes the essential features of his method: 'Philosophy is written in the immense Book of Nature which is constantly before our very eyes and which cannot be (humanly) understood unless one has previously learned the language and alphabet in which it is written. It is written in mathematical characters . . .'

We imagine it (mathematically) because it remains continually before our very eyes from the moment we first see the light of day. If, in this parabola, the duration of the visible seems simply to persist, geomorphology has disappeared or is at least reduced to an abstract language plotted on one of the first great industrial media (with all the artillery so vital to the disclosure of optical phenomena).

The celebrated Gutenberg Bible had by then been in print for nearly two centuries and the book trade in Europe, with a printing works in every town and a great number of them in the capitals, had already disseminated its products in the millions. Significantly, the 'art of writing artificially' as it was then called, was also, from its inception, placed at the service of religious propaganda, the Catholic Church at first, then the Reformation. But it was also an instrument of diplomatic and military propaganda, a fact that would later earn it the name *thought artillery*, well before Marcel L'Herbier labelled his camera a *rotary image press*.

A connoisseur of optical mirages, Galileo now no longer preferred to form images in the world directly in order to imagine it; he took up instead the much more limited oculomotor labour of reading.[10]

From Antiquity, a progressive simplification of written characters can be discerned, followed by a simplification of typographical composition which corresponded to an acceleration in the transmission of messages and led logically to the radical abbreviation of the contents of information. The tendency to make reading time as intensive as speaking time stemmed from the tactical necessities of military conquest and more particularly of the battlefield, that occasional field of perception, privileged space of the vision of the trooper, of rapid stimuli, slogans and other logotypes of war.

The battlefield is the place where social intercourse breaks off, where political rapprochement fails; making way for the inculcation of terror. The panoply of acts of war thus always tends to be organised at a distance, or rather, to organise distances. Orders, in fact speech of any kind, are transmitted by long-range instruments which, in any case, are often inaudible among combatants' screams, the clash of arms, and, later, the various explosions and detonations.

Signal flags, multicoloured pennants, schematic emblems then replace faltering vocal signals and constitute a *delocalised language* which can now be grasped via brief and distant glances, inaugurating a vectorisation that will become concrete in 1794 with the first aerial telegraph line between Paris and Lille and the announcement, at the Convention, of the French troops' victory at Condé-sur-l'Escaut. That same year, Lazare Carnot, organiser of the Revolution's armies, recorded the speed of transmission of military information that was at the very heart of the nation's political and social structures. He commented that if terror was the order of the day, it could thereafter hold sway at the front just as well and at the same time as behind the lines.

Some time later, at the moment when photography became instantaneous, messages and words, reduced to a few elementary signs, were themselves telescoped to the speed of light. On 6 January 1838 Samuel Morse, the American physicist and painter of battle-scenes, succeeded in sending the first electric-telegraph message from his workshop in New Jersey. (The term meaning *to write at a distance* was also used at the time to denote certain stagecoaches and other means of fast transport.)

The race between the *transtextual* and the *transvisual* ran on until the emergence of the *instantaneous ubiquity* of the audiovisual mix. Simultaneously tele-diction and television, this ultimate transfer finally undermines the age-old problematic of the *site where mental images are formed* as well as that of the consolidation of natural memory.

'The boundaries between things are disappearing, the subject and the world are no longer separate, time seems to stand still,' wrote the physicist Ernst Mach, known particularly for having established the role of the speed of sound in aerodynamics. In fact the *teletopological* phenomenon remains heavily marked by its remote beginnings in war, and does not *bring the subject closer* to the world. . . .

In the manner of the combatant of antiquity, it anticipates human movement, outstripping every displacement of the body and abolishing space.

With the industrial proliferation of visual and audiovisual prostheses and unrestrained use of instantaneous transmission equipment from earliest childhood onwards, we now routinely see the encoding of increasingly elaborate mental images together with a steady decline in retention rates and recall. In other words we are looking at the rapid collapse of mnemonic consolidation.

This collapse seems only natural, if one remembers *a contrario* that seeing, and its spatio-temporal organisation, precede gesture and speech and their co-ordination in knowing, recognising, making known (as images of our thoughts), our thoughts themselves and cognitive functions, which are never ever passive.[11]

Communicational experiments with newborn babies are particularly instructive. A small mammal condemned, unlike other mammals, to prolonged semi-immobility, the child, it seems, hangs on maternal smells (breast, neck . . .), but also on eye movements. In the course of an eye-tracking exercise that consists of holding a child of about three months in one's arms, at eye level and face to face, and turning it gently from right to left, then from left to right, the child's eyes 'bulge' in the reverse direction, as makers of old porcelain dolls clearly saw, simply because the infant does not want to lose sight of the smiling face of the person holding it. The child experiences this exercise in the expansion of its field of vision as deeply gratifying; it laughs and wants to go on doing it. Something very fundamental is clearly going on here, since the infant is in the process of forming a lasting communicational image by mobilising its eyes. As Lacan said, *communication makes you laugh* and so the child is in an ideally human position.

Everything I see is in principle within my reach, at least within reach of my sight, marked on the map of the 'I can'. In this important formulation, Merleau-Ponty pinpoints precisely what will eventually find itself ruined by the banalisation of a certain teletopology. The bulk of what I see is, in fact and in principle, no longer within my reach. And even if it lies within reach of my sight, it is no longer necessarily inscribed on the map of the 'I can'. The logistics of perception in fact destroy what earlier modes of representation preserved of this original, ideally human happiness, the 'I can' of sight, which kept art from being obscene. I have often been able to confirm this watching models who were perfectly happy to pose in the nude and submit to whatever painters and sculptors wanted them to do, but flatly refused to allow themselves to be photographed, feeling that that would amount to a pornographic act.

There is a vast iconography evoking this prime communicational image. It has been one of the major themes in Christian art, presenting the person of Mary (named *Mediator*) as the initial map of the Infant-God's '*I can*'. Conversely, the Reformation's rejection of consubstantiality and of such close physical proximity intervenes during the Renaissance, with the proliferation of optical devices. . . . Romantic poetry is one of the last movements to employ this type of cartography. In Novalis, the body of the beloved (having become profane) is the universe in miniature and the universe is merely the extension of the beloved's body.

So in spite of all this machinery of transfer, we get no closer to the *productive unconscious of sight*, something the surrealists once dreamed of in relation to photography and cinema. Instead, we only get as far as its *unconsciousness*, an annihilation of place and appearance, the future amplitude of which is still hard to imagine. *The death of art*, heralded from the beginning of the nineteenth century, turns out to be merely an initial, disquieting symptom of this process, despite being unprecedented in the history of human societies. This is the emergence of the deregulated world that Hermann Rauschning, the author of *The Revolution of Nihilism*, spoke about in November 1939 in relation to Nazism's project: *the universal collapse of all forms of established order, something never before seen in human memory*. In this unprecedented crisis of representation (bearing absolutely no relation to some kind of classic decadence), the age-old *act of seeing* was to be replaced by a regressive perceptual state, a kind of *syncretism*, resembling a pitiful caricature of the semi-immobility of early infancy, the sensitive substratum now existing only as a fuzzy morass from which a few shapes, smells, sounds accidentally leap out . . . more sharply perceived.

Thanks to work like that of W.R. Russell and Nathan (1946), scientists have become aware of the relationship of post-perceptual visual processes to time. The storage of mental images is never instantaneous; it has to do with the processing of perception. Yet it is precisely this storage process that is rejected today. The young American film-maker Laurie Anderson, among others, is able to declare herself *a mere voyeur interested only in details*; as for the rest, she says, '*I use computers that are tragically unable to forget, like endless rubbish dumps*.'[12]

Returning to Galileo's simile of deciphering the book of the real, it is not so much a question here of what Benjamin called the *image-illiteracy* of the photographers incapable of reading their own photographs. It is a question of *visual dyslexia*. Teachers have been saying for a long time now that the last few generations have great difficulty understanding what they read because they are incapable of *re-presenting* it to themselves. . . . For them, words have in the end lost their ability to come alive, since images, more rapidly perceived, were supposed to replace words according to the photographers, the silent film-makers, the propagandists and advertisers of the early twentieth century. Now there is no longer anything to replace, and the number of the visually illiterate and dyslexic keeps multiplying.

Here again, recent studies of dyslexia have established a direct connection between the subject's visual abilities, on the one hand, and language and reading on the other. They frequently record a weakening of central (foveal) vision, the site of the most acute sensation, along with subsequent enhancing of a more or less frantic peripheral vision – a dissociation of sight in which the heterogeneous swamps the homogenous. This means that, as in narcotic states, the series of visual impressions become meaningless. They no longer seem to belong to us, they just exist, as though the speed of light had won out, this time, over the totality of the message.

If we think about light, which has no image and yet creates images, we find that the use of light stimuli in crowd control goes back a long way. The inhabitant of the ancient city, for instance, was not the indoors type; he was out on the street, except at nightfall for obvious safety reasons. Commerce, craft, riots and daily brawls, traffic jams. . . . Bossuet was worried about this chronic lightweight who could not keep still, did not stop to think where he was going, who no longer even knew where he was and would soon be mistaking night for day. At the end of the seventeenth century, police lieutenant La Reynie came up with 'Lighting Inspectors' to reassure the Parisian public and encourage them to go out at night. When he quit his post in

1697, having been promoted chief of police, there were 6,500 lanterns lighting up the capital which would soon be known by contemporaries as the *city of light* for 'the streets are ablaze all through winter and even of a full moon', as the Englishman Lister wrote, comparing Paris to London which enjoyed no such privilege.

In the eighteenth century the by now rather shady population of Paris mushroomed and the capital became known as the *New Babylon*. The brightness of its lighting signalled not just a desire for security, but also individual and institutional economic prosperity, as well as the fact that 'brilliance is all the rage' among the new elites – bankers, gentlemen farmers and the *nouveaux riches* of dubious origins and careers. Whence the taste for garish lights which no lampshade could soften. On the contrary, they were amplified by the play of mirrors multiplying them to infinity. Mirrors turned into dazzling reflectors. A *giorno* lighting now spilled out of the buildings where it once helped turn reality into illusion – theatres, palaces, luxury hotels, princely gardens. Artificial light was in itself a spectacle soon to be made available to all, and street lighting, the democratisation of lighting, is designed to trick everyone's eyes. There is everything from old-fashioned fireworks to the light shows of the engineer Philippe Lebon, the inventor of the gaslight who, in the middle of a social revolution, opened the Seignelay Hotel to the public so they might appreciate the value of his discovery. The streets were packed at night with people gazing upon the works of lighting engineers and pyrotechnists known collectively as *impressionists*.[13]

But this constant straining after 'more light' was already leading to a sort of precocious disability, a blindness; the eye literally popped out of its socket. In this respect the delegation of sight to Nièpce's *artificial retinas*, took on its full meaning.[14] Faced with such a permanent regime of bedazzlement, the range of adaptability of the eye's crystalline lens was quickly lost. Madame de Genlis, then governess to the children of Louis-Philippe, pointed to the damage caused by the abuse of lighting: 'Since lamps have come into fashion, it is the young who are wearing glasses; good eyes are now only to be found among the old who have kept up the habit of reading and writing with a candle shaded by a candle guard.'

That perverted peasant and Paris pedestrian, Restif de la Bretonne, observing life with the rustic's sharp eye, soon gave way to a new, anonymous, ageless character who no longer took to the streets looking for *a man*, like Diogenes with his lantern burning in broad daylight. He now sought light itself, for where there is light there is the crowd. According to Edgar Allan Poe, our man no longer inhabited the big city strictly speaking (London, as it happens), but the dense throng. His only itinerary was that of the human stream wherever it was bound, wherever it was to be found. '*All was dark yet splendid*', Poe wrote, and the man's only terror was the risk of losing the crowd thanks to the strange light effects, 'to the speed with which the world of light vanishes. . . .' For this man, frowning furiously, shooting frantic looks here, there and everywhere towards all those swarming round him, drowning in the flood of images, one face constantly being gobbled up by another, the endless surging throng permitted only the briefest glance at any one face. When, having pursued him for hours, the exhausted author finally caught up and planted himself right in front of him, the man was pulled up short for a second, but looked straight through the author without even seeing him, then immediately flitted off on his merry manic way.[15]

In 1902 it was Jack London's turn to come to London and he too followed, step by step, the *people of the abyss*. Urban lighting had by then become a torture for the mass of social rejects of the capital of the world's most powerful Empire. The vast mob of the homeless represented more than 10 per cent of London's population of six million. They were not allowed to sleep at night anywhere, whether in parks, on benches or on the street; they had to keep walking till dawn, when they were finally allowed to lie down in places where there was little danger of anyone seeing them.[16]

No doubt because contemporary architects and town planners have no more than anyone else been able to escape such psychotropic disorders (the topographical amnesia described by neuropathologists as the *Elpenor Syndrome* or *incomplete awakening*[17]), one can say, with Agnès Varda, that *the most distinctive cities bear within them the capacity of being nowhere* . . . the dream décor of oblivion.

So, in Vienna, in 1908, Adolf Loos delivered his celebrated discourse *Ornament and Crime*, a manifesto in which he preaches the standardisation of *total functionalism* and waxes lyrical about the fact that 'the greatness of our age lies in its inability to produce a new form of decoration'. For, he claims, 'in fashioning ornaments human labour, money and material are ruined'. Loos considered this a real crime 'which we cannot simply shrug off'. This would be followed by Walter Gropius's 'industrial-building production standards', the ephemeral architecture of the Italian Futurist Fortunato Depero, the Berlin *Licht-Burg*, Moholy-Nagy's *space-light modulators*, Kurt Schwerdtfeger's *reflektorische Farblichtspiel* of 1922. . . .

In fact, the constructivist aesthetic would forever continue to hide behind the banalisation of form, the transparency of glass, the fluidity of vectors and the special effects of machines of transfer or transmission. When the Nazis came to power, busily persecuting 'degenerate artists' and architects and extolling the stability of materials and the durability of monuments, their resistance to time and to the obliviousness of history, they were actually putting the new psychotropic power to good use for propaganda purposes.

Hitler's architect, Albert Speer, organised the Nazi Zeppelin Field festivities and advocated the value of ruins. For the party rally at Nuremberg in 1935, he used 150 anti-aircraft searchlights with their beams pointing upwards, making a rectangle of light in the night sky. He wrote: 'Within these luminous walls, the first of their kind, the rally took place with all its rituals. . . . I now feel strangely moved by the idea that the most successful architectural creation of my life was a chimera, an immaterial mirage.'[18] Doomed to disappear at first light, leaving no more material trace than a few films and the odd photograph, the 'crystal castle' was especially aimed at Nazi militants who, according to Goebbels, *obey a law they are not even consciously aware of but which they could recite in their dreams*.

On the basis of 'scientific' analysis of the stenographic speed of his various speeches, Hitler's master of propaganda had invented, again in his own estimation, a *new mass language* which 'no longer has anything to do with archaic and allegedly popular forms of expression'. He added: 'This is the beginning of an *original aesthetic style*, a vivid and galvanising form of expression.'

At least he was good at self-promotion. Such declarations recall those of Futurists such as the Portuguese Mario de Sá-Carneiro (d.1916) celebrating *The Assumption of the Acoustic Waves*: 'Aaagh! Aaagh!/ The vibrating mass is pressing in.

. . . I can even feel myself being carried along by the air, like a ball of wool!' Or Marinetti who, as a war correspondent in Libya, was inspired by wireless telegraphy and all the other techniques of topographical amnesia besides – explosives, projectiles, planes, fast vehicles – to compose his poems.

The Futurist movements of Europe did not last. They disappeared in a few short years, nudged along by a bit of repression. In Italy they were responsible for anarchist and fascist movements – Marinetti was a personal friend of Il Duce – but all were quickly swept from the political stage.

No doubt they had come a little too close to the bone in exposing the conjunction between communication technologies and the totalitarianism that was then taking shape before '*Newly anointed eyes* – Futurist, Cubist, intersectionist eyes, which never cease to quiver, to absorb, to radiate all that spectral, transferred, substitute beauty, all that unsupported beauty, dislocated, standing out.'[19]

With *topographical memory*, one could speak of *generations of vision* and even of visual heredity from one generation to the next. The advent of the logistics of perception and its renewed vectors for delocalising geometrical optics, on the contrary, ushered in a eugenics of sight, a pre-emptive abortion of the diversity of mental images, of the swarm of image-beings doomed to remain unborn, no longer to see the light of day anywhere.

This problematic was beyond scientists and researchers for a long time. The work of the Vienna School, such as that of Riegl and Wickhoff, addressed the implied relations between modes of perception and the periods when they were on the agenda. But for the most part research remained limited to the investigation, *de rigueur* at the time, of the socio-economics of the image. Throughout the nineteenth century and for the first half of the twentieth, studies of human-memory processes were also largely functionalist, inspired in the main by the various learning processes and the conditioning of animals; here too, electrical stimuli played a part. The military supported such research and so, subsequently, did ideologues and politicians keen to obtain immediate practical social spin-offs. In Moscow, in 1920 a Russian committee was set up to promote collaboration between Germany and the Soviet Union in the area of racial biology. Among other things the work of the German neuropathologists sojourning in the Soviet capital was supposed to locate man's 'centre of genius' as well as the centre of mathematical learning. . . . The committee came under the authority of Kalinin, who was to be president of the praesidium of the Supreme Soviet Council from 1937 to 1946.

This was the real beginning, technically and scientifically speaking, of power based on hitherto unrecognised forms of postural oppression and, once again, the battlefield would ensure rapid deployment of the new physiological prohibitions.

As early as 1916, during the first great mediatised conflict in history, Doctor Gustave Lebon had remarked 'Old-fashioned psychology considered personality as something clearly defined, barely susceptible to variation. . . . This person endowed with a fixed personality now appears to be a figment of the imagination.'[20]

With the relentless churning up of the war's landscapes, he noted that the personality's alleged fixity had depended to a large extent, until then, on the permanence of the natural environment.

But what kind of permanence did he have in mind, and which environment? Is it the environment Clausewitz refers to, that battlefield where, beyond a certain threshold of danger, reason *thinks of itself differently*? Or, more precisely, is it the environment which is constantly targeted, intercepted by an optical arsenal going from the 'line of sight' of the firearm – cannons, rifles, machine guns, used on an unprecedented scale – to cameras, the high-speed equipment of aerial intelligence, projecting an image of a dematerialising world?

The origin of the word propaganda is well known: *propaganda fide*, propagation of the faith. The year 1914 not only saw the physical deportation of millions of men to the battlefields. With the apocalypse created by the deregulation of perception came a different kind of diaspora, the moment of panic when the mass of Americans and Europeans could no longer believe their eyes, when their *faith in perception* became slave to the faith in the technical *sightline* (line of faith): in other words, the visual field was reduced to the line of a sighting device.[21]

A little later the director Jacques Tourneur confirmed the truth of this: 'In Hollywood I soon learned that the camera never sees everything. I could see everything, but the camera only sees sections.'

But what does one see when one's eyes, depending on sighting instruments, are reduced to a state of rigid and practically invariable structural immobility? One can only see instantaneous sections seized by the Cyclops eye of the lens. *Vision, once substantial, becomes accidental.* Despite the elaborate debate surrounding the problem of the objectivity of mental or instrumental images, this revolutionary change in the regime of vision was not clearly perceived and the fusion-confusion of eye and camera lens, the passage from vision to visualisation, settled easily into accepted norms. While the human gaze became more and more fixed, losing some of its natural speed and sensitivity, photographic shots, on the contrary, became even faster. Today professional and amateur photographers alike are mostly happy to *fire off shot after shot*, trusting to the power of speed and the large number of shots taken. They rely slavishly on the contact sheet, preferring to observe their own photographs to observing some kind of reality. Jacques-Henri Lartigue, who called his camera his *memory's eye*, abandoned focusing altogether, knowing without looking what his Leica would see, even when holding it at arm's length, the camera becoming a substitute for both eye and body movements at once.

The reduction in mnesic choices which ensued from this dependence on the lens was to become the nodule in which the modelling of vision would develop and, with it, all possible standardisations of ways of seeing. Thanks to work on animal conditioning like that of Thorndike (1931) and McGeoch (1932), a new certainty was born. To retrieve a specific target attribute, it was no longer necessary to activate a whole array of attributes, *any single one of them being able to act independently*. This fact once again begged the frequently asked question of *the trans-situational identity of mental images*.[22]

From the beginning of the century the perceptual field in Europe was invaded by certain signs, representations and logotypes that were to proliferate over the next twenty, thirty, sixty years, outside any immediate explanatory context, like beak-nosed carp in the polluted ponds they depopulate. Geometric brand-images, initials, Hitler's swastika, Charlie Chaplin's silhouette, Magritte's blue bird or the red lips of Marilyn Monroe: parasitic persistence cannot be explained merely in terms of the power of technical reproducibility, so often discussed since the nineteenth century. We are in effect looking at the logical outcome of a system of message-intensification which has, for several centuries, assigned a primordial role to the techniques of visual and oral communication.

On a more practical note, Ray Bradbury remarked: 'Film-makers *bombard with images* instead of words and accentuate the details using special effects. . . . You can get people to swallow anything by intensifying the details.'[23]

The phatic image – a targeted image that forces you to look and holds your attention – is not only a pure product of photographic and cinematic focusing. More importantly it is the result of an ever-brighter illumination, of the intensity of its definition, singling out only specific areas, the context mostly disappearing into a blur.

During the first half of the twentieth century this kind of image immediately spread like wildfire in the service of political or financial totalitarian powers in acculturated countries, like North America, as well as in destructured countries like the Soviet Union and Germany, which were carved up after revolution and military defeat. In other words, in nations morally and intellectually in a state of least resistance. There the key words of poster ads and other kinds of posters would often be printed on a background in just as strong a colour. The difference between what was in focus and its context, or between image and text, was nevertheless stressed here as well, since the viewer had to spend more time trying to decipher the written message or simply give up and just take in the image.

Since the fifth century, Gérard Simon notes, the geometrical study of sight formed part of the pictorial techniques artists were bent on codifying. Thanks to the celebrated passage in Vitruvius, we also know that from Antiquity artists were at pains to give the illusion of depth, particularly in theatre sets.[24]

But in the Middle Ages *the background came to the surface* in pictorial representation. All the characters, even the most minute details – the context, if you like – remain on the same plane of legibility, of visibility. Only their exaggerated size, the way they loom forward suggesting pride of place, draws the observer's attention to certain important personages. Here everything is seen in the same light, in a transparent atmosphere, a brightness further highlighted by golds and halos, by ornaments. These are holy pictures, establishing a theological parallel between vision and knowledge, for which there are no blurred areas.

The latter make their first appearance with the Renaissance when religious and cosmogonical uncertainties begin to proliferate along with the proliferation of optical devices. Once you have smoke effects or distant mists, it is just a short step to the notion of the *non finito*, the unfinished vision of pictorial representation or statuary. In the eighteenth century, with the fashion in geological follies and the curling lines of the rococo and the baroque, architects like Claude Nicolas Ledoux at the Arc-et-Senans saltworks revelled in playing up the contrasts in the chaotic arrangement of matter, with untidy piles of stone blocks escaping the creator's grip on geometry. At the same time monumental ruins, real or fake, were very much in vogue.

Some sixty years later, chaos had taken over the entire structure of the painted work. *The composition decomposes*. The Impressionists deserted their studios and wandered off to catch real life in the act, the way the photographers were doing but with the advantage, soon to be lost, of colour.

With Edgar Degas, painter and amateur photographer, composition came close to framing, to positioning within the range of the viewfinder: the subjects seem decentred, segmented, viewed from above or below in an artificial, often harsh light, like the glare of the reflectors used by professional photographers at the time. 'We must free ourselves from nature's tyranny', Degas wrote of an art which, in his terms, *sums itself up rather than extends itself* . . ., and which also becomes more intense. This goes to show how apt was the nickname given to the new school of painting when Monet's canvas 'Impression Sunrise' was shown: *Impressionist*, like the pyrotechnists who created those eye-dazzling displays of flashing, flooding lights.

From the disintegration of composition we move on to that of sight. With pointillism, Georges Seurat reproduced the visual effect of the 'pitting' of the first daguerreotypes as well as applying a system of analogous dots to colour. In order to be restored, the image had to be seen at a certain distance, the observers doing their own focusing, exactly as with an optical apparatus, the dots then dissolving in the effect of luminance and vibrating within emerging figures and forms. It was not long before these too disintegrated and soon only a visual message worthy of morse code will survive, like Duchamp's retinal stimulator, or aspects of Op Art from Mondrian.

With the same implacable logic, publicity-seekers pop up on the art scene. Futurism is upon us, notably in the form of Depero's promotional architecture, followed by Dada in 1916 and then surrealism. In Magritte's view, painting and the traditional arts from this moment on lose *any sense of the sacred*. An advertising executive by profession, Magritte wrote:

> What Surrealism officially means is an advertising firm run with enough nous and conformism to be able to do as well as other businesses to which it is opposed only in certain details of pure form. Thus, 'surrealist woman' was just as stupid an invention as the *pin up girl* who has now taken her place. . . . I'm not much of a surrealist at all, then. To me, the term also signifies 'propaganda' (a dirty word) and all the inanity essential to the success of any 'propaganda'.[25]

But the syncretism, the nihilism, of which the techniques of the pseudo-communications company are carriers, are also to be found in Magritte as anxiety-producing symptoms. For Magritte, words are '*slogans that oblige us to think in a certain preordained order* . . . contemplation is a banal feeling of no interest.' As for 'the perfect painting', this could only produce an *intense effect* for a very short time. With the industrial multiplication of optical equipment, the artist's human vision is no more than one process among many of obtaining images. The following generation would attack 'the very essence of art', thereby putting the finishing touches to their own suicide.

In 1968 Daniel Buren explained to Georges Boudaille:

> It's funny when you realise that art was never a problem of depth but one of form. . . . The only solution lies in the creation – if the word can still be used – of something totally unconnected with what has gone

> before, completely unburdened by the past. This thing would thereby express itself just for the sake of it. Artistic communication is then cut off, no longer exists.[26]

Well before this, Duchamp wrote:

> I have never stopped painting. Every painting must exist in your mind before it is painted on the canvas and it always loses something in the painting. I'd rather see my painting without the murk.

'The painter takes his body with him,' Valéry said. Merleau-Ponty added: 'It's hard to see how a mind could paint'.[27] If art poses the enigma of the body, the enigma of technique poses the enigma of art. In fact devices for seeing dispense with the artist's body in so far as it is light that actually makes the image.

We have all had enough of hearing about the death of God, of man, of art and so on since the nineteenth century. What in fact happened was simply the progressive disintegration of a faith in perception founded in the Middle Ages, after animism, on the basis of the unicity of divine creation, the absolute intimacy between the universe and the God-man of Augustinian Christianity, a material world which loved itself and contemplated itself in its one God. In the West, the death of God and the death of art are indissociable; *the zero degree of representation* merely fulfilled the prophecy voiced a thousand years earlier by Nicephorus, Patriarch of Constantinople, during the quarrel with the iconoclasts: 'If we remove the image, not only Christ but the whole universe disappears.

Notes

1 Paul Gsell, *Auguste Rodin. L'Art: Entretiens réunis par Paul Gsell* (Paris: Grasset/Fasquelle, 1911). The quotation from Marmontel is adapted from his *Contes Moraux*: 'Music is the only talent that can be enjoyed by itself; all others require witnesses.'

2 Aldous Huxley, *The Art of Seeing* (London: Chatto & Windus, 1943).

3 Pascal, *Réflexions sur la géometrie en général*, vol. VII, no. 33. The studies of Marey and Muybridge fascinated Parisian artists of the period, particularly Kupka and Duchamp whose celebrated canvas *Nude Descending a Staircase*, was rejected in 1912 by the Salon des Indépendants. Already in 1911, when Gsell's interviews with Rodin appeared, Duchamp claimed to show *static compositions using static directions for the various positions taken by a form in motion without trying to create cinematic effects through painting*. If he too claimed that movement is in the eye of the beholder, he hoped to obtain it through *formal decomposition*.

4 Tristan Tzara, 'Le Photographe à l'envers Man Ray' in *Sept Manifestes DADA* (Paris, 1992) – modified.

5 Paul Virilio, *Esthétique de la disparition* (Paris: Balland, 1980).

6 The important work of Norman E. Spear, *The Processing of Memories: Forgetting and Retention* (Hillsdale, NJ: Laurence Erlbaum Associates, 1978).

7 ATX 414, Descartes does not completely spurn the imagination as is too often claimed.

8 Paul Virilio, *L'Espace critique* (Paris: Christian Bourgois, 1984) and *Guerre et cinéma 1: Logistique de la perception* (Paris: Editions de l'Etoile Cahiers du Cinéma, 1984; London: *War and Cinema*, Verso, 1986).

9 Jean-Louis Ferrier, *Holbein. Les ambassadeurs* (Paris: Denoël, 1977).

10 Oculomotor activity: the co-ordination of eye and body movements, especially the hands.

11 Jules Romains, *La Vision extra-rétinienne et le sens paroptique* (Paris: Gallimard, 1964). First published in 1920, this work was ahead of its time and was re-issued in 1964. 'Experiments on extra-retinal vision show that certain lesions of the eye (strabismic amblyopia for example) cause the subject to reject consciousness: the eye keeps its qualities, the image manages to form on it, but this is repelled more and more insistently by consciousness, sometimes to the point of complete blindness.'

12 W.R. Russell and Nathan, *Traumatic Amnesia* (Brain, 1946). Studies of forms of traumatism suffered by returned soldiers.

13 M.-J. Deribere, *Préhistoire et histoire de la lumière* (Paris: France-Empire, 1979).

14 Correspondence with Claude Nièpce, 1816.

15 Edgar Allan Poe, *The Man of the Crowd*. (First appeared in America in December 1840 in both *The Casket* and *Gentleman's Magazine*.)

16 Jack London, *The People of the Abyss* (London: Journeyman, 1977; originally published 1903). A report.

17 The Elpenor Syndrome, from the name of a hero of *The Odyssey* who fell off the roof of Circe's temple. Exercising normal automatic motor functions in waking up in an unfamiliar place, the subject was stricken with topographical amnesia. Because this often occurs on board fast transport, the General Secretary of the SNCF [French Rail], Vincent Bourrel, has called attention to the number of accidents resembling the historic one at the turn of the century when French President Deschanel fell from a train.

18 Albert Speer, *Inside the Third Reich* (London: Weidenfeld, 1970); *Spandau: The Secret Diaries* (London: Collins, 1976) (translation modified).

19 'Pessoa et le futurisme portuguais', *Action poétique*, 110, Winter 1987.

20 Gustave Lebon, *Enseignements psychologiques de la guerre européene* (Paris: Flammarion, 1916).

21 As Jean Rouch was later to write about the Russian film-maker: 'The Kino Eye is Dziga Vertov's gaze . . . left eyebrow down a little, nose tightly pinched so as not to get in the way of sight, *pupils open at 3.5 or 2.9*, but the focus on infinity, on vertigo . . . way past the soldiers on the attack.' In a few millennia, we lost '*that obscure faith in perception* which questions our mute life, *that combination of the world and ourselves which precedes reflection*'. Merleau-Ponty, *Le Visible et l'invisible* (Paris: Gallimard, 1964).

22 Watkins and Tulving, 'Episodic Memory: When Recognition Fails', *Psychological Bulletin*, 1974.

23 *Libération*, 24 November 1987.

24 Gérard Simon, *Le Regard, l'être et l'apparance* (Paris: Le Seuil, 1988).

25 Quoted by Georges Roque in his essay on Magritte and advertising, *Ceci n'est pas un Magritte* (Paris: Flammarion, 1983).,

26 'L'art n'est plus justifiable ou les points sur les i', interview with Daniel Buren recorded by Georges Boudaille in *Les lettres françaises*, March 1968.

27 Merleau-Ponty, *L'oeil et l'esprit* (Paris: Gallimard, 1964).

PART TWO

Visual culture and everyday life

Introduction to part two

■ Nicholas Mirzoeff

EVERYDAY LIFE IS THE KEY terrain for visual culture, just as it has been for cultural studies. This represents an ethical choice to concentrate on the culture of the majority rather than the elite practices of a few, for everyday life is the mass experience of modernity. Everyday need not mean banal or insignificant. On the contrary, as Henri Lefebvre argued in his influential *Everyday Life in the Modern World*, everyday life is a key site of the interaction between the everyday and the modern: 'two connected, correlated phenomena that are neither absolutes nor entities: everyday life and modernity, the one crowning and concealing the other, revealing it and veiling it' (Lefebvre 1971: 24). Lefebvre's terms suggest that a relationship between seeing and not-seeing is at the core of the everyday. In the present intensely visual age, everyday life is visual culture. The pre-eminence of the visual in everyday life is not merely a coincidence but rather the consequence of the intensity of modern capitalism in what the situationist Guy Debord called the 'society of the spectacle'. In this moment, Debord argued that 'the spectacle is *capital* to such a degree of accumulation that it becomes an image' (Debord 1977: 32). The essays in this part of the *Reader* show how visual culture intersects with commerce, law, education, technology and war in shaping our uneasy sense of a rapidly changing culture. They seek the points of resistance in everyday life to what can seem like the unstoppable juggernaut of global capitalism.

Marshall McLuhan has become widely accepted as the prophet of the global communications age, as frequently cited in *Wired* magazine as he is in communications and media studies. In this excerpt from his groundbreaking 1951 volume *The Mechanical Bride: Folklore of Industrial Man*, McLuhan appears far more sceptical about the promise of mass communications than he is often assumed to be (McLuhan 1951). McLuhan analyses an advertisement for Berkshire Nylon Stockings, noting that it employs the same technique as Pablo Picasso's *The Mirror* in creating 'symbolic unity among the most diverse and externally unconnected facts or situations'. He shows how the apparently casual juxtaposition of the female model based on the Hollywood 'good girl' type and a rearing stallion allows a sexualized message to be created that 'could never pass the censor of consciousness'. The 'suggestion of brutal violation' gives the superficial exaltation of '"refinement", "naturalness" and "girlish grace"' in the ad a powerful 'visceral wallop'. McLuhan sees this strategy as debasing the powerful modernist technique of montage but offers his own kind of reading pleasure in 'seeing through' the ad's superficial technique to its 'real' message. This type of reading has become a genre in itself, the subject of weekly columns in many publications and a staple of stand-up comedy. Ads themselves now seek to attract such sophisticated readers of mass culture, using slogans like this soft drink tag: 'Image is nothing. Thirst is everything.' This self-reflexivity in mass commercial culture was ironically made possible by critiques like that of McLuhan.

In her essay 'Visual Stories', revised for this volume, Ann Reynolds shows how mass media and public institutions combined to educate postwar consumers into making these 'extra-visual leaps' (Reynolds 1995). In magazines like *My Weekly Reader* and the museum displays at the American Museum of Natural History, viewers were taught to translate 'visible differences into markers of information that were literally invisible'. From 1946 onwards, Alfred Parr redesigned the Museum into a form of scientific story-telling that guided the visitor through a series of dioramas and display cases, building up a picture of the usually unseen workings of nature. In a close reading of the new entrance hall displays featuring upstate New York, Reynolds shows that Parr's efforts resulted not in his stated aim to 'tell the total story of the local landscape' but in the creation of a landscape designed for the visual pleasure of urban viewers. A series of unusual display techniques forced the visitor to pay close attention to specific aspects of the displays, while leaving the lives and work of local farmers and residents out of the picture. Just as the young readers of *My Weekly Reader* were asked to engage with the pictures to answer specific questions, so were the museum visitors expected to draw from the display what Parr called 'a total conception of the whole of nature as a balanced system'. Revisiting her discomfort with her childhood magazine, Reynolds sees it as a sign that, like all young women, she was not part of the 'targeted audience' for *My Weekly Reader* and concludes that 'an assumption of universal appeal always masks a much more considered selectivity'.

It was in such gaps between the carefully orchestrated patterns of modern urban living and the ways in which people actually live that the French historian Michel de Certeau located his influential analysis of the practice of everyday life (de Certeau 1984). De Certeau resisted writing a grand theory of everyday life, but in the excerpt reprinted here highlighted 'the possibility . . . of analyzing the immense field of an "art of practice" differing from the models that (in theory) reign from top to bottom in a culture certified by education'. Everyday life is in fact far from the regulated flow of procedures envisaged by the mass of regulations that administer what Michel Foucault called the 'disciplinary society'. Writing from a radical perspective in the aftermath of the failed May revolution of 1968, de Certeau expressed what is by now a commonplace disbelief in the Marxist-Leninist theory of revolutionary social change. He turned instead to what he called 'the resurgence of "popular" practices within industrial and scientific modernity'. These practices seek to 'trick' the actual order of things into easing the daily conditions of life. For example, French workers had a tactic they call *la perruque* (the wig) which 'actually diverts time . . . from the factory for work that is free, creative, and precisely not directed towards profit'. This could range from writing a letter on company time to using a factory tool for a domestic task – all those activities that come under the heading of 'making do'. Thus a North African immigrant to France adapts his housing development to the African way of life: 'by an art of being inbetween, he draws unexpected results from his situation'. De Certeau calls these tactics the resources of 'weak' power in the face of the strong that none the less alter the conditions of everyday life slightly in favour of the oppressed.

Media critic John Fiske has adapted many of de Certeau's theories to the consumption of mass media and technology, a change made necessary by the transformation of everyday life in the past fifteen years. The patterns of '[d]welling, moving about, speaking, reading, shopping and cooking' (de Certeau 1984: 40) that de Certeau saw as the unknown and unknowable domain of the consumer are now accurately and simply mapped by producers using ATMs, credit card records, and check-out scanners. Far from being unknown, patterns of consumption are mapped with remarkable precision. Even walking, a key mode of urban everyday life that 'affirms, suspects, tries out, transgresses, respects etc. the trajectories it speaks' (ibid.: 99) is now recorded on ubiquitous video cameras put up by banks, shopping malls, traffic control and the police. In his 1996 study of postmodern media, Fiske asserts that 'counterknowledge can never be repressed entirely' (Fiske 1996). Rather, it has simply changed its form. Instead of following de Certeau 'to make a kind of *perruque* of writing itself', postmodern everyday life finds ways to revisualize itself. In this excerpt, Fiske highlights the importance of lowtech video recordings, which he calls 'videolow' contrasted to the 'videohigh' of the media. Precisely because of its poor definition, lack of camera technique and editing resources, videolow has an authenticity that is often missing from videohigh. At one level, this credibility makes shows like *America's Funniest Home Videos* funny. At another, it is why George Halliday's videotape of Rodney King being beaten by the Los Angeles Police Department was so powerful. Fiske shows that in the first trial the defence was able to negate the effect of the video by transforming the tape using videohigh techniques of enhancement, slow-motion and shot-by-shot analysis. To a jury predisposed to take the police side, this was enough. Video, like other means of representation, is thus neither inherently progressive nor reactionary but the site of a contest over meaning. The increasing availability of video equipment at low prices, including broadcast quality machines, will undoubtedly raise the stakes in this contest in years to come.

For most people, photography and video are used as supplements to memory, recording family occasions, holidays and the progress of young children. This rise in the visual documentation of everyday life has generated a heightened public concern over the remembrance of national events. In her study of the Vietnam

Veterans Memorial adapted from her recent book *Tangled Memories*, Marita Sturken examines how the Memorial has become the focus for 'a contested form of remembrance' for issues as diverse as the war, modernist sculpture, race and gender (Sturken 1997). She shows that Maya Lin's wall of names was initially perceived as a 'black gash of shame', a comment in which 'a racially coded reading of the color black as shameful was combined with a reading of the feminized earth connoting a lack of power'. As a result, Frederick Hart was commissioned to create a realist monument to the soldiers that in turn prompted women service personnel to dedicate a Vietnam Women's Memorial. Yet the Wall has now come to be the most popular tourist destination in Washington, provoking a remarkable degree of interaction and involvement. On any given day you can see veterans, their families and friends taking rubbings of individual names, or leaving votive objects, photographs and texts. These artefacts have become part of the memorial itself and further, as Sturken perceptively remarks, 'the memorial is perceived as a site by visitors where they can speak to the dead (where, by implication, the dead are present)'. The Wall has in this sense become an altar. The official state commemoration of the war thus intersects with a variety of private narratives and memories, creating a complex screen of remembrance. None the less, this memorial is not complete. There is no mention of the three million Vietnamese who lost their lives during the conflict. This blind spot is not accidental but a necessary part of the successful American memorial.

Collectively, then, these essays show how the interpretation of visual culture in everyday life first became possible as a mode of critical activity in the post-war period until it is now one of the pre-eminent tasks confronting those de Certeau called the intellectuals. Paradoxically, it is those moments of everyday life that escape the totalizing gaze of global capital that constitute its most important points of resistance to that regime, whether in the mundane circumstances of office routing or the nightmarish extreme of war.

References and further reading

Debord, Guy (1977) *The Society of the Spectacle*, Detroit. Black and Red Press.

De Certeau, Michel (1984) *The Practice of Everyday Life*, Berkeley: University of California Press.

Featherstone, Mike (ed.) (1990) *Global Culture. Nationalism, Globalization and Modernity*, London: Sage.

Fiske, John (1996) *Media Matters: Race and Gender in US Politics*, Minneapolis: Minnesota University Press.

Friedlander, Saul (1992) *Probing the Limits of Representation: Nazism and the 'Final Solution'*, Cambridge, Mass.: Harvard University Press.

Hebdige, Dick (1979) *Subculture: The Meaning of Style*, London: Methuen.

—— (1988) *Hiding in the Light*, London: Routledge.

Lefebvre, Henri (1971) *Everyday Life in the Modern World*, New York: Harper & Row.

Marling, Karal Ann (1994) *As Seen on TV: the Visual Culture of Everyday Life in the 1950s*, Cambridge: Cambridge University Press.

McLuhan, Marshall (1951) 'Woman in a Mirror', from *The Mechanical Bride: Folklore of Industrial Man*, Boston: Beacon Press.

—— (1967) *The Medium is the Message*, New York: Random House.

McRobbie, Angela (1994) *Postmodernism and Popular Culture*, London: Routledge.

Reynolds, Ann (1995) 'Visual Stories' first appeared in different form in Lynne Cooke and Peter Wollen (eds), *Visual Display: Culture beyond Appearances*, Seattle: Bay Press.

Ross, Kristin (1995) *Fast Cars, Clean Bodies: Decolonization and the Reordering of French Culture*, Cambridge, Mass.: MIT Press.

Silverstone, Roger (1994) *Television and Everyday Life*, London: Routledge.

Sturken, Marita (1997) *Tangled Memories: The Vietnam War, the AIDS Epidemic, and the Politics of Remembering*, Berkeley: California University Press.

Chapter 11

Marshall McLuhan

WOMAN IN A MIRROR

Just another stallion and a sweet kid?

What was that sound of glass? A window
gone in the subconscious? Or was it Nature's
fire-alarm box?

The ad men break through the mind again?

The Senate sub-committee on mental
hygiene reports that it wasn't loaded?

The Greeks manage these matters in myths?

THIS AD (Figure 11.1) EMPLOYS the same technique as Picasso in *The Mirror*. The differences, of course, are obvious enough. By setting a conventional day-self over against a tragic night-self, Picasso is able to provide a time capsule of an entire life. He reduces a full-length novel (or movie) like *Madame Bovary* to a single image of great intensity. By juxtaposition and contrast he is able to 'say' a great deal and to provide much intelligibility for daily life. This artistic discovery for achieving rich implication by withholding the syntactical connection is stated as a principle of modern physics by A.N. Whitehead in *Science and the Modern World*.

> In being aware of the bodily experience, we must thereby be aware of aspects of the whole spatio-temporal world as mirrored within the bodily life. . . . my theory involves the entire abandonment of the notion that simple location is the primary way in which things are involved in space-time.

Which is to say, among other things, that there can be symbolic unity among the most diverse and externally unconnected facts or situations.

The layout men of the present ad debased this technique by making it a vehicle for 'saying' a great deal about sex, stallions, and 'ritzy dames' who are provided with custom-built allure.

Superficially, the ad shows a horse, which suggests classical sculpture, and a woman as serenely innocent as a coke-ad damsel. The opposition of the cool elements, phallic and ambrosial, provides a chain reaction. The girl in the ad is the familiar Hollywood Bergman type of 'somnambule,' or the dream walker. Stately, modest, and 'classical', she is the 'good girl,' usually counter-pointed against the 'good-time girl,' who is wide awake and peppy. The stately dream girl comes trailing clouds of culture as from some European castle. Effective adver-

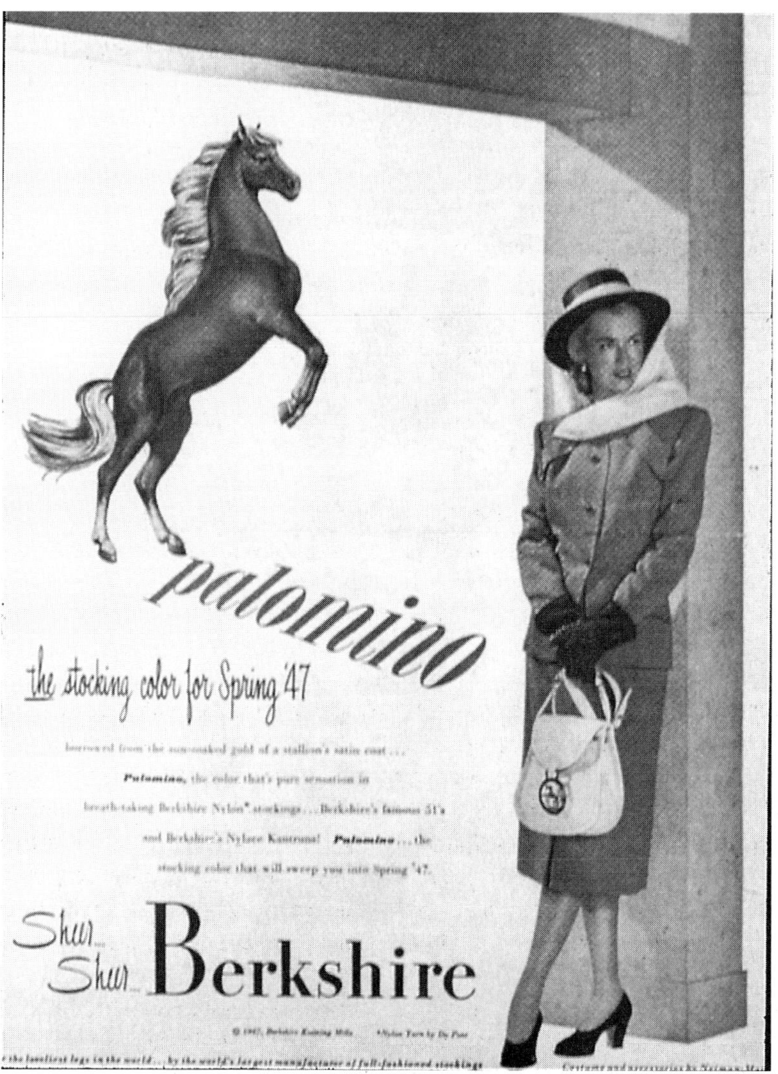

Figure 11.1 Advert for Berkshire Nylon Stockings, 1947

tising gains its ends partly by distracting the attention of the reader from its presuppositions and by its quiet fusion with other levels of experience. And in this respect it is the supreme form of cynical demagogic flattery.

The color in the original ad is described as 'borrowed from the sun-soaked gold of a stallion's satin coat . . . the color that's pure sensation . . . for the loveliest legs in the world.' The rearing horse completes the general idea. Many ads now follow this method of gentle, nudging 'subtlety.' Juxtaposition of items permits the advertiser to 'say,' by methods which *Time* has used to great effect, what could never pass the censor of consciousness. A most necessary contrast to 'raging animality' is that a girl should appear gentle, refined, aloof, and innocent. It's her innocence, her obvious 'class' that's terrific, because dramatically opposed to the suggestion of brutal violation. Describing his heroine in *The Great Gatsby*, Scott Fitzgerald notes:

> Her face was sad and lovely with bright things in it, bright eyes and a bright passionate mouth . . . a promise that she had done gay, exciting things just awhile since and that there were gay, exciting things hovering in the next hour.

She sits down at the table 'as if she were getting into bed.'

This sort of thing in Fitzgerald pretty well does what the present ad does. When Gatsby kisses this girl there is a kind of breathless round-up of the ad man's rhetoric.

> His heart beat faster and faster as Daisy's white face came up to his own. He knew that when he kissed this girl and forever wed his unutterable vision to her perishable breath, his mind would never romp again like the mind of God. So he waited, listening for a moment longer to the tuning-fork that had struck upon a star. Then he kissed her. At his lips' touch she blossomed for him like a flower, and the incarnation was complete.

It would seem to take a certain amount of theology to bring off these masterpieces of sentimental vulgarity. A kind of spectacular emptying out of established meanings and significances is necessary to the great thrills. Something important, a man or a thought, must be destroyed in order to deliver the supreme visceral wallop. In the present ad it is 'refinement,' 'naturalness,' and 'girlish grace' which are offered up. In one movie ad the woman says: 'I killed a man for this kiss, so you'd better make it good.' Romantic formula for fission?

Chapter 12

Ann Reynolds

VISUAL STORIES

> A working country is hardly ever a landscape. The very idea of landscape implies separation and observation. It is possible and useful to trace the internal histories of landscape painting, landscape writing, landscape gardening and landscape architecture, but in any final analysis we must relate these histories to the common history of a land and its society.
>
> (Raymond Williams, *The Country and the City*)

A *MY WEEKLY READER* 'Your Read and Study Guide' from 1966 posed these questions to nine-year-old schoolchildren: 'Study the designs of the superjets on this page and on the front page. How are the two planes alike? How do the two designs differ?' One child penciled in this answer: 'They are pointed on the front. They have different wings and engens [*sic*].'[1] She drew two of her conclusions from the visual evidence provided by the accompanying images, but her third answer required a conceptual leap since no significant differences between the engines of the two superjets are visible in either set of images. Evidently the student had been taught to attribute information to images through conceptually related visual cues, in this case the different shapes of the wings. This visible difference between the jets acted as a marker of an invisible difference, and allowed looking to yield information, although this information was not actually visible in the images.

Another *My Weekly Reader* article and study guide from the same year uses images in a similar manner. The article, entitled 'Packaged Power', contains illustrations of familiar objects such as clocks, cars, pencil sharpeners, and television sets. Each one is depicted as a simplified, blue silhouette while its battery appears as a black-and-white photographic image inside. The study guide asks students to

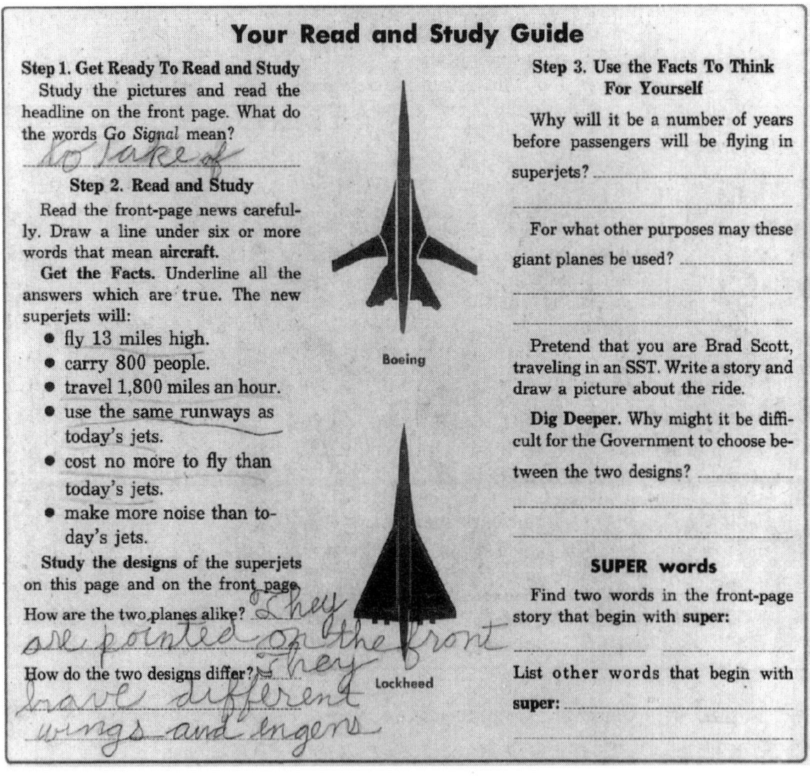

Your Read and Study Guide

Step 1. Get Ready To Read and Study
Study the pictures and read the headline on the front page. What do the words *Go Signal* mean? So take of

Step 2. Read and Study
Read the front-page news carefully. Draw a line under six or more words that mean **aircraft.**

Get the Facts. Underline all the answers which are true. The new superjets will:

- fly 13 miles high.
- carry 800 people.
- travel 1,800 miles an hour.
- use the same runways as today's jets.
- cost no more to fly than today's jets.
- make more noise than today's jets.

Study the designs of the superjets on this page and on the front page.
How are the two planes alike? They are pointed on the front
How do the two designs differ? They have different wings and engens

Step 3. Use the Facts To Think For Yourself
Why will it be a number of years before passengers will be flying in superjets? ....

For what other purposes may these giant planes be used? ....

Pretend that you are Brad Scott, traveling in an SST. Write a story and draw a picture about the ride.

Dig Deeper. Why might it be difficult for the Government to choose between the two designs? ....

SUPER words
Find two words in the front-page story that begin with **super:** ....

List other words that begin with **super:** ....

Figure 12.1 'Your Read and Study Guide', *My Weekly Reader*, 5 Oct. 1966 (Courtesy of Ann Reynolds)

name all the objects and then to extend their awareness of what was inside these objects to other objects used in their daily lives: 'What battery-driven toy have you enjoyed?' 'What other "cordless" products have you used?' and 'What electric products in your home may be "cordless" in the future?'[2] The last two questions imply that a product's cordlessness is visual evidence of the presence of a battery inside, but this evidence or marker makes sense only after students have been provided with the illustrated look inside the silhouetted objects. Again, the designers of *My Weekly Reader* translated visible differences into markers of information that was literally invisible. And students were expected to make conceptual leaps in order to put what they had learned to good use.

The steps involved in making the conceptual or extra-visual leaps prompted by 'marked' images need not be spelled out or even directly acknowledged in order for the lesson to be effective. In the case of the superjet example, the student made the connection between visible differences in wings and invisible differences in engines without needing any intermediary directions. Such successful leaps, when demanded and performed week after week, begin to seem self-evident, especially when the lessons provide no forum for students to challenge the way the questions and their appropriate responses connect images and information.

The enhancement of visual images with additional layers of information does not result, however, in seeing more, but only differently. Usually extra-visual leaps occur at the expense of aspects of these same images the lesson makers have determined to be irrelevant or detrimental to their educational aims. For example, a *My Weekly Reader* article on the Milwaukee Public Museum's soon-to-be completed diorama of a buffalo hunt provides an inventory of the items the diorama will contain, detailed descriptions of how each element and special effect is created, and general information on the importance of the buffalo to the Plains Indians.[3] The magazine also contains two photographic views of the diorama, completed and under construction. The study guide's choices of possible responses to its question 'If you could go to the new museum in Milwaukee, what might you see there?' are limited to those concerning how the diorama was created, such as 'a diorama with a painted foreground,' 'eight live buffalo,' and 'two horses made in papier-mâché.'[4] Another question, 'What sound effects might you hear at the exhibit?,' continues this line of inquiry, while others separately address the historical relationship between the buffalo and the Indian with no reference to the diorama at all, as if the subject of the diorama and the diorama itself had no related educational function. *My Weekly Reader*'s presentation of the diorama solely as a product of artifice unravels the diorama's illusionistic mysteries, but it ignores the museum curator's probable aim to teach the child about the subject of the diorama *through* the visual, audio, and textual elements of the diorama itself. As a result, the magazine's lesson on the buffalo seems more complete and direct than the museum curator's efforts because, in the former, visual fantasy appears to give way to hard 'facts.'

The articles and answers from *My Weekly Reader* that I have been using to describe the pedagogical process of extra-visual leaps come from my own copies of the magazine. I remember as a child I did not look forward to completing the 'Read and Study Guides' even though I usually answered them correctly. Their questions still make me uncomfortable, but as an adult, I am much better prepared to consider why this might be so.

The creators of the *My Weekly Reader* did not develop these questions and lessons for me alone. They reached a large number of elementary school students; many US public school systems subscribed to the magazine in the 1960s. Once one understands the basic principles behind these lessons – and the creators of *My Weekly Reader* certainly did not invent them – one can also begin to recognize these same pedagogical principles at work in many other places, albeit sometimes in either more complicated or less obvious configurations.

An examination of the pedagogical philosophy of one man, Alfred Parr, and his ground-breaking proposals for the Felix Warburg Man and Nature Hall at the American Museum of Natural History in New York illustrates the ways in which educational institutions encourage extra-visual leaps. The history of the development and refinement of Parr's basic educational aims and the hall designers' accommodation of them through several types of visual display provide striking examples of how and why public educational institutions addressed the complex relationship between vision and education during and after the Second World War in the United States. Through a historical analysis of such a well-documented case, the reasons why such lessons might have made at least some members of their audience uncomfortable can also be addressed.

Parr believed that many of the AMNH's public exhibits, particularly the dioramas, taught nothing at all and were hopelessly out of date in terms of contemporary scientific knowledge. Shortly after he took office as director of the museum in March 1942, he began to promote his ideas for a new introductory hall, which he believed would offer a totally new educational model for natural history museums. He stated in a letter to a colleague that his new hall, like the rest of the museum, should no longer depend on a strictly chronological format since such a model inevitably commences by taking the visitor 'back to the thing that occupies the remotest possible position in time and space from the moment and the place in which he is living and from the phenomena with which he is familiar and concerned in his own life'.[5] According to Parr, the introductory hall:

> should be the hall in which we meet our public on the basis of its common experience, which is a point from which we have to start if we wish to guide our visitor from his own knowledge into ours and from his own everyday experience into the new experience which science may have to offer him.[6]

Basically, Parr planned to ease the visitor's transition from a 'common' or shared set of everyday experiences to a new set of scientific experiences by explaining the latter in terms of the former. He described everyday experience as present and immediate, and not something consciously understood to be a result of or even a part of a historical continuum. He identified a corollary to this quality of 'presentness' in what he called the 'contemporary dynamics of nature,' which he also claimed could not be adequately apprehended through historical schemes:

> If you want to express it in terms of the physicist you may say that the historical rate of change (geologically speaking) is so slow in relation to the rates of change of contemporary dynamic processes that in historical perspective we can regard all the processes as being in instantaneous equilibrium with their own cause. Then the historical picture can, with more than adequate accuracy, be described as a series of equilibrium states, which means that to interpret any one of the states we can disregard the historical factor.[7]

For Parr, the 'contemporary dynamics of nature' were nature's own version of everyday experiences like those of museum visitors; these dynamics could be made to be immediately relevant without forcing visitors to deal with distant or abstract historical factors first.

Parr also used the term 'contemporary dynamics of nature' as a synonym for 'ecological subjects,' and early on, he often openly referred to the new introductory hall as an 'Ecological Hall.' This provisional title came as no surprise to his staff given his well-known commitment to ecology, but many of AMNH's scientists strongly opposed his decision to use ecology as the guiding organizational principle for public exhibition halls. One scientist claimed that such a principle lacked intrinsic unity, since it necessarily required information from various scientific disciplines and a grouping together of specimens usually displayed in separate halls. Parr countered this particular criticism with an alternate definition of unity and a restatement of his general educational aims:

> I have always been considerably disturbed by the lack of unity in the particular kind of *a priori* displays you suggest. It has always seemed to me that the introduction and importance of alfalfa at one point, rabbits in Australia, Japanese beetles, force of gravitation and so on at other points, merely give us tidbits of knowledge from all corners of the world and from all types of situations, which can never form an integrated totality in nature. . . . By showing all the disciplines in separate treatment it fails to show how they depend upon each other and how they supplement each other in the explanation of the totality of nature, which is very far from being merely the sum of its parts.[8]

As plans for the introductory hall progressed, Parr increasingly referred to the AMNH's explanation of the 'totality of nature' as the 'story' it should tell. The term 'story' makes one of its earliest appearances in the concluding paragraph to a lengthy, internal memo concerning the museum's exhibitions in general:

> We have a great story to tell, yet the simple truth of the matter is that we tell it so incredibly badly that few of our visitors ever get the idea that there is a story here at all. . . . In planning a hall the first question should be – not what objects do we want to place in the hall – but what STORY DO WE WANT THE HALL TO TELL. The objects should be used to drive home the salient points of the story and should (exceptions of course) no longer, except for study purposes, be regarded as sufficient unto themselves. The second question in planning a hall should be: what is the very best method we can devise for telling the particular story to the average visitor?[9]

This aim to tell a story, and to tell it so well that the visitor would recognize its unifying presence and message, goes hand in hand with Parr's desire to reveal the presence of science within and the relevance of science to everyday experience, since for him storytelling embodied the repetitive rhythm of the familiar and the everyday and could easily describe nature's cycles and systems. Such scientific storytelling would not need to refer to the complete sets of specimens or stages that taxonomic or evolutionary narratives did. In the new halls, fewer and more familiar objects would play multiple roles in depicting both the cyclical and historical events that comprise the total story of nature, which Parr believed the museum was obligated to tell.[10] The same objects and images would appear in more than one display case and in a variety of combinations, and their repeated appearances would encourage visitors physically to double back as well as move forward among the individual exhibits rather than to 'progress' sequentially through them. Through repeated viewings of these same objects and images from different perspectives and in various combinations, visitors would recognize that more was going on in these familiar things than met the eye. Gradually the pieces of the story of nature previously unknown or unacknowledged, such as evolutionary and geological changes, and other normally invisible processes, would come into view. And visitors would move beyond merely recognizing specific forms in a taxonomic chain to achieve an awareness of how the forms functioned within a total ecological system.

In keeping with his commitment to thread scientific understanding through the experiences of everyday life, Parr also determined early on that the new introductory hall should tell the story of the local landscape (see Figure 12.2). The idea, as Parr stated it in a memo, was to grasp the total story as it existed within a particular location but

> not to tie it [the hall] too specifically with the details of any particular location, but to design it so that it will give the visitor a feeling of familiarity with the landscape because it will represent any landscape he might be likely to see on a Sunday's drive.[11]

He did not want to provide a slavish copy of a specific place, but he insisted that the hall's designers work from a real landscape; otherwise they would fail to create the necessary 'true illusion.'[12]

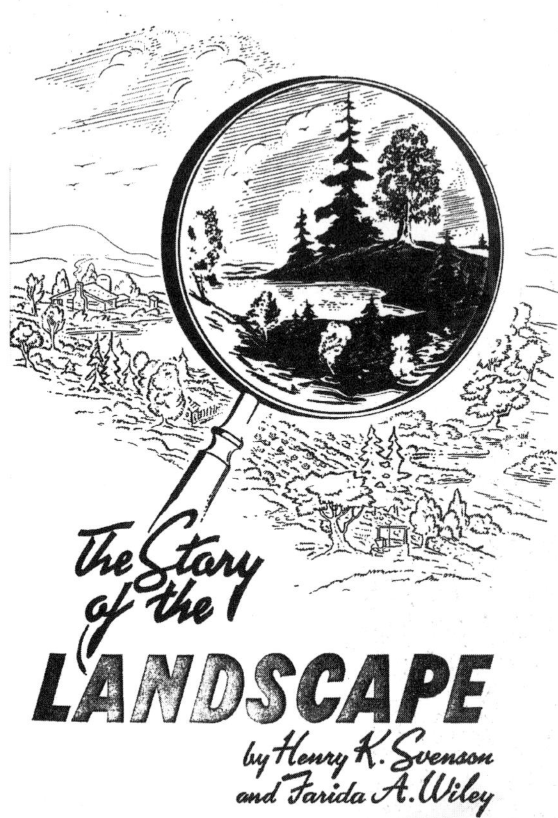

Figure 12.2 'The Story of the Landscape', cover of the guidebook to the Warburg Hall (Courtesy of the Department of Library Services, American Museum of Natural History)

By distinguishing between specificity of representation and true illusionism, Parr acknowledged the traditional goals of diorama construction. The chosen site was to be painstakingly reproduced in its particulars – local specimens, samples, and views – and these elements were to be artfully recombined in order to create a perfected totality that both generally alluded to the original site and convinced the visitor of its visual truth on its own illusionistic terms. But, in representing such a local and familiar site, one that could be visited over and over again, unlike the sites depicted in the museum's old dioramas, which were frequently remote and outside most visitors' everyday experience, Parr ensured that the hall's display images could never be regarded as just pretty pictures. Visitors would be motivated to learn more from the hall's images because they already had some experience of them as familiar places; they could more readily connect what they saw and learned in the hall to the actual places and things to which the hall's images referred. For Parr, telling the story of the local landscape provided the key to maintaining both a constant connection between representation and referent and a unity that many of his scientist colleagues feared would be lacking in an ecological hall.

By 1946, Parr had settled on the Pine Plains Valley and Mount Stissing area of upstate New York as his particular model for the new hall's local landscape, and the finished hall, called the Felix Warburg Memorial Hall of Man and Nature,

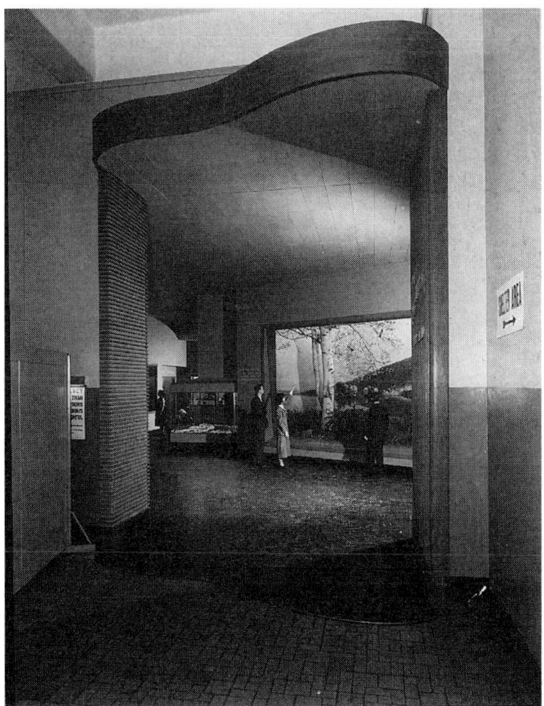

Figure 12.3 Entrance to the Warburg Hall
(Courtesy of the Department of Library Services, American Museum of Natural History)

opened on May 14, 1951.[13] All of the press releases and most newspaper reviews of the hall noted the innovative aspects of the hall's displays. Some of these displays were innovative for innovation's sake; after all, Parr wanted the new hall to provide a provocative first glimpse of the 'museum of natural history of the future' that would generate renewed outside financial support. But most of these innovations functioned as means toward Parr's stated educational aim to 'tell the total story of the local landscape.'

The hall's entrance directs the visitor in on a diagonal. A curve of wood panelling stretches out from the entrance door frame to promote this diagonal orientation, and the hall's initial diorama counters this diagonal with an orientation parallel to the lines suggested by the outward curve of the doorway. All of these axially aligned curves and diagonals initiate a rather unorthodox pattern of meandering movement through the hall. As for the visual aims of the individual displays, the deliberately 'off-kilter' framing of the entrance calls attention to the activity of framing itself and along with it, point of view.

The first diorama the visitor sees at the entrance is entitled *An October Afternoon near Stissing Mountain*. This group contains an image just as aesthetically pleasing and visually complex as many of the museum's earlier dioramas, and its brilliant, autumnal colors and picturesque composition are calculated to lure the museum visitor into the darkened hall. Yet the designers of this group are not aiming for the same kind of mysterious verisimilitude that they achieved in the earlier dioramas; the view depicted is obviously not equivalent to what the naked eye would perceive at the actual site, and the mechanics of the illusionistic process are also quite evident.

The animal, bird, insect, plant, and soil specimens occupy an unusually narrow strip of foreground space trapped between the background mural on the diorama's back wall and the glass front of the display case. And because the foreground area is so narrow, the mural is not much more than arm's length from the viewer. Even the artist's individual brush strokes are visible.

The illusionistic space depicted in the mural is also rather shallow because it recedes from right to left at a slight angle across and back, rather than gradually backward through an established middle ground to the mountains depicted in the background. When examining the mural artist's black-and-white preparatory photographs taken at the site one recognizes that he has mixed together several of the most picturesque views of the background and almost completely eliminated the middle ground areas, so that the space appears to move up from the foreground and diagonally across the background along several different orthogonals. These strategies for compressing several sweeping landscape views to fit the limited area of a showcase were commonly used in creating the background murals for the museum's earlier dioramas, but here the artist seems to push the distorting process beyond the point of creating a mysteriously real effect. The results of these distortions heighten the dramatic picturesqueness of the scene when visitors view it from the entrance, but when they move into the space of the hall and approach the display, parts of the scene appear to be closer than they would actually be at the site or even in an accomplished, highly illusionistic landscape painting. Even if the viewers cannot identify specifically what causes the spatial distortions in the diorama's overall image, the visual effects are slightly disorienting, and they call attention to the fact that what the viewer is looking at is a *landscape*, a construction made manifest through various points of view.

To eliminate the discomfort caused by the image's lack of visual coherence, visitors can either retreat to the entrance – not a very likely reaction – or move even closer to the display so that its overall image is no longer in view. Such close proximity invites inspection of the individual elements in the scene and their identifying labels which run along the lower edge of the case. Thus the diorama's artists used beauty as a device for drawing visitors in, made the slightly distanced space of purely aesthetic entertainment an uncomfortable one, and, as a result, encouraged a closer and longer inspection of both the image and its lessons. At least it is certain that the visitors were looking at the diorama differently, which was an important first step.

To quote again one of Parr's remarks made during the hall's early planning stages:

> The explanation of the totality of nature . . . is very far from being merely the sum of its parts. It seemed to me that the unity of the hall would be very plain, in that it was provided by the very landscape itself taken as a whole, as the visitor would first see it when he enters and would have it more or less before his eyes all the time in the form of a central topographic scale model. In other words, the central theme would be our effort to analyze and explain this landscape and all it contains.[14]

Visitors came to this topographic model of the Pine Plains Valley and Mount Stissing area immediately after viewing the initial diorama. This map was visible from many parts of the hall, and since the case it occupied was the only free-standing one in the hall, it anchored the other visual displays by its large physical presence and by offering the only complete view of the region. The rest of the displays are fragmentary, but through the foregrounding of the very devices of illusionism, each transformed the visitor's eyes into magnifying glasses, microscopes, or scalpels, which could reveal the invisible workings of a familiar yet superficially understood natural world. The story of the local landscape unfolded through the visitor's deepening visual understanding of this world.

For example, in a set of display cases entitled *Life in the Soil*, vertical cutaways of the soil strata underneath the surface of wood and farmlands offer little of the familiar space above ground for visitors to examine. But the display designers make up for this loss by providing visual access to this normally invisible world below the surface during winter and spring: earthworms, chipmunk and mole burrows and nests, a yellow jacket nest, an ant nest, a hibernating frog, and other forms of underground life and activity. These glimpses into life in the soil restore missing bits of the cyclical story of active and hibernating life of many species.

Other aspects of the soil's story are presented differently. Labeled, blown-up photographs of microscopic images of root systems detail the ways these systems absorb nutrients from the soil, and comparisons of soil profile specimens demonstrate the various effects of soil conservation. All of these displays contain enough formal similarities, such as the primarily vertical orientation of their images, the

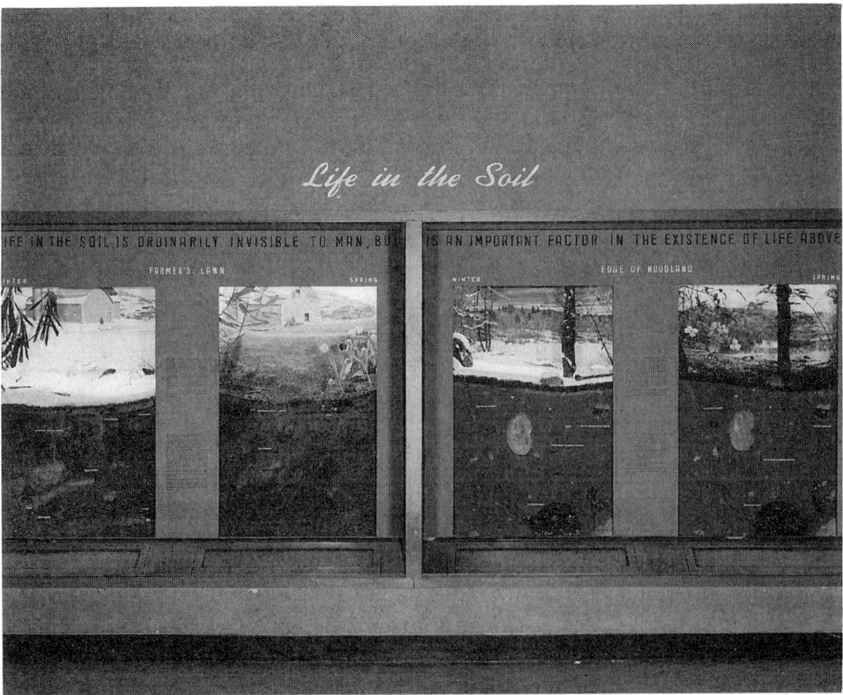

Figure 12.4 'Life in the Soil'
(Courtesy of the Department of Library Services, American Museum of Natural History)

identical colors of their backgrounds, and similar kinds of specimens, to encourage visitors to make visual and then conceptual associations back and forth across the space of the hall. These associations add up to a fairly complete understanding of the soil of the local landscape and of soil in general.

Another example – by far the most visually unsettling – of spatial manipulation used by the hall's artists, depended on a new type of visual display called a mirrorscope. Each of the mirrorscope display cases contains a miniature diorama mounted on the bottom of an individual case, directly below and behind a rectangular opening positioned in the wall at eye level. The visitor peers into the opening and down a dark, horizontal tunnel to view a tilted mirror-reflection of the diorama below. Viewers might not initially realize they are looking at a reflection. Eventually, they perceive how the mirrorscope works because of the unconventional diagonal orientation of the mirrored image. This contrived image calls attention to its reflective process, and reminds visitors that the dioramas are highly artificial images that indirectly reflect larger three-dimensional sites elsewhere.

From a distance these mirrorscopes appear to be small black holes, which disrupt the larger images in the displays that contain them. The viewer must move in quite close to these displays to see what is inside the holes; the mirrorscope images encourage, much more insistently, the same type of movement that the initial diorama does. The hall's designers also use this combination of two nested, but differently scaled, views to represent the relationship between local geological conditions and the overall trajectory of geological history and evolution. In one display, the former is represented by a cross-section of the Pine Plains Valley region running the entire length of the display case, and the latter consists of a timeline of the earth's history located under this cross-section, which also runs the length of the case. Small mirrorscope views of the local landscape during the Devonian, Pleistocene, and Triassic eras, located at the corresponding points on the timeline, physically link the general and the specific histories of the local landscape together. The contrasting visual experiences of the display indicate the local landscape's geological history, as well as geological history overall, and both kinds of history are given equal importance.

Another type of display could be called a 'picture diagram' because it consists of one or more miniature dioramas placed inside and set back behind a larger diagrammatic image painted on the outer display case wall. The diagrammatic components illustrate ubiquitous natural or agricultural processes which are either visually imperceptible or occur over an extended period of time and thus could not be represented in one view. This type of display aims to identify the presence and effects of such processes in the local landscape. For example, the hall's 'picture diagram' of the water cycle contains a miniature diorama depicting the Pine Plains Valley region inside a two-dimensional, diagrammatic picture of a similar, but more simplified landscape format. Both images contain an arrangement of clouds, a source of light coming from the right, a valley flanked by rises on either side, and a view of distant mountains in the background. In the outer diagram, the sun and its rays, clouds, precipitation, and evaporating water are schematically sketched in a limited range of colors on the blue background of the display case wall, and arrows indicate the counter-clockwise movements of water through the various stages that make up the water cycle. Both the central diorama and the surrounding diagrammatic picture are labeled at all of the same points; these labels, plus the general resemblance between the two compositions, link them together formally and then conceptually. Thus the presence of a 'contemporary dynamic of nature' in the local landscape is made visible through these formal analogies.

All of the exhibition strategies developed by the Warburg Hall designers offered museum visitors visual access to the normally unseen workings of nature or to the distant historical and geological past of the region through what were then deliberately unusual display techniques. These strategies were also meant to transform the daily activity of vision itself into a more self-conscious activity, extending it beyond its natural limits in time and space. Parr believed that the hall's lessons would be effective because they began with and always referred back to an already familiar site, the local landscape. But in order to benefit from these lessons, the museum visitors had to project what they had seen in the hall onto the local landscape itself, and these projections depended on conceptual associations or extra-visual leaps. One cannot see, for example, the life under the soil or the geological past of a particular site through looking alone; the soil and the landscape must be marked as carriers of this invisible information through related visual cues. The Warburg Hall displays, just like the lessons from *My Weekly Reader*, call attention to such cues and offer views of the usually unseen aspects of familiar objects and sites; the visitor may then extrapolate from what was seen when confronting the local landscape itself.

Although Parr selected 'common experience' as the starting point for his lessons, he did not assume that the AMNH's entire audience came to the museum with the same set of experiences. His early characterization of the visitor's 'feeling of familiarity with the landscape because it will represent any landscape he might be likely to see on a Sunday's drive' indicates that he had one particular group of visitors in mind: city dwellers. According to Parr, this group viewed the local landscape at a leisurely distance from their cars or picnic blankets, whereas the local inhabitants of the Pine Plains Valley and Mount Stissing area, whom Parr identified as mostly farmers, did not.[15] Thus his goal of creating a 'true illusion' of the local landscape from a generalized copy of a real landscape was based on an outsider's understanding of 'truth.' Parr had another reason for making the museum's landscape unrecognizable in specific terms: 'We do not wish to have any libel suits from the unintelligent farmer we propose to include.'[16] He knew that local farmers would be the only visitors able to recognize a slavish copy of property they owned; their particular familiarity with the local landscape was a liability if represented.

The city dweller's passive experience of the local landscape represented everything Parr believed to be wrong with the way museum visitors experienced the museum's old halls. So, by broadening and transforming their common experience into a more clearly self-conscious educational activity, he was able to address this old pedagogical problem of passivity. Parr's selection of the urban audience as his primary target group for the Warburg Hall was also strategic, since most of the wealthy former and potential donors to the museum belonged to this group.

Although Parr's choice of audience conformed to his general educational and financial goals for the AMNH, several crucial effects of his choice are troubling. His understanding of the urban visitor's experience of rural, upstate New York became the visual starting point for every museum visitor. And since this initial point of view was never explicitly identified with any particular segment of the museum's audience anywhere in the Warburg Hall, it seemed to be a self-evident choice, universally shared.

Because Parr was also committed to telling the 'total story of the local landscape,' he had to include man's participation in the appearance and productivity of the land. But he did not want to burden his targeted city audience with any but the most general aspects of these parts of the story because he realized that they would primarily still remain consumers of what they saw. The completed hall contained only a few displays dealing with crop cultivation and animal husbandry – but every one privileged general principles over detailed explanations of the farmer's practical problems, and most emphasized products over production. Even when production was the subject of a particular display, as in the presentation of the history of farming in New York State, all of the textual information was addressed to the layperson.

One might ask, at this point, 'What did the farmer learn when looking at these types of displays?' or 'How was his or her "common experience" as a producer or laborer being transformed?' Nowhere were these questions addressed in the hall. So, not only was the Warburg Hall's visual story of the local landscape partial, but the community of mutual understanding and interdependence promoted through the hall was limited, as it was based on the interests of residents of a single geographic region and, primarily, the middle and upper classes, who occupied only one position in the region's agricultural economy.[17]

Parr developed plans for the Warburg Hall long before the end of the Second World War; by the war's end, his pedagogical ambitions had outgrown teaching museum visitors about the relevance of science to their local, everyday lives. In his 1947 essay, 'Towards New Horizons,' published in the museum's annual report, he described the postwar moment in much the same terms as Karl Mannheim described the pre-war period in his text *Ideology and Utopia*, although where Mannheim identified *ideology*'s work in building a national and global community, Parr used *education*:

> The greater the mental confusion of the times, the greater the challenge to education, and the greater the value of teaching properly conceived and directed towards the elucidation of the problems which disturb the world. . . . In a world beset by hostility and want, the natural history museums have an opportunity, never before equaled, to serve the development of peace and of a better life for all by bringing their educational facilities and their scientific knowledge to bear upon the task of creating a better understanding of our own problems in relation to the country that surrounds us and supports us, and of the problems of other nations in relation to their natural circumstances, to one another, and to us.[18]

After the war was over, Parr and the museum president F.T. Davison increasingly described the ecological story of natural history as an antidote to totalitarianism.[19] Over and over again in his writings, Parr proposed 'a total conception of the whole of nature as a balanced system,' as a model for social cooperation which, when understood and 'cultivated' locally, could create a model for world peace. During this same period, Parr suggested that the term '"expedition," with its romantic associations with the idea of distant and long voyages' should be replaced by such works as '"survey" or "field work" to describe the manner in which the task of exploration is carried forward today,' since he felt that thorough scientific research could be conducted in one's own backyard.[20] There are even a few subtle indications of this larger purpose of global awareness in the Warburg Hall, though its displays ostensibly address only the problems of the local landscape.[21] Displayed world maps, for example, indicate where soil conditions in upstate New York occur globally as well as nationally.

The wedding of rarified science to everyday life in the design of the Warburg Hall represents a significant ideological shift in the museum's educational agenda, not just a simple effort toward better education. What Parr represented as an efficient or 'economical' model for understanding the total story of the local landscape, and ultimately of man and nature was, in fact, a model for naturalizing an economic structure of interdependence; twenty years of financial instability had demonstrated how much the museum depended on this economic structure for its own survival and growth.

Parr's desire to enlarge his public's visual understanding of the 'familiar' included social and political aims that could only be accomplished through dazzling, truly extra-visual and clearly ideological leaps, which started and ended with the experiences of only a segment of that public. Such disparities could easily have caused visitors some discomfort, especially if they were not members of that chosen segment of the public.

Perhaps the *My Weekly Reader* 'Read and Study Guides' made me uncomfortable because I wasn't among their ideal or 'targeted' audience.[22] When faced with an institutionalized and pervasive pedagogical device like extra-visual leaps, individuals are prone to blame themselves for feelings of discomfort, or to credit these feelings to those of inadequacy, especially since such devices do not value subjective responses, and thus provide no place for them. Part of my intention in this essay is to posit the value of using such subjective responses as the only way we have of differentiating ourselves and who we are from the institution's version of who we should be. Discomfort may be our only motivation to look harder at the agendas of pedagogical institutions and their devices, no matter how subtle. An assumption of universal appeal always masks a much more considered selectivity.

Notes

1 'U.S. Gives Go Signal for Superjets,' and 'Your Read and Study Guide,' *My Weekly Reader* 48, no. 4 (5 October 1966), pp.1, 8.
2 'Packaged Power,' and 'Your Read-Study Guide,' *My Weekly Reader* 48, no. 6 (19 October 1960), pp.1, 8.
3 'Where the Buffalo Roam,' *My Weekly Reader* 48, no. 7 (26 October 1966), p.1.
4 'Your Read-Study Guide: "Where the Buffalo Roam,"' *My Weekly Reader* 48, no. 7 (26 October 1966), p.8.
5 Alfred Parr, Letter to Dr Edwin H. Colbert, 9 September 1942, pp.1–2, Archives of AMNH.
6 Ibid., p.1.
7 Ibid., p.2.
8 Alfred Parr, letter to Dr William K. Gregory, 8 October 1942, p.1, Archives of AMNH.
9 Memo concerning exhibitions, Plan and Scope Committee, *c.* July 1942, pp.7-8, Archives of AMNH.
10 Alfred Parr, 'Towards New Horizons,' *American Museum of Natural History Annual Report* 78 (July 1946–June 1947),p.16.
11 Alfred Parr, 'Hall of the Local Landscape,' 25 September 1946, p.1, Archives of AMNH.
12 Alfred Parr, letter to Mrs Paul Moore (13 January 1943), p.1, Archives of AMNH.
13 The hall was named in memory of the father of the hall's major financial backer and a trustee of the museum, Frederick M. Warburg.
14 Alfred Parr, letter to Gregory, p.1.
15 Alfred Parr, letter to Moore, p.1.
16 Ibid., pp.1–2.
17 Alfred Parr shared his utopian faith in the capacity of storytelling to produce a unified community with Walter Benjamin, yet the differences in their explanations of the relationship between storytelling and the economic structure of the communities they shaped reveals the one-sided nature of Parr's understanding

of the practice. In 1936, Benjamin described storytelling as part of a pre-industrial past in which production and consumption were shared equally as experiences:

> 'the art of storytelling is coming to an end. Less and less frequently do we encounter people with the ability to tell a tale properly. More and more often there is embarrassment all around when the wish to hear a story is expressed. It is as if something that seemed inalienable to us, the securest among our possessions, were taken from us: the ability to exchange experiences.
>
> (Benjamin, 'The Storyteller,' *Illuminations*, New York, Schocken Books, 1969, p.83)

18 Alfred Parr, 'Towards New Horizons,' *American Museum of Natural History Annual Report* 78 (July 1946–June 1947), pp. 9–10.

19 F.T. Davison, 'Report of the President,' *American Museum of Natural History Annual Report* 81 (July 1949–June 1950).

20 Alfred Parr, 'The Museum Explores the World – Report of the Director,' *American Museum of Natural History Annual Report* 83 (July 1951–June 1952), pp.10–11.

21 The *My Weekly Reader* article 'U.S. Gives Go Signal for Superjets' contains some evidence of a similar, albeit unacknowledged, slide from national to global concerns. The title represents the competition between two companies to produce the jets as a national one, yet the article's author uses terms usually reserved for describing the then current international 'space race' to portray the stakes involved.

22 Even without the benefit of extensive research, I can draw some general conclusions concerning *My Weekly Reader*'s ideal audience in the 1960s based on the types of subjects consistently represented in the magazine and the manner in which they were addressed: enormous numbers of articles on NASA and technological innovations generally; studies of rural areas of the United States; and biographical essays on representational painters of the nineteenth century, such as Winslow Homer and contemporary artists, such as Norman Rockwell and the Wyeths. Examples of avant-garde culture, if mentioned at all, were treated as humorous curiosities akin to rare and odd-looking animals from exotic places. Girls like me, longing to learn about big cities and looking for images of how cultural life is lived there, particularly by women, could not help but be disappointed.

Chapter 13

Michel de Certeau

FROM *THE PRACTICE OF EVERYDAY LIFE*

A diversionary practice: 'la perruque'

[W]ITH THESE EXAMPLES of terrains on which one can locate the specific modalities of 'enunciative' practices (manipulations of imposed spaces, tactics relative to particular situations), the possibility is opened up of analyzing the immense field of an 'art of practice' differing from the models that (in theory) reign from top to bottom in a culture certified by education (from the universities to the elementary schools), models that all postulate the constitution of a space of their own (a scientific space or a blank page to be written on), independent of speakers and circumstances, in which they can construct a system based on rules ensuring the system's production, repetition, and verification. Two questions burden this inquiry. They concern, moreover, the two sides of a single political problem. First, on what grounds can we call this 'art' *different*? Second, *from what position* (from what distinct place) can we set out to analyze it? Perhaps by resorting to the very procedures of this art, we can revise our views on both its definition as 'popular' and our position as observers.

To be sure, there remain social, economic, historical differences between the practitioners (peasants, workers, etc.) of these ruses and ourselves as analysts. It is no accident that their culture is elaborated in terms of the conflictual or competitive relations between the stronger and the weaker, leaving no room for a legendary or ritual space that would be merely neutral. This difference can moreover be seen within the study itself, in the gap that separates the time of solidarity (marked by docility and gratitude toward one's hosts) from the time of writing; the latter reveals the institutional affiliations (scientific, social) and the profit (intellectual, professional, financial, etc.) for which this hospitality is objectively the means. The Bororos of Brazil sink slowly into their collective death, and Lévi-Strauss takes his seat in the French Academy. Even if this injustice disturbs him, the facts remain unchanged. This story is ours as much as his. In this one respect (which is an index of others that are more important), the intellectuals are still borne on the backs of the common people.

We need not stress here either the socioeconomic implications or the *locus* of ethnological or historical research, or the political situation that, from the very beginning of contemporary research, has inscribed the concept *popular* in a problematics of repression. But one pressing question must be confronted here: if one does not expect a revolution to transform the laws of history, how is it possible to foil here and now the social hierarchization which organizes scientific work on popular cultures and repeats itself in that work? The resurgence of 'popular' practices within industrial and scientific modernity indicates the paths that might be taken by a transformation of the object of our study and the place from which we study it.

The operational models of popular culture cannot be confined to the past, the countryside, or primitive peoples. They exist in the heart of the strongholds of the contemporary economy. Take, for examples, what in France is called *la perruque*, 'the wig.' *La perruque* is the worker's own work disguised as work for his employer. It differs from pilfering in that nothing of material value is stolen. It differs from absenteeism in that the worker is officially on the job. *La perruque* may be as simple a matter as a secretary's writing a love letter on 'company time' or as complex as a cabinetmaker's 'borrowing' a lathe to make a piece of furniture for his living room. Under different names in different countries this phenomenon is becoming more and more general, even if managers penalize it or 'turn a blind eye' to it in order not to know about it. Accused of stealing or turning material to his own ends and using the machines for his own profit, the worker who indulges in *la perruque* actually diverts time (not goods, since he uses only scraps) from the factory for work that is free, creative, and precisely not directed toward profit. In the very place where the machine he must serve reigns supreme, he cunningly takes pleasure in finding a way to create gratuitous products whose sole purpose is to signify his own capabilities through his *work* and to confirm his solidarity with other workers or his family through *spending* his time in this way. With the complicity of the other workers (who thus defeat the competition the factory tries to instill among them), he succeeds in 'putting one over' on the established order on its home ground. Far from being a regression toward a mode of production organized around artisans or individuals, *la perruque* reintroduces 'popular' techniques of other times and other places into the industrial space (that is, into the Present order).

Many other examples would show the constant presence of these practices in the most ordered spheres of modern life. With variations, practices analogous to *la perruque* are proliferating in governmental and commercial offices as well as in factories. No doubt they are just as widespread as formerly (though they ought still to be studied), just as widely suspected, repressed, or ignored. Not only workshops and offices, but also museums and learned journals penalize such practices or ignore them. The authority of ethnological or folklore studies permits some of the material or linguistic objects of these practices to be collected, labeled according to place of origin and theme, put in display cases, offered for inspection and interpretation, and thus that authority conceals, as rural 'treasures' serving to edify or satisfy the curiosity of city folk, the legitimization of an order supposed by its conservators to be immemorial and 'natural.' Or else they use the tools and products taken from a language of social operations to set off a display of technical gadgets and thus arrange them, inert, on the margins of a system that itself remains intact.

The actual order of things is precisely what 'popular' tactics turn to their own ends, without any illusion that it will change any time soon. Though elsewhere it is exploited by a dominant power or simply denied by an ideological discourse, here order is *tricked* by an art. Into the institution to be served are thus insinuated styles of social exchange, technical invention, and moral resistance, that is, an economy of the '*gift*' (generosities for which one expects a return), an aesthetics of '*tricks*' (artists' operations) and an ethics of *tenacity* (countless ways of refusing to accord the established order the status of a law, a meaning, or a fatality). 'Popular' culture is precisely that; it is not a corpus considered as foreign, fragmented in order to be displayed, studied and 'quoted' by a system which does to objects what it does to living beings.

The progressive partitioning of times and places, the disjunctive logic of specialization through and for work, no longer has an adequate counterpart in the conjunctive rituals of mass communications. This *fact* cannot become our *law*. It can be gotten around through departments that, 'competing' with the gifts of our benefactors, offer them products at the expense of the institution that divides and pays the workers. This practice of economic *diversion* is in reality the return of a sociopolitical ethics into an economic system. It is no doubt related to the *potlatch* described by Mauss, an interplay of voluntary allowances that counts on reciprocity and organizes a social network articulated by the 'obligation to give.' In our societies, the market economy is no longer determined by such an 'emulation': taking the abstract individual as a basic unit, it regulates all exchanges among these units according to the code of generalized equivalence constituted by money. This individualistic axiom is, of course, now surfacing as the question that disturbs the free market system as a whole. The *a priori* assumption of an historical Western option is becoming its point of implosion. However that may be, the *potlach* seems to persist within it as the mark of another type of economy. It survives in our economy, though on its margins or in its interstices. It is even developing, although held to be illegitimate, within modern market economy. Because of this, the politics of the 'gift' *also* becomes a diversionary tactic. In the same way, the loss that was voluntary in a gift economy is transformed into a transgression in a profit economy: it appears as an excess (a waste), a challenge (a rejection of profit), or a crime (an attack on property).

This path, relative to our economy, derives from another; it compensates for the first even though it is illegal and (from this point of view) marginal. The same pathway allows investigations to take up a position that is no longer defined only by an acquired power and an observational knowledge, with the addition of a pinch of nostalgia. Melancholy is not enough. Certainly, with respect to the sort of writing that separates domains in the name of the division of labor and reveals class affiliations, it would be 'fabulous' if, as in the stories of miracles, the groups that formerly gave us our masters and that are currently lodged in our corpus were to rise up and themselves mark their comings and goings in the texts that honor and bury them at the same time. This hope has disappeared, along with the beliefs which have long since vanished from our cities. There are no longer any ghosts who can remind the living of reciprocity. But in the order organized by the power of knowledge (ours), as in the order of the countryside or the factories, a diversionary practice remains possible.

Let us try to make a *perruque* in the economic system whose rules and hierarchies are repeated, as always, in scientific institutions. In the area of scientific research (which defines the current order of knowledge), working with its machines and making use of its scraps, we can divert the time owed to the institution; we can make textual objects that signify an art and solidarities; we can play the game of free exchange, even if it is penalized by bosses and colleagues when they are not willing to 'turn a blind eye' to it; we can create networks of connivances and sleights of hand; we can exchange gifts; and in these ways we can subvert the law that, in the scientific factory, puts work at the service of the machine and, by a similar logic, progressively destroys the requirement or creation and the 'obligation to give.' I know of investigators experienced in this art of diversion, which is a return of the ethical, of pleasure and of invention within the scientific institution. Realizing no profit (profit is produced by work done for the factory), and often at a loss, they take something from the order of knowledge in order to inscribe 'artistic achievements' on it and to carve on it the graffiti of their debts of honor. To deal with everyday tactics in this way would be to practice an 'ordinary' art, to find oneself in the common situation, and to make a kind of *perruque* of writing itself.

'Making do': uses and tactics

In spite of measures taken to repress or conceal it, *la perruque* (or its equivalent) is infiltrating itself everywhere and becoming more and more common. It is only one case among all the practices which introduce *artistic* tricks and competitions of *accomplices* into a system that reproduces and partitions through work or leisure. Sly as a fox and twice as quick: there are countless ways of 'making do.'

From this point of view, the dividing line no longer falls between work and leisure. These two areas of activity flow together. They repeat and reinforce each other. Cultural techniques that camouflage economic reproduction with fictions of surprise ('the event'), of truth ('information') or communication ('promotion') spread through the workplace. Reciprocally, cultural production offers an area of expansion for rational operations that permit work to be managed by dividing it (analysis), tabulating it (synthesis) and aggregating it (generalization). A distinction is required other than the one that distributes behaviors according to their *place* (of work or leisure) and qualifies them thus by the fact that they are located on one or another square of the social checkerboard – in the office, in the workshop, or at the movies. There are differences of another type. They refer to the *modalities* of action, to the *formalities* of practices. They traverse the frontiers dividing time, place, and type of action into one part assigned for work and another for leisure. For example, *la perruque* grafts itself onto the system of the industrial assembly line (its counterpoint, in the same place), as a variant of the activity which, outside the factory (in another place), takes the form of *bricolage*.

Although they remain dependent upon the possibilities offered by circumstances, these transverse *tactics* do not obey the law of the place, for they are not defined or identified by it. In this respect, they are not any more localizable than the technocratic (and scriptural) *strategies* that seek to create places in conformity with abstract models. But what distinguishes them at the same time concerns the *types of operations* and the role of spaces: strategies are able to produce, tabulate, and impose these spaces, when those operations take place, whereas tactics can only use, manipulate, and divert these spaces.

We must therefore specify the operational schemas. Just as in literature one differentiates 'styles' or ways of writing, one can distinguish 'ways of operating' – ways of walking, reading, producing, speaking, etc. These styles of action intervene in a field that regulates them at a first level (for example, at the level of the factory system), but they introduce into it a way of turning it to their advantage that obeys other rules and constitutes something like a second level interwoven into the first (for instance, *la perruque*). These 'ways of operating' are similar to 'instructions for use,' and they create a certain play in the machine through a stratification of different and interfering kinds of functioning. Thus a North African living in Paris or Roubaix (France) insinuates *into* the system imposed on him by the construction of a low-income housing development or of the French language the ways of 'dwelling' (in a house or a language) peculiar to his native Kabylia. He superimposes them and, by that combination, creates for himself a space in which he can find *ways of using* the constraining order of the place or of the language. Without leaving the place where he has no choice but to live and which lays down its law for him, he establishes within it a degree of *plurality* and creativity. By an art of being in between, he draws unexpected results from his situation.

These modes of use – or rather re-use – multiply with the extension of acculturation phenomena, that is, with the displacements that substitute manners or 'methods' of transiting toward an identification of a person by the place in which he lives or works. That does not prevent them from corresponding to a very ancient art of 'making do.' I give them the name of uses, even though the work most often designates stereotyped procedures accepted and reproduced by a group, its 'ways and customs.' The problem lies in the ambiguity of the word, since it is precisely a matter of recognizing in these 'uses' 'actions' (in the military sense of the word) that have their own formality and inventiveness and that discreetly organize the multiform labor of consumption.

[. . .]

Chapter 14

John Fiske

VIDEOTECH

THE RODNEY KING video was significant not just because its eighty-one seconds of electronic reality condensed four hundred years of racial history into the nation's experience of contemporary race relations, but also because, technologically, it operated at a crucial turning point in the flow of knowledge and visibility.

We live in a monitored society. In Liverpool, England, two youths abducted a two-year-old from a shopping mall. Video cameras in the mall watched and recorded their every move (as of every other shopper) and outside in the street more cameras recorded them (and all the other pedestrians). The videotapes played a vital role in helping police identify and catch the criminals. Thousands of other actions, interactions, and identities were also recorded by those cameras, a plethora of potential knowledge of people who did not know they were known. In Minneapolis, USA, the Mall of America uses 109 cameras to monitor its customers and staff: each of them can zoom in on an object as small as an ID card. David Guterson described in *Harper's* the giddy power he felt as he watched the bank of monitors in its security room.[1] Suddenly, a security guard noticed something of interest occurring in one of the parking lots, and zoomed in on a couple making love in their car: although their passion may have been all-consuming, they were not, so a guard was dispatched to put an end to such inappropriate behavior. Earlier, Guterson had himself been monitored, and had been chided by the mall's public relations officer, who had seen him talking to a garbage cleaner on one of the concourses. Not to be outdone by its famous mall, the city of Minneapolis plans to cover all its downtown streets with video monitoring to improve its traffic management. The cameras will see more than traffic jams.

Outside the Ronald Reagan Office Building in downtown Los Angeles, Mike Davis asked a homeless African-American why he never went into the shopping mall that occupied the building's lower floors. The answer was predictable: he knew that cameras would instantly identify him as an inappropriate person in that precisely monitored place, and that security guards would rapidly escort him outside.[2] Gated and guarded neighborhoods throughout L.A.'s suburbs have video cameras at their entries. An African-American professor told me how monitored he feels as he passes them, knowing that they see his Blackness and accord it special attention.

Information technology is highly political, but its politics are not directed by its technological features alone. It is, for instance, a technical feature of the surveillance camera that enables it to identify a person's race more clearly than his or her class or religion, but it is a racist society that transforms that information into knowledge. The video camera directs its gaze impartially on Black and white, the criminal and the law-abiding, the welcome and the unwelcome. But African-Americans entering a Korean grocery store or an exclusive housing development know that the impartiality stops at the moment when the electronic signal is turned into knowledge; they know that they are seen differently from whites. Social differences that are embodied, such as those of race and gender, are the ones that are most efficiently monitored; because in today's public life racial difference is seen to pose a greater threat to the dominant order than gender difference, video works particularly effectively in the monitoring of race relations.

The video camera is efficient in the information-gathering phases of surveillance, but in storage and retrieval the computer is king. As its sophistication increases, so does our power to know each individual and to track his or her movements through the places and times of ordinary life. The economics of everyday life are where this power is most efficiently applied. Our social security numbers document how much money we earn, and where and how we earn it; they record our loans, mortgages, and pension plans. In the sphere of consumption, our credit card numbers are routinely used to track our purchase of goods and services, and how we move around the neighborhood and the country as we make them; the last four numbers of our zip codes document where we live and the demographics of our neighbors. All this knowledge is combined to produce a 'consumer profile' that serves, in the domain of economics, as a social identity. If this surveillance is confined to the economic, its effects are unlikely to be worse than annoying (soliciting phone calls or junk mail) and may be helpful (catalogs matched to our tasted do save us trips to the mall).

A consumer profile, however, is only part of an individual's social identity; the same information technologies could readily supplement it with a 'political profile,' should one be needed. The magazines we subscribe to, the causes we donate to, the university courses we register for, the books we purchase and the ones we borrow from the library are all recorded, and recorded information is always potentially available. A Korean studying in the United States told me that agents of his government's secret police had warned him that his work was becoming too radical; one of the means by which they had identified him as worthy of special monitoring was through his library loans. Such a profile of what goes on inside our heads can be enhanced by knowledge of where our bodies move. Many parking garages record the license place numbers of every car that enters; some traffic lights are equipped with cameras to record those who run red lights; the City of London is planning to video-record every car entering it to improve its security against terrorists. In the United States, hydroponic gardening stores have been video-monitored by the DEA, and repeat customers have had their homes searched for marijuana plants. Any of our movements that the monitoring agency might consider abnormal could be fed into a political profile.

Norms are crucial to any surveillance system, for without them it cannot identify the abnormal. Norms are what enable it to decide what information should be turned into knowledge and what individuals need to be monitored. The massed information that is recorded about the majority may never be known in all its details, but it is still used to produce the norms that are necessary to identify the dissident and the dangerous. The power to produce and apply norms, as Foucault tells us, is a crucial social power. It is not hard to imagine circumstances in which political profiles of those who, by some standards, would be judged 'not normal' could be as useful to government agencies as consumer profiles are to commercial ones.

The monitoring of the conforming white middle classes may not bear too heavily upon us, for it is our behaviour that provides the norms against which others are evaluated. But the equivalent video tracking of African-Americans or Latino/as oppresses them every time they enter a store or shopping mall, or visit a gated neighborhood. Such monitoring does not need to be technological: Joe Soto, for instance, has filed a civil rights lawsuit against the Utah Highway Patrol, claiming that he has been stopped repeatedly solely because he is a Latino driving a Cadillac. In Tinicum, Pennsylvania, just outside Philadelphia, Black motorists have filed a similar class action suit against the local police department, and all Black motorists know that the odds of their being pulled over increase if they drive through white suburbs (it is worth recalling here that the Rodney King incident began with a traffic stop). Ice-T's anger at being pulled out of his car and made to kiss the pavement because he is Black is not just individual, but communal; not just personal, but political. To be seen to be Black or Brown, in all but a few places in the United States, is to be seen to be out of place, beyond the norm that someone else has set, and thus to be subject to white power. In these conditions being seen is, in itself, oppressive.

In no suburb is whiteness more thoroughly normalized than in Simi Valley. As its mayor has said, 'There is no question, in this community, that somebody out of the ordinary sticks out quickly. And people are very quick to report anything suspicious, very quick to call the police, and expect them to be there.'[3] He has no need to specify that being 'out of the ordinary' includes being Black when his constituents are as effective deniers and recoders of racism as the Arkins:

> 'We like living in a place with educated people, people who believe as we do,' said Brian Arkin, '. . . but I don't believe skin color is a criteria [*sic*] . . . There's a black person up our street and we say "Hi" like he's a normal person,' 'Mr. Arkin continued. 'This isn't about race, it's about whether you let your property run down.' 'Or whether you sell drugs out of your house,' his wife, Valerie interjected.[4]

We can now enlarge on William Buckley's comment: this cannot be a racist society if we love Bill Cosby, appoint Clarence Thomas, and say 'Hi' to a Black man as though he were a normal person.

Video technology may not be essential – Simi Valley residents can spot somebody out of the ordinary with their naked eyes – but it is efficient. It is particularly effective in racial surveillance, because racial difference from the white norm is so visible. Surveillance technology enhances the construction of whiteness as the space from which the other is viewed, and its development is so significant because it technologizes and thus extends a power application that is already widespread. A new technology does not, of itself, determine that it *will* be used or *how* it will. Similarly, technology may limit what can or cannot be seen but it does not dictate the way it is watched. Technology may determine what is shown, but society determines what is seen. The camera always shows racial difference, for instance; who sees it, however, is a function of social factors. Fewer European than African-Americans saw the race of Anita Hill and of Bill Cosby, but all whites saw the Blackness of Willie Horton. A general principle emerges here. When social difference advances the interests of the powerful it will be recognized by them; when, however, their interests are promoted by alliances that cross the social difference at issue, it will be overlooked by them. When it serves the interests of power to 'other' those whom it monitors, the social differences between the seer and the seen will loom large; when, however, the other is to be enrolled in a temporary alliance with 'us,' the differences shrink into insignificance.

Part of the reason for the rapid extension of surveillance technology is the perfect match between technology's ability to see racial difference and the need of whiteness to monitor it. Whiteness always needs to see its difference from the other, even when it suits its purposes to overlook or deny it, for, paradoxically, 'color blindness' can be strategically effective only if it sees what it pretends not to. While denying that Clarence Thomas's race had anything to do with his nomination, Bush used his 'color blindness' to advance his reactionary white strategy. Less intentionally, liberal white viewers of *The Cosby Show* and of the Thomas-Hill hearings could also be 'blind' to racial difference when it was in their interests to be so. Members of disempowered races, however, cannot afford the luxury of color blindness, for their social survival depends upon racial awareness. They need to see racial difference constantly in order to defend themselves against the power inscribed in it, and consequently they are at times able to make tactical uses of the technology whose strategy is normally hostile to them. Black viewers of both *The Cosby Show* and the hearings, therefore, were constantly aware of the Blackness of the figures on the screen, and of their difference from the whiteness of most television. Similarly, in the Murphy Brown-Dan Quayle debate, video technology showed racial difference to everyone in the audience, but who was 'blind' to it and who saw it was determined by social factors. Although the powerful have privileged access to technology, their access is not exclusive; although they exert powerful control over its social uses, their control is not total. Indeed, video technology often carries traces of the marginalized that verbal discourse represses more efficiently. Putting an event into any discourse always involves centering some elements and marginalizing or repressing others: because verbal language obeys no laws other than those that society has produced to organize it, putting an event into verbal discourse is a *purely* social process.

The camera, however, obeys the laws of optics and electronics as well as those of discourse. I do not wish to suggest that the laws of optics and electronics are objective and exist in nature only, for they are products of a particular scientific way of knowing: they have been 'discovered' and elaborated in order to enhance our ability to increase our control over nature and to understand those of its resources that we can turn to our own advantage. The power of scientific knowledge and its instrumental technologies is inextricably part of the domination of the world's physical and social resources by European-derived nations. No knowledge system is nonpolitical. But because the laws of optics or of physics have a grounding in nature, their politics are less immediate than those of discourse, and work rather on the level of the macropolitics of global capitalism as a system than on the more immediate level of the political struggles within it.

The laws of discourse, however, are more immediately political than those of optics and electronics. The saying 'The camera cannot lie' is inaccurate and out of date but not stupid, for it does point to key differences between words and photography in terms of the immediacy and totality of the social control that can be exerted over them. The fact that the optical camera is, in part, subject to the laws of nature does lend a sense of objectivity that carries an injunction to believe what it shows. The camera always tells us more than it needs to; a photograph always carries more information than is necessary to make its point. These bits of unnecessary information function to substantiate the 'truth injunction' of the photograph, but they also, simultaneously, undercut it: they can remind us that the event being photographed, like any other, can always be put into discourse differently. They are the traces through which the repressed alternatives can be recovered, and their inevitability makes the camera much less efficient than verbal discourse in repressing the stories it does not wish us to know. The camera finds it much harder than verbal discourse to keep the traces of these discursive alternatives on its unregarded margins.

Electronic photography may appear even more 'objective' than optical photography. When Roland Barthes wrote of the 'photographic paradox' by which the camera appeared to produce 'a message without a code,' he was writing of optical photography.[5] In his account, the truth injunction of photography results from the laws of optics appearing to overpower those of semiotics or discourse, which, until the invention of the camera, were in total control of every message. The camera, however, limited the semiotic control over encoding the message to two points of human intervention in the process – the choice of angle, framing, focus, or film stock when the photograph is taken, and the darkroom processes as it is developed and printed. In low-tech electronic photography even these choices appear to be reduced, for the darkroom is eliminated, and the choices at the moment of shooting are reduced to those of framing, angle, and distance (in most home video cameras, at least, everything else is taken care of automatically).

But even processes as technological as those of video never operate outside of social determinants. The credibility of video depends upon the social domain of its use. In the domain of the low (low capital, low technology, low power), video has an authenticity that results from its user's lack of resources to intervene in its technology. When capital, technology, and power are high, however, the ability to intervene, technologically and socially, is enhanced. The videohigh of Rodney King was a product of capital, technology, and social power that lay beyond the reach of the videolow. Because technology requires capital, it is never equally distributed or apolitical. George Holliday owned a camera, but not a computer enhancer; he could produce and replay an electronic image, but could not slow it, reverse it, freeze it, or write upon it, and his videolow appeared so authentic to so many precisely because he could not. The enhanced clarity of the videohigh lost the authenticity of the low but gained the power to tell its own truth in its own domain of the courtroom and the jury room. And that domain was, in this case, the limit of its victory.

The time gap between the writing and the reading of the previous paragraph may well have made it out of date. The video 'toaster' has already brought electronic manipulation of the image within the price range of many amateurs. And electronic manipulation leaves no trace of its operation. This has the legal profession worried, and many legal scholars would agree with Christine Guilshan when she writes, 'Today . . . the veracity of photographic evidence is being radically challenged. Computer imaging techniques are rapidly emerging which call into question the belief that photographs are neutral records of reality.'[6] When hooked up to a computer, the video camera provides not a photograph, but bits of visual information that can be undetectably enhanced, deleted, or rearranged – just like words. Guilshan's anxieties are those of the power bloc, not of the people: she is not concerned that powerful institutions such as the FBI or the media can manipulate images, for she has faith that their guidelines will prevent the ability being misused; what worries her is what might happen when the 'average citizen' has this capability.

It remains to be seen whether technological development will reduce the sense of authenticity that low-tech video still carries. We might hope that it does not, for this authenticity of the videolow allows the weak one of their few opportunities to intervene effectively in the power of surveillance, and to reverse its flow. George Holliday was not alone in grasping it. In Saint Paul, a Hmong teenager, Billy Her, was arrested for assaulting the police. Two days later, a videotape anonymously mailed to the police department resulted in the arresting officer's suspension from duty, because it showed him striking Billy Her repeatedly but gave no evidence of Billy Her attacking the police.[7] On her national talk show, Oprah Winfrey screened an amateur videotape showing Texas police punching Chon Soto as he was trying to attend his hometown city council meeting, where he was signed up to speak.[8] His friends told Oprah that they had expected the city council meeting to be heated, that they had had problems at previous meetings, and so they had asked Raoul Vasquez to bring his video camera to this one. Viewers never learned what was so heatedly disputed, not why only nineteen members of the public were to be allowed to attend the meeting. The camera showed, however, that the police were white and the citizens were Latino, and its microphone caught Latino-accented voices raised in protest. The police claimed that Chon Soto was trying to force his way into the meeting; the camera showed that the only force involved was applied by the police. Chon Soto was hospitalized, and, after the video was played on local TV stations, the chief of police was suspended.

Video plays such an important role in our culture because in its low- and high-tech forms it spreads far up and down our social hierarchy. But videolow does not always oppose videohigh; indeed, often the two work complicitly. Network television has developed a whole genre of programs to incorporate videolow into its high-capital, high-tech system. Shows such as *I Witness Videos* and *America's Funniest Home Videos* extend the reach of the high into the domain of the low, to turn it to a profit and to use its stories as they think best. Many of the *I Witness Videos* reproduce the forms of official news – people with video cameras are often present when disasters occur, whereas news crews typically arrive afterward. But like the Rodney King video, their lower-quality images, poor but closely involved vantage points, moments of loss of technical control (blurred focus, too-rapid pans, tilted or dropped cameras), and their reduced editing all serve to reveal the discursive control that official news exerts over the events it reports. Videolow shows that events can always be put into discourse differently from videohigh, and this enhances its sense of authenticity. Local news stations now solicit videolow from their viewers; they use their viewers' ubiquity to extend their monitoring reach and intensify our system of surveillance, to capture the immediate and the authentic, and to pull their viewers into an alliance with the station. Some are also experimenting with reducing the official 'news crew,' to a single reporter with a camcorder to cut costs, increase flexibility, and, they hope, gain a sense of authenticity.

Videolow is not only incorporable into the interests of the dominant, it often intentionally serves them and extends their surveillance. The day *The Oprah Winfrey Show* screened the videolow of the police roughing up Chon Soto it also screened others that were shot in order to assist in the policing of our society. A doctor who has mounted a video camera on his dashboard patrols the late-night roads of Chicago looking for drunk drivers. We watched him find one, follow them, videotaping all the time, and then call the police on his CB radio and offer them his video as evidence. The *New York Times* tells of a civilian video patrol in Methuen, Massachusetts, that tapes prostitutes and their clients as a community effort to clean up their neighborhood.[9] The report on their activities claims that everywhere individuals are using video cameras to document car thefts, drug deals, prostitution, and other unwelcome or illegal street activity. Gerald Arenberg, the director of the National Association of Chiefs of Police, told the reporter, 'Ever since the Rodney King incident, anyone who has a camcorder is using it.' Matt Reskin, director of a national organization that promotes community policing programs, agrees with police officers that video is a useful amateur policing tool. *The Oprah Winfrey Show* gave further examples, among them a video of a student party that got out of hand and vandalized a car, and, more to our point here, one showing the beating of Reginald Denny from ground level as the news helicopter videoed it from on high. The police used this videolow to help identify and arrest the suspects, and the cameraman, who was Black, had to go into hiding because, as he said, 'Threats started to come through the neighborhood, and gang members showed up looking for me.' Although the politics of technology itself may be distant, those of its uses are immediate.

The users of videolow to extend disciplinary surveillance can be countered, as we have seen, by those who turn the cameras back upon the surveillers. Across the nation, 'videoactivists' or 'videoguerrillas' are using the technology, particularly in conjunction with local-access cable channels, for explicit social criticism. The police are central agents in the surveillance system, so they are often the target of videoactivism. In Berkeley, California, for example, an organization called Copwatch uses video cameras and human eyes to monitor the police, particularly in their dealings with homeless people and African-Americans, in the belief that watching police behavior is the best way to prevent police brutality. The mainstream media can be as active surveillers as the police, and in Rochester, New York, a video collective followed local TV news crews, videoed them videoing events, talked to people they interviewed and to those they chose not to, and, on the local-access channel, showed not only that events could look very different but that the differences between high and low discourses were obviously political. The cops in Berkeley and the news crews in Rochester did all they could to prevent their actions being videoed.

A step higher up the technical, social, and institutional hierarchy is Paper Tiger Television, a video collective dedicated to criticizing the mainstream media, to providing alternate information, and to increasing popular skepticism about officially mediated knowledge. Longtime video activist Dee Dee Halleck describes the deliberately low-tech, low-budget style of Paper Tiger as it

> proudly flaunts the 'cheap art' of its graphics and its production 'values.' Paper Tiger uses hand-painted backdrops for sets, hastily scribbled felt-tip credits, and transitions that make no attempt to disguise the technology. On-air dialogue with the control room is amplified. 'Cue Herb, Daniel!' gets mixed into the overall sound track. The Paper Tiger aesthetic expanded from crayons and paints to include crude but inspired chroma key effects, such as Joan Braderman sliding down the Carrington banister in 'Joan Does Dynasty' and John Walden's hugging of Ted Koppel in 'From Woodstock to Tiananmen Square.' Many Paper Tiger programs that critique TV use simple TV effects in ways that expose mystified constructions in both television form and ideological content.[10]

Deep Dish Television has grown out of Paper Tiger; it brings satellite distribution to local video activists so that their work need not be limited to their local public-access channels. Of course, high-tech satellite time is high cost and Deep Dish can afford only two hours a week, which means that much low-tech communication by mail and telephone is needed to supplement it, to ensure that local stations are ready to receive and tape its offerings. Perhaps the biggest success of Deep Dish occurred during the Gulf War, when the official media were harnessed so closely to the White House and the Pentagon that echoes of dissenting voices and views were almost entirely eliminated from the nation's screens. Deep Dish called for other video coverage and received hundreds of tapes from all over the country. It organized them into four half-hour programs and uplinked them to the satellite nine days before the war began. It is impossible to know the full extent of the program's reach, because Deep Dish has no full record of who receives its programs and encourages people to dub them and show them whenever and wherever they wish. But it is known that many public access and public television stations screened the programs, often repeatedly; more than a thousand copies were mailed out in less than a month. In Britain, Channel 4 edited the programs into a one-hour special, which it aired in prime time; in Japan, the programs served as a focal point for antiwar activism.

The better access one has to capital and to the institutional power that goes with it, the better use one can make of video technology. But video has low-tech and high-tech forms and thus contradictory uses. It can be used both to bring us knowledge and to know us, to give us access to one system of power-knowledge while subjecting us to another. It is an instrument of both communication and surveillance. It can be used by the power bloc to monitor the comings and goings of the people, but equally its cameras can be turned 180 social degrees, to show the doings of the power bloc to the people.

Video monitoring and video knowledge are directed upon the body, for it is there that power is made visible. The strategizing of social alliances, the intentions and internal lives of people, and the abstract lines of social power all lie beyond video's capabilities. Video knowledge is that of the application of power to the body; its terrain is that in which broad social interests appear in their embodied form. Policing the social body is a paradigmatic example, for the physical contact between police officer and the individual suspect-citizen-disorderly body is an event that is both significant and videoknowable. The police use video surveillance for their purposes, from identifying bank robbers to monitoring Mayor Marion Barry receiving drugs and sex in their setup; they used it to identify the suspects in the Reginald Denny beating, and then, in the initial court hearing, they covertly videotaped a suspect's friends who attended in order to identify yet more potential suspect criminals (they knew, evidently, that friends of suspects were also suspect, particularly if Black).

Armies of law enforcement agencies and security services use millions of video cameras to monitor the places and the people they are hired to protect. But video technology still allows, on occasion, those who are normally monitored to monitor the monitors. This technological engagement in the social struggle never takes place on equal terms. Opportunistic tactics are set against strategically deployed power; the handheld home video camera has a mobility that makes it a good guerrilla weapon, whereas carefully located surveillance cameras are typical of a powerful strategy that is well planned and highly efficient, but cumbersome.

Notes

1 David Guterson (1993) 'Enclosed, Encyclopedic, Endured' *Harper's*, August, 55.

2 Mike Davis, *Junkyard of Dreams*, video for Channel 4, London (undated).

3 Quoted in *New York Times*, 4 May, 1992, A15; cited in Thomas Dunn (1993) 'The New Enclosures: Racism in the Normalized Community' in *Reading Rodney King Reading Urban Uprising*, Robert Gooding-Williams (ed.), New York: Routledge, p. 189.

4 Ibid.

5 Roland Barthes (1977) 'The Photographic Paradox' in *Image-Music-Text*, London: Fontana, pp. 15-32.

6 Christine Guilshan (1992) 'A Picture Is Worth a Thousand Lies: Electronic Imaging and the Future of the Admissibility of Photographs into Evidence', *Rutgers Computer and Technology Law Journal* 18 (1): 366.

7 *St. Paul Pioneer Press*, 20 December, 1992, C1.

8 *The Oprah Winfrey Show*, 26 February, 1993.

9 *New York Times*, 21 March, 1993, 15A.

10 Dee Dee Halleck, paper in *Leonardo: Journal of the International Society for the Arts, Sciences and Technology* (forthcoming).

Chapter 15

Marita Sturken

THE WALL, THE SCREEN AND THE IMAGE

The Vietnam Veterans Memorial

THE FORMS REMEMBRANCE takes indicate the status of memory within a given culture. In these forms, we can see acts of public commemoration as moments in which the shifting discourse of history, personal memory, and cultural memory converge. Public commemoration is a form of history-making, yet, it can also be a contested form of remembrance in which cultural memories slide through and into each other, merging and then disengaging in a narrative tangle.

With the Vietnam War, discourses of public commemoration are inextricably tied to the question of how war is brought to closure in American society. How, for instance, does a society commemorate a war for which the central narrative is one of division and dissent, a war whose history is still formative and highly contested? The Vietnam War, with its lack of a singular, historical narrative defining clear-cut purpose and outcome, has led to a unique form of commemoration.

Questions of public remembrance of the Vietnam War can be examined through the concept of the screen: a screen is a surface that is projected upon; it is also an object that hides something from view, that shelters or protects. The kinds of screens that converge in the case of the Vietnam Veterans Memorial in Washington, DC both shield and are projected upon: the black walls of the memorial act as screens for innumerable projections of memory and history – of the United States' participation in the Vietnam War and the experience of the Vietnam veterans since the war.

A singular, sanctioned history of the Vietnam War has not coalesced, in part because of the disruption of the standard narratives of American imperialism, technology, and masculinity that the war's loss represented. The history of the Vietnam War is still being composed from many conflicting histories, yet particular elements within the often opposing narratives are uncontested – the divisive effect the war had on American society and the marginalization of the Vietnam veteran. This essay is concerned with how narratives of the war have been constructed out of and within the cultural memory of the Vietnam Veterans Memorial. I shall examine how the screens of the memorial act to eclipse – to screen out – personal and collective memories of the Vietnam War in the design of history, and how the textures of cultural memory are nevertheless woven throughout, perhaps over and under, these screens.

The status of a memorial

Although now administered under the aegis of the National Parks Service of the federal government, the impetus for the creation of the Vietnam Veterans Memorial came from a group of Vietnam veterans who raised the funds and negotiated a site on the Washington Mall. Situated on the grassy slope of the Constitutional Gardens near the Lincoln Memorial, the Vietnam Veterans Memorial, which was designed by Maya Lin, consists of a V shape of two walls of black granite set into the earth at an angle of 125 degrees. Together, the walls extend almost 500 feet in length, with a maximum height of approximately 10 feet at the central hinge. These walls are inscribed with 58,196 names of men and women who died in the war, listed chronologically by date of death, with opening and closing inscriptions. The listing of names begins on the right-hand side of the hinge and continues to the end of the right wall; it then begins again at the far end of the left wall and ends at the center again. Thus, the name of the first American soldier killed in Vietnam, in 1959, is on a panel adjacent to that containing the name of the last American killed in 1975. The framing dates of 1959 and 1975 are the only dates listed on the wall; the names are listed alphabetically within each 'casualty day,' although those dates are not noted. Eight of the names on the wall represent women who died in the war. Since 1984 the memorial has been accompanied by a flag and a figurative sculpture of three soldiers, both facing the memorial from a group of trees south of the wall. In 1993 a statue commemorating the women who served in Vietnam was added 300 feet from the wall.

The memorial functions in opposition to the codes of remembrance evidenced on the Washington Mall. Virtually all the national memorials and monuments in Washington are made of white stone and constructed to be seen from a distance. In contrast, the Vietnam Veterans Memorial cuts into the sloping earth: it is not visible until one is almost upon it; if approached from behind, it seems to disappear into the landscape. Although the polished black granite walls of the memorial reflect the Washington Monument and face the Lincoln Memorial, they are not visible from the base of either structure. The black stone creates a reflective surface, one that echoes the reflecting pool of the Lincoln Memorial, and allows the viewers to participate in the memorial; seeing their own image reflected in the names, they are implicated in the listing of the dead. The etched surface of the memorial has a tactile quality, and viewers are compelled to touch the names and make rubbings of them.

Its status as a memorial, rather than a monument, situates the Vietnam Veterans Memorial within a particular code of remembrance. Monuments and memorials can often be used as interchangeable forms, but there are distinctions in intent between them. Arthur Danto writes: 'We erect monuments so that we shall always remember, and build memorials so that we shall never forget.'[1] Monuments are not generally built to commemorate defeats; the defeated dead are remembered in memorials. Whereas a monument most often signifies victory, a memorial refers to the life or lives sacrificed for a particular set of values. Memorials embody grief, loss, and tribute. Whatever triumph a memorial may refer to, its depiction of victory is always tempered by a foregrounding of the lives lost.

Memorials are, according to Charles Griswold, 'a species of pedagogy' that 'seeks to instruct posterity about the past and, in so doing, necessarily reaches a decision about what is worth recovering.'[2] The Lincoln Memorial is a funereal structure that gains its force from its implicit reference to Lincoln's untimely death. It embodies the man and his philosophy, with his words on its walls. The Washington Monument, by contrast, operates purely as a symbol, making no reference beyond its name to the mythic political figure. The distinction between the two outlines one of the fundamental differences between memorials and monuments: memorials tend to emphasize specific texts or lists of the dead, whereas monuments are usually anonymous.

The Vietnam Veterans Memorial is unmistakably representative of a particular period in Western art. In the uproar that accompanied its construction, it became the focus of a debate about the role of modernism in public sculpture. Just one month prior to the dedication of the memorial in November 1982, Tom Wolfe wrote a vitriolic attack on its design in the *Washington Post*, calling it a work of modern orthodoxy that was a 'tribute to Jane Fonda.'[3] Wolfe and other critics of modernism compared the memorial to two infamously unpopular, government-funded public sculptures: Carl Andre's *Stone Field Piece* (1980) in Hartford, Connecticut, and Richard Serra's *Tilted Arc* (1981) in downtown Manhattan. Andre's work, which consists of thirty-six large boulders positioned on a lawn near Hartford's city hall, is widely regarded with derision by residents as a symbol of the misguided judgements of their city government.[4] Serra's now notorious *Tilted Arc*, an oppressive, leaning slab of Cor-Ten steel that bisected the equally inhospitable Federal Plaza, inspired several years of intense debate and was dismantled in March 1989 after workers in the Federal Building petitioned to have it removed.[5] In the media, these two works came to symbolize the alienating effect of modern sculpture on the viewing public and people's questioning of the mechanisms by which tax-funded sculpture is imposed upon them.

In situating the Vietnam Veterans Memorial purely within the context of modernism, however, Wolfe and his fellow critics ignore fundamental aspects of this work, an omission which, it might be added, the sketches of the design may have aided. The memorial is not simply a flat, black, abstract wall; it is a wall inscribed with names. When members of the 'public' visit this memorial, they do not go to contemplate long walls cut into the earth but to see and touch the names of those whose lives were lost in this war. Hence, to call this a modernist work is to overemphasize its physical design and to negate its commemorative purpose.

Modernist sculpture has been defined by a kind of sitelessness. Yet, the Vietnam Veterans Memorial is a site-specific work that establishes its position within the symbolic history embodied in the national monuments on and around the Washington Mall. Pointing from its axis to both the Washington Monument and Lincoln Memorial, the Vietnam Veterans Memorial references, absorbs, and reflects these classical forms. Its black walls mirror not only the faces of its viewers and passing clouds but the obelisk of the Washington Monument, thus forming a kind of pastiche of monuments. The memorial's relationship to the earth shifts between context and decontextualization, between an effacement and an embracement of the earth; approached from above, it appears to cut into the earth; from below, it seems to rise from it. The site specificity of the Vietnam Veterans Memorial is crucial to its position as both subversive of and continuous with the nationalist discourse of the mall.

It is as a war memorial that the Vietnam Veterans Memorial most distinguishes itself from modernist sculpture. As the first national memorial to an American war built since the Second World War memorials, it makes a statement on war that diverges sharply from the traditional declarations of prior war memorials. The Vietnam Veterans Memorial Fund (VVMF), which organized the construction of the memorial, stipulated only two things in its design – that it contain the names of all of those who died or are missing in action, and that be apolitical and harmonious with the site. Implicit within these guidelines was the desire that the memorial offer some kind of closure to the debates on the war. Yet, with these stipulations, the veterans set the stage for the dramatic disparity between the message of this memorial and that of its antecedents. The stipulation that the work not espouse a political stand in regard to the war – a stipulation that, in the ensuing controversy, would ultimately appear naive – ensured that in the end the memorial would not glorify war.

The traditional war memorial achieves its status by enacting closure on a specific conflict. This closure contains the war within particular master narratives either of victory or the bitter price of victory, a theme dominant in the 'never again' texts of First World War memorials. In declaring the end of a conflict, this closure can by its very nature serve to sanctify future wars by offering a complete narrative with cause and effect intact. In rejecting the architectural lineage of monuments and contesting the aesthetic codes of previous war memorials, the Vietnam Veterans Memorial refuses to sanction the closure and implied tradition of those structures. Yet, it can be said to both condemn and justify future memorials.

The black gash of shame

Before the memorial was completed, its design came under attack not only because of its modernist aesthetics but, more significant, because it violated unspoken taboos about the remembrance of wars. When it was first unveiled, the design was condemned by certain veterans and others as a highly political statement about the shame of an unvictorious war. The memorial was termed the 'black gash of shame and sorrow,' a 'degrading ditch,' a 'tombstone,' a 'slap in the face,' and a 'wailing wall for draft dodgers and New Lefters of the future.' These dissenters included a certain faction of veterans and members of the 'New Right,' ranging from conservative activist Phyllis Schafly to future presidential candidate Ross Perot, who had contributed the money for the design contest. Many of these critics saw the memorial as a monument to defeat, one that spoke more directly to a nation's guilt than to the honor of the war dead and the veterans.

The criticism leveled at the memorial's design showed precisely how it was being 'read' by its opponents, and their readings compellingly reveal codes of remembrance of war memorials. Many saw its black walls as evoking shame, sorrow, and dishonor and others perceived its refusal to rise above the earth as indicative of defeat. Thus, a racially coded reading of the color black as shameful was combined with a reading of a feminized earth connoting a lack of power. Precisely because of its deviation from traditional commemorative codes – white stone rising above the earth – the design was read as a political statement. In a defensive attempt to counter aesthetic arguments, an editorial in the *National Review* stated:

> Our objection . . . is based upon the clear political message of this design. The design says that the Vietnam War should be memorialized in black, not the white marble of Washington. The mode of listing the names makes them individual deaths, not deaths in a cause: they might as well have been traffic accidents. The invisibility of the monument at ground level symbolizes the 'unmentionability' of the war . . . Finally, the V-shaped plan of the black retaining wall immortalizes the antiwar signal, the V protest made with the fingers.[6]

This analysis of the memorial's symbolism, indeed a perceptive reading, points to several crucial aspects of the memorial: its listing of names does emphasize individual deaths rather than the singular death of a body of men and women; the relationship of the memorial to the earth does refuse to evoke heroism and victory. Yet these conservative readings of the memorial, though they may have been accurate in interpreting the design, did not anticipate the effects of the inscription of names.

The angry reactions to the memorial design go beyond the accusation of the elite pretensions of abstraction – the uncontroversial Washington Monument itself is the epitome of abstraction. Rather, I believe that the memorial's primary (and unspoken) subversion of the codes of war remembrance is its antiphallic presence. By 'antiphallic' I do not mean to imply that the memorial is somehow a passive or 'feminine' form, but rather that it opposes the codes of vertical monuments symbolizing power and honor. The memorial does not stand erect above the landscape; it is continuous with the earth. It is contemplative rather than declarative. The V shape of the memorial has been interpreted by various commentators as V for Vietnam, victim, victory, veteran, violate, and valor. Yet one also finds here a disconcerting subtext in this debate in which the memorial is seen as implicitly evoking castration. The V of the two black granite walls, it seems, is also read as a female V. The 'gash' is not only a wound, it is slang for the female genitals. The memorial contains all the elements that have been associated psychoanalytically with the specter of woman – it embraces the earth; it is the abyss; it is death.

Indeed, some of the criticism of the memorial was direct in calling for a phallic memorial. James Webb, who was a member of the Fund's sponsoring committee, wrote:

> Watching then the white phallus that is the Washington Monument piercing the air like a bayonet, you feel uplifted. . . . That is the political

> message. And then when you peer off into the woods at this black slash of earth to your left, this sad, dreary mass tomb, nihilistically commemorating death, you are hit with that message also. . . . That is the tragedy of this memorial for those who served.[7]

To its critics, this antiphallus symbolized this country's castration in an unsuccessful war, a war that 'emasculated' the United States. The 'healing' of this wound would therefore require a memorial that revived the narrative of the United States as a technologically superior military power and rehabilitated the masculinity of the American soldier.

The person who designed this controversial, antiphallic memorial was unlikely to reiterate traditional codes of war remembrance. At the time her anonymously submitted design was chosen by a group of eight art experts, Maya Ying Lin was a 21-year-old undergraduate at Yale University. She had produced the design as a project for a funerary architecture course. She was not only young and uncredentialed but also Chinese-American and female. Initially, the veterans of the VVMF were pleased by this turn of events; they assumed that the selection of Lin's design would only show how open and impartial their design contest had been. However, the selection of someone with 'marginal' cultural status as the primary interpreter of a controversial war inevitably complicated matters. Eventually, Maya Lin was defined, in particular by the media, not as American but as 'other'. This otherness became an issue not only in the way she was perceived by the media and some of the veterans, it became a critical issue of whether or not that otherness had informed the design itself. Architecture critic Michael Sorkin wrote:

> Perhaps it was Maya Lin's 'otherness' that enabled her to create such a moving work. Perhaps only an outsider could have designed an environment so successful in answering the need for recognition by a group of people – the Vietnam vets – who are plagued by a sense of 'otherness' forced on them by a country that has spent ten years pretending not to see them.[8]

Lin's marginal status as a Chinese-American woman was thus seen as giving her insight into the marginal status experienced by Vietnam veterans, an analogy that noticeably erased other differences in race and age that existed between them.

When Lin's identity became known, there was a tendency in the press to characterize her design as passive, as having both a female and an Asian aesthetic. There is little doubt that in its refusal to glorify war, it is an implicitly pacifist work, and, by extension, a political work. In its form, the memorial is emphatically antiherioc. Yet as much as it is contemplative and continuous with the earth, it can also be seen as a violent work that cuts into the earth. Lin has said, 'I wanted to work with the land and not dominate it. I had an impulse to cut open the earth . . . an initial violence that in time would heal. The grass would grow back, but the cut would remain, a pure, flat surface, like a geode when you cut into it and polish the edge.'[9] The black walls cannot connote a healing wound without also signifying the violence that created that wound, cutting into the earth and splitting it open.

Trouble began almost immediately between Maya Lin and the veterans. 'The fund has always seen me as a female – as a child', she has said. 'I went in there when I first won and their attitude was – O.K. you did a good job, but now we're going to hire some big boys – boys – to take care of it.'[10] Lin was situated outside the veterans' discourse, because she was a woman and an Asian-American and because of her approach to the project. She had made a decision deliberately not to inform herself about the war's political history to avoid being influenced by debates about the war. According to veteran Jan Scruggs, who was the primary figure in getting the memorial built,

> She never asked, 'What was combat like?' or 'Who were your friends whose names we're putting on the wall?' And the vets, in turn, never once explained to her what words like 'courage,' 'sacrifice,' and 'devotion to duty' really meant'.[11]

In the larger political arena, discourses of aesthetics and commemoration were also at play. Several well-placed funders of the memorial, including Ross Perot, were unhappy with the design, and Secretary of the Interior James Watt withheld its permit. It became clear to the veterans of the VVMF that they had either to compromise or to postpone the construction of the memorial (which was to be ready by November 1982, in time for Veterans Day). Consequently, a plan was devised to erect a statue and flag close to the walls of the memorial; realist sculptor Frederick Hart was chosen to design it. (Hart was paid $330,000, compared to the $20,000 fee that Maya Lin received for her design from the same fund).[12]

Hart's bronze sculpture, placed in a grove of trees near the memorial in 1984, consists of three soldiers – one black, one Hispanic, and one white – standing and looking in the general direction of the memorial. The soldiers' military garb is realistically rendered, with guns slung over their shoulders and ammunition around their waists, and their expressions are somewhat bewildered and puzzled. Hart, one of the most vociferous critics of modernism in the debate over the memorial, said at the time:

> My position is humanist, not militarist. I'm not trying to say there was anything good or bad about the war. I researched for three years – read everything. I became close friends with many vets, drank with them in bars. Lin's piece is a serene exercise in contemporary art done in a vacuum with no knowledge of its subject. It's nihilistic – that's its appeal.[13]

Hart bases his credentials on a kind of 'knowledge' strictly within the male domain – drinking with the veterans in a bar – and unavailable to Maya Lin, whom he had on another occasion referred to as 'a mere student'. She describes the addition of his statue as 'drawing mustaches on other people's portraits'.[14] Hart characterizes Lin as having designed her work with no 'knowledge' and no 'research', as a woman who works with feeling and intuition rather than expertise. He ultimately defines realism as not only a male privilege but also an aesthetic necessity in remembering war. Ironically, the conflict over Lin's design forestalled any potential debate over the atypical expression of Hart's soldiers.

The battle over what kind of aesthetic style best represents the Vietnam War was, quite obviously, a battle of the discourse of the war itself. In striving for an 'apolitical' memorial, the veterans of the VVMF had attempted to separate the memorial, itself a contested narrative, from the contested narratives of the war, ultimately an impossible task. The memorial could not be a neutral site precisely because of the divisive effects of the Vietnam War. Later, Maya Lin noted the strange appropriateness of the two memorials: 'In a funny sense the compromise brings the memorial closer to the truth. What is also memorialized is that people still cannot resolve that war, nor can they separate issues, the politics, from it'.[15] However, after Lin's memorial had actually been constructed, the debate about aesthetics and remembrance surrounding its design simply disappeared. The controversy was eclipsed by a national discourse on remembrance and healing. The experience of viewing Lin's work was so powerful for the general public that criticism of its design vanished.

The Vietnam veteran: the perennial soldier

The incommunicability of the experience of the Vietnam veterans has been a primary narrative in Vietnam War representation. This silence has been depicted as a consequence of an inconceivable kind of war, one that fit no prior images of war, one that the American public would refuse to believe. The importance of the Vietnam Veterans memorial lies in its communicability, which in effect has mollified the incommunicability of the veterans' experience.

Though the Vietnam Veterans Memorial most obviously pays tribute to the memory of those who died during the war, it is a central icon for the veterans. It has been noted that the memorial has given them a place – one that recognizes their identities, a place at which to congregate and from which to speak. Vietnam veterans haunt the memorial, often coming at night after the crowds have dispersed. Many veterans regard the wall as a site where they visit their memories. Hence, the memorial is as much about survival as it is about mourning the dead. The construction of an identity for the veterans has become the most conspicuous and persistent narrative of the memorial. The central theme of this narrative is the veterans' initial marginalization, before the memorial's construction generated discussion about them.

Unlike the Second World War veterans, Vietnam veterans did not arrive home en masse for a celebration. Some of the most difficult stories of the veterans' experience are about their mistreatment upon their return, and these incidents serve as icons for the extended alienation and mistreatment felt by the veterans. Many veterans ended up in underfunded and poorly staffed Veterans' Administration Hospitals. They were expected to put their war experiences behind them and to assimilate quickly back into society. That many were unable to do so further exacerbated their marginalization – they were labeled social misfits and stereotyped as potentially dangerous men liable to erupt violently at any moment.

The scapegoating of the veteran as a psychopath absolved the American public of complicity and allowed the narrative of American military power to stand. Implied within these conflicting narratives is the question of whether or not the veterans are to be perceived as victims or complicit with the war. Peter Marin writes, 'Vets are in an ambiguous situation – they were the agents and victims of a particular kind of violence. That is the source of a pain that almost no one else can understand'.[16] Ironically, their stigma has resulted in many Vietnam veterans' assumption of hybrid roles; they are both, yet neither, soldiers and civilians.

Although the marginalization of the Vietnam veterans has been acknowledged in the current discourse of healing and forgiveness about the war, within the veterans' community another group has struggled against an imposed silence: the women veterans. Eight women military nurses were killed in Vietnam and memorialized on the wall. It is estimated that 11,500 women, half of whom were civilians and many of whom were nurses, served in Vietnam and that 265,000 women served in the military during the time period of the Vietnam War. The experience of the women who served in Vietnam was equally affected by the difference of the war: an unusually large proportion of them, three-quarters, were exposed to hostile fire. Upon their return, they were not only subject to post-traumatic stress like the male veterans but they were also excluded from the veteran community. Many have since revealed how they kept their war experience a secret, not telling even their husbands about their time in Vietnam.

These women veterans were thus doubly displaced, unable to speak as veterans or as women. In response, several women veterans began raising funds for their own memorial, and in November 1993, the Vietnam Women's Memorial was dedicated near the Vietnam Veterans Memorial. The statue, which was designed by Glenna Goodacre, depicts three uniformed women with a wounded soldier. The two women who direct the VWMP, Diane Carlson Evans and Donna Marie Boulay, say that it is Hart's depiction of three men who make the absence of women so visible, and that they would not have initiated the project had Lin's memorial stood alone. Says Evans, 'The wall in itself was enough, but when they added the men it became necessary to add women to complete the memorial'.[17] Hence, the singular narrative of Hart's realist depiction is one of both inclusion and exclusion.

One could argue that the widespread discourse of healing around the original memorial led women veterans to speak of their memorial as the beginning rather than the culmination of a healing process. Yet the radical message of commemorating women in war is undercut by the conventionality of the statue itself. A contemporary version of the *Pietà*, the statue presents one woman nurse heroically holding the body of a wounded soldier, one searching the sky for help, and one looking forlornly at the ground. Benjamin Forgery, who called this memorial in the *Washington Post* 'one monument too many', has criticized the women's memorial for cluttering up the landscape with 'blatheringly sentimental sculpture'. He wrote that the sculptor's 'ambition is sabotaged by the subject and the artist's limited talent – compared with Michelangelo's Christ figure, this GI is as stiff as a board. The result is more like an awkward still from a *M*A*S*H* episode'.[18]

The decision to build the women's memorial was not about aesthetics (except in so far as it reaffirms the representational aesthetic of Hart's statue) but about recognition and inclusion. However, by reinscribing the archetypal image of woman as caretaker, one that foregrounds the male veteran's body, the memorial reiterates the main obstacle to healing that women veterans face in recognizing their needs as veterans. Writes Laura Palmer, 'After all, these women had *degrees* in putting the needs of others before their own'.[19]

The difficulty of adequately and appropriately memorializing the women veterans falls within the larger issue of masculine identity in the Vietnam War. The Vietnam War is depicted as an event in which American masculinity was irretrievably damaged, and the rehabilitation of the Vietnam veteran is thus also a reinscription of American masculinity. This has also taken the form of re-enacting the war at the memorial itself, through the Veterans' Vigil of Honor, which keeps watch there, and the 'battles' over its construction and maintenance. As a form of re-enactment, this conflation of the memorial and the war is a ritual of healing, although one that appears to be stuck in its ongoing replay, with a resistance to moving beyond narratives of the war. For the men of the Veterans' Vigil, only the war can provide meaning. In refighting that war every day, they are also reinscribing narratives of heroism and sacrifice. But, for others, there is a powerful kind of closure at the memorial. The one story for which the memorial appears to offer resolution is that of the shame felt by veterans for having fought in an unpopular war, a story that is their primary battle with history.

The memorial as a shrine

The Vietnam Veterans Memorial has been the subject of an extraordinary outpouring of emotion since it was built. Over 150,000 people attended its dedication ceremony and some days as many as 20,000 people walk by its walls. It is presently the most visited site on the Washington Mall with an estimated 22 to 30 million visitors. People bring personal artifacts to leave at the wall as offerings, and coffee-table photography books document the experiences of visitors as a collective recovery from the war. It has also spawned the design or construction of at least 150 other memorials, including the Korean War Veterans Memorial, which was dedicated in July 1995.

The rush to embrace the memorial as a cultural symbol reveals not only the relief of voicing a history that has been taboo but also a desire to reinscribe that history. The black granite walls of the memorial act as a screen for myriad cultural projections; it is easily appropriated for a variety of interpretations of the war and of the experience of those who died in it. To the veterans, the wall makes amends for their treatment since the war; to the families and friends of those who died, it officially recognizes their sorrow and validates a grief that was not previously sanctioned; to others, it is either a profound antiwar statement or an opportunity to recast the narrative of the war in terms of honor and sacrifice.

The memorial's popularity must thus be seen in the context of a very active scripting and rescripting of the war and as an integral component in the recently emerged Vietnam War nostalgia industry. This sentiment is not confined to those who wish to return to the intensity of wartime; it is also felt by the news media, who long to recapture their moment of moral power – the Vietnam War was very good television. Michael Clark writes that the media nostalgia campaign,

> healed over the wounds that had refused to close for ten years with a balm of nostalgia, and transformed guilt and doubt into duty and pride. And with a triumphant flourish it offered us the spectacle of its most successful creation, the veterans who will fight the next war.[20]

Though the design of Maya Lin's memorial does not lend itself to marketable reproductions, the work has functioned as a catalyst for much of this nostalgia. The Vietnam Veterans Memorial is the subject of no fewer than twelve books, many of them photography collections that focus on the interaction of visitors with the names. The memorial has tapped into a reservoir of need to express in public the pain of this war, a desire to transfer the private memories of this war into a collective experience. Many personal artifacts have been left at the memorial: photographs, letters, poems, teddy bears, dog tags, combat boots and helmets, MIA/POW bracelets, clothes, medals of honor, headbands, beer cans, plaques, crosses, playing cards. At this site, the objects are transposed from personal to cultural artifacts, as items bearing witness to pain suffered.

Thus, a very rich and vibrant dialogue of deliberate, if sometimes very private, remembrance takes place at the memorial. Of the approximately 40,000 objects that have been left at the wall, the vast majority have been left anonymously. Relinquished before the wall, the letters tell many stories:

> Dear Michael: Your name is here but you are not. I made a rubbing of it, thinking that if I rubbed hard enough I would rub your name off the wall and you would come back to me. I miss you so.

> Dear Sir: For twenty-two years I have carried your picture in my wallet. I was only eighteen years old that day that we faced one another on that trail in Chu Lai, Vietnam. Why you didn't take my life I'll never know. You stared at me for so long, armed with your AK-47, and yet you did not fire. Forgive me for taking your life, I was reacting just the way I was trained, to kill VC.

Hence, the memorial is perceived by visitors as a site where they can speak to the dead (where, by implication, the dead are present). Many of these letters are addressed not to visitors but to the dead, though intended to be shared as cultural memory. Many of the artifacts at the memorial also represent a catharsis in releasing long-held objects to memory: a can of C-rations, a 'short stick', worn Vietnamese sandals, a grenade pin. For those who left these objects, the memorial represents their final destination and a relinquishing of memory.

The National Park Service, which is now in charge of maintaining the memorial, operates an archive of the materials that have been left at the memorial. Originally, the Park Service classified these objects as 'lost and found'. Later, Park Service officials realized the artifacts had been left intentionally, and they began to save them. The objects thus moved from the cultural status of being 'lost' (without category) to historical artifacts. They have now even turned into artistic artifacts; the manager of the archive writes:

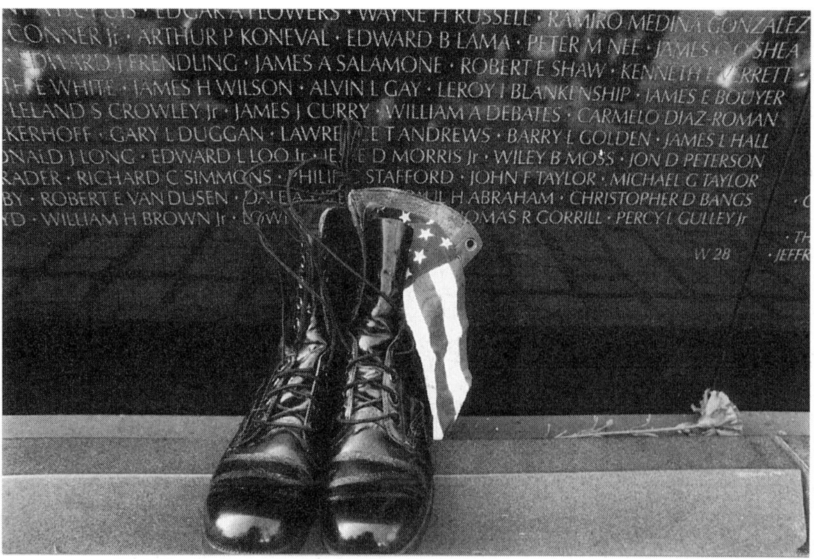

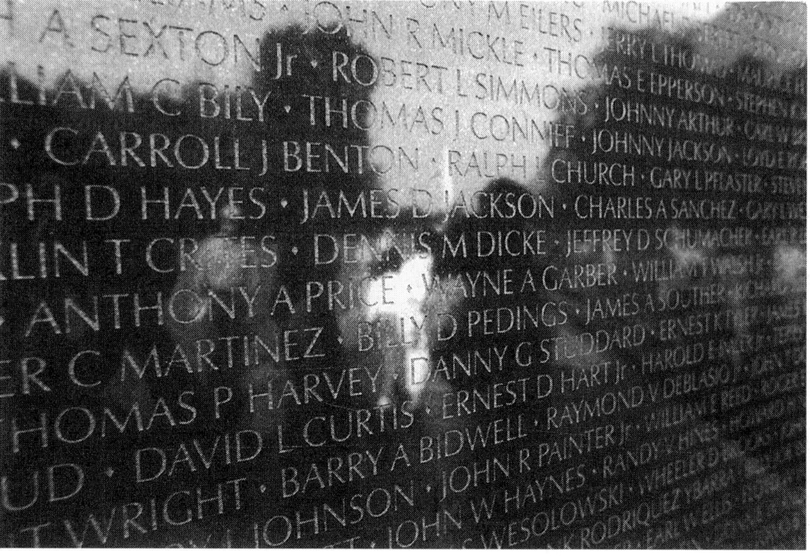

Figures 15.1–2 Vietnam Veterans Memorial, Washington DC (Photos courtesy: Marita Sturken)

These are no longer objects at the Wall, they are communications, icons possessing a subculture of underpinning emotion. They are the products of culture, in all its complexities. They are the products of individual selection. With each object we are in the presence of a work of art of individual contemplation. The thing itself does not overwhelm our attention since these are objects that are common and expendable. At the Wall they have become unique and irreplaceable, and, yes, mysterious.[21]

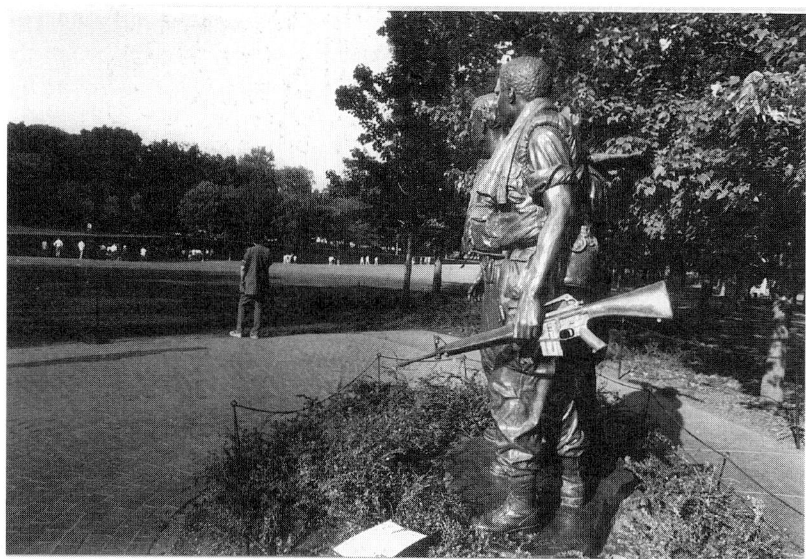

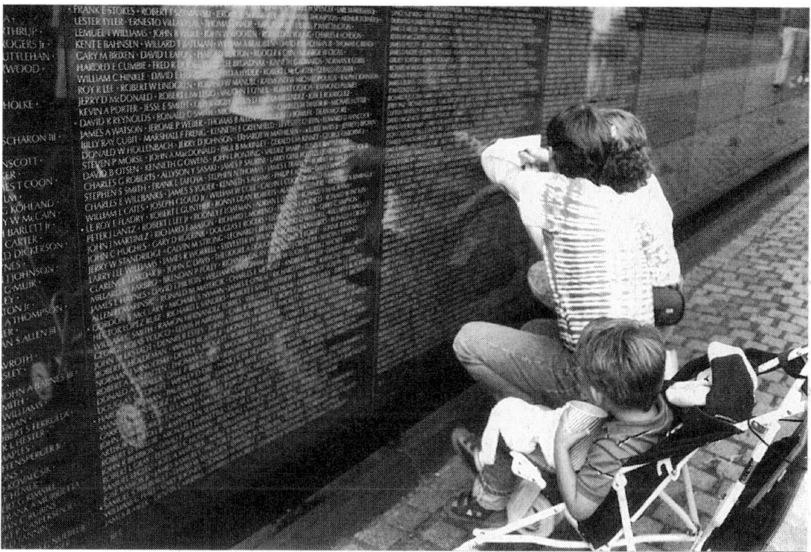

Figures 15.3–4 Vietnam Veterans Memorial, Washington DC (Photos courtesy: Marita Sturken)

Labeled 'mysterious', and thus coded as original works of art, these objects are given value and authorship. Some of the people who left them have since been traced. This attempt to tie these objects and letters to their creators reveals again the shifting realms of personal and cultural memory. Assigned authorship and placed in an historical archive, the objects are pulled from cultural memory, a realm in which they are presented to be shared and to participate in the memories of others.

The memorial has become not only the primary site of remembrance for the Vietnam War, but also a site where people pay homage to many current conflicts and charged public events. Artifacts concerning the abortion debate, the AIDS epidemic, gay rights, and the Persian Gulf War have all been left at the memorial. Hence, the memorial's collection inscribes a history not only of the American participation in the Vietnam War but also of national issues and events since the war. It is testimony to the memorial's malleability as an icon that both prowar and antiwar artifacts were left there during the Persian Gulf War.

One of the most compelling features of the Vietnam Veterans Memorial collection is its anonymity, mystery, and ambiguity. It appears that many of the stories behind a substantial number of artifacts may never be known, and that the telling of these stories to history was never the purpose of their being placed at the memorial. Though couched within an official history and held by a government institution, these letters and offerings to the dead will continue to assert individual narratives, strands of cultural memory that disrupt historical narratives. They resist history precisely through their obscurity, their refusal to yield specific meanings.

The construction of a history

The politics of memory and history of the Vietnam Veterans Memorial shift continuously in a tension of ownership and narrative complexity. Who, in actuality, is being allowed to speak for the experience of the war? Has the Vietnam Veterans Memorial facilitated the emergence of the voices of veterans and the families and friends of veterans in opposition to the voice of the media and the government? The process of healing can be an individual process or a national or cultural process; the politics of each is quite difference.

Much of the current embrace of the memorial amounts to historical revisionism. The period between the end of the war and the positioning of the memorial as a national wailing wall has been long enough for memories and culpability to fade. Ironically, the memorial allows for an erasure of many of the specifics of history. It is rarely noted that the discussion surrounding the memorial never mentions the Vietnamese people. This is not a memorial to their loss; they cannot even be mentioned in the context of the Mall. Nor does the memorial itself allow for their mention; though it allows for an outpouring of grief, it does not speak to the intricate reasons why the lives represented by the inscribed names were lost in vain.

Thus, remembering is in itself a form of forgetting. Does the remembrance of the battles fought by the veterans in Vietnam and at home necessarily screen out any acknowledgment of the war's effect on the Vietnamese? In its listing of the US war dead, and in the context of the Mall, the memorial establishes Americans, rather than Vietnamese, as the primary victims of the war. For instance, questions about the 1,300 American MIAs are raised at the memorial, yet in that space no mention can be made of the 300,000 Vietnamese MIAs. Does the process of commemoration necessitate choosing sides?

Artist Chris Burden created a sculpture in 1991, *The Other Vietnam Memorial*, in reaction to the memorial's nonacknowledgment of the Vietnamese. Burden's piece consists of large copper leaves, 12 by 8 feet, arranged as a kind of circular standing book, on which are engraved 3 million Vietnamese names to commemorate the 3 million Vietnamese who died in the war. He says: 'Even though I feel sorry for the individuals named on [the Vietnam Veterans Memorial], I was repulsed by the idea. I couldn't help but think that we were celebrating our dead, who were aggressors, basically, and wonder where were the Vietnamese names?'[22] Burden's listing of names is not unproblematic; he was unable to get the actual listing of names, so he took 4,000 names and repeated them over and over again. However, Burden's sculpture exposes a fundamental limit of commemoration within nationalism. Why must a national memorial re-enact conflict by showing only one side of the conflict? What is the memory produced by a national memorial?

The memorial's placement on the Washington Mall inscribes it within nationalism, restricting in many ways the kinds of memory it can provide. Its presence indicates both the limitations and the complexity of that nationalist discourse. Lauren Berlant writes:

> When Americans make the pilgrimage to Washington they are trying to grasp the nation in its totality. Yet the totality of the nation in its capital city is a jumble of historical modalities, a transitional space between local and national cultures, private and public property, archaic and living artifacts . . . it is a place of national *mediation*, where a variety of nationally inflected media come into visible and sometimes incommensurate contact.[23]

The memorial asserts itself into this 'jumble of historical modalities', both a resistant and compliant artifact. It serves not as a singular statement but a site of mediation, a site of conflicting voices and opposing agendas.

However, the act of commemoration is ultimately a process of legitimation and the memorial lies at the center of a struggle between narratives. It has spawned two very different kinds of remembrance: one a retrenched historical narrative that attempts to rewrite the Vietnam War in a way that reinscribes US imperialism and the masculinity of the American soldier; the other a textured and complex discourse of remembrance that has allowed the Americans affected by this war – the veterans, their families, and the families and friends of the war dead- to speak of loss, pain, and futility. The screens of the memorial allow for projections of a multitude of memories and individual interpretations. The memorial stands in a precarious space between these opposing interpretations of the war.

Notes

1 Arthur Danto, 'The Vietnam Veterans Memorial,' *The Nation*, August 31, 1985, p. 152.

2 Charles Griswold, 'The Vietnam Veterans Memorial and the Washington Mall,' *Critical Inquiry*, Summer 1986, p. 689.

3 Tom Wolfe, 'Art Disputes War,' *Washington Post*, October 13, 1982, p. B4.

4 Kenneth Baker, 'Andre in Retrospect,' *Art in America*, April 1980, pp. 88–94.

5 See Robert Storr, '"Tilted Arc": Enemy of the People,' in Arlene Raven (ed.), *Art in the Public Interest* (Ann Arbor: University of Michigan Press, 1989).
6 'Stop That Monument,' *National Review*, September 18, 1981, p. 1064.
7 Quoted in Mary McLeod, 'The Battle for the Monument,' in Helene Lipstadt (ed.), *The Experimental Tradition* (New York: Princeton Architectural Press, 1989), p. 125.
8 Michael Sorkin, 'What Happens When a Woman Designs a War Monument?', *Vogue*, May 1983, p. 122.
9 Quoted in 'America Remembers: Vietnam Veterans Memorial,' *National Geographic*, May 1985, p. 557.
10 'An Interview With Maya Lin,' in Reese Williams(ed.), *Unwinding the Vietnam War* (Seattle: Real Comet Press, 1987), p. 271.
11 Jan Scruggs and Joel Swerdlow, *To Heal a Nation* (New York: Harper & Row, 1985), p. 79.
12 Mary McLeod, op. cit., p. 127.
13 'An Interview With Frederick Hart,' in Reese Williams (ed.), *Unwinding the Vietnam War* (Seattle: Real Comet Press, 1987), p. 274.
14 Quoted in Rick Horowitz, 'Maya Lin's Angry Objections,' *Washington Post*, July 7, 1982, p. B1.
15 Quoted in Scruggs and Swerdlow, op. cit., p. 133.
16 Peter Marin, 'Conclusion,' in Harrison Salisbury (ed.), *Vietnam Reconsidered* (New York: Harper & Row, 1984), p. 213.
17 Quoted in Benjamin Forgery, 'Battle Won for War Memorials,' *Washington Post*, September 20, 1991.
18 Benjamin Forgery, 'One Monument Too Many,' *Washington Post*, November 6, 1993, p. D7.
19 Quoted in Laura Palmer, 'How to Bandage a War,' *New York Times Magazine*, November 7, 1993, p. 40.
20 Michael Clark, 'Remembering Vietnam,' *Cultural Critique* 3, Spring 1986, p. 49.
21 David Guynes, quoted in Lydia Fish, *The Last Firebase* (Shippensburg, Pa.: White Mane, 1987), p. 54.
22 Quoted in Robert Storr, 'Chris Burden,' *MoMA Members Quarterly*, Fall 1991, p. 5.
23 Lauren Berlant, 'The Theory of Infantile Citizenship,' *Public Culture* 5, 1993, p. 395.

PART THREE

Virtuality: virtual bodies, virtual spaces

Introduction to part three

■ Nicholas Mirzoeff

VIRTUALITY IS A BUZZWORD for the 1990s, a seemingly new way of experiencing the outside on the inside. It has become epitomized by the virtual reality helmet, worn by a user in order to interface with a three-dimensional, computer-generated environment. Some critics have wanted to call this a radical break with the past, heralding a transformation of everyday life unequalled since the Industrial Revolution. Others have insisted that there is relatively little new here, recalling a panoply of once-forgotten visual devices from the panorama to the stereoscope and zootrope that immersed the viewer in a seemingly real environment. For all the bluster, a middle way seems fairly clear. Virtuality has certainly been experienced before, perhaps as long as people have been sufficiently distracted by an artist's skill to take a picture briefly for reality. On the other hand, computer-generated environments offer the chance to interact with and change this illusory reality, an opportunity that no previous medium has been able to provide. At root, the question is the relationship between the human body and space, mediated by the sense of sight. What is the body in an age of virtuality? How can space be discussed as a changing medium rather than simply being considered as a void? These questions are addressed in the following sections.

(a) The virtual body

A decade ago, there was little published work available when I wanted to teach a thematic course on the body. Now there seems to be material on every aspect of the subject, so much so that it is hard to cover all aspects of the field. Thinking about and through the body has recast approaches to race and gender, as well as creating new fields like disability studies. In this section, I have chosen to focus on one of these new areas of research that has in turn generated many new ideas, namely feminist approaches to scientific and technical body imaging. Here feminist scholarship has sought to reclaim a number of areas that were not previously seen as central to feminism, especially the visual itself.

Donna Haraway, a pioneer of feminist research into scientific discourse, has sought to use vision and the visual to redefine the academic totem of objectivity. In a key section of her now-classic book *Simians, Cyborgs and Women* (1991), she replaced the 'conquering gaze from nowhere' with an insistence on the 'embodied nature of all vision', challenging the orthodoxies of observational science just as Descartes challenged the complacencies of scholasticism. Haraway argues that while vision is never found in the pure state suggested by the geometric lines used in Cartesian perspective, nor is everything simply relative. Instead, she aims at a redefinition of vision that would allow for the production of what she calls 'situated knowledges'. Replacing the disembodied view from above with the individual view from somewhere, she emphasizes that 'optics is a politics of positioning . . . Struggles over what will count as rational accounts of the world are struggles over *how* to see.' Like Descartes, Haraway recognizes that understanding vision is a key example of what will be accepted as rational method. Unlike him, she overtly acknowledges that vision is always about power and positioning, meaning that any method must be partial in both senses of the term.

Following Haraway's lead – and that of other feminist scholars like Sandra Harding and Chéla Sandoval – there has arisen an exciting re-examination of vision and its apparatuses, especially in relation to the body. In her important book *Screening the Body* (1995), Lisa Cartwright has set out an alternative history of film from these perspectives:

> The cinematic apparatus can be considered as a cultural technology for the discipline and management of the human body . . . [T]he long history of bodily analysis and surveillance in medicine and science is critically tied to the history of the development of cinema as a popular cultural institution and a technological apparatus.

In this extract, she shows how the photographs of the moving body produced by Etienne-Jules Marey and Eadweard Muybridge in the late nineteenth century, always a traditional starting point for film history, created a vital interaction between 'popular and professional representations of the body, as the site of human life and subjectivity'. Following the work of Michel Foucault, whose work will crop up time and again throughout this Reader, Cartwright shows that film and photography were used to demonstrate a shift in knowledge towards thinking about life in the abstract as opposed to individual living beings. The body on film revealed things that the eyes themselves could not see, using close-ups and frame enlargements to enhance natural vision. This virtual body acted in unexpected ways, providing both a source of cinematic pleasure for early twentieth-century audiences and an important source of medical knowledge.

The virtual body image presented in film, television and advertising has created an impossible standard against which real people have judged their own bodies. The essays by Susan Bordo and Anne Balsamo explore how women in particular have taken often drastic steps to try and close the gap between image and reality. In this excerpt from her essay 'Reading the Slender Body' (later to form part of her book *Unbearable Weight*) Susan Bordo looks at the role of the represented body in creating the new cult of slenderness (Bordo 1990, 1993). It is only within the last century that Westerners have come to value thinness, abstaining from food and now doing exercise in order to attain this goal. Quoting Foucault, Bordo shows that the representation of slenderness comes to form a 'set of *practical* rules and regulations (some explicit, some implicit) through which the living body is "trained, shaped, obeys and responds" '. She points out that slenderness has come to mean not just being thin but also having a taut, muscular body with no visible excess. Since the early twentieth century, 'excess body weight came to be seen as reflecting moral or personal inadequacy, or lack of will'. The shape of the body is thus seen as being indicative of 'the state of the soul'. These injunctions to discipline our own bodies have such effect because they encapsulate wider social goals – the slender muscular body is seen as socially mobile and successful – while also constraining gender roles to literally fixed boundaries.

New medical technology has transformed the ability to visualize the body to such an extent that, in Anne Balsamo's striking phrase, 'these new visualization techniques transform the material body into a visual medium'. In the extract from her essay 'On the Cutting Edge' (1992), Balsamo shows that the feminist analyses of the medical classification of the female body into a series of potentially pathological fragments now have to be supplemented with an interpretation of cosmetic and reconstructive surgery. For rather than trying to delve deeper into the body, these procedures provide a short-cut around the moral aspect of physical self-discipline. By concentrating solely on the surface, plastic surgery can make individual bodies conform to an aesthetic norm: 'In this way cosmetic surgery *literally* transforms the material body into a sign of culture.' While women have long had to contend with abstract standards of femininity and beauty, cosmetic surgeons now seek to apply these standards directly on to people's faces based, in the words of a standard text on the subject, on a 'scale of harmony and balance . . . The harmony and symmetry are compared to a mental, almost magical, ideal subject, which is our base concept of beauty.' Unsurprisingly, the 'ideal face' turns out to be white, Northern European.

Although many more men are now having these procedures, they are primarily aimed at women who are held to be responsible for the various 'defects' of their bodies. So strong is the pressure to 'get fixed' that some women have procedures over and again, becoming 'scalpel slaves' in their later thirties or forties. Often, these are women with a teenage history of anorexia, showing that the compulsion to correct the body highlighted by Bordo has now become technologized. Balsamo concludes that 'the body becomes . . . the site at which women, consciously or not, accept the meanings that circulate in popular culture about ideal beauty and, in comparison, devalue the material body.' However, looking at the widespread fashion for body-piercing, cyberpunk fantasies about technological prosthesis – and, one might add, the cosmetic surgery performance art of Orlan – she suggests that we may need to move beyond a 'neoromantic wistfulness about the natural, unmarked body' that is, after all, the guiding ideal of cosmetic surgery. Technology as a form of power is double-edged: it disciplines and empowers simultaneously. The question remains as to whether the new corporal technologies from laser eye-correction to imaging techniques and keyhole surgery can become part of a knowledge that helps individuals situate themselves physically or whether they become absorbed into the corporate medical establishment, creating an ever-more elusive and expensive version of the abstract 'normal' body.

(b) Virtual spaces

Space, it has been famously remarked, is the final frontier. If even the borders between the inside and the outside of the body are no longer as secure as they once were, the very space in which the rise of virtuality is taking place now comes into question. Space can no longer be seen as simply an empty backdrop but as a dynamic entity with a history and characteristics that vary from period to period and place to place. In his lecture 'Of Other Spaces' reprinted here (delivered in 1967 but not published until 1984), Michel Foucault called attention to the centrality of space in twentieth-century culture. Space is the key theme for 'the epoch of juxtaposition, the epoch of the near and the far, of the side-by-side, of the dispersed'. He outlined a rough history in which a medieval hierarchical notion of space was substituted by a modern theory of extended space that has in turn now been displaced by what he called the site.

Foucault's interest was especially caught by sites 'that have the curious property of being in relation with all the other sites, but in such a way as to suspect, neutralize, or invert the set of relations that they happen to designate, mirror, or reflect'. Influenced by Gaston Bachelard's ground-breaking work *The Poetics of Space*, Foucault was intrigued by certain sites that are at once central to a culture and set aside, like the cemetery, the prison, or the hospital. He called these places 'heterotopias', the opposite to utopias, which are unreal. In between the utopia and the heterotopia lies the mirror, which is both physically real and unreal:

> In the mirror, I see myself there where I am not, in an unreal virtual space that opens up behind the surface . . . But it is also a heterotopia in so far as the mirror does exist in reality, where it exerts a kind of counteraction on the position I occupy.

This self-recognition in the mirror played a key role in the work of psychoanalyst Jacques Lacan, who identified what he called the mirror stage as a key moment in the formation of the subject. Foucault steers away from such discussions of identity to think of the mirror as a mediation between different forms of space, real and virtual. As he later acknowledged, this spatial thinking set the agenda for his most famous work. *Discipline and Punish* (1977), which examines how the heterotopia of the disciplinary institution became the model for modern industrialized society.

The other essays in this section look at different historical moments of creating space and their implications, in the tradition established by Foucault's work. In his widely cited book *Techniques of the Observer* (1990), art historian Jonathan Crary identified a key model of modern extended space, the camera obscura. The camera obscura is literally a darkened room into which light is admitted through a small hole, often with a lens mounted in it. The result is that a picture of the outside world is formed upside-down on the far wall of the camera obscura, which became 'the compulsory site from which vision can be conceived or represented' from the mid-seventeenth to early nineteenth century. As such the camera obscura creates a division between the observer and the outside world: 'it is a figure for both the observer who is nominally a free sovereign individual and a privatized subject confined in a quasi-domestic space, cut off from a public exterior world.' The observer within does not see his or her own vision but a disembodied picture of the world, emphasizing the Enlightenment belief in a sharp distinction between the mind, which judges sensory perceptions, and the body, which merely registers them, just as the camera obscura admits light through its lens. In this view, the mind brings the results of perception into what philosopher Richard Rorty has called an 'inner area', sharply distinguished from the reality extending away from the eyes, which cannot be trusted to make accurate judgements by themselves.

Film critic Anne Friedberg has contrasted the immobility of the spectator in the camera obscura with the mobility of the gaze itself in nineteenth-century visual culture. In this extract from her remarkable book *Window Shopping: Cinema and the Postmodern* (1993), Friedberg examines what has been called the 'frenzy of the visible' that broke out in the period from the invention of photography to that of cinema (1839–95). She notes that in Foucault's analysis of the panopticon – a prison system where one guard could see all the prisoners without being seen – visibility became a system of discipline that contrasted to that of the camera obscura: 'The *seeing machine* was once a sort of dark room into which individuals spied; it has become a transparent building in which the exercise of power may be supervised by society as a whole.' Friedberg introduces two crucial complicating factors to this seemingly smooth transition. First, she notes that the 'controlled light' of the panopticon was also used to create the illusions of the panorama and diorama. These theatrical presentations used a combination of lighting and scenery to provide 'a spatial and temporal mobility – if only a virtual one'. The panorama provided views of domestic and foreign cities that had previously been available only to the wealthy tourists on the Grand Tour. It was no coincidence that Louis Daguerre, the proprietor of the diorama, was also the inventor of the first practical photographic method, known as the daguerreotype. Both devices offered an escape from the everyday constraints of space and time in distinction to the panopticon, which controlled both elements. Friedberg also argues that one cannot simply talk of 'the' observer as 'he or she', as Crary does. Following work such as that of Griselda Pollock (see Part One), she shows that critics like Charles Baudelaire sought to preserve a gaze that was mobile but not virtual, and masculine but not feminine. In short, the social ordering of space was and is contested within a particular period as well as changing from one period to the next.

It is noticeable that neither of these writers considers the possibility of a non-Western observer in Europe or of the European observer overseas. The latter figure was central to the modern understanding of space (the non-Western observer is discussed in the following section). However sceptical and divided European discourse on observation was at home, it was supremely self-confident overseas. As Europeans expanded their empires in Latin America, Africa and Asia in the nineteenth century, they came to rely above all on their individual observations of unknown landscapes. Literary critic Mary-Louise Pratt has usefully called this attitude 'the monarch-of-all-I-survey'. In the section from her book *Imperial Eyes* (1992) reprinted here, she discusses how British explorers seeking the source of the Nile in the 1860s provided extensive 'verbal paintings' of Central Africa for their readers at home. She shows that the explorers were always careful to mediate their reports by reference to familiar European sights. Here, for example, is the explorer Richard Burton describing Lake Tanganyika:

> Villages, cultivated lands, the frequent canoes of the fishermen on the waters . . . give something of a variety, of movement, of life to the landscape, which . . . wants but a little of the neatness and finish of art . . . to rival, if not to excel, the most admired scenery of the classic regions.

Burton's remarks show that the lake was far from the uncultivated wilderness of colonial propaganda but he none the less insists that its lack of aesthetics renders it inferior to the European landscape. As Pratt argues: 'Discovery in this context consisted of a gesture of converting local knowledges (discourses) into European national and continental knowledges associated with European forms and relations of power.' Just as the observer in the camera obscura corrects the simple observations of the sense of sight, so does the European rectify the raw African landscape by aestheticizing it. It was important to both reader and writer that this process be authenticated by the European author actually having seen what he described, for no African report could be trusted on its own. Pratt shows that even in the Victorian period, the immense pomposity required to maintain such attitudes was open to satire and ultimately to direct criticism. Colonialism constituted the greatest venture, and ultimately the greatest failure, of the modern European spatializing of the world.

With the creation of digital imagery, the relationship between observer and observed has changed. There is no longer any necessary or logical connection between a virtual image and exterior reality. However, Geoffrey Batchen argues in his essay '*Spectres of Cyberspace*' that 'to look ahead it might also be necessary to look back' (Batchen 1996). Did virtual reality begin with the development of palaeolithic tools or with that of the computer? Batchen highlights the role of the nineteenth-century stereoscope, a device that allowed the viewer to experience three-dimensional images by looking through a mask at a card with two images of the same scene printed side by side. The similarity between the stereoscopic viewer and the virtual reality helmet is enhanced by nineteenth-century accounts of this viewing experience which, in Batchen's words, 'appear to closely parallel the VR experience that so many commentators want to call "revolutionary"'. Following the theories of Foucault and Lacan, Batchen sees photography, stereoscopy and cyberspace alike as products of the modern crisis of subjectivity in which the 'never resolved assemblage of virtual and real is what makes up the very fabric of human subjectivity'. Rather than mourn that the computer Deep Blue has triumphed over the human chess champion Gary Kasparov, we should rather see it as the latest manifestation of an old encounter between humans, machines and animals that appears to be taking an intriguing new turn. New technology is aiding that discussion rather than causing it. None the less, the computer and its new virtual environments seem to be the most creative metaphor for the self to have been generated in over a century, whose consequences can as yet only be guessed at.

References and further reading

Bachelard, Gaston (1964) *The Poetics of Space*, New York: Orion.

Balsamo, Anne (1992) 'On the Cutting Edge: Cosmetic Surgery and the Technological Production of the Gendered Body', *Camera Obscura* 22, January.

—— (1996) *Technologies of the Gendered Body: Reading Cyborg Women*, Durham: Duke University Press.

Batchen, Geoffrey (1996) 'Spectres of Cyberspace', *Afterimage* 23(3), pp. 6–7.

Bordo, Susan (1990) 'Reading the Slender Body', in Mary Jacobus *et al.* (eds), *Body/Politics: Women and the Discourses of Science*, London and New York: Routledge.

—— (1993) *Unbearable Weight: Feminism, Western Culture and the Body*, Berkeley: University of California Press.

Braun, Marta (1992) *Picturing Time: the Work of Etienne-Jules Marey*, Chicago: University of Chicago Press.

Bukatman, Scott (1993) *Terminal Identity: The Virtual Subject in Postmodern Science Fiction*, Durham: Duke University Press.

Cartwright, Lisa (1995) *Screening the Body: Tracing Medicine's Visual Culture*, Minneapolis: University of Minnesota Press.

Charney, Leo, and Schwartz, Vanessa (1995) *Cinema and the Invention of Modern Life*, Berkeley: University of California Press.

Crary, Jonathan (1990) *Techniques of the Observer: On Vision and Modernity in the Nineteenth Century*, Cambridge, Mass.: MIT Press.

Foucault, Michael (1977) *Discipline and Punish: The Birth of the Prison*, New York: Vintage.

—— (1984) 'Of Other Spaces', *Diacritics* 16.

Friedberg, Anne (1993) *Window Shopping: Cinema and the Postmodern*, Berkeley: University of California Press.

Haraway, Donna (1991) *Simians, Cyborgs and Women: The Reinvention of Nature*, London and New York: Routledge.

Mirzoeff, Nicholas (1995) *Bodyscape: Art, Modernity and the Ideal Figure*, London and New York: Routledge.

Mitchell, William J. (1995) *City of Bits: Space, Place and the Infobahn*, Cambridge, Mass.: MIT Press.

Moser, Mary-Ann (ed.) (1996) *Immersed in Technology: Art and Virtual Environments*, Cambridge, Mass.: MIT Press.

Pratt, Mary-Louise (1992) *Imperial Eyes: Travel Writing and Transculturation*, London and New York: Routledge.

(a) The virtual body

Chapter 16

Donna Haraway

THE PERSISTENCE OF VISION

[I] WOULD LIKE to proceed by placing metaphorical reliance on a much maligned sensory system in feminist discourse: vision. Vision can be good for avoiding binary oppositions. I would like to insist on the embodied nature of all vision, and so reclaim the sensory system that has been used to signify a leap out of the marked body and into a conquering gaze from nowhere. This is the gaze that mythically inscribes all the marked bodies, that makes the unmarked category claim the power to see and not be seen, to represent while escaping representation. This gaze signifies the unmarked positions of Man and White, one of the many nasty tones of the word *objectivity* to feminist ears in scientific and technological, late industrial, militarized, racist, and male dominant societies, that is, there, in the belly of the monster, in the United States in the late 1980s. I would like a doctrine of embodied objectivity that accommodates paradoxical and critical feminist science projects: feminist objectivity means quite simply *situated knowledges*.

The eyes have been used to signify a perverse capacity – honed to perfection in the history of science tied to militarism, capitalism, colonialism, and male supremacy – to distance the knowing subject from everybody and everything in the interests of unfettered power. The instruments of visualization in multinationalist, postmodernist culture have compounded these meanings of dis-embodiment. The visualizing technologies are without apparent limit; the eye of any ordinary primate like us can be endlessly enhanced by sonography systems, magnetic resonance imaging, artificial intelligence-linked graphic manipulation systems, scanning electron microscopes, computer-aided tomography scanners, colour-enhancement techniques, satellite surveillance systems, home and office VDTs, cameras for every purpose from filming the mucous membrane lining the gut cavity of a marine worm living in the vent gases on a fault between continental plates to mapping a planetary hemisphere elsewhere in the solar system. Vision in the technological feast becomes unregulated gluttony; all perspective gives way to infinitely mobile vision, which no longer seems just mythically about the god-trick of seeing everything from nowhere, but to have put the myth into ordinary practice. And like the god-trick, this eye fucks the world to make techno-monsters. Zoe Sofoulis (1988) calls this the cannibal-eye of masculinist, extra-terrestrial projects for excremental second birthing.

A tribute to this ideology of direct, devouring, generative, and unrestricted vision, whose technological mediations are simultaneously celebrated and presented as utterly transparent, the volume celebrating the 100th anniversary of the National Geographic Society closes its survey of the magazine's quest literature, effected through its amazing photography, with two juxtaposed chapters. The first is on 'Space', introduced by the epigraph, 'The choice is the universe – or nothing' (Bryan 1987: 352). Indeed. This chapter recounts the exploits of the space race and displays the colour-enhanced 'snapshots' of the outer planets reassembled from digitalized signals transmitted across vast space to let the viewer 'experience' the moment of discovery in immediate vision of the 'object'. These fabulous objects come to us simultaneously as indubitable recordings of what is simply there and as heroic feats of techno-scientific production. The next chapter is the twin of outer space: 'Inner Space', introduced by the epigraph, 'The stuff of stars has come alive' (Bryan 1987: 454). Here, the reader is brought into the realm of the infinitesimal, objectified by means of radiation outside the wave lengths that 'normally' are perceived by hominid primates, i.e. the beams of lasers and scanning electron microscopes, whose signals are processed into the wonderful full-colour snapshots of defending T cells and invading viruses.

But of course that view of infinite vision is an illusion, a god-trick. I would like to suggest how our insisting metaphorically on the particularity and embodiment of all vision (though not necessarily organic embodiment and including technological mediation), and not giving in to the tempting myths of vision as a route to disembodiment and second-birthing, allows us to construct a usable, but not an innocent, doctrine of objectivity. I want a feminist writing of the body that metaphorically emphasizes vision again, because we need to reclaim that sense to find our way through all the visualizing tricks and powers of modern sciences and technologies that have transformed the objectivity debates. We need to learn in our bodies, endowed with primate colour and stereoscopic vision, how to attach the objective to our theoretical and political scanners in order to name where we are and are not, in dimensions of mental and physical space we hardly know how to name. So, not so perversely, objectivity turns out to be about particular and specific embodiment, and definitely not about the false vision promising transcendence of all limits and responsibility. The moral is simple: only partial perspective promises objective vision. This is an objective vision that initiates, rather than closes off, the problem of responsibility for the generativity of all visual practices. Partial perspective can be held accountable for both its promising and its destructive monsters. All Western cultural narratives about objectivity are allegories of the ideologies of the relations of what we call mind and body, of distance and responsibility, embedded in the science question in feminism. Feminist objectivity is about limited location and situated knowledge, not about transcendence and splitting of subject and object. In this way we might become answerable for what we learn how to see.

These are lessons which I learned in part walking with my dogs and wondering how the world looks without a fovea and very few retinal cells for colour vision, but with a huge neural processing and sensory area for smells. It is a lesson available from photographs of how the world looks to the compound eyes of an insect, or even from the camera eye of a spy satellite or the digitally transmitted signals of space probe-perceived differences 'near' Jupiter that have been transformed into coffee-table colour photographs. The 'eyes' made available in modern technological sciences shatter any idea of passive vision; these prosthetic devices show us that all eyes, including our own organic ones, are active perceptual systems, building in translations and specific *ways* of seeing, that is, ways of life. There is no unmediated photograph or passive camera obscura in scientific accounts of bodies and machines; there are only highly specific visual possibilities, each with a wonderfully detailed, active, partial way of organizing worlds. All these pictures of the world should not be allegories of infinite mobility and interchangeability, but of elaborate specificity and difference and the loving care people might take to learn how to see faithfully from another's point of view, even when the other is our own machine. That's not alienating distance; that's a *possible* allegory for feminist versions of objectivity. Understanding how these visual systems work, technically, socially, and psychically ought to be a way of embodying feminist objectivity.

Many currents in feminism attempt to theorize on the grounds for trusting especially the vantage points of the subjugated; there is good reason to believe vision is better from below the brilliant space platforms of the powerful (Hartsock 1983; Sandoval n.d.; Harding 1986; Anzaldúa 1987). Linked to this suspicion, this chapter is an argument for situated and embodied knowledges and against various forms of unlocatable, and so irresponsible, knowledge claims. Irresponsible means unable to be called into account. There is a premium on establishing the capacity to see from the peripheries and the depths. But here lies a serious danger of romanticizing and/or appropriating the vision of the less powerful while claiming to see from their positions. To see from below is neither easily learned nor unproblematic, even if 'we' 'naturally' inhabit the great underground terrain of subjugated knowledges. The positionings of the subjugated are not exempt from critical re-examination, decoding, deconstruction, and interpretation; that is, from both semiological and hermeneutic modes of critical enquiry. The standpoints of the subjugated are not 'innocent' positions. On the contrary, they are preferred because in principle they are least likely to allow denial of the critical and interpretative core of all knowledge. They are savvy to modes of denial through repression, forgetting, and disappearing acts – ways of being nowhere while claiming to see comprehensively. The subjugated have a decent chance to be on to the god-trick and all its dazzling – and, therefore, blinding – illuminations. 'Subjugated' standpoints are preferred because they seem to promise more adequate, sustained, objective, transforming accounts of the world. But *how* to see from below is a problem requiring at least as much skill with bodies and language, with the mediations of vision, as the 'highest' techno-scientific visualizations.

Such preferred positioning is as hostile to various forms of relativism as to the most explicitly totalizing versions of claims to scientific authority. But the alternative to relativism is not totalization and single vision, which is always finally the unmarked category whose power depends on systematic narrowing and obscuring.

The alternative to relativism is partial, locatable, critical knowledges sustaining the possibility of webs of connections called solidarity in politics and shared conversations in epistemology. Relativism is a way of being nowhere while claiming to be everywhere equally. The 'equality' of positioning is a denial of responsibility and critical enquiry. Relativism is the perfect mirror twin of totalization in the ideologies of objectivity; both deny the stakes in location, embodiment, and partial perspective; both make it impossible to see well. Relativism and totalization are both 'god-tricks' promising vision from everywhere and nowhere equally and fully, common myths in rhetorics surrounding science. But it is precisely in the politics and epistemology of partial perspectives that the possibility of sustained, rational, objective enquiry rests.

So, with many other feminists, I want to argue for a doctrine and practice of objectivity, that privileges contestation, deconstruction, passionate construction, webbed connections, and hope for transformation of systems of knowledge and ways of seeing. But not just any partial perspective will do; we must be hostile to easy relativisms and holisms built out of summing and subsuming parts. 'Passionate detachment' (Kuhn 1982) requires more than acknowledged and self-critical partiality. We are also bound to seek perspective from those points of view that can never be known in advance, which promise something quite extraordinary, that is, knowledge potent for constructing worlds less organized by axes of domination. In such a viewpoint, the unmarked category would *really* disappear – quite a difference from simply repeating a disappearing act. The imaginary and the rational – the visionary and objective vision – hover close together. I think Harding's plea for a successor science and for postmodern sensibilities must be read to argue that this close touch of the fantastic element of hope for transformative knowledge and the severe check and stimulus of sustained critical enquiry are jointly the ground of any believable claim to objectivity or rationality not riddled with breathtaking denials and repressions. It is even possible to read the record of scientific revolutions in terms of this feminist doctrine of rationality and objectivity. Science has been utopian and visionary from the start; that is one reason 'we' need it.

A commitment to mobile positioning and to passionate detachment is dependent on the impossibility of innocent 'identity' politics and epistemologies as strategies for seeing from the standpoints of the subjugated in order to see well. One cannot 'be' either a cell or molecule – or a woman, colonized person, labourer, and so on – if one intends to see and see from these positions critically. 'Being' is much more problematic and contingent. Also, one cannot relocate in any possible vantage point without being accountable for that movement. Vision is *always* a question of the power to see – and perhaps of the violence implicit in our visualizing practices. With whose blood were my eyes crafted? These points also apply to testimony from the position of 'oneself'. We are not immediately present to ourselves. Self-knowledge requires a semiotic-material technology linking meanings and bodies. Self-identity is a bad visual system. Fusion is a bad strategy of positioning. The boys in the human sciences have called this doubt about self-presence the 'death of the subject', that single ordering point of will and consciousness. That judgement seems bizarre to me. I prefer to call this generative doubt the opening of non-isomorphic subjects, agents, and territories of stories unimaginable from the vantage point of the cyclopian, self-satiated eye of the master subject. The Western eye has fundamentally been a wandering eye, a travelling lens. These peregrinations have often been violent and insistent on mirrors for a conquering self – but not always. Western feminists also *inherit* some skill in learning to participate in revisualizing worlds turned upside down in earth-transforming challenges to the views of the masters. All is not to be done from scratch.

The split and contradictory self is the one who can interrogate positionings and be accountable; the one who can construct and join rational conversations and fantastic imaginings that change history. Splitting, not being, is the privileged image for feminist epistemologies of scientific knowledge. 'Splitting' in this context should be about heterogeneous multiplicities that are simultaneously necessary and incapable of being squashed into isomorphic slots or cumulative lists. This geometry pertains within and among subjects. The topography of subjectivity is multidimensional; so, therefore, is vision. The knowing self is partial in all its guises, never finished, whole, simply there and original; it is always constructed and stitched together imperfectly, and *therefore* able to join with another, to see together without claiming to be another. Here is the promise of objectivity: a scientific knower seeks the subject position not of identity, but of objectivity; that is, partial connection. There is no way to 'be' simultaneously in all, or wholly in any, of the privileged (subjugated) positions structured by gender, race, nation, and class. And that is a short list of critical positions. The search for such a 'full' and total position is the search for the fetishized perfect subject of oppositional history, sometimes appearing in feminist theory as the essentialized Third World Woman (Mohanty 1984). Subjugation is not grounds for an ontology; it might be a visual clue. Vision requires instruments of vision; an optics is a politics of positioning. Instruments of vision mediate standpoints; there is no immediate vision from the standpoints of the subjugated. Identity, including self-identity, does not produce science; critical positioning does, that is, objectivity. Only those occupying the positions of the dominators are self-identical, unmarked, disembodied, unmediated, transcendent, born again. It is unfortunately possible for the subjugated to lust for and even scramble into that subject position – and then disappear from view. Knowledge from the point of view of the unmarked is truly fantastic, distorted, and so irrational. The only position from which objectivity could not possibly be practiced and honoured is the standpoint of the master, the Man, the One God, whose eye produces, appropriates, and orders all difference. No one ever accused the God of monotheism of objectivity, only of indifference. The god-trick is self-identical, and we have mistaken that for creativity and knowledge, omniscience even.

Positioning is, therefore, the key practice grounding knowledge organized around the imagery of vision, as so much Western scientific and philosophic discourse is organized. Positioning implies responsibility for our enabling practices. It follows that politics and ethics ground struggles for the contests over what may count as rational knowledge. That is, admitted or not, politics and ethics ground struggles over knowledge projects in the exact, natural, social, and human sciences. Otherwise, rationality is simply impossible, an optical illusion projected from nowhere comprehensively. Histories of science may be powerfully told as histories of the technologies. These technologies are ways of life, social orders, practices of visualization. Technologies are skilled practices. How to see? Where to see from? What limits to vision? What to see for? Whom to see with? Who gets to have more than one point of view? Who gets blinkered? Who wears blinkers? Who interprets the visual field? What other sensory powers do we wish to cultivate besides vision? Moral and political discourse should be the paradigm of rational discourse in the imagery and technologies of vision. Sandra Harding's claim, or observation, that movements of social revolution have most contributed to improvements in science might be read as a claim about the knowledge consequences of new technologies of positioning. But I wish Harding had spent more time remembering that social and scientific revolutions have not always been liberatory, even if they have always been visionary. Perhaps this point could be captured in other phrase: the science question in the military. Struggles over what will count as rational accounts of the world are struggles over *how* to see. The terms of vision: the science question in colonialism; the science question in exterminism (Sofoulis 1988); the science question in feminism.

The issue in politically engaged attacks on various empiricisms, reductionisms, or other versions of scientific authority should not be relativism, but location. A dichotomous chart expressing this point might look like this:

universal rationality	ethnophilosophies
common language	heteroglossia
new organon	deconstruction
unified field theory	oppositional positioning
world system	local knowledges
master theory	webbed accounts

But a dichotomous chart misrepresents in a critical way the positions of embodied objectivity which I am trying to sketch. The primary distortion is the illusion of symmetry in the chart's dichotomy, making any position appear, first, simply alternative and, second, mutually exclusive. A map of tensions and resonances between the fixed ends of a charged dichotomy better represents the potent politics and epistemologies of embodied, therefore accountable, objectivity. For example, local knowledges have also to be in tension with the productive structurings that force unequal translations and exchanges – material and semiotic – within the webs of knowledge and power. Webs *can* have the property of systematicity, even of centrally structured global systems with deep filaments and tenacious tendrils into time, space, and consciousness, the dimensions of world history. Feminist accountability requires a knowledge tuned to resonance, not to dichotomy. Gender is a field of structured and structuring difference, where the tones of extreme localization, of the intimately personal and individualized body, vibrate in the same field with global high-tension emissions. Feminist embodiment, then, is not about fixed location in a reified body, female or otherwise, but about nodes in fields, inflections in orientations, and responsibility for difference in material-semiotic fields of meaning. Embodiment is significant prosthesis; objectivity cannot be about fixed vision when what counts as an object is precisely what world history turns out to be about.

How should one be positioned in order to see in this situation of tensions, resonances, transformations, resistances, and complicities? Here, primate vision is not immediately a very powerful metaphor or technology for feminist political-epistemological clarification, since it seems to present to consciousness already processed and objectified fields; things seem already fixed and distanced. But the visual metaphor allows one to go beyond fixed appearances, which are only the end products. The metaphor invites us to investigate the varied apparatuses of visual production, including the prosthetic technologies interfaced with our biological eyes and brains. And here we find highly particular machineries for processing regions of the electromagnetic spectrum into our pictures of the world. It is in the intricacies of these visualization technologies in which we are embedded that we will find metaphors and means for understanding and intervening in the patterns of objectification in the world, that is, the patterns of reality for which we must be accountable. In these metaphors, we find means for appreciating simultaneously *both* the concrete, 'real' aspect and the aspect of semiosis and production in what we call scientific knowledge.

I am arguing for politics and epistemologies of location, positioning, and situating, where partiality and not universality is the condition of being heard to make rational knowledge claims. These are claims on people's lives; the view from a body, always a complex, contradictory, structuring and structured body, versus the view from above, from nowhere, from simplicity. Only the god-trick is forbidden. Here is a criterion for deciding the science question in militarism, that dream science/technology of perfect language, perfect communication, final order.

Feminism loves another science: the sciences and politics of interpretation, translation, stuttering, and the partly understood. Feminism is about the sciences of the multiple subject with (at least) double vision. Feminism is about a critical vision consequent upon a critical positioning in inhomogeneous gendered social space. Translation is always interpretative, critical, and partial. Here is a ground for conversation, rationality, and objectivity – which is power-sensitive, not pluralist, 'conversation'. It is not even the mythic cartoons of physics and mathematics – incorrectly caricatured in anti-science ideology as exact, hyper-simple knowledges – that have come to represent the hostile other to feminist paradigmatic models of scientific knowledge, but the dreams of the perfectly known in high-technology, permanently militarized scientific productions and positionings, the god-trick of a Star Wars paradigm of rational knowledge. So location is about vulnerability; location resists the politics of closure, finality, or, to borrow from Althusser, feminist objectivity resists 'simplification in the last instance'. That is because feminist embodiment resists fixation and is insatiably curious about the webs of differential positioning. There is no single feminist standpoint because our maps require too many dimensions for that metaphor to ground our visions. But the feminist standpoint theorists' goal of an epistemology and politics of engaged, accountable positioning remains eminently potent. The goal is better accounts of the world, that is, 'science'.

Above all, rational knowledge does not pretend to disengagement: to be from everywhere and so nowhere, to be free from interpretation, from being represented, to be fully self-contained or fully formalizable. Rational knowledge is a process of ongoing critical interpreation among 'fields' of interpreters and decoders. Rational knowledge is power-sensitive conversation (King 1987):

knowledge:community::knowledge:power
hermeneutics:semiology::critical interpretation:codes.

Decoding and transcoding plus translation and criticism: all are necessary. So science becomes the paradigmatic model not of closure, but of that which is contestable and contested. Science becomes the myth not of what escapes human agency and responsibility in a realm above the fray, but rather of accountability and responsibility for translations and solidarities linking the cacophonous visions and visionary voices that characterize the knowledges of the subjugated. A splitting of senses, a confusion of voice and sight, rather than clear and distinct ideas, become the metaphor for the ground of the rational. We seek not the knowledges ruled by phallogocentrism (nostalgia for the presence of the one true Word) and disembodied vision, but those ruled by partial sight and limited voice. We do not seek partiality for its own sake, but for the sake of the connections and unexpected openings that situated knowledges make possible. The only way to find a larger vision is to be somewhere in particular. The science question in feminism is about objectivity as positioned rationality. Its images are not the products of escape and transcendence of limits, i.e. the view from above, but the joining of partial views and halting voices into a collective subject position that promises a vision of the means of ongoing finite embodiment, of living within limits and contradictions, i.e. of views from somewhere.

References

Anzaldúa, Gloria (1987) *Borderlands/La Frontera*, San Francisco: Spinsters/Aunt Lute.

Bryan, C.D.B. (1987) *The National Geographic Society: 100 Years of Adventure and Discovery*, New York: Abrams.

Harding, Sandra (1986) *The Science Question in Feminism*, Ithaca: Cornell University Press.

Harding, Sandra and Merill, Hintikka (eds) (1983) *Discovering Reality: Feminist Perspectives on Epistemology, Metaphysics, and Philosophy of Science*, Dordrecht: Reidel.

Hartsock, Nancy (1983) 'The feminist standpoint: developing the ground for a specifically feminist historical materialism', in Harding and Hintikka (eds) (1983), pp. 283–310.

King, Katie (1987) 'Canons without innocence', University of California at Santa Cruz, PhD thesis.

Kuhn, Annette (1982) *Women's Pictures: Feminism and Cinema*, London: Routlege & Kegan Paul.

Mohanty, Chandra Talpade (1984) 'Under western eyes: feminist scholarship and colonial discourse', *Boundary* 2, 3 (12/13): 333–58.

Sandoval, Chela (n.d.) *Yours in Struggle: Women Respond to Racism, a Report on the National Women's Studies Association*, Oakland, CA: Center for Third World Organizing.

Sofoulis, Zoe (1988) 'Through the lumen: Frankenstein and the optics of re-origination', University of California at Santa Cruz, PhD thesis.

Chapter 17

Lisa Cartwright

SCIENCE AND THE CINEMA

IN THE BIOGRAPHICAL FILES of the New York Academy of Medicine, sharing a page with news entries documenting French claims to international railway speed and air flight records, appears a 1954 obituary for August Lumière, patriarch of the cinema. The appearance of Lumière's obituary among these items is not surprising. The Cinématographe, an instrument for the recording and projection of living motion invented by Lumière and his brother Louis in 1895, certainly would seem to deserve a place alongside these technologies of movement. However, the obituarist barely notes Lumière's reputation as a founder of the cinema. Instead, he extols his near-lifelong commitment to medical biology, pharmacology, and experimental physiology.

After 1900 Lumière's work, and much of the production of the Lumière plant in Lyons, turned toward medical research and production. The obituarist singles out as Lumière's most significant accomplishment not his work on the cinema but his laboratory research on tuberculosis and cancer, diseases that continue to elude scientific control even now, at the end of the twentieth century. By the end of his life, Lumière believed scientific medical research to be one of the most important areas of work in Western culture. In a text on the achievements of science published six years before his death, he attributes Western progress to advances in pharmaceutical and medical technology:

> It would be impossible to deny that the discoveries of Science always have affected Humanity's material progress . . . Formal proof of this is found in the fact that these discoveries have permitted the existence of man to be prolonged to the point that the average lifespan has tripled since the beginning of our century.[1]

Although he here cites the prolonged lifespan as proof of 'Humanity's material progress,' Lumière relegates the Cinématographe, an instrument of mass culture that can record but does not appear to alter the body physically, to a few anecdotal pages near the close of the book. Oddly, Lumière does not explain that many of his European and North American contemporaries regarded his popular invention as a key contribution to physiology – the very field of research through which he contributed to the advancement of French public health and the prolongation of the average lifespan. Certainly he was not unaware of the use of his invention in physiological research. In addition to the manufacture of products for a mass-audience cinema, the Lumière laboratory designed and produced specialized cameras and film stock for the laboratories of scientists and physicians – researchers for whom the Cinématographe was no less an instrument of physiological research than the microscope or the kymograph (a rotating drum-shaped apparatus used to inscribe movement in a wavelike linear trace).

Lumière's historical elision of his own popular invention from the history of science and medicine is symptomatic of a broader disregard for the cultural implications of the technological interdependency of science and forms of popular culture. It is a commonplace of film scholarship that the popularization of the serial motion photography of physiological movement produced by Etienne-Jules Marey in France and Eadweard Muybridge in the United States was key to the technological development of the cinema, and a few early film histories describe the scientific film as an important genre of the early cinema. However, what remains largely unconsidered is the extent to which the particular visual modes that were operative in laboratory techniques like kymography and chronophotography, or in the science film, are integral to other genres of the cinema and of popular visual culture.

Scholarly descriptions of many Lumière films as realist do underscore their indebtedness to the genre of the science film. Lumière films such as *La sortie des usines Lumière à Lyon* (1895) or *Arrivée d'un train en gare de Villefrance-sur-Saône* (1895) are cited often as precursors of documentary cinema. Alan Williams suggests that actuality films like these were implicated in the popular science genre of the 1890s media and press. His point is that the Lumière public 'was presumed to be interested in the question of the "realism" of the images, though certainly *not for the sake of the subjects represented* but for the demonstration they afforded of "scientific" interest and technical virtuosity.'[2] Williams implies that these films qualified as realist because they allowed living movement to be observed, and not because they depicted 'real' events. 'What was documented,' he explains, 'was the work of the apparatus itself.'[3]

In *Screening the Body* I examine closely the place of film in the scientific project of observing the movement of living bodies, in order to propose an alternative to the designation of the science film as a documentary and realist mode of representation. I suggest that the scientific analyses of living bodies conducted in laboratories of medicine and science were in fact based in a tradition that broke with the photographic and theatrical conventions that would inform both the documentary and the narrative cinema – a tradition that is linked to laboratory instruments of graphic inscription and measurement such as the myograph, the kymograph, and the electrocardiograph. Scientific interest in physiological movement and its technological instrumentation is indebted precisely to the modes and techniques of motion recording and observation developed by experimental physiologists in France and

Germany throughout the nineteenth century, those physiologists whose work falls within Auguste Lumière's 'other' field, medical science.

One of my primary claims here is that the cinematic apparatus can be considered as a cultural technology for the discipline and management of the human body, and that the long history of bodily analysis and surveillance in medicine and science is critically tied to the history of the development of the cinema as a popular cultural institution and a technological apparatus. Accounts of the prehistory of the cinema almost always begin with a description of the legacy of a science in the cinema *vis-à-vis* the physiological motion studies of Muybridge and Marey. It is by now a commonplace of film history that many of the techniques and instruments that contributed to the emergence of the cinema were designed and used by scientists, and that they were developed as a means of investigation into optics and physiology. As F.A. Talbot, the author of a 1912 history of the motion picture explains,

> In its very earliest stages the value of animated photography was conceded to be in the field of science rather than that of amusement. [Marey] realized the inestimable value of 'chronophotography' for the study and investigation of moving bodies, the rapidity in the changes of the position or form of which was impossible to follow otherwise.[4]

The historical narrative quickly shifts, however, from science to popular culture. Marey, the story goes, by failing to see the value of the Cinématographe, failed to bring the film motion study into the twentieth century. His rejection of the Cinématographe, an instrument so heavily laden with the promise of visual technology's future, coincides with the moment of the birth of the cinema in the public sphere, its availability to mass audiences in public screening halls. The prehistory of the cinema is conventionally told as a tale of early scientific experimentation marked by a break with science around 1895 with the emergence of a popular film culture and industry.

What this narrative leaves out is that the scientific film culture that contributed to the emergence of the popular cinema thrived beyond 1895, extending well into the twentieth century. This book traces the course of scientific cinema into the twentieth century, a history elided from most film history texts. But my aim here is not simply to set the film historical record straight. The history of the cinematic motion study is a crucial part of the history of the human body. Through such techniques as cinematic motion study the body was measured, regulated, and reconceptualized in medicine and science. My aim then is to trace the history of this reconfiguration of the body through scientific techniques of motion recording and analysis – techniques that were used to put forth a model of the body as a dynamic, distinctly living and moving system. A history of the film motion study is thus also a part of the history of twentieth-century scientific knowledge and power. *Screening the Body* seeks to uncover a history of the cinematic techniques that science has used to control, discipline, and construct the human body as a technological network of dynamic systems and forces. But it also seeks to demonstrate that this history is complexly interwoven with other areas of visual culture.

I argue throughout this book [viz. *Screening the Body*] that the importance of the film motion study is primarily neither its contribution to a singular dominant industry or optical paradigm nor its contribution to medical knowledge. Its greatest importance is its function as an intertext between popular and professional representations of the body as the site of human life and subjectivity. As a mode of knowledge, the film motion study is interesting less for what it showed researchers about the mechanics of human life than for what it tells us now about the cultural desires, pleasures, and fantasies surrounding the modernist dynamic model of 'life' generated in physiology and medical science and advanced through technologies like the cinema. The film body of the motion study thus is a symptomatic site, a region invested with fantasies about what constituted 'life' for scientists and the lay public in the early twentieth century, and anxieties about whether the 'life' scientists studied in the laboratory was something that could be seen, imaged, and ultimately controlled (whether by prolonging it, as Lumière wished to do, or by having the authority to determine the moment of death).

Throughout *Screening the Body* I consider instances in science in which film is implicated in the task of tracing the movements and changes of the body's systems and processes. I argue that, on one level, this cinematic tracking of the human body was a form of medical surveillance and social control. In this sense, the films I consider can be seen as a counterpart to the institutional practice of using photography to classify, to diagnose, and to maintain control over subjects deemed criminal, mentally ill, or otherwise aberrant. But I also show that these films contributed to the generation of a broad cultural definition of the body as a characteristically dynamic entity – one uniquely suited to motion recording technologies like the cinema, but also one peculiarly unsuited to static photographic observation because of its changeability and interiority. Many of the films described . . . were the culmination of years of effort on the part of scientists to glimpse a view of the body's interior systems in action. But, as I will try to show, this compulsion to reveal the interior technologies of the living body on motion-picture film involved a break with older conventions of photography and, perhaps paradoxically, instituted a crisis in scientific observation generally. The cinema I trace . . . then, is a cinema that is linked in important ways not only to the traditions of photography and the theater but also to a nonpictorial system of representation functioning in science throughout the nineteenth century, a tradition that emerged with physiology, the science devoted to the study of living systems in motion.

In the section that follows, I attempt to theorize this nonpictorial tradition of cinematic representation through accounts of the cinematic apparatus in order to ground my discussion of this distinctly nonpictorial, analytic, and surveillant cinema. My intention is to show that theories of the apparatus and spectatorship have not adequately accounted for the long-term impact of the scientific culture and economy so prevalent in the cinema's early history. Moreover, the techniques of scientific observation and analysis considered throughout *Screening the Body* constitute a mode of visuality that subtends some popular cinema genres in subtle but important ways. The pleasures of 'distanced' analytic viewing, I argue, are not peculiar to the genre of the motion study but have pervaded the popular cinema and other institutions. Surveillant looking and physiological analysis, then, are not just techniques of science. They are broadly practiced techniques of everyday public culture.

A scientific cinematic apparatus

Theories of the cinematic apparatus, centering on the writings of Christian Metz and Jean-Louis Baudry in the late 1960s and Jean-Louis Comolli in the early 1970s, opened up a space for the consideration of the cinema as a cultural technology. In summarizing this vein of film theory in 1978, Stephen Heath emphasizes the grounding of the concept of the apparatus in the historical framework of ideology. He thus distinguishes the approach to the subject informed by Marxism, psychoanalysis, and semiotics from the technological determinism that characterized the majority of previous historiographical accounts of cinematic technology. Heath takes as his example a program announcement for the historic Lumière screening at the Grand Café in 1895, a document that highlights cinematic technology at the expense of a description of the actual films whose showing it announces. Heath uses the term 'machine interest' to characterize the overriding public attention to the cinema's instrumentation apparent in this announcement:

> In the first moments of the history of the cinema, it is the technology which provides the immediate interest: what is promoted and sold is the experience of the machine, the apparatus.[5]

Heath suggests, like Williams, that this moment in cinema's history is marked by a fascination with the technology of movement rather than with the image itself. But with the rise of film narrative, interest in the complexities of content would soon surpass this simple fascination with the technology of movement. Heath suggests that Baudry, Metz, and Comolli, like the early film spectator, were also captivated with the technological apparatus when they theorized the cinema in their pivotal essays on the cinematic apparatus:

> As though returning to something of those first moments, theoretical work today has increasingly been directed towards posing the terms of the 'cinema-machine,' the 'basic apparatus,' the 'institution' of cinema, where 'cinema' is taken more widely than the habitual notion of the cinema industry to include the 'interior machine' of the psychology of the spectator.[6]

Among these theorists, Comolli goes farthest toward acknowledging the place of the economic and ideological within the cinema's technological history. However, he establishes a relation between technology and the social in a hierarchical chronology that effectively separates the technical from its post-1895 social context. Comolli argues that technical components of the cinema (camera, projector, a 'strip of images') were 'already there, more or less invented, a long time before the formal invention of the cinema.' With this prehistoric set of instruments in place, 'the cinema is born immediately as a social machine' in 1895 with verification of its profitability as public spectacle.[7] Comolli further asserts, 'One could just as well propose that it is the spectators who invent cinema.'[8] Comolli privileges the role of public exhibition in his account of the cinematic apparatus.

But how do we account for the epistemological and ideological baggage brought to the public cinema of 1895 through the 'prehistoric' set of instruments 'already there' at its origins? Or, to put this question another way, what techniques of power and knowledge were carried into the post-1895 popular cinema from the laboratories of our cinematic patriarchs (the Lumières, Edison, and Marey, for example)?

In his critique of myths of cinema origins, Comolli relies on the historian Jacques Deslandes to support his main argument that the cinema is finally determined not by disinterested science but by a commercial profit motive.[9] Questioning technological-determinist accounts that trace the cinema's history through a series of inventions and technologies that culminate in the public exhibitions of 1895, Comolli ultimately reasserts this date as a moment of last-instance economic determination. Interpreting the dictum that 'a machine is always social before it is technical' as a chronological scheme, Comolli views cinema technology after 1895 through the logic of this social moment. Its instruments and techniques 'already there, more or less ready,' the prehistory of the cinema is historically situated according to a singular future mark: The 'hundreds of little machines . . . destined for a more or less clumsy reproduction of the image and the movement of life' wait for the factor of exhibition, on which hinges the status of the cinema machine as a social technology.[10]

Comolli makes a crucial historical oversight in dismissing the 'hundreds of little machines' of the nineteenth century as props predestined for an end-of-century mass 'frenzy of the visible.' As Comolli himself has emphasized, cinema's prehistory is rife with inconsistencies, 'blanks and gaps.'[11] Yet there is an order and economy to this 'prehistoric' field. Many of these machines, the numerous cameras, projectors, and compound instruments that emerged over the course of the nineteenth century, in fact were no mere little machines, the silly contraptions of amateur inventors; they were fairly sophisticated instruments used in laboratories of physics, chemistry, and physiology. Understanding the social context of the laboratory – its technology, its economy, its own cultural modes of spectatorship – is no simple matter of evoking an unspecified artisanal science or a generalized technology. The cinema's emergence cannot be properly conceived without acknowledging the fascination with visibility that marked the preceding decades of nineteenth-century Western science.

Heath's emphatically uttered list '*camera, movement, projection, screen,*'[12] hints at the complex sliding between the psychological and the technological in theories of the cinematic apparatus. The terms signify mechanical aspects of the cinema while also evoking one of Freud's models for psychical processes. Baudry quotes Freud's comparison of the psyche to the instruments of photography or microscopy as indication of 'an optical construct which signals term for term the cinematographic apparatus.' The passage from Freud is as follows:

> What is presented to us in these words is the idea of a psychical locality. I shall entirely disregard the fact that the mental apparatus with which we are concerned is also known to us in the form of an anatomical preparation, and I shall carefully avoid the temptation to determine psychical locality in an anatomical fashion. I shall remain upon

> psychological ground, and I propose simply to follow the suggestion that we should picture the instrument which carries out our mental functions as resembling a compound microscope or a photographic apparatus, or something of the kind. On that basis, psychical locality will correspond to a point inside the apparatus at which one of the preliminary stages of an image comes into being. In the microscope and telescope, as we know, these occur in parts at ideal points, regions in which no tangible component to the apparatus is situated.[13]

Baudry justifies Freud's later exclusion of the camera from this model, and his turn to the telescope or microscope, by claiming that 'the cinema is already too technologically determined an apparatus for describing the psychical apparatus as a whole.' He then insists that the cinema and the Neoplatonic ocular subject it constructs should have remained an important reference point for Freud's historical subject. However, putting aside the fact that the compound microscope and the telescope were also highly overdetermined instruments at the time of Freud's writing, it remains that the camera, the microscope, and the telescope offer not one but three distinct optical models for a psychical apparatus. With their respective bases in representational structures very different from the pictorial and perspectival tradition on which the camera is based, the microscope and the telescope create some problems in Baudry's theory.

Baudry's rereading of the scene of Plato's cave privileges the cinema projector and not the camera. The use of firelight evokes the artificial light source within the projector. Shadow-images suggest the perspectival film image on the screen. The trancelike state of the cave occupants is linked to the passive state of the film viewer, not the mobile and controlling gaze of the cinematographer. In Baudry's account, the womblike cave becomes the site of an intermediary lens, a 'point inside the apparatus at which one of the preliminary stages of an image comes into being.' The subject is thus incorporated within the apparatus as a passive spectator.

As Joan Copjec has argued, theories of the cinematic apparatus present the cinema as an instrument of totalizing social control – a theoretical fantasy that is at bottom a 'delirium of clinical perfection.'[14] But what happens to Baudry's model if the camera is replaced with a different optical instrument – the compound microscope, for example, an instrument that the Lumières used in conjunction with the camera? The compound microscope contains not one but two lenses, an interior lens for magnification and a second for resolution. The microscope offers neither empirical nor interior view for comparison. The minute object viewed through it is not available to sight by eye; likewise, the magnified image on the interior lens is unresolved and therefore not empirically visible. The spectator incorporated within this apparatus would be implicated uncomfortably in the resolution of a rather startling and unfamiliar scene, a scene that must be made sense of, or resolved, without a profilmic, or promicroscopic, referent. The microscopic spectator would be compelled to perform a very different operation inside the apparatus, one that would involve a kind of interpretive analysis that would position the spectator in a much less secure relation to visual knowledge than Baudry's model of the filmic spectator suggests.

These speculations on the possibilities of a microscopic spectator in Plato's cave are put forth simply to demonstrate that the scientific cinema, its technical spectator, and its filmed bodies make up an aspect of the cinematic apparatus that breaks in crucial ways with paradigms of cinematic technology and spectatorship generated in film scholarship around narrative and pictorial film texts and genres. I would argue that medical and scientific film motion studies provide evidence of a mode of cinematic representation and spectatorship that is grounded in a Western scientific tradition of surveillance, measurement, and physical transformation through observation and analysis. The films I study in *Screening the Body* provide one of the few routes to rehistoricizing the cinema as an apparatus that historically has taken place in the emergence of Lumière's fantasmatic construction of 'human life' as a dynamic entity to be tracked, studied, and transformed in the social 'theater' of the laboratory.

The 'frenzy of the visible' in the cinema's prehistory

In a study on the relationship between science and the arts, the historian Jacob Opper suggests that changes in theories of nature from the eighteenth to the nineteenth century are best characterized by the shift from the logico-mathematical cosmology of the Enlightenment to the Darwinian biologico-evolutionary model. The example of the German physicist Ernst Mach's 'phenomenological physics' is cited to convey the move toward empirical, body-based models even within the physical sciences. Opper summarizes:

> The conspicuous feature of the change in theory of nature from the eighteenth to the nineteenth centuries is thus seen to involve a shift from mathematical physics to natural-history biology, from the noumenon to the phenomenon, from the '"logocentrism" of traditional epistemology' to '"biocentrically oriented" romantic thought.'[15]

Opper suggests that this biocentric orientation characterizes Western cultural production through the nineteenth century, the metaphor of the living, evolving organism replacing the metaphor of the mechanical, nonevolving, clock.

Foucault also remarks on the nonexistence of biology proper to the nineteenth century. However, he makes a critical distinction between natural history and biology, a distinction that has important implications for his descriptions of a scientific and medical gaze and, subsequently, for the cinema as a technology of medical and scientific representation by the late nineteenth century:

> Historians want to write histories of biology in the eighteenth century; but they do not realize that biology did not exist then, and that this pattern of knowledge that has been familiar to us for a hundred and fifty years is not valid for a previous period. And that, if biology was unknown, there was a very simple reason for it: that life itself did not exist. All that existed was living beings, which were viewed through a grid of knowledge constituted by natural history.[16]

In quoting Foucault I want to emphasize that the shift from natural history to biology entailed a shift in modes of visuality, and that with the emergence of a mode of representation specific to biology, we find the emergence of 'life' as a cultural concept. Foucault states that the shift from eighteenth-century natural history to nineteenth-century biology is marked by a change in relationship between representations and things. The emergence of 'life' thus is accompanied by the emergence of a new mode of representation. By the time of Lamarck, the 'grid of knowledge,' the table of representations through which living beings had been viewed, would no longer provide a foundation for Western thought:

> The space of order, which served as a *common place* for representations and for things, for empirical visibility and for the essential rules . . . which displayed the empirical sequence of representations in a simultaneous table, and made it possible to scan step by step, in accordance with a logical sequence, the totality of nature's elements thus rendered contemporaneous with one another – this space of order is from now on shattered: there will be things, with their own organic structures, their hidden veins, the space that articulates them, the time that produces them; and then representations, a purely temporal succession, in which those things address themselves (always partially) to a subjectivity, a consciousness, a singular effort of cognition, to the 'psychological' individual who from the depth of his own history . . . is trying to know. Representation is in the process of losing its power to define the mode of being common to things and to knowledge.[17]

Foucault suggests that biological representation no longer defines living beings descriptively but functions according to a structure that language cannot fully describe. This structure is 'the dark, concave, inner side' of the visibility of things/living beings.'[18] Whereas the grid of natural history brought living beings to full knowledge, biological representation seems to get at what cannot be seen in a process that makes all the more evident the disjuncture between representation and 'object' (or body). This formulation is far from the ideal of a romantic naturalism suggested in Opper's combined term 'natural-history biology,' by which nature, in direct correspondence with its science, serves as model for cultural form. It is even farther from both the space of the spectatorial cave and the pictorial space of Renaissance painting that Baudry suggests as models for cinematographic space. With the emergence of biological modes of representation, we find a historical break between observation (or image) and object of knowledge – a break in which the visualization of 'life' becomes all the more seductive to the scientific eye even as the limitations of representation are made plain.

The medical gaze Foucault describes is dependent on a history of empirical techniques of diagnosis or investigation – palpation and auscultation are precedents to the empirical investigation by sight of the body's interior surfaces in the process of autopsy. Palpation and observation are marked by a temporal immediacy: on one level, diagnosis takes the form of direct contact between the physician's eye, ear, or hand with the patient's body; on another level, disease is understood to leave a visible imprint on surface tissue, in a superimposing or mapping process.

In Foucault's account, even when the symptom is empirically seen, it is regarded as an indicator of a pathological condition at a different anatomical site. Paradoxically, as imaging becomes a more central means of diagnosis and study throughout the nineteenth century, sensory perception (including sight) is progressively destabilized as a source of anatomical knowledge.

It is important that the gaze Foucault identifies is tied to clinical, and not laboratory, medicine. The medical historian Robert G. Frank Jr points out that post-revolution France saw the development not only of clinical medicine but of pathology and physiology in laboratory medical research. Experimental physiology gained institutional prominence in early-nineteenth-century Germany through the laboratory research of figures such as Hermann von Helmholtz, Karl Ludwig, and Rudolph Virchow and their students. In France, physiology advanced as a specialized area of medical research in part distinct from the clinical sphere through the work of figures such as Marie-François-Xavier Bichat, Charles Edouard Brown-Séquard, and Claude Bernard. Bichat performed as a clinician; Bernard did not. This distinction is important in establishing methodological differences between practices confined to experimentation and those with more direct ties to the public sphere. Thus, the 'chemical gaze' Foucault describes, while not precisely that of the laboratory scientist alone, is not wholly congruent with the clinician's gaze.

A second and more crucial distinction must be noted. Although pathological anatomy, the area of Foucault's concern, centered its representations more closely on a static concept of morphology and structure, physiology – the discipline for which the film motion study was a crucial technique – regarded the body in terms of its living functions and processes, and its practitioners devised methods and techniques to facilitate a temporal, dynamic vision of the body in motion. While this progression from stasis to movement, from anatomy to physiology, seems to suggest a narrative of technological advance, it must be kept in mind that physiology did not replace anatomy but emerged as a related specialization in its own right. The continual exchange between these fields, like the interchange between photography and the cinema, informed the filmic elaboration of life as an entity that was both temporally and spatially constituted in modernist science.

In separate studies, the medical historians Merriley Borell and Stanley Reiser have shown that the institution of physiology as a medical discipline coincided with the development of mechanical techniques and instruments for the graphic registration of bodily processes. Well in advance of the development of cinematography, and independently from photography, physiologists developed visual instruments to gauge the course of normal and pathological processes qualitatively. During the decades before 1895, a highly sophisticated method of graphic visual representation took shape through German and French physiology. The use of photography for physiognomical measurement is well documented in the writings of Sander Gilman, Alan Sekula, and John Tagg. Tagg, in his account of the use of photography in nineteenth-century public institutions, summarizes concisely the argument that photography functioned as a representational strategy of corporeal control:

> We are dealing with the instrumental deployment of photography in privileged administrative practices and the professionalised discourses of the new social sciences – anthropology, criminology, medical

> anatomy, psychiatry, public health, urban planning, sanitation, and so on, all of them domains of expertise in which arguments and evidence were addressed to qualified peers and circulated only in certain limited institutional discourses. . . . In terms of such discourses, the working classes, colonized peoples, the criminal, poor, ill-housed, sick or insane were constituted as the passive – or, in this structure, 'feminised' – objects of knowledge. Subjected to a scrutinizing gaze, forced to emit signs, yet cut off from command of meaning, such groups were represented as, and wishfully rendered, incapable of speaking, acting, or organizing for themselves. The rhetoric of photographic documentation at this period . . . is therefore one of precision, measurement, calculation, and proof.[19]

Tagg's description can also be applied to the cinematic practices that are described throughout *Screening the Body*. But it is important to note that these films, as well as the photographic practices Tagg describes, supplemented a range of more commonly used scopes, recording devices, and measurement instruments in nineteenth-century institutions. Instruments like the sphygmoscope (a device for rendering the pulse visible), the myograph (an apparatus for recording muscular contractions), and the cardiograph (an instrument for tracing the heartbeat) were as crucial as photographic analysis to the scientific disciplining of bodies and communities. The technique of cinematography, however, was paradoxically grounded in a tradition of inscription that eschewed the visual and pictorial conventions of portraiture and representationalism that seem to have been so central to the legal, medical, and institutional photography that Tagg describes.

What is the historical basis for the scientific cinema's nonpictorial mode of representation? Frank suggests that Marey's techniques of motion recording and analysis, which came to be known as 'the graphic method,' had the stature of 'a new language,' the bearing of which is expressed in Borell's assertion that

> as the graphic method evolved, a new conception of the body emerged. Analysis of separate physiological events, the reductionist approach, revealed the interrelatedness of these events and the body's complex control mechanisms. By the second quarter of the twentieth century, in fact, these homeostatic mechanisms had become a major focus for biological research. Moreover, pharmacological studies had also matured: experimental analysis of the effect of drugs on physiological processes illuminated the nature of those processes, as well as suggested more precise biological tests for individual drugs.[20]

This 'language' of physiology incorporated Marey's technique of chronophotography and was the basis of Auguste Lumière's laboratory work in pharmacology and medical biology after 1901. From the perspective of film studies, the identification of physiology's methodology as a 'graphic language' has a certain resonance. It evokes the broad application of semiotics in the study of the cinema. However, the studies of Borell and others have tended to focus on the work process of physiologists and their methods and instruments rather than on texts (the images, graphs, charts, and analyses produced through the method) and their reception and use. Throughout *Screening the Body* I trace a history of the medical and scientific motion study that draws from both of these disciplines (film studies and the history of medicine and science). In order to underscore the place of the popular in this conjuncture, I conclude this chapter by returning to my claim that the film motion study is more than simply a technique of nineteenth-century science and medicine or a subgenre of the documentary tradition. As I demonstrate in this chapter's concluding discussion of the early cinema genre of the facial-expression film, the fascination with physiological and technological spectacles of 'life' was a transversal phenomenon, cutting across popular, public, and professional visual cultures.

Tom Gunning has made a case for a genre of the early cinema, which he calls a 'cinema of attractions,' that provides some useful ways of thinking about how the graphic method intersected with a physiological tradition of popular cinema. Gunning discusses the facial-expression film, a category that includes the Edison/Dickson 1894 *Kinetoscopic Record of a Sneeze*, as an example of this cinema of attraction. He suggests this mode is evident in pre-1906 films characterized in part by use of the close-up, the actor's look at the camera, and absence of narrative – a style centered on the performer's act of displaying bodily movement. 'A more primal fascination with the act of display' is the suggested cultural motivation for the reception of this type of film.[21]

Perhaps nowhere is the popular cinema's debt to experimental physiology and its surveillant gaze more clear than in the *Kinetoscopic Record of a Sneeze*. The film documents the moment of the physiological act of the sneeze, an event that induces the momentary cessation of the heartbeat. The sneeze perfectly suits physiology's interest in documenting the changes that occur in a physiological process. Further, it represents an instance of involuntary movement, an activity beyond the control of the observer. As Linda Williams notes (citing Gordon Hendricks), the film was made at the request of a reporter for *Harper's Weekly*, a request that specified, in Williams' words, 'a pretty young woman who would have lent prurient interest to the involuntary comic act of a sneeze.'[22] The film, which ultimately featured not a 'pretty woman' but Edison's laboratory assistant Fred Ott, was featured in *Harper's* in a series of frame enlargements. These images evoke no convention more than the film motion study reproduced for frame analysis in science and medical journals of the period (see Figure 17.1).

Gunning suggests that viewers experienced a physical response to this type of image, a visceral and immediate reaction that carried a certain immediacy and charge not elicited by, for example, films composed of long shots and less invested in the display of bodily events. He contrasts the 'primitive' spectatorial immediacy afforded by this kind of film with the hypothetically more distanced and analytical spectatorial position associated with the later narrative cinema. But here Gunning seems to confuse the immediacy of the act portrayed – the image of uncontrolled motor activity in the film body – with the production of perceptual immediacy 'in' the viewer. He assumes an identificatory link between images of physiological acts (sneezing, exercising, grimacing) and the spectator.

In the case of films such as the American Mutoscope and Biograph Company's *Female Facial Expressions* (1902) and *Photographing a Female Crook* (1904), or Edison's

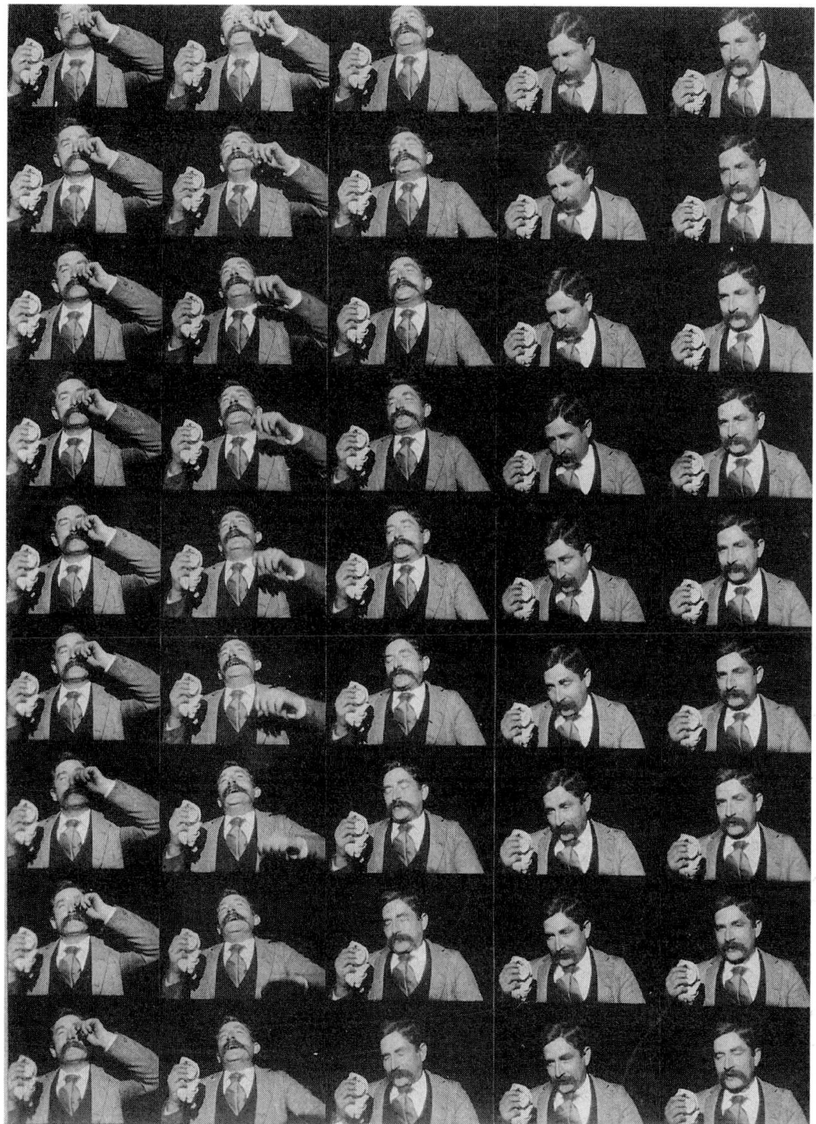

Figure 17.1 *Edison Kinetoscopic Record of a Sneeze*, 1894
(Courtesy of the Library of Congress Photography Archive)

Electrocuting an Elephant (1903), we also find physiological events presented in close-up as spectacles of corporeality. However, it can be argued that such close-ups and foregrounded bodily movement likely would have repelled their audiences. In *Female Facial Expressions* and *Photographing a Female Crook*, for example, we see female bodies resisting conformity to 'normal' physiology. In the former, a woman is shot in close-up as she contorts her face for the camera. In the latter, a woman 'crook' is restrained by male officers before the camera as she grimaces, distorting her features (presumably in order to render her photo ID unrecognizable). Whereas in the former film the grimacing of the woman demonstrates a resistance to standards of female beauty, the 'female crook' demonstrates the resistance of filmed subjects to the visual classification of their bodies as a mode of social control. One might say that this type of film might more accurately be dubbed a cinema of repulsion. Ironically, these popular expression films represent attempts to undercut the association between expression and meaning. The films both amuse and repel precisely because they represent subjects attempting to escape normative bodily conventions (for example, visual beauty and recognizability). In some ways, the spectator whose pleasure in the image hinges on an enjoyment of the spectacle of this refusal of representation, or on the thrill of repulsion (in the case of Edison's *Electrocuting an Elephant*, for example), is not unlike the spectator of the scientific film motion study, the scientist who takes pleasure in observing often aberrant and repulsive physiological processes. The films of Gunning's cinema of attractions ultimately seem to demand a spectator for whom disavowal undercuts the immediacy of the sight of a body that refuses self-regulation. The mode of the physiological motion study thus seems to appear, incongruously enough, in the popular cinema, where it invites the spectator to participate in the 'scientific' fascination with the execution of 'life'.

Notes

1 Auguste Lumière (1948) *La recherche scientifique*, Paris: Société d'Edition d'Enseignement Superieur, p. 5.

2 Alan Williams (1983) 'The Lumière Organization and Documentary Realism', in *Film before Griffith*, John Fell (ed.), Berkeley and Los Angeles: University of California Press, p. 158 (emphasis in original).

3 Ibid.

4 F.A. Talbot [1912] (1970) *Moving Pictures: How They Are Made and Worked*, New York: Arno Press, p. 18.

5 Stephen Heath (1980) 'Technology as Historical and Cultural Form', in *The Cinematic Apparatus*, Teresa de Laurentis and Stephen Heath (eds), New York: St. Martin's Press, p. 1.

6 Ibid., pp. 1–2.

7 See Jean-Louis Comolli, 'Machines of the Visible', in *The Cinematic Apparatus,* de Laurentis and Heath (eds), pp. 121–22.

8 Ibid., p. 122.

9 Ibid., pp. 137–38.

10 Ibid., pp. 121–22; Comolli (1977) 'Technique and Ideology: Camera, Perspective, Depth of Field', *Film Reader* 2: 137–38.

11 Comolli, 'Technique and Ideology', p. 132.

12 Heath, 'Technology as Historical and Cultural Form', p. 2.

13 Sigmund Freud (1965) *The Interpretation of Dreams*, New York: Avon, pp. 574–75; cited in Jean-Louis Baudry (1976) 'The Apparatus: Metapsychological Approaches to the Impression of Reality in the Cinema', *Camera Obscura* 1 Fall: 105.

14 Joan Copjec (1986) 'Cinematic Pleasure and Sexual Difference: The Delirium of Colinical Perfection', *Oxford Literary Review* 8: 57–65.

15 Jacob Opper (1973) *Science and the Arts: A Study of Relationships from 1600–1900*, Rutherford, NJ: Fairleigh Dickinson University Press, p. 35.

16 Michael Foucault (1973) *The Order of Things: An Archaeology of the Human Sciences*, New York: Vintage Books, pp. 129–30.

17 Foucault, *The Order of Things*, pp. 239–40 (my emphasis).

18 Ibid., p. 237.

19 John Tagg (1993) *The Burden of Representation: Essays on Photographies and Histories*, Minneapolis: University of Minnesota Press, p. 11.

20 Merrilly Borell (1986) 'Extending the Senses: The Graphic Method', *Medical Heritage* 2 (2) March/April: 46.

21 Tom Gunning (1989) '"Primitive" Cinema – A Frame Up? or, The Trick's on Us', *Cinema Journal* 28 (2) Winter: 9.

22 Linda Williams (1989) *Hard Core: Poweer, Pleasure, and the 'Frenzy of the Visible'*, Berkeley and Los Angeles: University of California Press, p. 52. Williams cites Hendricks, *Origins of the American Film*, 92–93.

Chapter 18

Susan Bordo

READING THE SLENDER BODY

IN THE LATE-VICTORIAN era, arguably for the first time in the West, those who could afford to eat well began systematically to deny themselves food in pursuit of an aesthetic ideal.[1] Certainly, other cultures had 'dieted.' Aristocratic Greek culture made a science of the regulation of food intake, in the service of the attainment of self-mastery and moderation.[2] Fasting, aimed at spiritual purification and domination of the flesh, was an important part of the repertoire of Christian practice in the Middle Ages.[3] These forms of 'diet' can clearly be viewed as instruments for the development of a 'self' – whether an 'inner' self, for the Christians, or a public self, for the Greeks – constructed as an arena in which the deepest possibilities for human excellence might be realized. Rituals of fasting and asceticism were therefore reserved for the select few, aristocratic or priestly in caste, deemed capable of achieving such excellence of spirit. In the late nineteenth century, by contrast, the practices of body management begin to be middle-class preoccupations, and concern with diet becomes attached to the pursuit of an idealized physical weight or shape; it becomes a project in service of 'body' rather than 'soul.' Fat, not appetite or desire, is the declared enemy, and people begin to measure their dietary achievements by the numbers on the scale rather than the level of their mastery of impulse and excess. The bourgeois 'tyranny of slenderness' (as Kim Chernin has called it[4]) had begun its ascendancy (particularly over women), and with it the development of numerous technologies – diet, exercise, and, later on, chemicals and surgery – aimed at a purely physical transformation.

Today, we have become acutely aware of the massive and multifaceted nature of such technologies and the industries built around them. To the degree that a popular critical consciousness exists, however, it has been focused largely (and not surprisingly) on what has been viewed as pathological or extreme – on the unfortunate minority who become 'obsessed' or go 'too far'. Television talk shows feature tales of disasters caused by stomach stapling, gastric bubbles, gastrointestinal bypass operations, liquid diets, compulsive exercising. Magazines warn of the dangers of fat-reduction surgery and liposuction. Books and articles about bulimia and anorexia nervosa proliferate. The portrayal of eating disorders by the popular media is often lurid and sensational; audiences gasp at pictures of skeletal bodies or at item-by-item descriptions of the volumes of food eaten during an average binge. Such presentations encourage a 'side show' experience of the relationship between the ('normal') audience and those on view ('the freaks'). To the degree that the audience may nonetheless recognise themselves in the behaviour or reported experiences of those on stage, they confront themselves as 'pathological' or outside the norm.

Of course, many of these behaviours *are* outside the norm, if only because of the financial resources they require. But preoccupation with fat, diet, and slenderness are not.[5] Indeed, such preoccupation may function as one of the most powerful 'normalizing' strategies of our century, ensuring the production of self-monitoring and self-disciplining 'docile bodies,' sensitive to any departure from social norms, and habituated to self-improvement and transformation in the service of those norms.[6] Seen in this light, the focus on 'pathology,' disorder, accident, unexpected disaster, and bizarre behaviour obscures the normalizing function of the technologies of diet and body management. For women, who are subject to such controls more profoundly and, historically, more ubiquitously than men, the focus on 'pathology' (unless embedded in a political analysis) diverts recognition from a central means of the reproduction of gender.

This essay is part of a larger analysis of the contemporary preoccupation with slenderness as it functions within a modern, 'normalizing' machinery of power in general, and, in particular, as it functions to reproduce gender-relations. For the purposes of this larger analysis, I make use of Foucault's distinction between two arenas of the social construction of the modern body – the 'intelligible body' and the 'useful body': (1) the representational, and (2) the practical, direct locus of social control, through which culture is converted into automatic, habitual bodily activity. The 'intelligible body' includes scientific, philosophic, and aesthetic representations of the body, norms of beauty, models of health, and so forth. These representations, however, may also be seen as legislating a set of *practical* rules and regulations (some explicit, some implicit), through which the living body is 'trained, shaped, obeys, and responds . . .'; becomes, in short, a socially adapted and 'useful body.'[7] So, for example, the seventeenth-century philosophic conception of body-as-machine arguably both mirrored and provided a metaphysical and technical model for an increasingly automated productive machinery of labor.

Understanding the 'political anatomy' (as Foucault would call it) of the slender body requires the interrogation of both 'useful' and 'intelligible' arenas – interrogation of the practices or 'disciplines' of diet and exercise which structure the organization of time, space, and the experience of embodiment for subjects; and, in our image-bedazzled culture, interrogation of the popular representations through which meaning is crystallized, symbolized, metaphorically encoded, and transmitted. My overall argument emphasizes the primacy of practice for evaluating the role of bodies in the nexus of power relations. In this light, we should certainly be 'politically' disturbed by recent statistics on the number of young girls (80 per cent of the 9 year-olds surveyed in one study[8]) who are making dedicated dieting the organizing principle of their days. This particular essay, however, will approach the normalizing role of diet and exercise via an examination of the representational body – the cultural imagery of ideal slenderness – which now reigns, increasingly across racial and ethnic boundaries, as the dominant body-standard of our culture.[9] More specifically, I wish to pursue here Mary Douglas's insight that images of the 'microcosm' – the physical body – may symbolically reproduce central vulnerabilities and anxieties of the macrocosm – the 'social body.'[10] I will explore this insight by 'reading' (as the text or surface on which culture is symbolically 'written') some dominant meanings that are connected, in our time, to the pursuit of slenderness.

Decoding cultural images is a complex business – particularly when one considers the wide variety of ethnic, racial, and class differences that intersect with, resist, and give distinctive meaning to dominant, normalizing imagery. Even on the level of homogenizing imagery (my focus in this essay), contemporary slenderness admits of many variants and has multiple and often mutually 'deconstructing' meanings. To give just one example, an examination of the photographs and copy of current fashion advertisements suggests that today's boyish body ideals, as in the 1920s, symbolize a new freedom, a casting off of the encumbrance of domestic, reproductive femininity. But when the same slender body is depicted in poses that set it off against the resurgent muscularity and bulk of the current male body-ideal, other meanings emerge. In these gender/oppositional poses, the degree to which slenderness carries connotations of fragility, defencelessness, and lack of power against a decisive male occupation of social space is dramatically represented.

Since it is impossible for any cultural analyst to do a full reading of the text of slenderness in the space of a single essay, I will instead attempt to construct an argument about some elements of the cultural context that has conditioned the flourishing of eating disorders – anorexia, bulimia, and obesity – in our time. The first step in that argument is a decoding of the contemporary slenderness ideal so as to reveal the psychic anxieties and moral valuations contained within it – valuations concerning the correct and incorrect management of impulse and desire . . . .

Slenderness and contemporary anxiety

In a recent edition of the magazine show *20/20*, several 10 year-old boys were shown some photos of fashion models. The models were pencil thin. Yet the pose was such that a small bulge of hip was forced, through the action of the body, into protuberance – as is natural, unavoidable on any but the most skeletal or the most tautly developed bodies. We bend over, we sit down and the flesh coalesces in spots. These young boys, pointing to the hips, disgustedly pronounced the models to be 'fat'. Watching the show, I was appalled at the boys' reaction. Yet I couldn't deny that I had also been surprised at my own current perceptions while re-viewing female bodies in movies from the 1970s; what once appeared slender and fit now seemed loose and flabby. *Weight* was not the key element in these changed perceptions – my standards had not come to favour *thinner* bodies – but rather, I had come to expect a tighter, smoother, more 'contained' body profile.

The self-criticisms of the anorexic, too, are usually focused on particular soft, protuberant areas of the body (most often the stomach) rather than on the body as a whole. Karen, in *Dying to Be Thin*, tries to dispel what she sees as the myth that the anorexic, even when emaciated, 'misperceives' her body as fat:

> I hope I'm expressing myself properly here, because this is important. You have to understand. I don't see my whole body as fat. When I look in the mirror, I don't really see a fat person there. I see certain things about me that are really thin. Like my arms and legs. But I can tell the minute I eat certain things that my stomach blows up like a pig's. I know it gets distended. And it's disgusting. That's what I keep to myself – hug to myself.[11]

Or Barbara:

> Sometimes my body looks so bloated, I don't want to get dressed. I like the way it looks for exactly two days each month: usually, the eighth and ninth days after my period. Every other day, my breasts, my stomach – they're just awful lumps, bumps, bulges. My body can turn on me at any moment; it is an out-of-control mass of flesh.[12]

Much has been made of such descriptions, from both psychoanalytic and feminist perspectives. But for now, I wish to pursue these images of unwanted bulges and erupting stomachs in another direction than that of gender symbolism. I want to consider them as a metaphor for anxiety about internal processes out of control – uncontained desire, unrestrained hunger, uncontrolled impulse. Images of bodily eruption frequently function symbolically in this way in contemporary horror movies – as in recent werewolf films *(The Howling, A Teen-Age Werewolf in London)* and in David Cronenberg's remake of *The Fly*. The original *Fly* imagined a mechanical joining of fly parts and person parts, a variation on the standard 'half-man, half-beast' image. In Cronenberg's *Fly*, as in the werewolf genre, a new, alien, libidinous, and uncontrollable self literally bursts through the seams of the victim's old flesh. (A related, frequently copied image occurs in *Alien*, where a parasite erupts from the chest of the human host.) While it is possible to view these new images as technically inspired by special-effects possibilities, I suggest that deeper psycho-cultural anxieties are being given form.

Every year, I present my metaphysics class with Delmore Schwartz's classic poem 'The Heavy Bear' as an example of a dualist imagination of self, in which the body is constructed as an alien, unconscious, appetitive force, thwarting and befouling the projects of the soul. Beginning with an epigraph from Alfred North Whitehead, 'The withness of the body,' Schwartz's poem makes 'the heavy bear who goes with [him]' into 'A caricature, a swollen shadow, A stupid clown of the spirit's motive.' Last year, for the first time, quite a few students interpreted the poem as describing the predicament of an obese man. This may indicate the increasing literalism of my students. But it also is suggestive of the degree to which the specter of 'fat' dominates their imaginations, and codes their generation's anxieties about the body's potential for excess and chaos. In advertisements, the construction of the body as an alien attacker, threatening to erupt in an unsightly display of bulging flesh, is an ubiquitous cultural image. Until the last decade, excess weight was the target of most ads for diet products; today, one is much more likely to find the enemy constructed as bulge, fat, or 'flab.' 'Now' (a typical ad runs), 'get rid of those embarrassing bumps, bulges, large stomach, flabby breasts and buttocks. Feel younger, and help prevent cellulite build-up. . . . Have a nice shape with no tummy.' To achieve such results (often envisioned as the absolute eradication of body: e.g., 'no tummy') a violent assault on the enemy is usually required; bulges must be 'attacked' and 'destroyed,' fat 'burned,' and stomachs (or, more disgustedly, 'guts') must be 'busted' and 'eliminated.' The increasing popularity of liposuction, a far from totally safe technique developed specifically to suck out the unwanted bulges of people of normal weight (it is not recommended for the obese), suggests how far our disgust with bodily bulges has gone. The ideal here is of a body that is absolutely tight, contained, 'bolted down,' firm (in other words, body that is protected against eruption from within, whose internal processes are under control). Areas that are soft, loose, or 'wiggly' are unacceptable, even on extremely thin bodies. Cellulite management, like liposuction, has nothing to do with weight loss, and everything to do with the quest for firm bodily margins.

This perspective helps illuminate an important continuity of meaning between compulsive dieting and bodybuilding in our culture, and reveals why it has been so easy for contemporary images of female attractiveness to oscillate back and forth between a spare 'minimalist' look and a solid, muscular, athletic look. The coexistence of these seemingly disparate images does not indicate that a postmodern universe of empty, endlessly differentiating images now reigns. Rather, the two ideals, though superficially very different, are united in battle against a common platoon of enemies: the soft, the loose; unsolid, excess flesh. It is perfectly permissible in our culture (even for women) to have substantial weight and bulk – so long as it is tightly managed. On the other hand, to be slim is simply not enough – so long as the flesh jiggles. Here, we arrive at one source of insight into why it is that the image of ideal slenderness has grown thinner and thinner over the last decade, and why women with extremely slender bodies often still see themselves as 'fat.' Unless one goes the route of muscle building, it is virtually impossible to achieve a flab-less, excess-less body unless one trims very near to the bone.

Slenderness and the state of the soul

This 'moral' (and, as we shall see, economic) coding of the fat/slender body in terms of its capacities for self-containment and the control of impulse and desire represents the culmination of a developing historical change in the social symbolism of body weight and size. Until the late nineteenth century, the central discriminations marked were those of class, race, and gender; the body indicated one's social identity and 'place.' So, for example, the bulging stomachs of successful mid-nineteenth-century businessmen and politicians were a symbol of bourgeois success, an outward manifestation of their accumulated wealth.[13] By contrast, the gracefully slender body announced aristocratic status; disdainful of the bourgeois

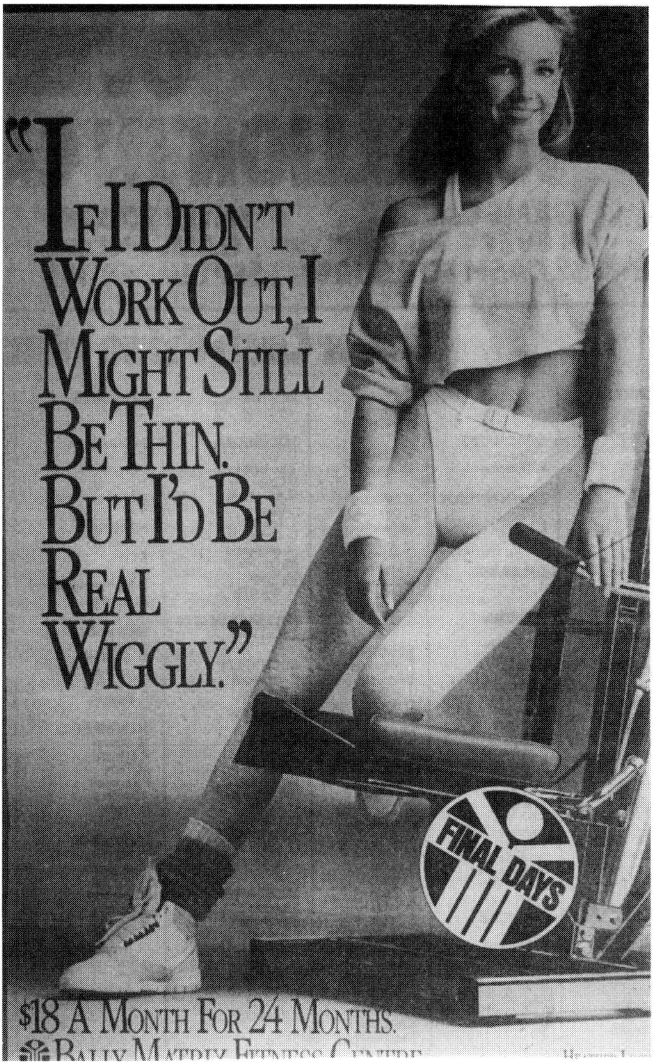

Figure 18.1 'If I didn't work out' advert

need to display wealth and power ostentatiously, it commanded social space invisibly rather than aggressively, seemingly above the commerce in appetite or the need to eat. Subsequently, this ideal began to be appropriated by the status-seeking middle class, as slender wives became the showpieces of their husbands' success.[14]

Corpulence went out of middle-class vogue at the end of the century (even William Howard Taft, who had weighed over 300 pounds while in office, went on a reducing diet); social power had come to be less dependent on the sheer accumulation of material wealth and more connected to the ability to control and manage the labor and resources of others. At the same time, excess body weight came to be seen as reflecting moral or personal inadequacy, or lack of will.[15] These associations are only possible in a culture of 'overabundance' (that is, in a society in which those who control the production of 'culture' have more than enough to eat). The moral requirement to diet depends upon the material preconditions that make the *choice* to 'diet' an option and the possibility of personal 'excess' a reality. Although slenderness has hitherto retained some of its traditional class-associations ('a woman can never be too rich or too thin'), the importance of this equation has eroded considerably over the last decade. Increasingly, the size and shape of the body has come to operate as a marker of personal, internal order (or disorder) – as a symbol for the state of the soul.

Consider one particularly clear example, that of changes in the meaning of the muscled body. Muscularity has had a variety of cultural meanings (until recently largely reserved for male bodies) which have prevented the well-developed body from playing too great a role in middle-class conceptions of attractiveness. Of course, muscles have symbolized masculine power. But at the same time, they have been associated with manual labor and chain-gangs (and thus with lower-class and even criminal status), and suffused with racial meaning (via numerous film representations of sweating, glistening bodies belonging to black slaves and prize-fighters). Given the racial and class biases of our culture, they were associated with the body as material, unconscious, or animalistic. Today, however, the well-muscled body has become a cultural icon; 'working out' is a glamorized and sexualized yuppie activity. No longer signifying lower-class status (except when developed to extremes, at which point the old association of muscles with brute, unconscious materiality surfaces once more), the firm, developed body has become a symbol of correct *attitude*; it means that one 'cares' about oneself and how one appears to others, suggesting willpower, energy, control over infantile impulse, the ability to 'make something' of oneself. 'You exercise, you diet,' says Heather Locklear, promoting Bally Matrix Fitness Centre on television, 'and you can do anything you want.' Muscles express sexuality, but controlled, managed sexuality that is not about to erupt in unwanted and embarrassing display.[16]

To the degree that the question of class still operates in all this, it relates to the category of social mobility (or lack of it) rather than class *location*. So, for example, when associations of fat and lower-class status exist, they are usually mediated by qualities of attitude or 'soul' – fat being perceived as indicative of laziness, lack of discipline, unwillingness to conform, and absence of all those 'managerial' abilities that, according to the dominant ideology, confer upward mobility. Correspondingly, in popular teen movies such as *Flashdance* and *Vision Quest*, the ability of the (working-class) heroine and hero to pare, prune, tighten, and master the body operates as a clear symbol of successful upward aspiration, of the penetrability of class boundaries to those who have 'the right stuff.' These movies (as one title explicitly suggests) are contemporary 'quest myths'; like their prototype, *Rocky*, they follow the struggle of an individual to attain a personal grail, against all odds, and through numerous trials. But unlike the film quests of a previous era (which sent Mr Smith to Washington and Mr Deeds to town to battle the respective social evils of corrupt government and big business), *Flashdance* and *Vision Quest* render the hero's and heroine's commitment, will, and spiritual integrity through the metaphors of weight loss, exercise, and tolerance of and ability to conquer physical pain and exhaustion. (In *Vision Quest,* for example, the audience is encouraged to admire the young wrestler's perseverance when he ignores the fainting spells and nosebleeds caused by his rigorous training and dieting.)

Not surprisingly, young people with eating disorders often thematize their own experience in similar terms, as in the following excerpt from an interview with a young woman runner:

> Well, I had the willpower. I could train for competition, and I could turn down food any time. I remember feeling like I was on a constant high. And the pain? Sure, there was pain. It was incredible. Between the hunger and the muscle pain from the constant workouts? I can't tell you how much I hurt.
>
> You may think I was crazy to put myself through constant, intense pain. But you have to remember. I was fighting a battle. And when you get hurt in a battle, you're proud of it. Sure, you may scream inside, but if you're brave and really good, then you take it quietly, because you know it's the price you pay for winning. And I needed to win. I really felt that if I didn't win, I would die . . . all these enemy troops were coming at me, and I had to outsmart them. If I could discipline myself enough – if I could keep myself lean and strong – then I could win. The pain was just a natural thing I had to deal with.[17]

As in *Vision Quest*, the external context is training for an athletic event. But here, too, that goal becomes subordinated to an internal one. The real battle, ultimately, is with the self. At this point, the limitations of the brief history that I presented in the opening paragraph of this essay are revealed. In that paragraph, the contemporary preoccupation with diet is contrasted to historical projects of body management suffused with moral meaning. In this section, however, I have suggested that examination of even the most 'shallow' representations (teen movies) discloses a moral ideology – one, in fact, seemingly close to the aristocratic Greek ideal described by Foucault in *The Use of Pleasure*. The central element of that ideal, as Foucault describes it, is 'an agnostic relation with the self' – aimed, not at the extirpation of desire and hunger in the interest of 'purity' (as in the Christian strain of dualism), but at a 'virile' mastery of desire through constant 'spiritual combat'.[18]

[. . .]

Notes

1 See Keith Walden, 'The Road to Fat City: An Interpretation of the Development of Weight Consciousness in Western Society,' *Historical Reflections* 12, 3 (1985) pp. 331–73.

2 See Michel Foucault, *The Use of Pleasure* (New York: Random House, 1986).

3 See Rudolph Bell, *Holy Anorexia* (Chicago: University of Chicago Press, 1985); and Carolyn Bynum, *Holy Feast and Holy Fast: The Religious Significance of Food to Medieval Women* (Berkeley: University of California Press, 1987), pp. 31–48.

4 See Kim Chernin, *The Obsession: Reflections on the Tyranny of Slenderness* (New York: Harper & Row, 1981).

5 See Thomas Cash, Barbara Winstead, and Louis Janda, 'The Great American Shape-up,' *Psychology Today*, April 1986; 'Dieting: The Losing Game,' *Time*, 20 January 1986, among numerous other general reports.

6 For Foucault on 'docile bodies,' see *Discipline and Punish* (New York: Vintage, 1979), pp. 135–69. For an application of Foucault's ideas to the practices of diet and fitness, see Walden, 'The Road to Fat City.' For a Foucauldian analysis of the practices of femininity, see Sandra Bartky, 'Foucault, Femininity, and the Modernization of Patriarchal Power,' in *Feminism and Foucault*, ed. Irene Diamond and Lee Quinby (Boston: Northeastern University Press, 1988), pp. 61–86.

7 Foucault, *Discipline and Punish*, p. 136.

8 'Fat or Not, 4th Grade Girls Diet Lest They Be Teased or Unloved,' *Wall Street Journal*, 11 February 1986 (based on a University of California study.) A still more recent study conducted at the University of Ottawa concluded that by age 7, a majority of young girls are anxious about their weight, and convinced they are much fatter than they are. ('Girls, at 7, Think Thin, Study Finds,' *New York Times*, 11 February, 1988)

9 On the 'spreading' nature of eating disorders, see Paul Garfinkel and David Garner, *Anorexia Nervosa: A Multidimensional Perspective* (New York: Bruner Mazel, 1982), pp. 102–3; and George Hsu, 'Are Eating Disorders Becoming More Common in Blacks?', *The International Journal of Eating Disorders* 6(1) (January 1987): pp. 113–24. Despite these trends, resistance to the slenderness ideal persists, and should not be overlooked as a source of insight into different cultural models of beauty and the conditions that promote them.

10 See Mary Douglas, *Natural Symbols* (New York: Pantheon, 1982); and *Purity and Danger* (London: Routledge & Kegan Paul, 1966).

11 Ira Sacker and Marc Zimmer, *Dying To Be Thin* (New York: Warner, 1987), p. 57.

12 Dalma Heyn, 'Body Vision?', *Mademoiselle*, April 1987, p. 213.

13 See Louis Banner, *American Beauty* (Chicago: University of Chicago Press, 1983), pp. 232.

14 Ibid., pp. 53–55.

15 See Walden, *Historical Reflections* 12 (3), pp. 334–35, 353.

16 I thank Mario Moussa for this point, and for the Heather Locklear quotation.

17 Ira Sacker and Marc Zimmer, op. cit., pp. 149–50.

18 Foucault, *The Use of Pleasure*, pp. 64–70.

Chapter 19

Anne Balsamo

ON THE CUTTING EDGE

Cosmetic surgery and the technological production of the gendered body

The biotechnological reproduction of gender

AMONG THE MOST intriguing new body technologies developed during the decade of the 1980s are techniques of visualization that redefine the range of human perception. New medical imaging technologies such as laparoscopy and computer tomography (CT) make the body visible in such a way that its internal status can be accessed before it is laid bare or opened up surgically. Like the techniques that enable scientists to encode and read genetic structures, these new visualization technologies transform the material body into the visual medium. In the process the body is fractured and fragmented so that isolated parts can be visually examined: the parts can be isolated by function, as in organs or neuron receptors, or by medium, as in fluids, genes, or heat. At the same time, the material body comes to embody the characteristics of technological images.

When the human body is fractured into organs, fluids, and genetic codes, what happens to gender identity? In a technologically deconstructed body, where is gender located? Gender, like the body, is a boundary concept; it is at once related to the physiological sexual characteristics of the human body (the natural order of the body) and to the cultural context within which that body 'makes sense.' The widespread technological refashioning of the 'natural' human body suggests that gender too would be ripe for reconstruction. Advances in reproductive technology already decouple the act of procreation from the act of sexual intercourse. Laparoscopy has played a critical role in the assessment of fetal development, with the attendant consequence that the fetal body has been metaphorically (and sometimes literally) severed from its natural association with the female body and is now proclaimed to be the new, and most important obstetric patient. What effects do these biotechnological advances have on cultural definitions of the female body? As is often the case when seemingly stable boundaries (human/artificial, life/death, nature/culture) are displaced by technological innovation, other boundaries are more vigilantly guarded. Indeed, the gendered boundary between male and female is one border that remains heavily guarded despite new technologized ways to rewrite the physical body in the flesh. So that it appears that while the body has been recoded within discourses of biotechnology and medicine as belonging to an order of culture rather than of nature, gender remains a naturalized point of human identity. As Judy Wajcman reminds us: 'technology is more than a set of physical objects or artefacts. It also fundamentally embodies a culture or set of social relations made up of certain sorts of knowledge, beliefs, desires, and practices.'[1] My concern here is to describe the way in which certain biotechnologies are ideologically 'shaped by the operation of gender interests' and, consequently, how these serve to reinforce traditional gendered patterns of power and authority. When Judith Butler describes the gendered body as 'a set of repeated acts within a highly rigid regulatory frame that congeal over time to produce the appearance of substance,' she identifies the mechanism whereby 'naturalized' gender identities are socially and culturally reproduced.[2]

Carole Spitzack suggests that cosmetic surgery actually deploys three overlapping mechanisms of cultural control: inscription, surveillance, and confession.[3] According to Spitzack, the physician's clinical eye functions like Foucault's medical gaze; it is a disciplinary gaze, situated within apparatuses of power and knowledge, that constructs the female figure as pathological, excessive, unruly, and potentially threatening. This gaze disciplines the unruly female body by first fragmenting it into isolated parts – face, hair, legs, breasts – and then redefining those parts as inherently flawed and pathological. When women internalize a fragmented body image and accept its 'flawed' identity, each part of the body then becomes a site for the 'fixing' of her physical abnormality. Spitzack characterizes this acceptance as a form of confession.

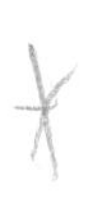

> In the scenario of the cosmetic surgeon's office, the transformation from illness to health is inscribed on the body of the patient. . . . The female patient is promised beauty and re-form in exchange for confession, which is predicated on an admission of a diseased appearance that points to a diseased (powerless) character. A failure to confess, in the clinical setting, is equated with a refusal of health; a preference for disease.[4]

But the cosmetic surgeon's gaze does not simply *medicalize* the female body, it actually redefines it as object for technological reconstruction. In her reading of the women's films of the 1940s, Mary Ann Doane employs the concept of the 'clinical eye' to describe how the technologies of looking represent and situate female film characters as the objects of medical discourse. In Doane's analysis, the medicalization of the female body relies on a surface/depth model of the body whereby the physician assumes the right and responsibility of divining the truth of the female body – to make visible her invisible depths. The clinical gaze of the physician reveals the truth of the female body in his act of looking through her to see the 'essence' of her illness. According to Doane, the clinical eye marks a shift in the signification of the female body, from a purely surface form of signification to a depth model of signification. She traces this shift through a reading of the difference between mainstream classical cinema and the woman's film of the 1940s.[5]

In examining the visualization technologies used in the practice of cosmetic surgery, we can witness the process whereby new biotechnologies are articulated with traditional and ideological beliefs about gender – an articulation that keeps the female body positioned as a privileged object of a normative gaze that is now not simply a medicalized gaze ('the clinical eye'), but also a technologized view. In the application of new visualization technologies, the relationship between the female body and the cultural viewing apparatus has shifted again; in the process, the clinical eye gives way to the deployment of a technological gaze. This application of the gaze does not rely on a surface/depth model of the material body, whereby the body has some sort of structural integrity as a bounded physical object. In the encounter between women and cosmetic surgeons, it is not so much the inner or essential woman that is looked at; her interior story has no truth of its own. Both her surface and her interiority are flattened and dispersed. Cosmetic surgeons use technological imaging devices to reconstruct the female body as a signifier of ideal feminine beauty. In this sense, surgical techniques literally enact the logic of assembly line beauty: 'difference' is made over into sameness. The technological gaze refashions the material body to reconstruct it in keeping with culturally determined ideals of feminine beauty.

Cosmetic surgery and the inscription of cultural standards of beauty

Cosmetic surgery enacts a form of cultural signification where we can examine the literal and material reproduction of ideals of beauty. Where visualization technologies bring into focus isolated body parts and pieces, surgical procedures carve into the flesh to isolate parts to be manipulated and resculpted. In this way cosmetic surgery *literally* transforms the material body into a sign of culture. The *discourse* of cosmetic surgery offers provocative material for a discussion of the cultural construction of the gendered body because, on the one hand, women are often the intended and preferred subjects of such discourse, and on the other, men are often the bodies doing the surgery. Cosmetic surgery is not then simply a discursive site for the 'construction of images of women,' but in actuality, a material site at which the physical female body is surgically dissected, stretched, carved, and reconstructed according to cultural and eminently ideological standards of physical appearance.

There are two main fields of plastic surgery. Whereas *reconstructive* surgery works on catastrophic, congenital or cancer-damage deformities, *cosmetic* or aesthetic surgery is often an entirely elective endeavour. And whereas reconstructive surgery is associated with the restoration of health, normalcy, and physical function, cosmetic surgery is said to improve self-esteem, social status, and sometimes even professional standing.

All cosmetic surgery implicitly involves aesthetic judgements of facial proportion, harmony, and symmetry. In fact, one medical textbook strongly encourages plastic surgeons to acquire some familiarity with classical art theory so that they are better prepared to 'judge human form in three dimensions, evaluate all aspects of the deformity, visualize the finished product, and plan the approach that will produce an optimal result.'[6] Codifying the aspects of such an 'aesthetic sense' seems counter-intuitive, but in fact, there is a voluminous literature that reports the scientific measurement of facial proportions in an attempt to accomplish the scientific determination of aesthetic perfection. According to one plastic surgeon, most cosmetic surgeons have some familiarity with the anthropological fields of anthropometry and human osteology. Anthropometry, which is defined in one source as 'a technique for the measurement of men, whether living or dead,' is actually a critically important science used by a variety of professional engineers and designers. One example of practical anthropometry is the collection of measurements of infants' and children's bodies for use in the design of automobile seat restraints. Of course it makes a great deal of sense that measurement standards and scales of human proportions are a necessary resource for the design of products for human use; in order to achieve a 'fit' with the range of human bodies that will eventually use and inhabit a range of products from office chairs to office buildings, designers must have access to a reliable and standardized set of body measurements. But when the measurement project identifies the 'object' being measured as the 'American negro' or the 'ideal female face,' it is less clear what practical use these measurements serve.

If anthropometry is 'a technique for the measurement of men,' the fascination of plastic surgeons is the measurement of the ideal. One well-cited volume in a series published by the American Academy of Facial Plastic and Reconstructive Surgery, titled *Proportions of the Aesthetic Face* (by Nelson Powell and Brian Humphreys) proclaims that it is a 'complete sourcebook of information on facial proportion and analysis.'[7] In the Preface the authors state:

> The face, by its nature, presents itself often for review. We unconsciously evaluate the overall effect each time an acquaintance is made. . . . This [impression] is generally related to some scale of beauty or balance. . . . The harmony and symmetry are compared to a mental, almost magical, ideal subject, which is our basic concept of beauty. Such a concept or complex we shall term the 'ideal face'.[8]

According to the authors, the purpose of this text is quite simple: to document, objectively, the guidelines for facial symmetry and proportion. Not inconsequentially, the 'Ideal Face' depicted in this book – both in the form of line drawings and in photographs – is of a white woman whose face is perfectly symmetrical in line and profile [Figure 19.1]. The authors claim that although the 'male's bone structure is sterner, bolder, and more prominent . . . the ideals of facial proportion and unified interplay apply to either gender.' And as if to prove the point, they provide an illustration of the ideal male face in the glossary. As I discuss later, this focus on the female body is prevalent in all areas of cosmetic surgery – from the determination of ideal proportions to the marketing of specific cosmetic procedures. The source or history of these idealized drawings is never discussed. But once the facial proportions of these images are codified and measured, they are reproduced by surgeons as they make modifications to their patients' faces. Even though they work

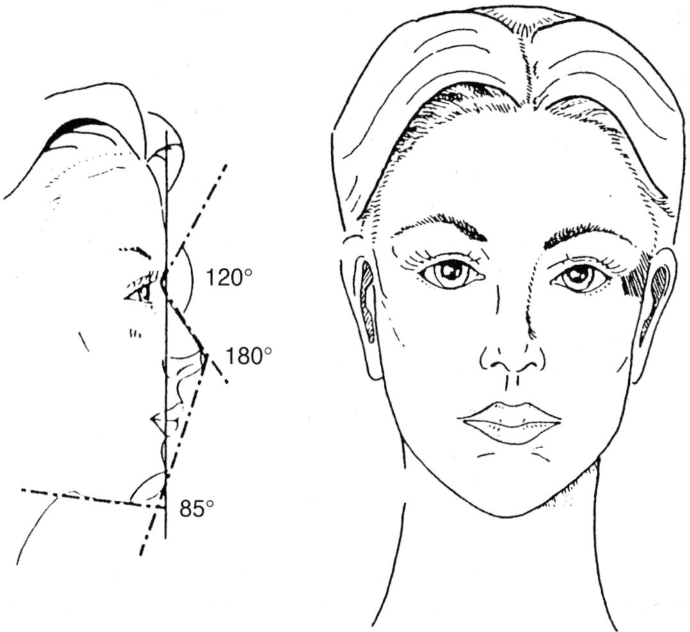

Figure 19.1 'Angles and proportions of the ideal female face' diagrams, 1984 (Courtesy of Thieme Medical Publishers)

with faces that are individually distinct, surgeons use the codified measurements as a guideline for the determination of treatment goals in the attempt to bring the distinctive face in alignment with artistic ideals of symmetry and proportion.

The treatment of race in this book on 'ideal proportions of the aesthetic face' reveals a preference for white, symmetrical faces that heal (apparently) without scarring. On the one hand the authors acknowledge that 'bone structure is different in all racial identities' and that 'surgeons must acknowledge that racial qualities are appreciated differently in various cultures,' but in the end they argue that 'the facial form [should be] able to confer harmony and aesthetic appeal regardless of race.'[9] It appears that this appreciation for the aesthetic judgement 'regardless of race' is not a widely shared assumption among cosmetic surgeons. Napoleon N. Vaughn reports that many cosmetic surgeons 'mindful of keloid formation and hyperpigmented scarring, routinely reject black patients.'[10] But the issue of scar tissue formation is entirely ignored in the discussion of the 'proportions of the aesthetic face.' Powell and Humphreys implicitly argue that black faces can be evaluated in terms of ideal proportions determined by the measurement of Caucasian faces, but they fail to address the issue of post-surgical risks that differentiate black patients from Caucasian ones. Although it is true that black patients and patients with dark ruddy complexions have a greater propensity to form keloid or hypertrophic scars than do Caucasian patients, many physicians argue that black patients who are shown to be prone to keloid formation in the lower body are not necessarily prone to such formations in the facial area and upper body; therefore a racial propensity for keloid formation should not be a reason to reject a black patient's request for facial cosmetic surgery. And according to Arthur Sumrall, even though 'postoperative dyschromic changes and surgical incision lines are much more visible in many black patients and races of color than their Caucasian counterpart,' these changes and incision lines greatly improve with time and corrective cosmetics.[11] As an abstraction the 'aesthetic face' is designed to assist surgeons in planning surgical goals; but as a cultural artifact, the 'aesthetic face' symbolizes a desire for standardized ideals of Caucasian beauty.

It is clear that any plastic surgery invokes standards of physical appearance and functional definitions of the 'normal' or 'healthy' body. Upon closer investigation we can see how these standards and definitions are culturally determined. In the 1940s and 1950s, women reportedly wanted 'pert, upturned noses,' but according to one recent survey this shape has gone out of style. 'The classic, more natural shape is the ultimate one with which to sniff these days.'[12] The obvious question becomes, what condition does the adjective 'natural' describe? In this case we can see how requests for cosmetic reconstructions show the waxing and waning of fashionable desires; in this sense, 'fashion surgery' might be a more fitting label for the kind of surgery performed for nonfunctional reasons. But even as high fashion moves toward a multiculturalism in the employ of nontraditionally beautiful models, it is striking to learn how great is the demand for cosmetic alterations that are based on Western markers of ideal beauty. In a *New York Times Magazine* feature, Ann Louise Bardach reports that Asian women often desire surgery to effect a more 'Western' eye shape.[13] Indeed, in several medical articles this surgery is actually referred to as 'upper lid Westernization,' and is reported to be 'the most frequently performed cosmetic procedure in the Orient.'[14] The surgeons explain:

> An upper lid fold is considered a sign of sophistication and refinement to many Orientals across all social strata. It is not quite accurate to say that Orientals undergoing this surgery desire to look Western or American; rather, they desire a more refined Oriental eye. . . . An upper lid Westernization blepharoplasty frequently is given to a young Korean woman on the occasion of her betrothal.

Although other surgeons warn that it is 'wise to discuss the Oriental and Occidental eye anatomy in terms of differences *not* defects,'[15] at least one other medical article on this type of surgery was titled 'Correction of the Oriental Eyelid.'[16] In terms of eyelid shape and design, the authors do not comment on how the 'natural' Oriental eye came to be described as having a 'poorly defined orbital and periorbital appearance;' thus, when their Oriental patients request 'larger, wider, less flat, more defined, more awake-appearing eyes and orbital surroundings,' these surgeons offer an operative plan for the surgical achievement of what is commonly understood to be a more Westernized appearance.[17] In discussing the reasons for the increased demand for this form of blepharoplasty 'among the Oriental,' Marwali Harahap notes that this technique became popular after the Second World War; this leads some surgeons to speculate that such a desire for Westernized eyes 'stem[s] from the influence of motion pictures and the increasing intermarriage of Asian women and Caucasian men.'[18]

[. . .]

Cosmetic surgery as a technology of the gendered body

In recent years, more men are electing cosmetic surgery than in the past, but often in secret. As one article reports: 'previously reluctant males are among the booming number of men surreptitiously doing what women have been doing for years: having their eyelids lifted, jowls removed, ears clipped, noses reduced, and chins tightened.' One cosmetic surgeon elaborates the reasons that men are beginning to seek elective cosmetic surgery:

> A middle-aged male patient – we'll call him Mr. Dropout – thinks he has a problem. He doesn't think he's too old for the lovely virgins he meets, but he wants to improve things. . . . When a man consults for aging, generally he is not compulsive about looking younger but he seeks relief from one or more specific defects incidental to aging: male pattern baldness . . . forehead wrinkling . . . turkey-gobbler neck. There are many things that can be done to help the aging man look younger or more virile.[19]

According to yet another cosmetic surgeon, the reason for some men's new concern about appearance is 'linked to the increasing competition for top jobs they face at the peak of their careers from women and Baby Boomers.'[20] Here the increase in male cosmetic surgery is explained as a shrewd business tactic: 'looking good' connotes greater intelligence, competence, and desirability as a colleague. Charges of narcissism, vanity, and self-indulgence are put aside; a man's choice to have cosmetic surgery is explained by appeal to a rhetoric of career enhancement: a better-looking body is better able to be promoted. In this case, cosmetic surgery is redefined as a body management technique designed to reduce the stress of having to cope with a changing work environment, one that is being threatened by the presence of women and younger people. While all of these explanations may be true in the sense that this is how men justify their choice to elect cosmetic surgery, it is clear that other explanations are not even entertained: for example, what about the possibility that men and women are becoming more alike with respect to 'the body beautiful,' that men are engaging more frequently in female body activities, or even simply that a concern with appearance is not solely a characteristic of women? What about the possibility that the boundary between genders is eroding? How is it that men avoid the pejorative labels attached to female cosmetic surgery clients?

In their ethnomethodological study of cosmetic surgery, Diana Dull and Candace West examine how surgeons and patients 'account' for their decisions to elect cosmetic surgery.[21] They argue that when surgeons divide the patient's body into component parts and pieces, it enables both 'surgeons and patients together [to] establish the problematic status of the part in question and its "objective" need of "repair"'.[22]

But Dull and West go on to argue that this process of fragmentation occurs in 'tandem with the accomplishment of gender' which, in relying upon an essentialist view of the female body as always 'needing repair,' understands women's choice for cosmetic surgery as 'natural' and 'normal' and as a consequence of their (natural) preoccupation with appearance. Because their 'essential' natures are defined very differently, men, on the other hand, must construct elaborate justifications for their decision to seek cosmetic alterations. This analysis illuminates one of the possible reasons why men and women construct different accounts of their decision to elect cosmetic surgery: the cultural meaning of their gendered bodies already determines the discursive rationale they can invoke to explain bodily practices. Where the bodies and faces of male farmers and construction workers, for example, are excessively 'tanned' due to their constant exposure to the sun as part of their work conditions, their ruddy, leathery skin is not considered a liability or deformity of their male bodies. In contrast, white women who display wrinkled skin due to excessive tanning are sometimes diagnosed with 'The Miami Beach Syndrome,' and as one surgeon claims: 'we find this type of overly tanned, wrinkled skin in women who not only go to Miami every year for three or four months, but lie on the beach with a sun reflector drawing additional rays to their faces.'[23] It is no surprise then, that although any body can exhibit the 'flaws' that supposedly justify cosmetic surgery, discussion and marketing of such procedures usually construct the female body as the typical patient. Such differential treatment of gendered bodies illustrates a by-now familiar assertion of feminist studies of the body and appearance: the meaning of the presence or absence of any physical quality varies according to the gender of the body upon which it appears. Clearly an apparatus of gender organizes our seemingly most basic, natural interpretation of human bodies, even when those bodies are technologically refashioned. Thus it appears that although technologies such as those used in cosmetic surgery can reconstruct the 'natural' identity of the material body, they do little to disrupt naturalization of essentialized gender identity.

Wendy Chapkis amplifies this point when she writes:

> However much the particulars of the beauty package may change from decade to decade – curves in or out, skin delicate or ruddy, figures fragile or fit – the basic principles remain the same. The body beautiful is woman's responsibility and authority. She will be valued and rewarded on the basis of how close she comes to embodying the ideal.[24]

In the popular media, advertisements for surgical services are rarely, if ever, addressed specifically to men. In a 1988 advertising campaign for the Liposuction Institute in Chicago, every advertisement features an illustration of a woman's (saddlebag) thighs as the 'before' image of liposuction procedures. And of course, many cosmetic alterations are designed especially for women: tattooed eyeliner marketed as 'the ultimate cosmetic;' electrolysis removal of superfluous hair; and face creams. An advertising representative for DuraSoft explains that the company has begun marketing their colored contact lenses specifically for black women, ostensibly because DuraSoft believes that 'black women have fewer cosmetic alternatives,' but a more likely reason is that the company wants to create new markets for its cosmetic lenses. So whereas 'being a real man requires having a penis and balls' and a concern with virility and productivity, being a real woman requires buying beauty products and services.[25]

And yet women who have too many cosmetic alterations are pejoratively labeled 'scalpel slaves' to identify them with their obsession for surgical fixes.

Women in their later thirties and forties are the most likely candidates for repeat plastic surgery. According to *Psychology Today* the typical 'plastic surgery junkie' is a woman who uses cosmetic surgery as an opportunity to 'indulge in unconscious wishes.'[26] *Newsweek* diagnoses the image problems 'scalpel slaves' have:

> Women in their 40s seem particularly vulnerable to the face-saving appeal of plastic surgery. Many scalpel slaves are older women who are recently divorced or widowed and forced to find jobs or date again. Others are suffering from the empty-nest syndrome. 'They're re-entry women,' says Dr. Susan Chobanian, a Beverly Hills cosmetic surgeon. 'They get insecure about their appearance and show up every six months to get nips and tucks. . . . Plastic-surgery junkies are in many ways akin to the anorexic or bulimic,' according to doctors. 'It's a body-image disorder,' says [one physician]. 'Junkies don't know what they really look like.' Some surgery junkies have a history of anorexia in the late teens, and now, in their late 30s and 40s, they're trying to alter their body image again.[27]

The naturalized identity of the female body as pathological and diseased is culturally reproduced in media discussions and representations of cosmetic surgery services. Moreover, the narrative obsessively recounted is that the female body is flawed in its distinctions and perfect when differences are transformed into sameness. But in the case of cosmetic surgery the nature of the 'sameness' is deceptive because the promise is not total identity reconstruction – such that a patient could choose to look like the media star of her choice – but rather the more elusive pledge of 'beauty enhancement.' When cosmetic surgeons argue that the technological elimination of facial 'deformities' will enhance a woman's 'natural' beauty, we encounter one of the more persistent contradictions within the discourse of cosmetic surgery: namely the use of technology to augment 'nature.'

[. . .]

Conclusion

Through the application of techniques of inscription, surveillance, and confession, cosmetic surgery serves as an ideological site for the examination of the technological reproduction of the gendered body. A primary effect of these techniques is to produce a gendered identity for the body at hand, techniques that work in different ways for male bodies than for female bodies. In its encounters with the cosmetic surgeon and the discourse of cosmetic surgery, the female body becomes an object of heightened personal surveillance; this scrutiny results in an internalized image of a fractured, fragmented body. The body becomes the vehicle of confession; it is the site at which women, consciously or not, accept the meanings that circulate in popular culture about ideal beauty and, in comparison, devalue the material body. The female body comes to serve, in other words, as a site of inscription, a billboard for the dominant cultural meanings that the female body is to have in postmodernity.

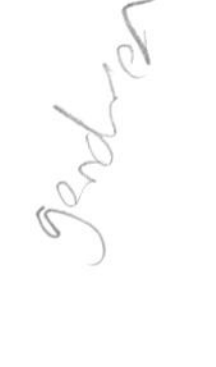

For some women, and for some feminist scholars, cosmetic surgery illustrates a technological colonization of women's bodies; for others, a technology women can use for their own ends. Certainly, as I have shown here, in spite of the promise cosmetic surgery offers women for the technological reconstruction of their bodies, such technologies in actual application produce bodies that are very traditionally gendered. Yet I am reluctant to accept as a simple and obvious conclusion that cosmetic surgery is simply one more site where women are passively victimized. Whether as a form of oppression or a resource of empowerment, it is clear to me that cosmetic surgery is a practice whereby women consciously act to make their bodies mean something to themselves and to others. A different way of looking at this technology might be to take seriously the notion I suggested earlier: to think of cosmetic surgery as 'fashion surgery.' Like women who get pierced-nose jewellery, tattoos, and hair sculptures, women who elect cosmetic surgery could be seen to be using their bodies as a vehicle for staging cultural identities. Even though I have argued that cosmetic surgeons demonstrate an unshakable belief in a Westernized notion of 'natural' beauty, and that the discourse of cosmetic surgery is implicated in reproducing such idealization and manipulation of 'the natural,' other domains of contemporary fashion cannot be so idealized. The anti-aesthetics of cyberpunk and slacker fashion, for example, suggest that feminists, too, might wish to abandon our romantic conceptions of the 'natural' body – conceptions that lead us to claim that a surgically refashioned face inevitably marks an oppressed subjectivity. As body piercing and other forms of prosthesis become more common – here I am thinking of Molly Million's implanted mirrorshades and Jael's naildaggers – we may need to adopt a perspective on the bodily performance of gender identity that is not so dogged by neoromantic wistfulness about the natural, unmarked body.

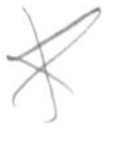

Notes

1 Judy Wajcman (1991) *Feminism Confronts Technology*, University Park: Pennsylvania State University Press, p. 149.
2 Judith Butler (1990) *Gender Trouble: Feminism and the Subversion of Identity*, London: Routledge.
3 Carole Spitzack (1988) 'The Confession Mirror: Plastic Images for Surgery', *Canadian Journal of Political and Social Theory*, 12 (1–2): 38–50.
4 Spitzack, p. 39.
5 Mary Ann Doane (1986) 'The Clinical Eye: Medical Discourses in the "Woman's Film" of the 1940s', in *The Female Body in Western Culture: Contemporary Perspectives*, Susan Suleiman (ed.), Cambridge, MA: Harvard University Press, pp. 152–74.
6 Stewart D. Fordham (1984) 'Art for Head and Neck Surgeons', in *Plastic and Reconstructive Surgery of the Head and Neck*, Paul H. Ward and Walter E. Berman (eds), Proceedings of the Fourth International Symposium of the American Academy of Facial Plastic and Reconstructive Surgery, *Volume 1: Aesthetic Surgery*, St Louis: C.V. Mosby Company, pp. 3–10, quotation is from p. 5.
7 Nelson Powell DDS, MD and Brian Humphreys MD (1984) *Proportions of the Aesthetic Face*, New York: Thieme-Stratton Inc.
8 Powell and Humphreys, p. 51.

9 Powell and Humphreys, p. 4.

10 Napoleon N. Vaughn (1982) 'Psychological Assessment for Patient Selection', *Cosmetic Plastic Surgery in Nonwhite Patients*, Harold E. Pierce MD (ed.), New York: Grune & Stratton, pp. 245–51.

11 Arthur Sumrall, 'An Overview of Dermatologic Rehabilitation: The Use of Corrective Cosmetics', in Pierce (ed.), pp. 141–54.

12 'Classic Schnozz is 80s nose', Jackie White, *Chicago Tribune*, 8 July 1988, section 2: 1, 3.

13 Ann Louise Bardach (1988) 'The Dark Side of Cosmetic Surgery: Long Term Risks are Becoming Increasingly Apparent', *The New York Times Magazine*, 17 April: 24–25, 51, 54–58.

14 Bradley Hall, Richard C. Webster and John M. Dobrowski, 'Blepharoplasty in the Oriental', in Ward and Berman (eds), pp. 210-25. Quotation is from p. 210.

15 Richard T. Farrior and Robert C. Jarchow, 'Surgical Principles in Face-Lift', in Ward and Berman (eds), pp. 297–311.

16 J.S. Zubiri (1981) 'Correction of the Oriental Eyelid', *Clinical Plastic Surgery* 8: 725.

17 Hall, Webster and Dobrowski, p. 210.

18 Marwali Harahap MD, 'Oriental Cosmetic Blepharoplasty', in Pierce (ed.), pp. 77–97. Quotation is from p. 78.

19 Michael M. Gurdin MD (1971) 'Cosmetic Problems of the Male', in *Cosmetic Surgery: What it Can Do for You*, Shirley Motter Linde MS (ed.), New York: Award Books, pp. 24–32.

20 Suzanne Dolezal (1988) 'More men are seeking their future in plastic – the surgical kind'. *Chicago Tribune*, 4 December, section 5: 13.

21 Diana Dull and Candace West (1991) 'Accounting for Cosmetic Surgery: The Accomplishment of Gender', *Social Problems* 38 (1), February: 54–70.

22 Dull and West: 67.

23 The quotation is from Blair O. Rogers MD, author of the chapter 'Management after Surgery in Facial and Eyelid Patients', in Linde (ed.), pp. 53–61.

24 Wendy Chapkis (1986) *Beauty Secrets: Women and the Politics of Appearance*, Boston, MA: South End Press, p. 14.

25 Carol Lynn Mithers (1987) 'The High Cost of Being a Woman', *Village Voice*, 24 March: 31.

26 Annette C. Hamburger (1988) 'Beauty Quest', *Psychology Today*, May: 28–32.

27 'Scalpel Slaves Just Can't Quit', *Newsweek*, 11 January 1988: 58–59.

(b) Virtual spaces

Chapter 20

Michel Foucault

OF OTHER SPACES[1]

THE GREAT OBSESSION of the nineteenth century was, as we know, history: with its themes of development and of suspension, of crisis and cycle, themes of the ever-accumulating past, with its great preponderance of dead men and the menacing glaciation of the world. The nineteenth century found its essential mythological resources in the second principle of thermodynamics. The present epoch will perhaps be above all the epoch of space. We are in the epoch of simultaneity: we are in the epoch of juxtaposition, the epoch of the near and far, of the side-by-side, of the dispersed. We are at a moment, I believe, when our experience of the world is less that of a long life developing through time than that of a network that connects points and intersects with its own skein. One could perhaps say that certain ideological conflicts animating present-day polemics oppose the pious descendants of time and the determined inhabitants of space. Structuralism, or at least that which is grouped under this slightly too general name, is the effort to establish, between elements that could have been connected on a temporal axis, an ensemble of relations that makes them appear as juxtaposed, set off against one another, implicated by each other – that makes them appear, in short, as a sort of configuration. Actually, structuralism does not entail a denial of time; it does involve a certain manner of dealing with what we call time and what we call history.

Yet it is necessary to notice that the space which today appears to form the horizon of our concerns, our theory, our systems, is not an innovation; space itself has a history in Western experience and it is not possible to disregard the fatal intersection of time with space. One could say, by way of retracing this history of space very roughly, that in the Middle Ages there was a hierarchic ensemble of places: sacred places and profane places; protected places and open, exposed places; urban places and rural places (all these concern the real life of men). In cosmological theory, there were the supercelestial places, as opposed to the celestial, and the celestial place was in its turn opposed to the terrestrial place. There were places where things had been put because they had been violently displaced, and then on the contrary places where things found their natural ground and stability. It was this complete hierarchy, this opposition, this intersection of places that constituted what could very roughly be called medieval space: the space of emplacement.

This space of emplacement was opened up by Galileo. For the real scandal of Galileo's work lay not so much in his discovery, or rediscovery, that the earth revolved around the sun, but in his constitution of an infinite, and infinitely open space. In such a space the place of the Middle Ages turned out to be dissolved, as it were; a thing's place was no longer anything but a point in its movement, just as the stability of a thing was only its movement indefinitely slowed down. In other words, starting with Galileo and the seventeenth century, extension was substituted for localization.

Today the site has been substituted for extension which itself had replaced emplacement. The site is defined by relations of proximity between points or elements; formally, we can describe these relations as series, trees, or grids. Moreover, the importance of the site as a problem in contemporary technical work is well known: the storage of data or of the intermediate results of a calculation in the memory of a machine; the circulation of discrete elements with a random output (automobile traffic is a simple case, or indeed the sounds on a telephone line); the identification of marked or coded elements inside a set that may be randomly distributed, or may be arranged according to single or to multiple classifications.

In a still more concrete manner, the problem of siting or placement arises for mankind in terms of demography. This problem of the human site or living space is not simply that of knowing whether there will be enough space for men in the world – a problem that is certainly quite important – but also that of knowing what relations of propinquity, what type of storage, circulation, marking, and classification of human elements should be adopted in a given situation in order to achieve a given end. Our epoch is one in which space takes for us the form of relations among sites.

In any case I believe that the anxiety of our era has to do fundamentally with space, no doubt a great deal more than with time. Time probably appears to us only as one of the various distributive operations that are possible for the elements that are spread out in space.

Now, despite all the techniques for appropriating space, despite the whole network of knowledge that enables us to delimit or to formalize it, contemporary space is perhaps still not entirely desanctified (apparently unlike time, it would seem, which was detached from the sacred in the nineteenth century). To be sure a certain theoretical desanctification of space (the one signaled by Galileo's work) has occurred, but we may still not have reached the point of a practical desanctification of space. And perhaps our life is still governed by a certain number of oppositions that remain inviolable, that our institutions and practices have not yet dared to break down. These are oppositions that we regard as simple givens: for example between private space and public space, between family space and social space, between cultural space and useful space, between the space of leisure and that of work. All these are still nurtured by the hidden presence of the sacred.

Bachelard's monumental work and the descriptions of phenomenologists have taught us that we do not live in a homogeneous and empty space, but on the contrary in a space thoroughly imbued with quantities and perhaps thoroughly fantasmatic as well. The space of our primary perception, the space of our dreams, and that of our passions hold within themselves qualities that seem intrinsic: there is a light, ethereal, transparent space, or again a dark, rough, encumbered space; a space from above, of summits, or on the contrary a space from below, of mud; or again a space that can be flowing like sparkling water, or a space that is fixed, congealed, like stone or crystal. Yet these analyses, while fundamental for reflection in our time, primarily concern internal space. I should like to speak now of external space.

The space in which we live, which draws us out of ourselves, in which the erosion of our lives, our time, and our history occurs, the space that claws and gnaws at us, is also, in itself, a heterogeneous space. In other words, we do not live in a kind of void, inside of which we could place individuals and things. We do not live inside a void that could be colored with diverse shades of light, we live inside a set of relations that delineates sites which are irreducible to one another and absolutely not superimposable on one another.

Of course one might attempt to describe these different sites by looking for the set of relations by which a given site can be defined. For example, describing the set of relations that define the sites of transportation, streets, trains (a train is an extraordinary bundle of relations because it is something through which one goes, it is also something by means of which one can go from one point to another, and then it is also something that goes by). One could describe, via the cluster of relations that allows them to be defined, the sites of temporary relaxation – cafes, cinemas, beaches. Likewise one could describe, via its network of relations, the closed or semi-closed sites of rest – the house, the bedroom, the bed, etc. But among all these sites, I am interested in certain ones that have the curious property of being in relation with all the other sites, but in such a way as to suspect, neutralize, or invert the set of relations that they happen to designate, mirror, or reflect. These spaces, as it were, which are linked with all the others, which however contradict all the other sites, are of two main types.

First there are the utopias. Utopias are sites with no real place. They are sites that have a general relation of direct or inverted analogy with the real space of society. They present society itself in a perfected form, or else society turned upside down, but in any case these utopias are fundamentally unreal spaces.

There are also, probably in every culture, in every civilization, real places – places that do exist and that are formed in the very founding of society – which are something like counter-sites, a kind of effectively enacted utopia in which the real sites, all the other real sites that can be found within the culture, are simultaneously represented, contested, and inverted. Places of this kind are outside of all places, even though it may be possible to indicate their location in reality. Because these places are absolutely different from all the sites that they reflect and speak about, I shall call them, by way of contrast to utopias, heterotopias. I believe that between utopias and these quite other sites, these heterotopias, there might be a sort of mixed, joint experience, which would be the mirror. The mirror is, after all, a utopia, since it is a placeless place. In the mirror, I see myself there where I am not, in an unreal, virtual space that opens up behind the surface; I am over there, there where I am not, a sort of shadow that gives my own visibility to myself, that enables me to see myself there where I am absent: such is the utopia of the mirror. But it is also a heterotopia in so far as the mirror does exist in reality, where it exerts a sort of counteraction on the position that I occupy. From the standpoint of the mirror, I discover my absence from the place where I am, since I see myself over there. Starting from this gaze that is, as it were, directed toward me, from the ground of this virtual space that is on the other side of the glass, I come back toward myself; I begin again to direct my eyes toward myself and to reconstitute myself there where I am. The mirror functions as a heterotopia in this respect: it makes this place that I occupy at the moment when I look at myself in the glass at once absolutely real, connected with all the space that surrounds it, and absolutely unreal, since in order to be perceived it has to pass through this virtual point which is over there.

As for the heterotopias as such, how can they be described, what meaning do they have? We might imagine a sort of systematic description – I do not say a science because the term is too galvanized now – that would, in a given society, take as its object the study, analysis, description, and 'reading' (as some like to say nowadays) of these different spaces, of these other places. As a sort of simultaneously mythic and real contestation of the space in which we live, this description could be called heterotopology. Its *first principle* is that there is probably not a single culture in the world that fails to constitute heterotopias. That is a constant of every human group. But the heterotopias obviously take quite varied forms, and perhaps no one absolutely universal form of heterotopia would be found. We can however classify them in two main categories.

In the so-called primitive societies, there is a certain form of heterotopia that I would call crisis heterotopias, i.e., there are privileged or sacred or forbidden places, reserved for individuals who are, in relation to society and to the human environment in which they live, in a state of crisis: adolescents, menstruating women, pregnant women, the elderly, etc. In our society, these crisis heterotopias are persistently disappearing, though a few remnants can still be found. For example, the boarding school, in its nineteenth-century form, or military service for young men, have certainly played such a role, as the first manifestations of sexual virility were in fact supposed to take place 'elsewhere' than at home. For girls, there was, until the middle of the twentieth century, a tradition called the 'honeymoon trip' which was an ancestral theme. The young woman's deflowering could take place 'nowhere' and, at the moment of its occurrence the train or honeymoon hotel was indeed the place of this nowhere, this heterotopia without geographical markers.

But these heterotopias of crisis are disappearing today and are being replaced, I believe, by what we might call heterotopias of deviation: those in which individuals whose behaviour is deviant in relation to the required mean or norm are placed. Cases of this are rest homes and psychiatric hospitals, and of course prisons; and one should perhaps add retirement homes that are, as it were, on the borderline between the heterotopia of crisis and the heterotopia of deviation since, after all, old age is a crisis, but is also a deviation since, in our society where leisure is the rule, idleness is a sort of deviation.

The *second principle* of this description of heterotopias is that a society, as its history unfolds, can make an existing heterotopia function in a very different fashion; for each heterotopia has a precise and determined function within a society and the same heterotopia can, according to the synchrony of the culture in which it occurs, have one function or another.

As an example I shall take the strange heterotopia of the cemetery. The cemetery is certainly a place unlike ordinary cultural spaces. It is a space that is however connected with all the sites of the city-state or society or village, etc., since each individual, each family has relatives in the cemetery. In Western culture the cemetery has practically always existed. But it has undergone important changes. Until the end of the eighteenth century, the cemetery was placed at the heart of the city, next to the church. In it there was a hierarchy of possible tombs. There was the charnel house in which bodies lost the last traces of individuality, there were a few individual tombs, and then there were the tombs inside the church. These latter tombs were themselves of two types, either simply tombstones with an inscription, or mausoleums with statues. This cemetery housed inside the sacred space of the church has taken on a quite different cast in modern civilizations, and curiously, it is in a time when civilization has become 'atheistic' as one says very crudely, that Western culture has established what is termed the cult of the dead.

Basically it was quite natural that, in a time of real belief in the resurrection of bodies and the immortality of the soul, overriding importance was not accorded to the body's remains. On the contrary, from the moment when people are no longer sure that they have a soul or that the body will regain life, it is perhaps necessary to give much more attention to the dead body, which is ultimately the only trace of our existence in the world and in language. In any case, it is from the beginning of the nineteenth century that everyone has a right to her or his own little box for her or his own little personal decay; but on the other hand, it is only from the start of the nineteenth century that cemeteries began to be located at the outside border of cities. In correlation with the individualization of death and the bourgeois appropriation of the cemetery, there arises an obsession with death as an 'illness'. The dead, it is supposed, bring illnesses to the living, and it is the presence and proximity of the dead right beside the houses, next to the church, almost in the middle of the street, it is this proximity that propagates death itself. This major theme of illness spread by the contagion in the cemeteries persisted until the end of the eighteenth century, until, during the nineteenth century, the shift of cemeteries toward the suburbs was initiated. The cemeteries then came to constitute, no longer the sacred and immortal heart of the city, but 'the other city,' where each family possesses its dark resting place.

Third principle. The heterotopia is capable of juxtaposing in a single real place several spaces, several sites that are in themselves incompatible. Thus it is that the theater brings onto the rectangle of the stage, one after the other, a whole series of places that are foreign to one another; thus it is that the cinema is a very odd rectangular room, at the end of which, on a two-dimensional screen, one sees the projection of a three-dimensional space; but perhaps the oldest example of these heterotopias that take the form of contradictory sites is the garden. We must not forget that in the Orient the garden, an astonishing creation that is now a thousand years old, had very deep and seemingly superimposed meanings. The traditional garden of the Persians was a sacred space that was supposed to bring together inside its rectangle four parts representing the four parts of the world, with a space still more sacred than the others that were like an umbilicus, the navel of the world at its center (the basin and water fountain were there); and all the vegetation of the garden was supposed to come together in this space, in this sort of microcosm. As for carpets, they were originally reproductions of gardens (the garden is a rug onto which the whole world comes to enact its symbolic perfection, and the rug is a sort of garden that can move across space). The garden is the smallest parcel of the world and then it is the totality of the world. The garden has been a sort of happy, universalizing heterotopia since the beginnings of antiquity (our modern zoological gardens spring from that source).

Fourth principle. Heterotopias are most often linked to slices in time – which is to say that they open onto what might be termed, for the sake of symmetry, heterochronies. The heterotopia begins to function at full capacity when men arrive at a sort of absolute break with their traditional time. This situation shows us that the cemetery is indeed a highly heterotopic place since, for the individual, the cemetery begins with this strange heterochrony, the loss of life, and with this quasi-eternity in which her permanent lot is dissolution and disappearance.

From a general standpoint, in a society like ours heterotopias and heterochronies are structured and distributed in a relatively complex fashion. First of all, there are heterotopias of indefinitely accumulating time, for example museums and libraries. Museums and libraries have become heterotopias in which time never stops building up and topping its own summit, whereas in the seventeenth century, even at the end of the century, museums and libraries were the expression of an individual choice. By contrast, the idea of accumulating everything, of establishing a sort of general archive, the will to enclose in one place all times, all epochs, all forms, all tastes, the idea of constituting a place of all times that is itself outside of time and inaccessible to its ravages, the project of organizing in this way a sort of perpetual and indefinite accumulation of time in an immobile place, this whole idea belongs to our modernity. The museum and the library are heterotopias that are proper to Western culture of the nineteenth century.

Opposite these heterotopias that are linked to the accumulation of time, there are those linked, on the contrary, to time in its most fleeting, transitory, precarious aspect, to time in the mode of the festival. These heterotopias are not oriented toward the eternal, they are rather absolutely temporal [*chroniques*]. Such, for example, are the fairgrounds, these marvelous empty sites on the outskirts of cities that teem once or twice a year with stands, displays, heteroclite objects, wrestlers, snakewomen, fortune-tellers, and so forth. Quite recently, a new kind of temporal heterotopia has been invented: vacation villages, such as those Polynesian villages that offer a compact three weeks of primitive and eternal nudity to the inhabitants of the cities. You see, moreover, that through the two forms of heterotopias that come together here, the heterotopia of the festival and that of the eternity of accumulating time, the huts of Djerba are in a sense relatives of libraries and museums. For the rediscovery of Polynesian life abolishes time; yet the experience is just as much the rediscovery of time, it is as if the entire history of humanity reaching back to its origin were accessible in a sort of immediate knowledge.

Fifth principle. Heterotopias always presuppose a system of opening and closing that both isolates them and makes them penetrable. In general, the heterotopic site is not freely accessible like a public place. Either the entry is compulsory, as in the case of entering a barracks or a prison, or else the individual has to submit to rites and purifications. To get in one must have a certain permission and make certain gestures. Moreover, there are even heterotopias that are entirely consecrated to these activities of purification – purification that is partly religious and partly hygienic, such as the hammam of the Moslems, or else purification that appears to be purely hygienic, as is Scandinavian saunas.

There are others, on the contrary, that seem to be pure and simple openings, but that generally hide curious exclusions. Everyone can enter into these heterotopic sites, but in fact that is only an illusion: we think we enter where we are, by the very fact that we enter, excluded. I am thinking, for example, of the famous bedrooms that existed on the great farms of Brazil and elsewhere in South America. The entry door did not lead into the central room where the family lives, and every individual or traveler who came by had the right to open this door, to enter into the bedroom and to sleep there for a night. Now these bedrooms were such that the individual who went into them never had access to the family's quarters; the visitor was absolutely the guest in transit, was not really the invited guest. This type of heterotopia, which has practically disappeared from our civilizations, could perhaps be found in the famous American motel rooms where a man goes with his car and his mistress and where illicit sex is both absolutely sheltered and absolutely hidden, kept isolated without however being allowed out in the open.

The last trait of heterotopias is that they have a function in relation to all the space that remains. This function unfolds between two extreme poles. Either their role is to create a space of illusion that exposes every real space, all the sites inside of which human life is partitioned, as still more illusory (perhaps that is the role that was played by those famous brothels of which we are now deprived). Or else, on the contrary, their role is to create a space that is other, another real space, as perfect, as meticulous, as well arranged as ours is messy, ill constructed, and jumbled. This latter type would be the heterotopia, not of illusion, but of compensation, and I wonder if certain colonies have not functioned somewhat in this manner. In certain cases, they have played, on the level of the general organization of terrestrial space, the role of heterotopias. I am thinking, for example, of the first wave of colonization in the seventeenth century, of the Puritan societies that the English had founded in America and that were absolutely perfect other places. I am also thinking of those extraordinary Jesuit colonies that were founded in South America: marvelous, absolutely regulated colonies in which human perfection was effectively achieved. The Jesuits of Paraguay established colonies in which existence was regulated at every turn. The village was laid out according to a rigorous plan around a rectangular place at the foot of which was the church; on one side, there was the school; on the other, the cemetery; and then, in front of the church, an avenue set out that another crossed at right angles; each family had its little cabin along these two axes and thus the sign of Christ was exactly reproduced. Christianity marked the space and geography of the American world with its fundamental sign. The daily life of individuals was regulated, not by the whistle, but by the bell. Everyone was awakened at the same time, everyone began work at the same time; meals were at noon and five o'clock; then came bedtime, and at midnight came what was called the marital wake-up, that is, at the chime of the churchbell, each person carried out her/his duty.

Brothels and colonies are two extreme types of heterotopia, and if we think, after all, that the boat is a floating piece of space, a place without a place, that exists by itself, that is closed in on itself and at the same time is given over to the infinity of the sea and that, from port to port, from tack to tack, from brothel to brothel, it goes as far as the colonies in search of the most precious treasures they conceal in their gardens, you will understand why the boat has not only been for our civilization, from the sixteenth century until the present, the great instrument of economic development . . . but has been simultaneously the greatest reserve of the imagination. The ship is the heterotopia *par excellence*. In civilizations without boats, dreams dry up, espionage takes the place of adventure, and the police take the place of pirates.

Notes

1 This text, entitled 'Des Espaces Autres,' and published by the French journal *Architecture-Mouvement-Continuité* in October 1984, was the basis of a lecture given by Michel Foucault in March 1967. Although not reviewed for publication by the author and thus not part of the official corpus of his work, the manuscript was released into the public domain for an exhibition in Berlin shortly before Michel Foucault's death. Attentive readers will note that the text retains the quality of lecture notes. It was translated by Jay Miskowiec.

Chapter 21

Jonathan Crary

THE CAMERA OBSCURA AND ITS SUBJECT

[B]EGINNING IN THE LATE 1500s the figure of the camera obscura beings to assume a pre-eminent importance in delimiting and defining the relations between observer and world. Within several decades the camera obscura is no longer one of the many instruments or visual options but instead the compulsory site from which vision can be conceived or represented. Above all it indicates the appearance of a new model of subjectivity, the hegemony of a new subject-effect. First of all the camera obscura performs an operation of individuation; that is, it necessarily defines an observer as isolated, enclosed, and autonomous within its dark confines. It impels a kind of *askesis*, or withdrawal from the world, in order to regulate and purify one's relation to the manifold contents of the now 'exterior' world. Thus the camera obscura is inseparable from a certain metaphysic of interiority: it is a figure for both the observer who is nominally a free sovereign individual and a privatized subject confined in a quasi-domestic space, cut off from a public exterior world.[1] (Jacques Lacan has noted that Bishop Berkeley and others wrote about visual representations as if they were private property.[2]) At the same time, another related and equally decisive function of the camera was to sunder the act of seeing from the physical body of the observer, to decorporealize vision. The monadic viewpoint of the individual is authenticated and legitimized by the camera obscura, but the observer's physical and sensory experience is supplanted by the relations between a mechanical apparatus and a pre-given world of objective truth. Nietzsche summarizes this kind of thought:

> The senses deceive, reason corrects the errors; consequently, one concluded, reason is the road to the constant; the least sensual ideas must be closest to the 'true world.' – It is from the senses that most misfortunes come – they are deceivers, deluders, destroyers.[3]

Among the well-known texts in which we find the image of the camera obscura and of its interiorized and disembodied subject are Newton's *Opticks* (1704) and Locke's *Essay on Human Understanding* (1690). What they jointly demonstrate is how the camera obscura was a model simultaneously for the observation of empirical phenomena *and* for reflective introspection and self-observation. The site of Newton's inductive procedures throughout his text is the camera obscura; it is the ground on which his knowledge is made possible. Near the beginning of the *Opticks* he recounts:

> In a very dark Chamber, at a round hole, about one third Part of an Inch, broad, made in the shut of a window, I placed a glass prism, whereby the Beam of the Sun's Light, which came in at that Hole, might be refracted upwards toward the opposite wall of the chamber, and there form a coloured image of the Sun.[4]

The physical activity that Newton describes with the first-person pronoun refers not to the operation of his own vision but rather to his deployment of a transparent, refractive means of representation. Newton is less the observer than he is the organizer, the stager of an apparatus from whose actual functioning he is physically distinct. Although the apparatus in question is not strictly a camera obscura (a prism is substituted for a plane lens or pinhole), its structure is fundamentally the same: the representation of an exterior phenomenon occurs within the rectilinear confines of a darkened room, a chamber, or, in Locke's words, an 'empty cabinet.'[5] The two-dimensional plane on which the image of an exterior presents itself subsists only in its specific relation of distance to an aperture in the wall opposite it. But between these two locations (a point and a plane) is an indeterminate extensive space in which an observer is ambiguously situated. Unlike a perspectival construction, which also presumed to represent an objectively ordered representation, the camera obscura did not dictate a restricted site or area from which the image presents its full coherence and consistency.[6] On one hand the observer is disjunct from the pure operation of the device and is there as a disembodied witness to a mechanical and transcendental re-presentation of the objectivity of the world. On the other hand, however, his or her presence in the camera implies a spatial and temporal simultaneity of human subjectivity and objective apparatus. Thus the spectator is a more free-flowing inhabitant of the darkness, a marginal supplementary presence independent of the machinery of representation. As Foucault demonstrated in his analysis of Velasquez's *Las Meninas*, it is a question of a subject incapable of self-representation as both subject and object.[7] The camera obscura *a priori* prevents the observer from seeing his or her position as part of the representation. The body then is a problem the camera could never solve except by marginalizing it into a phantom in order to establish a space of reason.[8] In a sense, the camera obscura is a precarious figurative resolution of what Edmund Husserl defined as the major philosophical problem of the seventeenth century: 'How a philosophizing which seeks its ultimate foundations in the subjective . . . can claim an objectively "true" and metaphysically transcendent validity.'[9]

Perhaps the most famous image of the camera obscura is in Locke's *Essay Concerning Human Understanding* (1690):

> External and internal sensations are the only passages that I can find of knowledge to the understanding. These alone, as far as I can discover, are the windows by which light is let into this *dark room*. For, methinks, the understanding is not much unlike a closet wholly shut from light, with only some little opening left . . . to let in external visible resemblances, or some idea of things without; would the pictures coming into such a dark room but stay there and lie so orderly as to be found upon occasion it would very much resemble the understanding of a man.[10]

An important feature of Locke's text here is how the metaphor of the dark room effectively distances us from the apparatus he describes. As part of his general project of introspection, Locke proposes a means of visualizing spatially the operations of the intellect. He makes explicit what was implied in Newton's account of his activity in his dark chamber: the eye of the observer is completely separate from the apparatus that allows the entrance and formation of 'pictures' or 'resemblances.' Hume also insisted on a similar relation of distance. 'The operations of the mind . . . must be apprehended in an instant by a *superior* penetration, derived from nature and improved by habit and reflection.'[11]

Elsewhere in Locke's text another meaning is given to the idea of the room, of what it literally meant in seventeenth-century England to be *in camera*, that is, within the chambers of a judge or person of title. Locke writes that sensations are conveyed 'from without to their audience in the brain – the mind's presence room, as I may so call it.'[12] In addition to structuring the act of observation as the process by which something is observed by a subject, Locke also gives a new juridical role to the observer within the camera obscura. Thus he modifies the receptive and neutral function of the apparatus by specifying a more self-legislative and authoritative function: the camera obscura allows the subject to guarantee and police the correspondence between exterior world and interior representation and to exclude anything disorderly or unruly. Reflective introspection overlaps with a regime of self-discipline.

It is in this context that Richard Rorty asserts that Locke and Descartes describe an observer fundamentally different from anything in Greek and medieval thought. For Rorty, the achievement of these two thinkers was

> the conception of the human mind as an inner space in which both pains and clear and distinct ideas passed in review before an Inner Eye. . . . The novelty was the notion of a single inner space in which bodily and perceptual sensations . . . were objects of quasi-observation.[13]

In this sense Locke can be linked with Descartes. In the *Second Meditation*, Descartes asserts that 'perception, or the action by which we perceive, is not a vision . . . but is solely an inspection by the mind.'[14] He goes on to challenge the notion that one knows the world by means of eyesight: 'It is possible that I do not even have eyes with which to see anything.'[15] For Descartes, one knows the world 'uniquely by perception of the mind,' and the secure positioning of the self within an empty interior space is a precondition for knowing the outer world. The space of the camera obscura, its enclosedness, its darkness, its separation from an exterior, incarnate Descartes' 'I will now shut my eyes, I shall stop my ears, I shall disregard my senses.'[16] The orderly and calculable penetration of light rays through the single opening of the camera corresponds to the flooding of the mind by the light of reason, not the potentially dangerous dazzlement of the senses by the light of the sun.

There are two paintings by Vermeer in which the paradigm of the Cartesian camera obscura is lucidly represented.[17] Consider *The Geographer* and *The Astronomer*, both painted around 1668. Each image depicts a solitary male figure absorbed in learned pursuits within the rectangular confines of a shadowy interior, an interior punctured apparently by only a single window. The astronomer studies a celestial globe, mapped out with the constellations; the geographer has before him a nautical map. Each has his eyes averted from the aperture that opens onto the outside. The exterior world is known not by direct sensory examination but through a mental survey of its 'clear and distinct' representation within the room. The somber isolation of these meditative scholars within their walled interiors is not in the least an obstacle to apprehending the world outside, for the division between interiorized subject and exterior world is a pre-given condition of knowledge about the latter. The paintings then are a consummate demonstration of the reconciling function of the camera obscura: its interior is the interface between Descartes' absolutely dissimilar *res cogitans* and *res extensa*, between observer and world.[18] The camera, or room, is the site within which an orderly projection of the world, of extended substance, is made available for inspection by the mind. The production of the camera is always a projection onto a two-dimensional surface – here maps, globes, charts, and images. Each of the thinkers, in a rapt stillness, ponders that crucial feature of the world, its extension, so mysteriously unlike the unextended immediacy of their own thoughts yet rendered intelligible to mind by the clarity of these representations, by their magnitudinal relations. Rather than opposed by the objects of their study, the earth and the heavens, the geographer and the astronomer engage in a common enterprise of observing aspects of a single indivisible exterior.[19] Both of them (and it may well be the same man in each painting) are figures for a primal and sovereign inwardness, for the autonomous individual ego that has appropriated to itself the capacity for intellectually mastering the infinite existence of bodies in space.

Descartes' description of the camera obscura in his *La dioptrique* (1637) contains some unusual features. Initially he makes a conventional analogy between the eye and the camera obscura:

> Suppose a chamber is shut up apart from a single hole, and a glass lens is placed in front of this hole with a white sheet stretched at a certain distance behind it so the light coming from objects outside forms images on the sheet. Now it is said that the room represents the eye; the hole the pupil; the lens the crystalline humour.[20]

But before proceeding further, Descartes advises his reader to conduct a demonstration involving 'taking the dead eye of a newly dead person (or, failing that, the eye of an ox or some other large animal)' and using the extracted eye as the lens in the pinhole of a camera obscura. Thus for Descartes the images observed within the camera obscura are formed by means of a disembodied cyclopean eye, detached from the observer, possibly not even a human eye. Additionally, Descartes specifies that one

> cut away the three surrounding membranes at the back so as to expose a large part of the humour without spilling any. . . . No light must enter this room except what comes through this eye, all of whose parts you know to be entirely transparent. Having done this, if you look at the white sheet you will see there, not perhaps without pleasure and wonder, a picture representing in natural perspective all the objects outside.[21]

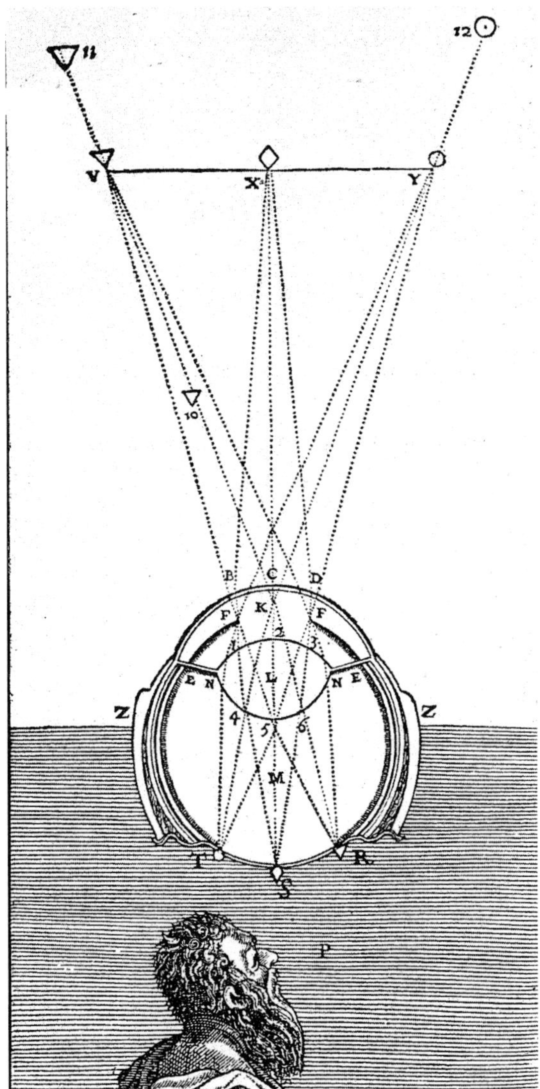

Figure 21.1 Diagram of the eye
(From René Descartes, *Discours de la Méthode*, 1637)

By this radical disjunction of eye from observer and its installation in this formal apparatus of objective representation, the dead, perhaps even bovine eye undergoes a kind of apotheosis and rises to an incorporeal status.[22] If at the core of Descartes' method was the need to escape the uncertainties of mere human vision and the confusions of the senses, the camera obscura is congruent with his quest to found human knowledge on a purely objective view of the world. The aperture of the camera obscura corresponds to a single, mathematically definable point, from which the world can be logically deduced by a progressive accumulation and combination of signs. It is a device embodying man's position between God and the world. Founded on laws of nature (optics) but extrapolated to a plane outside of nature, the camera obscura provides a vantage point onto the world analogous to the eye of God.[23] It is an infallible metaphysical eye more than it is a 'mechanical' eye.[24] Sensory evidence was rejected in favor of the representations of the monocular apparatus, whose authenticity was beyond doubt.[25] Binocular disparity is bound up in the physiological operation of human vision, and a monocular device precludes having to reconcile theoretically the dissimilar, and thus provisional, images presented to each eye. Descartes assumed that the pineal gland exercised a crucial monocular power:

> There must necessarily be some place where the two images coming through the eyes . . . can come together in a single image or impression before reaching the soul, so that they do not present to it two objects instead of one.[26]

At the same time, Descartes' instructions about removing the ocular membranes from the body of the eye is an operation ensuring the primal transparency of the camera obscura, of escaping from the latent opacity of the human eye.

Notes

1 Georg Lukács describes this type of artificially isolated individual in *History and Class Consciousness*, pp. 135–38. See also the excellent discussion of inwardness and sexual privatization in the seventeenth century in Francis Barker, *The Tremulous Private Body: Essays on Subjection* (London, 1984), pp. 9–69.

2 Jacques Lacan, *The Four Fundamental Concepts of Psycho-Analysis*, trans. Alan Sheridan (New York, 1978), p. 81.

3 Friedrich Nietzsche, *The Will to Power*, p. 317.

4 Sir Isaac Newton, *Opticks, or a Treatise of the Reflections, Refractions, Inflections and Colours of Light*, 4th edn (1730; rpt. New York, 1952), p. 26.

5 John Locke, *An Essay Concerning Human Understanding*, ed. Alexander Campbell Fraser (New York, 1959), I, ii, 15. On some of the epistemological implications of Newton's work, see Stephen Toulmin, 'The Inwardness of Mental Life,' *Critical Inquiry* (Autumn 1979), pp. 1–16.

6 Hubert Damisch has stressed that late quattrocento perspectival constructions allowed a viewer a limited field of mobility from within which the consistency of the painting was maintained, rather than from the immobility of a fixed and

single point. See his *L'origine de la perspective* (Paris, 1988). See also Jacques Aumont, 'Le point de vue,' *Communications* 38, 1983, pp. 3–29.

7 Foucault, *The Order of Things*, pp. 3–16. See also Hubert Dreyfus and Paul Rabinow, *Michel Foucault: Beyond Structuralism and Hermeneutics* (Chicago, 1982), p. 25.

8 On Galileo, Descartes, and 'the occultation of the enunciating subject in discursive activity,' see Timothy J. Reiss, *The Discourse of Modernism* (Ithaca, 1982), pp. 38–43.

9 Edmund Husserl, *The Crisis of European Science and Transcendental Phenomenology*, trans. David Carr (Evanston, Ill., 1970), p. 81.

10 Locke, *An Essay Concerning Human Understanding*, II, xi, 17.

11 David Hume, *An Inquiry Concerning Human Understanding* (1748; New York, 1955), p. 16 (emphasis mine). A similar setup is noted in Descartes by Maurice Merleau-Ponty, where space is a 'network of relations between objects such as would be seen by a witness to my vision or by a geometer looking over it and reconstructing it from the outside.' 'Eye and Mind,' *The Primacy of Perception*, ed. James M. Edie (Evanston, Ill., 1964), p. 178. Jacques Lacan discusses Cartesian thought in terms of the formula 'I see myself seeing myself,' in *Four Fundamental Concepts of Psycho-Analysis*, pp. 80–81.

12 Locke, *An Essay Concerning Human Understanding*, II, iii, 1.

13 Richard Rorty, *Philosophy and the Mirror of Nature* (Princeton, 1979), pp. 49–50. For an opposing view, see John W. Yolton, *Perceptual Acquaintance from Descartes to Reid* (Minneapolis, 1984), pp. 222–23.

14 René Descartes, *The Philosophical Writings of Descartes*, 2 vols., trans. John Cottingham, Robert Stoothoff, and Dugald Murdoch (Cambridge, 1984), vol. 2, p. 21.

15 Descartes, *Philosophical Writings*, vol. 2, p. 21.

16 Descartes, *Philosophical Writings*, vol. 2, p. 24.

17 My discussion of Vermeer clearly does not engage any of the extensive art historical speculation about his possible use of the camera obscura in the making of his pictures . . . Did he in fact use one, and if so, how did it affect the makeup of his paintings? While these are interesting questions for specialists, I am not concerned here with the answers one way or the other. Such investigations tend to reduce the problem of the camera obscura to one of optical effects and ultimately painterly style. I contend that the camera obscura must be understood in terms of how it defined the position and possibilities of an observing subject; it was *not* simply a pictorial or stylistic option, one choice among others for a neutral and ahistorical subject. Even if Vermeer never touched the mechanical apparatus of the camera obscura and other factors explain his halation of highlights and accentuated perspective, his paintings are nonetheless profoundly embedded in the larger epistemological model of the camera.

18 The affinity between Vermeer and Cartesian thought is discussed in Michel Serres, *La Traduction* (Paris, 1974), pp. 189–96.

19 Descartes rejected the scholastic distinction between a sublunary or terrestrial world and a qualitatively different celestial realm in his *Principles of Philosophy*, first published in Holland in 1644. 'Similarly, the earth and the heavens are composed of one and the same matter; and there cannot be a plurality of worlds.' *The Philosophical Writings of Descartes*, vol. 1, p. 232. Cf. Arthur K. Wheelock, *Vermeer* (New York, 1988), Abrams, p. 108.

20 Descartes, *The Philosophical Writings of Descartes*, vol. 1, p. 166; *Oeuvres philosophiques*, vol. 1, pp. 686–87.

21 Descartes, *The Philosophical Writings*, vol. 1, p. 166.

22 See the chapter 'L'oeil de boeuf: Descartes et l'après-coup idéologique,' in Sarah Kofman, *Camera obscura de l'idéologie*, pp. 71–76.

23 Classical science privileges a description as objective 'to the extent that the observer is excluded and the description is made from a point lying de jure outside the world, that is, from the divine viewpoint to which the human soul, created as it was in God's image, had access at the beginning. Thus classical science still aims at discovering the unique truth about the world, the one language that will decipher the world of nature.' Ilya Prigogine and Isabelle Stengers, *Order out of Chaos: Man's New Dialogue with Nature* (New York, 1984), p. 52.

24 On Descartes' fear of the distorting power of perspective, see Karsten Harries, 'Descartes, Perspective and the Angelic Eye,' *Yale French Studies* 49 (1973), pp. 28–42. See also Paul Ricoeur, 'The Question of the Subject: The Challenge of Semiology,' in his *The Conflict of Interpretations*, trans. Don Ihde (Evanston, Ill., 1974), pp. 236–66. Cartesian thought, for Ricoeur, 'is contemporaneous with a vision of the world in which the whole of objectivity is spread out like a spectacle on which the *cogito* casts its sovereign gaze' (p. 236).

25 The theological dimension of monocularity is suggested in Daniel Defoe, *The Consolidator: or, Memoirs of sundry transactions from the world in the moon* (London, 1705), p. 57: 'A generation have risen up, who to solve the difficulties of super-natural systems, imagine a mighty vast something who has no form but what represents him to them as one Great Eye. This infinite Optik they imagine to be Natura Naturans . . . the soul of man therefore, in the opinion of these naturalists, is one vast Optik Power . . . From hence they resolve all Beings to Eyes.'

26 *The Philosophical Writings of Descartes*, vol. 1, p. 340.

Chapter 22

Anne Friedberg

THE MOBILIZED AND VIRTUAL GAZE IN MODERNITY

Flâneur/Flâneuse

The second half of the nineteenth century lives in a sort of *frenzy of the visible*. It is, of course, the effect of the *social multiplication of images:* ever wider distribution of illustrated papers, waves of print, caricatures, etc. The effect also, however, of something of a geographical extension of the *field of the visible* and the representable: by journies, explorations, colonizations, the whole world becomes visible at the same time that it become appropriatable.

(Jean-Louis Comolli, 'Machines of the Visible' (emphasis added))

In societies where modern conditions of production prevail, all of life presents itself as *an immense accumulation of spectacles. Everything that was directly lived has moved away into a representation.*

(Guy Debord, *Society of the Spectacle* (emphasis added))

[I]N THE NINETEENTH century, a wide variety of apparatuses extended the 'field of the visible' and turned visualized experience into commodity forms. As print was disseminated widely, new forms of newspaper illustration emerged; as lithography was introduced, the caricatures of Daumier, Grandville, and others burgeoned; as photography became more widespread, the evidentiary means of public and family record were transformed. The telegraph, the telephone, and electricity increased the speed of communications, the railroad and steamship changed concepts of distance, while the new visual culture – photography, advertising, and shop display – recast the nature of memory and experience. Whether a 'frenzy of the visible,' or 'an immense accumulation of spectacles,' everyday life was transfigured by the 'social multiplication of images.'

Yet there remains a historiographical debate about whether this new predominance of the visible produced a crisis of confidence in the eye itself, or whether it was the coincident increase in optical research which produced this frenzy of visual cultures. The same historiographic debate pervades the history of the arts; either the invention of photography produced a crisis that led to continued optical research, or the nineteenth-century obsession with optical research produced a crisis that led to photography. In order to organize the vast historical process that led to the emergence of the cinema it is necessary to enter into this debate, a dispute that festers at the roots of modernity.

In this chapter, I begin by describing the 'observer' in modernity, situating the emergence of the cinema in the historical framework of precinematic mobile and virtual gazes. Such a 'situated' approach to the cinematic apparatus necessitates an account of the imbrication of images in the social relations of looking. The flâneur will serve as a model for an observer who follows a style of visuality different from the model of power and vision so frequently linked with modernity – what Michel Foucault dramatically described as 'un régime panoptique.'[1] The trope of flânerie delineates a mode of visual practice coincident with – but antithetical to – the panoptic gaze. Like the panopticon system, flânerie relied on the visual register – but with a converse instrumentalism, emphasizing mobility and fluid subjectivity rather than restraint and interpellated reform.

The panoptic gaze has been invoked by feminist theorists to underline the one-way power of gendered looking, where women have internalized the voyeuristic gaze and are always subjectively 'objects of the look.'[2] As we examine divergent models of the observer in modernity, a refutation of theories of the panoptic gaze will have significant ramifications on accounts of gendered spectatorship. The panoptic gaze may indeed suggest a model for the increased priority of the visual register, but there were alternative gazes that, while still reordering the importance of the visual, produced different – more fluid – forms of subjectivity.

Gender, to follow Teresa de Lauretis's recent formulation, 'is the product of various social technologies' that include '*cinema* . . . institutionalized discourses, epistemologies, and critical practices, *as well as practices of daily life*' (emphasis added).[3] And although gender seems a necessary component of debates about the role of vision in modernity and postmodernity, genealogies of the nineteenth-century observer have, as we shall see, retained a resistance to the gendered subject. Once we establish the flâneur's mobility, we will see the necessity of charting the origins of his female equivalent, the flâneuse.

Modernity and the 'panoptic' gaze

It is in this *episteme*, as Foucault would have it, that new modes of social and political control were institutionalized by 'un régime panoptique.' Foucault places the panoptic model in a pivotal position in the epistemological shift from eighteenth-century empiricism to the invention of a transcendental concept of 'man.' In a dramatic passage in *The Order of Things*, he describes this transition as 'the threshold of modernity.' Foucault finds the origins of modernity in the reordering of power and knowledge and the visible.[4]

The panopticon

Jeremy Bentham's panopticon device (1791) provided the model for Foucault's characterization of panoptic power and the 'disciplines' of imagined scrutiny.[5] (*Discipline* has been the common English translation for Foucault's term, *surveiller.*) Invoked as a philosophic model for the scopic regime of power through the visual register, the panopticon was an apparatus – a 'machine of the visible,' to use Comolli's phrase – which controlled the seer–seen relation. In the panopticon, an *unseen seer* surveys a confined and controlled subject. The panopticon produces a subjective effect, a 'brutal dissymmetry of visibility'[6] for both positions in this dyad: the *seer* with the sense of omnipotent voyeurism and the *seen* with the sense of disciplined surveillance.

Foucault described the panopticon as an 'architectural mechanism,'[7] a 'pure architectural and optical system' that did not need to use force because the 'real subjection is born *mechanically* from a *fictitious relation*.'[8] The panopticon structure was then, in a sense, a 'building-machine' that, through its spatial arrangement, established scopic control over its inhabitants.

The architectural system of the panopticon restructured the relation of jailer to inmate into a scopic relation of power and domination. The panopticon building was a twelve-sided polygon. Using iron as a skeleton, its internal and external skin was glass. The central tower was pierced by windows that provided a panoramic

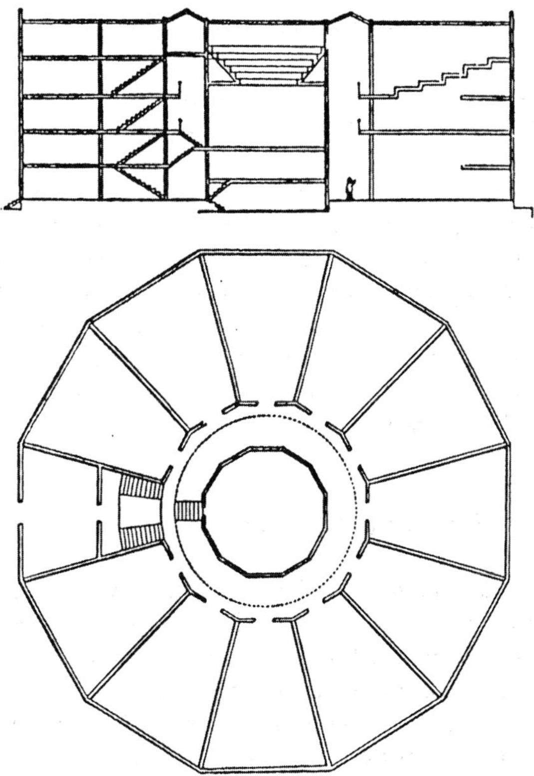

Figure 22.1 Jeremy Bentham, section and plan of Panopticon Building, 1791

view of separate peripheral cells. Light from the outer walls illuminated each cell. The panoptic subject was placed in a state of 'conscious and permanent visibility.'[9] The panopticon prison was thought of as a spatial reformatorium that could change and 'correct' subjectivity by architectural means. As Foucault describes it:

> The *seeing machine* was once a sort of dark room into which individuals spied; it has become a transparent building in which the exercise of power may be supervised by society as a whole.[10]

Prisoners were objects of an *imagined* scrutiny, where the internalized sense of surveillance changed the disposition of external power:

> He who is subjected to a field of visibility, and who knows it, assumes responsibility for the constraints of power . . . he becomes the principle of his own subjection. By this very fact, the external power may throw off its physical weight; *it tends to the non-corporeal;* and, the more it approaches this limit, the more constant, profound and permanent are its effects.[11]
>
> (emphasis added)

Foucault uses the panoptic model to illustrate how, when power enters the visual register, it 'tends to the non-corporeal.' In the panopticon prison, confinement was successfully maintained by the barrier walls of the prison, but the subjective changes in the inmate were to be produced by the incorporation of the imagined and permanent gaze of the jailer. Bentham's panopticon was designed for other uses than the prison – the factory, the asylum, the hospital – but all of these uses were for institutions where enclosure was a priority.

Hence, the panopticon model has served as a tempting originary root for the inventions that led to the cinema, an apparatus that produces an even more 'mechanically . . . fictitious relation' and whose 'subjection' is equally internalized. Feminist theorists have invoked the 'panoptic' implant as a model for the ever-present 'male gaze,' while 'apparatus' film theories relied more on the immobility and confined spatial matrix of the prison. The prisoners in Plato's cave provide, in Jean-Louis Baudry's emphatic account, an origin for cinematic spectatorship with immobility as a necessary condition.

As an analogy for cinematic spectation, the model of the panoptic guard (the *unseen seer* in the position of omnipotent voyeurism) is not literal, but figurative and metaphoric. Like the central tower guard, the film spectator is totally invisible, absent not only from self-observation but from surveillance as well. But unlike the panoptic guard, the film spectator is not in the position of the central tower, with full scopic range, but is rather a subject with a limited (and preordained) scope. The film spectator's position is one of such *imaginary* visual omnipotence. It is the condition of invisibility which is the premise, in the argument of Baudry, for the spectator-subject's confusion of representation and self-generated perception, what Baudry deemed an 'over-cathexsis' with representation, a position that guarantees the dependence on the constructed view provided by representation.[12] The panoptic model emphasizes the subjective effects of imagined scrutiny and 'permanent visibility' on the *observed*, but does not explore the subjectivity of the *observer*.

In re-examining the emergence of the cinema, one can trace the roots of an instrumentalization of visual culture which is coincident with, but also different from, the paradigm of panoptic visuality. A brief comparison of the panopticon (1791) with two other important devices – the panorama (1792) and the diorama (1823) – will suggest alternative models for visuality.

The panorama and the diorama were building-machines with a different objective: designed to *transport* – rather than to *confine* – the spectator-subject. As we shall see, these devices produced a spatial and temporal mobility – if only a 'virtual' one. The panoramic and dioramic observer was deceptively accorded an *imaginary* illusion of mobility. In Walter Benjamin's conversely demonstrative rhetoric, cinematic spectatorship functioned as an explosive ('dynamite of a tenth of a second') that freed the spectator from the 'prison-world' (*Kerkerwelt*) of nineteenth-century architectural space.[13]

Modernity and the 'virtual' gaze

The panorama

> At leisure let us view from day to day,
> As they present themselves, *the spectacles*
> *Within doors:* troops of wild beast, bird and beasts
> Of every nature from all climes convened,
> And, next to these, *those mimic sights that ape*
> *The absolute presence of reality*
> Expressing as in mirror sea and land,
> And what earth is, and what she hath to shew –
> *I do not here allude to subtlest craft*,
> By means refined attaining purest ends,
> But imitations fondly made in plain
> Confession of man's weakness and his loves.
> Whether the painter – *fashioning a work*
> *To Nature's circumambient scenery*
>
> (William Wordsworth, *Prelude*, 1805,
> Seventh Book, lines 244–57, emphasis added)

As Wordsworth notes, the panorama was not the 'subtlest craft' for presenting 'the absolute presence of reality.' But its 'spectacles/Within doors' of 'every nature from all climes' used 'circumambient scenery' to create an artificial elsewhere for the panoramic spectator.

The panorama was a 360-degree cylindrical painting, viewed by an observer in the center. The illusion presented by the panorama was created by a combination of realist techniques of perspective and scale with a mode of viewing that placed the spectator in the center of a darkened room surrounded by a scene lit from above. The panorama was first patented by the Irishman Robert Barker, who took out a patent for panoramic painting in Edinburgh in 1787 and opened the first completely circular panorama in Leicester Square in London in 1792. (Recall the years of Bentham's work on the panopticon, from 1787 to 1791.) Barker's inspiration for the panorama came, according to an anecdote told by historian Olive Cook, in a manner worthy of comparison to Bentham's panopticon prison:

> The invention of the Panorama is usually attributed to Robert Barker, an Edinburgh painter. In about 1785 he was put into prison for debt and was confined to a cell lit by a grating let into the wall at the junction of wall and ceiling. One day he was reading a letter and to see more clearly carried it below the grating. *The effect when the paper was held in the shaft of light falling from the opening was so astonishing that Barker's imagination was set working on the possibilities of controlled light flung from above upon pictures of large dimensions.*[14]
>
> (emphasis added)

If 'controlled light' served to survey and measure the wards in the panopticon prison, in an opposite way it also served to create the visual illusions of the panorama.

The panorama did not physically *mobilize* the body, but provided virtual spatial and temporal mobility, bringing the country to the town dweller, transporting the past to the present. The panoramic spectator lost, as Helmut Gernsheim described, 'all judgement of distance and space' and 'in the absence of any means of comparison with real objects, a perfect illusion was given.'[15] The panorama offered a spectacle in which all sense of time and space was lost, produced by the combination of the observer in a darkened room (where there were no markers of place or time) and presentation of 'realistic' views of other places and times.

The ideology of representation in the panoramic painting must be placed in the context of the concurrent reconceptualization of the idea of the horizon and of perspective (the first hot air balloon was launched in 1783 and aerial balloonists found vistas that radically changed the landscape perspective) and the 'cult of immensity' in painting, where scale was a factor in the concept of illusionist immersion. In addition, the panorama developed out of the context of earlier 'screen' entertainments.

The 'magic lantern' devices of Athanasius Kircher, Johannes Zahn, and others introduced a form of projected entertainment spectacle that relied on controlled light projected through glass slides: drawn figures of skeletons, demons, and ghosts appeared on a screen surface. In his text of 1646, *Ars Magna Lucis et Umbrae*, Kircher (1601–80) – a Roman Catholic priest – published his procedures for projecting ghostly apparitions. Whether, as Musser argues, Kircher sought to demystify the 'magic' of the lantern or whether, to the contrary, he trained a new legion of mystifiers, the eerie effects produced by these luminous projections established an early link between two potentially competing systems of subjective interpellation: religion and optics. Kircher concealed the lantern from his audiences by placing it on the other side of the screen. He could change the distance of the lantern, vary the sizes of his figures. Musser traces the roots of cinema in these forms of late eighteenth-century forms of 'screen practice.' These entertainments – shadow plays, phantasmagorias, lantern displays – relied on dark rooms and projected light.

Philip Jacob de Loutherbourg, a French-born painter and stage designer who came to England in 1771, had designed a viewing system, the *eidophusikon* (1781), which also relied on spectators in a darkened auditorium viewing an illuminated (10 foot by 6 foot) translucent screen, with light projected from behind. The eidophusikon spectacle produced simulations of sunsets, fog, and dawn accompanied by sound effects and harpsichord music. In Paris, a device called the phantasmagoria similarly relied on a lantern with lens to project drawings of celebrities from Voltaire to Rousseau to Marat. Étienne-Gaspard Roberton – a self-styled *aéronaute* to whom the invention of the parachute is attributed – devised a magic lantern show set in a Capuchin monastery. The phantasmagoria made its début in Paris from 1797 to 1800, traveled to London from 1801 to 1803, and arrived in New York in 1803.

Phantasmagorias, panoramas, dioramas – devices that concealed their machinery – were dependent on the relative immobility of their spectators, who enjoyed the illusion of presence of virtual figures. These apparatuses produced an illusion of presence of virtual figures. These apparatuses produced an illusion of unmediated referentiality. Other optical entertainments that required viewing devices – the stereoscope, the phenakistoscope – were dependent on quite different optical principles and hence produced diverse subjective effects.

Benjamin saw a direct relation between the panoramic observer and the flâneur:

> The city-dweller . . . attempts to introduce the countryside into the city. In the panoramas the city dilates to become landscape, as it does in a subtler way for the *flâneur*.[16]

Before the advent of illustrated print journalism in the 1840s, the panorama supplied a visual illustration of places and events that one could read about in print. The panorama not only appealed to the public interest in battles and historical illustration, but also to a fascination with landscape art, travel literature, and travel itself. As Richard Altick argues, the panorama was the 'bourgeois public's substitute for the Grand Tour'.[17]

Dolf Sternberger has emphasized that the lure of these entertainments was not in their verisimilitude with reality, but rather in their deceptive skills, their very artificiality.[18] As an early epitome of the lure of artificiality, in 1823 Yorkshireman Thomas Hornor climbed the top of St Paul's with sketching implements and telescopes and sketched London in 360-degree detail. Hornor's gigantic rendering was housed in Decimus Burton's Colosseum. The building took years to build (1824–29) but, when finished, encased a panorama of remarkable verisimilitude: a simulated London viewed from the top of a simulated St Paul's. The rooftop location of this panorama necessitated a new design feature: the first hydraulic passenger lift ('ascending room') carried spectators who did not wish to climb the stairs. The elevator was a mechanical aid to mobility; the gaze at the end of this 'lift' was virtual.

The panorama was taken to Paris in 1799 by Robert Fulton, who had purchased the foreign patent rights. Two rotundas for the panorama were built in Paris on Boulevard Montmartre. In the interior were two paintings, one that displayed a view of Paris from the Tuilleries and another that showed the British evacuation during the Battle of Toulon in 1793. The immediate city – the Paris of only blocks away – was presented to itself; but so was a distant city (Toulon) at a distant time (six years before). Sternberger has aptly named these panoramic paintings, 'captured historical moments(s).'[19]

In 1800, the Passage des Panoramas was built to connect the Palais Royal to the panorama on Boulevard Montmartre. The cylindrical panorama building was connected directly to the Passsage des Panoramas – one entered through the arcade. The panorama was lit from above by the same glass and iron skylight as the arcade. . . .

The diorama

Louis Jacques Mandé Daguerre, later famed for his 1839 invention of a photographic process he named the daguerreotype, began his career as an assistant to the celebrated panorama painter, Pierre Prévost. In 1822, Daguerre debuted a viewing device that expanded upon the panorama's ability to transport the viewer, an apparatus he called the diorama.

Like the *diaphanorama* – in which translucent watercolors were illuminated from behind – the dioramic illusion relied on the manipulation of light through a transparent painting. Daguerre's visitors looked through a proscenium at a scene composed of objects arranged in front of a backdrop; after a few minutes, the auditorium platform was rotated 73 degrees to expose another dioramic opening. The diorama was designed to construct and restructure – through light and movement – the relation of the viewer to the spatial and temporal present. A scene was transformed through the manipulation of daylight, which shifted the temporal mood. The diorama differed significantly from the panorama: the diorama spectator was immobile, at the center of the building, and the 'views' were mobilized as the entire diorama building with its pulleys, cords, and rollers became a machine for changing the spectator's view.

When the diorama opened in Paris in 1822, it displayed two distant tableaux: 'The Valley of Sarnen,' a scene from Switzerland, and 'Interior of Trinity Church – Canterbury Cathedral,' a scene from England. Of the thirty-two scenes exhibited during the seventeen years of its existence, ten of the paintings were interiors of distant chapels or cathedrals. As a local newspaper account indicated: 'We cannot sufficiently urge Parisians who like pleasure without fatigue to make the journey to Switzerland and to England without leaving the capital.'[20]

Helmut and Alison Gernsheim extend this description of the diorama as a substitute for travel: 'The many foreign views, too, no doubt had a special appeal to the general public who, before the days of Cook's Tours, had little chance of travelling abroad.'[21]

Dioramas opened in other cities, in Breslau in 1826, in Berlin in 1827, in Stockholm in 1846, and in Frankfurt in 1852. (Thomas Cook's first guided tours of the continent were in 1855.) There were other variations on the diorama. The *pleorama*, which opened in Berlin in 1832, had the audience seated in a ship and taken for an hour's 'voyage,' as the illusion of movement was created by the backcloth moving slowly across the stage. This device emphasized the equation otherwise implicit between travel and viewing scenes of the distant and of the past.

In 1839, Daguerre's diorama on Rue Sanson in Paris was destroyed by fire. In that same year, he patented a technique for *fixing* images on copper plates, the 'daguerreotype.' Few dioramic or panoramic paintings survive. The illusions produced were dependent on the effects of artificial light, and many of the paintings, and the buildings which housed them, ended in flames. The 'captured historical moment' could be more securely impounded on a photographic plate. Benjamin will remark on this historical coincidence; photography emerged from the ashes of the diorama.

Both the panorama and its successor, the diorama, offered new forms of virtual mobility to its viewer. But a paradox here must be emphasized: as the 'mobility' of the gaze became more 'virtual' – as techniques were developed to paint (and then to photograph) realistic images, as mobility was implied by changes in lighting (and then cinematography) – the observer became more immobile, passive, ready to receive the constructions of a virtual reality placed in front of his or her unmoving body.

The panopticon versus the diorama

Like the panopticon, the diorama-building was an architectural arrangement with a center position for the *seer* with a view to 'cells' or 'galleries.' Yet unlike the observation tower of the panopticon, the diorama platform turned (the auditorium rotated 73 degrees) to mobilize the viewer. The diorama had a *collective observer*, a shared audience on the moving platform. Dioramas and panoramas were not directly instruments of social engineering (cf. Fourier's phalanstery) but were, nevertheless, conceived of as satisfying a social desire or curiosity – a desire to have visual mastery over the constraints of space and time. The technology of the diorama relied on spectator immobility, but offered a visual excursion and a virtual release from the confinements of everyday space and time.

But if the panopticon was dependent on the enclosure of the look, the inward measure of confined but visible subjects, the diorama was dependent on the imaginary expansion of that look. Unlike the jailer-surveyor, the dioramic spectator was not attempting mastery over human subjects, but was instead engaged in the pleasures of mastery over an artificially constructed world, the pleasure of immersion in a world not present.

In the diorama, the spectator sat on a darkened center platform and looked toward the brightness of the peripheral scenes: transparent paintings where light was manipulated to give the effect of time passing – a sunset, or the changing light of the day. In the panopticon, the role of light was to indict, to measure. In the diorama, light played a deceptive role. In the panopticon, there was no spatial illusion, no fooling with time. Both panoptic and dioramic systems required a degree of spectator immobility and the predominance of the visual function. And it is this notion of the confined *place* combined with a notion of *journey* that is present simultaneously in cinematic spectation.

[. . .]

Notes

1 Michel Foucault (1979) *Discipline and Punish*, translated by Alan Sheridan, New York: Pantheon Books. Originally published as *Surveiller et Punir* [Paris, 1975].
2 See Mary Ann Doane, Patricia Mellencamp, and Linda Williams (eds) (1984) *Re-vision*, Los Angeles: AFI, p. 14. John Berger (1972) *Ways of Seeing*, London: Penguin Books. Laura Mulvery (1975) 'Visual Pleasure and Narrative Cinema', *Screen* 16 (3), Autumn, Joan Copjec (1989) 'The Orthopsychic Subject', *October* 49, Summer: 53–71.
3 Teresa de Lauretis (1987) *Technologies of Gender*, Bloomington: Indiana University Press, p. 2.
4 Michel Foucault (1970) *The Order of Things: An Archaeology of the Human Sciences*, translated from *Les Mots et Les Choses*, New York: Random House, p. 319.
5 Jeremy Bentham (1962) *Panopticon, Works of Jeremy Bentham Published under the Superintendence of His Executor, John Bowring*, 11 vols, New York: Russell and Russell.
6 Jacques-Alain Miller (1987) 'Jeremy Bentham's Panoptic Device', translated by Richard Miller, *October* 41, Summer: 4.
7 Foucault, *Discipline and Punish*, p. 204.
8 Ibid., p. 205.
9 Ibid., p. 201.
10 Ibid., p. 207.
11 Ibid., pp. 202–3.
12 Jean-Louis Baudry, 'The Apparatus: Metapsychological Approaches to the Impression of Reality in the Cinema', translated by Jean Andrews and Bertrand Augst in *Narrative, Apparatus, Ideology*, p. 316.
13 Walter Benjamin (1969) 'The Work of Art in the Age of Mechanical Reproduction', in *Illuminations*, translated by Harry Zorn, New York: Schocken Books, p. 236.
14 Olive Cook (1963) *Movement in Two Dimensions*, London: Hutchinson and Co., p. 32.
15 Helmut Gernsheim and Alison Gernsheim (1968) *L.J.M. Daguerre: The History of the Diorama and the Daguerrotype*, New York: Dover Publications, p. 6.
16 'Paris – Capital of the Nineteenth Century', translated by Edmund Jephcott, in *Reflections*, New York: Harcourt Brace and Jovanovich, 1979, p. 150.
17 Richard D. Altick (1978) *The Shows of London*, Cambridge, MA: Harvard University Press, p. 180.
18 Dolf Sternberger (1977) *Panorama of the Nineteenth Century*, translated by Joachim Neugroschel, New York: Urizen Books, p. 13.
19 Ibid., p. 13.
20 Gernsheim and Gernsheim, *L.J.M. Daguerre*, p. 18.
21 Ibid.

Chapter 23

Mary-Louise Pratt

FROM THE VICTORIA NYANZA TO THE SHERATON SAN SALVADOR

> To land at this airport . . . is to plunge directly into a state in which no ground is solid, no depth of field reliable, no perception so definite that it might not dissolve into its reverse.
>
> (Joan Didion, *Salvador* (United States, 1983))

> They put me in a room and the first thing I saw when they uncovered my eyes was the United States flag and on the other side the Bolivian flag, and a framed picture with two hands that said 'Alliance for Progress.' [. . .] The desk was full of rubber stamps.
>
> (Domitila Barrios de Chungara, *Let Me Speak* (Bolivia, 1978))

The monarch of all I survey

NO ONE WAS BETTER at the monarch-of-all-I-survey scene than the string of British explorers who spent the 1860s looking for the source of the Nile. As the Linnaeans had their labeling system, and the Humboldtians their poetics of science, the Victorians opted for a brand of verbal painting whose highest calling was to produce for the home audience the peak moments at which geographical 'discoveries' were 'won' for England. Ironized and modernized, their vivid imperial rhetoric endures today in the writings of their postcolonial heirs, for whom there is little left on the planet to pretend to conquer.

One of my favorites in the monarch-of-all-I-survey genre comes from Richard Burton's *Lake Regions of Central Africa*, which appeared in 1860 and achieved considerable renown in that prolific and highly competitive era of travel writing. Here in a descriptive *tour de force* Burton renders the dramatic moment of his discovery of Lake Tanganyika:

> Nothing in sooth, could be more picturesque than this first view of the Tanganyika Lake, as it lay in the lap of the mountains, basking in the gorgeous tropical sunshine. Below and beyond a short foreground of rugged and precipitous hill-fold, down which the foot-path zigzags painfully, a narrow strip of emerald green, never sere and marvellously fertile, shelves towards a ribbon of glistening yellow sand, here bordered by sedgy rushes, there cleanly and clearly cut by the breaking wavelets. Further in front stretch the waters, an expanse of the lightest and softest blue, in breadth varying from thirty to thirty-five miles, and sprinkled by the crisp east-wind with tiny crescents of snowy foam. The background in front is a high and broken wall of steel-coloured mountain, here flecked and capped with pearly mist, there standing sharply pencilled against the azure air; its yawning chasms, marked by a deeper plum-colour, fall towards dwarf hills of mound-like proportions, which apparently dip their feet in the wave. To the south, and opposite the long, low point, behind which the Malagarazi River discharges the red loam suspended in its violent stream, lie the bluff headlands and capes of Uguhha, and, as the eye dilates, it falls upon a cluster of outlying islets, speckling a sea horizon. Villages, cultivated lands, the frequent canoes of the fishermen on the waters, and on a nearer approach the murmurs of the waves breaking upon the shore, give a something of variety, of movement, of life to the landscape, which, like all the fairest prospects in these regions, wants but a little of the neatness and finish of art – mosques and kiosks, palaces and villas, gardens and orchards – contrasting with the profuse lavishness and magnificence of nature, and diversifying the unbroken *coup d'oeil* of excessive vegetation to rival, if not to excel, the most admired scenery of the classic regions.[1]

Promontory descriptions are of course very common in Romantic and Victorian writing of all kinds. . . . In the context of exploration writing, the device is called upon to accomplish a particular meaning-making task that at first blush must seem quite a challenge. The verbal painter must render momentously significant what is, especially from a narrative point of view, practically a non-event. As a rule the 'discovery' of sites like Lake Tanganyika involved making one's way to the region and asking the local inhabitants if they knew of any big lakes, etc. in the area, then hiring them to take you there, whereupon with their guidance and support, you proceeded to discover what they already knew.

Crudely, then, discovery in this context consisted of a gesture of converting local knowledges (discourses) into European national and continental knowledges associated with European forms and relations of power. To put the matter this way is, of course, to set aside rather aggressively what actually constituted the heroic dimension of this kind of discovery, namely the overcoming of all the geographical, material, logistical, and political barriers to the physical and official presence of Europeans in places such as Central Africa. I wish to foreground the contradictions in the heroic perspective. In the end, the act of discovery itself, for which all the untold lives were sacrificed and miseries endured, consisted of what in European culture counts as a purely passive experience – that of seeing. In

Burton's situation at Lake Tanganyika, the heroics of discovery were particularly problematic. Burton had been so ill he had to be carried much of the way by African assistants. His companion John Speke, though able to walk, had been blinded by fever and was therefore at the crucial moment unable in a literal way to discover anything. While the ordeal required to make the discovery is unforgettably concrete, in this mid-Victorian paradigm the 'discovery' itself, even within the ideology of discovery, has no existence of its own. It only gets 'made' for real after the traveler (or other survivor) returns home, and brings it into being through texts: a name on a map, a report to the Royal Geographical Society, the Foreign Office, the London Mission Society, a diary, a lecture, a travel book. Here is language charged with making the world in the most singlehanded way, and with high stakes. As the explorers found out, lots of money and prestige rode on what you could convince others to give you credit for.

Analyzing Victorian discovery rhetoric, I have found it useful to identify three conventional means which create qualitative and quantitative value for the explorer's achievement. The Burton text just quoted illustrates them well. First, and most obvious, the landscape is *estheticized*. The sight is seen as a painting and the description is ordered in terms of background, foreground, symmetries between foam-flecked water and mist-flecked hills, and so forth. In the Burton text there is a whole binary rhetoric at work playing off large and small, back and front. It is important to note that within the text's own terms the esthetic *pleasure* of the sight singlehandedly constitutes the value and significance of the journey. At the end of the passage quoted, Burton sums it all up: 'Truly it was a revel for

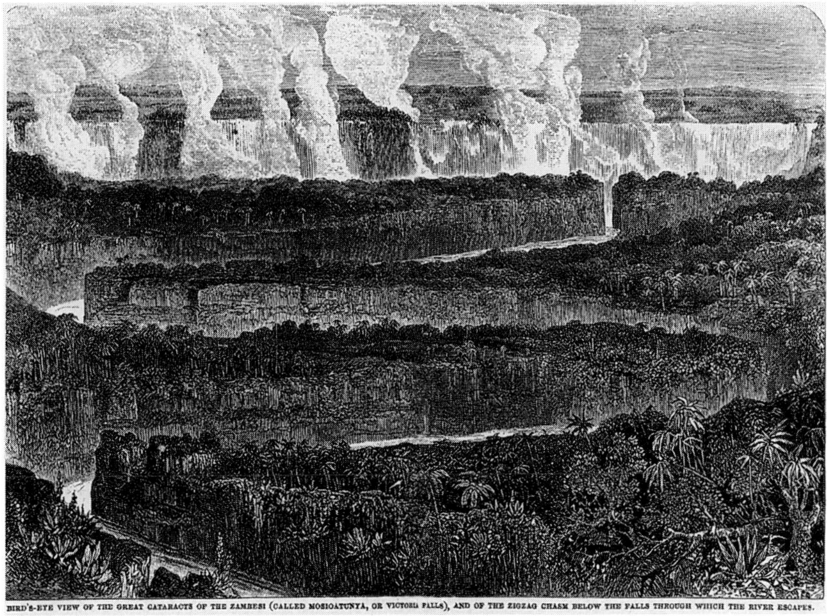

Figure 23.1 Victoria Falls, 1865
(Frontispiece of David Livingstone's *Narrative of an Expedition to the Zambesi*, 1865)

soul and sight! Forgetting toils, dangers, and the doubtfulness of return, I felt willing to endure double what I had endured; and all the party seemed to join with me in joy.'

Second, *density of meaning* in the passage is sought. The landscape is represented as extremely rich in material and semantic substance. This density is achieved especially through a huge number of adjectival modifiers – scarcely a noun in the text is unmodified. Notice, too, that many of the modifiers are derived from nouns (like 'sedgy,' 'capped,' or 'mound-like') and thus add density by introducing additional objects or materials into the discourse. Of particular interest in this respect is a series of nominal color expressions: '*emerald* green,' '*snowy* foam,' '*steel*-coloured mountain,' '*pearly* mist,' '*plum*-colour.' Unlike plain color adjectives, these terms add material referents into the landscape, referents which all, from steel to snow, tie the landscape explicitly to the explorer's home culture, sprinkling it with some little bits of England. Scientific vocabulary is completely absent.

The third strategy at work here [is] . . . the relation of *mastery* predicated between the seer and the seen. The metaphor of the painting itself is suggestive. If the scene is a painting, then Burton is both the viewer there to judge and appreciate it, and the verbal painter who produces it for others. From the painting analogy it also follows that what Burton sees is all there is, and that the landscape was intended to be viewed from where he has emerged upon it. Thus the scene is deictically ordered with reference to his vantage point, and is static.

The viewer–painting relation also implies that Burton has the power if not to possess, at least to evaluate this scene. Conspicuously, what he finds lacking is more Art, where Art (mosques and kiosks, palaces, gardens) is equated with Mediterranean high culture and institutions. Evidently, the African villages and cultivations already mentioned are not enough *esthetically*. The non-Christian Mediterranean esthetics here reflect nonconformist Burton's deep ambivalences about Victorian English culture, its rigid family and class bases, its repressive morality and arrogant colonial designs. (He had sealed his fame already by making a pilgrimage to Mecca disguised as an Arab, at a time when detection would likely have cost him his life.) At the same time, depicting the civilizing mission as an esthetic project is a strategy the West has often used for defining others as available for and in need of its benign and beautifying intervention. Another Nile explorer, James Grant, in an account written a year or two after Burton's, actually supplied the missing elements in one of his discovery scenes. Reaching Lake Victoria Nyanza, he reported, he was inspired to make a sketch, 'dotting it with imaginary steamers and ships riding at anchor in the bay,' in addition to the African boats he has already mentioned. Often in such scenes the indigenous labor pool is called upon to verify the European's achievement. Burton asserts above that 'all the party seemed to join with me in joy' at Lake Tanganyika; Grant observes that 'even the listless Wanyamuezi came to have a look. . . . The Seedees were in raptures.'[2] African members of 'the party' doubtless did get caught up in the excitement of the quest on expeditions such as these. The writing convention that marshals their reactions to confirm the European's achievement subordinates their response, assigns them the task of carrying their masters' emotional baggage along with the rest of their stuff.

The monarch-of-all-I-survey scene, then, would seem to involve particularly explicit interaction between esthetics and ideology, in what one might call a rhetoric of presence. In Burton's rendering, if we take it literally, the esthetic qualities of the landscape constitute the social and material value of the discovery to the explorers' home culture, at the same time as its esthetic deficiencies suggest a need for social and material intervention by the home culture. Burton's partner and younger rival John Speke drew on the same equation to express his disappointment when one of his discoveries let him down. While accompanying Burton on his Nile expedition, Speke became convinced that the source of the Nile would be found in Lake Victoria N'yanza (as it was later called). In a famous dispute his mentor Burton soundly rejected the proposal, which later proved true. To confirm his hypothesis, Speke made a second expedition in the company of James Grant. The results were quite decisive, but because this second expedition was unable to map the entire circumference of the Victoria N'yanza, Speke's claim remained technically open to question. Many readers will be familiar with the vicious polemic which ensued back in England between Burton and Speke, resulting in Speke's apparent suicide. Speke's account of the expedition (*Journal of the Discovery of the Source of the Nile*, 1863) was written in the midst of this polemic. In a startingly schematic way, Speke wrote his disappointment and filial anguish into the scene of discovery that culminates his narrative. The passage quoted below displays many elements of the monarch-of-all-I-survey trope: the value of the sight is expressed in terms of esthetic pleasure, the party spontaneously bears witness, the sketch book is mentioned, but the sight itself is expressed as a letdown (my italics):

> We were well rewarded; for the 'stones' as the Waganda call the falls, was by far *the most interesting sight* I had seen in Africa. *Everybody ran to see them* at once, though the march had been long and fatiguing, and even *my sketch-book* was called into play. *Though beautiful*, the scene was *not exactly what I had expected*: for the broad surface of the lake was *shut out from view* by a spur of hill, and the falls, about 12 feet deep, and 400–500 feet broad, were *broken by rocks*. Still it was a sight that attracted one to it for hours – the roar of the waters, the thousands of passenger-fish, leaping at the falls with all their might, the Wasoga and Waganda fishermen coming out in boats and taking post on all the rocks with rod and hook, hippopotami and crocodiles lying sleepily on the water, the ferry at work above the falls, and cattle driven down to drink at the margin of the lake – made all in all, with the *pretty nature* of the country – small hills, grassy-tipped, with trees in the folds, and gardens on the lower slopes – as *interesting a picture* as one could wish to see.
>
> The expedition had now performed its functions. I saw that old father Nile without any doubt rises in the Victoria N'yanza, and as I foretold, that lake is the great source of the holy river which cradled the first expounder of our religious belief. I mourned, however, when I thought of how much I had lost by the delays in the journey which had *deprived me of the pleasure* of going to look at the northeast corner.[3]

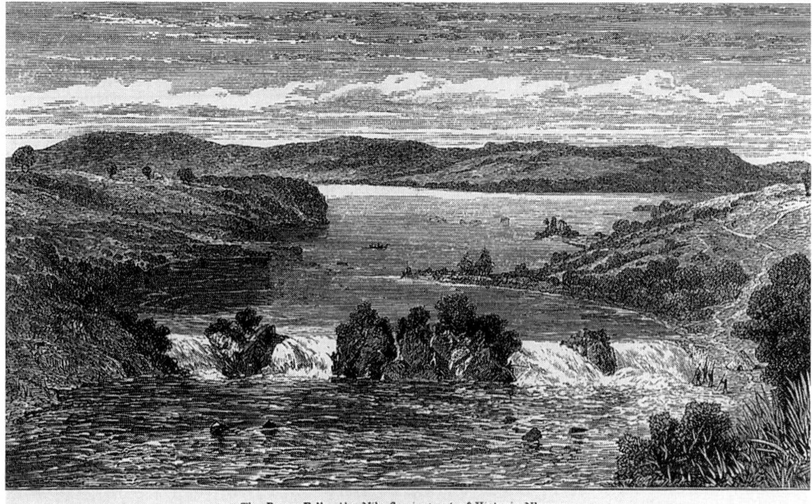

The Ripon Falls—the Nile flowing out of Victoria N'yanza.

Figure 23.2 Ripon Falls, 1863
(From John Hanning Speke's *Journal of the Discovery of the Source of the Nile*, 1863)

Speke's esthetic disappointment exactly duplicates his logistical one. Obstacles block the view; the river's smooth flow, like the explorer's own movement, is interrupted. Behind the rocks, the falls and the hill, Lake Victoria N'yanza undoubtedly lies, as Lake Tanganyika did for Burton, 'basking in the gorgeous tropical sunshine,' but Speke cannot see it/(her) – yet only the seeing, and the writing of the seeing, can fully constitute the discovery. Locked into the rhetoric, and locked at the same time into a public Oedipeal battle with Burton, Speke displays his failure here even as he claims the achievement. The rhetoric uses him, and he it. Estheticization is reduced to the mundane categories of the interesting and attractive, not the sublime; neither metaphors nor adjectives nor European allusion provide density of meaning. The European's claim to mastery and will to intervention are also absent here. Speke writes the scene of fish, fishermen, livestock, and ferries as a complete whole that in no way belongs or even beckons to him. If anything, mastery resides with the Wasoga and Waganda fishermen, and Speke is one of the thousands of passenger-fish leaping hopelessly up the falls. And indeed, in the final paragraph, Speke moves out of the monarchic trope to find meaning for his act in a series of Oedipeal images: old father Nile, his religious forebear Jesus, and the unmentioned, unforgiving father, Burton.

Hyphenated white men and the critique from within

The solemnity and self-congratulatory tone of the monarch-of-all-I-survey scene are a virtual invitation to satire and demystification. Congo explorer Paul Du Chaillu, a contemporary of Speke and Burton, was one explorer-writer who accepted the invitation, writing a travel book in 1861 that wildly disturbed the esthetic-ideological matrix of art-and-empire. Du Chaillu was a Franco-American whose father had been in trade in West Africa. While the British sought to 'win' the source of the Nile, Du Chaillu took on another enigma: the gorilla. Reports of a huge, man-like animal had emanated from the Congo ever since anyone could remember, but Western curiosity about the creature had been quenched by equally vivid reports of cannibalism throughout the region. Fever was also a major deterrent, as well as the inland African traders on the Congo, who seem to have been particularly adept at protecting their business from European encroachment. With the advent of evolutionary thinking and modern race theories in the 1850s, however, the possibility of the gorilla acquired extraordinary new significances (for instance as the lower beast to whom Africans would be more closely related than Europeans). It became imperative for Europeans to confirm or discount the creature's existence. At about the same time, medical advances made African travel safer for Europeans. Though not everyone believed him, Du Chaillu did 'discover' the gorilla and wrote it up in his popular and sensational *Explorations and Adventures in Equatorial Africa* (1861). It is a discovery so ideologically charged that Westerners have had to re-enact it at regular intervals ever since. (A 1980s re-enactment took place in the film *Gorillas in the Mist*, based on the life of primatologist Dian Fossey.)

Du Chaillu's 'discovery' of the gorilla made him famous, and his highly entertaining travel books gained him notoriety – as a satirist, a sensationalist, and a liar. Like Henry Morton Stanley, another hyphenated (in this case Anglo-) American who would soon turn up in the Congo, Du Chaillu challenged head-on the literary decorum of the British gentlemen travelers and their legitimating rhetoric of presence, substituting it with what one might call a rhetoric of illegitimate presence. Consider, for instance, what happens to the monarch-of-all-I-survey scene in this excerpt from Du Chaillu's vivid exploration narrative. It begins like an echo of Burton, then evolves into parody:

> From this elevation – about 5000 feet above the ocean level – I enjoyed an unobstructed view as far as the eye could reach. The hills we had surmounted the day before lay quietly at our feet, seeming mere mole-hills. On all sides stretched the immense virgin forests, with here and there the sheen of a water-course. And far away in the east loomed the blue tops of the farthest range of the Sierra del Cristal, the goal of my desires. The murmur of the rapids below filled my ears, and as I strained my eyes toward those distant mountains which I hoped to reach, I began to think how this wilderness would look if only the light of Christian civilization could once be fairly introduced among the black children of Africa. I dreamed of forests giving way to plantations of coffee, cotton, spices; of peaceful negroes going to their contented daily tasks; of farming and manufactures; of churches and schools; and luckily, raising my eyes heavenward at this stage of my thoughts, saw pendant from the branch of a tree beneath which I was sitting an immense serpent, evidently preparing to gobble up this dreaming intruder on his domains.[4]

Again, many standard elements of the imperial trope are present: the mastery of the landscape, the estheticizing adjectives, the broad panorama anchored in the seer. But as soon as the explorer's eyes light on the 'goal of his desires,' an interventionist fantasy completely displaces the reality of the landscape before him and becomes the content of the vision. Unlike Burton and Grant's fantasies of adding a little something here and there to perfect the scene (a mosque here, a steamship there), Du Chaillu orchestrates a wholesale transformation unabashedly colonialist (and American) in character. Then along comes the serpent to ironize the guilty fantasy, and point to its guilt. Simultaneously a double of the dreamer and a symbol of the other, the serpent (not snake, mind you) has come directly from the Garden of Eden, bringing among other things the unwelcome (but also welcome) knowledge that the cozy pastoral-plantation fantasy is forbidden fruit likely to lead to expulsion from the garden. Who might know this better than an American in the aftermath of the Civil War?

In the face of the serpentine intrusion, Du Chaillu, the original sinner/intruder, abandons his visionary role and grabs onto the fundamental material instrument of the civilizing mission: 'My dreams of future civilization vanished in a moment,' we read; 'Luckily my gun lay at hand.' That is the end of the serpent ('my black friend,' he calls it), but not the satire, for now, 'the Christian civilization of which I had mused so pleasantly a few minutes before received another shock':

> My men cut off the head of the snake, and dividing the body into proper pieces, roasted it and ate it on the spot; and I poor, starved, but civilized mortal, stood by, longing for a meal, but unable to stomach this. So much for civilization, which is a very good thing in its way, but has no business in an African forest when food is scarce.[5]

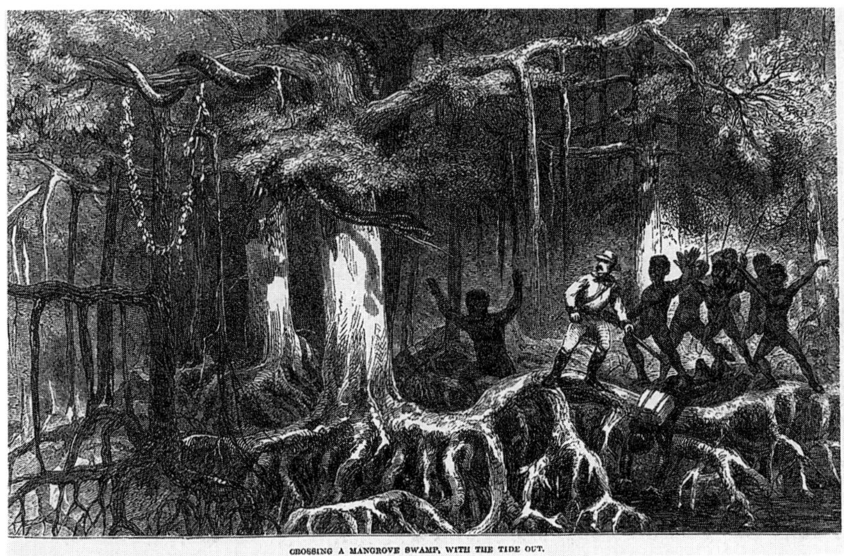
CROSSING A MANGROVE SWAMP, WITH THE TIDE OUT.

Figure 23.3 'Crossing a mangrove swamp, with the tide out', 1861
(From Du Chaillu's *Explorations and Adventures in Equatorial Africa*, 1861)

The scene has all the overtones of a communion or last supper, except that the Messiah is an outsider who will not share the meal, and could become part of it. Far from sharing and reflecting the explorer's paradigms of value and desire, 'the party' in Du Chaillu's depiction act on values of their own which, in a very overdetermined way, are incompatible with Du Chaillu's. Throughout his book, Du Chaillu repeatedly tells us he does not eat snake or gorilla. Why not? Symbolically, it seems, to eat snake ('my black friend') is to eat Satan (alias the African as other), while eating gorilla raises the specter of cannibalism (alias the self as African).

'Civilized' impractical practices anchored in 'uncivilized' white supremacist assumptions – so the imperial project is displayed by Du Chaillu. So the imperial subject splits in his writing: Du Chaillu is now parodist, now parodied; now dreamer, now demystifier of his own dream; now Adam, now serpent; now provider of civilization, now deprived of it; now hunter, now hunted. His discourse here achieves its semantic density through the very contradictions of the European's presence in Africa. This perverse perspective is very likely connected with the fact that Du Chaillu is himself neither European nor African, but a Franco-American. A hyphenated white man writing at the height of civilizing mission, Du Chaillu is indeed an early serpent in the African imperial garden. Thirty years later, it was right there in the Congo that the civilizing mission unmasked itself in the sadistic, genocidal drama of the Congo rubber boom. From their mountain retreats, the gorillas perhaps looked on while Europeans became, and watched each other become, white barbarians as wild and ruthless as those they had always imagined for themselves in Africa. Relayed back to Europe through the intervention of critical intellectuals, European barbarism in the Congo became one of the great political scandals of the turn of the century. Among the European witnesses were several

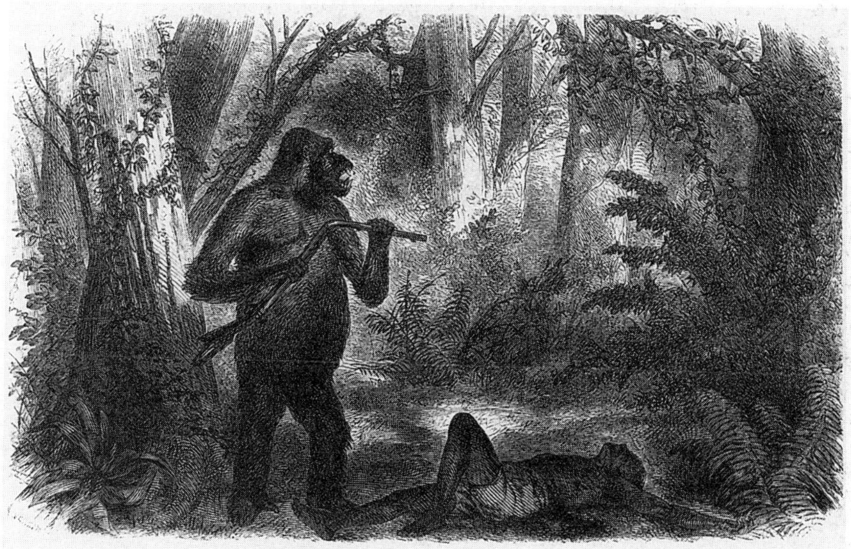

Figure 23.4 'Death of my hunter', 1861
(From Du Chaillu's *Explorations and Adventures in Equatorial Africa*, 1861)

hyphenated white men armed with pens and paper: Henry Stanley, the Anglo-American who led the scramble for Africa and transformed English exploration writing to fit the bill; Roger Casement, the Anglo-Irishman who worked tirelessly to expose the horrors Stanley had set in motion; and Joseph Conrad, the Anglo-Pole who made the Congo debacle into the allegory of the failure of Europe. Each was a white man whose national and civic identifications were multiple and often conflicted; each had lived out in deep personal and social histories the raw realities of Euro-expansionism, white supremacy, class domination, and heterosexism. The hyphenated white men are principal architects of the often imperialist internal critique of empire.

[. . .]

Notes

1 Richard Burton (1961) *The Lake Regions of Central Africa: A Picture of Exploration* (1860) Volume III, New York: Horizon Press, p. 43.

2 James Augustus Grant (1864) *A Walk Across Africa or, Domestic Scenes from my Nile Journal*, Edinburgh, p. 196.

3 John Hanning Speke (1863) *Journal of the Discovery of the Source of the Nile*, Edinburgh: Blackwoods, p. 466.

4 Paul Du Chaillu (1861) *Explorations and Adventures in Equatorial Africa*, New York, p. 83.

5 Ibid., p. 84.

Chapter 24

Geoffrey Batchen

SPECTRES OF CYBERSPACE

A NEW SPECTRE is haunting Western culture – the spectre of Virtual Reality. Not here yet but already a force to be reckoned with, the apparition of VR is ghost-like indeed. Even the words themselves have a certain phantom quality. Virtual Reality – a reality which is apparently true but not *truly* True, a reality which is apparently real but not *really* Real. The term has been coined to describe an imagined assemblage of human and machine so intertwined that the division between the two is no longer discernible. In VR, so it is said, the human will be irresistibly melded to the morphology of its technological supplement. The resulting biomorph will inhabit a world beyond the surface of the screen, living behind or perhaps even *within* that boundary which has traditionally been thought to separate reality from its representation. The cybernaut won't just step into the picture; he/she/it will become the picture itself.

Various combinations of technology promise to induce this assemblage, but its principal spatial and temporal horizons are provided by a computer-generated, interactive virtual environment known as cyberspace. It is the three-dimensional simulation offered by this cyberspace that seemingly lies at the heart of VR's projected field of dreams. For, according to at least one critic: 'these new spaces instantiate the collapse of the boundaries between the social and technological, biology and machine, natural and artificial that are part of the postmodern imaginary.'

This particular imaginary has tended to attract contradictory responses, sometimes from the same commentators. One response laments the possible loss of the human, the body, community, sexual difference, reality, and all those other privileged foundations of a modern Cartesian epistemology. The other celebrates this same loss on behalf of the disabled, the military, world communication, the sexually promiscuous, the leisure industry, medicine, and a host of other presumed benefactors.

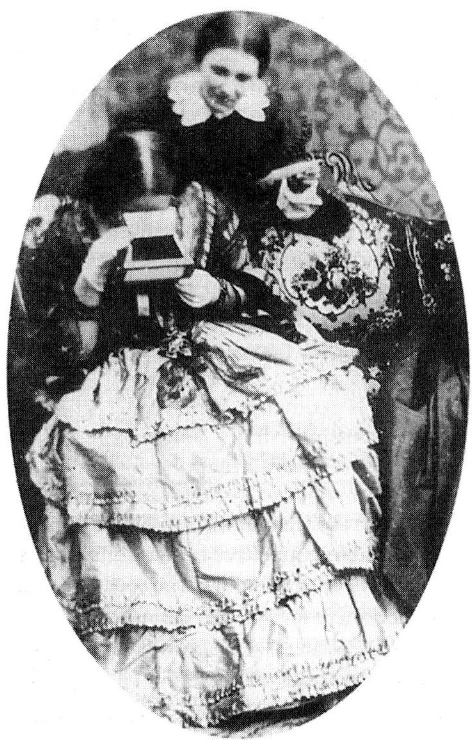

Figure 24.1 'Cybernauts of the nineteenth century'

What is interesting about both arguments is the assumption that VR's promised implosion of reality and representation is in some way a new, even revolutionary phenomenon. It is, after all, only because a completely plausible VR is not yet here, not yet actual, that critics feel moved to speak about its *potential* for social change, whether they think that change is likely to be destructive or liberatory. The inference is that, even in the imaginary, cyberspace represents the possibility of a distinctive and definitive move beyond the modern era. Postmodernism has at last been given a technological face, the inscrutable space-age visage of the VR headset. But what character can be ascribed to this particular physiognomy? What is new about a desire that already seems so strangely familiar? How is a virtual reality different from the one which for so long we have simply and complacently called 'the Real'?

Such questions suggest that, to look ahead, it might also be necessary to look back – an analytical gesture that would of course replicate the forward but inward stare of the fully equipped VR cybernaut. Conjoining a future that is already here with a past that continually returns, the spectral matter of cyberspace is perhaps something that can be conjured only through a reflexive repetition of its own peculiar trajectory through space and time.

However, this trajectory is itself a matter of some debate. In *Cyberspace: First Steps* Michael Benedikt, for example, wants us to go back beyond William Gibson's *Neuromancer* of 1984 and seek the historical origins of cyberspace in our culture's displacement from 'the temperate and fertile plains of Africa two million years ago – from Eden if you will.' David Tomas looks a little closer to home, measuring cyberspace against the 'master space' of a Euclidean world-view that is as much social as it is geometric. While conceding that VR is 'new' and 'postindustrial,' Tomas argues that cyberspace also represents a ritual process of contesting cultural knowledge that is as old as society itself. In a 1995 essay for the Canadian journal *Public*, Dale Bradley also points to the generative accumulations of the postindustrial state, insisting that:

> it is the social space of late capitalism which . . . constitutes the surface of emergence for cyberspace. . . . cyberspace is the embodiment or concretization of a logic of control already existent in the power relations that define late capitalism and the modern welfare state.

Some of VR's historians prefer to concentrate on the story of its technological rather than its social development. This doesn't necessarily make the tale any simpler. Howard Rheingold, for example, traces 'the first virtual reality' to the development of tools 30,000 years ago in an upper paleolithic cave. Nevertheless, he then goes on to spend most of his book, *Virtual Reality*, recounting his personal experience of more recent experiments involving computers and scientific visualization. Allucquère Rosanne Stone also concentrates on questions of technology. She is perhaps the most ubiquitous of VR's historians, having already provided the medium with a number of informative if competing 'origin myths.' In one of these, she divides the history of cyberspace into four successive epochs, beginning with the introduction of printed texts in the mid-1600s, then jumping to the development of electronic communication systems like the telegraph in the first years of the twentieth-century. This is followed by the rapid expansion of computerized information technology in the 1960s and then finally by the new sense of community given representation by Gibson's 1984 science fiction novel. Not content with this already complex historical stratification, Stone provided yet another at a 1991 symposium in San Francisco. In this case she specifically traced the genealogy of Virtual Reality back to the invention of the stereoscope in 1838.

This last point of origin is a particularly intriguing one. Conceived in the 1830s by Charles Wheatstone and David Brewster (who in 1815 had also invented the kaleidoscope), the stereoscope was, according to Jonathan Crary, 'the most significant form of visual imagery in the nineteenth century, with the exception of photographs.' American critic Oliver Wendell Holmes provides us with a number of stirring accounts of stereoscopy written in the 1850s and 1860s. These descriptions speak of the stereograph as producing 'a dream-like exaltation in which we seem to leave the body behind us and sail away into one strange scene after another, like disembodied spirits.' Holmes describes this cyber-like stereoscopic experience in equally ecstatic detail in an essay published in 1859:

> Oh, infinite volumes of poems that I treasure in this small library of glass and pasteboard! I creep over the vast features of Rameses, on the face of his rockhewn Nubian temple; I scale the huge mountain-crystal that calls itself the Pyramid of Cheops. I pace the length of the three Titanic stones of the wall of Baalbec, – mightiest masses of quarried

> rock that man has lifted into the air. . . . [I] leave my outward frame in the arm-chair at my table, while in spirit I am looking down upon Jerusalem from the Mount of Olives.

Here we have a description of an early nineteenth-century technology of seeing that would appear to parallel closely the VR experience that so many commentators want to call 'revolutionary' and 'altogether new.' Nor do the parallels end there. Charles Babbage (1792–1871), inventor of the first analytical machine or computer (based in turn on his 1822 Difference Machine), was also the first person to sit for a stereoscopic portrait (taken by Henry Collen, probably in 1841, for Charles Wheatstone). We can presume that he was therefore also one of the earliest stereo-cybernauts. But what was the nature of the space he explored? And how does this stereo-space relate to the computer-induced environment we now want to privilege with the name of cyberspace?

Julian Bleecker is one critic who argues that the implications of stereoscopy and VR are 'fundamentally different.' While agreeing that there are some 'initial similarities' between the two, in a 1992 essay for *Afterimage* he draws a contrast between the stereoscope's emergence out of scientific investigations of vision physiology and VR's involvement with the computerized organization and dissemination of information. Bleecker takes a dark view of VR's easy assimilation into military, corporate, and consumerist machinations, concluding that it has become a 'metonym for the influential and hegemonic state of the information distribution apparatus.' Predictably enough, this simplistic sketch of the relationship between power and technology ends with a paean to the anti-technological innocence of the Australian Aborigine – or at least to those virtual primitives portrayed in Wim Wenders' 1991 film *Until the End of the World*.

The problem with Bleecker's account is that it leaves no room for complexity; for the complexity of the operations of both power and history, for the complexity and diversity of cyberspace itself (in which systems established by the Pentagon have already been taken over by undergraduates and Chiapis rebels alike as Multiple User Dialogue and e-mail services), and, last but not least, for the complexity of Aboriginal culture (which has for some time been quietly producing some of the most interesting film and television in Australia).

Nevertheless, Bleecker's dire warnings do at least turn our discussion to the question of cyberspace and politics, to the question of cyberspace *as* a politics. In this regard, it is interesting to note that technologies such as stereoscopy are but one manifestation of a general dissolution in the years around 1800 of the boundaries between observer and observed, subject and object, self and other, virtual and actual, representation and real – the very dissolution which some want to claim is peculiar to a newly emergent and postmodern VR. We can find this same disruption, for example, inscribed within apparently 'realist' image-making processes like photography. Conceived in the 1790s but only placed on the market in 1839, the concept-metaphor of photography centered on the virtual image produced by a mirrored surface exposed to the perspectival order of the camera's optical geometry. However photography's many inventors never seemed able to define satisfactorily exactly what the photograph was. For with photography they found themselves having to describe something altogether new to them, an apparently interconstitutive relationship involving both a viewer and a thing viewed, representing and being represented, fixity and transience, nature and culture – such that all of these terms are radically reconfigured. This conundrum is embodied in the eventual choice of 'photography' as the word for this relationship. Operating simultaneously as verb and noun, photography describes a form of 'writing' that produces while being produced, inscribing even as it is inscribed. It is as if photography can only be properly represented by way of a Mobius-like enfoldment of One within its Other.

Seen in the context of its own convoluted etymological history, photography is in its turn strikingly reminiscent of the paradoxical play of disciplinary power that Michel Foucault has associated with panopticism. Conceived by Jeremy Bentham in 1791 (i.e. in the same decade that photography is also conceived), the Panopticon is, for Foucault, the exemplary technological metaphor for the operations of modern systems of power. The circular architecture of this new notion of the prison allowed each prisoner to be continually surveyed by a single viewer standing in a central tower. Thanks to a bright light shining from the top of the tower, the warder remained invisible to those in the cells. The tower could even be left empty with no detrimental effect on the process of surveillance. As the prisoner never knows if he is being watched or not, he must assume that it is always so. He is thereby forced to survey and discipline himself. Continually projecting himself into a space between tower and cell, the panoptic subject becomes both the prisoner and the one who imprisons, both the subject and the object of his own gaze. As Foucault says, 'he becomes the principle of his own subjection.'

Remember that, for Foucault, panopticism is not just an efficient piece of prison design but also 'the diagram of a mechanism of power reduced to its ideal form.' His own work returned again and again to such diagrams of power, always finding within them a peculiarly modern configuration of human subjectivity. Positioned as both the subject and object of knowledge, this modern human is, he says, an undoubtedly 'strange empirico-transcendental doublet.' As an effect of and vehicle for the exercise of power/knowledge, the modern human subject is, in other words, a being produced within the interstices of a continual negotiation of virtual and real.

Such a notion is hardly peculiar to Foucault. Jacques Lacan reiterates something of this same conceptual economy in his 1936 meditations on the 'Mirror Stage.' This is what he called that inevitable phase in our infant development where, by being brought face to face with the image of a virtual Other, we learn to recognize ourselves as a self. According to Lacan's description of the Mirror Stage, our unconscious efforts to incorporate a perceived difference between real and virtual result in our becoming an irretrievably split being, a creature always in the process of being divided from itself. The way Lacan tells it, the production of this split subjectivity centers on

> a series of gestures in which [the child] experiences in play the relation between the movements assumed in the image and the reflected environment, and between this virtual complex and the reality it reduplicates – the child's own body, and the persons and things, around him.

To become a complete subject in a world of differentiations, the child has no choice but to invent a cyberspace of which it becomes the convulsive possession. Thus, in Lacan's schema, a never-resolved assemblage of virtual and real is what makes up the very fabric of human subjectivity.

This story is surely rehearsed every time we, as adults, confront ourselves in an actual mirror, there to be faced with an apparently real but completely inverted replica. We raise a hand and find ourselves in perfect harmony with the opposite hand of our replicant self, the one floating before us in virtual space. This replicant is a separate entity, but is also inseparable from our other 'real' self. In order to coincide with this self-same simulacra, the body must break the boundary of its skin and simultaneously occupy both sides of its senses. It must somehow incorporate this divided self and be both before and behind the mirror, be both subject and object of its own gaze. When we move through the world, it is as the embodied enactment of this continual double gesture.

These selected examples, no more than cursorily sketched here, suggest that a comprehensive account of the history and cultural implications of cyberspace has yet to be written. However, one could already argue that the problematic of a 'virtual reality' (and the threatened dissolution of boundaries and oppositions it is presumed to represent) is not something peculiar to a particular technology or to postmodern discourse but is rather one of the fundamental conditions of modernity itself. Thus, those that lament VR's destruction of the body, the human, and so on, are in fact mourning a Cartesian reality and subject that have already been under erasure for nigh on 200 years.

This image of cyberspace as something that has for some time already been with us returns my paper to its beginnings, to VR's present haunting of Western cultural discourse. For if we are properly to characterize cyberspace as a postmodern phenomenon, it must be as part of a postmodernism that does not come after the modern so much as assertively re-enacts modernism's desire to fold back in on itself. Like VR, this viral postmodernism takes nourishment from an inseparable host, replicating itself as an aberrant form of the other and thereby leaving us with a troubling because all too faithful repetition of the same. It is here then, here in the complex interweave of this entanglement – here within the spacing of One with its Other – that the political and historical identity of cyberspace might best be sought.

PART FOUR

Race and identity in colonial and postcolonial culture

Introduction to part four

■ Nicholas Mirzoeff

ONE OF THE DEFINING features of the modern era has been the experience of colonialism and slavery. The colonial efforts that began as soon as Columbus landed in the Caribbean, culminated in 1914 with a staggering 85 per cent of the globe being a colonial possession of one sort or another. The expansion of Europe was made possible in material terms by the Atlantic slave trade which flourished from the seventeenth to the early nineteenth centuries, forcibly removing ten to fifteen million Africans and killing many more in the attempt. Slavery was the unspoken guarantor of European racial supremacy. Its abolition led to the growth of 'scientific' racism that claimed to be able to prove the inferiority of other 'races' as a given fact. From the skull researches of Blumenbach in the eighteenth century to recent efforts to define blacks as genetically inferior, all such attempts have failed. It is impossible to create rational sense out of the irrationalities of racism. None the less, the futile quest to visualize racial difference was a key part of Western visual culture throughout the modern period and its effects are only too apparent in contemporary everyday life. Are there non-racialized ways of looking at people? This question has to be considered both within the former colonial powers and in the postcolonial nations themselves. Indeed, the African philosopher V.Y. Mudimbe has argued that the system of nations and colonies constructed by the Great Powers of the nineteenth century has only very recently come to a close. While many nations have had independence for decades, the end of the Cold War and the restructuring of global and local power that has accompanied it, make a truly postcolonial culture now possible for the first time. What will the postcolony look like to former colonizers and colonized?

(a) Visual colonialism

The colonial powers always claimed that their role centred on the three Cs enumerated by the missionary David Livingstone: commerce, Christianity and civilization. What the French called the 'civilizing mission' may seem like a mere excuse for the development of trade, but the colonialists took their self-appointed role very seriously. One of the consequences was an immensely productive visual colonialism, ranging from maps, photographs and paintings to collections of indigenous arts and crafts. These objects were assembled in vast collections like that of the Musée de l'Homme in Paris, the Museum of Mankind in London, the Musée du Congo Belge in Terveruen and so on. Collectively, the visual culture of colonialism had a significant role to play in both explaining and defining the colonial order.

The anthropologist Johannes Fabian argues that conventional anthropology, which grew in direct relation to European colonies, was so visually oriented that 'the ability to "visualise" a culture or society almost becomes synonymous for understanding it' (Fabian 1983). He names this system 'visualism', closely allied to the Enlightenment notion of observational science as defined by John Locke: 'The perception of the mind [is] most aptly explained by words relating to the sight'. For Fabian and other anthropologists, the solution to this problem lies in turning away from an exclusive reliance on visual observation to incorporate the evidence of all the senses. It is hard to agree completely with this conclusion. No researcher can actually function as a purely visual being, disregarding all other sensory information. Blaming the visual aspect to anthropology conveniently ignores that visualism aspired to create a racialized system of distinguishing humans by means of an evolutionary 'ladder' stretching from the 'primitive' to the 'civilized'.

In the extract from his fascinating essay 'Orientalism and the Exhibitionary Order', Timothy Mitchell shows how nineteenth-century anthropological exhibitions were dedicated to displaying what he calls 'Orientalist reality' (Mitchell 1992). Orientalism was the name given to the Western study of the imaginary place known as the Orient that was based on the European colonies in the Middle East and North Africa but corresponded to a notion of the Orient as everything exotic and Other. This Orientalist reality was defined 'as the product of unchanging racial or cultural essences' which were held to be diametrically opposed to those of the 'West'. The Oriental was necessarily marked by an absence of certain Western qualities, which the repeated world's fairs and universal exhibitions of the period constantly sought to display to their visitors. Mitchell uses the accounts of Arab visitors to these exhibitions to argue that 'the world itself [was] being ordered up as an endless exhibition'. Middle Eastern visitors found it curious that Westerners were so obsessed with 'spectacle' – a word for which they could find no equivalent. No effort was spared to render the displays of Oriental life and culture 'realistic' but their value was only to serve as what one catalogue called 'an object lesson'. The lesson taught that, as Mitchell puts it,

> objectiveness was a matter not just of visual arrangement around a curious spectator, but of representation. What reduced the world to

> a system of objects was the way their careful organization enabled them to evoke some larger meaning, such as History or Empire or Progress.

These disparate meanings were in themselves linked by the discourse of race and racial difference. The exhibitionary order certainly relied on visualism but that was not its goal. It sought to use visual imagery to represent the grand narratives of the imperial world-view both to domestic populations and also to subject peoples.

The exhibitionary order of visual colonialism extended into the everyday lives of both Europeans and indigenous peoples. No product could seem more innocent and everyday than the humble bar of soap. In this extract from her acclaimed book *Imperial Leather*, Anne McClintock shows that the remarkable growth of soap as a commodity in the nineteenth century was due to its being perceived as the very essence of imperial culture: 'Soap flourished not only because it created and filled a spectacular gap in the domestic market but also because, as a cheap and portable domestic commodity, it could persuasively mediate the Victorian poetics of racial hygiene and imperial progress' (McClintock 1995). A repeated theme in mass advertising of the period showed a black child being washed with soap in the first frame and then becoming white below the neck in the second. Imperialism literally washes away the stains of primitivism and 'the purification of the domestic body becomes a metaphor for the regeneration of the body politic'. Protestantism, commerce and civilization were thus all mobilized by the bar of soap, selling both the product and the political culture of imperialism.

Malek Alloula takes another everyday object – the postcard – and shows how it was a classic locus of Orientalism, which has long been a phantasm of the West: 'There is no phantasm, though, without sex, and in this Orientalism . . . a central figure emerges, the very embodiment of the obsession: the harem' (Alloula 1986). In Arabic *harim* means forbidden and thus also refers to the women's quarters of an Islamic household. Embroidering from four centuries of stories concerning the Imperial harem in Istanbul, the Western imagination had transformed every harem into a hotbed of sensuality and sexuality. France colonized Algeria in 1830, an operation documented by artists like Eugène Delacroix and later Horace Vernet. In the first decades of the twentieth century, the fine art genre of the odalisque, or Oriental nude, was displayed by a flood of popular postcards depicting the *algérienne*, the Algerian woman. Alloula, himself Algerian, studied this mass of now-discarded visual material in his volume *The Colonial Postcard* in which he attempts to 'return this immense postcard to its sender', showing how the veiled Algerian woman was a provocation to the photographer as her white clothing produced a 'whiteout', a technical failure of the photograph. The women's peephole gaze from behind the veil recalls the photographer's own gaze and in a sense 'the photographer feels photographed . . . *he is dispossessed of his own gaze*'. Perhaps predictably the response is clear: 'he will unveil the veiled and give figural expression to the forbidden'. Thus from the seemingly innocent postcards showing a woman slightly lifting her veil to the popular image of the half-naked Algerian woman there is hardly a step. The colonial gaze must see and make an exhibition of these women. The erotic effect, such as it is, is beside the point, for this is an operation of colonial power.

African art historian Suzanne Preston Blier gives a striking account of how the operations of colonial power transformed one evocative genre of African art, the Fon *bocio* figure (Blier 1995). In this region of West Africa, slavery did not disappear with the end of the Atlantic slave trade but continued domestically in order to supply labour for the palm-oil plantations that supplied the soap industry described by Anne McClintock. By 1900, as many as one-third of the population in the Danhome area were plantation slaves. The violence of slavery was powerfully expressed in the gagged and bound *bocio* figure that was in sharp contrast to the smoothly rounded sculpture produced for the Fon nobility of the period. As Blier explains in this extract from her prize-winning book *African Vodun: Social History and the Slave Trade*, these sculptures 'offered a way of both accepting and refusing the negative by helping their users to "think-through-terror", as [Michael] Taussig would say. . . . Art provides one way of uttering what is otherwise unutterable.' While Alloula regrets that the gaze of the Algerian women is nowhere represented in the postcards, the subaltern experience is given visible expression in the Fon *bocio* figure, as it is in Kongo *minkisi* power figures. As important as it has been to analyse the visual culture of imperial nations, this kind of dialogue with the experience of the colonized themselves has still to be fully developed in scholarly accounts. Disciplinary constraints of language skills and fieldwork experience have been deployed to restrict research into these encounters. These border experiences will be a vital field for visual culture studies.

(b) Visualizing race and identity

In 1735 the Swedish botanist Karl Linnaeus applied the classificatory schemes he had devised for plants to humans. He divided humanity into four separate types: the European, the African, the Asian and the American (meaning the indigenous peoples of the Americas). Ever since, Western culture has sought to visualize these differences, despite the now-overwhelming scientific evidence that there are no essential biological distinctions between peoples. The idea that there were different human types gradually became codified as distinct races, although there was never a consensus as to how race could be defined. At different periods, race theorists looked to the skull, the brain, art, and now the gene to find a visible and permanent mark of race. Often, despite grandiose denials that this was the case, only skin colour could be found to serve as an absurdly imprecise means of categorizing people.

However, despite the consistent failure to explain race biologically, race can also be considered as culture, terms that were virtually synonymous in the eighteenth century. Nineteenth-century anthropology redefined culture to mean the entire way of life in a particular society, as in the expression 'Jewish culture', but continued to use it in a racialized context. The question is how and whether race can be kept out of culture. Recent writing on this subject has stressed that culture should not be seen as a given but as something constantly in flux and whose borders are always in dispute. For Antonio Benítez-Rojo: 'Culture is a discourse, a language, and as such it has no beginning or end, and is always in transformation since it is always looking to signify what it cannot manage to signify.' The essays in this section look at the challenges posed by such an approach both within and without a particular culture.

In his essay on black British art reprinted here, entitled 'Art of Darkness', Paul Gilroy argues from the perspective of cultural studies that in contemporary Britain 'the politics of race has changed' (Gilroy 1993b). He has sought to shift the debate away from narrow anti-racist politics towards the wider complexities of culture and belonging. In a series of publications, perhaps most notably *The Black Atlantic* (Gilroy 1993a), Gilroy has explored what it means to be both black and British. Even to ask this question is to expose the fiction that Britishness is somehow natural and reveals it to refer predominantly to (white) Englishness, rather than to the Scots, Welsh or Irish, let alone the many ethnic minorities that make up Britain's past and present population. Gilroy argues that Britain needs to be understood as part of the black Atlantic, a cultural geography created by the forced movement of enslaved Africans and the diaspora of their free descendants, as well as by the routes taken by the commercial products of colonial culture, like sugar, cotton, tea and coffee. Black British artists are participating in this rewriting of history and are moving beyond the first, necessary reclamation of the black experience 'to re-compose understanding of English culture, and their creativity needs to be complemented by a re-reading of that culture's history which places the idea of "race" at the centre rather than the margin.' Gilroy contributes to this re-reading by showing that J.M.W. Turner's famous painting *The Slave Ship*, which depicts the slave ship *Zong* throwing Africans overboard in a storm in order to lighten the load and claim insurance on the deceased, was indeed understood by his contemporaries as addressing the issue of slavery and not just as a beautiful seascape. Gilroy sees Sonia Boyce's painting *She Ain't Holding Them Up, She's Holding On (Some English Rose)* as a contemporary interrogation of Britain's 'hybrid cultural heritage'. Her painting depicts a young black British woman 'holding up' her family, including her partner, children, and mother, against a non-realistic background incorporating African and Caribbean motifs. For Boyce the question of Englishness is conceptually and compositionally subordinate to the gender politics of everyday life.

As the tension between Boyce's painting and Gilroy's interpretation suggests, sustaining such discussions is by no means easy. Different groups may approach the same cultural artifact and have very different responses. bell hooks describes one such case in her reading of Wim Wenders' film *Wings of Desire* (1988), taken from her collection of essays entitled *Yearnings* (hooks 1990). Set in Berlin before the fall of Eastern Europe, many acclaimed the film for its message of hope and compassion; hooks, by contrast, saw it as 'another in a series where postmodern white culture looks at itself somewhat critically, revising here and there, then falling in love with itself all over again.' hooks points out that all the angels are unproblematically portrayed as white, while Berlin's substantial non-white population are relegated to background shots. While Wenders saw his film as reopening a discussion about historical memory, especially that of the Third Reich, hooks notes that 'the film's implied critique of oppressive masculinity is undercut by the re-inscription of sexist male bonding as regards sexual desire'. She shows that Marion, the trapeze artist, is presented as an object for the male gaze, retelling an old story of male desire for sex, female desire for love. In *Wings of Desire*, 'it is only white people who are angels, only white men who dialogue with one another, only white people who interpret and revise old scripts.' Quoting the artist and theorist Coco Fusco, hooks concludes: 'To ignore white ethnicity is to redouble its hegemony by naturalizing it. Without specifically addressing white ethnicity, there can be no critical evaluation of the construction of the other.' In the time since this essay was first published, there has been the discussion that Wenders wanted about German history. Whiteness is now a hot academic topic, in part at least because it allows white academics the cachet of working on ethnicity. Yet the mutual construction of otherness by blacks and whites is still a highly charged topic.

Such alterities can arise within ethnic groups as well as across them. In his essay 'The Gangsta and the Diva', the leading cultural studies theorist Andrew Ross argues that black popular culture has 'two current polarities of "fierceness" ', one represented by gangsta rappers like Treach of Naughty by Nature and the other by cross-dressing model and singer Ru Paul (Ross 1994). While there is little public acknowledgement of this connection, the 'houses' represented in the film *Paris Is Burning* (see Butler's essay below) can be usefully compared to the familial structures of gangs. The rapper Ice-T has described LA gangland as 'ghetto male love being pushed to its limits'. In both domains, 'realness' is a key aesthetic. For the rapper, realness represents staying true to the ghetto, even at the cost of death, as Tupac Shakur and the Notorious B.I.G. both discovered. In the cross-dressed world, 'realness' means the ability to pass for whatever category is being imitated, although the imitation must still be recognized as such – 'almost straight but not quite', as Homi Bhabha nearly put it. Ross further argues that hardcore rap is 'just about the only medium in which ghetto life attains something approaching authentic recognition'. When one considers how often the dilemmas of suburban life are replayed on television, it is clear that such representation is central to identity in the atomized postmodern world. The popularity of gangsta rap amongst the children of the suburbs suggests that many such youth are 'propelled by the prospect of their economic redundancy, and thus committed to the ultimate desertion of a white parental culture that can't even offer them a future with the dignity of employment.' The rapper and the drag queen represent different aspects of a conflicted black – and increasingly white – masculinity, whose diversity Ross argues should be the starting-point for a new 'cultural politics of masculinity'. Perhaps the embrace of the cross-dressing basketball player Dennis Rodman by the notoriously racially divided city of Chicago is a sign that this discussion is finally at least possible.

(c) Identity and transculture

As the twentieth century draws to an unmourned close, a striking historical development of its latter years has been the simultaneous globalization and localization of culture and identity. The nation state, so central to politics and identity for the past two centuries, seems to be waning in the face of this joint pressure. New transnational economic power blocs like the European Union and the North

American Free Trade Agreement have substantially limited the nation state. Increasingly, workers in the developed nations have found their negotiating position undermined by the ability of capital to relocate in 'underdeveloped' nations. Labour everywhere has been forced to become migrant, so that the new symbol of the American working class is the Ryder moving truck rather than the shining Thunderbird of the 1950s. One response to this weakening of the national has been an increased attention to what one might call micro-identity, exemplified by the gruesome absurdity of the Balkan War. Artists, critics and intellectuals have tried to resist this new essentialism by seeking to define what Cuban critic Fernando Ortiz called 'transculture', a fusion of old, new and borrowed cultural practices (Ortiz 1947). Transcultural studies concentrates on those places where the carefully defined borders of identity become confused and overlapping, a task that requires both new histories and new means of representation.

In her essay 'Passing for White, Passing for Black', the artist and philosopher Adrian Piper uses her personal difficulties as an African-American who also has European ancestry to consider the interaction of ethnic groups in America (Piper 1992). It so happens that she has light skin, causing many Euramericans to doubt her ethnicity: 'Their ridicule and accusations then function to both disown and degrade you from their status, to mark you not as having *done* wrong but as *being* wrong.' Interspersing her memoir with quotations from a wide range of literature and criticism, Piper shows that the question of 'passing' has been critical to American identity since slavery. Her essay raises the question of how identity is to be defined and what its markers are. To be considered Native American, at least one-eighth of your ancestors must be Native American, while any African ancestry at all will mark you as black. On the other hand, 95 per cent of white Americans have some African ancestry that is unacknowledged because they are not 'visibly' black: 'the primary issue for them is not what they might have to give away by admitting that they are in fact black, but rather what they have to lose.' This dilemma is re-enacted time and time again in American culture from movies like *Jungle Fever* and *A Family Thing* to the controversy over the ethnicity of the golfer Tiger Woods. When he pointed out after winning the 1997 US Masters tournament that he was not simply of African descent but a complicated hybrid of Thai, African and Native American, he caused a storm of controversy. It seems that, despite 500 years of experience to the contrary, the sight of miscegenation is still the ultimate taboo in American culture, to be denied or repressed at all costs.

The construction of a monolithic Euramerican identity has depended on an exotic Other, whose existence has been repeatedly confirmed by the ethnographic display of human beings. To mark the quincentennial of Columbus's voyage to America in 1992, performance artists Coco Fusco and Guillermo Gómez-Peña created a satirical re-enactment of such displays by placing themselves on display in a cage, labelled as 'Two Undiscovered Amerindians', supposedly hailing from an unknown island in the Gulf of Mexico called Guatinau. As Coco Fusco reports in this extract from her book *English Is Broken Here*, the consequences were not as they expected:

> a substantial portion of the pubic believed that our fictional identities were real ones. . . . a substantial number of intellectuals, artists and cultural bureaucrats sought to deflect attention from the substance of our experiment to the 'moral' implications of our dissimulation.
>
> (Fusco 1995)

Once again, the question of 'realness' and identity displaced all others. While some viewers were simply willing to accept that any such display in a museum or public space must be 'real', others were aware of the performance yet quickly 'felt entitled to assume the role of the colonizer'. Museum curators and other professionals wanted to question only the 'authenticity' of the performance rather than treat it as a piece of theatre. While the performance had been designed as a comment on past relations, Fusco concludes that 'the constant concern about our "realness" revealed a need for reassurance that a "true primitive" *did* exist, whether we fit the bill or not, and that she or he [be] visually identifiable.' The prevalence of such attitudes undercuts both what Fusco calls 'happy multiculturalism' and the denial that ethnicity has any place in the world of art.

The Latin American critic Néstor García Canclini has written extensively about the place of visual culture in the global culture of postmodernism. In his essay 'Remaking Passports' reprinted here, Canclini notes that for many Western critics,

> Latin America continues to be interesting only as a continent of a violent nature, of an archaism irreducible to modern nationality, an earth fertilized by an art conceived as tribal or national dreaming and not as thinking about the global and the complex.
>
> (Canclini 1994)

In a context where most art history has been written as the 'history of the art of nations', this has the effect of excluding Latin America from art history except as an example of the primitive or exotic. Canclini emphasizes that not only is this an ignorant account of Latin American culture, it is now an irrelevance in an age in which the globalization of the economy has deterritorialized art. He asserts, in conjunction with the artist Luis Felipe Noé, that art 'doesn't need a passport'. Works like the 'airmail' paintings of Eugenio Dittborn seek to be 'polyglot and migrant, they can function in diverse and multiple contexts and permit divergent readings from their hybrid constitution'. In order to understand such work, we need to turn to the kind of polycentric approach called for by Robert Stam and Ella Shohat in this volume rather than a naïve multiculturalism in which difference is simply subsumed into a vague notion of 'culture'.

In her essay 'Engendering New Worlds', taken from the special edition of *Art and Design* on 'New Art from Latin America', art historian Oriana Baddeley pursues a similar argument to that of Canclini, examining the changing meanings of the sexualized allegory of the 'encounter' between Europeans and indigenous peoples in Latin America: 'Traditionally, the encounter is discussed in ostensibly sexual terms. The eroticised Indian nude greeting the arrival of the Spanish conqueror with equanimity . . . has functioned as a powerful metaphor within Latin American culture' (Baddeley 1994). While early twentieth-century Latin American art presented the encounter as a rape, more recent renditions see it in more ambiguous terms: 'To put it simply, the definition of what is imposed and what is inherited in cultural terms has shifted. Colonialism is not denied but clearly defined criteria of cultural identity are replaced by a series of questions.' Rather than assume that precolonial Amerindian cultures can still offer a sense of cultural identity in the late twentieth-century in the fashion of the Mexican muralist Diego Rivera, contemporary artists have moved away from a binary mode – male/female; colonizer/colonized; evil/good – to explore the complex 'legacy of pain and cruelty' with which the continent has to deal daily. Culture is no longer a source of certainty but the place where the remarkable hybridity of Latin American life can be approached.

While it is possible to argue, in the title of Nathan Glazer's 1997 book, that 'we are all multiculturalists now', it is still unclear what real change has been effected. In the art world, it is now fashionable to denounce 'political' art, which of course has the result of remarginalizing work concentrating on issues of gender and race. Television continues to show us the only group of *Friends* living in New York City who do not know any people of colour. *Seinfeld* went so far as to devote an entire episode to George's inevitably unsuccessful search for an African-American friend in order to prove a point at work. At the same time, universities in California and Texas, where affirmative action has been banned, have seen a dramatic drop in applications from black and Latina/o candidates. There is no doubt that diaspora, displacement and hybridity are key factors of contemporary everyday life. What is at stake in much contemporary cultural work of all kinds is whether the move towards transculture is embraced or rejected.

References and further reading

Alloula, Malek (1986) *The Colonial Harem*, Minneapolis: Minnesota University Press.

Baddeley, Oriana (1994) *New Art from Latin America: Expanding the Continent*, Art and Design Profile No. 37, *Art and Design*.

Benítez-Rojo, Antonio (1996) *The Repeating Island: The Caribbean and the Postmodern Perspective*, Durham: Duke University Press.

Bhabha, Homi (1994) *The Location of Culture*, London: Routledge.

Blier, Suzanne Preston (1995) *African Vodun: Art, Psychology and Power*, Chicago: Chicago University Press.

Canclini, Néstor García (1994) 'Remaking Passports: Visual Thought in the Debate on Multiculturalism', *Third Text* 28/29 (Autumn/Winter 1994).

Fabian, Johannes (1983) *Times and the Other*, New York: Columbia University Press.

Fanon, Frantz (1967) *Black Skin, White Masks*, New York: Grove.

Fusco, Coco (1995) *English Is Broken Here: Notes on Cultural Fusion in the Americas*, New York: New Press.

Gilroy, Paul (1993a) *The Black Atlantic: Modernity and Double-Consciousness*, Cambridge, Mass.: Harvard University Press.

—— (1993b) *Small Acts: Thoughts on the Politics of Black Cultures*, London: Serpent's Tail.

hooks, bell (1990) *Yearning: Race, Gender and Cultural Politics*, Boston: South End Press.

—— (1996) *Reel to Real: Race, Sex and Class at the Movies*, New York: Routledge.

McClintock, Anne (1995) *Imperial Leather: Race, Gender and Sexuality in the Colonial Contest*, London and New York: Routledge.

MacGaffey, Wyatt (1993) *Astonishment and Power*, Washington DC: National Museum of African Art.

Mesquita, Ivo (1993) *Cartographies*, Winnipeg: Winnipeg Art Gallery.

Mitchell, Timothy (1992) 'Orientalism and the Exhibitionary Order', in Nicholas Dirks (ed.), *Colonialism and Culture*, Ann Arbor: University of Michigan Press.

Mudimbe, V.Y. (1988) *The Invention of Africa: Gnosis, Philosophy and the Order of Knowledge*, Bloomington: Indiana University Press.

Ortiz, Fernando (1947) *Cuban Counterpoint: Tobacco and Sugar*, New York: Knopf.

Pakenham, Thomas (1991) *The Scramble for Africa*, New York: Random House.

Piper, Adrian (1992) 'Passing for White, Passing for Black', in Joanna Frueh, Cassandra L. Langer, and Arlene Raven (eds), *New Feminist Criticism: Art, Identity, Action*, New York: Icon Editions.

Read, Alan (1996) *The Fact of Blackness: Frantz Fanon and Visual Representation*, Seattle: Bay Press.

Ross, Andrew (1994) 'The Gangsta and the Diva,' first published in Thelma Golden (ed.), *Black Male: Representations of Masculinity in Contemporary American Art*, New York: Abrams.

Said, Edward (1978) *Orientalism*, New York: Vintage.

—— (1993) *Culture and Imperialism*, New York: Knopf.

Shelton, Antony (1995) *Fetishism: Visualizing Power and Desire*, London: South Bank Centre.

Spivak, Gayatri Chakravorty (1994) 'Can the Subaltern Speak?', reprinted in P. Williams and L. Chrisman (eds), *Colonial Discourse and Postcolonial Theory*, New York: Columbia University Press.

Stocking, George (1987) *Victorian Anthropology*, London: Free Press.

Vogel, Susan (ed.) (1991) *Africa Explores: 20th Century African Art*, New York: Center for African Art.

Ware, Vron (1992) *Beyond the Pale: White Women, Racism and History*, London: Verso.

Young, Robert J.C. (1995) *Colonial Desire: Hybridity in Theory, Culture and Race*, London and New York: Routledge.

(a) Visual colonialism

Chapter 25

Timothy Mitchell

ORIENTALISM AND THE EXHIBITIONARY ORDER

IT IS NO LONGER unusual to suggest that the construction of the colonial order is related to the elaboration of modern forms of representation and knowledge. The relationship has been most closely examined in the critique of Orientalism. The Western artistic and scholarly portrayal of the non-West, in Edward Said's analysis, is not merely an ideological distortion convenient to an emergent global political order but a densely imbricated arrangement of imagery and expertise that organizes and produces the Orient as a political reality.[1] Three features define this Orientalist reality: it is understood as the product of unchanging racial or cultural essences; these essential characteristics are in each case the polar opposite of the West (passive rather than active, static rather than mobile, emotional rather than rational, chaotic rather than ordered); and the Oriental opposite or Other is, therefore, marked by a series of fundamental absences (of movement, reason, order, meaning, and so on). In terms of these three features – essentialism, otherness, and absence – the colonial world can be mastered, and colonial mastery will, in turn, reinscribe and reinforce these defining features.

Orientalism, however, has always been part of something larger. The nineteenth-century image of the Orient was constructed not just in Oriental studies, romantic novels, and colonial administrations, but in all the new procedures with which Europeans began to organize the representation of the world, from museums and world exhibitions to architecture, schooling, tourism the fashion industry, and the commodification of everyday life. In 1889, to give an indication of the scale of these processes, 32 million people visited the Exposition Universelle, built that year in Paris to commemorate the centenary of the Revolution and to demonstrate French commercial and imperial power.[2] The consolidation of the global hegemony of the West, economically and politically, can be connected not just to the imagery of Orientalism but to all the new machinery for rendering up and laying out the meaning of the world, so characteristic of the imperial age.

The new apparatus of representation, particularly the world exhibitions, gave a central place to the representation of the non-Western world, and several studies have pointed out the importance of this construction of otherness to the manufacture of national identity and imperial purpose.[3] But is there, perhaps, some more integral relationship between representation, as a modern technique of meaning and order, and the construction of otherness so important to the colonial project? One perspective from which to explore this question is provided by the accounts of non-Western visitors to nineteenth-century Europe. An Egyptian delegation to the Eighth International Congress of Orientalists, for example, held in Stockholm in the summer of 1889, traveled to Sweden via Paris and paused there to visit the Exposition Universelle, leaving us a detailed description of their encounter with the representation of their own otherness. Beginning with this and other accounts written by visitors from the Middle East, I examine the distinctiveness of the modern representational order exemplified by the world exhibition. What Arab writers found in the West, I will argue, were not just exhibitions and representations of the world, but the world itself being ordered up as an endless exhibition. This world-as-exhibition was a place where the artificial, the model, and the plan were employed to generate an unprecedented effect of order and certainty. It is not the artificiality of the exhibitionary order that matters, however, so much as the contrasting effect of an external reality that the artificial and the model create – a reality characterized, like Orientalism's Orient, by essentialism, otherness, and absence. In the second half of the article, I examine this connection between the world-as-exhibition and Orientalism, through a rereading of European travel accounts of the nineteenth-century Middle East. The features of the kind of Orient these writings construct – above all its characteristic absences – are not merely motifs convenient to colonial mastery, I argue, but necessary elements of the order of representation itself.

La rue du Caire

The four members of the Egyptian delegation to the Stockholm Orientalist conference spent several days in Paris, climbing twice the height (as they were told) of the Great Pyramid in Alexandre Eiffel's new tower, and exploring the city and exhibition laid out beneath. Only one thing disturbed them. The Egyptian exhibit had been built by the French to represent a street in medieval Cairo, made of houses with overhanging upper stories and a mosque like that of Qaitbay. 'It was intended,' one of the Egyptians wrote, 'to resemble the old aspect of Cairo.' So carefully was this done, he noted, that 'even the paint on the buildings was made dirty.'[4] The exhibit had also been made carefully chaotic. In contrast to the geometric layout of the rest of the exhibition, the imitation street was arranged in the haphazard manner of the bazaar. The way was crowded with shops and stalls, where Frenchmen, dressed as Orientals, sold perfumes, pastries, and tarbushes. To complete the effect of the Orient, the French organizers had imported from Cairo fifty Egyptian donkeys, together with their drivers and the requisite number of grooms, farriers, and saddlers. The donkeys gave rides (for the price of one franc) up and down the street, resulting in a clamor and confusion so lifelike, the director of the exhibition was obliged to issue an order restricting the donkeys to a certain number at each hour of the day. The Egyptian visitors were disgusted by all this and stayed away. Their final embarrassment had been to enter the door of the mosque and discover that, like the rest of the street, it had been erected as what the Europeans called a façade. 'Its external form was all that there was of the mosque. As for the interior, it had been set up as a coffee house, where Egyptian girls performed dances with young males, and dervishes whirled.'[5]

After eighteen days in Paris, the Egyptian delegation traveled on to Stockholm to attend the Congress of Orientalists. Together with other non-European delegates, the Egyptians were received with hospitality – and a great curiosity. As though they were still in Paris, they found themselves something of an exhibit. '*Bona fide* Orientals,' wrote a European participant in the Congress, 'were stared at as in a Barnum's all-world show: the good Scandinavian people seemed to think that it was a collection of *Orientals*, not of *Orientalists*.'[6] Some of the Orientalists themselves seemed to delight in the role of showmen. At an earlier congress, in Berlin, we are told that

> the grotesque idea was started of producing natives of Oriental countries as illustrations of a paper: thus the Boden Professor of Sanskrit at Oxford produced a real live Indian Pandit, and made him go through the ritual of Brahmanical prayer and worship before a hilarious assembly. . . . Professor Max Müller of Oxford produced two rival Japanese priests, who exhibited their gifts; it had the appearance of two showmen exhibiting their monkeys.[7]

At the Stockholm Congress, the Egyptians were invited to participate as scholars, but when they used their own language to do so they again found themselves treated as exhibits. 'I have heard nothing so unworthy of a sensible man,' complained an Oxford scholar, 'as . . . the whistling howls emitted by an Arabic student of El-Azhar of Cairo. Such exhibitions at Congresses are mischievous and degrading.'[8]

The exhibition and the congress were not the only examples of this European mischief. As Europe consolidated its colonial power, non-European visitors found themselves continually being placed on exhibit or made the careful object of European curiosity. The degradation they were made to suffer seemed as necessary to these spectacles as the scaffolded facades or the curious crowds of onlookers. The facades, the onlookers, and the degradation seemed all to belong to the organizing of an exhibit, to a particularly European concern with rendering the world up to be viewed. Of what, exactly, did this exhibitionary process consist?

An object-world

To begin with, Middle Eastern visitors found Europeans a curious people, with an uncontainable eagerness to stand and stare. 'One of the characteristics of the French is to stare and get excited at everything new,' wrote an Egyptian scholar who spent five years in Paris in the 1820s, in the first description of nineteenth-century

Europe to be published in Arabic.[9] The 'curiosity' of the European is encountered in almost every subsequent Middle Eastern account. Toward the end of the nineteenth century, when one or two Egyptian writers adopted the realistic style of the novel and made the journey to Europe their first topic, their stories would often evoke the peculiar experience of the West by describing an individual surrounded and stared at, like an object on exhibit. 'Whenever he paused outside a shop or showroom,' the protagonist in one such story found on his first day in Paris, 'a large number of people would surround him, both men and women, staring at his dress and appearance.'[10]

In the second place, this curious attitude that is described in Arabic accounts was connected with what one might call a corresponding *objectness*. The curiosity of the observing subject was something demanded by a diversity of mechanisms for rendering things up as its object – beginning with the Middle Eastern visitor himself. The members of an Egyptian student mission sent to Paris in the 1820s were confined to the college where they lived and allowed out only to visit museums and the theater – where they found themselves parodied in vaudeville as objects of entertainment for the French public.[11]

> They construct the stage as the play demands. For example, if they want to imitate a sultan and the things that happen to him, they set up the stage in the form of a palace and portray him in person. If for instance they want to play the Shah of Persia, they dress someone in the clothes of the Persian monarch and then put him there and sit him on a throne.[12]

Even Middle Eastern monarchs who came in person to Europe were liable to be incorporated into its theatrical machinery. When the Khedive of Egypt visited Paris to attend the Exposition Universelle of 1867, he found that the Egyptian exhibit had been built to simulate medieval Cairo in the form of a royal palace. The Khedive stayed in the imitation palace during his visit and became a part of the exhibition, receiving visitors with medieval hospitality.[13]

Visitors to Europe found not only themselves rendered up as objects to be viewed. The Arabic account of the student mission to Paris devoted several pages to the Parisian phenomenon of '*le spectacle*,' a word for which its author knew of no Arabic equivalent. Besides the Opéra and the Opéra-Comique, among the different kinds of spectacle he described were 'places in which they represent for the person the view of a town or a country or the like,' such as 'the Panorama, the Cosmorama, the Diorama, the Europorama and the Uranorama.' In a panorama of Cairo, he explained in illustration, 'it is as though you were looking from on top of the minaret of Sultan Hasan, for example, with al-Rumaila and the rest of the city beneath you.'[14]

The effect of such spectacles was to set the world up as a picture. They ordered it up as an object on display to be investigated and experienced by the dominating European gaze. An Orientalist of the same period, the great French scholar Sylvestre de Sacy, wanted the scholarly picturing of the Orient to make available to European inspection a similar kind of object-world. He had planned to establish a museum, which was to be

> a vast depot of objects of all kinds, of drawings, of original books, maps, accounts of voyages, all offered to those who wish to give themselves to the study of [the Orient]; in such a way that each of these students would be able to feel himself transported as if by enchantment into the midst of, say, a Mongolian tribe or of the Chinese race, whichever he might have made the object of his studies.[15]

As part of a more ambitious plan in England for 'the education of the people,' a proposal was made to set up 'an ethnological institution, with very extensive grounds', where 'within the same enclosure' were to be kept 'specimens in pairs of the various races.' The natives on exhibit, it was said,

> should construct their own dwellings according to the architectural ideas of their several countries; their . . . mode of life should be their own. The forms of industry prevalent in their nation or tribe they should be required to practise; and their ideas, opinions, habits, and superstitions should be permitted to perpetuate themselves. . . . To go from one division of this establishment to another would be like travelling into a new country.[16]

The world exhibitions of the second half of the century offered the visitor exactly this educational encounter, with natives and their artifacts arranged to provide the direct experience of a colonized object-world. In planning the layout of the 1889 Paris Exhibition, it was decided that the visitor 'before entering the temple of modern life' should pass through an exhibit of all human history, 'as a gateway to the exposition and a noble preface.' Entitled 'Histoire du Travail,' or, more fully, 'Exposition retrospective du travail et des sciences anthropologiques,' the display would demonstrate the history of human labor by means of 'objects and things themselves.' It would have 'nothing vague about it,' it was said, 'because it will consist of an *object lesson*.'[17]

Arabic accounts of the modern West became accounts of these curious object-worlds. By the last decade of the nineteenth century, more than half the descriptions of journeys to Europe published in Cairo were written to describe visits to a world exhibition or an international congress of Orientalists.[18] Such accounts devote hundreds of pages to describing the peculiar order and technique of these events – the curious crowds of spectators, the organization of panoramas and perspectives, the arrangement of natives in mock colonial villages, the display of new inventions and commodities, the architecture of iron and glass, the systems of classification, the calculations of statistics, the lectures, the plans, and the guidebooks – in short, the entire method of organization that we think of as representation.

The world-as-exhibition

In the third place, then, the effect of objectness was a matter not just of visual arrangement around a curious spectator, but of representation. What reduced the world to a system of objects was the way their careful organization enabled them to evoke some larger meaning, such as History or Empire or Progress. This machinery of representation was not confined to the exhibition and the congress. Almost everywhere that Middle Eastern visitors went they seemed to encounter the arrangement of things to stand for something larger. They visited the new museums, and saw the cultures of the world portrayed in the form of objects arranged under glass, in the order of their evolution. They were taken to the theater, a place where Europeans represented to themselves their history, as several Egyptian writers explained. They spent afternoons in the public gardens, carefully organized 'to bring together the trees and plants of every part of the world,' as another Arab writer put it. And, inevitably, they took trips to the zoo, a product of nineteenth-century colonial penetration of the Orient, as Theodor Adorno wrote, that 'paid symbolic tribute in the form of animals.'[19]

The Europe one reads about in Arabic accounts was a place of spectacle and visual arrangement, of the organization of everything and everything organized to represent, to recall, like the exhibition, a larger meaning. Characteristic of the way Europeans seemed to live was their preoccupation with what an Egyptian author described as '*intizam almanzar*,' the organization of the view.[20] Beyond the exhibition and the congress, beyond the museum and the zoo, everywhere that non-European visitors went – the streets of the modern city with their meaningful facades, the countryside encountered typically in the form of a model farm exhibiting new machinery and cultivation methods, even the Alps once the funicular was built – they found the technique and sensation to be the same.[21] Everything seemed to be set up before one as though it were the model or the picture of something. Everything was arranged before an observing subject into a system of signification, declaring itself to be a mere object, a mere 'signifier of' something further.

The exhibition, therefore, could be read in such accounts as epitomizing the strange character of the West, a place where one was continually pressed into service as a spectator by a world ordered so as to represent. In exhibitions, the traveler from the Middle East could describe the curious way of addressing the world increasingly encountered in modern Europe, a particular relationship between the individual and a world of 'objects' that Europeans seemed to take as the experience of the real. This reality effect was a world increasingly rendered up to the individual according to the way in which, and to the extent to which, it could be made to stand before him or her as an exhibit. Non-Europeans encountered in Europe what one might call, echoing a phrase from Heidegger, the age of the world exhibition, or rather, the age of the world-as-exhibition.[22] The world-as-exhibition means not an exhibition of the world but the world organized and grasped as though it were an exhibition.

The certainty of representation

'England is at present the greatest Oriental Empire which the world has ever known,' proclaimed the president of the 1892 Orientalist Congress at its opening session. His words reflected the political certainty of the imperial age. 'She knows not only how to conquer, but how to rule.'[23] The endless spectacles of the world-as-exhibition were not just reflections of this certainty but the means of its production, by their technique of rendering imperial truth and cultural difference in 'objective' form.

Three aspects of this kind of certainty can be illustrated from the accounts of the world exhibition. First there was the apparent realism of the representation. The model or display always seemed to stand in perfect correspondence to the external world, a correspondence that was frequently noted in Middle Eastern accounts. As the Egyptian visitor had remarked, 'Even the paint on the buildings was made dirty.' One of the most impressive exhibits at the 1889 exhibition in Paris was a panorama of the city. As described by an Arab visitor, this consisted of a viewing platform on which one stood, encircled by images of the city. The images were mounted and illuminated in such a way that the observer felt himself standing at the center of the city itself, which seemed to materialize around him as a single, solid object 'not differing from reality in any way.'[24]

In the second place, the model, however realistic, always remained distinguishable from the reality it claimed to represent. Even though the paint was made dirty and the donkeys were brought from Cairo, the medieval Egyptian street at the Paris exhibition remained only a Parisian copy of the Oriental original. The certainty of representation depended on this deliberate difference in time and displacement in space that separated the representation from the real thing. It also depended on the position of the visitor – the tourist in the imitation street or the figure on the viewing platform. The representation of reality was always an exhibit set up for an observer in its midst, an observing European gaze surrounded by and yet excluded from the exhibition's careful order. The more the exhibit drew in and encircled the visitor, the more the gaze was set apart from it, as the mind (in our Cartesian imagery) is said to be set apart from the material world it observes. The separation is suggested in a description of the Egyptian exhibit at the Paris Exhibition of 1867.

> A museum inside a pharaonic temple represented Antiquity, a palace richly decorated in the Arab style represented the Middle Ages, a caravanserai of merchants and performers portrayed in real life the customs of today. Weapons from the Sudan, the skins of wild monsters, perfumes, poisons and medicinal plants transport us directly to the tropics. Pottery from Assiut and Aswan, filigree and cloth of silk and gold invite us to touch with our fingers a strange civilization. All the races subject to the Vice-Roy [*sic*] were personified by individuals selected with care. We rubbed shoulders with the fellah, we made way before the Bedouin of the Libyan desert on their beautiful white dromedaries. This sumptuous display spoke to the mind as to the eyes; it expressed a political idea.[25]

The remarkable realism of such displays made the Orient into an object the visitor could almost touch. Yet to the observing eye, surrounded by the display but excluded from it by the status of visitor, it remained a mere representation, the picture of some further reality. Thus, two parallel pairs of distinctions were maintained, between the visitor and the exhibit and between the exhibit and what it expressed. The representation seemed set apart from the political reality it claimed to portray as the observing mind seems set apart from what it observes.

Third, the distinction between the system of exhibits or representations and the exterior meaning they portrayed was imitated, within the exhibition, by distinguishing between the exhibits themselves and the plan of the exhibition. The visitor would encounter, set apart from the objects on display, an abundance of catalogs, plans, signposts, programs, guidebooks, instructions, educational talks, and compilations of statistics. The Egyptian exhibit at the 1867 exhibition, for example, was accompanied by a guidebook containing an outline of the country's history – divided, like the exhibit to which it referred, into the ancient, medieval, and modern – together with a 'notice statistique sur le territoire, la population, les forces productives, le commerce, l'effective militaire et naval, l'organisation financière, l'instruction publique, etc. de l'Egypte' compiled by the Commission Impériale in Paris.[26] To provide such outlines, guides, tables, and plans, which were essential to the educational aspect of the exhibition, involved processes of representation that are no different from those at work in the construction of the exhibits themselves. But the practical distinction that was maintained between the exhibit and the plan, between the objects and their catalog, reinforced the effect of two distinct orders of being – the order of things and the order of their meaning, of representation and reality.

Despite the careful ways in which it was constructed, however, there was something paradoxical about this distinction between the simulated and the real, and about the certainty that depends on it. In Paris, it was not always easy to tell where the exhibition ended and the world itself began. The boundaries of the exhibition were clearly marked, of course, with high perimeter walls and monumental gates. But, as Middle Eastern visitors continually discovered, there was much about the organization of the 'real world' outside, with its museums and department stores, its street facades and Alpine scenes, that resembled the world exhibition. Despite the determined efforts to isolate the exhibition as merely an artificial representation of a reality outside, the real world beyond the gates turned out to be more and more like an extension of the exhibition. Yet this extended exhibition continued to present itself as a series of mere representations, representing a reality beyond. We should think of it, therefore, not so much as an exhibition but as a kind of labyrinth, the labyrinth that, as Derrida says, includes in itself its own exits.[27] But then, maybe the exhibitions whose exits led only to further exhibitions were becoming at once so realistic and so extensive that no one ever realized that the real world they promised was not there.

The labyrinth without exits

To see the uncertainty of what seemed, at first, the clear distinction between the simulated and the real, one can begin again inside the world exhibition, back at the Egyptian bazaar. Part of the shock of the Egyptians came from just how real the street claimed to be: not simply that the paint was made dirty, that the donkeys were from Cairo, and that the Egyptian pastries on sale were said to taste like the real thing, but that one paid for them with what we call '*real* money.'

The commercialism of the donkey rides, the bazaar stalls, and the dancing girls seemed no different from the commercialism of the world outside. With so disorienting an experience as entering the façade of a mosque to find oneself inside an Oriental café that served real customers what seemed to be real coffee, where, exactly, lay the line between the artificial and the real, the representation and the reality?

Exhibitions were coming to resemble the commercial machinery of the rest of the city. This machinery, in turn, was rapidly changing in places such as London and Paris, to imitate the architecture and technique of the exhibition. Small, individually owned shops, often based on local crafts, were giving way to the larger apparatus of shopping arcades and department stores. According to the *Illustrated Guide to Paris* (a book supplying, like an exhibition program, the plan and meaning of the place), each of these new establishments formed 'a city, indeed a world in miniature.'[28] The Egyptian accounts of Europe contain several descriptions of these commercial worlds-in-miniature, where the real world, as at the exhibition, was something organized by the representation of its commodities. The department stores were described as 'large and well organized,' with their merchandise 'arranged in perfect order, set in rows on shelves with everything symmetrical and precisely positioned.' Non-European visitors would remark especially on the panes of glass, inside the stores and along the gas-lit arcades. 'The merchandise is all arranged behind sheets of clear glass, in the most remarkable order. . . . Its dazzling appearance draws thousands of onlookers.'[29] The glass panels inserted themselves between the visitors and the goods on display, setting up the former as mere onlookers and endowing the goods with the distance that is the source, one might say, of their objectness. Just as exhibitions had become commercialized, the machinery of commerce was becoming a further means of engineering the real, indistinguishable from that of the exhibition.

Something of the experience of the strangely ordered world of modern commerce and consumers is indicated in the first fictional account of Europe to be published in Arabic. Appearing in 1882, it tells the story of two Egyptians who travel to France and England in the company of an English Orientalist. On their first day in Paris, the two Egyptians wander accidentally into the vast, gas-lit premises of a wholesale supplier. Inside the building they find long corridors, each leading into another. They walk from one corridor to the next, and after a while begin to search for the way out. Turning a corner they see what looks like an exit, with people approaching from the other side. But it turns out to be a mirror, which covers the entire width and height of the wall, and the people approaching are merely their own reflections. They turn down another passage and then another, but each one ends only in a mirror. As they make their way through the corridors of the building, they pass groups of people at work. 'The people were busy setting out merchandise, sorting it and putting it into boxes and cases. They stared at the two of them in silence as they passed, standing quite still, not leaving their places or interrupting their work.' After wandering silently for some time through the building, the two Egyptians realize they have lost their way completely and begin going from room to room looking for an exit. 'But no one interfered with them,' we are told, 'or came up to them to ask if they were lost.' Eventually they are rescued by the manager of the store, who proceeds to explain to them how it is organized, pointing out that, in the objects being sorted and packed, the produce of every country in the world is represented. The West, it appears is a place organized as a system of commodities, values, meanings, and representations, forming signs that reflect one another in a labyrinth without exits.

[. . .]

Notes

This is a revised and extended version of 'The World as Exhibition,' *Comparative Studies in Society and History* 31, (2) (April, 1989): 217–36, much of which was drawn from the first chapter of *Colonising Egypt* (Cambridge: Cambridge University Press, 1988). I am indebted to Lila Abu-Lughod, Stefania Pandolfo, and the participants in the Conference on Colonialism and Culture held at the University of Michigan in May, 1989, for their comments on earlier versions.

1 Edward Said, *Orientalism* (New York: Pantheon, 1978).
2 Tony Bennett, 'The Exhibitionary Complex,' *New Formations* 4 (Spring, 1988): 96. Unfortunately, this insightful article came to my attention only as I was completing the revisions to this article.
3 See especially Robert W. Rydell, *All the World's a Fair: Visions of Empire at American International Expositions, 1876–1916* (Chicago: University of Chicago Press, 1984); see also Bennett, 'Exhibitionary Complex,' op. cit.
4 Muhammad Amin Fikri, *Irshad al-alibba' ila mahasin Urubba* (Cairo, 1892), 128.
5 Fikri, *Irshad*, 128–29, 136.
6 R.N. Crust, 'The International Congresses of Orientalists,' *Hellas* 6 (1897): 359.
7 Ibid.: 351.
8 Ibid.: 359.
9 Rifa 'a al-Tahtawi, *al-A'mal al-kamila* (Beirut: al-Mu'assasa al-Arabiyya li-l-Dirasat wa-l-Nashr, 1973), 2: 76.
10 Ali Mubarak, *Alam al-din* (Alexandria, 1882), 816. The 'curiosity' of the European is something of a theme for Orientalist writers, who contrast it with the 'general lack of curiosity' of non-Europeans. Such curiosity is assumed to be the natural, unfettered relation of a person to the world, emerging in Europe once the loosening of 'theological bonds' had brought about 'the freeing of human minds' (Bernard Lewis, *The Muslim Discovery of Europe* [London: Weidenfeld & Nicholson, 1982], 299). See Mitchell, *Colonising Egypt*, 4–5, for a critique of this sort or argument and its own 'theological' assumptions.
11 Alain Silvera, 'The First Egyptian Student Mission to France under Muhammad Ali,' in *Modern Egypt: Studies in Politics and Society*, ed. Elie Kedourie and Sylvia G. Haim (London: Frank Cass, 1980), 13.
12 Tahtawi, *al-A'mal*, 2: 177, 119–20.
13 Georges Douin, *Histoire du règne du Khédive Ismaïl* (Rome: Royal Egyptian Geographical Society, 1934), 2: 4–5.
14 Tahtawi, *al-A'mal*, 2: 121.
15 Quoted in Said, *Orientalism*, 165.
16 James Augustus St John, *The Education of the People* (London: Chapman and Hall, 1858), 82–83.

17 'Les origins et le plan de l'exposition,' in *L'Exposition de Paris de 1889*, 3 (December 15, 1889): 18.

18 On Egyptian writing about Europe in the nineteenth century, see Ibrahim Abu-Lughod, *Arab Rediscovery of Europe* (Princeton: Princeton University Press, 1963); Anouar Louca, *Voyageurs et écrivains égyptiens en France au XIXe siècle* (Paris: Didier, 1970); Mitchell, *Colonising Egypt*, 7–13, 180 n. 14.

19 Theodor Adorno, *Minima Moralia: Reflections from a Damaged Life* (London: Verso, 1978), 116; on the theater, see, for example, Muhammad al-Muwaylihi, *Hadith Isa ibn Hisham, aw fatra min al-zaman*, 2nd edn (Cairo: al-Maktaba al-Azhariyya, 1911), 434, and Tahtawi, *al-A'mal*, 2: 119–20; on the public garden and the zoo, Muhammad al-Sanusi al-Tunisi, *al-Istitla 'at al-barisiya fi ma'rad sanat 1889* (Tunis: n.p., 1891), 37.

20 Mubarak, *Alam al-din*, 817.

21 The model farm outside Paris is described in Mubarak, *Alam al-din*, 1008–42; the visual effect of the street in Mubarak, *Alam al-din*, 964, and Idwar Ilyas, *Mashahid Uruba wa-Amirka* (Cairo: al-Muqtataf, 1900), 268; the new funicular at Lucerne and the European passion for panoramas in Fikri, *Irshad*, 98.

22 Martin Heidegger, 'The Age of the World Picture,' in *The Question Concerning Technology and Other Essays* (New York: Harper & Row, 1977).

23 International Congress of Orientalists, *Transactions of the Ninth Congress, 1892* (London: International Congress of Orientalists, 1893), 1: 35.

24 Al-Sanusi, *al-Istitla 'at*, 242.

25 Edmond About, *Le fellah: souvenirs d'Egypte* (Paris: Hachette, 1869), 47–48.

26 Charles Edmond, *L'Egypte à l'exposition universelle de 1867* (Paris: Dentu, 1867).

27 Jacques Derrida, *Speech and Phenomena and Other Essays on Husserl's Theory of Signs* (Evanston, Ill.: Northwestern University Press, 1973), 104. All of his subsequent writings, Derrida once remarked, 'are only a commentary on the sentence about a labyrinth' ('Implications: Interview with Henri Ronse,' in *Positions* [Chicago: University of Chicago Press, 1981], 5). My article, too, should be read as a commentary on that sentence.

28 Quoted in Walter Benjamin, 'Paris, Capital of the Nineteenth Century,' in *Reflections: Essays, Aphorisms, Autobiographical Writings* (New York: Harcourt Brace Jovanovich, 1978), 146–47.

29 Mubarak, *Alam al-din*, 818; Ilyas, *Mashahid Uruba*, 268.

Chapter 26

Anne McClintock

SOFT-SOAPING EMPIRE
Commodity racism and imperial advertising

Soap is Civilization.

(Unilever company slogan)

Doc: My, it's so clean.
Grumpy: There's dirty work afoot.

(Snow White and the Seven Dwarfs)

Soap and civilization

AT THE BEGINNING of the nineteenth century, soap was a scarce and humdrum item and washing a cursory activity at best. A few decades later, the manufacture of soap had burgeoned into an imperial commerce; Victorian cleaning rituals were peddled globally as the God-given sign of Britain's evolutionary superiority, and soap was invested with magical, fetish powers. The soap saga captured the hidden affinity between domesticity and empire and embodied a triangulated crisis in value: the *undervaluation* of women's work in the domestic realm, the *overvaluation* of the commodity in the industrial market and the *disavowal* of colonized economies in the arena of empire. Soap entered the realm of Victorian fetishism with spectacular effect, notwithstanding the fact that male Victorians promoted soap as the icon of nonfetishistic rationality.

Both the cult of domesticity and the new imperialism found in soap an exemplary mediating form. The emergent middle-class values – monogamy ('clean' sex, which has value), industrial capital ('clean' money, which has value), Christianity ('being washed in the blood of the lamb'), class control ('cleansing the great unwashed') and the imperial civilizing mission ('washing and clothing the savage') – could all be marvelously embodied in a single household commodity. Soap advertising, in particular the Pears soap campaign, took its place at the vanguard of Britain's new commodity culture and its civilizing mission.

In the eighteenth century, the commodity was little more than a mundane object to be bought and used – in Marx's words, 'a trivial thing.'[1] By the late nineteenth century, however, the commodity had taken its privileged place not only as the fundamental form of a new industrial economy but also as the fundamental form of a new cultural system for representing social value.[2] Banks and stock exchanges rose up to manage the bonanzas of imperial capital. Professions emerged to administer the goods tumbling hectically from the manufactories. Middle-class domestic space became crammed as never before with furniture, clocks, mirrors, paintings, stuffed animals, ornaments, guns, and myriad gewgaws and knick-knacks. Victorian novelists bore witness to the strange spawning of commodities that seemed to have lives of their own, and huge ships lumbered with trifles and trinkets plied their trade among the colonial markets of Africa, the East, and the Americas.[3]

The new economy created an uproar not only of things but of signs. As Thomas Richards has argued, if all these new commodities were to be managed, a unified system of cultural representation had to be found. Richards shows how, in 1851, the Great Exhibition at the Crystal Palace served as a monument to a new form of consumption: 'What the first Exhibition heralded so intimately was the complete transformation of collective and private life into a space for the spectacular exhibition of commodities.'[4] As a 'semiotic laboratory for the labor theory of value,' the World Exhibition showed once and for all that the capitalist system had not only created a dominant form of exchange but was also in the process of creating a dominant form of representation to go with it: the voyeuristic panorama of surplus as spectacle. By exhibiting commodities not only as goods but as an organized system of images, the World Exhibition helped fashion 'a new kind of being, the consumer and a new kind of ideology, consumerism.'[5] The mass consumption of the commodity spectacle was born.

Victorian advertising reveals a paradox, however, for, as the cultural form that was entrusted with upholding and marketing abroad those founding middle-class distinctions – between private and public, paid work and unpaid work – advertising also from the outset began to confound those distinctions. Advertising took the intimate signs of domesticity (children bathing, men shaving, women laced into corsets, maids delivering nightcaps) into the public realm, plastering scenes of domesticity on walls, buses, shopfronts, and billboards. At the same time, advertising took scenes of empire into every corner of the home, stamping images of colonial conquest on soap boxes, matchboxes, biscuit tins, whiskey bottles, tea tins and chocolate bars. By trafficking promiscuously across the threshold of private and public, advertising began to subvert one of the fundamental distinctions of commodity capital, even as it was coming into being.

From the outset, moreover, Victorian advertising took explicit shape around the reinvention of racial difference. Commodity kitsch made possible, as never before, the mass marketing of empire as an organized system of images and attitudes. Soap flourished not only because it created and filled a spectacular gap in the domestic market but also because, as a cheap and portable domestic commodity, it could persuasively mediate the Victorian poetics of racial hygiene and imperial progress.

Commodity racism became distinct from scientific racism in its capacity to expand beyond the literate, propertied elite through the marketing of commodity spectacle. If, after the 1850s, scientific racism saturated anthropological, scientific and medical journals, travel writing, and novels, these cultural forms were still relatively class-bound and inaccessible to most Victorians, who had neither the means nor the education to read such material. Imperial kitsch as consumer spectacle, by contrast, could package, market, and distribute evolutionary racism on a hitherto unimagined scale. No pre-existing form of organized racism had ever before been able to reach so large and so differentiated a mass of the populace. Thus, as domestic commodities were mass marketed through their appeal to imperial jingoism, commodity jingoism itself helped reinvent and maintain British national unity in the face of deepening imperial competition and colonial resistance. The cult of domesticity became indispensable to the consolidation of British national identity, and at the center of the domestic cult stood the simple bar of soap.[6]

Yet soap has no social history. Since it purportedly belongs in the female realm of domesticity, soap is figured as beyond history and beyond politics proper.[7] To begin a social history of soap, then, is to refuse, in part, to accept the erasure of women's domestic value under imperial capitalism. It cannot be forgotten, moreover, that the history of European attempts to impose a commodity economy on African cultures was also the history of diverse African attempts either to refuse or to transform European commodity fetishism to suit their own needs. The story of soap reveals that fetishism, far from being a quintessentially African propensity, as nineteenth-century anthropology maintained, was central to industrial modernity, inhabiting and mediating the uncertain threshold zones between domesticity and industry, metropolis and empire.

Soap and commodity spectacle

Before the late nineteenth century, clothes and bedding washing was done in most households only once or twice a year in great, communal binges, usually in public at streams or rivers.[8] As for body washing, not much had changed since the days when Queen Elizabeth I was distinguished by the frequency with which she washed: 'regularly every month whether she needed it or not.'[9] By the 1890s, however, soap sales had soared. Victorians were consuming 260,000 tons of soap a year, and advertising had emerged as the central cultural form of commodity capitalism.[10]

Before 1851, advertising scarcely existed. As a commercial form, it was generally regarded as a confession of weakness, a rather shabby last resort. Most advertising was limited to small newspaper advertisements, cheap handbills, and posters. After midcentury, however, soap manufacturers began to pioneer the use of pictorial advertising as a central part of business policy.

The initial impetus for soap advertising came from the realm of empire. With the burgeoning of imperial cotton on the slave plantations came the surplus of cheap cotton goods, alongside the growing buying power of a middle class that could afford for the first time to consume such goods in large quantities. Similarly, the sources for cheap palm oil, coconut oil, and cottonseed oil flourished in the imperial plantations of West Africa, Malay, Ceylon, Fiji, and New Guinea. As rapid changes in the technology of soapmaking took place in Britain after mid-century, the prospect dawned of a large domestic market for soft body soaps, which had previously been a luxury that only the upper class could afford.

Economic competition with the United States and Germany created the need for a more aggressive promotion of British products and led to the first real innovations in advertising. In 1884, the year of the Berlin Conference, the first wrapped soap was sold under a brand name. This small event signified a major transformation in capitalism, as imperial competition gave rise to the creation of monopolies. Henceforth, items formerly indistinguishable from each other (soap sold simply as soap) would be marketed by their corporate signature (Pears, Monkey Brand, etc.). Soap became one of the first commodities to register the historic shift from myriad small businesses to the great imperial monopolies. In the 1870s, hundreds of small soap companies plied the new trade in hygiene, but by the end of the century, the trade was monopolized by ten large companies.

In order to manage the great soap show, an aggressively entrepreneurial breed of advertisers emerged, dedicated to gracing each homely product with a radiant halo of imperial glamor and racial potency. The advertising agent, like the bureaucrat, played a vital role in the imperial expansion of foreign trade. Advertisers billed themselves as 'empire builders' and flattered themselves with 'the responsibility of the historic imperial mission.' Said one: 'Commerce even more than sentiment binds the ocean-sundered portions of empire together. Anyone who increases these commercial interests strengthens the whole fabric of the empire.[11] Soap was credited not only with bringing moral and economic salvation to Britain's 'great unwashed' but also with magically embodying the spiritual ingredient of the imperial mission itself.

In an ad for Pears, for example, a black and implicitly racialized coalsweeper holds in his hands a glowing, occult object. Luminous with its own inner radiance, the simple soap bar glows like a fetish, pulsating magically with spiritual enlightenment and imperial grandeur, promising to warm the hands and hearts of working people across the globe.[12] Pears, in particular, became intimately associated with a purified nature magically cleansed of polluting industry (tumbling kittens, faithful dogs, children festooned with flowers) and a purified working class magically cleansed of polluting labor (smiling servants in crisp white aprons, rosy-cheeked match girls and scrubbed scullions).[13]

None the less, the Victorian obsession with cotton and cleanliness was not simply a mechanical reflex of economic surplus. If imperialism garnered a bounty of cheap cotton and soap oils from coerced colonial labor, the middle-class Victorian fascination with clean, white bodies and clean, white clothing stemmed not only from the rampant profiteering of the imperial economy but also from the realms of ritual and fetish.

Soap did not flourish when imperial ebullience was at its peak. It emerged commercially during an era of impending crisis and social calamity serving to preserve, through fetish ritual, the uncertain boundaries of class gender and race identity in a social order felt to be threatened by the fetid effluvia of the slums, the belching smoke of industry, social agitation, economic upheaval, imperial competition, and anticolonial resistance. Soap offered the promise of spiritual salvation and regeneration through commodity consumption, a regime of domestic hygiene that could restore the threatened potency of the imperial body politic and the race.

The Pears' campaign

In 1789 Andrew Pears, a farmer's son, left his Cornish village of Mevagissey to open a barbershop in London, following the trend of widespread demographic migration from country to city and the economic turn from land to commerce. In his shop, Pears made and sold the powders, creams, and dentifrices used by the rich to ensure the fashionable alabaster purity of their complexions. For the elite, a sun-darkened skin stained by outdoor manual work was the visible stigma not only of a class obliged to work under the elements for a living, but also of far-off, benighted races marked by God's disfavor. From the outset, soap took shape as a technology of social purification, inextricably entwined with the semiotics of imperial racism and class denigration.

In 1838 Andrew Pears retired and left his firm in the hands of his grandson, Francis. In due course, Francis' daughter, Mary, married Thomas J. Barratt, who became Francis' partner and took the gamble of fashioning a middle-class market for the transparent soap. Barratt revolutionized Pears by masterminding a series of dazzling advertising campaigns. Inaugurating a new era of advertising, he won himself lasting fame, in the familiar iconography of male birthing, as the 'father of advertising.' Soap thus found its industrial destiny through the mediation of domestic kinship and that peculiarly Victorian preoccupation with patrimony.

Through a series of gimmicks and innovations that placed Pears at the center of Britain's emerging commodity culture, Barratt showed a perfect understanding of the fetishism that structures all advertising. Importing a quarter of a million French centime pieces into Britain, Barratt had the name Pears stamped on them and put the coins into circulation – a gesture that marvelously linked exchange value with the corporate brand name. The ploy worked famously, arousing much publicity for Pears and such a public fuss that an Act of Parliament was rushed through to declare all foreign coins illegal tender. The boundaries of the national currency closed around the domestic bar of soap.

Georg Lukács points out that the commodity lies on the threshold of culture and commerce, confusing the supposedly sacrosanct boundaries between aesthetics and economy, money, and art. In the mid-1880s, Barratt devised a piece of breathtaking cultural transgression that exemplified Lukács' insight and clinched Pears' fame. Barratt bought Sir John Everett Millais' painting '*Bubbles*' (originally entitled 'A Child's World') and inserted into the painting a bar of soap stamped with the totemic word *Pears*. At a stroke, he transformed the artwork of the best-known painter in Britain into a mass-produced commodity associated in the public mind with Pears.[14] At the same time, by mass reproducing the painting as a poster ad, Barratt took art from the elite realm of private property to the mass realm of commodity spectacle.[15]

In advertising, the axis of possession is shifted to the axis of spectacle. Advertising's chief contribution to the culture of modernity was the discovery that by manipulating the semiotic space around the commodity, the unconscious as a public space could also be manipulated. Barratt's great innovation was to invest huge sums of money in the creation of a visible aesthetic space around the commodity. The development of poster and print technology made possible the mass reproduction of such a space around the image of a commodity.[16]

In advertising, that which is disavowed by industrial rationality (ambivalence, sensuality, chance, unpredictable causality, multiple time) is projected onto image space as a repository of the forbidden. Advertising draws on subterranean flows of desire and taboo, manipulating the investment of surplus money. Pears' distinction, swiftly emulated by scores of soap companies including Monkey Brand and Sunlight, as well as countless other advertisers, was to invest the aesthetic space around the domestic commodity with the commercial cult of empire.

Empire of the home: racializing domesticity

The soap

Four fetishes recur ritualistically in soap advertising: soap itself, white clothing (especially aprons), mirrors, and monkey. A typical Pears' advertisement figures a black child and a white child together in a bathroom (Fig. 26.1). The Victorian bathroom is the innermost sanctuary of domestic hygiene and by extension the private temple of public regeneration. The sacrament of soap offers a reformation allegory whereby the purification of the domestic body becomes a metaphor for the regeneration of the body politic. In this particular ad, a black boy sits in the bath, gazing wide-eyed into the water as if into a foreign element. A white boy,

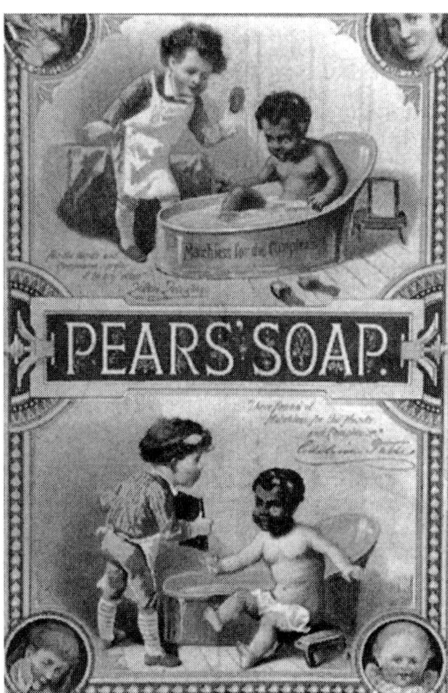

Figure 26.1 Advert for Pears' soap, 1880s

clothed in a white apron – the familiar fetish of domestic purity – bends benevolently over his 'lesser' brother, bestowing upon him the precious talisman of racial progress. The magical fetish of soap promises that the commodity can regenerate the Family of Man by washing from the skin the very stigma of racial and class degeneration.

Soap advertising offers an allegory of imperial progress at spectacle. In this ad, the imperial topos that I call panoptical time (progress consumed as a spectacle from a point of privileged invisibility) enters the domain of the commodity. In the second frame of the ad, the black child is out of the bath and the white boy shows him his startled visage in the mirror. The black boy's body has become magically white, but his face – for Victorians the seat of rational individuality and self-consciousness – remains stubbornly black. The white child is thereby figured as the agent of history and the male heir to progress, reflecting his lesser brother in the European mirror of self-consciousness. In the Victorian mirror, the black child witnesses his predetermined destiny of imperial metamorphosis but remains a passive racial hybrid, part black, part white, brought to the brink of civilization by the twin commodity fetishes of soap and mirror. The advertisement discloses a crucial element of late Victorian commodity culture: the metaphoric transformation of imperial *time* into consumer *space* – imperial progress consumed at a glance as domestic spectacle.

The monkey

The metamorphosis of imperial time into domestic space is captured most vividly by the advertising campaign for Monkey Brand Soap. During the 1880s, the urban landscape of Victorian Britain teemed with the fetish monkeys of this soap. The monkey with its frying pan and bar of soap perched everywhere, on grimy hoardings and buses, on walls and shop fronts, promoting the soap that promised magically to do away with domestic labor: 'No dust, no dirt, no labor.' Monkey Brand Soap promised not only to regenerate the race but also to erase magically the unseemly spectacle of women's manual labor.

In an exemplary ad, the fetish soap-monkey sits cross-legged on a doorstep, the threshold boundary between private domesticity and public commerce – the embodiment of anachronistic space (Figure 26.2). Dressed like an organ-grinder's minion in a gentleman's ragged suit, white shirt, and tie, but with improbably human hands and feet, the monkey extends a frying pan to catch the surplus cash of passersby. On the doormat before him, a great bar of soap is displayed, accompanied by a placard that reads: 'My Own Work.' In every respect the soap-monkey is a hybrid: not entirely ape, not entirely human; part street beggar, part gentleman; part artist, part advertiser. The creature inhabits the ambivalent border of jungle and city, private and public, the domestic and the commercial, and offers as its handiwork a fetish that is both art and commodity.

Monkeys inhabit Western discourse on the borders of social limit, marking the place of a contradiction in social value. As Donna Haraway has argued: 'the primate body, as part of the body of nature, may be read as a map of power.'[17] Primatology, Haraway insists, 'is a Western discourse . . . a political order that works by the negotiation of boundaries achieved through ordering

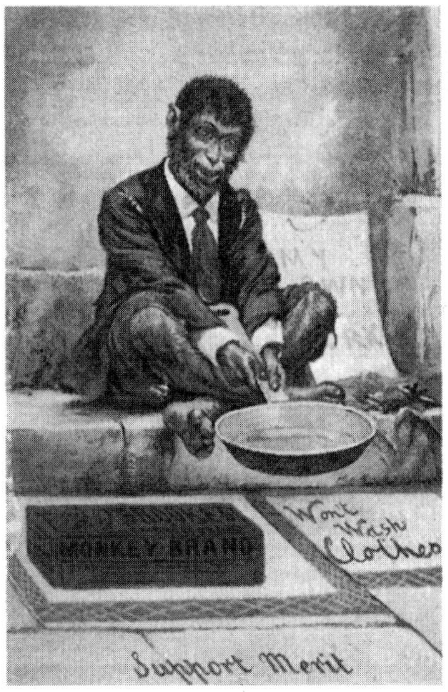

Figure 26.2 Advert for Monkey Brand Soap, 1880s

differences.'[18] In Victorian iconography, the ritual recurrence of the monkey figure is eloquent of a crisis in value and hence anxiety at possible boundary breakdown. The primate body became a symbolic space for reordering and policing boundaries between humans and nature, women and men, family and politics, empire and metropolis.

Simian imperialism is also centrally concerned with the problem of representing *social change*. By projecting history (rather than fate, or God's will) onto the theater of nature, primatology made nature the alibi of political violence and placed in the hands of 'rational science' the authority to sanction and legitimize social change. Here, 'the scene of origins,' Haraway argues, 'is not the cradle of civilization, but the cradle of culture . . . the origin of sociality itself, especially in the densely meaning-laden icon of the family.'[19] Primatology emerges as a theater for negotiating the perilous boundaries between the family (as natural and female) and power (as political and male).

The appearance of monkeys in soap advertising signals a dilemma: *how to represent domesticity without representing women at work*. The Victorian middle-class house was structured around the fundamental contradiction between women's paid and unpaid domestic work. As women were driven from paid work in mines, factories, shops, and trades to private, unpaid work in the home, domestic work became economically undervalued and the middle-class definition of femininity figured the 'proper' woman as one who did not work for profit. At the same time, a *cordon sanitaire* of racial degeneration was thrown around those women who did work publicly and visibly for money. What could not be incorporated into the industrial formation (women's domestic economic value) was displaced onto the invented domain of the primitive, and thereby disciplined and contained.

Monkeys, in particular, were deployed to legitimize social boundaries as edicts of nature. Fetishes straddling nature and culture, monkeys were seen as allied with the dangerous classes: the 'apelike' wandering poor, the hungry Irish, Jews, prostitutes, impoverished black people, the ragged working class, criminals, the insane, and female miners and servants, who were collectively seen to inhabit the threshold of racial degeneration. When Charles Kingsley visited Ireland, for example, he lamented:

> I am haunted by the human chimpanzees I saw along that hundred miles of horrible country. . . . But to see white chimpanzees is dreadful; if they were black, one would not feel it so much, but their skins, except where tanned by exposure, are as white as ours.[20]

In the Monkey Brand advertisement, the monkey's signature of labor ('My Own Work') signals a double disavowal. Soap is masculinized, figured as a male product, while the (mostly female) labor of the workers in the huge, unhealthy soap factories is disavowed. At the same time, the labor of social transformation in the daily scrubbing and scouring of the sinks, pans and dishes, labyrinthine floors and corridors of Victorian domestic space vanishes – refigured as anachronistic space, primitive, and bestial. Female servants disappear and in their place crouches a phantasmic male hybrid. Thus, domesticity – seen as the sphere most separate from the marketplace and the masculine hurly-burly of empire – takes shape around the invented ideas of the primitive and the commodity fetish.

In Victorian culture, the monkey was an icon of metamorphosis, perfectly serving soap's liminal role in mediating the transformation of nature (dirt, waste, and disorder) into culture (cleanliness, rationality, and industry). Like all fetishes, the monkey is a contradictory image, embodying the hope of imperial progress through commerce while at the same time rendering visible deepening Victorian fears of urban militancy and colonial misrule. The soap-monkey became the emblem of industrial progress and imperial evolution, embodying the double promise that nature could be redeemed by consumer capital and that consumer capital could be guaranteed by natural law. At the same time, however, the soap-monkey was eloquent of the degree to which fetishism structures industrial rationality.

The mirror

In most Monkey Brand advertisements, the monkey holds a frying pan, which is also a mirror. In a similar Brooke's Soap ad, a classical female beauty with bare white arms stands draped in white, her skin and clothes epitomizing the exhibition value of sexual purity and domestic leisure, while from the cornucopia she holds flows a grotesque effluvium of hobglobin angels. Each hybrid fetish embodies the doubled Victorian image of woman as 'angel in the drawing room, monkey in the bedroom,' as well as the racial iconography of evolutionary progress from ape to angel. Historical time, again, is captured as domestic spectacle, eerily reflected in the frying pan/mirror fetish.

In this ad, the Brooke's Soap offers an alchemy of economic progress, promising to make 'copper like gold.' At the same time, the Enlightenment idea of linear, rational time leading to angelic perfection finds its antithesis in the other time of housework, ruled by the hobgoblins of dirt, disorder, and fetishistic, nonprogressive time. Erupting on the margins of the rational frame, the ad displays the irrational consequences of the idea of progress. The mirror/frying pan, like all fetishes, visibly expresses a crisis in value but cannot resolve it. It can only embody the contradiction, frozen as commodity spectacle, luring the spectator deeper and deeper into consumerism.

Mirrors glint and gleam in soap advertising, as they do in the culture of imperial kitsch at large. In Victorian middle-class households, servants scoured and polished every metal and wooden surface until it shone like a mirror. Doorknobs, lamp stands and banisters, tables and chairs, mirrors and clocks, knives and forks, kettles and pans, shoes and boots were polished until they shimmered, reflecting in their gleaming surfaces other object-mirrors, an infinity of crystalline mirrors within mirrors, until the interior of the house was all shining surfaces, a labyrinth of reflection. The mirror became the epitome of commodity fetishism: erasing both the signs of domestic labor and the industrial origins of domestic commodities. In the domestic world of mirrors, objects multiply without apparent human intervention in a promiscuous economy of self-generation.

Why the attention of surface and reflection? The polishing was dedicated, in part, to policing the boundaries between private and public, removing every trace of labor, replacing the disorderly evidence of working women with the exhibition of domesticity as veneer, the commodity spectacle as surface, the house arranged as a theater of clean surfaces for commodity display. The mirror/commodity renders the value of the object as an exhibit, a spectacle to be consumed, admired, and displayed for its capacity to embody a twofold value: the man's market worth and the wife's exhibition status. The house existed to display femininity as bearing exhibition value only, beyond the marketplace and therefore, by natural decree, beyond political power.

An ad for Stephenson's Furniture Cream figures a spotless maid on all fours, smiling up from a floor so clean that it mirrors her reflection. The cream is 'warranted not to fingermark.' A superior soap should leave no telltale smear, no fingerprint of female labor. As Victorian servants lost individuality in the generic names their employers imposed on them, so soaps erased the imprint of women's work on middle-class history.

Domesticating empire

By the end of the century, a stream of imperial bric-a-brac had invaded Victorian homes. Colonial heroes and colonial scenes were emblazoned on a host of domestic commodities, from milk cartons to sauce bottles, tobacco tins to whiskey bottles, assorted biscuits to toothpaste, toffee boxes to baking powder.[21] Traditional national fetishes such as the Union Jack, Britannia, John Bull, and the rampant lion were marshaled into a revamped celebration of imperial spectacle. Empire was seen to be patriotically defended by Ironclad Porpoise Bootlaces and Sons of the Empire soap, while Henry Morton Stanley came to the rescue of the Emin of Pasha laden with outsize boxes of Huntley and Palmers Biscuits.

Late Victorian advertising presented a vista of Africa conquered by domestic commodities.[22] In the flickering magic lantern of imperial desire, teas, biscuits, tobaccos, Bovril, tins of cocoa and, above all, soaps bench themselves on far-flung shores, tramp through jungles, quell uprisings, restore order and write the inevitable legend of commercial progress across the colonial landscape. In a Huntley and Palmers' Biscuits ad, a group of male colonials sit in the middle of a jungle on biscuit crates, sipping tea. Moving toward them is a stately and seemingly endless procession of elephants, loaded with more biscuits and colonials, bringing teatime to the heart of the jungle. The serving attendant in this ad, as in most others, is male. Two things happen in such images: women vanish from the affair of empire, and colonized men are feminized by their association with domestic servitude.

Liminal images of oceans, beaches, and shorelines recur in cleaning ads of the time. An exemplary ad for Chlorinol Soda Bleach shows three boys in a soda box sailing in a phantasmic ocean bathed by the radiance of the imperial dawn. In a scene washed in the red, white, and blue of the Union Jack, two black boys proudly hold aloft their boxes of Chlorinol. A third boy, the familiar racial hybrid of cleaning ads, has presumably already applied his bleach, for his skin is blanched an eerie white. On red sails that repeat the red of the bleach box, the legend of black people's purported commercial redemption in the arena of empire reads: 'We are going to use "Chlorinol" and be like de white nigger.'

The ad vividly exemplifies Marx's lesson that the mystique of the commodity fetish lies not in its use value but in its exchange value and its potency as a sign: 'So far as "the commodity" is a value in use, there is nothing mysterious about it.' For three naked children, clothing bleach is less than useful. Instead, the whitening agent of bleach promises an alchemy of racial upliftment through historical contact with commodity culture. The transforming power of the civilizing mission is stamped on the boat-box's sails as the objective character of the commodity itself.

More than merely a *symbol* of imperial progress, the domestic commodity becomes the *agent* of history itself. The commodity, abstracted from social context and human labor, does the civilizing work of empire, while radical change is figured as magical, without process or social agency. Hence the proliferation of ads featuring magic. In similar fashion, cleaning ads such as Chlorinol's foreshadow the 'before and after' beauty ads of the twentieth century: a crucial genre directed largely at women, in which the conjuring power of the product to alchemize change is all that lies between the temporal 'before and after' of women's bodily transformation.

The Chlorinol ad displays a racial and gendered division of labor. Imperial progress from black child to 'white nigger' is consumed as commodity spectacle – as panoptical time. The self-satisfied, hybrid 'white nigger' literally holds the rudder of history and directs social change, while the dawning of civilization bathes his enlightened brow with radiance. The black children simply have exhibition value as potential consumers of the commodity, there only to uphold the promise of capitalist commerce and to represent how far the white child has evolved – in the iconography of Victorian racism the condition of 'savagery' is identical to the condition of infancy. Like white women, Africans (both women and men) are figured not as historic agents but as frames for the commodity, valued for *exhibition* alone. The working women, both black and white, who spent vast amounts of energy bleaching the white sheets, shirts, frills, aprons, cuffs, and collars of imperial clothes are nowhere to be seen. It is important to note that in Victorian advertising, black women are very seldom rendered as consumers of commodities, for, in imperial lore, they lag too far behind men to be agents of history. Imperial domesticity is therefore a domesticity without women.

In the Chlorinol ad, women's creation of social value through housework is displaced onto the commodity as its own power, fetishistically inscribed on the children's bodies as a magical metamorphosis of the flesh. At the same time, military subjugation, cultural coercion, and economic thuggery are refigured as benign domestic processes as natural and healthy as washing. The stains of Africa's disobligingly complex and tenacious past and the inconvenience of alternative economic and cultural values are washed away like grime.

Incapable of themselves actually engendering change, African men are figured only as 'mimic men,' to borrow V.S. Naipaul's dyspeptic phrase, destined simply to ape the epic white march of progress to self-knowledge. Bereft of the white raiments of imperial godliness, the Chlorinol children appear to take the fetish literally, content to bleach their skins to white. Yet these ads reveal that, far from being a quintessentially African propensity, the faith in fetishism was a faith fundamental to imperial capitalism itself.

[. . .]

Notes

1 Karl Marx, 'Commodity Fetishism,' *Capital*, vol. 1 (New York: Vintage Books, 1977), p. 163.

2 See Thomas Richards' excellent analysis, *The Commodity Culture of Victorian Britain: Advertising and Spectacle, 1851–1914* (London: Verso, 1990), especially the introduction and ch. 1.

3 See David Simpson's analysis of novelistic fetishism in *Fetishism and Imagination: Dickens, Melville, Conrad* (Baltimore: Johns Hopkins University Press, 1982).

4 Richards, *The Commodity Culture*, p. 72.

5 Ibid., p. 5.

6 In 1889, an ad for Sunlight Soap featured the feminized figure of British nationalism, Britannia, standing on a hill and showing P.T. Barnum, the famous circus manager and impresario of the commodity spectacle, a huge Sunlight Soap factory stretched out below them. Britannia proudly proclaims the manufacture of Sunlight Soap to be: 'The Greatest Show On Earth.' See Jennifer Wicke's excellent analysis of P.T. Barnum in *Advertising Fiction: Literature, Advertisement and Social Reading* (New York: Columbia University Press, 1988).

7 See Timothy Burke, ' "Nyamarira That I Loved": Commoditization, Consumption and the Social History of Soap in Zimbabwe,' *The Societies of Southern Africa in the 19th and 20th Centuries: Collected Seminar Papers*, no. 42, vol. 17 (London: University of London, Institute of Commonwealth Studies, 1992), pp. 195–216.

8 Leonore Davidoff and Catherine Hall, *Family Fortunes: Men and Women of the English Middle Class* (London: Routledge 1992).

9 David T.A. Lindsey and Geoffrey C. Bamber, *Soap-Making. Past and Present, 1876–1976* (Nottingham: Gerard Brothers Ltd, 1965), p. 34.

10 Lindsey and Bamber, *Soap-Making*, p. 38. Just how deeply the relation between soap and advertising became embedded in popular memory is expressed in words such as 'soft-soap' and 'soap opera.' For histories of advertising, see also Blanche B. Elliott, *A History of English Advertising* (London: Business Publications Ltd., 1962); and T.R. Nevett, *Advertising in Britain. A History* (London: Heinemann, 1982).

11 Quoted in Diana and Geoffrey Hindley, *Advertising in Victorian England, 1837–1901* (London: Wayland, 1972), p. 117.

12 Mike Dempsey (ed.) *Bubbles: Early Advertising Art from A. & Pears Ltd.* (London: Fontana, 1978).

13 Laurel Bradley, 'From Eden to Empire: John Everett Millais' Cherry Ripe,' *Victorian Studies* vol. 34, no. 2 (Winter 1991), pp. 179–203. See also, Michael Dempsey, *Bubbles*.

14 Barratt spent £2,200 on Millais' painting and £30,000 on the mass production of millions of individual reproductions of the painting. In the 1880s, Pears was spending between £300,000 and £400,000 on advertising alone.

15 Furious at the pollution of the sacrosanct realm of art with economics, the art world lambasted Millais for trafficking (publicly instead of privately) in the sordid world of trade.

16 See Jennifer Wicke, *Advertising Fiction*, p. 70.

17 Donna Haraway, *Primate Visions: Gender, Race, and Nature in the World of Modern Science* (London: Routledge, 1989), p. 10.

18 Ibid., p. 10.

19 Ibid., pp. 10–11.

20 Charles Kingsley, Letter to his wife, 4 July 1860, in *Charles Kingsley: His Letters and Memories of His Life*, Frances E. Kingsley, ed., (London: Henry S. King and Co., 1877), p. 107. See also Richard Kearney (ed.) *The Irish Mind* (Dublin: Wolfhound Press, 1985); L.P. Curtis Jr, *Anglo-Saxons and Celts: A Study of Anti-Irish Prejudice in Victorian England* (Bridgeport: Conference on British Studies of University of Bridgeport, 1968); and Seamus Deane, 'Civilians and Barbarians,' *Ireland's Field Day* (London: Hutchinson, 1985), pp. 33–42.

21 During the Anglo-Boer War, Britain's fighting forces were seen as valiantly fortified by Johnston's Corn Flour, Pattison's' Whiskey and Frye's Milk Chocolate. See Robert Opie, *Trading on the British Image* (Middlesex: Penguin, 1985) for an excellent collection of advertising images.

22 In a brilliant chapter, Richards explores how the imperial conviction of the explorer and travel writer, Henry Morton Stanley, that he had a mission to civilize Africans by teaching them the value of commodities, 'reveals the major role that imperialists ascribed to the commodity in propelling and justifying the scramble for Africa.' Richards, *The Commodity Culture*, p. 123.

Chapter 27

Malek Alloula

FROM *THE COLONIAL HAREM*

The Orient as stereotype and phantasm

ARRAYED IN THE BRILLIANT colors of exoticism and exuding a full-blown yet uncertain sensuality, the Orient, where unfathomable mysteries dwell and cruel and barbaric scenes are staged, has fascinated and disturbed Europe for a long time. It has been its glittering imaginary but also its mirage.

Orientalism, both pictorial and literary, has made its contribution to the definition of the variegated elements of the sweet dream in which the West has been wallowing for more than four centuries. It has set the stage for the deployment of phantasms.

There is no phantasm, though, without sex, and in this Orientalism, a confection of the best and of the worst – mostly the worst – a central figure emerges, the very embodiment of the obsession: the harem. A simple allusion to it is enough to open wide the floodgate of hallucination just as it is about to run dry.

For the Orient is no longer the dreamland. Since the middle of the nineteenth century, it has inched closer. Colonialism makes a grab for it, appropriates it by dint of war, binds it hand and foot with myriad bonds of exploitation, and hands it over to the devouring appetite of the great mother countries, ever hungry for raw materials.

Armies, among them the one that landed one fine 5 July 1830 a little to the east of Algiers, bring missionaries and scholars with their impedimenta as well as painters and photographers forever thirsty for exoticism, folklore, Orientalism. This fine company scatters all over the land, sets up camp around military messes, takes part in punitive expeditions (even Théophile Gautier is not exempt), and dreams of the Orient, its delights and its beauties.

What does it matter if the colonized Orient, the Algeria of the turn of the century, gives more than a glimpse of the other side of its scenery, as long as the phantasm of the harem persists, especially since it has become profitable? Orientalism leads to riches and respectability. Horace Vernet, whom Baudelaire justly called the Raphael of barracks and bivouacs, is the peerless exponent of this smug philistinism. He spawns imitators. Vulgarities and stereotypes draw upon the entire heritage of the older, precolonial Orientalism. They reveal all its presuppositions to the point of caricature.

It matters little if Orientalistic painting begins to run out of wind or falls into mediocrity. Photography steps in to take up the slack and reactivates the phantasm at its lowest level. The postcard does it one better; it becomes the poor man's phantasm: for a few pennies, display racks full of dreams. The postcard is everywhere, covering all the colonial space, immediately available to the tourist, the soldier, the colonist. It is at once their poetry and their glory captured for the ages; it is also their pseudo knowledge of the colony. It produces stereotypes in the manner of great seabirds producing guano. It is the fertilizer of the colonial vision.

The postcard is ubiquitous. It can be found not only at the scene of the crime it perpetrates but at a far remove as well. Travel is the essence of the postcard, and expedition is its mode. It is the fragmentary return to the mother country. It straddles two spaces: the one it represents and the one it will reach. It marks out the peregrinations of the tourist, the successive postings of the soldier, the territorial spread of the colonist. It sublimates the spirit of the stopover and the sense of place; it is an act of unrelenting aggression against sedentariness. In the postcard, there is the suggestion of a complete metaphysics of uprootedness.

It is also a seductive appeal to the spirit of adventure and pioneering. In short, the postcard would be a resounding defense of the colonial spirit in picture form. It is the comic strip of colonial morality.

But it is not merely that; it is more. It is the propagation of the phantasm of the harem by means of photography. It is the degraded, and degrading, revival of this phantasm.

The question arises, then, how are we to read today these postcards that have superimposed their grimacing mask upon the face of the colony and grown like a chancre or a horrible leprosy?

Today, nostalgic wonderment and tearful archeology (Oh! those colonial days!) are very much in vogue. But to give in to them is to forget a little too quickly the motivations and the effects of this vast operation of systematic distortion. It is also to lay the groundwork for its return in a new guise: a racism and a xenophobia titillated by the nostalgia of the colonial empire.

Beyond such barely veiled apologias that hide behind aesthetic rationalizations, another reading is possible: a symptomatic one.

To map out, from under the plethora of images, the obsessive scheme that regulates the totality of the output of this enterprise and endows it with meaning is to force the postcard to reveal what it holds back (the ideology of colonialism) and to expose what is represented in it (the sexual phantasm).

The Golden Age of the colonial postcard lies between 1900 and 1930. Although a latecomer to colonial apologetics, it will quickly make up for its belatedness and come to occupy a privileged place, which it owes to the infatuation it elicits, in the preparations for the centennial of the conquest, the apotheosis of the imperial epoch.

In this large inventory of images that History sweeps with broad strokes out of its way, and which shrewd merchants hoard for future collectors, one theme especially seems to have found favor with the photographers and to have been accorded privileged treatment: the *algérienne*.

History knows of no other society in which women have been photographed on such a large scale to be delivered to public view. This disturbing and paradoxical fact is problematic far beyond the capacity of rationalizations that impute its occurrence to ethnographic attempts at a census and visual documentation of human types.

Behind this image of Algerian women, probably reproduced in the millions, there is visible the broad outline of one of the figures of the colonial perception of the native. This figure can be essentially defined as the practice of a right of (over)sight that the colonizer arrogates to himself and that is the bearer of multiform violence. The postcard fully partakes in such violence; it extends its effects; it is its accomplished expression, no less efficient for being symbolic. Moreover, its fixation upon the woman's body leads the postcard to paint this body up, ready it, and eroticize it in order to offer it up to any and all comers from a clientele moved by the unambiguous desire of possession.

To track, then, through the colonial representations of Algerian women – the figures of a phantasm – is to attempt a double operation: first, to uncover the nature and the meaning of the colonialist gaze; then, to subvert the stereotype that is so tenaciously attached to the bodies of women.

A reading of the sort that I propose to undertake would be entirely superfluous if there existed photographic traces of the gaze of the colonized upon the colonizer. In their absence, that is, in the absence of a confrontation of opposed gazes, I attempt here, lagging far behind History, to return this immense postcard to its sender.

What I read on these cards does not leave me indifferent. It demonstrates to me, were that still necessary, the desolate poverty of a gaze that I myself, as an Algerian, must have been the object of at some moment in my personal history. Among us, we believe in the nefarious effects of the evil eye (the evil gaze). We conjure them with our hand spread out like a fan. I close my hand back upon a pen to write *my* exorcism: *this text*.

Women from the outside: obstacle and transparency

> The reading of public photographs is always, at bottom, a private reading.
> (Roland Barthes, *Camera Lucida*, 1981)

The first thing the foreign eye catches about Algerian women is that they are concealed from sight.

No doubt this very obstacle to sight is a powerful prod to the photographer operating in urban environments. It also determines the obstinacy of the camera operator to force that which disappoints him by its escape.

The Algerian woman does not conceal herself, does not play at concealing herself. But the eye cannot catch hold of her. The opaque veil that covers her intimates clearly and simply to the photographer a refusal. Turned back upon himself, upon his own impotence in the situation, the photographer undergoes an *initial experience of disappointment and rejection*. Draped in the veil that cloaks her to her ankles, the Algerian woman discourages the *scopic desire* (the voyeurism) of the photographer. She is the concrete negation of this desire and thus brings to the photographer confirmation of a triple rejection: the rejection of his desire, of the practice of his 'art,' and of his place in a milieu that is not his own.

Algerian society, particularly the world of women, is forever forbidden to him. It counterposes to him a smooth and homogeneous surface free of any cracks through which he could slip his indiscreet lens.

The whiteness of the veil becomes the symbolic equivalent of blindness: a leukoma, a white speck on the eye of the photographer and on his viewfinder. *Whiteness is the absence of a photo, a veiled photograph, a whiteout, in technical terms.* From its background nothing emerges except some vague contours, anonymous in their repeated resemblance. Nothing distinguishes one veiled woman from another.

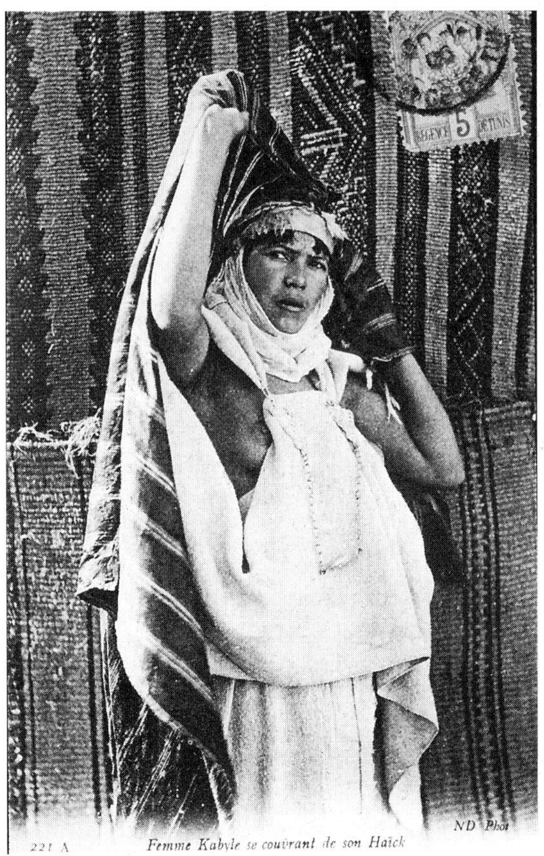

Figure 27.1 Kabyl woman covering herself with the haik
(From Mallek Alloula, *The Colonial Harem*, Manchester University Press, 1985)

The veil of Algerian women is also seen by the photographer as a sort of perfect and generalized mask. It is not worn for special occasions. It belongs to the everyday, like a uniform. It instills uniformity, the modality of the impossibility of photography, its disappointment and deficiency of expression.

It will be noted that whenever a photographer aims his camera at a veiled woman, he cannot help but include in his visual field several instances of her. As if to photograph one of them from the outside required the inclusion of a *principle of duplication* in the framing. For it is always a group of veiled women that the photographer affixes upon his plate.

One may well wonder about this peculiarity since it could easily be overcome by technical means through the isolation and the enlargement of a detail. This everyday technique of printmaking is never used, however. Does this indicate, perhaps, that the photographer's frustration is generalized and not amenable to being directed toward one individual in the group? Does this mean that his frustration is an induced effect? The society he observes reveals to him the instinctual nature of his desire (voyeurism) and challenges him beyond the defenses of his professional alibi. The exoticism that he thought he could handle without any problems suddenly discloses to him a truth unbearable for the further exercise of his craft.

Here there is a sort of ironic paradox: the veiled subject – in this instance, the Algerian woman – becomes the purport of an unveiling.

But the veil has another function: to recall, in individualized fashion, the closure of private space. It signifies an injunction of no trespassing upon this space, and it extends it to another space, the one in which the photographer is to be found: public space.

These white islets that dot the landscape are indeed aggregates of prohibition, mobile extensions of an imaginary harem whose inviolability haunts the

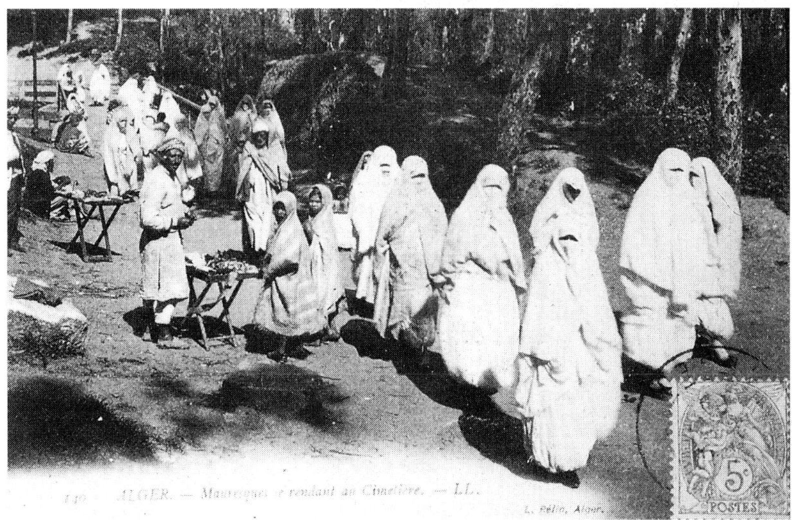

Figure 27.2 Moorish women on their way to the cemetery
(From Mallek Alloula, *The Colonial Harem*, Manchester University Press, 1985)

photographer-voyeur. They are scandalous, or at least perceived as being so. By their omnipresence, they revive frustration. They also recall the existence of the well-known pseudo-religious taboo of the Muslims: the figural depiction of the human body prohibited by Islam.

These veiled women are not only an embarrassing enigma to the photographer but an outright attack upon him. It must be believed that the feminine gaze that filters through the veil is a gaze of a particular kind: concentrated by the tiny orifice for the eye, this womanly gaze is a little like the eye of a camera, like the photographic lens that takes aim at everything.

The photographer makes no mistake about it: he knows this gaze well; it resembles his own when it is extended by the dark chamber or the viewfinder. Thrust in the presence of a veiled woman, the photographer feels photographed; having himself become an object-to-be-seen, he loses initiative: *he is dispossessed of his own gaze.*

This varied experience of frustration is turned by the photographer into the sign of his own negation. Algerian society, particularly the feminine world within it, threatens him in his being and *prevents him from accomplishing himself as gazing gaze.*

The photographer will respond to this quiet and almost natural challenge by means of a double violation: he will unveil the veiled and give figural representation to the forbidden. This is the summary of his only program or, rather, his symbolic revenge upon a society that continues to deny him any access and questions the legitimacy of his desire. The photographer's studio will become, then, a pacified microcosm where his desire, his scopic instinct, can find satisfaction.

And so, now in the studio, adorned for the occasion, is one of the numerous models whom the photographer will have wear the veil. As if it were at once part of an exorcism or an act of propitiation, she is drawing the veil aside with both hands in a gesture of inaugural invitation that the photographer has staged (richness of dress, jewelry, smile, etc.), first for himself, and second for the viewer. Separated from the group that rendered her nondescript, the model is holding a pose, haloed in artistic soft focus, the metaphorical equivalent of intense exultation.

This is a determinant moment for what follows because this is where the machinery, or rather the machination, is set in motion. The entire distorting enterprise of the postcard is given here in schematic form. It is contained in the gesture of drawing the veil aside – a gesture executed at the photographer's command and destined to be followed by others. When she completes them, the *algérienne* will no longer have anything to hide.

Chapter 28

Suzanne Preston Blier

VODUN ART, SOCIAL HISTORY AND THE SLAVE TRADE

A man without force is without the essential dignity of humanity.
(Frederick Douglass, *Life and Times*)

To have seen a country is not the same as to have lived it.
[Edumɛ kpokpo a, me edumɛ yiyi o]
(Gen proverb)

BETWEEN 1710 AND 1810 over a million slaves (principally of Fon, Aja, Nago, Mahi, Ayizo, and Gedevi descent) were exported on English, French, and Portuguese vessels out of the Bight of Benin and what was then called the Slave Coast of Africa (Curtin 1969: 228; Manning 1982: 335). This trade, which continued from the region in varying degrees through the end of the nineteenth century, contributed to one of the greatest intercontinental migrations in world history (Curtin 1967; Polanyi 1966; Law 1991). Many of those who were sent from this area were brought to Brazil and various Caribbean islands. The slave trade had dire consequences not only for the men and women who crossed the Atlantic but also for many of those who remained in Africa. In the kingdom of Danhomɛ the acquisition and trading of slaves had assumed dimensions of a national industry. To a large extent, the Danhomɛ state economy was based upon annual raids and military expeditions against neighboring groups and villages, the primary purpose of which was to capture men, and to a lesser extent women and children, who could be sold for profit.

In the course of these campaigns, which often took place soon after harvest, many people lost their lives immediately in confrontations with the Danhomɛ troops; others lost their freedom, homelands, and dignity when they were taken prisoner and were brought to the Danhomɛ capital, where they were either sold into slavery or were kept as prisoners, later to be killed in state ceremonies or forced into involuntary life-long servitude in the state militia, court harems, plantation labor groups, or households of the governing elite.

Those fortunate enough to flee the advancing Danhomɛ armies also suffered greatly. Most returned to their homes to find their farms burned, their granaries emptied, their animals stolen, or slaughtered, and their houses and temples destroyed. For them the answer often was further flight and hiding. With the famines that often followed, medical problems, infertility, and high infant mortality were rampant (see Manning 1982). The prime targets of the slave raids, primarily young men, were precisely the ones who would have been essential in providing the labor needed to rebuild and sustain the community. Without them, survival was tenuous. Although the situation often was dire, it would have been intolerable without a viable means of both comprehending and coping with the difficult conditions. This included the prominent use of *bocið* and *bo*. No matter what the misfortune, works of this type provided a means of personal and social response to the attendant problems or concerns.

The physical and psychological suffering experienced by persons living in (or near) the Danhomɛ state during the period of international slavery was not to any degree dissipated when the slave trade was outlawed by European states in the nineteenth century. Coinciding with this ban was a new European demand for palm oil to be used in the industrial production of soap. This need was accompanied by the setting up of large oil palm plantations in Africa. In Danhomɛ these plantations were worked by slaves overseen by the kings and other powerful persons. The slaves were obtained, as before, through warfare and raids. Thus at the same time that European states sought to end the horrors of international slavery, they simultaneously encouraged the acquisition and extensive use of slave labor within Africa for palm oil production. The social impact of this economic change was great, for by 1900 fully one-quarter to one-third of the population in the Danhomɛ area were first- or second-generation slaves, many of whom were working on plantations (Manning 1982: 192).

With the French conquest of Danhomɛ in 1894, the difficult conditions of rural peoples appear to have been little improved. Although the French were able to enforce a cessation of the slave raids that had been used to acquire plantation labor, colonial officials to a large degree reinforced and gave legitimacy to essential conditions of the past by allowing princes and newly appointed *cercle* chiefs to retain control over many of their former slaves and the lands they worked. As late as the 1930s, when Herskovits, along with several members of the Danhomɛ aristocracy, visited a village of slave descendants, the latter showed clear indications of fear and discomfort (Herskovits 1967, 1: 103–4; Blier 1988: 140). As Patrick Manning points out in reference to the above incident (1982: 192), 'The heritage of slavery in this region where slavery and slave trade were so much a part of life for centuries is deeply and subtly ingrained.'

The fundamental links between individual disempowerment and emotional expressions thereof find ample evidence in *bocið*. Often bound tightly in cords, these works evoke the image of a prisoner. They suggest what the Fon call *kannumon*, 'thing belonging [in] cords,' i.e., the enslaved person. Such individuals, themselves signifiers of personal demise, were potent reminders of the disturbing effects of war, poverty, insecurity, and loss of freedom. As Ahanhanzo Glélé, a descendant of the powerful nineteenth-century ruler King Glélé, notes (1974: 158): 'The *kannumon* came from several sources: regular wars (war prisoners), commerce (individuals bought from Hausa, Bariba, and Nago merchants), the ravaging of populations not under Agbomɛ domination, and generally poor people in the state of dependence.'

The prominence of cords and binding in commoner *bocIↄ* traditions is a poignant reference to the trauma which resulted from state-induced or supported violence. If slaves, ex-slaves, and the many others who were fearful of enslavement suggest what W.B. Friedman (1956: 175) calls potent 'bundles of power,' *bocIↄ* can be said to represent these bundles in manifestly visual ways. *BocIↄ* arts, I maintain, were not merely intended to be reflections of violence and danger, but rather were thought to offer important strategies for responding to the difficult social conditions in which people found themselves at this time. These sculptures were not indifferent or adiaphoric to the sufferer's plight, but served as a means of readdressing wrongs and dissipating attendant anxiety.

Yet resolution of individual and social tension represents but one aspect of each sculpture's textual meaning, for these works also are provocative signifiers of the danger of leaving difficulties unresolved. Such works offered a way of both accepting and refusing the negative by helping their users to objectify conflict and to 'think-through-terror,' as Taussig would say (1987: 5). As Marcuse suggests (1978: 9), art provides one with a way of uttering what is otherwise unutterable, allowing one to escape from one's bondage however defined. *BocIↄ* through this means enabled area residents to gain a certain sense of control over the sometimes grave social, political, and physical conditions around them.

In several impassioned books on the difficulties of colonialism in Algeria, psychiatrist Frantz Fanon has argued (1968) that the psychological ills suffered by Algerians during their war for independence often were attributable to the horrors of the political situation in which they found themselves. In both precolonial and postcolonial Danhomɛ, many inhabitants also suffered from various forms of psychological trauma. *BocIↄ* functioned in a certain sense as counterfoils and complements to such problems, responses to what Clifford Geertz discussed (1983: 55–70) in terms of psychopathology encouraged by social disorder. The visual power of *bocIↄ* objects reveal in key respects the social and personal impact of such insecurity and disempowerment. This is an art in which a full range of anxieties is manifestly felt. And in so far as anxiety derives from the feeling of helplessness that fear evokes, *bocIↄ* help to relieve related concerns in the face of life's lesser and greater traumas. Works of this sort no doubt were made and used prior to the slave trade. Indeed the specific problems which these works are commissioned to address include a range of personal and familial concerns which sometimes had little relation to war or slavery. None the less, these sculptures appear to have assumed special poignancy and meaning in the area owing to the often difficult circumstances promoted by the slave trade. Related images express what Marcuse calls (1978: 19–20) a 'consciousness of crisis' (*Krisenbewusstein*).

The power of *bociɔ* counteraesthetics

Questions of the social and psychological grounding of *bociɔ* arts are addressed in provocative ways in the potent aesthetic concerns which they define. *Bociɔ* aesthetic criteria accordingly offer a unique ground against which to explore questions of art, power, and expression generally. Perhaps not surprising in light of the above discussion of political difference and distance, *bociɔ* aesthetic signification is closely bound up with societal (and countersocietal) values such as dissonance, force, destruction, decay, and danger. *Bociɔ* arts, as we will see, express not only an aesthetic of negativity, but also what Kristeva calls *frappe* or shock.

With these works, as in any art corpus identified so closely with social and psychological expression the aesthetic criteria used in sculptural evaluation are complex. The 'strong' object, explains Sagbadju (7.1.86), 'is not something of beauty.' Ayido observes similarly (5.2.86) that 'one does not need to carve a sculpture so that it is attractive in order to have it work.' In art as in life, two terms are employed by the Fon to indicate general attractiveness: *acɔ* and *dɛkpɛ*. The former refers to things which are ornamental, delicate, refined, decorative, dressed, and tidy, and the latter designates ideas of beauty, elegance, and attractiveness generally. The vast majority of commoner *bociɔ* clearly stand out in marked contrast to these two aesthetic ideals. These sculptures are not ornamental, refined, elegant, or attractive in any standard sense of the words. Nor do these figures conform to the variant secondary aesthetic criteria that are said by Fon artists to be important to them in evaluating beauty in sculptural form. The latter include qualities such as youthfulness (*ɖekpe* – beauty in Fon is synonymous with youth), smoothness (*ɖiɖi*), completeness (*bisese*), and correctness (*pɛpɛ*). As we have seen within commoner *bociɔ*, there also is little to suggest youthful grace, surface polish, a sense of finish, or exacting anatomical detail.

These lacks are all the more striking in view of the strong emphasis in the kingly *bociɔ* arts which is given to refined features and attributes which are elegant, ornamental, polished, and exacting in form. Thus whereas Fon royal *bociɔ* arts conform in essential ways to local beauty criteria, commoner works emphasize counteraesthetic, even antiaesthetic values and features of ugliness. The counteraesthetics of commoner *bociɔ* arts are of considerable interest in this light because they constitute in essence the aesthetic of choice of the subaltern groups living in this area – the rural residents, nonroyals, and those generally suffering from the effects of disempowerment.

What is suggested here is that artists of commoner *bociɔ*, aware of the diminished political statuses of their patrons, to some extent reified the latter's positions by emphasizing certain counteraesthetic features in their arts. The two Fon terms used to indicate a negation or lack of beauty, *magnon* (which also signifies 'ignorant' and 'unschooled') and *gnlan kan* (designating 'bad' or 'beastly' – literally 'bad cord'), suggest a complementary emphasis on attributes perceived to be rural or outside the encultured mainstream, as defined by the elite. The artists, activators, and users of commoner *bociɔ*, by intentionally avoiding qualities associated with beauty and refinement in royal art contexts, promoted status difference through privileging antithetical forms of aesthetic expression. While associated concerns were never discussed by local artists or *bociɔ* users, the visual differences between commoner and royal *bociɔ* aesthetic expression are striking.

Secondary aesthetic criteria employed to designate the lack or negation of beauty (*magnon* and *gnlan kan*) underscore these status differences in interesting ways. One feature said to characterize works showing a lack or negation of beauty is messiness (*gudu gudu*: disorderly, piggish, mixed up, troubled; from *gu*, designating things which are spoiled, corrupted, inutile, wasted, or negated). Commoner *bociɔ*, in conforming to this counteraesthetic of messiness and disorder, may in some way be seen to complement the confusion and disorder that defined many of their users' lives. In local divination sessions in which commoner *bociɔ* are discussed, these concerns come up with considerable frequency).

Three other values said to characterize commoner *bociɔ* counteraesthetics also have important sociopolitical and psychological complements. These include fury (*adan*), strength (*sien*, 'resistant,' 'solid'), and force (*hlon hlon*). Associated qualities are revealed most importantly in audience responses to *bociɔ* . . . Like *gudu*, 'disorderly,' the above also offer insight into *bociɔ* signification. Accordingly, *adanwatɔ*, 'father of fury,' is the term frequently used to describe powerful people in the community who are able to bring their influence to bear on others living around them. . . . Each *bociɔ* serves similarly as an 'object of fury,' something which accords its users considerable power. Ancillary meanings of the term *adan*, the most important of which are audaciousness, anger, intrepidness, hardness, courage, coerciveness, and scolding (Segurola 1963: 4), also are of interest. In their roles as aggressive and protective forces, *bociɔ* display similar values. Supplemental associations of the Fon term *hlon hlon* ('force') carry provocative secondary meanings as well, in this case, of violence, vengeance, and vindictiveness (Segurola 1963: 227). These attributes complement at once the sometimes embattled social and political contexts in which such objects are made and the force that is thought to be necessary to counter danger and difficulties that lie in life's path.

The selection of *bociɔ* materials for their physical and metaphoric strength and the emphasis in these works on knotting and tying suggest in turn the strength (*sien*) which these objects are intended to express through their forms and functioning. The prominent use of raffia cord, with its characteristic solidity and resistance, is significant too, for comparable strength is essential to *bociɔ* roles in turning away danger and discord from their various owners. Appropriately ancillary meanings of the counteraesthetic term *sien* designate things which are courageous, insistent, secure, resistant, persevering, tenacious, forceful, severe, opinionated, hardheaded, and hardened (Segurola 1963: 471). Similar qualities are vital to *bociɔ* in their roles in helping one to survive or better one's condition in life. Seeing these and related visual properties within sculptural form no doubt gave local viewers a sense of assurance and security in the face of various difficulties. Through emphasizing aesthetics of shock which in various ways privilege conflict, contradiction, chaos, obscurity, mystery, and brute force, these works convey an emotional energy of considerable potency.

[. . .]

References

Blier, Suzanne Preston (1988) 'Melville J. Herskovits and the Arts of Ancient Dahomey', *Res* 16 (Autumn): 124–42.

Curtin, Philip D. (ed.) (1967) *Africa Remembered: Narratives by West Africans from the Era of the Slave Trade*, Madison: University of Wisconsin Press.

Curtin, Philip D. (1969) *The Atlantic Slave Trade: A Census*, Madison: University of Wisconsin Press.

Douglass, Frederick ([1883] 1972) *The Life and Times of Frederick Douglass*, New York: Bonanza Books.

Fanon, Frantz (1968) *The Wretched of the Earth*, trans. Constance Farrington, New York: Grove Press.

Friedman, W.B. (1956) 'Changes in Property Relations', *Transactions of the Third World Congress of Sociology*: 1–2.

Geertz, Clifford (1983) *Local Knowledge: Further Essays in Interpretive Anthropology*, New York: Basic Books.

Glélé, Maurice Ahanhanzo (1974) *Le Danxomè: Du pouvoir Aja à la nation Fon*, Paris: Nubia.

Herskovits, Melville J. [1938] (1967) *Dahomey: An Ancient West African Kingdom*, vols 1 and 2, Evanston, Ill: Northwestern University Press.

Law, Robin (1991) *The Slave Coast of West Africa 1550–1750: The Impact of the Atlantic Slave Trade on an African Society*, Oxford: Clarendon Press.

Manning, Patrick (1982) *Slavery, Colonialism, and Economic Growth in Dahomey, 1640–1960*, New York: Cambridge University Press.

Marcuse, Herbert (1978) *The Aesthetic Dimension: Toward a Critique of Marxist Aesthetics*, Boston: Beacon Press.

Polanyi, Karl, with Abraham Rotstein (1966) *Dahomey and the Slave Trade: An Analysis of an Archaic Economy*, Seattle: University of Washington Press.

Segurola, R. Père B. (1963) *Dictionnaire Fon-Française*, Cotonou, Republic du Ben Procure de L'Archidiocèse.

Taussig, Michael (1987) *Shamanism, Colonialism and the Wild Man*, Chicago: University of Chicago Press.

(b) Visualizing race and identity

Chapter 29

Paul Gilroy

ART OF DARKNESS

Black art and the problem of belonging to England

THE POLITICS OF RACE has changed. The idea of a narrow anti-racism, for example, is no longer tenable. This situation has not come about because racism is less pernicious or because the long-term goal of racial justice is any less worthy. This change is not a result of the political ineptitude of anti-racist work in local authorities, or of the trivialization of black life which often characterized that work, nor even of the way that the idea of anti-racism has itself been dragged through the mud by moralism and discredited yet further by the excesses of its evangelical cadres. None of these noxious features announces the end of anti-racism as we have known it. It is the issue of culture and the failings of anti-racist practice to deal effectively with the cultural dimensions of racial politics in this country that confirm its redundancy.

Well before *The Satanic Verses* underscored this critical deficiency, organized anti-racism had been unable to respond to the varieties of racist discourse that linked understanding of race to *cultural* difference rather than biological hierarchy. Anti-racism was confidently able to define racism in the sum of prejudice and power but could not define race apart from the cultural characteristics which sometimes give 'racial' groups their cohesion. Anti-racism could not theorize the relationship between 'race' and culture because these two ideas were not effectively distinguished. Anti-racists colluded with their New Right opponents by reducing the former to the latter. They remained inert while ideas of race and nation became ever more closely associated in a new popular, patriotic brew. Their own covert reliance on ethnic absolutes made it hard to deny coherently the legitimacy of the ethnic absolutism when it appeared in the Honeyford brand of reasoned British nativism.

In this climate, to be both black and British was thought to be an impossibly compound identity. To be British is, in any case, to contract into a category of administrative convenience rather than an ethnic identity. It's an ambiguous word which often refuses its own obvious cultural referents. The term 'English', which is often mistakenly substituted for it, acts as a partial and manifestly inadequate cultural counterpart. The disjuncture between the two terms is a continual reminder not just of English dominance over Scots, Welsh and Irish people, but also that a British state can exist comfortably without the benefit of a unified British culture. The idea of an authentic cultural content of our national life is therefore constructed through an appeal to Englishness rather than to Britishness. It is around this concept that the difficult tasks of creating a more pluralistic sense of national identity and a new conception of national culture revolve.

These problems have a special significance for the artists of Britain's emergent black vernacular. They echo through musician Jazzie B's boast that he is proud to be both black and English and even resound when Ian Wright, the national B-team striker, confides to the *Daily Star* that he weeps as he pulls on his white England shirt. There is, however, no more striking example of the manner in which these vital conflicts are resolved by blacks in this country than painter Sonia Boyce's ironic re-figuration of herself in the guise of an English rose. All these actions are part of a wider cultural struggle to affiliate with England and, in so doing, to change what it means to be English. These young, gifted and black Britons are not naïve. The impact of a diaspora sensibility on their lives means that they can readily comprehend the limitations of national identities as such. Contemporary racism forces the most sensitive of them to try to understand the enduring appeal of national belonging. Their tentative but none the less insubordinate gestures signify an approach that has moved far beyond the typical anti-racist practice of peering into the murky pool of English culture in order to locate evidence of its monolithically racist character. The desire to make art out of being both black and English has become a major issue in the black art movement and should be seen as part of the long, micro-political task of recoding the cultural core of national life. In this light, the fissures, stress cracks and structural fatigue in the edifices of Englishness become more interesting and acquire their own beauty. With ethnic absolutism left behind, the tasks of demolition and reconstruction may also provide an opportunity to create a division of political labour in which white radicals can share.

The burgeoning musical distinctiveness of black England has provided the easiest means to explore this process of cultural exchange and transformation. However, during the 1980s the movement of black artists encompassed a variety of other expressive forms. The recent exhibition at the Hayward Gallery in which Sonia Boyce's picture is featured has provided an overdue occasion to reflect on the development of black visual arts, the distinct place they occupy in the art establishment, and their importance for the black communities. This exhibition – 'The Other Story' – has also performed the valuable role of flushing out the ethnocentric attitudes of a number of critics who have secreted the discourse of white supremacy in their commentaries on the show. Visual art currently constitutes a significant battleground because aesthetic issues are particularly close to the surface of individual judgements and, above all, because the majority of its critics are bound by the common-sense view that good art is universally recognizable and cultural background is not a factor either in its production or its appreciation. This position has remained largely unaffected by any relativist fallout from anti-racist orthodoxy.

It is important to appreciate that the idea of universality on which aesthetic judgements depend was itself constructed out of debates in which racial difference was a central issue. In Hegel's influential work, for example, blacks were incorporated directly into the discussion of aesthetics.[1] The capacity to make art was identified as a sign of the progress of non-Europeans out of their prehistoric state and into both history and culture. Writing before scientific racism gained its intellectual grip, Hegel identified the major difference between blacks and whites as a cultural or perceptual one. He denied blacks the ability to appreciate the necessary mystery involved in the creation of truly symbolic art and placed them outside the realm of authentic aesthetic sensibility. Unlike the American Indians whom he saw as effectively destroyed by the exposure to the culture and values of the West, he endowed blacks with the potential to progress into culture, even if they were often viewed as a childlike group that could perceive higher values, but were incapable of objectifying them as artistic abstractions. Where these higher values were perceived, the childlike blacks transferred 'them to the next best stone, which they thus make their fetish'.[2] Blacks perceive the divine objects they have created as sublime, but Europeans see them as 'hideous' just as they hear non-European music as 'the most detestable noise.'

The distinctively English idioms of art criticism also rest on aesthetic principles produced during a period when slavery was still part of Western civilization and therefore a fundamentally political concept. Here too, the image of the black played an important role in debates over taste, judgement and the role of culturally specific experience in grounding aesthetic principles. Burke's discussion of the sublime is striking for its association of darkness with the 'blackness' of a black woman's skin. Some of the reviews of the Hayward exhibition suggest that assimilating the work of black artists to a concept of the primitive, and declaring it bad modern art on that basis, is an enduring strategy. In his catalogue the show's curator, Rashid Araeen, counters it by arguing that it is necessary to rewrite the history of modern art. This is to be achieved mainly through a tried and tested anti-racist approach: black creativity has been excluded from the aesthetic citadels of modernity and post-modernity and this wrong can be redressed by the corrective reconstruction of the Western canon. No doubt there are many good reasons for this to be done. Successive generations of black artists have suffered from the contempt and hostility of critics, galleries and potential patrons. But if this process of rewriting art history along multicultural lines is not to degenerate into a crude debate over who did what first, there are significant problems to be faced. The first of these is the need to produce new concepts and a *non-narrative* periodization of Western art. Despite its title, 'The Other Story' is an important contribution to this long-term task.

The necessary but insufficient tactic of corrective inclusion that Araeen advocates leaves dominant notions of art and artistic creativity entirely unscathed. Furthermore, it attempts to force a wide range of postcolonial and non-European art practice into the rigid sequence that leads from modernism to postmodernism. This is not always possible, let alone desirable. Most importantly, this approach seems to accept the idea that 'race' is something that enters English culture from the outside during the postwar period. It shrinks before the wider obligation to adapt and transform understanding of English culture as a whole so that being black and English is no longer either a curiosity or an outrage. Araeen appreciates that the mere existence of black artists in the West challenges art history's sense of where the modern begins, let alone its line between the modern and the post-modern, but his argument remains somehow too internal to the institutional world of art. Perhaps moving outside it would expose the enormous generational and political differences between the artists who contributed to 'The Other Story'.

Black artists are now in a position to attempt a more ambitious project than simply filling in the spaces that racism has left blank in the history of art. They are already working to recompose understanding of English culture, and their creativity needs to be complemented by a rereading of that culture's history which places the idea of 'race' at the centre rather than the margin. The visual arts will play a key role in this, not just because of the tremendous vitality of the black fine art during the last decade, but because architecture, aesthetics and art have recently re-emerged as politically significant issues. As the principal public means to mark out and signify the cultural limits of national life, they will have a direct bearing on what the cultural order of a new Europe will be.

An editorial in a recent issue of the journal *Modern Painters*,[3] which pleaded for Prince Charles to extend his well-known ideas about architecture into a discussion of art, offered an important insight into this. Though sometimes cited as evidence of his eccentricity, Charles's interest in his black subjects-to-be is well known. These views should not, however, distract us from the less wholesome ways in which some of his supporters would link the relationship between what is national and what is natural in a political discourse which offers the black English very little. The newer, culturally focused varieties of racism I have described make no appeal whatsoever to biology but they view the nation as a *natural* unit formed spontaneously from the association of families. The national frontier around authentic English culture marks the boundaries of the national community as naturally and as finally as the white cliffs of Dover.

The *Modern Painters* editorial identified the things 'for which the Prince has so eloquently argued' as 'the replenishment of traditional skills, a renewed sense of the spiritual dimensions of aesthetic life' and 'imaginative involvement with the natural landscape.' These great themes were given a narrowly national currency and linked to 'the historic achievements of the British School'. There are plenty of clues here that we are dealing with a notion of national culture that is as homogeneous as it is ethnically undifferentiated. It becomes necessary to ask whether the aesthetic that underlies these suggestions would view blacks as a natural and acceptable presence in the English landscapes it reveres? The black presence in cities is novel and symptomatic of their postwar decline but it is somehow appropriate. Contemporary racism has identified black settlers with the cities in which most of them live and their cultural distinctiveness with its urban setting. Black life discovered amidst urban chaos and squalor has contributed new images of dangerousness and hedonism to the anti-urbanism of much English cultural commentary. How much less congruent is a black presence with the natural landscapes within which historically authentic English sensibility has been formed?

Here, the issue of black settlement needs to be separated from consideration of how blacks have been pictured in England's own imagination. The imagery of race has a much longer lineage in English cultural life than the aura of postwar novelty allows us to see. The theme of racial difference has also been extensively addressed from within that tradition. It should not be surprising that the relationship between the forces of nature and the human processes that culminate in racial exploitation has been explored before. It can even be found in what the editors of *Modern Painters* would probably regard as the exalted point in the artistic inventory of English national culture represented by John Ruskin and his first mentor, J.M.W. Turner.

Turner's famous tragic picture *Slavers Throwing Overboard the Dead and Dying: Typhoon Coming On* (also known as *The Slave Ship*) draws these strands together. The picture deploys the imagery of wrathful nature and of dying slaves as powerful means to highlight the degenerate and irrational nature of English civil society as it entered the 1840s. This work can provide a small illustration both of the extent to which race has been tacitly erased from discussion of English culture and how a 'racial' theme, relocated at the heart of national self-understanding, can contribute to a new, more pluralistic conceptualization of both England and Britain.

Turner and Ruskin, who owned *The Slave Ship* for twenty-eight years, currently enjoy special status in contemporary cultural life. Turner is a leading player in the unfolding drama of our national heritage, while Ruskin's social thought was an important inspiration in the development of New Left thinking about English intellectual history. More recently, his aesthetic ideas have supplied the raw material for precisely the ambiguous, organicist conception of English culture celebrated in the reborn *Modern Painters* and its royalist editorial. Turner's picture was first publicly shown in London in 1840, a few weeks before the World Anti-slavery Convention met in the Strand's Exeter Hall. Its immediate inspiration seems to have been James Thomson's poem 'The Seasons', although it may also have been inspired by Thomas Clarkson's accounts of barbaric events aboard the slave ships *Zong* and *Rodeur*. The artist's apparent alignment with the abolitionist cause has been queried by some commentators, but the lines which accompanied the painting illuminate his elemental despair for which the morality of the traffic in slaves offered a striking and appropriate symbol: 'hope hope fallacious hope where is thy market now?'

The picture was not well received, opinion being divided as to whether it was absurd rather than sublime. *The Times* ridiculed it and drew attention to 'the leg of a negro, which is about to afford a nibble to a John Dory, a pair of soles and a shoal of whitebait'. Writing in *Fraser's Magazine*, Thackeray was not slow to query the use to which the images of the trade had been put:

> the slaver throwing its cargo overboard is the most tremendous piece of colour that ever was seen. . . . The sun glares down upon a horrible sea of emerald and purple, into which chocolate coloured slaves are plunged, and chains that will not sink; and round these are floundering such a race of fishes as was never seen in the saeculum Pyrrhae . . . horrid spreading polypi, like huge, slimy, poached eggs, in which hapless niggers, plunge and disappear. Ye gods what a 'middle passage'!

Ruskin's father gave him the picture in January 1844 as a New Year's present to celebrate the publication of the first volume of the original *Modern Painters*. An entry in his diary a couple of days before the painting was delivered conveys his excitement and something of his early responses to the picture:

> Suspense about Slaver. My heart is all on eyes of *fish* now – it knew something of other kind of eyes once, and of slavery too, in its way. Its slavery now is colder like being bound to the dead, as in old Spanish cruelty.[4]

These private acknowledgements of the metaphysical potency of the painting's theme contrast quite sharply with the famous description of the painting he had penned previously for *Modern Painters*.[5] Here, Ruskin's evaluation of the painting forms part of his discussion of how water should be painted. He praised Turner's picture because it includes 'the noblest sea that Turner has ever painted' which is also 'the noblest certainly ever painted by man'. He continues: 'if I were reduced to rest Turner's immortality upon any single work, I should choose this.' The celebrated passage is too long to be quoted here but it is significant that Ruskin relegates the information that 'the guilty ship', 'girded with condemnation', is a slaver, to an extraordinary footnote: 'she is a slaver, throwing her slaves overboard. The near sea is encumbered with corpses.' One of Ruskin's biographers tells us that William Morris, Burne-Jones and other members of their set at Oxford were so deeply moved by the 'weltering oceans of eloquence' found in Ruskin's description of the ship that Morris would 'chant' the passage in his mighty singing voice. We are not told if the crucial footnote featured in these dramatic presentations.[6] It seems legitimate to draw attention to Ruskin's inability to integrate his aesthetic commentary on the painting with an open acknowledgement of its 'racial' content. Why was the 'racial' theme, which contributes directly to the conspicuous power of the work, given no aesthetic significance of its own? Three years after his notorious involvement in the campaign to defend Governor Eyre's brutal handling of the Morant Bay rebellion in Jamaica, Ruskin put the painting up for sale at Christie's. It is said that he had begun to find the subject matter of his father's gift too painful to live with. No buyer was found at that time and he eventually sold the picture to an American three years later. The painting has remained in the United States ever since and is now exhibited at the Museum of Fine Arts in Boston. Its exile also raises significant questions for the cultural historian as to the apparently un-English nature of its content.

It would be simplistic, even absurd, to characterize any of the complex exchanges around Turner's extraordinary painting as racist in the modern sense of the term. It is exciting to discover how the imagery of race and slavery appears centrally in Victorian debates over what England had been and what it was to become. The painting offers one opportunity to appreciate that English art and aesthetics are not simply in place alongside English thinking about race. Thinking about England is being conducted through the 'racial' symbolism that artistic images of black suffering provide. These images were not an alien or unnatural presence that had somehow intruded into English life from the outside. They were an integral means with which England was able to make sense of itself and its destiny.

The picture and its strange history pose a challenge to the black English today. It demands that we strive to integrate the different dimensions of our hybrid cultural heritage more effectively. If we are to change England by being English in addition to everything else that we are, our reflections on it and other comparable controversies in national art and letters must be synthesized with the different agenda of difficulties that emerges from our need to comprehend a phenomenon like the Hayward exhibition and the movement that produced it. In doing this, we may discover that our story is not the *other* story after all but *the* story of England in the modern world. The main danger we face in embarking on this difficult course is that these divergent political and aesthetic commentaries will remain the exclusive property of two mutually opposed definitions of cultural nationalism: one black, one white. Each has its own mystical sense of the relationship between blood, soil and seawater. Neither of them offers anything constructive for the future.

Notes

1 Sander Gilman. 'The Figure of the Black in German Aesthetic Theory', *Eighteenth Century Studies*, vol. 8, 1975, pp. 373–91.
2 See the discussion of the fetish in the section on the geographical basis of history which introduces Hegel's lectures on *The Philosophy of History*, New York, Dover, 1956, pp. 91–99.
3 *Modern Painters*, vol. 2, no. 3, Autumn 1989.
4 *Diaries of John Ruskin*, ed. Joan Evans and J.H. Whitehouse, entry for 27 December 1843, Oxford, Clarendon Press, 1956.
5 Vol. 1 section 5, ch. III, section 39.
6 E.T. Cook, *Life of Ruskin*, 2 vols, London, George Allen, 1911, p. 147.

Chapter 30

bell hooks

REPRESENTING WHITENESS
Seeing *Wings of Desire*

WIM WENDERS' 1988 FILM *Wings of Desire* received much critical acclaim and was loved by movie-goers everywhere, yet I found the film very stylized, so intent to impress its seriousness upon the audience that there were moments when I just wanted to laugh, and there were tedious moments when I was just plain bored. Arriving at the cinema early, I took a seat which allowed me to watch folks coming to see this much talked-about film. Seated around me were viewers who had seen the film many times. They were praising Wenders even as they munched popcorn and searched for seats. As is often the case at this type of artsy film, there were few black viewers (three of us). I was curious to know how the two black women saw the film but did not dare ask (after all, they might not 'see' themselves as black).

Seeing the film with a politically aware white feminist friend who loved it and was seeing it a second time, I could not resist teasing her by saying, 'How come you love this film when all the male stars are angels and the female star is a trapeze artist? I mean, isn't this every straight male's fantasy?' She didn't get it. I said, 'You know, the woman who can twist her body into any position, like those Modigliani paintings.' Later I said, 'So why didn't you tell me this was a film about white German angst?' She didn't get it. 'You know,' I declared, 'It's another in a series where postmodern white culture looks at itself somewhat critically, revising here and there, then falling in love with itself all over again.' She didn't get it. I gave up and began to speak English, that is to say, to speak a language she could understand (no more subaltern black codes).

Seriously, this film made me think deeply about white culture, though not simply in terms of skin color – rather whiteness as a concept underlying racism, colonization, and cultural imperialism. Wenders' earlier film *Paris, Texas* (a work I find interesting and problematic) did not raise whiteness as an issue. *Wings of Desire* evoked images of that imperialist colonizing whiteness that has dominated much of the planet. This image was reinforced by the use of nonwhite people as colorful backdrop in the film, a gesture that was in no way subversive and undermining in that much of the film was an attempt to represent white culture in a new light. Encountering white friends raving about the magic of this film, I would respond by saying it was just 'too white.' They would give me that frustrated 'no racism again, please' look that is so popular these days and explain to me that, after all, Berlin is a white city. Of course I had to remind them about those black and brown people in the background – none of whom were either angels or trapeze artists. And that no, Berlin is not exclusively a 'white city.'

Talking to serious black movie-goers who also could not get into this film, I was relieved. There was one exception, a fellow black woman 'cultural terrorist' (a name we jokingly call ourselves), who liked the film's focus on history and memory. I could not see how she missed linking those concerns to white culture. I was surprised that she did not ponder the basic question of why all the angels were white. Here response was to ask me if I 'could really imagine black angels.' I thought immediately of the black angels (handmade dolls) hanging in my kitchen. I was surprised that she had never seen the brown-faced angels in Ethiopian talismanic art, work much older than figurative drawing.

'Why,' I exclaimed, 'I have one of those angels painted on a scroll in my living room! I see black angels every day.' We continued to talk about the film, about the way in which ethnicity does or does not shape out viewing sensibility. We even tried to explore whether I had experienced some racist trauma the day I saw the film which might have made me more acutely aware of the issue. My insistence was that the issue was there in the work.

Filmmaker Wim Wenders does place this work in a decidedly white European context with an underlying focus on Western civilization and history. In an interview with *Cineaste*, Wenders discusses the importance of not forgetting history, relating it to the film: 'If there is any response to my parents' generation or to the one before it, it is the way they treated history after 1945. They tend to make everyone forget, which made it impossible to deal with.'

Incorporating footage of war-torn Berlin and Nazism, Wenders compels audiences to remember. If, as he suggests, the angels are 'a metaphor for history, a particular memory,' we would all have seen these angels differently had they not been predominantly male and all white. In many ways, the film attempts to create a space of otherness, where white masculinity can be reconceptualized and white patriarchal imperialist history critiqued. Such a project raises questions about whether the alternative narrative Wenders constructs actually subverts or challenges the old. Wenders' work represents a trend in white avant-garde aesthetic circles toward revisioning old narratives of opposition. *Wings of Desire* does not fulfill this promise. It does not tell a new story.

Homer, the aged writer/storyteller, asserts his longing for another narrative even as we witness his nostalgia for sentimental aspects of the old. He recovers himself through memory, through the act of storytelling. Interviewed in *Film Quarterly*, Wenders talks about his fascination and renewed interest in storytelling:

> It is one of the most reassuring things. It seems its very basis is that it reassures you that there is a sense to things. Like the fact that children want to hear stories when they go to sleep. I mean not so much that

> they want to know this or that, but that they want it as it gives them a security. The story creates a form and the form reassures them so that you can almost tell them any story – which you can actually do. So there is something very powerful in stories, something that gives you security and a sense of identity and meaning.

To many audiences watching *Wings of Desire*, the reassuring story may be that narrative which promises the possibility of radical change in European history, in white culture. It's important, then, that the primary signifier of that change is the rejection by white males (the old storytellers, the main angels Damiel and Cassiel) of destructive violence symbolized by war and genocidal holocaust. Imperialist masculinity is negated, and the new vision evoked by angelic style is of a world wherein the visionary white men exude divine presence and regard life as sacred. They do so as angels. They do so as men. Peter Falk (playing himself), in Berlin to make a detective movie, bonds with Damiel, sharing that he had once been an angel. His retention of the capacity to recognize divine presence links the insight of angels to that of mortals. Through much of the film, male angels use their bodies in ways that subvert traditional masculine physicality; their movements suggest tenderness and gentleness, never aggressiveness or brutality. However, the film's implied critique of oppressive masculinity is undercut by the reinscription of sexist male bonding as regards sexual desire.

Only the male angels repudiate this form of bonding. Capable of compassionate empathy and abundant generosity, Damiel and Cassiel move about the city making connections with sensitive mortals, with hurt individuals who need healing. We witness their caring gestures, the way they appear to understand one another's longings, their bond expressed in deep penetrating glances at each other. At times they gaze at each other sensually, evoking an aura of angelic homoerotic bonding. However, their friendship changes as Damiel pursues Marion, the desired 'mortal' female. Toward the end of *Wings of Desire*, Damiel meets Marion for the first time at a rock concert. Cassiel appears to be anguished by the pending separation from his friend. There is a powerful moment when he turns toward the wall, hands covering his face as though deeply wounded. On the other side of the wall the erotic bond between Marion and Damiel is forming. The loss of meaningful connection between the angels suggests that homosocial bonding, however innocent, must become secondary to the fulfillment of heterosexual desire.

In essence, the relationship between Damiel and Marion is a romantic reassertion of the primacy of heterosexual love. Ironically, despite his angelic past, Damiel approaches heterosexual desire in ways that are too familiar. His desire for Marion is first expressed via the objectifying gaze; she is the object of his look. Watching him watch her, I was reminded of that often quoted statement of John Berger in *Ways of Seeing*:

> Men act and women appear. Men look at women. Women watch themselves being looked at. This determines not only most relations between men and women but also the relation of women to themselves. The surveyor of woman in herself is male; the surveyed female. Thus she turns herself into an object of vision: a sight.

Wenders certainly does not rewrite this script. He graphically dramatizes it. The audience first sees Marion working as a trapeze artist, every movement of her body watched by males. Their voyeuristic gaze is upon her and so is ours. She is scantily clothed; they are fully dressed. We in the onlooking audience are fully dressed. Since her movements on the trapeze are difficult exertions of physical skill, we are all the more mesmerized. Her attire and the men watching deflect attention away from physical effort and her body movements are sexualized.

Berger's comments on male presence suggest that it is defined by power, by what 'he is capable of doing to you or for you.' Throughout much of the film we are impressed by the way Damiel carries himself, by what he does. We watch his actions. His repeated touching of bodies is not sexualized. In contrast, Marion's every movement on stage or off is sexualized. As Berger suggests, her female presence is determined by attitude: 'A woman must continually watch herself . . . From earliest childhood she has been taught and persuaded to survey herself continually.' When Marion stops working and returns to her trailer, we watch as she surveys herself, as she examines her face in the mirror. We are placed in the position of voyeurs, as is the angelic Damiel. His watching her (unidentified and unseen) in her private space can be seen as benevolent since he is an angel. In this scene he can be viewed as guardian, as protector. This is one way to look at it. Another is that the embedded message here is that the angelic cloak is a disguise marking the potential reality of his gaze, especially as we later witness that gaze turn into an intense lustful stare. Constructing a male angel who both protects and ultimately desires the innocent unsuspecting female is a gesture more fundamentally linked to patriarchal valuation of dissimulation than a radical rethinking of coercive masculinity.

Casting the men as angels without wings is not an unambiguous gesture. We watch them knowing they are to be seen as figures of innocence though we simultaneously recognize their embodiment as men. Every time their hands were placed on people's bodies, I contrasted that caring touch with the reality of white male disregard and violation of other people's body space. Throughout the film, viewers are to believe that angelic status diffuses their power so it is in no way harmful. Yet it is difficult to see subverse content in this imagery when white male agencies like the FBI and CIA as well as their Berlin counterparts would have us believe that their surveillance of the planet is for our own good. How can this imagery be trusted when the male gaze which begins as benevolent ends as a self-interested stare, expressed as longing for sexual possession? When the potential lovers finally meet at the bar, Marion wants to talk and Damiel wants to consume her physically (he is all over her). His acquiescence to her demands is not a gesture that transforms the dominating positioning of his desire. Much of the film centers on his enthrallment with her, which is so intense he surrenders being an angel to make contact.

Yet Wenders can say in *Film Quarterly* that he thought 'it would be fatal for the film if she had been the object of his desire.' It is disturbing that he is convinced that the film represents a change in his treatment of female subjectivity, that he can claim that Marion is 'the leading character.' Even the title *Wings of Desire* emphasizes the primacy of Damiel's character. His desire is central. Marion's sexuality is never fulfilled. Contrary to critics who interpret the voice-over where she expresses her point of view as a declaration of subjectivity, it is solely an expression of her ideas about love distinct from sexual desire. Again an old script is rewritten – women want love, men want sex.

Both *Wings of Desire* and Wenders' earlier film *Paris, Texas* explore male erotic fantasy, portraying male inability to acknowledge the subjectivity of women. Though scenes in *Paris, Texas* moved me deeply, from a feminist perspective it was a problematic film. The film was groundbreaking in that it portrayed a male character coming to understand the degrees to which clinging to male domination and coercive control damages his primary love relationship. Yet that understanding is undercut when expressed in the context of a scene which reinscribes structures of domination. During the 'peepshow' scene, which is the climactic point in the film, the male character tells the story of his sexist abuse and exploitation of his young wife, speaking to her. She is working in the booth. He watches her; she cannot see him. He knows her identity; she cannot recognize him until he identifies himself (sound familiar? – we could be speaking about Damiel and Marion). While naming coercive male control as destructive, he does not surrender control, only the coercive element. However touching this confession and her ultimate recognition, it is not a scene of female empowerment; just as the scene where Marion speaks to Damiel does not change the dominating power of his presence. *Wings of Desire* ends with a scene where Marion performs, the object of Damiel's gaze. Despite her earlier insistence on will, knowledge, and choice, nothing has changed their physical placement in the film. The visual image that remains is of a woman performing for male pleasure. Presumably her non-erotic desire has been satisfied, her longing to be touched by 'a wave of love that stirs.'

That this 'love story,' like *Cinderella, Sleeping Beauty*, and many others, satisfies and reassures is no cause for celebration. Perhaps it is dangerous that Wenders and the white male who interviewed him in *Film Quarterly* were so congratulatory and confident that this film had a 'feminist' message, though they do not use that word. And even more dangerous, they do not question their vantage point. Are they so well informed about feminist thinking that they are able to determine whether Marion is portrayed as subject or object? It is as though the stage of acquiring the feminist standpoint that would be a basis for constructing different images of women and critically examining that construction, though unnamed, is presumed to have occurred; the same might be said of race. Representations of both gender and race in the film suggest otherwise. Current trends in avant-garde cultural production by white people, which presume to challenge the status quo regarding race and gender, are ethically and politically problematic. While it is exciting to witness a pluralism that enables everyone to have access to the use of certain imagery, we must not ignore the consequences when images are manipulated to appear 'different' while reinforcing stereotypes and oppressive structures of domination.

In *Wings of Desire*, the library as storehouse of knowledge is the meeting place of angelic visionaries. It is only white people who are angels, only white men who dialogue with one another, only white men who interpret and revise old scripts (benevolently reading people's minds, touching them in their intimate body space). Wenders' imaginative offering of an alternative to destructive white masculinity is appealing, yet he does not fulfill the promise of his own creative assertions.

White avant-garde artists must be willing openly to interrogate work which they or critics cast as liberatory or oppositional. That means they must consider the role whiteness plays in the construction of their identity and aesthetic visions, as well as the way it determines reception of their work. Coco Fusco explains the importance of such awareness in her essay 'Fantasies of Oppositionality,' published in *Afterimage:*

> Racial identities are not only black, Latino, Asian, Native American, and so on; they are also white. To ignore white ethnicity is to redouble its hegemony by naturalizing it. Without specifically addressing white ethnicity, there can be no critical evaluation of the construction of the other.

If the current fascination with otherness is an authentic expression of our desire to see the world anew, then we must be willing to explore the cultural blindness of the many people who saw *Wings of Desire* and who did not see whiteness represented there as sign and symbol.

Chapter 31

Andrew Ross

THE GANGSTA AND THE DIVA

In 1994, Daytona Beach city elders refused to play host to MTV's Spring Break, a weeklong televised spree of lascivious beach games organized around live musical interludes. A year earlier, in its customary Florida venue, they had taken offence to the hedonistic goings-on, including the now-famous drag queen performer Ru Paul's fierce debut at this event. There, at the forefront of commercial youth culture, in the midst of all the dating games involving cross-dressing, suddenly, whoomp! Ru Paul was the real thing on the runway. The mostly white college jock audience in Daytona that spring responded with seriously muted applause – a reaction that was probably part embarrassment, part homophobia, and part jaw-dropped amazement at just how damned good he was. This was the same crowd that had bayed with co-sexual appreciation for the other black men on the bill – Shabba Ranks, the sexed-up Jamaican toaster, and Naughty by Nature, featuring Treach, with masculinity to spare in his minimalist moves.

Treach's street-bad machete and Ru Paul's supermodel sashay represent two polarities of 'fierceness' in black popular culture. The first attitude is a reduced, deadpan burlesque of menace-to-society rap, the second a camp alchemist's transmutation of black female assertiveness into diva-rich parody. Either way – whether in the ghetto street or in the nightclub version – being fierce is a theatrical response to the phenomenal social pressure exerted upon black males in the waning years of the twentieth century. Blaine and Antoine, those over-the-top queens from 'Men on Film,' on Fox TV's *In Living Color*, may have been crude, even offensive caricatures, but it's probably fair to say that the figure of the black snap queen rules over camp sectors of queer culture and holds uncontested sway over club nightlife, where Ru Paul's dance-floor injunction, 'You Bettuh Work!' is one of the wittiest inflections of the Puritan work ethic to have penetrated weekend leisure time. As for the gangsta rapper, whether he was kicking back the day with smooth laconic beats, Cali-style, or 'wrecking the mic' with motormouth rhymes, East

Coast-style, he likewise established his dominion over male youth culture in a field where competition runs high.

The dialogue between these two figures is not supposed be acknowledged publicly, and their relation to each other has been entirely ignored in the recent flap about gangsta rap, attended by so much moralizing. But it is worth examining. Ru Paul's song 'Back to My Roots' – a wickedly funny tribute to black hair culture – was reportedly suggested, and then rejected, as soundtrack for hardcore rapper Tupac Shakur's beauty salon scenes with Janet Jackson in John Singleton's film *Poetic Justice* – a symptom of the homophobic response to any combination of this kind. Nonetheless, voguers – those ghetto performance queens, popularized by Jennie Livingston's documentary *Paris is Burning*, whose spectacular dance-floor competitions were based upon dressy impersonations of 'real' social types quite removed from their own lives – subtly honored the gangsta with a drag category of bhanjee realness all their own. Voguers belonged to 'houses,' whose mode of affiliation and social rivalry are not at all dissimilar to the loyalty structure of gangs. Ice-T described LA gangland as 'ghetto male love being pushed to its limit,' and there is no shortage of testimony within hip hop culture to the intense homosociality of the crews, posses and clans that dominate the scene with their all-boyz blood-oath families, sworn to the cult of ultramasculinity. While there is no lack of cut-throat spirit to the voguer's one-upping art of 'throwing shade' on the dance floor, there's more than a little fussy styling to the ghettocentric iconography of swagger-and-scowl associated the world over with hardcore rap. As for the black pop mainstream, now that transvestism has become American apple pie à la mode, it's time to ask where the likes of Little Richard, Michael Jackson, Jimi Hendrix, Eddie Murphy, Prince, Martin, and Arsenio would be if they had not had a showbiz repertoire of draggy gestures to feed off in shaping their own personal style. With the mercurial rise of the cross-dressing Dennis Rodman at the very core of sports celebrity culture, all bets are off.

The profile of the reality rapper, scaled down to the ultimate, low metabolism vibe of Dr Dre (who had pursued an earlier glam-with-eyeliner singing career) and Snoop Doggy Dogg, evokes an affectless masculinity, conceived under siege and resonating with the long history of presenting a neutral face as a mask of inscrutability to the white gaze. (Snoop's video retreat into the harmless poses of the playful, late adolescent prankster, or the retro soulboy could similarly be seen as a tactical response to white disapproval of the gangsta as public enemy.) Alternately, when the voguer uses an imaginary compact to 'put on a face,' or when the snap queen feigns the composed hauteur of the style aristocrat or hams the high-eyed shock of bourgeois outrage, the extravagant use of 'face' is plain to see. Whether underplayed or overplayed, these theatrical versions of black masculinity are as much methods of deflecting or neutralizing white disapproval as modes of expressing black traditions. White culture has always compelled black males to perform, usually as entertainers or as athletes. Performance has typically been the obverse of black invisibility in a society of white privilege. Today, however, the underlying trend points beyond invisibility, and towards disappearance.

Efforts to evacuate young black men from the public sphere have proceeded on every front. As dropouts from the educational system, as victims of suicides, homicides, and the penal system, as casualties of the incredible shrinking welfare state, as fatalities of the crack economy and the AIDS emergency, and as targets of new and more virulent forms of racism, black male youth are quite systematically being driven toward social obsolescence. It is from this context – the absent existential status of an entire social cohort – that the brouhaha about gangster rap took its political significance. Those who reduced rap to a discussion of its most disturbing misogynistic or anti-social lyrics ignore how both this context, and the way in which the culture that springs from it, merely exacerbates, rather than creates, forms of social prejudice long rife in white, patriarchal America. Those politicians and black preachers who took the high ground against gangsta rap have profited, as their professional status dictates, from media grandstanding. The broad left (black and white) has no excuse for indulging in this lazy moralizing, least of all when it chooses rap as a vehicle to bash the cause of cultural politics in general.

In these apocalyptic years, before the first batch of the crack-baby generation came of age, hardcore rap was just about the only medium in which ghetto life attained something approaching authentic recognition. Hence the distinction hotly debated among hip-hop audiences between rappers who 'front' and those who 'represent.' The distinction separates the pretenders from those who exemplify the true hardcore spirit of hip-hop (rather like an athlete who represents a nation in competition) or the ethos of a community: Brooklyn, Compton. But, above all, 'representing' involves a demonstrated loyalty to the storytelling genre itself. In rap, genre justice, earned at the microphone, determines how respect is distributed. The rapper's aim is to convince an audience that his 'shit is real,' but this is a much more complex task than simply proving that the events he describes actually happened to him. For middle-class performers, this is a form of downwardly mobile 'passing,' no less performative than the upward aspirations of the voguer's role-playing. The rap debate in the public media entirely missed such evolved and highly competitive aspects of the genre and instead revolved simply around whether gangsta lyrics represent reality or shape reality – in other words, induce criminal behavior. In the long run, both debates may be pretty inconsequential but they do demonstrate (a) the level of desperation among poor black youth; and (b) the sad lack of understanding among the larger public about the political nature of cultural events.

Links have to be made. At the very least, we ought to temper the moral panic about drugs with the knowledge that marijuana is now overwhelmingly the hip-hop drug of choice, and that its advocacy among rappers not only challenged the chokehold of the crack economy but also reinforced the arguments for legalizing hemp as a versatile industrial crop – arguments hitherto only associated with white, countercultural voices. Second, we ought to connect the moral panic about guns with demands to demilitarize police divisions up and down the country. The fact that LA gangstas are armed was quite possibly one of the few obstacles to the partial realization of a police state in Southern California. Just as the Black Panthers made theatrical appearances with guns in public, rap's romance with the gangsta consciously contested the official taboo against images of armed black males (with the exception of black policemen). Of course, much of this was the politics of symbolism, but it also relates to a reality in which the street-cleaning of the gangsta guns would be seen as near-genocidal if it were actually being executed by police weapons. If the recent East-West Coast wars between the Death Row and Bad Boy companies (allegedly linked to the Tupac and Biggie Small killings) proved anything, it was not about how lyrical violence inevitably overflows into real homicides, but rather about the aggressive outcome of cut-throat commercial competition.

The gangs I grew up around in the industrial Scottish lowlands were, by comparison, low tech in their cult of the flick knife. The gang in my own hometown was called Young Bowery, a parochial imitation of the notorious Glasgow gangs, and, I suppose, the result of some long-lost tribute to the first Irish gangs of Lower Manhattan. In its Scottish form, the dominant gangster pose of the 'hard man' touched a deep vein in industrial working-class culture, where the strongest manifestations of this personality were often reserved for anti-colonial flights of animus against the English. As an outlawed collectivity, the gang had its place then as a minor vehicle for the virility-testing Scottish proletarianism that was losing its muscle, even in my youth. Its more warlike sensibility fed the romance of pre-capitalist, clannish resistance to the English while, at the same time, providing fresh fuel to the London media for racist stereotypes of the barbarous Scottish male. As models of masculinity, the small-time thugs I knew had few qualities that would be thought of as 'progressive' by the standards of modern sexual politics. Their pathologies did not belong to them, however, but were the cultural frames that defined how, where, and when they were permitted to announce their anger. Whereas in North America social divisions are most sharply determined by race, in the West of Scotland they were almost entirely the result of Protestant/Catholic antagonisms, as hate-bound as in Northern Ireland and much more meaningful than the weak socio-economic segmentation that existed within a broadly working-class culture. Actual religious belief had almost nothing to do with this, of course. For the most part, Protestant and Catholic were simply banners to fight under, marking pseudo-ethnicities that retained their popularity because they were not defined wholly by economic conditions, and consequently were regarded as if they were properties belonging to 'the people.' By contrast, then, when Pakistani families formed the first substantial community of color in the 1980s, their perceived otherness was as much socioeconomic and religious – a petty-bourgeois shopkeeper class that did not observe Sunday closing hours – as it was ethnic.

The point here is that while socially denied people do not express rage just as they please, or under circumstances of their choosing, they do tend to opt for vehicles that are the least likely to be culturally influenced by the powerful. That is why, incongruous as it often seems, gangsta rap came to provide the most articulate frame for black anger available for its young devotees. After a quarter-century of sell-out black politicians and almost ceaseless economic warfare, it's no surprise that kids believed they could locate sincerity only in a musical genre, top-heavy with humor and creativity, that delivers fantasies much closer to home than the distant middle-class dreamworld of affirmative action politics. As for the white youth who affiliated themselves with the hip-hop nation, their identification might not be the ephemeral, and thus comfortable, choice it was for their forebears in the bohemian tradition of the white Negro. The emergence of legions of white hip-hop junkies – termed 'wiggers' by the tabloid press – may well testify to a significant reversal in the politics of integration. The shoe is now on the other foot, as white kids seek to integrate into black-and-brown culture in ways that their civil rights-generation parents find difficult to understand. Sure, there is a sizeable proportion of suburbanites in this movement, bent, as always, on driving their parents crazy, but just as many are youth propelled by the prospect of their economic redundancy, the ultimate desertion of a white parental culture that can't even offer them the certainty of employment at a living wage. When they are not making some kind of common sense of these conditions with black and brown youth (often by wearing 'infantile' fashion as if to defer the future), all they have to fall back on is a parody of white trash; how to look awful and still look good is still the favorite style pursuit of the post-grunge crowd.

Outside of its persistence in Levi ads, where does the injunction, 'Got To Be Real,' come to rest? The hardcore rapper's steady loyalty to ghetto realism (the appearance of being totally determined by one's social environment) finds its counterpoint in the vogue queen's 'realness' (the ability to impersonate anything but that which you are). The gangsta MC needs the ghetto to justify his every move and rhyme; without that constant appeal, he falls off, his career is over, he becomes a tired studio gangsta. By contrast, the snap queen only refers to elsewhere; her utopia is to be entirely free of the constraints of class, race, and gender that define ghetto life. Along the way, she will become fodder for the talk shows, just as the gangsta's career trajectory leads him to flirt perilously with the penal system. For both, the ultimate aim is to 'get paid,' in terms of wealth or glamor, all the while retaining respect from their respective marginal undergrounds: the street and the after-hours nightclub.

These are not positive NAACP role models, nor are they meant to be. Bill Cosby and Michael Jordan have that field covered. Neither are they militant advocates of the sort desired by radicals. We look to the preach-and-teach rapper and the gay black activist for that. Rather, they are semi-outlawed, institutional archetypes, each carrying a rich history of meanings, some ugly, some exquisite, for communities for whom poverty and performance have been daily horizons of existence since slavery days. Like barometric pressure systems, separate but equal, in a prevailing weather front, the gangsta and the diva both command center stage in black popular culture, even if they rarely appear on the same stage. Perhaps this is the latest version of what Amiri Baraka, in a famous, and relentlessly homophobic essay, referred to as 'the changing same,' when he proposed a unity vibe between street R&B and free, avant-garde jazz in the 1960s. Just as that fusion was never realized, it is unlikely that the gangsta and the diva will ever make common cause, despite the remarkable capacity of hip-hop and drag to reinvent themselves almost every year. It is no more likely that the beauty, anger, intelligence, prejudice, compassion, and pain of young black men will be found in any one individual type. Why should they be? The full range of masculinity is not individual, it is cultural. A major part of the women's movement has been devoted to arguing this much about femininity. This is not to say that sexism and homophobia should be accepted as part of the 'diversity' of masculine culture. But we cannot expect these powerful masculine legacies to disappear simply by denouncing their most powerless manifestations (as in rap lyrics) in the name of moral hygiene, least of all when the offenders in question are drawn from, or represent some of the most economically denied sectors of the population. The flowering of fully fashioned types like the gangsta and the diva, with their respective mimicry of extremes of 'masculine' and 'feminine' behavior, is evidence of the complex challenges faced by proponents of sexual politics today. Listening to the incomplete dialogue between these figures might serve as one starting point, and not a conclusion, for a cultural politics of masculinity that is willing to view sexual justice as a radical struggle, and not simply as a liberal, consensual limit to intolerance. Perhaps Isaac Julien had it right in his film *The Darker Side of Black*, when he imagined the following scenario:

> Saturday night in downtown Manhattan. A bhanji boy and his boyfriend give a homeboy face. 'We're here, we're black, and we're queer, get over it,' they tell him. The homeboy turns to them, makes his hand into the shape of a gun, and fires it at them. The bhanji boy replies, 'Its not me you want to kill, but yourself that you see in me.' Somewhere behind every homie exterior lies a homo interior.

(c) Identity and transculture

Chapter 32

Adrian Piper

PASSING FOR WHITE, PASSING FOR BLACK

IT WAS THE NEW Graduate Student Reception for my class, the first social event of my first semester in the best graduate department in my field in the country. I was full of myself, as we all were, full of pride at having made the final cut, full of arrogance at our newly recorded membership among the privileged few, the intellectual elite, this country's real aristocracy, my parents told me; full of confidence in our intellectual ability to prevail, to fashion original and powerful views about some topic we represented to ourselves only vaguely. I was a bit late, and noticed that many turned to look at – no, scrutinize me as I entered the room. I congratulated myself on having selected for wear my black velvet, bell-bottomed pants suit (yes, it was that long ago) with the cream silk blouse and crimson vest. One of the secretaries who'd earlier helped me find an apartment came forward to greet me and proceeded to introduce me to various members of the faculty, eminent and honorable faculty, with names I knew from books I'd studied intensely and heard discussed with awe and reverence by my undergraduate teachers. To be in the presence of these men and attach faces to names was delirium enough. But actually to enter into casual social conversation with them took every bit of poise I had. As often happens in such situations, I went on automatic pilot. I don't remember what I said; I suppose I managed not to make a fool of myself. The most famous and highly respected member of the faculty observed me for a while from a distance and then came forward. Without introduction or preamble he said to me with a triumphant smirk, 'Miss Piper, you're about as black as I am.'

One of the benefits of automatic pilot in social situations is that insults take longer to make themselves felt. The meaning of the words simply don't register right away, particularly if the person who utters them is smiling. You reflexively respond to the social context and the smile rather than to the words. And so I automatically returned the smile and said something like, 'Really? I hadn't known that about you' – something that sounded both innocent and impertinent, even though that was not what I felt. What I felt was numb, and then shocked and terrified, disoriented, as though I'd been awakened from a sweet dream of unconditional support and approval and plunged into a nightmare of jeering contempt. Later those feelings turned into wrenching grief and anger that one of my intellectual heroes had sullied himself in my presence and destroyed my illusion that these privileged surroundings were benevolent and safe; then guilt and remorse at having provided him the occasion for doing so.

Finally, there was the groundless shame of the inadvertent impostor, exposed to public ridicule or accusation. For this kind of shame, you don't actually need to have done anything wrong. All you need to do is care about others' image of you, and fail in your actions to reinforce their positive image of themselves. Their ridicule and accusations then function to both disown and degrade you from their status, to mark you not as having *done* wrong but as *being* wrong. This turns you into something bogus relative to their criterion of worth, and false relative to their criterion of authenticity. Once exposed as a fraud of this kind, you can never regain your legitimacy. For the violated criterion of legitimacy implicitly presumes an absolute incompatibility between the person you appeared to be and the person you are now revealed to be; and no fraud has the authority to convince her accusers that they merely imagine an incompatibility where there is none in fact. The devaluation of status consequent on such exposure is, then, absolute; and the suspicion of fraudulence spreads to all areas of interaction.

[. . .]

> She walked away. . . . The man followed her and tapped her shoulder.
>
> 'Listen, I'd really like to get to know you,' he said, smiling. He paused, as if expecting thanks from her. She didn't say anything. Flustered, he said, 'A friend of mine says you're black. I told him I had to get a close-up look and see for myself.'
>
> (Perry, *Another Present Era*, p. 19)

The irony was that I could have taken an easier entry route into this privileged world. In fact, on my graduate admissions application I could have claimed alumni legacy status and the distinguished family name of my paternal great-uncle, who had not only attended that university and sent his sons there, but had endowed one of its buildings and was commemorated with an auditorium in his name. I did not because he belonged to a branch of the family from which we had been estranged for decades, even before my grandfather – his brother – divorced my grandmother, moved to another part of the country, and started another family. My father wanted nothing more to do with my grandfather or any of his relatives. He rejected his inheritance and never discussed them while he was alive. For me to have invoked his uncle's name in order to gain a professional advantage would have been out of the question. But it would have nullified my eminent professor's need to tell me who and what he thought I was.

Recently I saw my great-uncle's portrait on an airmail stamp honoring him as a captain of industry. He looked so much like family photos of my grandfather and father that I went out and bought two sheets' worth of these stamps. He had my father's and grandfather's aquiline nose, and their determined set of the chin. Looking at his face made me want to recover my father's estranged family, particularly my grandfather, for my own. I had a special lead: A few years previously, in the South, I'd included a phototext work containing a fictionalized narrative about my father's family – a history chock-full of romance and psychopathology – in an exhibition of my work. After seeing the show, a white woman with blue eyes, my father's transparent rosy skin and auburn-brown hair, and that dominant family nose walked up to me and told me that we were related. The next day she brought photographs of her family, and information about a relative who kept extensive genealogical records on every family member he could locate. I was very moved, and also astounded that a white person would voluntarily acknowledge blood relation to a black. She was so free and unconflicted about this. I just couldn't fathom it. We corresponded and exchanged family photos. And when I was ready to start delving in earnest, I contacted the relative she had mentioned for information about my grandfather, and initiated correspondence or communication with kin I hadn't known existed and who hadn't known that I existed or that they or any part of their family was black. I embarked on this with great trepidation, anticipating with anxiety their reaction to the racial identity of these long-lost relatives, picturing in advance the withdrawal of warmth and interest, the quickly assumed impersonality and the suggestion that there must be some mistake.

> The dread that I might lose her took possession of me each time I sought to speak, and rendered it impossible for me to do so. That moral courage requires more than physical courage is no mere poetic fancy. I am sure I should have found it easier to take the place of a gladiator, no matter how fierce the Numidian lion, than to tell that slender girl that I had Negro blood in my veins.
>
> (James Weldon Johnson, *The Autobiography of an Ex-Coloured Man*, (1912), p. 200)

These fears were not unfounded. My father's sister had, in her youth, been the first black woman at a Seven Sisters undergraduate college and the first at an Ivy League medical school; had married into a white family who became socially, politically and academically prominent; and then, after taking some family mementos my grandmother had given my father for me, had proceeded to sever all connections with her brothers and their families, even when the death of each of her siblings was imminent. She raised her children (now equally prominent socially and politically) as though they had no maternal relatives at all. We had all been so very proud of her achievements that her repudiation of us was devastating. Yet I frequently encounter mutual friends and colleagues in the circles in which we both travel, and I dread the day we might find ourselves in the same room at the same time. To read or hear about or see on television her or any member of her immediate family is a source of personal pain for all of us. I did not want to subject myself to that again with yet another set of relatives.

> Those who pass have a severe dilemma before they decide to do so, since a person must give up all family ties and loyalties to the black community in order to gain economic and other opportunities.
> (F. James Davis, *Who Is Black? One Nation's Definition* (1991), p. 143)

Trying to forgive and understand those of my relatives who have chosen to pass for white has been one of the most difficult ethical challenges of my life, and I don't consider myself to have made very much progress. At the most superficial level, this decision can be understood in terms of a cost-benefit analysis: Obviously, they believe they will be happier in the white community than in the black one, all things considered. For me to make sense of this requires that I understand – or at least accept – their conception of happiness as involving higher social status, entrenchment within the white community and corresponding isolation from the black one, and greater access to the rights, liberties and privileges the white community takes for granted. What is harder for me to grasp is how they could want these things enough to sacrifice the history, wisdom, connectedness and moral solidarity with their family and community they must sacrifice in order to get them. It seems to require so much severing and forgetting, so much disowning and distancing, not simply from one's shared past, but from one's former self – as though one had cauterized one's long-term memory at the moment of entry into the white community.

But there is, I think, more to it than that. Once you realize what is denied you as an African-American simply because of your race, your sense of the unfairness of it may be so overwhelming that you may simply be incapable of accepting it. And if you are not inclined toward any form of overt political advocacy, passing in order to get the benefits you know you deserve may seem the only way to defy the system. Indeed, many of my more prominent relatives who are passing have chosen altruistic professions that benefit society on many fronts. They have chosen to use their assumed social status to make returns to the black community indirectly, in effect compensating for the personal advantages they have gained by rejecting their family.

Moreover, your sense of injustice may be compounded by the daily humiliation you experience as the result of identifying with those African-Americans who, for demanding their rights, are punished and degraded as a warning to others. In these cases, the decision to pass may be more than the rejection of a black identity. It may be the rejection of a black identification that brings too much pain to be tolerated.

> All the while I understood that it was not discouragement or fear or search for a larger field of action and opportunity that was driving me out of the Negro race. I knew that it was shame, unbearable shame. Shame at being identified with a people that could with impunity be treated worse than animals.
> (Johnson, *The Autobiography of an Ex-Coloured Man*, (1912), p. 191)

The oppressive treatment of African-Americans facilitates this distancing response, by requiring every African-American to draw a sharp distinction between the person he is and the person society perceives him to be; that is, between who he is as an individual, and the way he is designated and treated by others.

> The Negro's only salvation from complete despair lies in his belief, the old belief of his forefathers, that these things are not directed against him personally, but against his race, his pigmentation. His mother or aunt or teacher long ago carefully prepared him, explaining that he as an individual can live in dignity, even though he as a Negro cannot.
>
> (John Howard Griffin, *Black Like Me* (1960), p. 48)

This condition encourages a level of impersonality, a sense that white reactions to one have little or nothing to do with one as a person and an individual. Whites often mistake this impersonality for aloofness or unfriendliness. It is just one of the factors that make genuine intimacy between blacks and whites so difficult. Because I have occasionally encountered equally stereotypical treatment from other blacks and have felt compelled to draw the same distinction there between who I am and how I am perceived, my sense of impersonality pervades most social situations in which I find myself. Because I do not enjoy impersonal interactions with others, my solution is to limit my social interactions as far as possible to those in which this restraint is not required. So perhaps it is not entirely surprising that many white-looking individuals of African ancestry are able to jettison this doubly alienated and alienating social identity entirely, as irrelevant to the fully mature and complex individuals they know themselves to be. I take the fervent affirmation and embrace of black identity to be a countermeasure to and thus evidence of this alienation, rather than incompatible with it. My family contains many instances of both attitudes.

There are no proper names mentioned in this account of my family. This is because in the African-American community, we do not 'out' people who are passing as white in the European-American community. Publicly to expose the African ancestry of someone who claims to have none is not done. There are many reasons for this, and different individuals cite different ones. For one thing, there is the vicarious enjoyment of watching one of our own infiltrate and achieve in a context largely defined by institutionalized attempts to exclude blacks from it. Then there is the question of self-respect: If someone wants to exit the African-American community, there are few blacks who would consider it worth their while to prevent her. And then there is the possibility of retaliation: not merely the loss of credibility consequent on the denials by a putatively white person who, by virtue of his racial status, automatically has greater credibility than the black person who calls it into question; but perhaps more deliberate attempts to discredit or undermine the messenger of misfortune. There is also the instinctive impulse to protect the wellbeing of a fellow traveler embarked on a particularly dangerous and risky course. And finally – the most salient consideration for me in thinking about those many members of my own family who have chosen to pass for white – a person who seeks personal and social advantage and acceptance within the white community so much that she is willing to repudiate her family, her past, her history, and her personal connections within the African-American community in order to get them is someone who is already in so much pain that it's just not possible to do something that you know is going to cause her any more.

> Many colored Creoles protect others who are trying to pass, to the point of feigning ignorance of certain branches of their families. Elicited genealogies often seem strangely skewed. In the case of one very good informant, a year passed before he confided in me that his own mother's sister and her children had passed into the white community. With tears in his eyes, he described the painful experience of learning about his aunt's death on the obituary page of the *New Orleans Times-Picayune*. His cousins failed to inform the abandoned side of the family of the death, for fear that they might show up at the wake or the funeral and thereby destroy the image of whiteness. Total separation was necessary for secrecy.
>
> (Virginia R. Domínguez, *White by Definition: Social Classification in Creole Louisiana* (1986), p. 161)

> She said: 'It's funny about "passing." We disapprove of it and at the same time condone it. It excites our contempt and yet we rather admire it. We shy away from it with an odd kind of revulsion, but we protect it.'
>
> 'Instinct of the race to survive and expand.'
>
> 'Rot! Everything can't be explained by some general biological phrase.'
>
> 'Absolutely everything can. Look at the so-called whites, who've left bastards all over the known earth. Same thing in them. Instinct of the race to survive and expand.'
>
> (Nella Larsen, *Passing* (1929), pp. 185–86)

Those of my grandfather's estranged relatives who welcomed me into dialogue instead of freezing me out brought tears of gratitude and astonishment to my eyes. They seemed so kind and interested, so willing to help. At first I couldn't accept for what it was their easy acceptance and willingness to help me puzzle out where exactly we each were located in our sprawling family tree. It is an ongoing endeavor, full of guesswork, false leads, blank spots and mysteries. For just as white Americans are largely ignorant of their African – usually maternal – ancestry, we blacks are often ignorant of our European – usually paternal – ancestry. That's the way our slavemaster forebears wanted it, and that's the way it is. Our names are systematically missing from the genealogies and public records of most white families, and crucial information – for example, the family name or name of the child's father – is often missing from our black ancestors' birth certificates, when they exist at all.

> A realistic appreciation of the conditions which exist when women are the property of men makes the conclusion inevitable that there were many children born of mixed parentage.
>
> (Joe Gray Taylor, *Negro Slavery in Louisiana* (1963), p. 20)

> Ownership of the female slave on the plantations generally came to include owning her sex life. Large numbers of white boys were socialized to associate physical and emotional pleasure with the black women who nursed and raised them, and then to deny any deep feelings for them. From other white males they learned to see black girls and women as legitimate objects of sexual desire. Rapes occurred, and many slave women were forced to submit regularly to white males or suffer harsh consequences. . . . as early as the time of the American Revolution there were plantation slaves who appeared to be completely white, as many of the founding fathers enslaved their own mixed children and grandchildren.
>
> (Davis, *Who Is Black?*, (1991) pp. 38, 48–49)

So tracing the history of my family is detective work as well as historical research. To date, what I *think* I know is that our first European-American ancestor landed in Ipswich, Massachusetts, in 1620 from Sussex; another in Jamestown, Virginia, in 1675 from London; and another in Philadelphia, Pennsylvania, in 1751, from Hamburg. Yet another was the first in our family to graduate from my own graduate institution in 1778. My great-great-grandmother from Madagascar, by way of Louisiana, is the known African ancestor on my father's side, as my great-great-grandfather from the Ibo of Nigeria is the known African ancestor on my mother's, whose family has resided in Jamaica for three centuries.

I relate these facts and it doesn't seem to bother my newly discovered relatives. At first I had to wonder whether this ease of acceptance was not predicated on their mentally bracketing the implications of these facts and restricting their own immediate family ancestry to the European side. But when they remarked unselfconsciously on the family resemblances between us I had to abandon that supposition. I still marvel at their enlightened and uncomplicated friendliness, and there is a part of me that still can't trust their acceptance of me. But that is a part of me I want neither to trust nor to accept in this context. I want to reserve my vigilance for its context of origin: the other white Americans I have encountered – even the bravest and most conscientious white scholars – for whom the suggestion that they might have significant African ancestry as the result of this country's long history of miscegenation is almost impossible to consider seriously.

> She's heard the arguments, most astonishingly that, statistically . . . the average white American is 6 percent black. Or, put another way, 95 percent of white Americans are 5 to 80 percent black. Her Aunt Tyler has told her stories about these whites researching their roots in the National Archives and finding they've got an African-American or two in the family, some becoming so hysterical they have to be carried out by paramedics.
>
> (Perry, *Another Present Era*, p. 66)

> Estimates ranging up to 5 percent, and suggestions that up to one-fifth of the white population have some genes from black ancestors, are probably far too high. If these last figures were correct, the majority

> of Americans with some black ancestry would be known and counted as whites!
>
> (Davis, *Who Is Black?*, (1991), pp. 21–22)

The detailed biological and genetic data can be gleaned from a careful review of *Genetic Abstracts* from about 1950 on. In response to my request for information about this, a white biological anthropologist once performed detailed calculations on the African admixture of five different genes in British whites, American whites, and American blacks. American whites had from 2 per cent of one gene to 81.6 per cent of another. About these results he commented, 'I continue to believe 5 per cent to be a reasonable estimate, but the matter is obviously complex. As you can see, it depends entirely on which genes you decide to use as racial "markers" that are supposedly subject to little or no relevant selective pressure.' Clearly, white resistance to the idea that most American whites have a significant percentage of African ancestry increases with the percentage suggested.

> 'Why, Doctor,' said Dr. Latimer, 'you Southerners began this absorption before the war. I understand that in one decade the mixed bloods rose from one-ninth to one-eighth of the population, and that as early as 1663 a law was passed in Maryland to prevent English women from intermarrying with slaves; and, even now, your laws against miscegenation presuppose that you apprehend danger from that source.'
>
> (Harper, *Iola Leroy*, p. 228)

> (That legislators and judges paid increasing attention to the regulation and punishment of miscegenation at this time does not mean that interracial sex and marriage as social practices actually increased in frequency; the centrality of these practices to legal discourse was instead a sign that their relation to power was changing. The extent of uncoerced miscegenation before this period is a debated issue.)
>
> (Eva Saks, 'Representing Miscegenation Law,' *Raritan* (1991), pp. 43–44)

The fact is, however, that the longer a person's family has lived in this country, the higher the probable percentage of African ancestry that person's family is likely to have – bad news for the D.A.R., I'm afraid. And the proximity to the continent of Africa of the country of origin from which one's forebears emigrated, as well as the colonization of a part of Africa by that country, are two further variables that increase the probability of African ancestry within that family. It would appear that only the Lapps of Norway are safe.

In Jamaica, my mother tells me, that everyone is of mixed ancestry is taken for granted. There are a few who vociferously proclaim themselves to be 'Jamaican whites' having no African ancestry at all, but no one among the old and respected families takes them seriously. Indeed, they are assumed to be a bit unbalanced, and are regarded with amusement. In this country, by contrast, the fact of African ancestry among whites ranks up there with family incest, murder, and suicide as one of the bitterest and most difficult pills for white Americans to swallow.

> 'I had a friend who had two beautiful daughters whom he had educated in the North. They were cultured, and really belles in society. They were entirely ignorant of their lineage, but when their father died it was discovered that their mother had been a slave. It was a fearful blow. They would have faced poverty, but the knowledge of their tainted blood was more than they could bear.'
>
> (Harper, *Iola Leroy*, p. 100)

> There was much apprehension about the unknown amount of black ancestry in the white population of the South, and this was fanned into an unreasoning fear of invisible blackness. For instance, white laundries and cleaners would not accommodate blacks because whites were afraid they would be 'contaminated' by the clothing of invisible blacks.
>
> (Davis, *Who Is Black?*, (1991) p. 145)

> Suspicion is part of everyday life in Louisiana. Whites often grow up afraid to know their own genealogies. Many admit that as children they often stared at the skin below their fingernails and through a mirror at the white of their eyes to see if there was any 'touch of the tarbrush'. Not finding written records of birth, baptism, marriage, or death for any one ancestor exacerbates suspicions of foul play. Such a discovery brings glee to a political enemy or economic rival and may traumatize the individual concerned.
>
> (Domínguez, *White by Definition*, (1986), p. 159)

A number of years ago I was doing research on a video installation on the subject of racial identity and miscegenation, and came across the Phipps case of Louisiana in the early 1980s. Susie Guillory Phipps had identified herself as white and, according to her own testimony (but not that of some of her black relatives), had believed that she was white, until she applied for a passport, when she discovered that she was identified on her birth records as black in virtue of having 1/32 African ancestry. She brought suit against the state of Louisiana to have her racial classification changed. She lost the suit, but effected the overthrow of the law identifying individuals as black if they had 1/32 African ancestry, leaving on the books a prior law identifying an individual as black who had any African ancestry – the 'one-drop' rule that uniquely characterizes the classification of blacks in the United States in fact, even where no longer in law. So according to this longstanding convention of racial classification, a white who acknowledges any African ancestry implicitly acknowledges being black – a social condition, more than an identity, that no white person would voluntarily assume, even in imagination. This is one reason why whites, educated and uneducated alike, are so resistant to considering the probable extent of racial miscegenation.

This 'one-drop' convention of classification of blacks is unique not only relative to the treatment of blacks in other countries but also unique relative to the treatment of other ethnic groups in this country. It goes without saying that no one, either white or black, is identified as, for example, English by virtue of having some small fraction of English ancestry. Nor is anyone free, as a matter of social convention, to do so in virtue of that fraction, although many whites do. But even in the case of other disadvantaged groups in this country, the convention is different. Whereas any proportion of African ancestry is sufficient to identify a person as black, an individual must have *at least* one-eighth Native American ancestry in order to identify legally as Native American.

Why the asymmetry of treatment? Clearly, the reason is economic. A legally certifiable Native American is entitled to financial benefits from the government, so obtaining this certification is difficult. A legally certifiable black person is *disentitled* to financial, social and inheritance benefits from his white family of origin, so obtaining this certification is not just easy, but automatic. Racial classification in this country functions to restrict the distribution of goods, entitlements and status as narrowly as possible, to those whose power is already entrenched. Of course this institutionalized disentitlement presupposes that two persons of different racial classifications cannot be biologically related, which is absurd.

> [T]his [one-drop] definition of who is black was crucial to maintaining the social system of white domination in which widespread miscegenation, not racial purity, prevailed. White womanhood was the highly charged emotional symbol, but the system protected white economic, political, legal, education and other institutional advantages for whites. . . . American slave owners wanted to keep all racially mixed children born to slave women under their control, for economic and sexual gains. . . . It was intolerable for white women to have mixed children, so the one-drop rule favored the sexual freedom of white males, protecting the double standard of sexual morality as well as slavery. . . . By defining all mixed children as black and compelling them to live in the black community, the rule made possible the incredible myth among whites that miscegenation had not occurred, that the races had been kept pure in the South.
>
> (Davis, *Who Is Black?*, pp. 62–63, 113–14, 174)

But the issues of family entitlements and inheritance rights are not uppermost in the minds of most white Americans who wince at the mere suggestion that they might have some fraction of African ancestry and therefore be, according to this country's entrenched convention of racial classification, black. The primary issue for them is not what they might have to give away by admitting that they are in fact black, but rather what they have to lose. What they have to lose, of course, is social status; and, in so far as their self-esteem is based on their social status as whites, self-esteem as well.

> 'I think,' said Dr. Latrobe, proudly, 'that we belong to the highest race on earth and the negro to the lowest.'
>
> 'And yet,' said Dr. Latimer, 'you have consorted with them till you have bleached their faces to the whiteness of your own. Your children nestle in their bosoms; they are around you as body servants, and yet if one of them should attempt to associate with you your bitterest scorn and indignation would be visited upon them.'
>
> (Harper, *Iola Leroy*, p. 227)

[. . .]

Chapter 33

Coco Fusco

THE OTHER HISTORY OF INTERCULTURAL PERFORMANCE

IN THE EARLY 1900S, Franz Kafka wrote a story that began, 'Honored members of the Academy! You have done me the honor of inviting me to give your Academy an account of the life I formerly led as an ape.' Entitled 'A Report to an Academy,' it was presented as the testimony of a man from the Gold Coast of Africa who had lived for several years on display in Germany as a primate. That account was fictitious and created by a European writer who stressed the irony of having to demonstrate one's humanity; yet it is one of many literary allusions to the real history of ethnographic exhibition of human beings that has taken place in the West over the past five centuries. While the experiences of many of those who were exhibited is the stuff of legend, it is the accounts by observers and impresarios that constitute the historical and literary record of this practice in the West. My collaborator, Guillermo Gómez-Peña, and I were intrigued by this legacy of performing the identity of an Other for a white audience, sensing its implications for us as performance artists dealing with cultural identity in the present. Had things changed, we wondered? How would we know, if not by unleashing those ghosts from a history that could be said to be ours? Imagine that I stand before you then, as did Kafka's character, to speak about an experience that falls somewhere between truth and fiction. What follows are my reflections on performing the role of a noble savage behind the bars of a golden cage.

Our original intent was to create a satirical commentary on Western concepts of the exotic, primitive Other; yet we had to confront two unexpected realities in the course of developing this piece: (a) a substantial portion of the public believed that our fictional identities were real ones; and (b) a substantial number of intellectuals, artists, and cultural bureaucrats sought to deflect attention from the substance of our experiment to the 'moral implications' of our dissimulation, or in their words, our 'misinforming the public' about who we were. The literalism implicit in the interpretation of our work by individuals representing the 'public interest' bespoke their investment in positivist notions of 'truth' and depoliticized, ahistorical notions of 'civilization.' This 'reverse ethnography' of our interactions with the public will, I hope, suggest the culturally specific nature of their tendency toward a literal and moral interpretation.

When we began to work on this performance as part of a counter-quincentenary project, the Bush administration had drawn clear parallels between the 'discovery' of the New World and his 'New World Order.' We noted the resemblance between official quincentenary celebrations in 1992 and the ways that the 1892 Columbian commemorations had served as a justification for the United States' then new status as an imperial power. Yet, while we anticipated that the official quincentenary celebration was going to form an imposing backdrop, what soon became apparent was that for both Spain and the United States, the celebration was a disastrous economic venture, and even an embarrassment. The Seville Expo went bankrupt; the US Quincentenary Commission was investigated for corruption; the replica caravels were met with so many protestors that the tour was canceled; the Pope changed his plans and didn't hold mass in the Dominican Republic until after October 12; American Indian Movement activist Russell Means succeeded in getting Italian Americans in Denver to cancel their Columbus Day parade; and the film super-productions celebrating Columbus – from *1492: The Discovery* to *The Conquest of Paradise* – were box office failures. Columbus, the figure who began as a symbol of Eurocentrism and the American entrepreneurial spirit, ended up being devalued by excessive reproduction and bad acting.

As the official celebrations faded, it became increasingly apparent that Columbus was a smokescreen, a malleable icon to be trotted out by the mainstream for its attacks on 'political correctness.' Finding historical justification for Columbus's 'discovery' became just another way of affirming Europeans' and Euro-Americans 'natural right' to be global cultural consumers. The more equitable models of exchange proposed by many multiculturalists logically demanded a more profound understanding of American cultural hybridity, and called for redefinitions of national identity and national origins. But the concept of cultural diversity fundamental to this understanding strikes at the heart of the sense of control over Otherness that Columbus symbolized, and was quickly cast as un-American. Resurrecting the collective memory of colonial violence in America that has been strategically erased from the dominant culture was described consistently throughout 1992 by cultural conservatives as a recipe for chaos. More recently, as is characterized by the film *Falling Down*, it is seen as a direct threat to heterosexual, white male self-esteem. It is no wonder that contemporary conservatives invariably find the focus on racism by artists of color 'shocking' and inappropriate, if not threatening to national interests, as well as to art itself.

Our of this context arose our decision to take a symbolic vow of silence with the cage performance, a radical departure from Guillermo's previous monologue work and my activities as a writer and public speaker. We sought a strategically effective way to examine the limits of the 'happy multiculturalism' that reigned in cultural institutions, as well as to respond to the formalists and cultural relativists who reject the proposition that racial difference is absolutely fundamental to aesthetic interpretation. We looked to Latin America, where consciousness of the repressive limits on public expression is far more acute than it is here, and found many examples of how popular opposition has for centuries been expressed through the use of satiric spectacle. Our cage became the metaphor for our condition, linking the racism implicit in ethnographic paradigms of discovery with the exoticizing rhetoric of 'world beat' multiculturalism. Then came a perfect opportunity: In 1991, Guillermo and I were invited to perform as part of the Edge '92 Biennial, which was to take place in London and also in Madrid as the capital of European culture. We took advantage of Edge's interest in locating art in public spaces to create a site-specific performance for Columbus Plaza in Madrid, in commemoration of the so-called Discovery.

Our plan was to live in a golden cage for three days, presenting ourselves as undiscovered Amerindians from an island in the Gulf of Mexico that had somehow been overlooked by Europeans for five centuries. We called our homeland Guatinau, and ourselves Guatinauis. We performed our 'traditional tasks,' which ranged from sewing voodoo dolls and lifting weights to watching television and working on a lap-top computer. A donation box in front of the cage indicated that, for a small fee, I would dance (to rap music), Guillermo would tell authentic Amerindian stories (in a nonsensical language), and we would pose for Polaroids with visitors. Two 'zoo guards' would be on hand to speak to visitors (since we could not understand them), take us to the bathroom on leashes, and feed us sandwiches and fruit. At the Whitney Museum in New York we added sex to our spectacle, offering a peek at authentic Guatinaui male genitals for $5. A chronology with highlights from the history of exhibiting non-Western peoples was on one didactic panel and a simulated Encyclopedia Britannica entry with a fake map of the Gulf of Mexico showing our island was on another. After our three days in May 1992, we took our performance to Covent Garden in London. In September, we presented it in Minneapolis, and in October, at the Smithsonian's National Museum of Natural History. In December, we were on display in the Australian Museum of Natural History in Sydney, and in January 1993, at the Field Museum of Chicago. In early March, we were at the Whitney for the opening of the Biennial, the only site where we were recognizably contextualized as artwork. Prior to our trip to Madrid, we did a test run under relatively controlled conditions in the Art Gallery of the University of California, Irvine.

Our project concentrated on the 'zero degree' of intercultural relations in an attempt to define a point of origin for the debates that link 'discovery' and 'Otherness.' We worked within disciplines that blur distinctions between the art object and the body (performance), between fantasy and reality (live spectacle), and between history and dramatic re-enactment (the diorama). The performance was interactive, focusing less on what we did than on how people interacted with us and interpreted our actions. Entitled *Two Undiscovered Amerindians Visit . . .*, we chose not to announce the event through prior publicity or any other means, when it was possible to exert such control; we intended to create a surprise or 'uncanny' encounter, one in which audiences had to undergo their own process of reflection as to what they were seeing, aided only by written information and parodically didactic zoo guards. In such encounters with the unexpected, people's defense mechanisms are less likely to operate with their normal efficiency; caught off guard, their beliefs are more likely to rise to the surface.

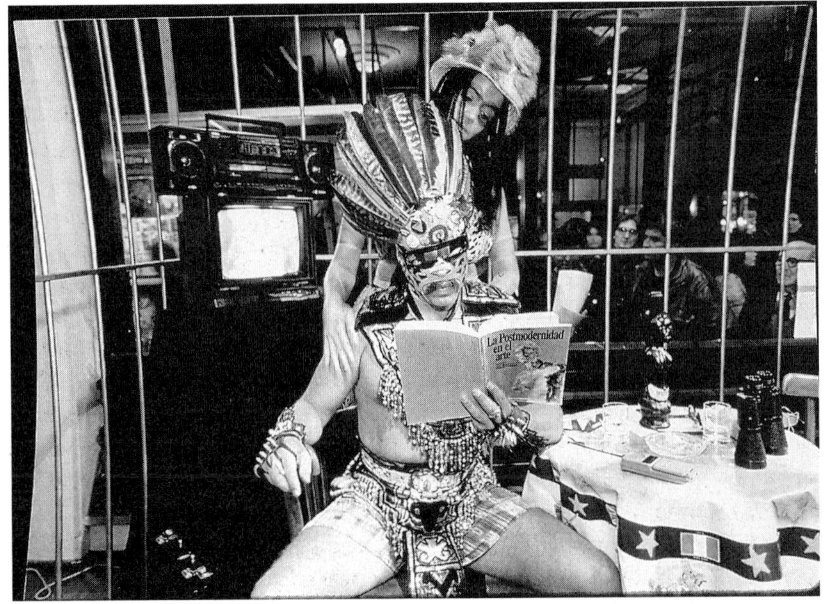

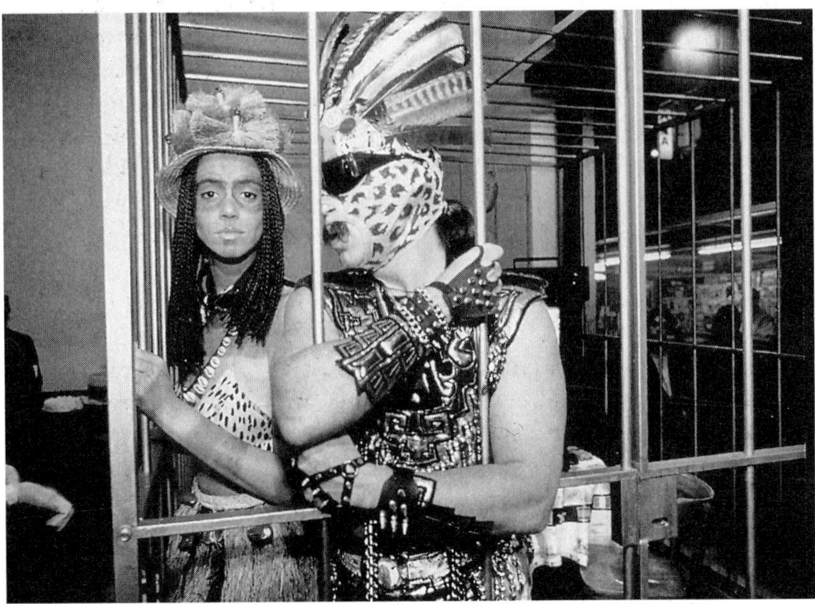

Figures 33.1 and 33.2 *Two Undiscovered Amerindians Visit Buenos Aires*, 1994 (Photos courtesy: Coco Fusco)

Our performance was based on the once popular European and North American practice of exhibiting indigenous people from Africa, Asia, and the Americas in zoos, parks, taverns, museums, freak shows, and circuses. While this tradition reached the height of its popularity in the nineteenth century, it was actually begun by Christopher Columbus, who returned from his first voyage in 1493 with several

Arawaks, one of whom was left on display at the Spanish Court for two years. Designed to provide opportunities for aesthetic contemplation, scientific analysis, and entertainment for Europeans and North Americans, these exhibits were a critical component of a burgeoning mass culture whose development coincided with the growth of urban centers and populations, European colonialism, and American expansionism.

In writing about these human exhibitions in America's international fairs from the late nineteenth and early twentieth centuries, Robert W. Rydell (author of *All the World's a Fair*; *Visions of Empire at American International Exhibitions, 1876–1916*) explains how the 'ethnological' displays of nonwhites – which were orchestrated by impresarios but endorsed by anthropologists – confirmed popular racial stereotypes and built support for domestic and foreign policies. In some cases, they literally connected museum practices with affairs of state. Many of the people exhibited during the nineteenth century were presented as the chiefs of conquered tribes and/or the last survivors of 'vanishing' races. Ishi, the Yahi Indian who spent five years living in the Museum of the University of California at the turn of the century, is a well-known example. Another lesser-known example comes from the US–Mexico War of 1836, when Anglo-Texan secessionists used to exhibit their Mexican prisoners in public plazas in cages, leaving them there to starve to death. The exhibits also gave credence to white supremacist worldviews by representing nonwhite peoples and cultures as being in need of discipline, civilization, and industry. Not only did these exhibits reinforce stereotypes of 'the primitive' but they served to enforce a sense of racial unity as whites among Europeans and North Americans, who were divided strictly by class and religion until this century. Hence, for example, at the Columbian Exhibition of 1893 in Chicago, ethnographic displays of peoples from Africa and Asia were set up outside 'The White City,' an enclosed area celebrating science and industry.

[. . .]

Our cage performances forced these contradictions out into the open. The cage became a blank screen onto which audiences projected their fantasies of who and what we are. As we assumed the stereotypical role of the domesticated savage, many audience members felt entitled to assume the role of the colonizer, only to find themselves uncomfortable with the implications of the game. Unpleasant but important associations have emerged between the displays of old and the multicultural festivals and ethnographic dioramas of the present. The central position of the white spectator, the objective of these events as a confirmation of their position as global consumers of exotic cultures, and the stress on authenticity as an aesthetic value, all remain fundamental to the spectacle of Otherness many continue to enjoy.

The original ethnographic exhibitions often presented people in a simulation of their 'natural' habitat, rendered either as an indoor diorama, or as an outdoor recreation. Eyewitness accounts frequently note that the human beings on display were forced to dress in the European notion of their traditional 'primitive' garb, and to perform repetitive, seemingly ritual tasks. At times, nonwhites were displayed together with flora and fauna from their regions, and artifacts, which were often fakes. They were also displayed as part of a continuum of 'outsiders' that included 'freaks,' or people exhibiting physical deformities. In the nineteenth and early twentieth centuries, many of them were presented so as to confirm social Darwinist ideas of the existence of a racial hierarchy. Some of the more infamous cases involved individuals whose physical traits were singled out as evidence of the bestiality of nonwhite people. For example, shortly after the annexation of Mexico and the publication of John Stephens' account of travel in the Yucatan, which generated popular interest in pre-Columbian cultures, two microcephalics (or 'pinheads') from Central America, Maximo and Bartola, toured the United States in P.T. Barnum's circus; they were presented as Aztecs. This set off a trend that would be followed by many other cases into the twentieth century. From 1810–15, European audiences crowded to see the Hottentot Venus, a South African woman whose large buttocks were deemed evidence of her excessive sexuality. In the United States, several of the 'Africans' exhibited were actually black Americans, who made a living in the nineteenth century by dressing up as their ancestors, just as many Native Americans did dressing up as Sioux whose likenesses, thanks to the long and bloody Plains Wars of the late nineteenth century, dominate the American popular imagination.

For Gómez-Peña and myself, the human exhibitions dramatize the colonial unconscious of American society. In order to justify genocide, enslavement, and the seizure of lands, a 'naturalized' splitting of humanity along racial lines had to be established. When rampant miscegenation proved that those differences were not biologically based, social and legal systems were set up to enforce those hierarchies. Meanwhile, ethnographic spectacles circulated and reinforced stereotypes, stressing that 'difference' was apparent in the bodies on display. Thus they naturalized fetishized representations of Otherness, mitigating anxieties generated by the encounter with difference.

In his essay, 'The Other Question', Homi Bhabha explains how racial classification through stereotyping is a necessary component of colonialist discourse, as it justifies domination and masks the colonizer's fear of the inability to always already know the Other. Our experiences in the cage suggested that even though the idea that America is a colonial system is met with resistance – since it contradicts the dominant ideology's presentation of our system as a democracy – the audience reactions indicated that colonialist roles have been internalized quite effectively.

The stereotypes about nonwhite people that were continuously reinforced by the ethnographic displays are still alive in high culture and the mass media. Imbedded in the unconscious, these images form the basis of the fears, desires, and fantasies about the cultural Other. In 'The Negro and Psychopathology,' Frantz Fanon discusses a critical stage in the development of children socialized in Western culture, regardless of their race, in which racist stereotypes of the savage and the primitive are assimilated through the consumption of popular culture: comics, movies, cartoons, and so forth. These stereotypical images are often part of myths of colonial dominion (for example, cowboy defeats Indian, conquistador triumphs over Aztec Empire, colonial soldier conquers African chief, and so on). This dynamic also contains a sexual dimension, usually expressed as anxiety about white male (omni)potence. In *Prospero and Caliban: The Psychology of Colonization*, Octave Mannoni coined the term 'Prospero complex' to describe the white colonial patriarch's continuous fear that his daughter might be raped by a nonwhite male. Several colonial stereotypes also nurture these anxieties, usually representing a white woman whose 'purity' is endangered by black men with oversized genitals, or suave Latin lovers, or wild-eyed Indian warriors; and the common practice of publicly lynching black men in the American South is an example of a ritualized white male response to such fears. Accompanying these stereotypes are counterparts that humiliate and debase women of color, mitigating anxieties about sexual rivalry between white and nonwhite women. In the past, there was the subservient maid and the overweight and sexless Mammy; nowadays, the hapless victim of a brutish or irrational dark male whose tradition is devoid of 'feminist freedoms' is more common.

These stereotypes have been analyzed endlessly in recent decades, but our experiences in the cage suggest that the psychic investment in them does not simply wither away through rationalization. The constant concern about our 'realness' revealed a need for reassurance that a 'true primitive' *did* exist, whether we fit the bill or not, and that she or he be visually identifiable. Anthropologist Roger Bartra sees this desire as being part of a characteristically European dependence on an 'uncivilized other' in order to define the Western self. In his book *El Salvaje en el Espejo/The Savage in the Mirror*, he traces the evolution of the 'savage' from mythological inhabitants of forests to 'wild' and usually hairy men and women who even in the modern age appeared in freak shows and horror films. These archetypes eventually were incorporated into Christian iconography and were then projected onto peoples of the New World, who were perceived as either heathen savages capable of reform or incorrigible devils who had to be eradicated.

While the structure of the so-called primitive may have been assimilated by the European avant-garde, the function of the ethnographic displays as popular entertainment was largely superceded by industrialized mass culture. Not unsurprisingly, the popularity of these human exhibitions began to decline with the emergence of another commercialized form of voyeurism – the cinema – and the assumption by ethnographic film of their didactic role. Founding fathers of the ethnographic filmmaking practice, such as Robert Flaherty and John Grierson, continued to compel people to stage their supposedly 'traditional' rituals, but the tasks were now to be performed for the camera. One of the most famous of the white impresarios of the human exhibits in the United States, William F. 'Buffalo Bill' Cody, actually starred in an early film depicting his Wild West show of Native American horsemen and warriors, and in doing so gave birth to the 'cowboy and Indian' movie genre, this country's most popular rendition of its own colonial fantasy. The representation of the 'reality' of the Other's life, on which ethnographic documentary was based and still is grounded, is this fictional narrative of Western culture 'discovering' the negation of itself in something *authentically* and *radically* distinct. Carried over from documentary, these paradigms also became the basis of Hollywood filmmaking in the 1950s and 1960s that dealt with other parts of the world in which the United States had strategic military and economic interests, especially Latin America and the South Pacific.

The practice of exhibiting humans may have waned in the twentieth century, but it has not entirely disappeared. The dissected genitals of the Hottentot Venus are still preserved at the Museum of Man in Paris. Thousands of Native American remains, including decapitated heads, scalps, and other body parts taken as war booty or bounties, remain in storage at the Smithsonian. Shortly before arriving in Spain, we learned of a current scandal in a small village outside Barcelona, where a visiting delegation had registered a formal complaint about a desiccated, stuffed Pygmy man that was on display in a local museum. The African gentleman in the delegation who had initiated the complaint was threatening to organize an African boycott of the 1992 Olympics, but the Catalonian townspeople defended what they saw as the right to keep 'their own black man.' We also learned that Julia Pastrana, a bearded Mexican woman who was exhibited throughout Europe until her death in 1862, is still available in embalmed form for scientific research and loans to interested museums. This past summer, the case of Ota Benga, a Pygmy who was exhibited in the primate cage of the Bronx Zoo in 1906, gained high visibility as plans for a Hollywood movie based on a recently released book were made public. And at the Minnesota State Fair last summer, we saw 'Tiny Teesha, the Island Princess,' who was in actuality a black woman midget from Haiti making her living going from one state fair to another.

While the human exhibition exists in more benign forms today – that is, the people in them are not displayed against their will – the desire to look upon predictable forms of Otherness from a safe distance persists. I suspect after my experience in the cage that this desire is powerful enough to allow audiences to dismiss the possibility of self-conscious irony in the Other's self-presentation; even those who saw our performance as art rather than artifact appeared to take great pleasure in engaging in the fiction, by paying money to see us enact completely nonsensical or humiliating tasks. A middle-aged man who attended the Whitney Biennial opening with his elegantly dressed wife insisting on feeding me a banana. The zoo guard told him he would have to pay $10 to do so, which he quickly paid, insisting that he be photographed in the act. After the initial surprise of encountering caged beings, audiences invariably revealed their familiarity with the scenario to which we alluded.

We did not anticipate that our self-conscious commentary on this practice could be believable. We underestimated public faith in museums as bastions of truth, and institutional investment in that role. Furthermore, we did not anticipate that literalism would dominate the interpretation of our work. Consistently from city to city, more than half of our visitors believed our fiction and thought we were 'real'; at the Whitney, however, we experienced the art world equivalent of such misperceptions: some visitors assumed that we were not the artists, but rather actors who had been hired by another artist. As we moved our performance from public site to natural history museum, pressure mounted from institutional representatives obliging us didactically to correct audience misinterpretations. We found this particularly ironic, since museum staffs are perhaps the most aware of the rampant distortion of reality that can occur in the labeling of artifacts from other cultures. In other words, we were not the only ones who were lying; our lies simply told a different story. For making this manifest, we were perceived as either noble savages or evil tricksters, dissimulators who discredit museums and betray public trust. When a few uneasy staff members in Australia and Chicago realized that large groups of Japanese tourists appeared to believe the fiction, they became deeply disturbed, fearing that the tourists would go home with a negative impression of the museum. In Chicago, just next to a review of the cage performance, the daily *Sun-Times* ran a phone-in questionnaire asking readers if they thought the Field Museum *should* have exhibited us, to which 47 per cent answered no, and 53 per cent yes. We seriously wonder if such weighty moral responsibilities are leveled against white artists who present fictions in nonart contexts.

Chapter 34

Néstor García Canclini

REMAKING PASSPORTS

Visual thought in the debate on multiculturalism

HOW DO WE INTERPRET the changes in contemporary visual thought? One of the greatest difficulties rests in the fact that tendencies do not develop from one paradigm to the next. We are not displacing ourselves from one type of rationality and visuality to another as in the Renaissance or in the transition from classicism to romanticism, nor as in the substitution that happened amongst the avant-gardes throughout the twentieth century. A real reorganisation has emerged from the intersection of multiple, simultaneous processes. Rather than changing, art appears to be vacillating. I am going to linger over one of those fluctuations which I consider to be crucial in the debate on identities: I am referring to the oscillation between a national visuality and the deterritorialised and transcultural forms of art and communication. Concerning the basis of this analysis, we might ask ourselves what type of visual thinking can speak today significantly in the discordant dialogue between fundamentalism and globalisation.

How are artists thinking?

This is difficult to answer if we consider that the polemic at the core of the modern aesthetic, that opposition between romanticism and classicism, persists even into postmodernity. For the romantics, art is a production of the intuitive and solitary genius; in the same way, reception is defined as an act of unconditional contemplation, the empathy of an individual sensitive disposition which allows itself to be penetrated by the mysterious eloquence of the work. Classical thought, by contrast, always works to subordinate sensibility and intuition to the order of reason: artistic production should be a way of presenting multiple meanings and expand the world in relation to its forms; we the spectators see those images in diverse ways – from the different codes imprinted in us by our social and educational structures – searching for the geometry of the real or expressionistically lamenting its loss.

The history of modern art, written as the history of avant-gardes, has contributed to the maintenance of this disjunction: on one hand, Surrealism, Pop Art and 'Bad Painting', for example; and on the other, Constructivism, the Bauhaus, Geometricism and all the self-reflexive artists from Marcel Duchamp to the Conceptualists, for whom art is a mental activity. The disillusioned farewell to the avant-gardes did not end this dichotomy; some postmoderns nostalgically pursue the order of Hellenic or Renaissance symmetry (even if it is under the sceptical-ironic form of the ruin); others place their irrationalist vocation in the enigmatic exuberance of rituals and tribal objects. In the former case, the artist as archaeologist or restorer of classical harmony; in the second, as a 'magician of the earth'. Such work, part of the hypothesis of contemporary epistemology, at least since Gaston Bachelard and Claude Lévi-Strauss, argues that the theory of art stems from the dilemma between rationalism and irrationalism. I agree with Michel Serres when he said that Bachelard is the last romantic (his cultural psychoanalysis adopted a non-positivist polysemy of meaning) and the first Neo-classicist (because he reunited 'the clarity of form for freedom and the density of content for understanding').[1] His new scientific spirit coincides, up to a point, with that of Lévi-Strauss when he demonstrated that the difference between science and magic, or between science and art, is not the distance between the rational and the pre-rational, but between two types of thought, one expressed in concepts and the other submerged in images. Magic and art are not weak or babbling forms of science, but – together with it – strategic and distinct levels in which nature and society allow themselves to be attacked by questions of knowledge.[2]

The second hypothesis is that a theory of art capable of transcending the antagonism between thought and intuition could contribute to a re-elaboration of the dilemmas of the end of the century, when all the sociocultural structures are destabilized and we ask ourselves if it is possible to construct imaginaries that do not empty into irrational arguments. We need to discover if the actual organisation of the aesthetic field (producers, museums, galleries, historians, critics and the public) contributes, and in what way, to the elaboration of shared imaginaries. It is not only the wit of a picture or the will of the artist that is inserted in or isolated from social history; it is also the interaction between the diverse members of the field (as both cultural system and market) which situates the significance of art in the vacillating meaning of the world.[3] In posing the problem in this way, it is possible to include in the question something about how art thinks today, even its innovative gestures: what capacity to think about a world orphaned of paradigms do transgressive or deconstructive works possess that are submitted to the order of the museums and the market?

Our third hypothesis is that this contribution of art is enabled by tendencies which are not only dedicated to thinking about the national but also to multiculturalism and globalisation. It seems unattractive to elaborate this theme from the perspective of Latin American art, because many artists are moving in that direction; but the strategies of the market, of international exhibitions and of the critics almost always banish it to the margins as the magic realism of local colour. Even when our people migrate extensively and a large part of our art work and literature is dedicated to *thinking* about the multicultural, Latin America continues to be interesting only as a continent of a violent nature, of an archaicism irreducible to modern nationality, an earth fertilised by an art conceived as tribal or national dreaming and not as thinking about the global and the complex.

How is the nation thinking, how is the market thinking?

Are the artists thinking the nation or thinking for it? When one observes, for example, the stylistic uniformity of French Baroque, Mexican Muralism or American Pop, one might ask if the artists of those currents thought the nation in their work or if they left the pre-existing cultural structure to shape the configuration. Individual differences in creative gestures are undeniable, but in the larger trajectory of these movements there has prevailed the enunciation of an 'ideology of images', a national community, that has proclaimed the heroism of the citizen, from David and Duplessis in pre-Revolutionary France,[4] across the reiterations of Diego Rivera, Siqueiros and their innumerable followers in Mexican legends, and through the work of Jasper Johns, Claes Oldenburg, Rauschenberg and others in the imaginary of the American consumer.

It is not possible to enter here into a debate on how far the possessions or patrimony of a nation condition fine art discourses and to what degree personal innovations evade such conditioning.[5] Rather, I am interested in emphasising that the modern history of art has been practised and written, to a great extent, as a history of the art of nations. This way of suppressing the object of study was mostly a fiction, but it possessed a verisimilitude over several centuries because the nations appeared to be the 'logical' mode of organisation of culture and the arts. Even the vanguards that meant to distance themselves from the sociocultural codes are identified with certain countries, as if these national profiles would help to define their renovative projects: thus, one talks about Italian Futurism, Russian Constructivism and the Mexican Muralist School.

A large amount of actual artistic production is made as an expression of national iconographic traditions and circulates only in its own country. In this way fine art remains one of the nuclei of the national imaginary, scenarios of the dedication and communication of signs of regional identities. But a sector, increasingly more extensive in the creation, the diffusion and the reception of art, is happening today in a deterritorialised manner. Many painters whom critical favour and cultural diplomacy promote as the 'big national artists', for example Tamayo and Botero, manifest a sense of the cosmopolitan in their work, which partly contributes to their international resonance. Even those chosen as the voices of more narrowly defined countries – Tepito or the Bronx, the myths of the Zapotecos or the Chicano Frontier – become significant in the market and in the exhibitions of American art in so far as their work is a 'transcultural quotation'.[6]

It is not strange that time and again international exhibitions subsume the particularities of each country under conceptual transnational networks. The shows in the Georges Pompidou Centre, 'Paris–Berlin' and 'Paris–New York', for example, purported to look at the history of contemporary art not suppressing national patrimonies but distinguishing axes that run through frontiers. But it is above all the art market that declassifies national artists, or at least subordinates the local connotations of the work, converting them into secondary folkloric references of an international, homogenised discourse. The internal differences of the world market point less to national characteristics than to the aesthetic currents monopolised by the leading galleries, whose headquarters in New York, London, Paris, Milan and Tokyo circulate work in a deterritorialised form and encourage the artists to adapt to different 'global' publics. The art fairs and the biennials also contribute to this multicultural game, as one could see in the last Venice Biennale, where the majority of the fifty-six countries represented did not have their own pavilion: most of the Latin Americans (Bolivia, Chile, Colombia, Costa Rica, Cuba, Ecuador, El Salvador, Mexico, Panama, Paraguay and Peru) exhibited in the Italian section, but that mattered little in a show dedicated, under the title 'Puntos cardinales del arte/Cardinal Points of Art', to exhibiting what today is constituted as 'cultural nomadism'.[7]

As these international events and the art magazines, the museums and the metropolitan critics manage aesthetic criteria homologous to the criteria of the market, so the artists who insist on national particularity rarely get recognition. The incorporation for short periods of some territorial movements into the mainstream, as happened with Land Art, or recently, with marginal positions, such as the Chicanos and Neomexicanists, does not negate the above analysis. The short-term speculations of the art market and their 'innovative and perpetual turbulence'[8] is as harmful in the long run to national cultures as to the personal and lengthy productions of artists; only a few can be adopted for a while to renovate the attraction of the proposition. It is in this sense that thinking today for much visual art means to be thought by the market.

From cosmopolitanism to globalisation

References to foreign art accompany the whole history of Latin American art. Appropriating the aesthetic innovations of the metropolises was a means for much art to rethink its own cultural heritage: from Diego Rivera to Antonio Berni, innumerable painters fed on Cubism, Surrealism and other Parisian vanguards to elaborate national discourses. Anita Malfatti found in New York Expressionism and Berlin Fauvism the tools to reconceptualise Brazilian identity, analogous to the way Oswald de Andrade utilised the Futurist Manifesto to re-establish links between tradition and modernity in São Paulo.

This cosmopolitanism of Latin American artists resulted, in most cases, in the affirmation of the self. A national consciousness has existed, torn by doubts about our capacity to be moderns, but capable of integrating into the construction of repertoires of images the journeys, the itinerant glances, which would differentiate each people. The foreign 'influences' were translated and relocated in national matrices, in projects which united the liberal, rationalist aspiration for modernity with a nationalism stamped with the Romantic, by which the identity of each people could be one, distinctive and homogeneous.

The pretension of constructing national cultures and representing them by specific iconographies is challenged in our time by the processes of an economic and symbolic transnationalisation. Arjun Appadurai groups these processes into five tendencies:

1 the population movements of emigrants, tourists, refugees, exiles and foreign workers;
2 the flows produced by technologies and transnational corporations;
3 the exchanges of multinational financiers;
4 the repertoires of images and information distributed throughout the planet by newspapers, magazines and television channels;
5 the ideological models representative of what one might call Western modernity: concepts of democracy, liberty, wellbeing and human rights, which transcend the definitions of particular identities.[9]

Taking into account the magnitude of this change, the deterritorialisation of art appears only partly the product of the market. Strictly speaking, a part is formed by a greater process of globalisation of the economy, communications and cultures. Identities are constituted now not only in relation to unique territories, but in the multicultural intersection of objects, messages and people coming from diverse directions.

Many Latin American artists are participating in the elaboration of a new visual thought which corresponds to this situation. There is no single pathway for this search. One is amazed that the preoccupation with decentring the artistic discourse from national niches crosses as much through the expressionistic Romantics as those who cultivate rationalism in conceptual practices and installations.

I agree with Luis Felipe Noé and his defence of an aesthetic that 'doesn't need a passport'. We cannot, he says, interrogate identity as a simple reaction against cultural dependency: to pose it in that way is like proposing 'to reply to a policeman who requires documents of identity or like a functionary who asks for a birth certificate'. For this reason, he affirms that the question whether there exists a Latin American art is one that is 'absurdly totalitarian'.[10]

Rather than devote ourselves to the nostalgic 'search for a non-existent tradition' he proposes we take on the diverse Baroque nature of our history, reproduced in many contemporary painters by 'an incapacity to make a synthesis faced with the excess of objects'.[11] He pleads for an expressionistic painting, like that of his own work: trying to feel oneself primitive in the face of the world, but transcended not so much by nature as by the multiplicity and dispersion of cultures. In this way, his paintings escape from the frame, reach from ceiling to floor, in tempestuous lands that 'rediscover' the Amazons, historical battles, the glance of the first conquistador.

In another way, of a conceptual character, Alfredo Jaar realises an analogical search. He invented a Chilean passport, in which only the covers replicated the official document. Inside, each double page opened to show the barbed wire of a concentration camp which receded towards an infinity uninterrupted by the mountains. The scene could be in his native Chile or in Hong Kong – where he made a documentary for the Vietnamese exiles – or in any of those countries where people speak seven languages and which repeat the phrase 'opening new doors', written in the sky of this closed horizontal: English, Cantonese, French, Italian,

Spanish, German and Japanese. They correspond to certain nations with harder migration problems and with a more restrictive politics of migration. As the document of identification, at the same time national and individual, the passport is made to locate the origin of the traveller. It enables the passage from one country to another, but also stamps people by their place of birth and at times impedes them from change. The passport, as a synthesis of access entrapment, serves as a metaphor to men and women of a multicultural age, and amongst them to artists for whom 'their place is not within any particular culture, but in the interstices between them, in transit'.[12]

How can we study this delocalised art? By contrast to those explanations referring to a geographic milieu or a social unity, many actual artistic works need to be seen 'as something transported'. Guy Brett used this formula for the 'airmail' paintings of Eugenio Dittborn, those 'fold-up and compartmented rafts' that one receives in order to return: they are for 'seeing between two journeys'.[13] They are supported by a poetic of the transitory, in which their own peripheric nation – in this case Chile, the same as Jaar – can be the point of departure, but not the destination. Neither is any metropolis, as believed by some cosmopolitan Latin Americans, because the 'airmail' paintings, said Roberto Merino, also change metropolises into places of transit. Without centre, without hierarchical trajectories, these works, like those of Felipe Ehrenberg, Leon Ferrari and many others who make postal art, speak about Chile, Mexico or Argentina but overflow their own territories, because the works' journeys make its external resonance a component of the message.

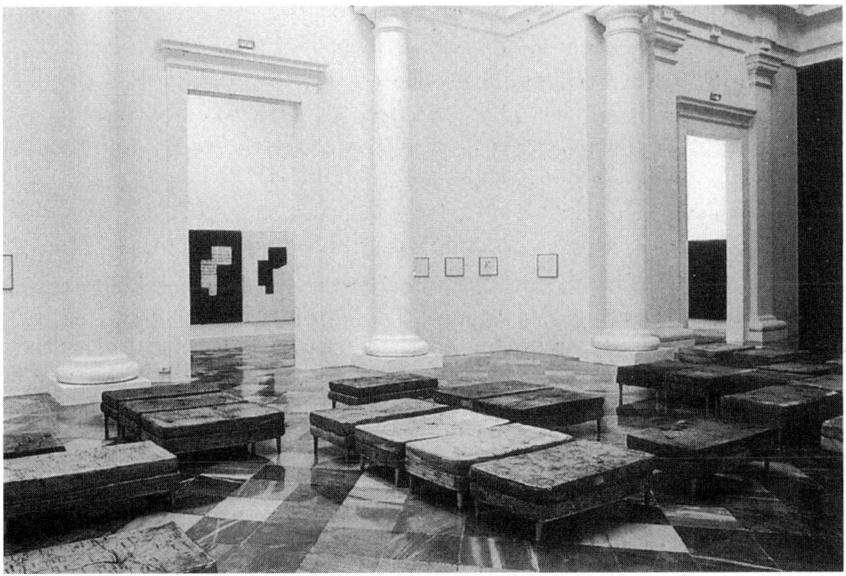

Figure 34.1 Guillermo Kuitca, Installation at IVAM Centro del Carme, Valencia, Spain, 1993
(From *Third Text: Third World Perspectives on Contemporary Art and Culture*, 28/29 Autumn/Winter 1994)

Dittborn used to include little houses in his paintings. The same tension between the journey and the period of residence is encountered in the maps and beds of Guillermo Kuitca. His images name at the same time the relation between particular territories and deterritorialisation. On one hand, street maps like that of Bogotá, whose streets are not drawn in lines but in syringes, or the maps of apartments made with bones, reflectors which illuminate uninhabited beds, the recording machines and the microphones without personages which allude to the terror in Argentina. 'During the time of the Malvinas I started to paint little beds . . . it was a period of depression and what I wanted to transmit in the work was that I was staying quiet with the paintbrush in my hand, and, to produce the painting, what was moving was the bed.'[14]

The quietude of the brush while the context was transformed, while people travel. In painting over the mattress maps of Latin America and Europe, Kuitca reconfigures the tensions of many exiles: from Europe to America, from one America to another, from America again to Europe. Is it for this reason that the 'beds are without homes'?[15] To organise the world, Kuitca poses it at the same time as travel and rest: the maps of cities on the mattresses seem intended to disrupt rest. He wants to reconcile the romantic sense, uncertain or simply a painful journey with the organised space of a regular mattress, or conversely, exasperate the rigorous geometry of the maps, superimposing them over the territory of dreams. The map as a ghost, or the bed as a root: bedmaps, in this way migrates the person who looks for roots.

Who gives passports?

These works do not allow us to interrogate them for social identities and the identity of art. But they attempt to be an art that recognises the exhaustion of ethnic or national mono-identities, which thinks to represent very little but talks about local and non-temporal essences. The material that creates their icons are not uniquely persistent objects, the monuments and rituals that gave stability and distinction to the culture are also related to passports, the beds with maps, the vibrant images of the media. Like today's identities, their works are polyglot and migrant, they can function in diverse and multiple contexts and permit divergent readings from their hybrid constitution.

But these multicultural reformulations of visual thinking are in conflict with at least three tendencies in the artistic camp/context. In the first place, in front of the inertia of the artist, intermediaries and public that continue to demand from art that it is representative of a pre-nationalised globalised identity. In the second place, the artist who relativises national traditions has difficulty being accommodated by state promotion which expects work from its creators that has the capacity to show to the metropolis the splendour of many centuries of national history.

Finally, the Latin American artists who work with globalisation and multiculturalism interact with the strategy of museums, galleries and critics of the metropolis who prefer to keep them as representatives of exotic cultures, of ethnic alterity and Latin otherness, that is, in the margins. In the US, George Yúdice observes, the multicultural politics of the museums and universities has been useful

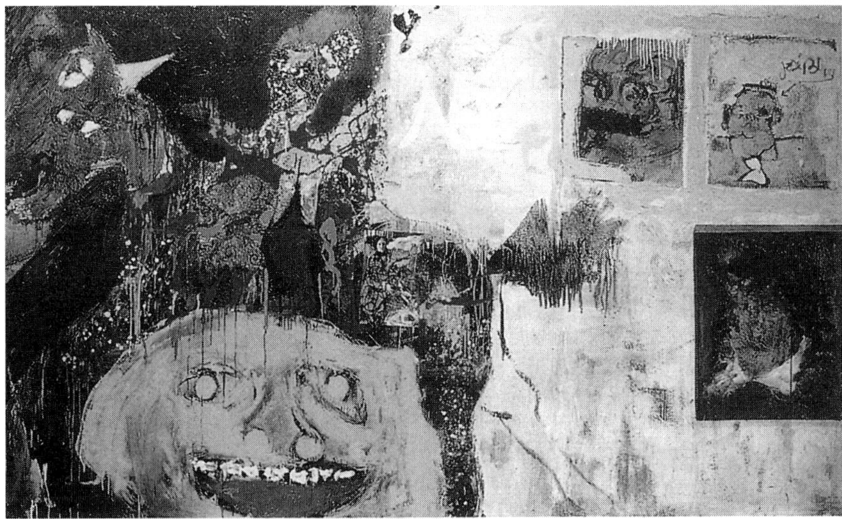

Figure 34.2 Luis Felipe Noé, *Algún día de estos* [One of These Days], 1963 (Courtesy of the Museo de Arte Contemporánea, Buenos Aires)

more to the recognition of difference than as an interlocutor in a dialogue of equality, to situate them as a subaltern corner of the *American way of life*. 'If before, they asked Latin Americans to illustrate pure surrealism, as in the case of Alejo Carpentier, with his "marvellous realism" or his *santería*, now today they are asking that Latin Americans become something like "Chicano" or "Latino".'[16] Also, in Europe, the mechanisms of determination of artistic value hope that Latin Americans act and illustrate their difference: in a recent multicultural exhibition that took place in Holland, *Het Klimaat* (The Climate), the catalogue maintained that 'for the non-Western artist or intellectual it is above all essential to create and recreate the historical and ideological conditions that more or less provide the possibility to exist'. The Argentinian artist Sebastián López challenged this 'condescending point of view' which relegates foreign artists to exhibiting their work in the alternative circuits:

> While the European artist is allowed to investigate other cultures and enrich their own work and perspective, it is expected that the artist from another culture only works in the background and with the artistic traditions connected to his or her place of origin (even though many Dutch managers of cultural politics, curators, dealers were ignorant of these traditions and their contemporary manifestations). If the foreign artist does not conform to this separation, he is considered inauthentic, Westernised, and an imitator copyist of 'what we do'. The universal is 'ours, the local is yours'.[17]

Thinking today is, as always, thinking difference. In this time of globalisation this means that visual thinking transcends as much the romantic conceit of nationalism as the geometric orders of a homogeneous transnationalism. We need images of transits, of crossings and interchanges, not only visual discourses but also open, flexible reflections, which find a way between these two intense activities: the nationalist fundamentalism which seeks to conjure magically the uncertainties of multiculturalism, and on the other, the globalising abstractions of the market and the mega exhibitions, where one loses the will and desire for reformulating the manner in which we are thought.[18]

Notes

This paper was first presented at the 17th Symposium of Art History, hosted by the Instituto de Investigaciones Estéticas de la UNAM and the Comité Internacional de Historia del Arte, in Zacatecas, 23–28 September, 1993.

1 Michel Serres, 'Análisis simbólico y método estructural', in Andrea Bonomi *et al.* (Eds) *Estructuralismo y filosofía*, Nueva Vision, Buenos Aires, 1969, p. 32.

2 Claude Lévi-Strauss, *El pensamiento salvaje*, FCE, Mexico, 1964, pp. 30–33.

3 For this form of enquiry we should not forget the founding work of Rudolf Arnheim, *El pensamiento visual*, Eudeba, Buenos Aires, 1971, which connects well with the contributions of Howard S. Becker, Pierre Bourdieu and Fredric Jameson, whose possible complement I discussed in *Culturas híbridas: Estrategías para entrar y salir de la modernidad*, Grijalbo-CNCA, Mexico, 1990, chs 1 and 2.

4 As expressed by Nicos Hadjinicolau (*Historia del arte y lucha de clases*, 5th edn, Siglo Veintuno, Mexico, 1976, ch. 5), but this author relates 'ideology in the image' to social class and dismisses the nationalist differences that also have an effect on styles. Although I do not have space here to develop this critique, I want to say at least that a non-reductionist sociological reading, besides social class, ought to take into account other groups that organise social relations: nation, ethnicity, generation, etc.

5 I analysed this theme in 'Memory and Innovation in the Theory of Art', in *South Atlantic Quarterly*, Duke University Press, vol. 92, no. 3, 1993.

6 See *Art from Latin America: The Transcultural Meeting*, exhibition catalogue; exhibition curated by Nellie Richard, the Museum of Contemporary Art, Sydney, 10 March–13 June 1993.

7 The formula belongs to the curator of the Biennial Achille Bonito Oliva, quoted by Lilia Driben, 'La XLV Bienal de Venecia, los puntos cardinales del arte nómada de 56 países', *La Jornada*, 23 August 1993, p. 23.

8 See the illuminating chapter on this theme, 'Le marché et le musée', in Raymonde Moulin, *L'Artiste, l'institution et le marché*, Flammarion, Paris, 1992.

9 Arjun Appadurai, 'Disjuncture and Difference in the Global Cultural Economy', in Mike Featherstone (ed.), *Global Culture: Nationalism, Globalization and Modernity*, Sage Publications, London, Newburg Park-New Delhi, 1990.

10 Luis Felipe Noé, 'Does Art from Latin America Need a Passport?' in Rachel Weiss and Alan West (eds), *Being America, Essays on art, literature and identity from Latin America*, White Pine Press, New York, 1991.

11 Luis Felipe Noé, 'La nostalgia de la historia en el proceso de imaginacíon plástica de América Latina', in *Encuentro artes visuales e identidad en América Latina*, Foro de Arte Contemporáneo, Mexico, 1982, pp. 46–51.

12 Adriana Valdés, 'Alfredo Jaar: imágenes entre culturas', *Arte en Colombia Internacional*, 42, December 1989, p. 47.

13 Guy Brett and Sean Cubitt, *Camino Way. Las pinturas aeropostales de Eugenio Dittborn*, Santiago de Chile, 1991.

14 Martín Rejtman, 'Guillermo Kuitca, Mirada interior', *Claudia*, Buenos Aires, November 1992, no. 3, p. 68. Reproduced by Marcelo B. Pacheco in 'Guillermo Kuitca: inventario de un pintor', *Un libro sobre Guillermo Kuitca*, IVAM Centre del Carme, Valencia, 1993, p. 123.

15 The phrase is from Jerry Saltz, 'El toque humano de Guillermo Kuitca', in *Un libro sobre Guillermo Kuitca*, op. cit.

16 George Yúdice, 'Globalizacíon y nuevas formas de intermediacíon cultural', paper presented at the conference 'Identidades, políticas e integración regional', Montevideo, 22–23 July 1993.

17 Sebastián López, 'Identity: Reality or Fiction', *Third Text*, 18, 1992, pp. 332–34, cited by Yúdice, op. cit. See also the issue of *Les Cahiers du Musée National d'Art Moderne* dedicated to the exhibition 'Les magiciens de la terre', no 28, 1989, especially the articles by James Clifford and Lucy Lippard.

18 Translated from the Spanish by E.P. Quesada.

Chapter 35

Oriana Baddeley

ENGENDERING NEW WORLDS
Allegories of rape and reconciliation

THE NEED TO discuss the nature of the Latin American context, to deal with the disjunctions and incongruities of a post-colonial culture has become one of the most readily recognisable characteristics of twentieth century art from Latin America. Complex metaphors and symbolic languages have developed to define the interdependency of European and Latin American cultures, to offer some sort of explanation for the hybrid nature of Latin America. Within this category of cultural production, traditions of allegory have formed an important element. Allegory as a discursive medium is part of the heritage of Catholic evangelisation but also remains part of the visual vocabulary of many contemporary practitioners. In some ways the Renaissance appropriation of the classical past, from which many of our uses of allegory descend, was itself a model of cultural 'interaction'. As a model, it also puts an interesting gloss on the definitions of originality and replication so frequently of interest to artists working outside the defined mainstream. Re-using and re-ordering the visual languages of a distant culture to the needs of a different time and place cannot be seen as specific to Latin America but rather as symptomatic of an awareness of cultural multiplicity.

1992–1492

In the wake of 1992's quincentennial of the 'encounter', attention has been focused anew on the point of contact between Europe and what Europeans called the 'New World'. To many artists, such as Maria Sagradini, the event served to highlight the continuing contradictions and inequality of this relationship. However, from whichever of the numerous complex and often conflicting perspectives adopted towards this historical moment, the quincentennial was a reminder of the essentially hybrid nature of Latin American culture.

Neither indigenous, nor European, Latin American culture has been balanced between a sense of belonging and of exclusion since the 'encounter.' The visualising of this finely poised relationship has traditionally encompassed the recognition of both conflict and power, a tipping of the scales in the direction of one ideological camp or the other. The art of the region's diverse constituencies determined that whichever visual language was adopted, it would carry a set of meanings beyond that of the artists' personal aesthetic. From the very first moments of contact between the two worlds; the power of visual languages to speak to the continent's different constituent cultures – the Spanish, the indigenous and the ever increasing 'mestizo' – was acknowledged. At the same time, the differing traditions of representation and symbolism remained recognisably culturally specific. In the period after the Mexican Revolution, a highly rhetorical stand was taken to the notion of interdependency, as artists such as the muralists attempted to construct what they saw as a new, assertively anti-colonial art form. For many contemporary artists, however, the notion of both conflict and affiliation goes deeper than the rights and wrongs of colonialism.

The rape of America

Traditionally, the encounter is discussed in ostensibly sexual terms. The eroticised Indian nude greeting the arrival of the Spanish conqueror with equanimity, represents a longstanding tradition of allegorical renderings of the colonial enterprise in the Americas. In a work such as Jan van de Straet's engraving from *c.*1600 of *Vespucci Discovering America*, the naked fertile America is quite literally discovered by the explorer Vespucci; the clothed, civilised European, Vespucci, bringing technology and knowledge to the available, desirable but primitive Americas.

This fantasy of colonial relations, intersecting as it does with traditional gender roles – Woman/passive vs Man/active; Woman/Nature vs Man/Technology – has functioned as a powerful metaphor within Latin American culture. In one form or other this gendering of the 'encounter' appears in many different Latin American contexts as an explanation of the hybrid nature of the post-colonial culture; the Indian mother taken by force by the European father, giving birth to the 'illegitimate', mixed race, 'mestizo', culture of Latin America.

The most famous version of this allegory of cultural origins is that of the Spanish conqueror Hérnan Cortes and his Indian interpreter/mistress, Malinche. From the sixteenth century on, the realities of Mexican colonial culture could be visualised via this relationship. The problematic figure of Malinche, half collaborator, half victim, manifests the ambivalent interrelationship of the conquered to the conqueror. In Antonio Ruiz's intricate, small painting, *The Dream of Malinche* (1939), Malinche's sleeping body metamorphoses into a microcosm of colonial Mexico. Traditionally, she is both pitied and despised but none the less she embodies the territories of the colonised. She forms part of the complex amalgam of allegorical Indian women referred to by Octavio Paz in his seminal discussion of the Mexican psyche *The Labyrinth of Solitude* (1950).[1] In this work Paz links the figure of Malinche to that of the 'Chingada', a raped and beaten mother of popular slang, and discusses the cultural ramifications of the collective mother/victim/nation image.

It is this allegory of injured 'motherland' that is frequently referred to in the work of Frida Kahlo, who elides the notion of personal injury with that of the collective trauma of colonisation.[2] In *The Two Fridas* (1939) Kahlo depicts herself as the allegorical body of Mexico, literally split into two, yet interdependent; the injured infertile colonial body gaining strength from that of the strong fertile Indian woman. This Indian woman is not the compromised and despised 'mother' Malinche, but Kahlo's iconic image of the inviolate spirit of the Americas, the Tehuana.

In the period after the Mexican Revolution, the Tehuana came to represent an assertively post-colonial culture, the fertile unbowed body, closer in spirit to the 'Amazons' of sixteenth-century travellers' tales. She existed in direct opposition to the image of the brutalised Indian woman, raped by the European colonisers. She represented a pride in the indigenous past and a denial of cultural dependency. This glorification of the 'un-raped' Indian woman emerged simultaneously to the appropriation of the visual languages of popular art into the construction of an oppositional culture to that of the Eurocentric high art tradition.

In Diego Rivera's *Dream of a Sunday Afternoon in the Alameda Park*, the artist produced a work which constituted a personal manifesto for a new art. Rivera paints himself as a child (the art of the revolutionary future) nursed by the Tehuana (Kahlo) but parented by the 'popular' (in the form of the printer José Guadalupe Posada and his most famous creation, the skeletal lady 'La Caterina'). This allegorical 'family' is used to lay claim to a set of cultural values that conformed to Rivera's anti-colonialist aspirations. Past conflicts epitomised by the skeletal yet living figure of the Caterina, are seen as engendering a new, more positive future.

Contemporary Mexican artists appear highly conscious of the work of their predecessors and the use of allegory remains a important tool. But the mood has radically changed. Rivera's use of the popular and the indigenous to represent the dynamics of national identity is savagely inverted in Julio Galan's *Tehuana* (1990). Here the familiar costume of the Tehuana becomes an empty, bitter reminder of the hollowness of nationalist rhetoric. The blank gap for the face beckons like a fairground painting, waiting to be filled by any passing visitor, still a reference to the popular, but evoking a more random, less controllable force. Galan's is a world where 'authentic identity' has become something to buy at a souvenir shop. This is not so much a transformation of the allegorical body of the Tehuana, as a knowing rejection of the traditions of visualising the 'Latin American' identity. In this play upon the traditions of asserting a 'purer' identity, Galan attempts to escape the endlessly polarised positions of the gendered allegories of cultural interaction.

In a similarly bleak vein, Enrique Chagoya's *LA-K-LA-K* (1987), takes Posada's 'La Caterina' and unites her with a skeletal Mickey Mouse in a parody of Rivera's *Alameda* . . . self-portrait. The 'mother' culture claimed by Rivera has the bleak emptiness of Galan's *Tehuana*, the 'new art of the revolution', the sterility of Disney. Here again we are forced to recognise the mass marketing of the notion of authenticity, the impossibility of the 'pure' inviolate culture.

The battle seems no longer to be the simpler rejection of colonial culture espoused by the generation of Diego Rivera and the proponents of nationalist cultures within Latin America. The stark blacks and whites of Rivera's more jingoistic 'good Indians/bad Spaniards' have blurred to grey. To put it simply, the definition of what is imposed and what is inherited in cultural terms has shifted.

Colonialism is not denied but clearly defined criteria of cultural identity are replaced by a series of questions.

Guilt and reconciliation

The 'encounter/Rape/conquest' and its ensuing progeny, so often a theme within Latin American art, remains more than just a reference to a distant if crucial moment in history; it also becomes an allegorical reworking of the problematic position of the Latin American artist to the visual languages of a Eurocentric 'high art' tradition.

This tradition of the 'great artist' as the signifier of civilisation has itself been a focus of attention during the 1980s, an intrinsic part of the selfconscious games of postmodernism. However, in the work of Latin American artists, such as Alberto Gironella or Alejandro Colunga, these references are given an added meaning.

The roots of Latin America's colonial past grow from the same soil as Spain's 'golden age of painting'; for every Columbus, Cortes and Pissaro there was also a Titian, El Greco and Velázquez. As representative of Spanish culture at one of the most dramatic points in colonial history, the work of these 'Great Masters' takes on an added political dimension within a Latin American context.

In Colunga's *The Marriage of Chamuco & La Llorona*, the deliberately 'El Grecoesque' style of the artist's earlier work is present if subdued, while the theme is again that of hybrid identity. As with Chagoya, this work parodies the claims of the earlier generation and denies the notion of a transcendent culture emerging from the ashes of colonialism. Instead we are shown a 'family' of the insane and the vicious; Chamuco, the Christian devil imported by the Spaniards; and La Llorona, the 'Weeping Woman', a figure descended from an Aztec death goddess, whose annual festival represents the trauma of conquest. This is not just the injured Chingada but an altogether more dangerous and uncontrollable 'mother' figure, who is said to roam the streets at night stealing children to revenge the loss of her own murdered offspring. Colunga's dark allegory points to the shared heritage of horror, a sort of 'a curse on all your houses'. There is no heroic victim, just a legacy of pain and cruelty.

The assigning of blame is also deliberately avoided by Alberto Gironella. His numerous reworkings of Velázquez's *Queen Mariana* dissect and reconstitute the body of this colonial queen, transforming aggressor into victim. In *Queen of Yokes*, the ghost of the Velázquez portrait fights with the vitality of the collage of popular references, as if trapped forever within the wrong painting. In inverting the traditions of the male/Spanish/coloniser allegory, Gironella also humanises the notion of power, focusing on more subtle notions of freedom and oppression. The Spanish Queen becomes as much a victim of her birth and her particular historical moment as Malinche.

While in Mexico the point of contact between the 'old world' and the 'new', and the metaphorical debate surrounding that moment has a continuing relevance. It is obvious that the conditions of the present have changed. Within other parts of Latin America the relationship to the history of colonialism has not always been so vociferous and yet this move towards a less polarised position is equally evident.

In a work such as *El Compromiso* (1982) by the Uruguayan painter José Gamarra, the scene is set in a fantasy coastline jungle *somewhere in Latin America*. The style of the painting is deliberately 'old master' with only its scale alerting the observer to its 'modernity'. In this faraway unreachable place the representatives of indigenous and colonial worldviews are locked in violent conflict. The priest cuts the throat of the feathered serpent while the native child stares unconcerned at a pet parrot. As an audience we are not asked to judge or take sides, we merely observe the progress of history. We cannot judge events taking place in a world created by writers and explorers, this lush jungle painted Rousseau-like by Gamarra from his studio in Paris. For Gamarra, the past is indeed another country, a place where injury and cruelty co-exist with hope and innocence. His Latin America is an Eden-like paradise on the point of corruption; the conquest a sort of 'fall of man'. Yet the event is inevitable and offered in explanation of the chaos and hurt of the present times, a distant starting point. This point is made not just by the subject matter but by the manipulation of the traditions of representing the unknown. Gamarra's bitter-sweet Utopias evoke the Latin America of European fantasy, it is a place without tangible existence yet is somehow familiar.

This same sense of familiarity pervades the work of the Argentine Miguel D'Arienzo. In his *La Conquista* [The Conquest] (1992), the violence of the

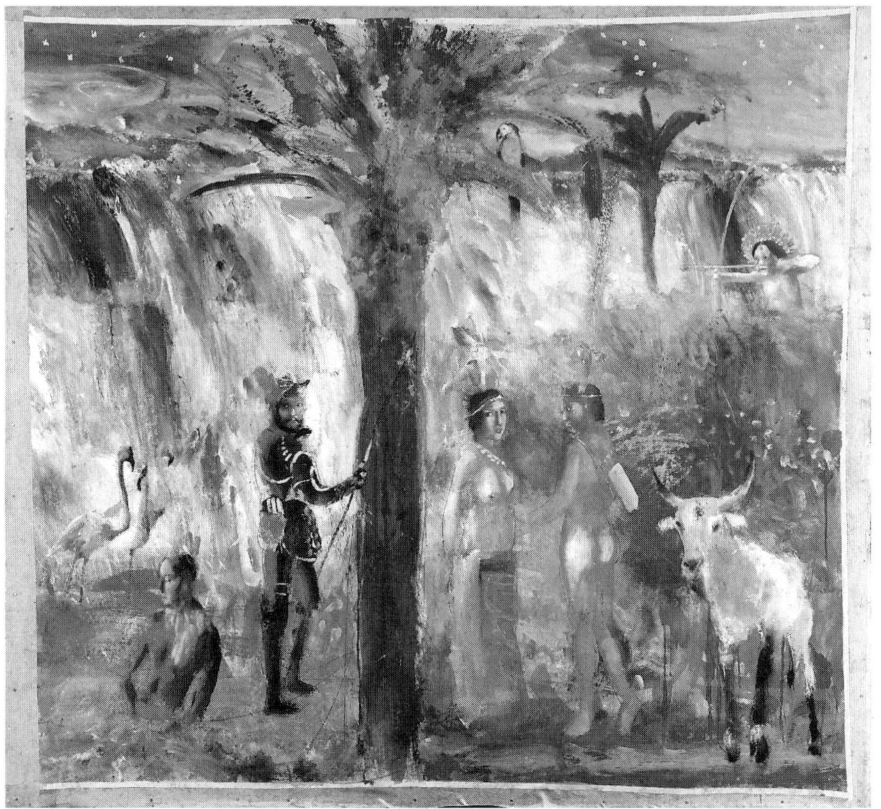

Figure 35.1 Miguel d'Arienzo, *The Conquest of America* (Courtesy of Miguel d'Arienzo)

'encounter' is only passingly referred to in the figure of the Indian child aiming his bow at the distracted *conquistador*. Even this reference is ambivalent: is this an attack or are we observing the antics of some indigenous Cupid, whose magic arrow will turn the heart of the homesick Spaniard towards the Indian woman who gazes so solemnly at the spectator? 'See what is about to happen', she seems to say, as we are confronted with the amoral inevitability of history. D'Arienzo's work is not, however, about Latin America's colonial past in any direct sense. Even more strongly than in Gamarra's work we are asked not to assign blame. The Spaniard arrives almost like Ulysses on the island of Circe, he is about to forget his past to lose himself in his 'new world'. In this sense D'Arienzo's work is all about memory and loss, his characters as they move from painting to painting (and many of his works pick up on the same characters), act out semi-forgotten moments in a past they no longer recall. Did they once belong to Titian or Goya? Was that gesture once played out in a painting by Velázquez or Tintoretto? Like a company of provincial players performing *The Tempest* in the Pampas, they act out a narrative, the meaning of which they have forgotten, while the lines and parts remain and are reconstituted into a new set of meanings. For D'Arienzo this seems to be the crux of the matter – that within replication there is also a reordering, a reconstituting of meaning which makes the alien, familiar; the distant, close.

The allegorical nature of D'Arienzo's work is made even more evident in his *Rape of America*, acting as it does as a conceptual counterpiece to the more traditional 'Rape of Europa' theme. The classical explanation of the origins of 'Europe' linked the notions of history, myth and sexuality into a complex allegory. In D'Arienzo's painting the power relations of the original are inverted. The transgressive lustful figure of the disguised Zeus, the bull, is still the central focus of the allegory. Here, however, he becomes not just the godly antagonist but the Spanish presence. D'Arienzo's bull seems more tragic than aggressive, his America a temptress not a victim. The scene evokes the spirit of the bullfight (a sport imported with enthusiasm by the Spaniards to their colonies) rather than that of

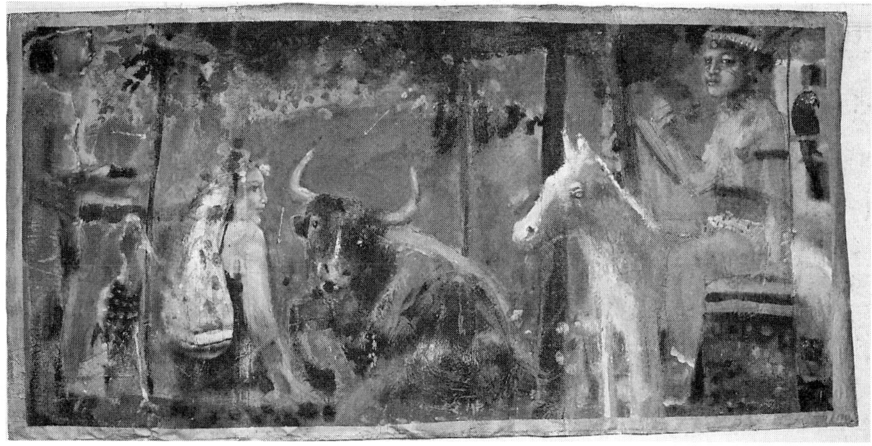

Figure 35.2 Miguel d'Arienzo, *The Rape of America* (Courtesy of Miguel d'Arienzo)

an abduction and rape. The bull appears confused and wounded, dying a victim of its own obsession.

If the languages of allegory have formed an important part of the dialogue between the 'old world' and the 'new', they have also served to highlight the culturally specific meanings of the power relations within the traditions of metaphor. In a time of changing valuations of identity, both sexual and ethnic, the shifting focus of these contemporary Latin American artists represents a complex and sensitive response to a world of change and uncertainty.

Notes

1 Octavio Paz, 'The Sons of La Malinche', in his *The Labyrinth of Solitude*, trans. L. Kemp, Harmondsworth, Penguin, 1985.

2 Frida Kahlo, 'Body and Soul: Women and Post Revolutionary Messianism', in J. Franco (ed.) *Plotting Women: Gender and Representation in Mexico*, London, Verso, 1989.

PART FIVE

Gender and sexuality

Introduction to part five

■ Nicholas Mirzoeff

(a) The gaze and sexuality

NO TERM HAS BEEN more important to the various visual disciplines over the last twenty years than the gaze. The gaze creates and recreates the identity of the gazer by at once making us aware of visual perception and also that others can see us. The re-evaluation of looking as the gaze by feminist and queer theory in the past twenty-five years has transformed our understanding of issues as wide-ranging as the painted nude, the Hollywood film and advertising. For it allows us to think about the ways in which looking is a form of power and how that power can be gendered. Thus much argument has centred on whether the gaze is in itself male, objectifying and subordinating women. These debates were indebted to psychoanalysis, especially in the work of Jacques Lacan. Lacan saw the gaze as a key element in the formation of the ego in his famous mirror stage, during which the infant learns both to distinguish itself from its parents and to place itself in gendered relationship to each parent according to the dynamics of the Oedipus complex. Thus the male child desires the mother but is restrained by what Lacan called the Name of the Father. Despite a great deal of complex argument, his theory never seemed to work as well for female children. Lacanian schemes of vision end up being reduced to an opposition between male or female within a heterosexual, some might say heterosexist, framework. The male position was the privileged place from which to look, while the female place was simply to be looked at.

For both intellectual and political reasons, finding new ways to theorize the gaze that build on these important insights but go beyond the restrictions of the binary couple has become crucial to any interpretation of visual culture. In rethinking the gaze, critics have made it central to reformulations of the constitution of gender, race and sexuality themselves. It might seem that this move takes us away from culture into the 'real' but as we shall see, the definition of the real is precisely what is at stake.

The modern period can be distinguished from all earlier history in the area of gender and sexuality. As the historian Thomas Lacquer has shown (Lacquer 1990), medical science came to describe a fundamental difference between the two sexes by around 1800, breaking with the classical tradition of seeing the human body as essentially one type with two variations. In an essay taken from her forthcoming study *Art and Anatomy from Albinus to Charcot*, Anthea Callen quotes the physician Pierre Roussel to this effect: 'The essence of sex is not confined to a single organ but extends, through more or less perceptible nuances, into every part.' What had previously been a simple inversion of genitalia (male/outside, female/inside) had become a distinguishing mark of every part of the human anatomy. At the same time, this science came to believe that the human body was fully legible, that is to say, its physical condition could be interpreted visually. It followed that the sexual difference between men and women must be fully visible. In a careful study of the content of form, Callen examines how the eighteenth-century anatomist Albinus made sexual difference a key aspect of his obsessively careful engravings of the human skeleton that none the less seemed to lack a practical application. Its pose was drawn from the classical statue known as the Apollo Belvedere

> suggest[ing] an authority based on command both of the self, and of knowledge; a mutually reinforcing self-control and control of the environment. These ideas are rehearsed by anatomist and engraver in the actual making of this image which, through the very process of its materialization, enacts a man's claim to rational authority over (feminine) nature.

Far from being a dispassionate assemblage of artistic and medical knowledge, the skeleton engravings represent an incorporation of the new sexual distinction into the very structures of life itself.

From a psychoanalytic standpoint, such manoeuvres are no surprise, for reality is in the eye of the beholder. Art historian Tamar Garb shows how Freudian notions of difference can be used to explain historical dilemmas over the gaze in her interdisciplinary study of women artists and their reception in the late nineteenth century (Garb 1993). Women artists successfully claimed the right to equal art education, only to be denied access to the life class where students drew the nude male figure. For the possibility of the female gaze awakened the fear of castration, through what Freud called 'the sight of something' – the phallus – and the absence of something else – the mother's phallus. In an art world that prized the capacity of art to 'transcend the physical', women – the very definition of the physical – threatened to overturn an already fragile aesthetic doctrine. For Freud it was axiomatic that 'probably no male human being is spared the terrifying shock of threatened castration at the sight of the female genitals' (Freud 1959). Garb shows how these anxieties were safely resolved in a popular short story of the period, telling how a woman artist did come to draw the male figure but with no dangerous consequences. The story is all the more revealing of contemporary attitudes for its lack of artistic merit or pretension. Without giving anything away, let it just be said that masculinity is safely restored to its throne by the bloodthirsty conclusion. Ironically, the fear of male arousal under the female artist's gaze was the subject of a 1997 British advertisement for perfume, showing that such anxieties are a long time in dying.

Freud's scheme established men as the possessors of the phallus and women as constituted by their lack of same. As Callen and Garb show, this supposedly anatomical distinction had pronounced cultural effects, especially as translated into the field of vision. Subsequent critics have noted that all these oppositions rest upon the heterosexual binary itself. In her landmark study *Gender Trouble* (1990), philosopher Judith Butler sought to challenge the very status of gender as a category of analysis by challenging its dependence on such normative notions of (hetero) sexuality. In this extract, she considers how the Freudian analyst Joan Riviere came to arrive at her notion that womanliness is masquerade. Butler notes that Riviere is concerned about the distinction between heterosexual and homosexual women. In 1997 there was a remarkable public discussion of this kind surrounding the comedian Ellen Degeneres in the United States. Lifestyle commentators, TV critics and lesbian activists all had their say both on Degeneres' own sexuality and that of her character Ellen Morgan. The 'is she or isn't she?' question became the barely concealed theme of the entire series, ending with the narrative climax of the 'coming out' episode. Degeneres embodies the problem that concerned Riviere in 1929. While many then and now assumed that lesbian women would 'plainly display strong features of the other sex', Riviere counters that 'women who wish for masculinity may put on a mask of womanliness to avert anxiety and the retribution feared from men'. Paradoxically, the greatest display of masculinity and femininity may then come from homosexual men and women. Riviere then made a leap outside the psychoanalytic gender system by concluding: 'The reader may now ask . . . where I draw the line between genuine womanliness and the "masquerade". My suggestion is not, however, that there is any such difference; whether radical or superficial, they are the same thing.' Butler concludes that the very 'cultural production of gender' is at stake in such discussions, and challenges the binary oppositions set up by many psychoanalytic critics. Her book steps aside from two centuries of the medical gaze by concluding that 'gender is not written on the body' but is a 'stylized repetition of acts'. Gender becomes understood not as a physical essence or even cultural construct but as a performance which becomes naturalized through constant repetition. Butler's performative theory of identity challenges both the early modern notion of the legible body and the psychoanalytic construction of what she calls 'compulsory heterosexuality' (see following section). While these constructions will not simply curl up and die just because they have been outed as constructions, Butler's theoretical work none the less offers us the possibility that these long-lasting binaries can gradually be displaced, affecting our notion of femininity, masculinity and the very idea that sex is in itself an identity.

(b) Queering the visual

One way to challenge the heterosexual binary created by psychoanalytic approaches to the gaze is simply to ask what might happen if a gay or lesbian spectator were to look or be represented. That was the first move of gay and lesbian studies in the 1970s and 1980s, just as it had been for feminism and African-American studies: to assert the existence of gay and lesbian people as creators, consumers and subjects of visual imagery and to reclaim their place in the historical record. That work of course continues, but it has been joined by a striking new approach to identity and sexuality known as queer theory. Rather than see sexuality as identity, forming a neat unit, 'queer' turns towards what Eve Kosofsky Sedgwick (1993: 18) has called: 'the open mesh of possibilities, gaps, overlaps, dissonances, and resonances, lapses and excesses of meaning when the constituent elements of anyone's gender, of anyone's sexuality aren't made (or can't be made) to signify monolithically.' Sexual and gender identity are seen to overlap with race, ethnicity and nationality in ways that question how identity itself, a very privileged term in the last decade, should be conceived. Queer theory thus does for sexuality what deconstruction did for philosophy. In the 1960s and subsequently, Jacques Derrida has proposed that philosophy created *différance* rather than a system of binary difference, a neologism he created from a fusion of the French terms for differing and deferring. While Derrida's work has often been dismissed by Anglo-American critics as lacking relevance to the real world, his concepts are now informing the re-evaluation of identity politics in very practical ways, as the essays in this section attest.

In his review of gay male spectatorship in photography and film from the nineteenth century to the present, Thomas Waugh shows that, while classic narrative cinema may deny the presence of the spectator, gay cinema is always aware of its audience (Waugh 1993). He argues that three types of male body are offered to the homoerotic gaze. First was the ephebe, the young man with a slender androgynous figure who was highly popular in Victorian imagery but has fallen under suspicion in the age of moral panics concerning child sexuality. Second was the 'he-man' the muscular figure of the mature athlete as familiar from neo-classical images of the body as from contemporary 'clones'. The third body 'the looking, representing subject, stood in for the authorial self as well as for the assumed gay spectator'. Waugh thus centres his discussion on the gay subject, possessor of the gaze, rather than its object. However, he does not argue that in itself the creation of a gay subject takes us beyond the received patterns of sexuality. On the contrary, 'the same-sex imaginary preserves and even heightens the structures of sexual difference inherent in Western (hetero) patriarchal culture but usually stops short of those structures' customary dissolution in narrative closure'. Rather than binary difference, there is the *différance* that leaves us without a wedding at the end. Waugh delineates a 'taxonomy of gay-authored narrative cinema' created by directors exploiting the 'built-in ambiguity of the narrative codes of the art cinema'.

Moving away from such coded representations of queer culture, Judith Butler looks at one of the most controversial documentaries of the early 1990s in her essay on Jennie Livingston's *Paris is Burning* (1991), in which gay sexuality is very much on display yet out of sight of the 'mainstream' (Butler 1993). A classic 'fly-on-the-wall' documentary, the film details the lives of black and Latino gay men on the cross-dressing scene in New York later appropriated by Madonna for her song 'Vogue' and its accompanying video. This subculture centred around cross-dressed balls where contestants competed in a series of different categories of cross-dressing, ranging from *haute couture* fashion to the straight male businessman. The goal was to achieve a level of 'realness' that resists the possibility of a 'read', or critique. Butler reiterates her case that drag reveals the ' "imitation" . . . at the heart of the *heterosexual* project and its gender binarisms'. Like Waugh, she recognizes that the appropriation of drag is not necessarily subversive. In films like *Mrs Doubtfire,* it is a cosy part of the heterosexual imaginary. Drag can act, however, as a displacement of gender norms. The question in *Paris is Burning* is: who is appropriating whom? For some radical feminists, the answer was men appropriating women and a white filmmaker appropriating black subculture. Butler insists that 'identification is always an ambivalent process'. In her view, the lesson of *Paris is Burning* is not a familiar restatement of oppressions but an insight into the overly precise way that visual and cultural studies have defined identity:

> The order of sexual difference is not prior to that of race or class in the constitution of the subject; indeed, the symbolic is also and at once a racializing set of norms and th[e] norms of realness by which the subject is produced are racially informed conceptions of 'sex'.

Of course, the film itself produces a version of even this level of 'realness' in accord with Livingston's own agenda. In a culture where there is no bedrock identity to be claimed, appearance and 'look' are more important, not to mention more confused, than ever.

One way to track this shifting terrain of identity is to look at the different responses to women's magazines. In 'Looking Good', Reina Lewis examines how lesbian imagery works in publications explicitly aimed at a lesbian audience (Lewis 1997). For some time, mainstream magazines like *Vogue* have played with sexually ambivalent imagery, such as the *Vanity Fair* cover showing k.d. lang getting a 'shave' from Cindy Crawford. Images like this can be read in hetero- or homosexual ways, depending on the reader's own disposition and are now termed 'gay-vague' by the advertising industry. As Lewis emphasizes, when two men in a Volkswagen get taken to be a gay couple: 'It is the act of interpretation itself that is eroticized.' As a result, she no longer speaks of 'the' lesbian gaze but a variety of viewpoints that might be taken by different women (and even, some would add, men) that can produce what she calls 'lesbian pleasure, a pleasure that would be available to anyone able to exercise a similar competency, whether lesbian or not'. At the same time, the development of a 'pink economy' – lesbian and gay consumerism – brought with it magazines explicitly intended for a lesbian readership that have taken on fashion as part of their editorial policy. Lewis examines how such fashion imagery works where same-sex pleasure is the overt rather than covert goal of the publication. However, the cultural politics of the lesbian community are in many ways hostile to the fashion industry, leading to a realist mode of representation in such photography – a careful balance of ethnicities, ages, body types and so on – that leads her to conclude that 'some lesbian and gay readers demand unambiguous politically or aesthetically "safe" images in the gay press whereas they revel in transgressive, contradictory and subversive pleasures in the mainsteam.' Lewis emphasizes the provisional nature of her conclusions, yet her work opens up a series of new ways of thinking about the sexuality of looking. Rather than seeking to find a grand unifying theory of the gaze that so often seems inadequate to particular cultural moments, Lewis suggests that 'the problem becomes one of the relationships between meanings'. Neither an aesthetic nor a theoretical formalism will address such complexities that may find the same person adopting totally different positions in relation to visually similar material, depending upon the context in which it is published or read. Such an approach may lack the pleasurable neatness of formalism but it feels much closer to the actual complexities of looking.

Further reading and references

Bad Object Choices (1991) *How Do I Look? Queer Film and Video*, Seattle: Bay Press.

Brod, Harry (1995) 'Masculinity as Masquerade', in Andrew Perchuch and Helaine Posner (eds), *The Masculine Masquerade: Masculinity and Representation*, Cambridge, Mass.: MIT Press.

Butler, Judith (1990) *Gender Trouble: Feminism and the Subversion of Identity*, London and New York: Routledge.

—— (1993) *Bodies That Matter*, London and New York: Routledge.

Callen, Anthea (1995) *The Spectacular Body: Science, Method and Meaning in the Work of Edgar Degas*, New Haven: Yale University Press.

De Lauretis, Teresa (1987) *Technologies of Gender: Essays on Theory, Film and Fiction*, Bloomington: Indiana University Press.

Doane, Mary Ann (1987) *The Desire to Desire*, Bloomington: Indiana University Press.

Epstein, Julia (1990) 'Either/Or – Neither/Both: Sexual Ambiguity and the Ideology of Gender', *Genders*, 7, Spring: 99–143.

Foucault, Michel (1980) *A History of Sexuality*, vol. 1, New York: Vintage.

Freud, Sigmund (1959) 'Fetishism', *Sigmund Freud: Collected Papers*, vol. V, New York: Basic Books.

Fuss, Diana (1991) *Inside/Out: Lesbian Theories, Gay Theories*, London and New York: Routledge.

Garb, Tamar (1993) 'The Forbidden Gaze: Women Artists and the Male Nude in Late Nineteenth-Century France', in Kathleen Adler and Marcia Pointon (eds), *The Body Imaged: The Human Form and Visual Culture since the Renaissance*, Cambridge: Cambridge University Press.

Haraway, Donna (1991) *Simians, Cyborgs, and Women: The Reinvention of Nature,* London and New York: Routledge.

Horne, Peter and Lewis, Reina (1996) *Outlooks: Lesbian and Gay Sexualities and Visual Cultures,* London and New York: Routledge.

Jordanova, Ludmilla (1989) *Sexual Visions: Images of Gender in Science and Medicine between the Eighteenth and Twentieth Centuries,* Madison: University of Wisconsin Press.

Lacan, Jacques (1977) *Four Fundamental Concepts of Psychoanalysis,* New York: Norton.

Lacquer, Thomas (1990) *Making Sex: Body and Gender from the Greeks to Freud,* Cambridge, Mass: Harvard University Press.

Lewis, Reina (1997) 'Looking Good: The Lesbian Gaze and the Fashion Industry', *Feminist Review* 55, Spring.

Mayne, Judith (1993) *Cinema and Spectatorship,* London and New York: Routledge.

Miller, D.A. (1990) 'Anal Rope', *Representations* 32, Fall.

Mulvey, Laura (1989) *Visual and Other Pleasures,* Bloomington: Indiana University Press.

Pollock, Griselda (ed.) (1996) *Generations and Geographies in the Visual Arts: Feminist Readings,* London and New York: Routledge.

Rose, Jacqueline (1986) *Sexuality in the Field of Vision,* London: Verso.

Scott, Joan (1988), *Gender and the Politics of History,* New York: Columbia University Press.

Sedgwick, Eve Kosofsky (1993) *Tendencies,* Durham: Duke University Press.

Spivak, Gayatri (1988) 'Can the Subaltern Speak?', in C. Nelson (ed.), *Marxism and the Interpretation of Culture,* Urbana: University of Illinois.

Trinh T. Minh-ha (1989) *Woman, Native, Other,* Bloomington: Indiana University Press.

Waugh, Thomas (1993) 'The Third Body: Patterns in the Construction of the Subject in the Gay Male Narrative Film,' in Martha Gever (ed.), *Queer Looks: Perspectives on Lesbian and Gay Film and Video,* New York: Routledge.

(a) The gaze and sexuality

Chapter 36

Anthea Callen

IDEAL MASCULINITIES
An anatomy of power[1]

IN THE SEARCH for an affirmative answer to Montesquieu's question 'Does natural law submit women to men?', the question of the 'nature' of woman became a priority of Enlightenment research in the eighteenth century.[2] Human anatomy was an important focus of this preoccupation in medical science: the male body provided an anatomical norm against which femaleness could be construed.

The terms 'male' and 'female' here refer to biological distinctions of gender, with the proviso that the sciences are, in themselves, culturally produced and by no means ideologically neutral or trans-historical. I link the terms 'masculine' and 'feminine' to the cultural naming and attribution of human characteristics according to binary principles: they work to define difference with respect to gender in ways that valorise particular qualities over others. This process of differentiation is cultural, serving to position men and women within a hierarchical social order.

Visual representations of the body are particularly powerful in this respect: their impact is direct and immediate. They depend upon a common visual vocabulary – of marks, of lines, shading, and sometimes colour – a vocabulary learned and as such admitting those with educational privilege to shared view and meaning which excludes others; all may look (if they have access to the image) but for some the body is 'foreign', undecipherable. In the present context I look here specifically at classicism – the language of an educated elite – as a style, and of the messages it contains. Visual images are, then, potent mediators of the lived experience of the body, our own and others, giving us ways of conceptualising and describing the bodily. In pictorial images we recognise likeness or difference; we identify ourselves, or find a different 'other', an other which, equally powerfully, serves to reinforce our image of our own bodily existence. Yet however carefully observed, the represented body is an abstracted body: the product of ideas that are culturally and historically specific, and in which the social formation of the producer determines the appearance and meanings of the body; its meanings are then further modified in the act of consumption. The making and meaning of the visual body's cultural message is, therefore, a dynamic process under constant re-vision.

My argument therefore assumes that there is no such thing as a 'natural' body: all bodies – whether an historical anatomy or a Raphael nude – are socially constructed; all are representations which embody a complex web of cultural ideas, including notions of race, class and gender difference. Our own bodies, and our experience of them are also culturally mediated. My particular interest is in the overlap between art and medicine in visualising the body, and most notably in anatomies which could serve the needs of both disciplines – anatomies which focused on the outwardly visible structures: the skeleton and superficial muscles. This essay concentrates on the skeleton, and my principal example for analysis is an Albinus *Human Skeleton*, published in Leiden in 1747.[3] The fact that 'human skeleton' refers to a male skeleton is symptomatic of the normative function of the male body in anatomical paradigms. My interest is in decoding the visual language of anatomies: the messages contained not simply in their subject matter, but in the choice and use of medium, of pose types, proportions, setting and accessories. What view of masculinity was constructed in medical and artistic anatomies, and how was that view materially embodied? In a close visual analysis of the Albinus, I want to show what such material can reveal.

In sixteenth- and seventeenth-century anatomies sexual difference was not a principal concern. Early eighteenth-century thinkers still considered the only anatomical differences between men and women were to be found in their sexual organs. Yet it is clear from extant examples that differentiation appears both in the choice of the sex of the subject depicted, and in the dissected examples selected for illustration. Thus the vast majority of 'in depth' dissections – of internal organs, veins, nervous system, etc. – depicted the male body, whereas the female body was used almost exclusively to illuminate woman's sexual difference – her reproductive organs and the gravid uterus.[4] The assumption implicit here was that male and female bodies are essentially the same, and that the male anatomy could represent both in all respects apart from reproduction.

However, by the mid-eighteenth century this assumption came under attack, as physiological bases for gender difference – for man's 'natural' superiority – were sought. In 1775, for example, the French physician Pierre Roussel reproached his colleagues for considering woman similar to man: 'The essence of sex is not confined to a single organ but extends, through more or less perceptible nuances, into every part.'[5]

Up until the early seventeenth century, then, the human skeleton was synonymous with the male skeleton. Thus, although *gravida* images were common, the first known illustration of a female skeleton dates from 1583, in a crude engraving by Platter, redrawn and reversed in 1605 by Bauhin.[6] Detailed investigation of a distinctively female anatomy only began in the second half of the eighteenth century. As has been shown in respect of the Scot William Hunter's obstetrical atlas, published in 1774, 'seeing was knowing':[7] the visual held primacy, and illustrations of natural phenomena were taken to constitute reality. Thus the visual evidence of skeletons – or rather, and crucially, of their culturally mediated form as *illustrations* of skeletons – came to be used as objective scientific proof of woman's 'natural

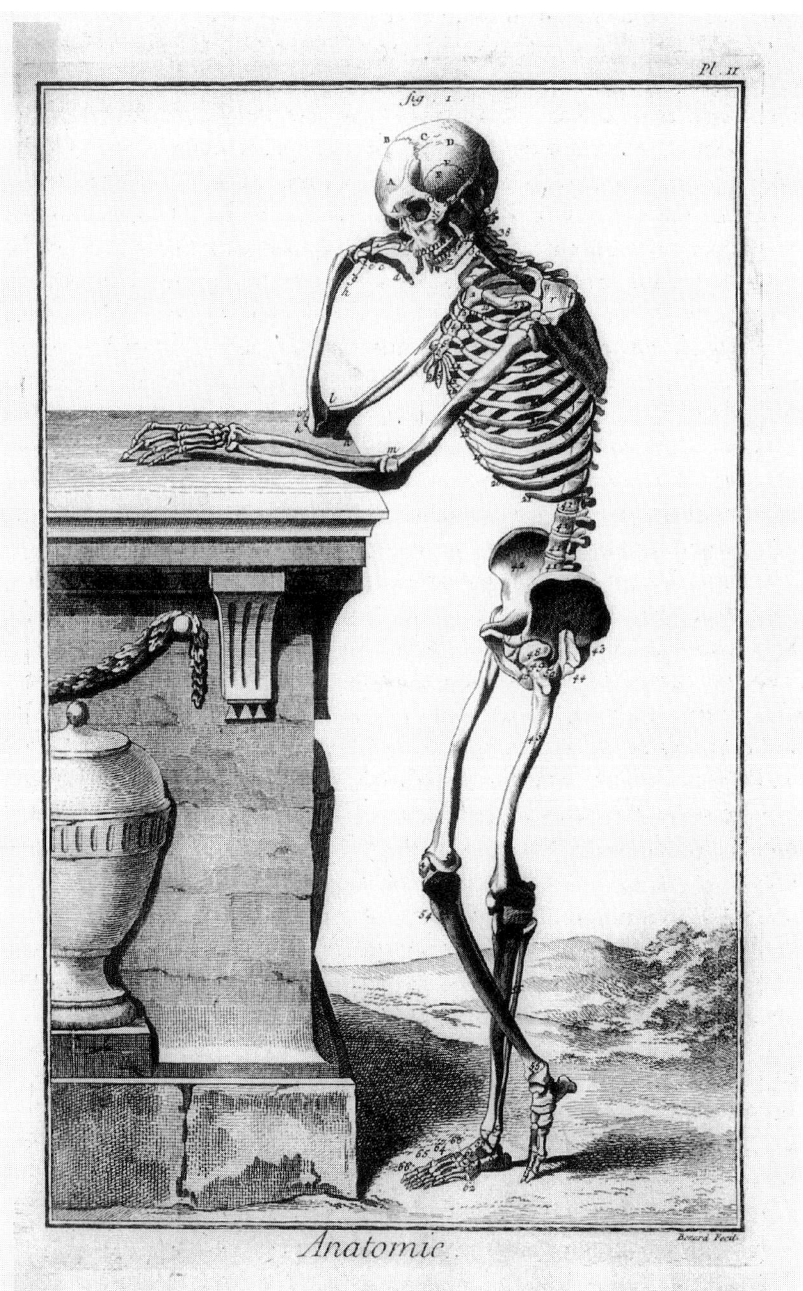

Figure 36.1 Lateral view of the human male skeleton, by Bernard, after Andrea Vesalius (Courtesy the Wellcome Institute Library, London)

difference'. Given its long and unquestioned visual history and hegemony, the male skeleton provided an established norm; it was thus against a male skeletal paradigm that the female skeleton came to be measured – and found wanting. In particular, medical and artistic authorities accepted the male skeleton by the Netherlandish anatomist Bernard Siegfried Albinus (Figure 36.1), which remained unsurpassed for at least three-quarters of a century. My analysis depends upon the view that anatomical prints, like all other visual images, work actively in the production of cultural values – in this case ideals of the male body and of masculinity.

Pose and proportions

Anatomies are, of course, representations of the human body – albeit bodies stripped in varying degrees to the skeleton. This Albinus figure – it is constructed as such – stands upright and gestures evocatively as if still living. The pose is meaningful both in the practical sense, in that it displays the skeletal structure in an informative manner, and discursively through its iconographic references. Set in a landscape, the figure's eloquent left index finger, the spread right hand, the tilt of the head and the classical *contrapposto* communicate the graceful melancholy of a Poussinesque *et in arcadia ego* (Figure 36.2). Such symbolism was common in anatomical prints, and can be seen even more explicitly in the Vesalius *memento mori* anatomy, 'Bones of the human body', in which the male skeleton reflects upon a tomb (Figure 36.1).

The pose chosen for the Albinus figure is not accidental. Drawn directly from the classical tradition, in a form which would have been immediately recognisable to his elite, classically educated Enlightenment audience, it is based on the Apollo Belvedere (Figure 36.3) – according to Winckelmann the 'highest ideal of art among the works of antiquity that have escaped destruction':

> His build is sublimely superhuman, and his stance bears witness to the fullness of his grandeur. An eternal springtime, as if in blissful Elysium, clothes the charming manliness of maturity with grace and youthfulness, and plays with soft tenderness on the proud build of his limbs.[8]

A French writer following Winckelmann echoed these sentiments, finding the Apollo the Greek statue which, 'by his air of grandeur, stirs your passion, penetrates you and makes you sense the flash and brilliance of a super-human majesty which he sheds . . . all around him.'[9] Albinus's choice of pose thus intentionally imbued the male anatomical ideal with connotations of the Sun God – the god of intellectual, moral and, according to eighteenth-century thinkers, (homo)erotic en*light*enment.[10] Kenneth Clark was more circumspect in his admiration than his eighteenth-century precursors:

> [Apollo] was beautiful because his body conformed to certain laws of proportion and so partook of the divine beauty of mathematics . . . Since justice can only exist when facts are measured in the light of reason, Apollo is the god of justice, vanquisher of darkness.[11]

And hence ignorance. The Albinus anatomy thus signals reason dispelling ignorance, and simultaneously, the dark shadow of the other, the feminine. Commonly taken to represent the moment after the youthful Apollo's slaughter of the Pythian serpent with an arrow, for Winckelmann the sculpture was 'an ideal conflation of the austerely sublime and sensuously beautiful', with the 'potential to be the focus of competing fantasies of unyielding domination and exquisite desirability'.[12] The combination of supreme power and vulnerability identified in the Apollo Belvedere by eighteenth-century writers, is reinforced in the image of the skeleton, where an ambiguous mortality suggests both vulnerability and power.

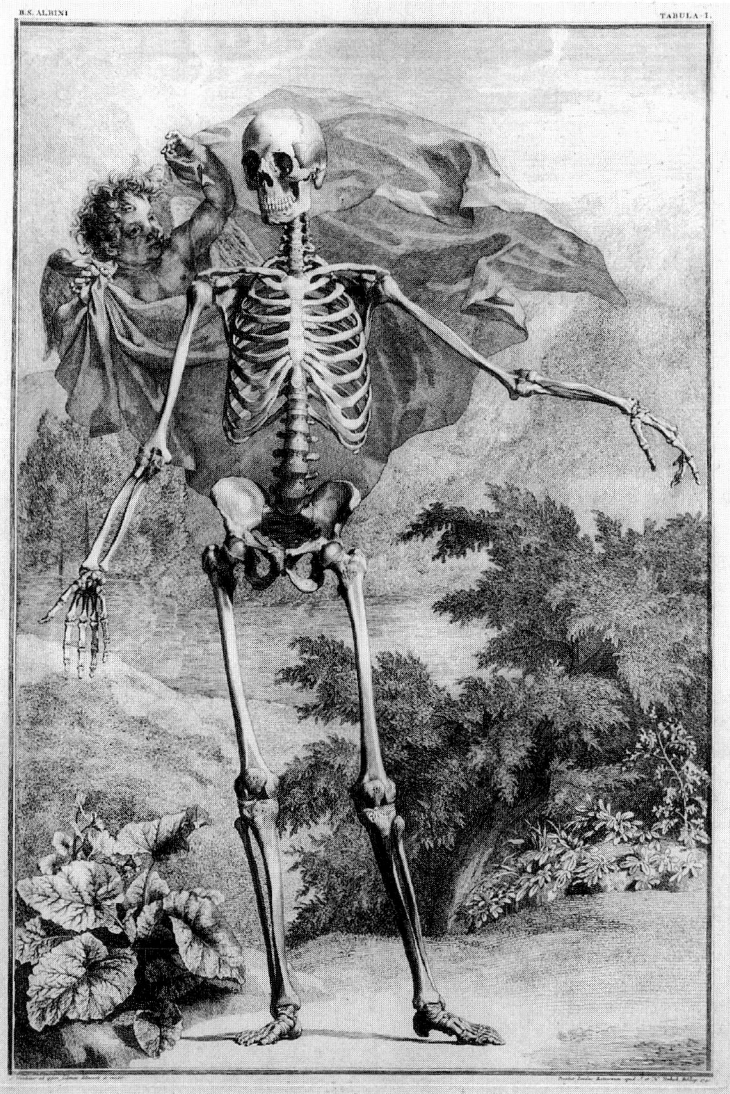

Figure 36.2 Bernard Albinus, 'The Bones of the Human Body' (From *Tabulae sceleti et musculorum corporis humani*, Leyden, 1747. Courtesy the Wellcome Institute Library, London)

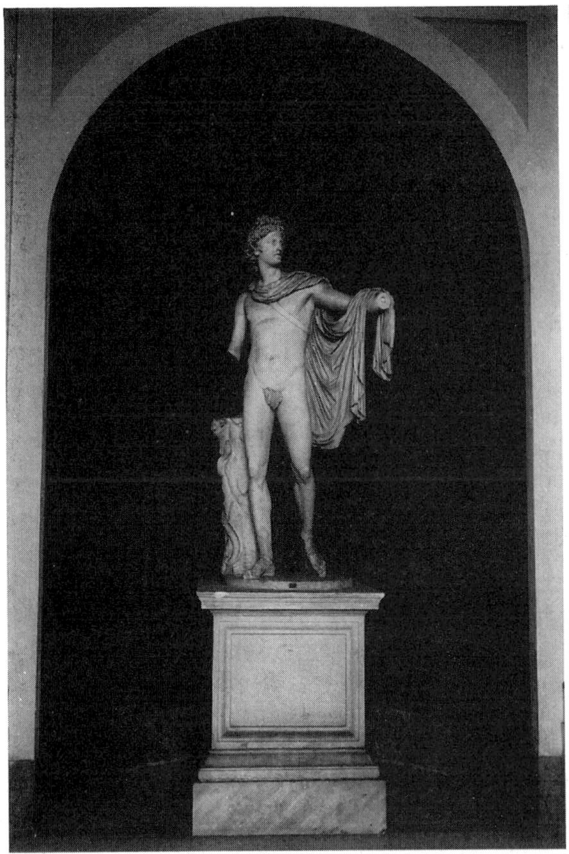

Figure 36.3 Apollo Belvedere, Vatican Museum, Rome (Courtesy of the Conway Library, Courtauld Institute of Art)

Just as the Apollo was based on carefully calculated, 'mathematical' proportions, so too – in the Renaissance Humanist tradition – was the Albinus skeleton. The anatomist's approach fused a classical aesthetic with an almost obsessive Netherlandish scientific empiricism. He was explicit about his methods in the introduction to the 1747 volume, *Tabulae sceleti et musculorum corporis humani*, pirated, in translation, in London in 1749.[13] Albinus chose his dead subject on the basis of two criteria. First, the body's beauty – 'I cannot help congratulating my good fortune' on finding the right corpse, he wrote. He emphasised the need for the subject to be 'elegant and at the same time not too delicate; so as neither to show a juvenile or feminine roundness and slenderness; nor on the contrary an unpolished roughness and clumsiness'. Here is clear evidence of gender- and class-specific determinants guiding Albinus's selection of an ideal, a Platonic ideal, rather than purely scientific concerns. The second criterion was Albinus's ideals of male proportion. These he then explicitly improved upon in the manner of classical art:

> As therefore painters, when they draw a handsome face . . . render the likeness the more beautiful [by removing blemishes]; so these things which

> were less perfect, [in the skeleton] were mended in the figures . . . care being taken at the same time that they should be altogether just.[14]

Just – 'fit, proper, accurate, precise, impartial'; the *just*ice of Apollo.

The wish for a selective, idealised beauty was combined with a desire for mathematical precision in the accurate recording of the skeleton. Albinus's methods were novel, and extravagant in their cost and rigour. He suspended his anatomical example by a complex arrangement of ropes and pulleys, with rings in the ceiling, to establish the pose with its weight on the right foot: the classical *contrapposto*. A live model of comparable stature was posed alongside the skeleton, to enable Albinus to set up and correct its lifelike pose; by pulling the cords and using wedges, the position of the naturally articulated skeleton could be adjusted – a procedure which took some days to complete. 'Naturally articulated' means the bones still held together by the bodily materials, cartilage, etc., which held them together in life.

Albinus's engraver was Jan Wandelaar, and the artistic product of such a collaboration clearly depends greatly on both the skills of the artist and the quality of his relationship with the anatomist. The *Tabulae sceleti* took over twenty years to complete, so the two men worked closely over an extended period. Wandelaar lived in Albinus's house and was very much under the anatomist's direct authority: he was evidently a hard taskmaster. The copper plates were preceded by careful drawings. In order to save the engraver from stooping while working in front of his subject, his work was positioned on a tripod on a table. Effectively this also meant that the engraver did not have constantly to change his angle of vision and move his eyes from the line of the model when transferring his observations to the plate – hence the arrangement was designed to improve the accuracy of his pictorial record.

Albinus considered taking measurements from the skeleton too time-consuming:

> I foresaw that the . . . [drawing] would be very incorrect . . . if it was taken off by merely viewing the original, as ingravers [*sic*] commonly do . . . [to take a measurement of every part] was an infinite task, nor could it possibly be done without some certain infallible rule to direct the ingraver.[15]

Albinus's solution was to use a more sophisticated version of Dürer's perspectival grid (Figure 36.4): in place of a single grid, Albinus used two nets, or grids of small cords. One grid was placed directly in front of the skeleton, the other, with squares a tenth the size, was positioned four 'Rhenish feet' (30.8 cm × 4) away from the skeleton.

> The ingraver [*sic*] placing himself in the most proper situation near the skeleton . . . endeavoured to make some point where the cords of the lesser [net] . . . coincide to the eye with the corresponding decussating point in the cords of the greater one; and the part of the skeleton which was directly behind these points, he drew upon his plate . . . which was similarly marked out. [He] was to find out a proper

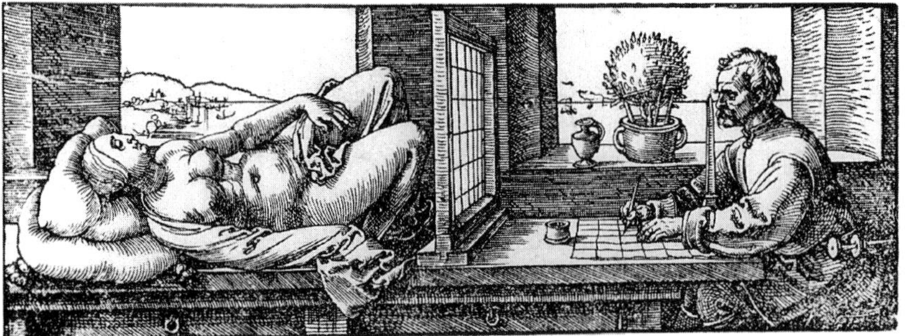

Figure 36.4 Albrecht Dürer's perspectival grid, 1525
(Courtesy of the Whit Library, Courtauld Institute of Art, and Graphische Sammlung Albertina, Vienna)

> place for viewing [the skeleton] through the [nets], by means of a fixed hole, not very large; which by applying his eye to, he could see what parts of the skeleton answered to [the cords of the grid] . . . According to this method then (which as it answered the intention, so it occasioned an incredible deal of trouble to the ingraver) a fore view of the skeleton was first drawn as it stood.

This was followed by back and side views, at which point the skeleton was disarticulated and the bones cleaned completely, each one then being drawn to natural size, which served, he said, as practice for the artist.[16] This grid technique would, given the constraints of observing the subject with a single eye through a small hole (as in the Dürer), have required the engraver to adjust the positioning of the hole – his viewpoint – a number of times, sideways, and up and down, in order to piece together a view of the complete skeleton as a whole.[17] Simultaneously, Wandelaar would have had to maintain an equal viewing distance on the vertical skeleton, from top to toe: any change in the perpendicular angle of vision – and hence to the viewing distance from the skeleton – which would result from gazing up, down or across, would have produced distortions (parallax) in the final image. Albinus's method would have further complicated Wandelaar's work because of the need to take the eye from the hole while transferring the observed data to the depiction, and then to re-focus at the eye-hole.

It is clear from these meticulous procedures the degree of Albinus's concern with scientific precision in his anatomical figures. Of course, the chosen methods themselves also carry meaning. However accurate the grid system may in fact have been – and its success depended greatly on the talents of the engraver – Albinus's methods endowed him with the authority of a man of science. His search for precision was, as we have seen, wholly in keeping with eighteenth-century ideals of classical beauty: the divine beauty of mathematics, the beauty of harmony and symmetry and, in this context, the beauty of the masculine. The chosen proportions of the skeleton also conform to classical ideals of perfection: it is a figure of eight heads; in other words, the head divides seven times into the length of the body.

Composition and medium

Compositionally, the Albinus skeleton is positioned to fill the pictorial space. Placed close to the picture plane, it makes full use of the engraved surface of the plate. In the print, the skeleton's extremities reach close to the framing edge on all four sides, giving optimum display while creating a dynamic tension between figure and frame which heightens the sense of figural animation. Obviously the disposition of the figure is partly determined by the scientific purposes of the print – the need to inform the viewer by exposing the maximum information possible in a two-dimensional image. The pose permits a fair degree of empirical detail, but the limitations of the print medium and flatness exclude much of medical interest, not least the forms in-the-round of the bones: a series of different views (front, side and rear) of a skeleton are required to 'add up' to a fuller anatomical picture. Three-dimensional examples of human anatomy, like those in wax, can be far more informative but were primarily used for representing internal organs: the technical limits of the wax medium constrain its use in complete skeletons. Apart from the plaster cast reproductions after sculpted flayed figures (*écorchés*) which were in widespread use for teaching, anatomical sculptures, whether in wax or wood, were costly one-offs which did not offer the same potential for dissemination as the printed image.

The question of dissemination is in itself highly pertinent here, and a grand volume such as this initiated by Albinus himself (engraved surface of the plates in this series *c.*56 × 40 cm) were by no means cheap to produce or buy: the *Tabulae* took an estimated twenty-two years to complete; the engraving alone took eight years.[18] As far as professional medical usage was concerned, the most successful volumes tended to be the practical anatomies like Bauhin's *Theatrum anatomicum* . . . of 1605, a chunky quarto of 1,300 pages, which were relatively small and portable. The audience for anatomies like the Albinus was by no means exclusively medical; such exquisite images were greatly sought-after for gentlemen's cabinets of curiosities: well-off physicians, surgeons, men of letters, aristocrats and connoisseur-collectors acquired such tomes, but not medical students. Indeed, although human anatomy promised a greater understanding of the body's constituent parts, it had only limited practical application for the medical profession (with the exception of obstetricians and midwives) before the advent of anaesthetics, antiseptics and deep surgery in the late nineteenth century;[19] thus anatomical prints like those of Albinus were chiefly of intellectual, taxonomic and curiosity interest. And, I would argue, of great ideological importance.

Medical science and scientific accuracy were not the exclusive motives behind the Albinus print's conception. It does represent, however, a prototypical male nude. Whether nude or skeletal, the male figure in art is consistently shown as inhabiting and defining its own space. Here, the full-frontal view, the out-turned feet, the spread-eagled arms, all extend the male body to show man's ownership of the world around him.

The commanding pose of the Apollo Belverderesque skeleton communicates an expansive openness; but it is not open in the sense of receptive, rather of complacent self-assurance – notably paradoxical given that it is a skeleton. The pose suggests an authority based on command both of the self, and of knowledge; a mutually reinforcing self-control and control of the environment. These ideas are rehearsed by anatomist and engraver in the actual making of this image which, through the very process of its materialisation enacts man's claim to rational authority over (feminine) nature: nature cleaned up, perfected, ordered and reduced to the cool engraver's medium – the crisp burin mark in copper, the classical certainties of line: 'black and white', as we say. Engraving requires absolute precision, for mistakes are not readily changed or erased: burnishing can be used to efface only the shallowest of cuts. The engraver's tool stands for the scalpel, its incision a metaphor for the process of dissection itself. The resulting engraved lines, paradoxically a mirror-image of the original subject reversed in the printing process, form a language connoting clarity, cleanliness and objectivity which gives the viewer an illusion of control over the 'natural' body in all its gory unpredictability. Equally, the physical disorder of the medium, the oily black printer's ink which gets everywhere and filthies the (craftsman) engraver's hands in the process of printing, is a gory mess contained in the workshop and rendered invisible in the perfection of the finished print: the viewer is intended to register the message rather than the medium. Such images, then, rehearse a macabre pantomime of human frailty; terror of the material body and its functions is laid bare and simultaneously contained within the reassuring conventions of the classical idiom: hence the body is returned to man's ownership.

The Apollo Belvedere embodies the notion of masculine authority: alert and commanding, he is literally a man of vision. Although the skull and 'gaze' of the Albinus figure are lowered, suggesting a more introspective demeanour, a greater interiority, reflection is posited as the product of *knowledge* (in this case of man's mortality) and knowledge ensures authority. Hence the historical link to the Belvedere provides, in this *memento mori*, an assurance of spiritual immortality thanks to man's enlightened state. The early Christian iconographic tradition, in which Apollo transforms into Christ, reinforces this reading of the Albinus skeleton. At the same time, the erect stature and almost arrogant dignity of the skeleton's pose ensure its embodiment of the Belvederesque ideal of a dominating masculinity. This is reinforced in the spatial arrangement of the skeleton in its setting. Where Albinus's elaborate copying methods eliminate a specific viewing position on the figure itself, Wandelaar's landscape setting – with its low horizon and thus viewpoint – constructs the spectator's eyeline as well below that of the skeleton. Thereby inscribed in a position of pictorial, and thence social and moral, inferiority, the spectator 'looks up' to/at the super-human perfection of the skeleton. However, where in the Belvedere the elegantly twisting torso is achieved by non-alignment of hips and shoulders, and sensual vitality is enhanced in the accentuated spinal 'S' curve, the Albinus is more squarely frontal and 'grounded', suggesting a greater civic *gravitas*. In the equation domination–desirability which Winckelmann found exquisitely balanced in the Apollo Belvedere, the Albinus skeleton tips the balance away from the sensual (which arguably depends on flesh and muscle) and towards the powerful. Thus masculine power is idealised through the male anatomical figure's embodiment and subtle modification of particular classical associations, reminding the spectator to identify a normative masculinity with that formal idea.

By naturalising the Belvedere pose within a medical discourse which also served to inform artists and their patrons, Albinus underwrote the ideal physique of the classical statue with an authenticity guaranteed by the natural sciences. In this reflexive relationship of meaning, the two figures are mutually validated and ensure each other's authority; so, too, the professional status of the anatomist himself. Artists sought both to give anatomical conviction to the forms of their male figures, and to imbue them with higher meaning; the Albinus–Apollo pose was thus the outstanding exemplar for full-length male portraiture of the period. The Apollo Belvedere had already been assigned this role in seventeenth-century France, when Charles Lebrun, Director of the Académie Royale de Peinture, adopted its pose for a victorious Louis XIV. Lebrun thus elaborated an iconography of the Absolute Monarch as sun-god which simultaneously affirmed the statue's privileged status while recuperating its authority within the visual language of the Académie. Democratised during the course of the eighteenth-century, aristocrats, professionals, politicians and bourgeois patriarchs alike were portrayed in this meaningful guise, which ascribed to them an elevated power and civic *gravitas* by association with classical authority. Employed throughout the West, the Belvedere was equally exploited in painted and sculpted portraits to authorise the power of, for example, politicians and the landed gentry in Britain (Ramsey, Reynolds and Gainsborough),[20] French Revolutionary heroism (David)[21] and New World leaders (Figure 36.5).

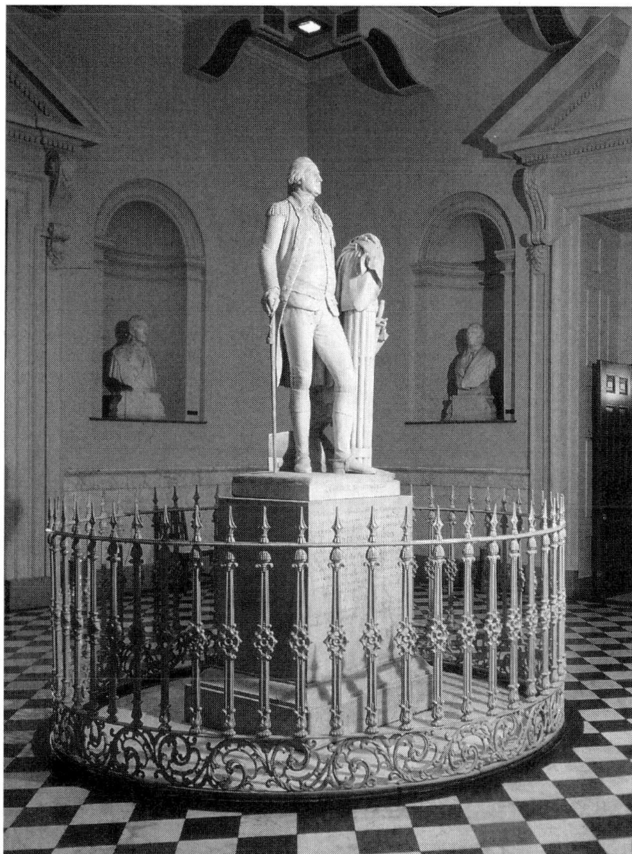

Figure 36.5 J.A. Houden, Statue of George Washington, 1788–92 (Courtesy Bridgeman Art Library)

Thus, although the political inflection of the embodied meaning might be diametrically opposed according to time and place, the ubiquity of the Belvedere and its seemingly transparent legibility made it readily adaptable within a formula whose common denominator was partriarchal dominance.

Accessories

The Albinus print is not atypical in its inclusion of accessories not strictly required in a purely anatomical study; the anatomist argued that the landscape setting improved the illusion of relief in the skeleton, which certainly looks flatter in impressions printed without it. Thus Albinus explained that his backgrounds were not only to 'fill up the empty spaces . . . and make them appear more agreeable' but that they ensured 'the light and shade of the figures might be preserved and heightened and the figures themselves appear more raised and rounded.' He suggested that the plates be looked at through the cupped hand 'in the manner of a spy-glass',[22] an idea which has parallels in the classical tradition of viewing Claudian landscapes. Not surprisingly, Albinus used Claudian pastoral settings, often complete with classical architecture; these motifs depended again on the particular skills of his engraver. Jan Wandelaar was also a botanical illustrator, and the accuracy of his empirical studies notable in the foreground details of the Albinus prints derived from this expertise. However, these elements also add a further layer of ideological meaning.

Setting the skeleton in a landscape has the effect of figuratively 'naturalising' the anatomist's vision: linking it with the natural world thereby makes it authentic; the 'natural world' in this context is, of course that of the natural sciences, a world ordered by masculine reason and not 'untamed' nature. The scientific authority of the image is further validated by the inclusion of Wandelaar's detailed, precise renderings of natural flora and fauna in the Enlightenment manner of the botanical taxonomist; their very abundance stands in poignant contrast to the skeleton. Their iconographic significance adds weight to the anatomist's theme – the thorns of gorse and bramble are a reminder of Christ's Passion.

Most startling, however, is a small winged putto or angel holding a dark billowing shroud; like a sinister cloud of shading, which throws the pale skeleton into relief, the putto unveils for the viewer this fascinating, macabre, but at the same time wholly convincing scientific display. The shadow of death falls, quite literally, across the infant face, plunging it into obscurity in yet another reminder of mortality. It is significant that female skeletons were rarely represented as embodying the *memento mori* theme (we have seen the Platter/Bauhin example which carries an hourglass); they were commonly represented as not privy to knowledge: the female skeleton bore the material, the reproductive, rather than the productive, spiritually or intellectually meaningful symbolism.

Ideal scientific anatomies such as the Albinus skeleton were rarely divorced from connotations of the *memento mori*; as Ludmilla Jordanova argues,

> Lessons about death are often contained in the gesture and position of the figure, and the background and accompanying objects. These are

> far from extraneous to the image: on the contrary, it is they that render it meaningful. They frame the image, give it a location and guide the viewer as to what he should attend to.[23]

In such images the artist/anatomist dissects the dead, she argues, 'in order to reveal, lay bare and ultimately comprehend the living'. But their meaning goes beyond straight revelation, or even the 'unveiling' of some pre-existing cultural construct: these images are directly implicated in the production of cultural meaning. Thus I would posit a much more active ideological role for pictorial anatomies, which here can be seen to construct a certain ideal of masculinity as universal and normal – and such ideals of masculinity have a formative impact on the ordering or reinforcing of hierarchical or social roles. Anatomies like the Albinus, then, worked actively within the complex socio-historical developments which, by the final years of the eighteenth century, culminated in a polarisation of cultural gender distinctions.

Notes

1 I am particularly grateful to Michael Rosenthal for sharing his ideas with me, and for reading and suggesting changes to the present essay. Beyond the remit here, the links between anatomy and race are addressed in A. Callen, *The Spectacular Body: Science, Method and Meaning in the Work of Degas*, New Haven and London, 1995, ch. 1, and will be pursued in greater depth in A. Callen, *Art and Anatomy from Albinus to Charcot* (Yale, in preparation).

2 Quoted in L. Schiebinger, 'Skeletons in the Closet: The First Illustrations of the Female Skeleton in Eighteenth-Century Anatomy', in C. Gallagher and T. Lacquer (eds), *The Making of the Modern Body*, California, 1987, p. 43.

3 Analysis here refers to the text of the shorter, London reprinted edition in English of Albinus's *Tables of the Skeleton and Muscles of the Human Body* (1749).

4 For example, Guidi, *De anatome*, 1611, title-page.

5 Schiebinger, op. cit., p. 51.

6 See K.B. Roberts and J.D.W. Tomlinson, *The Fabric of the Body: European Traditions of Anatomical Illustration*, Oxford, pp. 220–25 and plate 54, pp. 23–1.

7 L. Jordanova, 'Gender, Generation and Science: William Hunter's Obstetrical Atlas', in W.F. Bynum and R. Porter (eds), *William Hunter and the Eighteenth-Century Medical World*, Cambridge, 1985, p. 385.

8 *Geschichte*, p. 392, quoted in A. Potts, *Flesh and the Ideal: Winckelmann and the Origins of Art History*, New Haven and London, 1994, p. 118.

9 François Raguenet on the Apollo Belvedere, 1700, quoted in F. Haskell, *Rediscoveries in Art,* London, 1976, p. 109, n. 71 (my translation).

10 See Potts's discussion of the homoerotic in relation to classical sculpture in eighteenth-century France, in Potts, *Flesh and the Ideal*; on the Apollo Belvedere, esp. pp. 118ff.; beyond the bounds of the present essay, I pursue the theme of the homoerotic in relation to male anatomies in *Art and Anatomy from Albinus to Charcot* (Yale, in preparation).

11 K. Clark, *The Nude*, Harmondsworth, 1970, p. 26.

12 Potts, op. cit., p. 118.
13 It is on this edition that the present discussion depends.
14 Albinus, London edn 1749, quoted in Roberts and Tomlinson, op. cit., pp. 324–25.
15 Quoted in ibid., p. 324.
16 Quoted and paraphrased in ibid.
17 For his eye to take in the complete figure, Wandelaar needed to be placed at a distance from his subject equivalent to three times its height: e.g. for a 6-foot figure, 18 feet away.
18 Roberts and Tomlinson, op. cit., p. 322.
19 Ibid., p. 623.
20 Cf. D. Solkin, 'Great Pictures or Great Men? Reynolds, Male Portraiture, and the Power of Art', *Oxford Art Journal*, vol. 9, no. 2, pp. 42ff., and A. Smart, *Allan Ramsey*, 1992, pp. 81ff.
21 See Potts, op. cit., esp. pp. 223–30.
22 Roberts and Tomlinson, op. cit., pp. 326–27.
23 Jordanova, 'William Hunter . . .', op. cit., pp. 411–12.

Chapter 37

Tamar Garb

THE FORBIDDEN GAZE

Women artists and the male nude in late nineteenth-century France

IN 1883 CHARLES AUBERT, author of mildly titillating, sometimes smutty pulp fiction, published a short story with a woman artist as its central character. This was one of thirteen tales of sex and seduction by the same author, entitled *Les Nouvelles amoureuses*, which were to be collated into one volume in 1891 and illustrated by Jul. Hanriot, the engraver who had provided a frontispiece and engraving to accompany the 1883 publication (Figure 37.1).

The story begins as a conversation between the narrator and a prim, self-righteous, older woman who expresses outrage at the request of the wealthy young Isabelle, the heroine of the tale, to see the body of a naked man. She, and the reader, are assured of the innocence of the heroine's motive by the revelation that she is an artist, incarcerated in her luxurious Parisian *hôtel* and closely guarded by her mother-in-law, while her husband, a captain, is away at sea. To pass away her time in her husband's absence she has turned to painting religious scenes and has been thrown into a state of utter confusion and distress by being offered a commission to paint a St Sebastian.

From the beginning, therefore, the story invokes a range of anxieties and potential threats. What is primarily articulated at this stage in the narrative, albeit in a disingenuous tone of concern, is the threat to the modesty of the woman artist, representative here of upper-middle-class femininity, who is caught in an impossible situation in which she is bound to be compromised. A classic staging of resistance (her piety, innocence and loneliness are stressed) and the inevitable path to seduction (beneath the veil is a rampant and unfulfilled desire) is set up. What subtends the linear narrative thrust, which in itself has only the richness of banality as its defence, are subtle and deeply rooted anxieties which invoke the power structures at stake in the scopic field as encoded in narrative and image in *fin-de-siècle* Paris.

One cannot underestimate the banal or the repetitive as historical material. For in the clichéd resolutions and cheap gratifications offered by much caricature

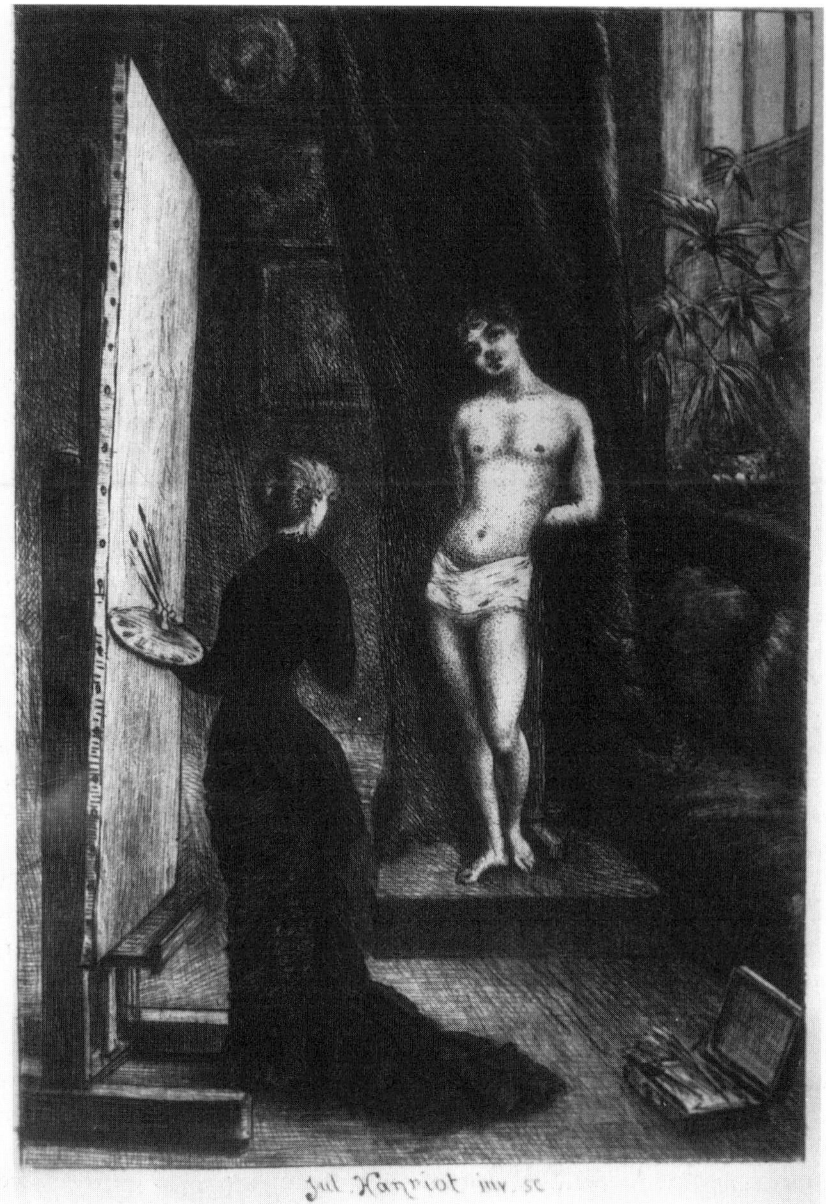

Figure 37.1 Jul. Hanriot, frontispiece of Book V, *Les Nouvelles amoureuses*, 1883

and popular fiction, of which this story is a typical example, lies a form of cultural repression which renders anxieties manageable even as it veils and occludes them.

The potentially comic situation of the woman artist in close proximity to an undressed or semi-dressed male figure offered ample opportunity for smutty humour and caricature throughout the century. In an early nineteenth-century image a young woman with eyes modestly downcast is told to remember that she is painting history by her stern and rather lecherous-looking teacher as she is confronted by the full frontal nudity of the less-than-ideal male model. In a much later caricature from *Gil Blas*, the predictable scene of seduction and deception is staged in the temporary absence of the older male chaperone/authority figure. Here the power of the woman artist to possess the world with her sight is contained by the reinscription of her as object of seduction, admired and exchanged, often unconsciously, between men. In keeping with contemporary narrative structures, the expectation which is set up in our story is that Isabelle, after some resistance, will be seduced.

The prohibition which gave Aubert's story its frisson was tenaciously defended by the art establishment during this period. But the disquiet that the prospect of a woman viewing the body of a naked man provoked is surely based on more than the protection of women's chastity required for their exchange and circulation in the interests of the bourgeois family. At any rate, even if this lies at the heart of the social order, it is not primarily the protection of women and their modesty which is at stake here but the preservation of masculinity as it is lived out in different social spheres. Discursively this may, of course, masquerade as beneficence towards women.

Aubert's story was published during a period of heated debate over women's involvement in art and their exclusion from state-funded Fine Art education. The Union des femmes peintres et sculpteurs, founded in 1881, campaigned vigorously for women's admission to the Ecole des Beaux-Arts, and women journalists and artists poured scorn on what they saw as a reactionary and exclusive art establishment. There were those who saw no sense in the case which apparently sought to protect women by their exclusion from the life-class whilst they were free to visit the art galleries of the world and behold, unscathed, the painted image of the male nude. The debates raged in the Ecole, in the press and in the Chamber of Deputies itself. Many reasons were given for women's exclusion from the Ecole, including their ostensible innate inability to work in the higher genres because of their limited powers of abstraction. Other reasons cited were the overcrowding of the artistic profession, the expense that the provision of Fine Art education for women would entail, the need for women to contribute to the threatened industries of luxury goods, decorative arts and traditional light crafts, and even the threat of depopulation which the advent of the professional woman would, it was believed, only exacerbate, if not by her refusal to have children then by the deterioration of her reproductive capacities which would inevitably result from excessive mental stimulation.

But the problem to which many commentators returned, and on which the teachers and administrators of the Ecole des Beaux-Arts and even the deputies in the Chamber were to dwell repeatedly, was the issue of the life-class. Why was the prospect of mixed life-classes such a threat during this period and how could the anxieties they provoked be resolved? The ready-made solution of fiction, that of seduction in the interests of salacious humour, mild sexual excitation or the appeasement of anxiety, available to the predictable Aubert were, of course, not on offer as strategies of containment in the realm of public debate, however, much their concerns occupied the same dialogical field.

The devices mobilised by Aubert to assure the minimum disruption to the phallic order in the face of threat are not quite as simple as one might expect. The focus of anxiety in the story centres on the problematics of looking and sight, for it is through these that power is encoded or subverted. It is through the usurping of a culturally forbidden look that the gaze, which polices looking, is momentarily threatened and rendered vulnerable. But it is not only the woman's look that is potentially dangerous. In the man's beholding of the *woman who looks* lies a much deeper threat, for it is through the unveiling of the threat of castration, linked here, as in the case of the Medusa's head, 'to the sight of something', to quote Freud, that masculinity is potentially at risk. The effect of Medusa's power, her 'evil look', is that it not only kills or devours but blinds as well (Freud 1955).

Isabelle's problem when first mooted by Aubert, is framed as a problem of sight: 'elle desirait voir un jeune homme' (Aubert 1883: 10). The obstacles facing her seemed insurmountable. The house in which she was confined was guarded by her mother-in-law and no young man would have been allowed to enter her private quarters, although she had had no problem in having women models to sit for her. More difficult even than such practical problems were the fears and resistances which she built up in the processes of thinking about the prospect of beholding a naked man. Would she have the courage to look at the model, would she dare to confront his body with her eye? Would he not triumph at her discomfort and delight in her difficulties, and how would she cope with her own inadmissible desires which must be repressed at all costs? These are the thoughts, according to our narrator, which go through the young woman's mind but, instead of dissuading her from her course, make her obsessed by it. At this point Aubert introduces an intermediary male figure, a corrupt old picture seller from Montmartre who supplies Isabelle with equipment and models. He is brought in to resolve the conflict and promises, at a considerable cost, to smuggle a male model into her quarters for her. He is described as 'a superb young man, the ideal of beauty and elegance, gentle and well brought up' (Aubert 1883: 21). At first Isabelle resists resolutely but she is persuaded to accept him by the vital piece of information that, though possessed of magnificent eyes, the young man has been blind from birth. This fills her with comfort and relief: 'Elle pourrait voir sans être vue' (Aubert 1883: 22). This is perhaps the moment to reveal that the title of the story is, appropriately, *L'aveugle*.

Momentarily we are offered a complete inversion of traditional power relations in the visual field: a woman in possession of the gaze, a beautiful male body providing the unthreatening spectacle. But this fantasy, at least on behalf of the reader, is short lived, for no sooner are we offered this vision of a world turned upside down than we are assured that patriarchy is still intact and an elaborate trick is about to be played on the vulnerable and unknowing Isabelle. The model turns out, of course, to be a starving artist called Charles Morose, in the debt of our dealer/intermediary, who is promised to be released from his debts if he agrees to pretend to be blind and be smuggled in a crate, for a period of thirty days, into the studio of the beautiful woman who is too modest to dare view a model who can see her.

It is this symbolic inversion of the natural order which the story must both play out and undermine. The tempering of Isabelle's power comes early on in this potentially dangerous scenario and is achieved by the usual means. Overcome by the young man's beauty as he strips down in order to put on his drapery, Isabelle faints and is caught in his arms, coming to with her head on his naked breast.

From very early on, therefore, the woman's power as an artist, as encoded in the engraving at the beginning of the 1883 edition, is contained by her weakness as a woman. The model's vulnerability, his nakedness, the 'effeminate' pose which he is forced to adopt and his incapacitating blindness, is assuaged by the power beneath his masquerade which even the innocent Isabelle suspects but never admits. At the same time, however, the relationship of looks in an engraving like that in Figure 37.1 points to a source of anxiety which is never quite articulated in this context but surfaces, as we shall see, elsewhere. Whilst the play-acting of the model requires the adoption of the ethereal, abstracted expression of the St Sebastian, traditionally constructed in representation as a feminised male, the attention of the woman artist is firmly fixed on his covered genitals.

Which are the forbidden gazes at stake here? On the one hand the story must contain and police female sexuality, reinscribe it as lack, and subordinate it to male desire if order is to be maintained. The inevitable seduction, Isabelle's transformation from artist into amorous woman, will assure this and invest in masculinity the power which is its due. The seduction scene itself is ultimately dependent upon the reinscription of Isabelle as the object of the look. At the beginning of the story, the artist is described as being dressed formally, in black silk and firmly corseted in keeping with the laws of etiquette. Gradually, however, the heat of the studio and the knowledge that her model is blind allow her to discard the corset and to dress less formally.

This makes for her easy narrative objectification as we are treated to long descriptions of the gradual slipping of her gown off her shoulder and the slow but climactic revelation of her nipple, while she, unawares, is absorbed in her work. All that she notices is a movement in the model's drapery, the origins of which she does not quite understand, but which unsettles her. Her power is further undermined by the reinscription of the model as artist. In her absence he corrects her drawing and improves the painting so that it turns out by the end to be the best work she has ever done. The model/artist transcends his objectification by becoming master of his own image. The man transcends his humiliation by having an erection.

But the frightening spectacle of a woman who usurps power, whilst able to be diffused effectively in fiction through the fantasy of seduction, is not quite so easily contained within the discourses of art education and administration. One of the ways in which fear in men is managed, according to Freud, is via the erection: 'it offers consolation to the spectator: he is still in possession of a penis, and the stiffening reassures him of the fact'. Or put another way: 'To display the penis (or any of its surrogates) is to say: "I am not afraid of you. I defy you. I have a penis"' (Freud 1955: 273–74). The erection therefore can function as a defence in a situation where power is usurped or horror is invoked. The objectification of the male model and the empowerment of the woman artist is discursively constructed as one such situation.

The entry of women into the life-class at the Ecole des Beaux-Arts would, it was felt, lead to a major disruption. As Gérôme stated in 1890 (p. 318), it was impossible to admit women and men into the same classes as work would suffer. Proof of this was the fact that when the art students had, approximately once a month, to work from a female model, they worked much less well. The very presence of women, even in this subordinate role, was disruptive to the high seriousness of an all-male community and its commitment to the transcendent qualities of art. But the appearance of a female art student, an equal, was potentially much more threatening than the presence of working-class women used as models in relation to whom the young male art students could unite in predictable pranks and sexual innuendoes. The form of male bonding perceived to be under threat by women's entry to the Ecole is encoded in contemporary photographs of the ateliers of the Ecole. In [one] . . . the young art students pose in serried ranks, anonymous in their masculine costume, together with their teacher who kneels in the front row. Behind them on the walls are their nude studies, draped or naked. In this representation, the life studies can be read as the referent to the art which ostensibly draws these men together. It was this apparent harmony which the entry of women threatened. Pedagogical principles and lofty aspirations required, therefore, that in the Ecole itself and the associated School at Rome, women be almost entirely excluded.

Amongst the traditionalists, what needed to be preserved was the capacity of art, conceived in this context in terms of the threatened academic doctrine of idealism to transcend the physical. What was needed to perform this transformation was serious training, developed powers of intellectual abstraction and an ability to see beyond immediate visceral experience. There was serious doubt as to whether women were capable of this. In their presence art risked being reduced while the model's physicality would be emphasised. In a contemporary caricature, the absurd underpants, portly figure and Venus-like pose of the [male] model are juxtaposed with the artists, represented as shrewish wife and skinny daughter, who are rendered as incapable of transforming nature into art as the model is of evoking the great hero Achilles.

Supporters of women's entry to the Ecole, like Jules Antoine of *L'Art et Critique*, argued that the situation of the life-class 'gives a sort of impersonality to the model which becomes no more than the object to be drawn' (Antoine 1890: 344). In their view, the sex of the artist should not affect this. Art transformed the naked into the nude, and thereby occluded its sexual connotations. It came rather to signify the pure, the ideal.

But others were not so easily reassured. They felt that for this basic but fragile tenet of academic doctrine to be sustained, the person who would need protecting was not the woman artist and her modesty, but the male model. The writer for the *Moniteur des Arts* explained the resistance to women's entry as stemming from 'a concern for the male models, who in front of the pretty little faces, blonde hair and laughing eyes of the young women artists, would not be able to conserve their "sang froid"' (Sainville 1890: 325). It was the gaze of the model that had to be forbidden. For if the model was to become aroused, who would testify to the transcendence of the nude over the naked? One deputy speaking in the Chamber in 1893 even alluded to an allegedly American practice of making the male model wear a mask as a way out of a tricky situation.

In this context the memoirs of Virginie Demont-Breton, one of the chief campaigners for the entry of women into the Ecole, are instructive. Reporting on a meeting of the sub-commission set up at the Ecole itself in 1890 to debate the issue, the conflicting claims of the transcendent powers of Art on the one hand,

and the assertion of male virility on the other, come into open conflict. Mme Demont-Breton recounts that while she was addressing the meeting, the architect Charles Garnier suddenly cried out that it was absolutely impossible to put men and women under the same roof at all: 'this would put the fire near to the powder . . . and would produce an explosion in which art would be completely annihilated.' He was quickly attacked by the sculptor Guillaume, who allegedly exclaimed: 'You don't know what you are saying. When an artist works, does he think about anything else but the study in which he is passionately engaged . . . ? In the school we envisage, there will be no men and women, but artists animated by a noble and pure spirit.' Garnier was not satisfied with this vision and retorted: 'It is possible that you, O Great Sculptor, you are made of marble and wood like your statues, but if I had seen a pretty little feminine face next to my easel at twenty years, to hell with my drawing. O! Guillaume. You are not a man!' To which Guillaume is said to have exclaimed: 'O! Garnier. You are not an artist!' (Demont-Breton 1926: 198–99).

It is the presence of women who apparently bring this otherwise harmonious conjunction of art and masculinity into conflict. To assuage castration anxiety, male virility must assert itself. But in so doing the edifice of the already waning academic establishment and the repression on which its pedagogy is founded is at risk. Masculinity needs the erection as reassurance. Art needs an occlusion/diminution of the penis if the phallic order/ideal is to remain intact. When women were finally admitted into the Ecole in 1897, after having been hounded out of the school by some of their future colleagues with cries of 'Down with women', the ateliers still remained closed to them, and life drawing and anatomy lessons were segregated, with male models neatly tucked into their much maligned underpants.

It is only in the fantasy world of fiction that resolution is potentially absolute. Scolded by Isabelle for the strange movement in his drapery, Charles is armed with one of her absent husband's arrows and told to keep still. The humiliation is too much for him. In a dramatic gesture he wounds himself in the chest with the arrow. Finally castrated, the model appears about to become the martyr he has been imitating. But his masculinity is restored by a contrite Isabelle who prostrates herself before him and declares her love. The charade is over. The danger is gone. All that is needed now is the annihilation of the absent sea-captain. In a gruesome narrative twist which invokes the implicit violences involved in the maintenance of social order, he is conveniently devoured by a band of savage negresses. The story is ultimately haunted and framed therefore by the excessive fantasy of an untamed voracious femininity, out there on the margins of civilisation, but one which threatens to invade its closely policed boundaries. At the moment of the tale's resolution, this grotesque disposal of the final obstacle, the legitimate husband, reveals the fear of feminine power that the story has done everything to contain but which seeps out, in a displaced form, at its edges.

References

Antoine, J. (1890) *L'Art et critique*, reprinted in *Moniteur des Arts*, 1917.

Aubert, C. (1883) 'L'aveugle', *Les Nouvelles amoureuses*, Paris.

Demont-Breton, V. (1926) *Les Maisons que j'ai connues*, Paris.
Freud, S. (1955) 'Medusa's Head' (1940/1922), in *The Standard Edition of the Complete Psychological Works of Sigmund Freud*, J. Strachey (ed.), volume XVIII, London.
Gérôme, J.L. (1890) 'Les Formes à l'Ecole des Beaux-Arts', *Moniteur des Arts*, 12 September: 318.
Sainville (1890) 'Chronique de la semaine', *Moniteur des Arts*, 1913, 325.

Chapter 38

Judith Butler

PROHIBITION, PSYCHOANALYSIS AND THE HETEROSEXUAL MATRIX

[P]UBLISHED IN 1929, Joan Riviere's essay, 'Womanliness as a Masquerade'[1] introduces the notion of femininity as masquerade in terms of a theory of aggression and conflict resolution. This theory appears at first to be far afield from Lacan's analysis of masquerade in terms of the comedy of sexual positions. She begins with a respectful review of Ernest Jones's typology of the development of female sexuality into heterosexual and homosexual forms. She focuses, however, on the 'intermediate types' that blur the boundaries between the heterosexual and the homosexual and, implicitly, contest the descriptive capacity of Jones's classificatory system. In a remark that resonates with Lacan's facile reference to 'observation', Riviere seeks recourse to mundane perception or experience to validate her focus on these 'intermediate types': 'In daily life types of men and women are constantly met with who, while mainly heterosexual in their development, plainly display strong features of the other sex'. What is here most plain is the classifications that condition and structure the perception of this mix of attributes. Clearly, Riviere begins with set notions about what it is to display characteristics of one's sex, and how it is that those plain characteristics are understood to express or reflect an ostensible sexual orientation. This perception or observation not only assumes a correlation among characteristics, desires, and 'orientations,' but creates that unity through the perceptual act itself. Riviere's postulated unity between gender attributes and a naturalized 'orientation' appears as an instance of what Wittig refers to as the 'imaginary formation' of sex.

And yet, Riviere calls into question these naturalized typologies through an appeal to a psychoanalytic account that locates the meaning of mixed gender attributes in the 'interplay of conflicts'. Significantly, she contrasts this kind of psychoanalytic theory with one that would reduce the presence of ostensibly 'masculine' attributes in a woman to a 'radical or fundamental tendency.' In other words, the acquisition of such attributes and the accomplishment of a heterosexual or homosexual orientation are produced through the resolution of conflicts that have as their aim the suppression of anxiety. Citing Ferenczi in order to establish an analogy with her own account, Riviere writes:

> Ferenczi pointed out . . . that homosexual men exaggerate their heterosexuality as a 'defence' against their homosexuality. I shall attempt to show that women who wish for masculinity may put on a mask of womanliness to avert anxiety and the retribution feared from men.
>
> (Riviere 1986: 35)

It is unclear what is the 'exaggerated' form of heterosexuality the homosexual man is alleged to display, but the phenomenon under notice here might simply be that gay men simply may not may not look much different from their heterosexual counterparts. This lack of an overt differentiating style or appearance may be diagnosed as a symptomatic 'defense' only because the gay man in question does not conform to the idea of the homosexual that the analyst has drawn and sustained from cultural stereotypes. A Lacanian analysis might argue that the supposed 'exaggeration' in the homosexual man of whatever attributes count as apparent heterosexuality is the attempt to 'have' the Phallus, the subject position that entails an active and heterosexualized desire. Similarly, the 'mask' of the 'women who wish for masculinity' can be interpreted as an effort to renounce the 'having' of the Phallus is order to avert retribution by those from whom it must have been procured through castration. Riviere explains the fear of retribution as the consequence of a woman's fantasy to take the place of men, more precisely, of the father. In the case that she herself examines, which some consider to be autobiographical, the rivalry with the father is not over the desire of the mother, as one might expect, but over the place of the father in public discourse as speaker, lecturer, writer – that is, as a user of signs rather than a sign-object, an item of exchange. This castrating desire might be understood as the desire to relinquish the status of woman-as-sign in order to appear as a subject within language.

Indeed, the analogy that Riviere draws between the homosexual man and the masked woman is not, in her view, an analogy between male and female homosexuality. Femininity is taken on by a woman who 'wishes for masculinity,' but fears the retributive consequences of taking on the public appearance of masculinity. Masculinity is taken on by the male homosexual who, presumably, seeks to hide – not from others, but from himself – an ostensible femininity. The woman takes on a masquerade knowingly in order to conceal her masculinity from the masculine audience she wants to castrate. But the homosexual man is said to exaggerate his 'heterosexuality' (meaning a masculinity that allows him to pass as heterosexual?) as a 'defence,' unknowingly, because he cannot acknowledge his own homosexuality (or is it that the analyst would not acknowledge it, if it were his?). In other words, the homosexual man takes unconscious retribution on himself, both desiring and fearing the consequences of castration. The male homosexual does not 'know' his homsexuality, although Ferenczi and Riviere apparently do.

But does Riviere know the homosexuality of the woman in masquerade that she describes? When it comes to the counterpart of the analogy that she herself sets up, the woman who 'wishes for masculinity' is homosexual only in terms of sustaining a masculine identification, but not in terms of a sexual orientation or desire. Invoking Jones's typology once again, as if it were a phallic shield, she formulates a 'defense' that designates as asexual a class of female homosexuals understood as the masquerading type: 'his first group of homosexual women who, while taking no interest in other women, wish for "recognition" of their masculinity from men and claim to be the equals of men, or in other words, to be men themselves' (Riviere 1986: 37). As in Lacan, the lesbian is here signified as an asexual position, as indeed, a position that refuses sexuality. For the earlier analogy with Ferenczi to become complete, it would seem that this description enacts the 'defence' against female homosexuality *as sexuality* that is nevertheless understood as the reflexive structure of the 'homosexual man.' And yet, there is no clear way to read this description of a female homosexuality that is not about a sexual desire for women. Riviere would have us believe that this curious typological anomaly cannot be reduced to a repressed female homosexuality or heterosexuality. What is hidden is not sexuality, but rage.

One possible interpretation is that the woman in masquerade wishes for masculinity in order to engage in public discourse with men and as a man as part of a male homoerotic exchange. And precisely because that male homoerotic exchange would signify castration, she fears the same retribution that motivates the 'defences' of the homosexual man. Indeed, perhaps femininity as masquerade is meant to deflect from male homosexuality – that being the erotic presupposition of hegemonic discourse, the 'hommo-sexuality' that Irigaray suggests. In any case, Riviere would have us consider that such women sustain masculine identifications not to occupy a position in a sexual exchange, but, rather, to pursue a rivalry that has no sexual object or, at least, that has none that she will name.

Riviere's text offers a way to reconsider the question: What is masked by masquerade? In a key passage that marks a departure from the restricted analysis demarcated by Jones's classificatory system, she suggests that 'masquerade' is more than the characteristic of an 'intermediate type,' that it is central to all 'womanliness':

> The reader may now ask how I define womanliness or where I draw the line between genuine womanliness and the 'masquerade'. My suggestion is not, however, that there is any such difference; whether radical or superficial, they are the same thing.
>
> (Riviere 1986: 38)

This refusal to postulate a femininity that is prior to mimicry and the mask is taken up by Stephen Heath in 'Joan Riviere and the Masquerade' as evidence for the notion that 'authentic womanliness is such a mimicry, *is* the masquerade.' Relying on the postulated characterization of libido as masculine, Heath concludes that femininity is the denial of that libido, the 'dissimulation of a fundamental masculinity.'[2]

Femininity becomes a mask that dominates/resolves a masculine identification, for a masculine identification would, within the presumed heterosexual matrix of desire, produce a desire for a female object, the Phallus; hence, the donning of femininity as mask may reveal a refusal of a female homosexuality and, at the same time, the hyperbolic incorporation of that female Other who is refused – an odd form of preserving and protecting that love within the circle of the melancholic and negative narcissism that results from the psychic inculcation of compulsory heterosexuality.

One might read Riviere as fearful of her own phallicism – that is, of the phallic identity she risks exposing in the course of her lecture, her writing, indeed, the writing of this phallicism that the essay itself both conceals and enacts. It may, however, be less her own masculine identity than the masculine heterosexual desire that is its signature that she seeks both to deny and enact by becoming the object she forbids herself to love. This is the predicament produced by a matrix that accounts for all desire for women by subjects of whatever sex or gender as originating in a masculine, heterosexual position. The libido-as-masculine is the source from which all possible sexuality is presumed to come.

Here the typology of gender and sexuality needs to give way to a discursive account of the cultural production of gender. If Riviere's analysand is a homosexual without homosexuality, that may be because that option is already refused her; the cultural existence of this prohibition is there in the lecture space, determining and differentiating her as speaker and her mainly male audience. Although she fears that her castrating wish might be understood, she denies that there is a contest over a common object of desire without which the masculine identification that she does acknowledge would lack its confirmation and essential sign. Indeed, her account presupposes the primacy of aggression over sexuality, the desire to castrate and take the place of the masculine subject, a desire avowedly rooted in a rivalry, but one which, for her, exhausts itself in the act of displacement. But the question might usefully be asked: What sexual fantasy does this aggression serve, and what sexuality does it authorize? Although the right to occupy the position of a language user is the ostensible purpose of the analysand's aggression, we can ask whether there is not a repudiation of the feminine that prepares this position within speech and which, invariably, re-emerges as the Phallic-Other that will phantasmatically confirm the authority of the speaking subject?

We might then rethink the very notions of masculinity and femininity constructed here as rooted in unresolved homosexual cathexes. The melancholy refusal/domination of homosexuality culminates in the incorporation of the same-sexed object of desire and re-emerges in the construction of discrete sexual 'natures' that require and institute their opposites through exclusion. To presume the primacy of bisexuality or the primary characterization of the libido as masculine is still not to account for the construction of these various 'primacies.' Some psychoanalytic accounts would argue that femininity is based in the exclusion of the masculine, where the masculine is one 'part' of a bisexual psychic composition. The coexistence of the binary is assumed, and then repression and exclusion intercede to craft discretely gendered 'identities' out of this binary, with the result that identity is always already inherent in a bisexual disposition that is, through repression, severed into its component parts. In a sense, the binary restriction on culture postures as the precultural bisexuality that sunders into heterosexual familiarity through its advent into 'culture.' From the start, however, the binary restriction on sexuality shows clearly that culture in no way postdates the bisexuality that it purports to repress: It constitutes the matrix of intelligibility through which primary bisexuality itself becomes thinkable. The 'bisexuality' that is posited as a psychic foundation and is said to be repressed at a later date is a discursive production that claims to be prior to all discourse, effected through the compulsory and generative exclusionary practices of normative heterosexuality.

[. . .]

Notes

1 Joan Riviere (1986) 'Womanliness as a Masquerade', in Victor Burgin, James Donald, Cora Kaplan (eds), *Formations of Fantasy*, London: Methuen, pp. 35–44.

2 Stephen Heath, 'Joan Riviere and the Masquerade', ibid., pp. 45–61.

(b) Queering the visual

Chapter 39

Thomas Waugh

THE THIRD BODY

Patterns in the construction of the subject in gay male narrative film

Prelude: Victorian gay photography and its invisible subject

NINETEENTH-CENTURY HOMOEROTIC photography established a constellation of three types in its construction of the male body. The three bodies can be glimpsed through the photographs of Wilhelm von Gloeden, the Prussian aesthete and archetypal gay Victorian who worked in Taormina, Sicily, until his death in 1931. Two objects of the homoerotic gaze, the ephebe and the 'he-man' (the adolescent youth and the mature athlete, respectively) constituted polar figures in his work. The ephebe, Ganymede, was by far the most popular body type in the erotic repertory of the Victorian gay imaginary. He reflected both cultural justifications derived from the classical pastoral model, and economic and social realities of the period. The ephebe in drag was an important subcategory: cross-gender motifs offered not only an image of nineteenth-century sexological theories of the 'Urning,' or the 'third sex,' a biological in-between, but also a matter-of-fact acknowledgement of the marketplace scale of erotic tastes. The cross-dressed ephebe may also have functioned as an alibi for that homosexuality that dared not fully assume the dimensions of same-sex desire, a reassurance for the masculine-gendered body and identity of the discreet spectator (not to mention the producer and censor).

The ephebe was predominant in von Gloeden, and there were only occasional appearances of the 'he-man,' the Hercules who substitutes maturity for pubescence, squareness for roundness, stiff, active, untouchability for soft, passive accessibility. Apparently not von Gloeden's cup of tea, the he-man was nevertheless very popular with other Victorian photographers, and omnipresent in other cultural spheres, from the Academy to the popular press and postcard industry, that is, in media that were on the surface more respectably homosocial than homosexual.

These two bodies together predicated in turn a third body, an implied gay subject, the invisible desiring body of the producer-spectator – behind the camera, in front of the photograph, but rarely visualized within the frame. The third body, the looking, representing subject, stood in for the authorial self as well as for the assumed gay spectator.

The Victorian homoerotic pattern of visualized objects and invisible subjects replicated those structures of Otherness and sexual difference inherent in all patriarchal Western culture. In fact, in gay culture, as we shall see, those structures seemed even exaggerated, as if to offset the sameness of the same-sex relation, to unbalance the tedious symmetry of the Narcissus image. The ephebe addressed the phallic spectator as older, stronger, more powerful, active, just as surely as the female photographic object addressed its gender opposite, the heterosexual male spectator. At the same time, the he-man object addressed the more 'feminized,' passive body of the homoerotic spectator. As for all the other variables entering Victorian gay iconography, from implied distinctions of class, age, and gender role to Orientalist and classical trappings, these clearly accentuated and elaborated on the basic built-in structures of difference.

In Victorian gay photography the third body, the gay subject, became visible only in the minor genre of the self-portrait. Von Gloeden and his American contemporary Holland Day, both adopting the drag of Christ, anticipated the element of costume and disguise in the gay self-portrait in its later photographic manifestations of our century (think of George Platt Lynes and Robert Mapplethorpe).

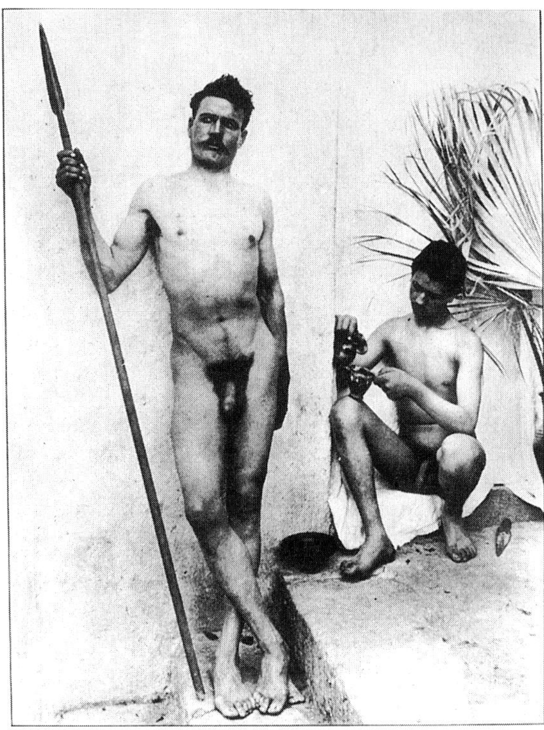

Figure 39.1 A rare convergence of ephebe and he-man in the photography of Wilhelm von Gloeden

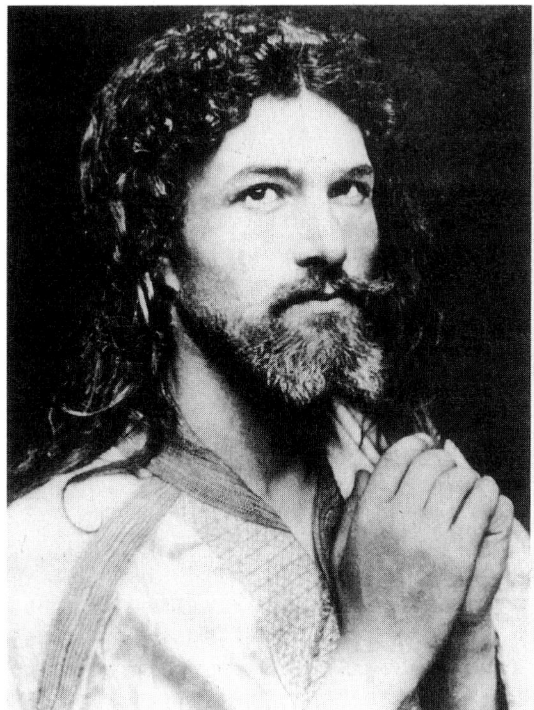

Figure 39.2 Self-portrait of von Gloeden as a Christ in disguise

Twentieth-century gay cinema and its visible subject

In the twentieth century, it is gay male filmmakers, competing with photographers as prophets of the homosexual body, who most definitely take up the job of constructing the gay subject. In the gay-authored narrative cinema, as gay themes become more and more explicit after the Second World War, filmmakers replace the alibis of their photographer precursors with an agenda of self-representation and self-definition. At the same time, they unfreeze the iconicity of the photographic body with the identificatory drive of narration and characterization. From his obscure corner in the photographic corpus, the third body finally enters the foreground of the image, alongside the ephebe and the he-man, the objects of his desire. In the new configuration of character types, the cinema provides two points of entry for the gay spectator: a site for identification with the narrative subject, and a site for specular erotic pleasure in his object.

Within a gay narrative universe that remains remarkably constant across the seventy-five year span of my cinematic corpus, 1916–90, the gay subject consistently accomplishes twin functions. On the one hand, he enacts a relationship of desire – constituted through the specular dynamics basic to the classical narrative cinema, the diegetic and the extra-diegetic gaze – and on the other, he enacts certain narrative functions that are more specific to the gay imaginary. These functions often have a literally *discursive* operation within the diegetic world. To be specific, the gay subject takes on one of, or a combination of, several recurring social roles, namely those of the artist, the intellectual, and/or the teacher. In other words, to complete the mythological triangle, Ganymede and Hercules are figured alongside, and are imagined, represented, and desired by, a third body type that is a hybrid of oracle, centaur, mentor . . . and satyr.

The gay subject looks at and desires the object within the narrative. As artist-intellectual he also bespeaks him, constructs him, projects him, fantasizes him, in short, *represents* him. He fucks with him rarely, alas, seldom consummating his desire as he would within the master narrative of the (hetero) partriarchal cinema built on the conjugal drive. The dualities set up by both photographers and film-makers – mind and body, voice and image, subject and object, self and other, site for identification and site for pleasure – these dualities remain literally separate. For the most part, narrative denouements, far from celebrating union, posit separation, loss, displacement, sometimes death, and, at the very most, open-endedness. Yet, at the same time, the denouement may also involve an element of identity transformation or affirmation. In fact the assertion of identity, the emergence from the closet (to use a post-Stonewall concept), is often a basic dynamic of the plot, usually paired with an acceptance of the above separation, and signalled by telling alterations in the costumes that we shall come to in a moment. Through all of these patterns, the same-sex imaginary preserves and even heightens the structures of sexual difference inherent in Western (hetero) patriarchal culture but usually stops short of those structures' customary dissolution in narrative closure. In other words, the protagonists of this alternative gay rendering of the conjugal drive, unlike their hetero counterparts, seldom end up coming together. We don't establish families – we just wander off looking horny, solitary, sad, or dead. Or, as I said with denunciatory fervor along with everyone else in the 1970s, gay closures are seldom happy endings (Waugh 1977).

Costumes

The physicality of the gay subject is cloaked, like Grandfather von Gloeden in various corporal, vestimentary, and narrative costumes, which are in sharp contrast to the sensuous idealized bareness of his object, whether the he-man's squareness or the ephebe's androgynous curves. The third body puts on costumes as readily as the objects of his desire take them off. The element of costume has several resonances. First, it is obviously a disguise, a basic term of homosexuals' survival as an invisible, stigmatized minority. Second, it operates to desexualize the subject within an erotophobic regime in which nudity articulates sexual desirability. Finally, costume is a cultural construction, which sets up the nudity of the object as some kind of idealized natural state, but at the same time acknowledges the historical contingency and discursive provenance of sociosexual identity, practice, and fantasy.

The costumes of the gay subject are familiar markers from the repertory of cinematic realism, drawing singly or in combination from a roster of attributes, each attribute predicating its opposite in the narrative object of desire. Thus we have:

1 *age* as opposed to the greater *youth* of the object (e.g. *Mikael* or *Montreal Main*);

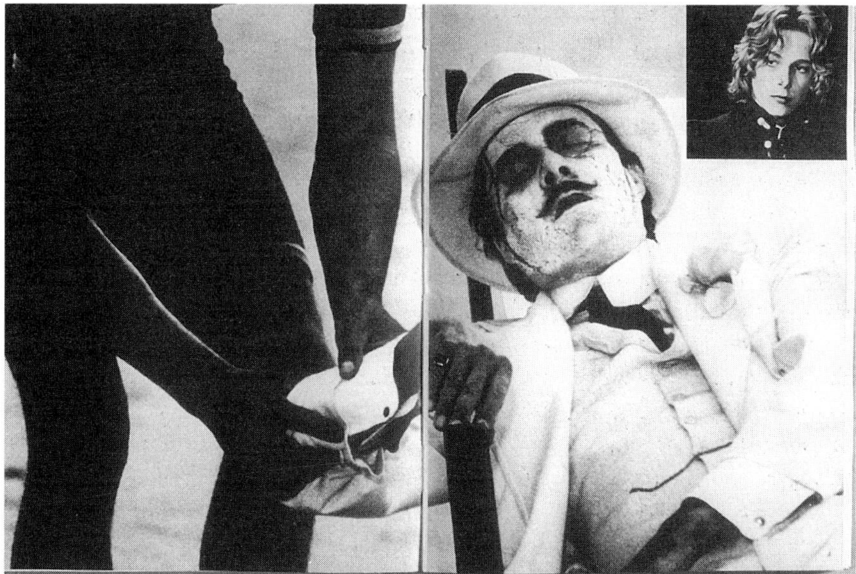

Figure 39.3 The disguise and mortality of the gay subject in *Death in Venice*, 1971 (Dir. Luchino Visconti; Courtesy Warner Bros)

2 *class privilege* as opposed to *peasant, proletarian or lumpen* affinities e.g. *Ludwig* or *Ernesto*);
3 *cultural-racial privilege* as opposed to identities that are *less white*, or *less European* (e.g. *Arabian Nights*, *Prick Up Your Ears*, and *Mala Noche*);
4 *clothing* connoting all of the above, as opposed to *nudity* (e.g. *A Bigger Splash* or *Flesh*);
5 *bodily condition*, by which I mean markers such as eyeglasses, makeup, obesity, disease, and mortality, as opposed to *beauty*, *strength*, and *health* (e.g. *Death in Venice*, *Caravaggio*);
6 *gender role* as opposed to its complement (this pair is a reversible term; if the subject is feminized, the object is often masculinized, and vice versa, with narrative oppositions of active–passive or powerful–submissive assigned either in the traditional gender configuration (e.g. *Flesh*, *The Naked Civil Servant*); or
7 its *inverse*, that is, with the object exerting control over the subject (e.g. *Querelle*, *Sebastiane*).

Shifting ground

All of these narrative functions and layers of narrative costumes constitute a mosaic of the gay self, the third body, which subtends the corpus of the gay-authored narrative cinema from the First World War to the present. Certain films stand out as prototypes of successive generations of the gay imaginary. Under the shadow of the German civil rights campaign of the Scientific Humanitarian Committee (1897–1933), the pair of films based on the gay novel *Mikael*, by Mauritz Stiller

(1916) and Carl Dreyer (1924) respectively, together with the German social-reform narrative feature *Anders als die Anderen* (1919), produce the jilted artist and the violinist blackmail victim as the first gay subjects of the cinema.

In the considerably more repressed period after the Second World War, the works of Anger, Fontaine, and Warhol elaborate obliquely on the pattern. They tease out heightened and ambiguous tensions with spectator voyeurism and construct a gay subject that is partly obscured, displaced, or off-screen. In the early 1970s, Visconti's *Death in Venice* and Pasolini's 'Trilogy of Life' converge as a final celebration of a departed (fantasized?) sexual regime, as if to deny the rumblings of Stonewall (not to mention the women's movement) on the other side of the Atlantic. Their younger contemporaries, like Larkin, Hazan, Peck, Fassbinder (*Germany in Autumn*), and Benner situate the gay subject within a complex, curiously antiseptic universe where visions of post-Stonewall affirmation are often achieved at a cost. Interestingly, in all of these latter films, the gay subjects' strong nonsexual relationships with women rival the inter-male subject–object sexuality for dramatic space.

Finally, the flood of 1980s updates – the British pair *Caravaggio* and *Looking for Langston* dispelling the shadow of Section 28, the Canadian *Urinal*, the Dutch *A Strange Love Affair*, the Spanish *Law of Desire*, the numerous American entries from *Abuse* to *Torch Song Trilogy* – are all eclectic, postmodern renditions of the traditional configuration of the gay artist-intellectual, situated on various strata of the cultural hierarchy and in different relations to gay subcultural constituencies. These entries of the last prolific decade all reflect (implicitly or explicitly) shifting sensibilities and cultural-political strategies in the face of the antigay backlash and the Pandemic. Significantly, all reclaim the sensuous Pasolinian eroticism which the Stonewall pioneers had somehow downplayed.

As for the object types, Victorian iconography has undergone a radical shift as twentieth-century gay male culture has evolved. The predominant icon of the modern gay erotic imaginary, the he-man (in his postwar ghetto incarnations as 'trade,' 'clone,' and bodybuilder) has gradually supplanted the ephebe, in both his straight and 'in-betweenist' shapes. Aside from some important exceptions, the ephebe is now relegated to stigmatized specialty tastes within gay culture. When young Thomas Mann imagined an ephebe at the center of his novella *Death in Venice* in 1911, he was in stride with his generation, but when old Luchino Visconti translated that vision literally onto the screen sixty years later, it now seemed nostalgic and anachronistic within the rapidly changing gay cultural context. It is symbolically apt that the professorial protagonist of *A Strange Love Affair* supplants his original ephebe object with the latter's decidedly bearish old dad. The decline of the ephebe stems perhaps from the tightening taboos on pedophilia within sociomedical-juridical discourse, but no doubt more fundamentally from changing conceptions of the economic role and sexual identity of the child, and the emergence of youth culture with its (post-)pubescent subject. No doubt as well, the gay imaginary has dared more and more to desire (and represent the desire for) objects with with no alibi of femininity, but the trend away from the ephebe was clear well before Gay Liberation took hold. One perhaps symptomatic development of postwar gay sensibilities is the emergence of a hybrid object, the body of the he-man with the mind of the ephebe, incarnated archetypally by (Little!) Joe

Dallesandro and the cowboy hustlers of *The Boys in the Band* and *Midnight Cowboy* (the last decade may have mercifully reversed that trend). Regardless, the object type of our dreams may have fluctuated, but the figure of the artist-intellectual remains an all-embracing constant.

The queen

One important variation of the gay artist figure is the queen, whether aggressively lustful or passively pining. Though the queen does not always have the obvious discursive narrative function of the artist-intellectual, no one will deny that she discourses in her active way in the construction of gender, body, and identity. The queen inherits gender markers from her Victorian third-sex precursor, the ephebe in drag, but these markers now adorn the gay subject rather than the gay object. In some manifestations, the queenly subject may even push gender markers into the realm of biology, whether real or silicone, whether as transvestite, transsexual, or even as heterosexual woman, all incarnating to a greater or lesser degree the desiring gay male subject. Though Molly Haskell (1974) and Pauline Kael (1981) thought they'd cleverly unmasked the insidious phenomenon of gay men hiding in the bodies of heterosexual heroines in Tennessee Williams and George Cukor respectively, in fact the most vivid recurring example in the corpus comes from the Warhol-Morrissey oeuvre. Here, queens as biologically diverse as Taylor Meade and Holly Woodlawn join 'real women' Jane Goforth and Viva in playing the gay male subject, often competing for (though never obtaining) the films' limp and sleepy dreamboat objects like Joe Dallesandro.

The artist

What does it mean for the gay subject to be translated so often as a figure operating diegetically as a discursive agent, namely as artist or intellectual or queen? No doubt many factors are in play. On the one hand, two ideals are inherited from precinematic gay literary traditions: first the ideal of pedagogic Eros, the Socratic intergenerational initiation (the two silent adaptations of *Mikael* present a mentor relationship where the sexual object is simultaneously artistic apprentice and model), and second the aesthete or dandy, member of a refined and sensitive elite. Wilde's *Picture of Dorian Gray* may not have been the first work to posit artistic representation as some kind of metaphoric analogue of gay identity, and the artist-intellectual as the gay prototype, but it is undoubtedly the Ur-text of the third body narratives.

On the other hand, a documentary dimension to the artist figure is also significant in so far as he embodies a sociological acknowledgment of a sector where gays traditionally are disproportionately visible, sheltered, and nurtured. More specifically, an autobiographical discourse can be read on a quite literal level. What else to make of Visconti, in his sixties, undertaking his final progression of portraits of aging artistic figures: composer, patron, and connoisseur, respectively in *Death in Venice*, *Ludwig*, and *Conversation Piece*? The autobiographical possibility is dramatically foregrounded in that small group of 'avant-garde' works, mostly nonfiction, by Werner Schroeter, R.W. Fassbinder, George Kuchar, Rosa von Praunheim, Derek Jarman, and Curt McDowell, where the filmmaker plays himself as gay artist literally integrating sexual expression and artistic creation. Of course, Pasolini's performance as artist in two installments of his trilogy is a unique and sublime variation of this pattern in narrative fiction. The autobiographical reading of the gay artist figure may be better understood by comparing it with the important role of autobiographical writing in the cultural affirmations of other disenfranchised groups, from women to blacks.

Another perspective on the artist figure assumes an analogy between the Romantic moment of artistic inspiration/crisis and the gay ritual of coming out. Pasolini's *Teorema* does exactly that, when aspiring painter Pietro has sex with Terence Stamp and calls into question his entire vocation: Action Painting becomes Piss Art (Stamp as homoerotic object has had a similar devastating impact in other films as well, from *Billy Budd* to *Far from the Madding Crowd*, and his androgynous compatriots, Dirk Bogarde and Michael York, have shown similar propensities – there's a thesis in there somewhere).

Perhaps at a more profound psychosexual level is the issue of empowerment, both individual and collective. Does the artistic control of model and scenario, guaranteed by professional protocol, social status and/or class privilege, translate into a fantasy of general sexual empowerment in a hostile social setting? Does specific sexual control of the body of the loved one represent a symbolic victory over repression?

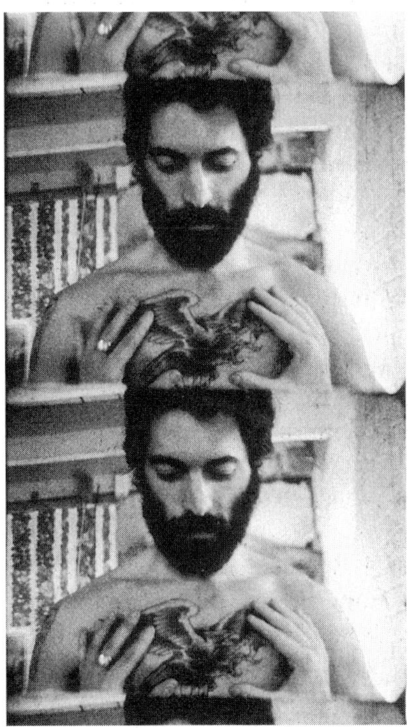

Figure 39.4 Autobiography: the filmmaker Curt McDowell's hands in *Loads*

The incarnation of the gay subject as artist connotes a sense of presence in the world that is one of thought and feeling as opposed to action; of desire rather than consummation; of representing as if in revenge for the nonrepresentation of gayness in official culture; of observation as if in retaliation for the increasing surveillance we have been subjected to from the start of this chronology.

Narrative role: the look and the voice

Sexual looking is, of course, a highly charged activity in our culture, all the more so for the same-sex look that ventures outside of certain carefully controlled areas (such as sport). The artist figure, then, at the most pragmatic level, has recourse to a traditional high-status alibi, and thereby legitimizes sexual looking and representation. Furthermore, the artist-intellectual is traditionally an outsider type in our culture (as is the queen in her simultaneous embrace and rejection of disguise). The artist's outsider vantage point fuses with that of the sexual outlaw in patriarchal culture. The image of Caravaggio watching the goings-on of the papal court, or of Aschenbach on the porch of the Venice hotel, is that of both the alienated artist charting the machinations of social power from the wings, and the gay man tuning into the sexual undercurrents of his surroundings. The gay artist figure exposes and concentrates the networks of sexual looking and being-looked-at within gay narrative and within gay culture, and, in fact, within Western patriarchal culture as a whole.

Two interesting variations in the scenario of the look must also be noted:

1 *The return of the look of the sexual object.* The subject's model, initiate, or sexual object looking back can be a key moment in the narrative of the third body, hinting tantalizingly at the possible union of subject and object. Remember Tadzio's complicit look back as *Death in Venice* draws to a close – a look of acceptance and reciprocity, perhaps a challenge to the act of voyeurism as well (this look back is incidentally a key addition that Visconti brought to the Mann novella). In some cases, the returned look of the object can so dominate or unsettle or overturn the narrative structure that an entirely new narrative mythos emerges, the object as subject – as in Fassbinder's groundbreaking *Querelle* or its realist precursor *Fox and His Friends*, or in Derek Jarman's *Sebastiane*. More literal instances are those moments in 1980s' works like *Looking for Langston* and *Law of Desire*, where the object looks directly at the camera and the spectator, thus subverting both the subject-object dynamic and the narrative syntax of voyeuristic pleasure.
2 *The voice of the subject.* In many cases, the look of the gay subject is activated by or signified by his voice, namely through the mechanism of disembodied voice-over narration. It might be argued that the preponderance of voice-over narrations in gay fictional cinema reflects only the low-budget artisanal level of the production, as in *My Hustler* or *Loads*, or in physique movie mogul Dick Fontaine's overdubbing of his classic erotic shorts with a giddy voice-over by queenly commentator Glory Holden. However, the voice-over has lingered as an aesthetic strategy in nonartisanal cinema, throughout entire

films such as *Looking for Langston* or in key moments such as the porn-dubbing opening sequence of *Law of Desire*.

The voice-over, emitting from the body of author-subject as he retreats once more behind the camera, may impart a level of retroactive self-reflexivity, as in *Caravaggio* and *Loads*. This voice may also enact a simultaneous sportscasting relationship to the erotic action of the camera's gaze, as in *My Hustler*, or the gay cable video genre represented by a mid-1980s New York work like *How to Seduce a Preppie* (Rick X). With both options, the effect is to amplify the outsider status of the gay subject, to cement the irreconcilability of subject and object, and to indulge in a deliriously self-conscious game of voyeurism that at the same time problematizes and exults in the subject's look. In *Langston* and *Querelle*, external and literary voices engage in a multivocal address of and by the gay subject. The often disembodied quotations and overlapping voices create a distancing, multivalent effect.

The erotic cinema

Many of the foregoing titles, because of the oblique or direct eroticism of their address, call for a momentary digression to consider how the third body pattern pertains to that disreputable mirror of the narrative cinema, the erotic cinema proper. Since no gay fiction is far from the erotic impulse that is central to all gay (popular) culture, it is not surprising that the third body makes an appearance in the erotic cinema as well, yet with an important inflection. Here, the gay subject is both absent and present: absent as in the erotic photograph, even in the pinup layout's narrative modes, for the gay subject seems invisible and is assumed to be off-screen. Yet the gay subject is also present, in the sense that subject and object within the diegesis are often fused, and these roles are dispersed interchangeably among all the bodies within the frame. It is a question, to paraphrase Mingus, the legendary, pseudonymous, porn reviewer of the *New York Native*, of confusion and ambiguity between the men we want to be and the men we want to love, in other words, between subject and object. Mingus goes on to argue that this confusion emerged with what I've called the decline of the ephebe, which he situates in the late 1950s, before which there was a clear dichotomy between adolescent object and 'dirty old john over thirty' (the exact point of this historical threshold needs further study at the very least). Nevertheless, this current (con)fusion of subject and object is highlighted by the artist-intellectual figures who people the porno formulas. For they are indeed stock characters in gay film, including the writer-researcher (usually of porno novels), the photographer, and the journalist. The list expands if one includes the porno world's variations on the Socratic mentor: the track coach, the sex doctor, and the Marine officer. With these figures, who are homoerotic objects as well as subjects, most of the tensions of difference that structure the licit fiction disappear; artist and model, subject and object, self and other, he-man and third body, become all but indistinguishable in bodily construction (except for the occasional differences in race, age, body, consciousness, and sometimes other factors that recall but usually don't replicate the original structures of opposition). In this minimization of difference, it is interesting to locate gay eroticism's most essential distinctiveness alongside heterosexual eroticism, in whose narrative world difference is always visualized at its most extreme form, that is, as *gender* difference.

Positive image/happy ending, or the failure of gay liberation criticism

The foregoing attempt at a taxonomy of gay-authored narrative cinema as a trans-historical, transcultural corpus, this project of defining the gay subject as third body, as incarnation of difference and enactor of representation, is not without methodological stresses. Aside from the dangers of gay essentialism lurking in any cross-cultural and transhistorical study, does this taxonomy in fact constitute genre criticism without a genre (in the sense that the necessary continuing dialogue between genre author and genre audience would seem missing with this retroactively constructed, discontinuous corpus that is the gay art cinema)? Is this auteur criticism without an auteur (in the sense that the gay author is constructed collectively and retroactively on the basis of thematic consistence and biographical knowledge that in many cases are invisible to the ordinary spectator)? Or is this a structuralist inventory of narrative archetypes and functions without the necessary mythological coherence of a discrete host culture (unless the international network of gay subcultures that are the pillar of the 'art cinema' constituency can be considered a coherent 'culture')? (Of course, these problems tend to dissolve with the 1980s corpus, since the new breed of young gay directors have been very much plugged into their gay constituency, and the international circuit of gay festivals has begun to consolidate something like real gay genres, gay audiences, and gay authors, arguably for the first time in our history.)

What is clear amid this methodological tentativeness is that traditional gay liberation criticism, as exemplified in the post-Stonewall decade by the ethic-aesthetic of the positive image, would see, and has usually seen, the foregoing corpus as irredeemable traffic in negative stereotypes. A familiar litany of 'bad images' can readily be drawn up from the films I've discussed: the young, silenced, and objectified sex object, attracting but never reciprocating the lustful gaze of the aging, bourgeois, libertine predator; the sensitive yet self-destructive artist; the wilting pansy; the dead queer.

In short, the 'positive image' perspective founders before this corpus assembled around authorship and sexual orientation, and has no power to explain the irresistible attraction by gay authors to images that seem harmful in the viewfinders of movement ideologues. Is the attraction to the 'negative image' by the the gay author simply a question of self-oppression, as we assumed in the 1970s? Or is it a kind of existential reappropriation of stigma, a Genetesque, defiant inoculation against the denigration of the stereotype? Is it a preference for the exclusive marginality of the damned, rather than the anonymous absorption entailed by the civil rights/gay liberation platform? Is it a Pasolinian refusal of the consumerism and conformism of the liberal utopia? Or is it simply, as Dyer would have it, the adaptation by an invisible minority of the only available system of coding for self-definition (Dyer, 'Homosexuality and Film Noir' 1977)? All of these possibilities no doubt enter into play, but too often we have avoided them, relying instead on reductive moralism instead of criticism.

For all of the indisputable magnitude of the late Vito Russo's contribution to gay cultural history, as a populist polemicist he did have certain blind spots around gay authors of the art cinema. Russo's famous 'Necrology' of the cinema's dead queers in *The Celluloid Closet* contains not a few gay authors (though several obvious entrants have inexplicably been sifted out, such as Fassbinder and Pasolini). His dismissal of *Ludwig* ('Sleeping with a stable boy rots your teeth') is a scandalous rejection of one of the few serious, gay-authored works to attempt to imagine nineteenth-century cultural and sexual sensibilities (Russo 1987: 336). But Russo was not alone: remember the fierce polemics in many gay community newspapers around Fassbinder's *Fox*, around semi-mainstream films, from *La Cage aux Folles* to *Kiss of the Spider Woman*, and around Dyer's and Jack Babuscio's useful articles on 'camp'. Even Dyer seemed to contradict his own sensible discussion of stereotypes and a social typing strategically useful for the gay liberation project of self-definition by his later uncharacteristically moralistic broadside against Pasolini's *Arabian Nights* (Dyer, 'Stereotyping,' 1977; Dyer, 'Pasolini,' 1977). My own record is by no means spotless in this regard: I still cringe when I remember my 1978 denunciation of *Sebastiane* for its 'cloyingly pompous stylization, visual and dramatic vacuum,' and 'tawdry jumble of s-m formulae,' with the parting shot that 'the only thing that distinguishes *Sebastiane* from the realm of the soft core is the honesty of the latter.' In short, while the positive-image gay critic has usually been dead-on in his targeting of the *Cruisings* of the (hetero) patriarchal entertainment industry and has effectively revolutionized the reception of mainstream media within gay culture, he has too often gunned for the fragile butterflies of gay expression within the art cinema as well, and with counterproductive effect. Of course, feminists, too, have had to grapple with the negative image issue: for example, over the past decade, New York lesbian independents Lizzie Borden, Sheila McLaughlin, and Su Friedrich have insisted on dealing upfront in their films with previously 'negative' iconography of woman as victim, sex worker, butch/femme, and nun respectively.

Our uneasy relationships with the tragic or ironic sensibilities of the great gay art-house filmmakers of the post-Stonewall generation continue – from Visconti and Pasolini to Fassbinder and Almodovar (our relationship with cult gay authors from Morrissey-Warhol to Waters has been only marginally better). Our reluctance to become the gay constituency they deserved has been due in no small way to the failure of a whole generation of gay critics to understand the contradictions of the international art cinema marketplace within which so many of these authors were circulated.

The institution of the art cinema stalled the development of a discrete gay constituency in two ways: through the ambivalence of its discourse, and through the crossover constitution of its audience. Textually speaking, the art house/film festival product usually offers a something-for-everyone blend of intellectualism and ambiguity, and an aura of recuperable marginality. The 'exotic' articulation of taboo desire alongside its simultaneous disavowal, this cinema hovers on a tightrope between high-cultural status and subversive subcultural chic. Gay cinephiles are offered a mixed package, just the right blend of melodramatic catharsis, social justification provided through visibility alone, and finally an adequate dose of skin, albeit ultimately frustrated through the forever-receding closure of the open ending.

The demographic mosaic of the art house audience also enters the picture. If the gay spectator cements his identification with the gay subject through the voyeuristic sighting of the gay object, non-gay spectators, one can speculate, attach their voyeuristic fix on the gay subject himself, shaped through discourses of stereotype, freakshow, and pathos/victimization. For non-gay constituencies and critics, gay directors' tragic sensibilities seemed a tautological adjunct of marginality. Meanwhile, straight critics actively stifled gay discourses around these films, either through homophobic panic, liberal tolerance ('I'm so matter-of-fact and cool that sexual orientation doesn't have to be mentioned'), or allegorical exegesis ('This film is not about gayness, it's about fill-in-the-blank'). If the built-in ambiguity of the narrative codes of the art cinema allowed gay authors space to create, it denied them the chance to nurture a continuous and coherent gay audience. Instead, we remained invisible and covert spectators, a divided and discontinuous audience.

The inadequate critical context set the tone for the expectations and tastes of gay audiences in the rare moments when they were constituted as a discrete group, most often through the gay festivals that started cropping up in large markets in the 1970s (a similar abdication of critical responsibility affected the other discrete gay market, the porno scene). Even seasoned gay festival audiences still lean towards the happy-ending, positive-image standard, with a preference for *intimiste* domestic or romantic melodramas with open – but not *too* open – endings; and this after almost two decades of gay programming. Some post-Liberation gay filmmakers have excelled within the melodrama genre – think of Frank Ripploh, the late Bill Sherwood, the late Artie Bressan, or Quebec's Michel Tremblay (in his screenwriter's hat) – namely through developing strong and authentic emotional hooks on lifestyle issues within the ghetto. The melodrama's validity as a format of gay popular culture is without question, having delivered some of the 1980s' undisputed masterpieces. However, the development of the gay melodrama hardly constituted the appearance 'at last' of *the* gay cinema, as each successive new work from *Taxi Zum Klo* to *Longtime Companion* was greeted by both gay and straight blurbists. As for the Pandemic's impact on the mythic landscape, ACT UP's exemplary cultural politics may have stimulated a new creative energy in the cultural margins and on community levels, but the health crisis's impact on feature-length independent fiction has been largely to enrich this important melodrama tradition – think of *Buddies*, *Death in the Family*, and *Parting Glances*, all precursors of that mother of all melodramas, *Longtime Companion*.

Reinventing the third body/gay subjects in the 1980s and 1990s

Aside from this healthy melo current, the third body pattern maintained its currency at the end of the 1980s, and is still in the process of being reinvented by the young, post-Stonewall authors (who are still incidentally far ahead of their critical constituency for the most part, though the gap may be closing). In another context, Richard Dyer describes this work as 'post-affirmation,' 'films that manage to deconstruct without auto-destructing, that leave behind without anguish the fixed identifiers affirmed by earlier films, that seem to enjoy the struggle with definitions of identity as an ongoing process' (Dyer 1990: 284). In the recent renditions of the third body films, the separation of subject and object is no longer a given, nor is the fixity of observer status, the immutability of difference, or the infinite deferral of closure. The gay subject emerges now dialectically, for example, as a comic subject rather than tragic, through parodic quotation or through reversals. Risks are taken with 'dangerous' or negative imagery (I am sure that for Almodovar the concept of the positive image is an inscrutable aberration of Protestantism), sexual pleasure is reclaimed and celebrated as much as it is problematized, humor and anger are as characteristic as the melancholy of yore.

Fassbinder's relentless exploration of the subjectivity of the object and the power dynamics of desire in *Fox*, *In a Year of Thirteen Moons*, and *Querelle*, and Jarman's not-dissimilar experiment in *Sebastiane*, have now proven to be prophetic of a whole spectrum of work, from the haunting *L'Homme Blessé* (Patrice Chéreau, 1983) to the infuriating *A Virus Knows No Morals*. Meanwhile, Jarman's idols Genet and Pasolini reawaken as the presiding spirits of the end of the century.

Jarman's two non-white compatriots Hanif Kureishi and Isaac Julien both explode the patterns of subject–object difference predicated on white, middle-class subject and racial Other, superimposing contradictory grids of identity, involving race, class, gender, and sex, and making new connections and coalitions from grid to grid. Julien goes further than Kureishi's fundamentally populist, realist framework to disperse the subject, and yet collectivize him at the same time, disallowing the individualist readings encouraged by art cinema's fetishization of psychological realism.

While Julien reclaims the gay subject from buried racial, cultural, and sexual history, John Greyson reclaims dozens of them, offering his historical reconstructions of everyone from Aschenbach and Kipling to Foucault and (Rock) Hudson. This video artist offers essayistic hypernarrative formats, mattter-of-factly peopled by self-conscious and lascivious gay artist-intellectual subjects from the pre-Stonewall era, who have come back to haunt the post-Liberation gay sensibility. Is this recuperation of gay history or a tongue-in-cheek postmodern version of the old gay community ritual of citing the famous fags of history from Plato to Liberace (a self-affirming ritual which in any case has undoubtedly been more responsible for the momentum of the 'third body' narrative than I have acknowledged)? Whatever, in *Urinal*, Greyson's first feature film, Sergei Eisenstein tries to seduce not an object type but another subject, Langston Hughes. More at home in the toilet stall than the art house, he squints through a glory hole, not at an ephebe or he-man, but at the parade of gay artist subjects who now become recycled as postmodern pastiche, at the ferment of sexual politics in the cultural horizon of the present, at the collapse of the public and the private and, at the same time, happily, at the still-undiminished, infinite, and delirious possibilities of the (homo)sexual body.

Three of Greyson's subjects are lesbian artists, sketched with his traditionally impeccable gender parity. Greyson however certainly did not invent the lesbian third body narrative. In fact the sudden emergence of a flood of lesbian-authored variants of the form in the mid-1980s, each with its own incarnation of the artist-intellectual subject, made a major contribution to its reinvention. The list includes works by Su Friedrich, Patricia Rozema, Elfi Mikesch, Lizzie Borden, Sheila McLaughlin, Léa Pool, Chantal Akerman, and perhaps Sally Potter, with associate status for Liliana Cavani and Jill Godmilow (for her non-lesbian-authored, nonsexual Gertie and Alice). Donna Deitch has a place, albeit tenuous, in our category as well, since *Desert Hearts* occupies the borderland between art film narrative and pop romance, and Helen Shaver's status as an intellectual is more a question of script exposition and wardrobe than of narrative function. Léa Pool's *A Corps Perdu* (*Straight to the Heart*, 1988), her follow-up to *Anne Trister*, may also belong as a lesbian-authored version of the gay male third body narrative, with the subject this time a photographer. This is not to say that the specularization of eroticism, the problematization of subject–object relations, or the autobiographical resonances in the lesbian films are identical to the gay male formulations – far from it. Whether the lesbian films constitute a transmigration or spontaneous combustion, whether or not they confirm the pattern as a basic cultural structure of same-sex sexuality, or as just a genre of art cinema with a new lease on life, they clearly second Greyson's demonstration that the third body narrative – the subject as artist-intellectual and gender transgressor – is large and flexible enough to absorb each generation's and each constituency's particular mythic projection and political challenges.

The continuous thread from von Gloeden and Stiller on through Jarman and Greyson is of course neither as continuous or as threadlike as might be inferred. The new breed of the 1980s notwithstanding, the battles are far from over. The spurts and starts sometimes seem as uneven as ever, especially as the crisis in non-Hollywood film financing deepens around the world, gay or straight, and the flourishing gay festival circuit still can't finance a single feature budget. The lures of success are also as insidious as ever (will the *Poison* of today become the *Tie Me Up Tie Me Down* of tomorrow?), and the bowdlerization of gay history in the mainstream biopic seems as obnoxious as ever (was Charlton Heston's Michelangelo in *The Agony and the Ecstasy* really any worse than the recent Canadian Whitman travesty *Beautiful Dreamers* or the Hollywood 'straightening out' of Sir Richard Burton in *Mountains of the Moon*?). Still, for all the continued lurching back and forth, in and out of the closet threshold zone of self-censorship dictated by state-supported art film financing, for all the occasional rubbing thin of the 'third body' thread, it shows surprisingly little danger of unraveling in the 1990s. For gay and now lesbian artists and audiences, the narrative art cinema, poised halfway between the quagmires of Hollywood and the uncompromising nontheatrical fringes of the radical avant-garde, continues to be an indispensable forum for confronting the world and ourselves.

The third body: a select filmography of the gay male subject as artist, intellectual, and queen

Titles are in approximate chronological order; works are presumed gay- or bisexual-authored, with authorship sometimes defined to include scriptwriter or, in the case of adaptations, author of original source material.

Mauritz Stiller, *The Wings* (*Vingarne*) (Sweden, 1916); sculptor – first adaptation of Herman Bang's gay novel *Mikael*.

Richard Oswald and Magnus Hirschfeld, *Anders als die Anderen* [*Different from the Others*] (Germany, 1919); musician.

Carl Dreyer and Herman Bang, *Mikael* (Germany, 1924); painter – second adaptation of *Mikael*.

Jean Cocteau, *Blood of a Poet* (France, 1930); *Orphée* (1949); *Le Testament D'Orphée* (1959); more-or-less autobiographical variations on gay artist as subject.

S.M. Eisenstein, *Ivan the Terrible* (USSR, 1944–46); Czar as proto-gay subject/looker, bodyguards as objects.

Kenneth Anger, *Fireworks* (US, 1948); hybrid formula includes photo-object protagonist.

Dick Fontaine (US, 1950s–60s); physique narrative shorts, many with artist subjects, some narrated by queen voice-over.

Andy Warhol and Paul Morrissey, *My Hustler* (US, 1965); queens compete for object.
Lonesome Cowboys (US, 1968); queens compete for cowboy object.
Flesh (US, 1968); hustler object surrounded by queens and photographer.
Trash (US, 1969); queen and hustler.

Pier Paolo Pasolini, *Teorema* (Italy, 1968); episode around painter/son Pietro.
'Trilogy of Life' (Italy):
The Decameron (1971); PPP as Giotto.
The Canterbury Tales (1972); PPP as Chaucer.
Arabian Nights (1974); episode around Arab poet Abu-Nuwas, etc.

Luchino Visconti, *Death in Venice* (Italy, 1971); composer.
Ludwig (Italy, 1973); patron.
Conversation Piece (Italy, 1974); connoisseur/collector.

John Schlesinger, *Midnight Cowboy* (US, 1969); hybrid melodrama includes gay object as protagonist.
Sunday Bloody Sunday (UK, 1971); hybrid melodrama includes doctor/art-lover as gay subject.

R.W. Fassbinder, *Beware the Holy Whore* (Germany, 1970); filmmaker.
Fox and His Friends (Germany, 19975); prole underdog as object-protagonist surrounded by subject types.
Germany in Autumn (Germany, 1978); RWF episode has real-life filmmaker as subject.
In the Year of Thirteen Moons (Germany, 1978); transsexual.
Querelle (Germany, 1982); sailor as object–protagonist, officer as subject/representer/looker.

Frank Vitale, *Montreal Main* (Canada, 1974); photographer and ephebe.

Jack Hazan, *A Bigger Splash* (UK, 1974); painter and model.

Ryan Larkin, *A Very Natural Thing* (US, 1974); a romantic melodrama with both photographer and teacher as protagonists.

Derek Jarman, *Sebastiane*, (UK, 1976); hybrid includes centurion as gay subject and martyr as gay object/protagonist.
The Tempest (UK, 1979); magician/impresario.
Caravaggio (UK, 1986); painter.

Richard Benner, *Outrageous* (Canada, 1977); *Too Outrageous* (1988); drag performer.

Arturo Ripstein, *A Limitless Place* (Mexico, 1977); drag queen subject.

Jack Gold and Quentin Crisp, *The Naked Civil Servant* (UK, 1977); queen.

Ron Peck, *Nighthawks* (UK, 1978); teacher.

Rosa von Praunheim, *Army of Lovers or the Revolt of the Perverts* (Germany, 1979); documentary author as subject.

Guy Hocquenghem and Lionel Soukaz, *Race d'Ep* (France, 1979); episodes around von Gloeden and Hirschfeld.

Salvatore Samperi and Umberto Saba, *Ernesto* (Italy, 1979); student subject, autobiographical core.

Curt McDowell, *Loads* (US, 1980); documentary author as subject.

Frank Ripploh, *Taxi Zum Klo* (Germany, 1980); domestic melo with teacher subject.

Werner Schroeter, *La Répétition Generale* (France, 1980); documentary author as subject.

The Rose King (Germany, 1986); mother and son compete for ephebe.

Arthur Bressan, *Abuse* (US, 1982); filmmaker and ephebe.

Paul Verhoeven and Gerard Reve, *The Fourth Man* (Netherlands, 1983); writer.

Gus Van Sant, *Mala Noche* (US, 1985); countercultural subject and Chicano ephebe.

Hector Babenco and Herman Puig, *Kiss of the Spider Woman* (US/Brazil, 1985); queen/cinephile as gay subject.

Takis Spetsiotis, *Meteor and Shadow* (Greece, 1985); poet.

Eric de Kuyper, *A Strange Love Affair* (Netherlands, 1985); film studies teacher and ephebe.

Stephen Frears and Hanif Kureishi, *My Beautiful Laundrette* (UK, 1985); entrepreneur.

Bill Sherwood, *Parting Glances* (US, 1986); musician, editor, porn writer.

Michel Tremblay and Jean-Yves Laforce, *Le Coeur Découvert* [*The Heart Exposed*] (Québec, 1987); domestic melo, teacher and actor subjects, child object?

Stephen Frears and Joe Orton, *Prick Up Your Ears*, (UK, 1987); non-gay adaptation of playwright's diaries.

Pedro Almodovar, *Law of Desire* (Spain, 1987); filmmaker.

Isaac Julien, *Looking for Langston* (UK, 1988); poet.

John Greyson, *Urinal* (Canada, 1988); Eisenstein, Mishima, Hughes, Wilde, etc.

Harvey Fierstein, *Torch Song Trilogy* (US, 1989); drag performer.

Marlon Riggs, *Tongues Untied* (US, 1990); autobiographical elements, poet persona.

References

Dyer, Richard. 'Homosexuality and Film Noir,' *Jump Cut* 16 (1977), pp. 18–21.

—— *Now You See It: Studies on Lesbian and Gay Film* (London: Routledge, 1990).

—— 'Pasolini and Homosexuality,' in Paul Willemen (ed.), *Pier Paolo Pasolini* (London: BFI, 1977) pp. 57–63.

—— 'Stereotyping,' in Dyer (ed.), *Gays and Film* (London: BFI, 1977) pp. 27–39.

Haskell, Molly. *From Reverence to Rape: The Treatment of Women in the Movies* (New York: Holt, Rinehart and Winston, 1974).

Kael, Pauline. Review of *Rich and Famous*, in *The New Yorker*, October 26, 1981, rpt. Kael, *Taking It All In* (New York: Holt, Rinehart and Winston, 1984) pp. 247–48.

Mingus (pseud.). *The New York Native*, undated, untitled clipping, *c.*1985.

Russo, Vito. *The Celluloid Closet*, revised edn (New York: Harper and Row, 1987).

Waugh, Thomas. 'Films by Gays for Gays,' *Jump Cut* 16 (1977), pp. 14–16.

—— '*Sebastiane*', *The Body Politic* (March, 1978).

Chapter 40

Judith Butler

GENDER IS BURNING
Questions of appropriation and subversion

> We all have friends who, when they knock on the door and we ask, through the door, the question, 'Who's there?,' answer (since 'it's obvious') 'It's me.' And we recognize that *'it is him,'* or '*her*' [my emphasis]
> (Louis Althusser, 'Ideology and Ideological State Apparatuses')

> The purpose of 'law' is absolutely the last thing to employ in the history of the origin of law: on the contrary . . . the cause of the origin of a thing and its eventual utility, its actual employment and place in a system of purposes, lie worlds apart; whatever exists, having somehow come into being, is again and again reinterpreted to new ends, taken over, transformed, and redirected.
> (Friedrich Nietzsche, *On the Genealogy of Morals*)

IN ALTHUSSER'S NOTION of interpellation, it is the police who initiate the call or address by which a subject becomes socially constituted. There is the policeman, the one who not only represents the law but whose address 'Hey you!' has the effect of binding the law to the one who is hailed. This 'one' who appears not to be in a condition of trespass prior to the call (for whom the call establishes a given practice as a trespass) is not fully a social subject, is not fully subjectivated, for he or she is not yet reprimanded. The reprimand does not merely repress or control the subject, but forms a crucial part of the juridical and social *formation* of the subject. The call is formative, if not *per*formative, precisely because it initiates the individual into the subjected status of the subject.

Althusser conjectures this 'hailing' or 'interpellation' as a unilateral act, as the power and force of the law to compel fear at the same time that it offers recognition at an expense. In the reprimand the subject not only received recognition, but attains as well a certain order of social existence, in being transferred from an outer region of indifferent, questionable, or impossible being to the discursive or social domain of the subject. But does this subjectivation take place as a direct effect of the reprimanding utterance or must the utterance wield the power to compel the fear of punishment and, from that compulsion, to produce a compliance and obedience to the law? Are there other ways of being addressed and constituted by the law, ways of being occupied and occupying the law, that disarticulate the power of punishment from the power of recognition?

Althusser underscores the Lacanian contribution to a structural analysis of this kind, and argues that a relation of misrecognition persists between the law and the subject it compels. Although he refers to the possibility of 'bad subjects,' he does not consider the range of *disobedience* that such an interpellating law might produce. The law might not only be refused, but it might also be ruptured, forced into a rearticulation that calls into question the monotheistic force of its own unilateral operation. Where the uniformity of the subject is expected, where the behavioral conformity of the subject is commanded, there might be produced the refusal of the law in the form of the parodic inhabiting of conformity that subtly calls into question the legitimacy of the command, a repetition of the law into hyperbole, a rearticulation of the law against the authority of the one who delivers it. Here the performative, the call by the law which seeks to produce a lawful subject, produces a set of consequences that exceed and confound what appears to be the disciplining intention motivating the law. Interpellation thus loses its status as a simple performative, an act of discourse with the power to create that to which it refers, and creates more than it ever meant to, signifying in excess of any intended referent.

It is this constitutive failure of the performative, this slippage between discursive command and its appropriated effect, which provides the linguistic occasion and index for a consequential disobedience.

Consider that the use of language is itself enabled by first having been *called a name*; the occupation of the name is that by which one is, quite without choice, situated within discourse. This 'I,' which is produced through the accumulation and convergence of such 'calls,' cannot extract itself from the historicity of that chain or raise itself up and confront that chain as if it were an object opposed to me, which is not me, but only what others have made of me; for that estrangement or division produced by the mesh of interpellating calls and the 'I' who is its site is not only violating, but enabling as well, what Gayatri Spivak refers to as 'an enabling violation.' The 'I' who would oppose its construction is always in some sense drawing from that construction to articulate its opposition; further, the 'I' draws what is called its 'agency' in part through being implicated in the very relations of power that it seeks to oppose. To be *implicated* in the relations of power, indeed, enabled by the relations of power that the 'I' opposes is not, as a consequence, to be reducible to their existing forms.

You will note that in the making of this formulation, I bracket this 'I' in quotation marks, but I am still here. And I should add that this is an 'I' that I produce here for you in response to a certain suspicion that this theoretical project has lost the person, the author, the life; over and against this claim, or rather in response to having been called the site of such an evacuation, I write that this kind of bracketing of the 'I' may well be crucial to the thinking through of the constitutive ambivalence of being socially constituted, where 'constitution' carries both the enabling and violating sense of 'subjection.' If one comes into discursive life through being called or hailed in injurious terms, how might one occupy the interpellation by which one is already occupied to direct the possibilities of resignification against the aims of violation?

This is not the same as censoring or prohibiting the use of the 'I' or of the autobiographical as such; on the contrary, it is the inquiry into the ambivalent relations of power that makes that use possible. What does it mean to have such uses repeated in one's very being, 'messages implied in one's being,' as Patricia Williams claims, only to repeat those uses such that subversion might be derived from the very conditions of violation. In this sense, the argument that the category of 'sex' is the instrument or effect of 'sexism' or its interpellating moment, that 'race' is the instrument and effect of 'racism' or its interpellating moment, that 'gender' only exists in the service of heterosexism, does *not* entail that we ought never to make use of such terms, as if such terms could only and always reconsolidate the oppressive regimes of power by which they are spawned. On the contrary, precisely because such terms have been produced and constrained within such regimes, they ought to be repeated in directions that reverse and displace their originating aims. One does not stand at an instrumental distance from the terms by which one experiences violation. Occupied by such terms and yet occupying them oneself risks a complicity, a repetition, a relapse into injury, but it is also the occasion to work the mobilizing power of injury, of an interpellation one never chose. Where one might understand violation as a trauma which can only induce a destructive repetition compulsion (and surely this is a powerful consequence of violation), it seems equally possible to acknowledge the force of repetition as the very condition of an affirmative response to violation. The compulsion to repeat an injury is not necessarily the compulsion to repeat the injury in the same way or to stay fully within the traumatic orbit of that injury. The force of repetition in language may be the paradoxical condition by which a certain agency – not linked to a fiction of the ego as master of circumstance – is derived from the *impossibility* of choice.

It is in this sense that Irigaray's critical mime of Plato, the fiction of the lesbian phallus, and the rearticulation of kinship in *Paris Is Burning* might be understood as repetitions of hegemonic forms of power which fail to repeat loyally and, in that failure, open possibilities for resignifying the terms of violation against their violating aims. Cather's occupation of the paternal name, Larsen's inquiry into the painful and fatal mime that is passing for white, and the reworking of 'queer' from abjection to politicized affiliation will interrogate similar sites of ambivalence produced at the limits of discursive legitimacy.

The temporal structure of such a subject is chiasmic in this sense: in the place of a substantial or self-determining 'subject,' this juncture of discursive demands is something like a 'crossroads,' to use Gloria Anzaldúa's phrase, a crossroads of cultural and political discursive forces, which she herself claims cannot be understood through the notion of the 'subject.' There is no subject prior to its constructions, and neither is the subject determined by those constructions; it is always the nexus, the nonspace of cultural collision, in which the demand to resignify or repeat the very terms that constitute the 'we' cannot be summarily refused, but neither can they be followed in strict obedience. It is the space of this ambivalence which opens up the possibility of a reworking of the very terms by which subjectivation proceeds – and fails to proceed.

Ambivalent drag

From this formulation, then, I would like to move to a consideration of the film *Paris Is Burning*, to what it suggests about the simultaneous production and subjugation of subjects in a culture which appears to arrange always and in every way for the annihilation of queers, but which nevertheless produces occasional spaces in which those annihilating norms, those killing ideals of gender and race, are mimed, reworked, resignified. As much as there is defiance and affirmation, the creation of kinship and of glory in that film, there is also the kind of reiteration of norms which cannot be called subversive, but which lead to the death of Venus Xtravaganza, a Latina/preoperative transsexual, cross-dresser, prostitute, and member of the 'House of Xtravaganza.' To what set of interpellating calls does Venus respond, and how is the reiteration of the law to be read in the manner of her response?

Venus, and *Paris Is Burning* more generally, calls into question whether parodying the dominant norms is enough to displace them; indeed, whether the denaturalization of gender cannot be the very vehicle for a reconsolidation of hegemonic norms. Although many readers understood *Gender Trouble* to be arguing for the proliferation of drag performances as a way of subverting dominant gender norms, I want to underscore that there is no necessary relation between drag and subversion, and that drag may well be used in the service of both the denaturalization and reidealization of hyperbolic heterosexual gender norms. At best, it seems, drag is a site of a certain ambivalence, one that reflects the more general situation of being implicated in the regimes of power by which one is constituted and, hence, of being implicated in the very regimes of power that one opposes.

To claim that all gender is like drag, or is drag, is to suggest that 'imitation' is at the heart of the *heterosexual* project and its gender binarisms, that drag is not a secondary imitation that presupposes a prior and original gender, but that hegemonic heterosexuality is itself a constant and repeated effort to imitate its own idealizations. That it must repeat this imitation, that it sets up pathologizing practices and normalizing sciences in order to produce and consecrate its own claim on originality and propriety, suggests that heterosexual performativity is beset by an anxiety that it can never fully overcome, that its effort to become its own idealizations can never be finally or fully achieved, and that it is consistently haunted by that domain of sexual possibility that must be excluded for heterosexualized gender to produce itself. In this sense, then, drag is subversive to the extent that it reflects on the imitative structure by which hegemonic gender is itself produced and disputes heterosexuality's claim on naturalness and originality.

But here it seems that I am obliged to add an important qualification: heterosexual privilege operates in many ways, and two ways in which it operates include naturalizing itself and rendering itself as the original and the norm. But these are not the only ways in which it works, for it is clear that there are domains in which heterosexuality can concede its lack of originality and naturalness but still hold on to its power. Thus, there are forms of drag that heterosexual culture produces for itself – we might think of Julie Andrews in *Victor, Victoria* or Dustin Hoffmann in *Tootsie* or Jack Lemmon in *Some Like It Hot*, where the anxiety over a possible homosexual consequence is both produced and deflected within the narrative trajectory of the films. These are films which produce and contain the homosexual excess of any given drag performance, the fear that an apparently heterosexual contact might be made before the discovery of a nonapparent homosexuality. This is drag as high het entertainment, and though these films are surely important to read as cultural texts in which homophobia and homosexual panic are negotiated, I would be reticent to call them subversive. Indeed, one might argue that such films are functional in providing a ritualistic release for a heterosexual economy that must constantly police its own boundaries against the invasion of queerness, and that this displaced production and resolution of homosexual panic actually fortifies the heterosexual regime in its self-perpetuating task.

In her provocative review of *Paris Is Burning*, bell hooks criticized some productions of gay male drag as misogynist, and here she allied herself in part with feminist theorists such as Marilyn Frye and Janice Raymond. This tradition within feminist thought has argued that drag is offensive to women and that it is an imitation based in ridicule and degradation. Raymond, in particular, places drag on a continuum with cross-dressing and transsexualism, ignoring the important differences between them, maintaining that in each practice women are the object of hatred and appropriation, and that there is nothing in the identification that is respectful or elevating. As a rejoinder, one might consider that identification is always an ambivalent process. Identifying with a gender under contemporary regimes of power involves identifying with a set of norms that are and are not realizable, and whose power and status precede the identifications by which they are insistently approximated. This 'being a man' and this 'being a woman' are internally unstable affairs. They are always beset by ambivalence precisely because there is a cost in every identification, the loss of some other set of identifications, the forcible approximation of a norm one never chooses, a norm that chooses us, but which we occupy, reverse, resignify to the extent that the norm fails to determine us completely.

The problem with the analysis of drag as only misogyny is, of course, that it figures male-to-female transsexuality, cross-dressing, and drag as male homosexual activities – which they are not always – and it further diagnoses male homosexuality as rooted in misogyny. The feminist analysis thus makes male homosexuality *about* women, and one might argue that at its extreme, this kind of analysis is in fact a colonization in reverse, a way for feminist women to make themselves into the center of male homosexual activity (and thus to reinscribe the heterosexual matrix, paradoxically, at the heart of the radical feminist position). Such an accusation follows the same kind of logic as those homophobic remarks that often follow upon the discovery that one is a lesbian: a lesbian is one who must have had a bad experience with men, or who has not yet found the right one. These diagnoses presume that lesbianism is acquired by virtue of some failure in the heterosexual machinery, thereby continuing to install heterosexuality as the 'cause' of lesbian desire; lesbian desire is figured as the fatal effect of a derailed heterosexual causality. In this framework, heterosexual desire is always true, and lesbian desire is always and only a mask and forever false. In the radical feminist argument against drag, the displacement of women is figured as the aim and effect of male-to-female drag; in the homophobic dismissal of lesbian desire, the disappointment with and displacement of men is understood as the cause and final truth of lesbian desire. According to these views, drag is nothing but the displacement and appropriation of 'women,' and hence fundamentally based in a misogyny, a hatred of women; and lesbianism is nothing but the displacement and appropriation of men, and so fundamentally a matter of hating men – misandry.

These explanations of displacement can only proceed by accomplishing yet another set of displacements: of desire, of phantasmatic pleasures, and of forms of love that are not reducible to a heterosexual matrix and the logic of repudiation. Indeed, the only place love is to be found is *for* the ostensibly repudiated object, where love is understood to be strictly produced through a logic of repudiation; hence, drag is nothing but the effect of a love embittered by disappointment or rejection, the incorporation of the Other whom one originally desired, but now hates. And lesbianism is nothing other than the effect of a love embittered by disappointment or rejection, and of a recoil from that love, a defense against it or, in the case of butchness, the appropriation of the masculine position that one originally loved.

This logic of repudiation installs heterosexual love as the origin and truth of both drag and lesbianism, and it interprets both practices as symptoms of thwarted love. But what is displaced in this explanation of displacement is the notion that there might be pleasure, desire, and love that is not solely determined by what it repudiates. Now it may seem at first that the way to oppose these reductions and degradations of queer practices is to assert their radical specificity, to claim that there is a lesbian desire radically different from a heterosexual one, with *no* relation to it, that is neither the repudiation nor the appropriation of heterosexuality, and that has radically other origins than those which sustain heterosexuality. Or one might be tempted to argue that drag is not related to the ridicule or degradation or appropriation of women: when it is men in drag as women, what we have is the destabilization of gender itself, a destabilization that is denaturalizing and that calls into question the claims of normativity and originality by which gender and sexual oppression sometimes operate. But what if the situation is neither exclusively one nor the other; certainly, some lesbians have wanted to retain the notion that their sexual practice is rooted in part in a repudiation of heterosexuality, but also to claim that this repudiation does not account for lesbian desire, and cannot therefore be identified as the hidden or original 'truth' of lesbian desire. And the case of drag is difficult in yet another way, for it seems clear to me that there is both a sense of defeat and a sense of insurrection to be had from the drag pageantry in *Paris Is Burning*, that the drag we see, the drag which is after all framed for us, filmed for us, is one that both appropriates and subverts racist, misogynist, and homophobic norms of oppression. How are we to account for this ambivalence? This is not first an appropriation and then a subversion. Sometimes it is both at once; sometimes it remains caught in an irresolvable tension, and sometimes a fatally unsubversive appropriation takes place.

Paris Is Burning (1991) is a film produced and directed by Jennie Livingston about drag balls in New York City, in Harlem, attended by, performed by 'men' who are either African-American or Latino. The balls are contests in which the contestants compete under a variety of categories. The categories include a variety of social norms, many of which are established in white culture as signs of class, like that of the 'executive' and the Ivy League student; some of which are marked as feminine, ranging from high drag to butch queen; and some of them, like that of the 'bangie,' are taken from straight black masculine street culture. Not all of the categories, then, are taken from white culture; some of them are replications of a straightness that is not white, and some of them are focused on class, especially those that almost require that expensive women's clothing be 'mopped' or stolen for the occasion. The competition in military garb shifts to yet another register of legitimacy, which enacts the performative and gestural conformity to a masculinity which parallels the performative or reiterative production of femininity in other categories. 'Realness' is not exactly a category in which one competes; it is a standard that is used to judge any given performance within the established categories. And yet what determines the effect of realness is the ability to compel belief, to produce the naturalized effect. This effect is itself the result of an embodiment of norms, a reiteration of norms, an impersonation of a racial and class norm, a norm that is at once a figure, a figure of a body, which is no particular body, but a morphological ideal that remains the standard which regulates the performance, but which no performance fully approximates.

Significantly, this is a performance that works, that effects realness, to the extent that it *cannot* be read. For 'reading' means taking someone down, exposing what fails to work at the level of appearance, insulting or deriding someone. For a performance to work, then, means that a reading is no longer possible, or that a reading, an interpretation, appears to be a kind of transparent seeing, where what appears and what it means coincide. On the contrary, when what appears and how it is 'read' diverge, the artifice of the performance can be read as artifice; the ideal splits off from its appropriation. But the impossibility of reading means that the artifice works, the approximation of realness appears to be achieved, the body peforming and the ideal performed appear indistinguishable.

But what is the status of this ideal? Of what is it composed? What reading does the film encourage, and what does the film conceal? Does the denaturalization of the norm succeed in subverting the norm, or is this a denaturalization in the service of a perpetual reidealization, one that can only oppress, even as, or precisely when, it is embodied most effectively? Consider the different fates of Venus Xtravanganza. She 'passes' as a light-skinned woman, but is – by virtue of a certain failure to pass completely – clearly vulnerable to homophobic violence; ultimately, her life is taken presumably by a client who, upon the discovery of what she calls her 'little secret,' mutilates her for having seduced him. On the other hand, Willi Ninja can pass as straight; his voguing becomes foregrounded in het video productions with Madonna *et al.*, and he achieves post-legendary status on an international scale. There is passing and then there is passing, and it is – as we used to say – 'no accident' that Willi Ninja ascends and Venus Xtravaganza dies.

Now Venus, Venus Xtravaganza, she seeks a certain transubstantiation of gender in order to find an imaginary man who will designate a class and race privilege that promises a permanent shelter from racism, homophobia, and poverty. And it would not be enough to claim that for Venus gender is *marked by* race and class, for gender is not the substance or primary substrate and race and class the qualifying attributes. In this instance, gender is the vehicle for the phantasmatic transformation of that nexus of race and class, the site of its articulation. Indeed, in *Paris Is Burning*, becoming real, becoming a real woman, although not everyone's desire (some children want merely to 'do' realness, and that, only within the confines of the ball), constitutes the site of the phantasmatic promise of a rescue from poverty, homophobia, and racist delegitimation.

The contest (which we might read as a 'contesting of realness') involves the phantasmatic attempt to approximate realness, but it also exposes the norms that regulate realness as *themselves* phantasmatically instituted and sustained. The rules that regulate and legitimate realness (shall we call them symbolic?) constitute the mechanism by which certain sanctioned fantasies, sanctioned imaginaries, are insidiously elevated as the parameters of realness. We could, within conventional Lacanian parlance, call this the ruling of the symbolic, except that the symbolic assumes the primacy of sexual difference in the constitution of the subject. What *Paris Is Burning* suggests, however, is that the order of sexual difference is not prior to that of race or class in the constitution of the subject; indeed, that the symbolic is also and at once a racializing set of norms, and that norms of realness by which the subject is produced are racially informed conceptions of 'sex' (this underscores the importance of subjecting the entire psychoanalytic paradigm to this insight).

This double movement of approximating and exposing the phantasmatic status of the realness norm, the symbolic norm, is reinforced by the diagetic movement of the film in which clips of so-called 'real' people moving in and out of expensive stores are juxtaposed against the ballroom drag scenes.

In the drag ball productions of realness, we witness and produce the phantasmatic constitution of a subject, a subject who repeats and mimes the legitimating norms by which it itself has been degraded, a subject founded in the project of mastery that compels and disrupts its own repetitions. This is not a subject who stands back from its identifications and decides instrumentally how or whether to work each of them today; on the contrary, the subject is the incoherent and mobilized imbrication of identifications; it is constituted in and through the iterability of its performance, a repetition which works at once to legitimate and delegitimate the realness norms by which it is produced.

In the pursuit of realness this subject is produced, a phantasmatic pursuit that mobilizes identifications, underscoring the phantasmatic promise that constitutes any identificatory move – a promise which, taken too seriously, can culminate only in disappointment and disidentification. A fantasy that for Venus, because she dies – killed apparently by one of her clients, perhaps after the discovery of those remaining organs – cannot be translated into the symbolic. This is a killing that is performed by a symbolic that would eradicate those phenomena that require an opening up of the possibilities for the resignification of sex. If Venus wants to become a woman, and cannot overcome being a Latina, then Venus is treated by the symbolic in precisely the ways in which women of color are treated. Her death thus testifies to a tragic misreading of the social map of power, a misreading orchestrated by that very map according to which the sites for a phantasmatic self-overcoming are constantly resolved into disappointment. If the signifiers of whiteness and femaleness – as well as some forms of hegemonic maleness constructed through class privilege – are sites of phantasmatic promise, then it is clear that women of color and lesbians are not only everywhere excluded from this scene, but constitute a site of identification that is consistently refused and abjected in the collective phantasmatic pursuit of a transubstantiation into various forms of drag, transsexualism, and uncritical miming of the hegemonic. That this fantasy involves becoming in part like women and, for some of the children, becoming like black women, falsely constitutes black women as a site of privilege; they can catch a man and be protected by him, an impossible idealization which of course works to deny the situation of the great numbers of poor black women who are single mothers without the support of men. In this sense, the 'identification' is composed of a denial, an envy, which is the envy of a phantasm of black women, an idealization that produces a denial. On the other hand, in so far as black men who are queer can become feminized by hegemonic straight culture, there is in the performative dimension of the ball a significant *reworking* of that feminization, an occupation of the identification that is, as it were, *already* made between faggots and women, the feminization of the faggot, the feminization of the black faggot, which is the black feminization of the faggot.

The performance is thus a kind of talking back, one that remains largely constrained by the terms of the original assailment: If a white homophobic hegemony considers the black drag ball queen to be a woman, that woman, constituted already by that hegemony, will become the occasion for the rearticulation of its terms; embodying the excess of that production, the queen will out-woman women, and in the process confuse and seduce an audience whose gaze must to some degree be structured through those hegemonies, an audience who, through the hyperbolic staging of the scene, will be drawn into the abjection it wants both to resist and to overcome. The phantasmatic excess of this production constitutes the site of women not only as marketable goods within an erotic economy of exchange, but as goods which, as it were, are also privileged consumers with access to wealth and social privilege and protection. This is a full-scale phantasmatic transfiguration not only of the plight of poor black and Latino gay men, but of poor black women and Latinas, who are the figures for the abjection that the drag ball scene elevates as a site of idealized identification. It would, I think, be too simple to reduce this identificatory move to black male misogyny, as if that were a discrete typology, for the feminization of the poor black man and, most trenchantly, of the poor, black, gay man, is a strategy of abjection that is already underway, originating in the complex of racist, homophobic, misogynist, and classist constructions that belong to larger hegemonies of oppression.

These hegemonies operate, as Gramsci insisted, through *rearticulation*, but here is where the accumulated force of an historically entrenched and entrenching rearticulation overwhelms the more fragile effort to build an alternative cultural configuration from or against that more powerful regime. Importantly, however, that prior hegemony also works through and as its 'resistance' so that the relation between the marginalized community and the dominative is not, strictly speaking, oppositional. The citing of the dominant norm does not, in this instance, displace that norm; rather, it becomes the means by which that dominant norm is most painfully reiterated as the very desire and the performance of those it subjects.

Clearly, the denaturalization of sex, in its multiple senses, does not imply a liberation from hegmonic constraint: when Venus speaks her desire to become a whole woman, to find a man and have a house in the suburbs with a washing machine, we may well question whether the denaturalization of gender and sexuality that she performs, and performs well, culminates in a reworking of the normative framework of heterosexuality. The painfulness of her death at the end of the film suggests as well that there are cruel and fatal social constraints on denaturalization. As much as she crosses gender, sexuality, and race performatively, the hegemony that reinscribes the privileges of normative femininity and whiteness wields the final power to *re*naturalize Venus's body and cross out that prior crossing, an erasure that is her death. Of course, the film brings Venus back, as it were, into visibility, although not to life, and thus constitutes a kind of cinematic performativity. Paradoxically, the film brings fame and recognition not only to Venus but also to the other drag ball children who are depicted in the film as able only to attain local legendary status while longing for wider recognition.

The camera, of course, plays precisely to this desire, and so is implicitly installed in the film as the promise of legendary status. And yet, is there a filmic effort to take stock of the place of the camera in the trajectory of desire that it not only records, but also incites? In her critical review of the film, bell hooks raises the question not only of the place of the camera, but also that of the filmmaker, Jennie Livingston, a white lesbian (in other contexts called 'a white Jewish lesbian from Yale,' an interpellation which also implicates this author in its sweep), in relation to the drag ball community that she entered and filmed, hooks remarks that,

> Jennie Livingston approaches her subject matter as an outsider looking in. Since her presence as white woman/lesbian filmmaker is 'absent' from *Paris Is Burning*, it is easy for viewers to imagine that they are watching an ethnographic film documenting the life of black gay 'natives' and not recognize that they are watching a work shaped and formed from a perspective and standpoint specific to Livingston. By cinematically masking this reality (we hear her ask questions but never see her) Livingston does not oppose the way hegemonic whiteness 'represents' blackness, but rather assumes an imperial overseeing position that is in no way progressive or counterhegemonic.

Later in the same essay, hooks raises the question of not merely whether or not the cultural location of the filmmaker is absent from the film, but whether this absence operates to form tacitly the focus and effect of the film, exploiting the colonialist trope of an 'innocent' ethnographic gaze:

> Too many critics and interviewers . . . act as though she somehow did this marginalized black gay subculture a favor by bringing their experience to a wider public. Such a stance obscures the substantial rewards she has received for this work. Since so many of the black gay men in the film express the desire to be big stars, it is easy to place Livingston in the role of benefactor, offering these 'poor black souls' a way to realize their dreams.

Although hooks restricts her remarks to black men in the film, most [are] . . . members of the House of Xtravaganza, who are Latino, some of whom are light-skinned, some of whom engage in crossing and passing, some of whom only do the ball, some [of whom] . . . are engaged in life projects to effect a full transubstantiation into femininity and/or into whiteness. The 'houses' are organized in part along ethnic lines. This seems crucial to underscore precisely because neither Livingston nor hooks considers the place and force of ethnicity in the articulation of kinship relations.

To the extent that a transubstantiation into legendary status, into an idealized domain of gender and race, structures the phantasmatic trajectory of the drag ball culture, Livingston's camera enters this world as the promise of phantasmatic fulfillment: a wider audience, national and international fame. If Livingston is the white girl with the camera, she is both the object and vehicle of desire; and yet, as a lesbian, she apparently maintains some kind of identificatory bond with the gay men in the film and also, it seems, with the kinship system, replete with 'houses,' 'mothers,' and 'children,' that sustains the drag ball scene and is itself organized by it. The one instance where Livingston's body might be said to appear allegorically on camera is when Octavia St Laurent is posing for the camera, as a moving model would for a photographer. We hear a voice tell her that she's terrific, and it is unclear whether it is a man shooting the film as a proxy for Livingston, or Livingston herself. What is suggested by this sudden intrusion of the camera into the film is something of the camera's desire, the desire that motivates the camera, in which a white lesbian phallically organized by the use of the camera (elevated to the status of disembodied gaze, holding out the promise of erotic recognition) eroticizes a black male-to-female transsexual – presumably preoperative – who 'works' perceptually as a woman.

What would it mean to say that Octavia is Jennie Livingston's kind of girl? Is the category or, indeed, 'the position' of white lesbian disrupted by such a claim? If this is the production of the black transsexual for an exoticizing white gaze, is it not also the transsexualization of lesbian desire? Livingston incites Octavia to become a woman for Livingston's own camera, and Livingston thereby assumes the power of 'having the phallus,' i.e., the ability to confer that femininity, to anoint Octavia as model woman. But to the extent that Octavia receives and is produced by that recognition, the camera itself is empowered as phallic instrument. Moreover, the camera acts as surgical instrument and operation, the vehicle through which the transubstantiation occurs. Livingston thus becomes the one with the power to turn men into women who, then, depend on the power of her gaze to become and remain women. Having asked about the transsexualization of lesbian desire, then, it follows that we might ask more particularly: what is the status of the desire to feminize black and Latino men that the film enacts? Does this not serve the purpose, among others, of a visual pacification of subjects by whom white women are imagined to be socially endangered?

Does the camera promise a transubstantiation of sorts? Is it the token of that promise to deliver economic privilege and the transcendence of social abjection? What does it mean to eroticize the holding out of that promise, as hooks asks, when the film will do well, but the lives that they record will remain substantially unaltered? And if the camera is the vehicle for that transubstantiation, what is the power assumed by the one who wields the camera, drawing on that desire and exploiting it? Is this not its own fantasy, one in which the filmmaker wields the power to transform what she records? And is this fantasy of the camera's power not directly counter to the ethnographic conceit that structures the film?

hooks is right to argue that within this culture the ethnographic conceit of a neutral gaze will always be a white gaze, an unmarked white gaze, one that passes its own perspective off as the omniscient, one that presumes upon and enacts its own perspective as if it were no perspective at all. But what does it mean to think about this camera as an instrument and effect of lesbian desire? I would have liked to have seen the question of Livingston's cinematic desire reflexively thematized in the film itself, her intrusions into the frame as 'intrusions,' the camera *implicated* in the trajectory of desire that it seems compelled to incite. To the extent that the camera figures tacitly as the instrument of transubstantiation, it assumes the place of the phallus, as that which controls the field of signification. The camera thus trades on the masculine privilege of the disembodied gaze, the gaze that has the power to produce bodies, but which is itself no body.

But is this cinematic gaze only white and phallic, or is there in this film a decentered place for the camera as well? hooks points to two competing narrative trajectories in the film, one that focuses on the pageantry of the balls and another that focuses on the lives of the participants. She argues that the spectacle of the pageantry arrives to quell the portraits of suffering that these men relate about their lives outside the ball. And in her rendition, the pageantry represents a life of pleasurable fantasy, and the lives outside the drag ball are the painful 'reality' that the pageantry seeks phantasmatically to overcome. hooks claims that,

> at no point in Livingston's film are the men asked to speak about their connections to a world of family and community beyond the drag ball. The cinematic narrative makes the ball the center of their lives. And yet who determines this? Is this the way the black men view their reality or is this the reality that Livingston constructs?

Clearly, this *is* the way that Livingston constructs their 'reality,' and the insights into their lives that we do get are still tied in to the ball. We hear about the ways in which the various houses prepare for the ball, we see 'mopping;' and we see the differences among those who walk in the ball as men, those who do drag inside the parameters of the ball, those who cross-dress all the time in the ball and on the street and, among the cross-dressers, those who resist transsexuality, and those who are transsexual in varying degrees. What becomes clear in the enumeration of the kinship system that surrounds the ball is not only that the 'houses' and the 'mothers' and the 'children' sustain the ball, but that the ball is itself an occasion for the building of a set of kinship relations that manage and sustain those who belong to the houses in the face of dislocation, poverty, homelessness. These men 'mother' one another, 'house' one another, 'rear' one another, and the resignification of the family through these terms is not a vain or useless imitation, but the social and discursive building of community, a community that binds, cares, and teaches; that shelters and enables. This is doubtless a cultural re-elaboration of kinship that anyone outside of the privilege of heterosexual family (and those within those 'privileges' who suffer there) needs to see, to know, and to learn from; a task that makes none of us who are outside of heterosexual 'family' into absolute outsiders to this film. Significantly, it is in the elaboration of kinship forged through a resignification of the very term terms which effect our exclusion and abjection that such a resignification creates the discursive and social space for community, that we see an appropriation of the terms of domination that turns them toward a more enabling future.

In these senses, then, *Paris Is Burning* documents neither an efficacious insurrection nor a painful resubordination, but an unstable coexistence of both. The film attests to the painful pleasures of eroticizing and miming the very norms that wield their power by foreclosing the very reverse occupations that the children nevertheless perform.

This is not an appropriation of dominant culture in order to remain subordinated by its terms, but an appropriation that seeks to make over the terms of domination; a making over which is itself a kind of agency, a power in and as discourse, in and as performance, which repeats in order to remake – and sometimes succeeds. But this is a film that cannot achieve this effect without implicating its spectators in the act; to watch this film means to enter into a logic of fetishization which installs the ambivalence of that 'performance' as related to our own. If the ethnographic conceit allows the performance to become an exotic fetish, one from which the audience absents itself, the commodification of heterosexual gender ideals will be, in that instance, complete. But if the film establishes the ambivalence of embodying – and failing to embody – that which one sees, then a distance will be opened up *between* that hegemonic call to normativizing gender and its critical appropriation.

Symbolic reiterations

The resignification of the symbolic terms of kinship in *Paris Is Burning* and in the cultures of sexual minorities represented and occluded by the film raises the question of how precisely the apparently static workings of the symbolic order become vulnerable to subversive repetition and resignification. To understand how this resignification works in the fiction of Willa Cather, a recapitulation of the psychoanalytic account of the formation of sexed bodies is needed. The turn to Cather's fiction involves bringing the question of the bodily ego in Freud and the status of sexual differentiation in Lacan to bear on the question of naming and, particularly, the force of the name in fiction. Freud's contention that the ego is always a bodily ego is elaborated with the further insight that this bodily ego is projected in a field of visual alterity. Lacan insists that the body as a visual projection or imaginary formation cannot be sustained except through submitting to the name, where the 'name' stands for the Name of the Father, the law of sexual differentiation. In 'The Mirror Stage,' Lacan remarks that the ego is produced 'in a fictional direction,' that its contouring and projection are psychic works of fiction; this fictional directionality is arrested and immobilizied through the emergence of a symbolic order that legitimates sexually differentiated fictions as 'positions.' As a visual fiction, the ego is inevitably a site of *méconnaissance*; the sexing of the ego by the symbolic seeks to subdue this instability of the ego, understood as an imaginary formation.

Here it seems crucial to ask where and how language emerges to effect this stabilizing function, particularly for the fixing of sexed positions. The capacity of language to fix such positions, that is, to enact its symbolic effects, depends upon the permanence and fixity of the symbolic domain itself, the domain of signifiability or intelligibility. If, for Lacan, the name secures the bodily ego in time, renders it identical through time, and this 'conferring' power of the name is derived from the conferring power of the symbolic more generally, then it follows that a crisis in the symbolic will entail a crisis in this identity-conferring function of the name, and in the stabilizing of bodily contours according to sex allegedly performed by the symbolic. *The crisis in the symbolic, understood as a crisis over what constitutes the limits of intelligibility, will register as a crisis in the name and in the morphological stability that the name is said to confer.*

The phallus functions as a synecdoche, for in so far as it is a figure of the penis, it constitutes an idealization and isolation of a body part and, further, the investment of that part with the force of symbolic law. If bodies are differentiated according to the symbolic positions that they occupy, and those symbolic positions consist in either having or being the phallus, bodies are thus differentiated and sustained in their differentiation by being subjected to the Law of the Father, which dictates the 'being' and 'having' positions; men become men by approximating the 'having of the phallus,' which is to say they are compelled to approximate a 'position' which is itself the result of a synecdochal collapse of masculinity into its 'part' and a corollary idealization of that synecdoche as the governing symbol of the symbolic order. According to the symbolic, then, the assumption of sex takes place through an approximation of this synecdochal reduction. This is the means by which a body assumes sexed integrity as masculine or feminine: the sexed integrity of the body is paradoxically achieved through an identification with its reduction into idealized synecdoche ('having' or 'being' the phallus). The body which fails to submit to the law or occupies that law in a mode contrary to its dictate, thus loses its sure footing – its cultural gravity – in the symbolic and reappears in its imaginary tenuousness, its fictional direction. Such bodies contest the norms that govern the intelligibility of sex.

Is the distinction between the symbolic and the imaginary a stable distinction? And what of the distinction between the name and the bodily ego? Does the name, understood as the linguistic token which designates sex, only work to *cover over* its fictiveness, or are there occasions in which *the fictive and unstable status of that bodily ego trouble the name, expose the name as a crisis in referentiality*? Further, if body parts do not reduce to their phallic idealizations, that is, if they become vectors for other sorts of phantasmatic investments, then to what extent does the synecdochal logic through which the phallus operates lose its differentiating capacity? In other words, the phallus itself presupposes the regulation and reduction of phantasmatic investment such that the penis is either idealized as the phallus or mourned as the scene of castration, and desired in the mode of an impossible compensation. If these investments are deregulated or, indeed, diminished, to what extent can having/being the phallus still function as that which secures the differentiation of the sexes?

In Cather's fiction, the name not only designates a gender uncertainty, but produces a crisis in the figuration of sexed morphology as well. In this sense, Cather's fiction can be read as the foundering and unraveling of the symbolic on its own impossible demands. What happens when the name and the part produce divergent and conflicting sets of sexual expectations? To what extent to the unstable descriptions of gendered bodies and body parts produce a crisis in the referentiality of the name, the name itself as the very fiction it seeks to cover? If the heterosexism of the Lacanian symbolic depends on a set of rigid and prescribed identifications, and if those identifications are precisely what Cather's fiction works through and against the symbolically invested name, then the contingency of the symbolic – and the heterosexist parameters of what qualifies as 'sex' – undergo a rearticulation that works the fictive grounding of what only appears as the fixed limits of intelligibility.

Cather cites the paternal law, but in places and ways that mobilize a subversion under the guise of loyalty. Names fail fully to gender the characters whose femininity and masculinity they are expected to secure. The name fails to sustain the identity of the body within the terms of cultural intelligibility; body parts disengage from any common center, pull away from each other, lead separate lives, become sites of phantasmatic investments that refuse to reduce to singular sexualities. And though it appears that the normativizing law prevails by forcing suicide, the sacrifice of homosexual eroticism, or closeting homosexuality, the text exceeds the text, the life of the law exceeds the teleology of the law, enabling an erotic contestation and disruptive repetition of its own terms.

Chapter 41

Reina Lewis

LOOKING GOOD

The lesbian gaze and fashion imagery

Abstract

THIS PAPER IS CONCERNED with the different forms of pleasure and identification activated in the consumption of dominant and subcultural print media. It centres on an analysis of the lesbian visual pleasures generated through the reading of fashion editorial in the new lesbian and gay lifestyle magazines. This consideration of the lesbian gaze is contrasted to the lesbian visual pleasures obtained from an against the grain reading of mainstream women's fashion magazines. The development of the lesbian and gay lifestyle magazines, in the context of the pink pound, produces a situation in which an eroticized lesbian visual pleasure is the overt remit of the magazine, rather than a clandestine pleasure obtained through a transgressive reading of dominant cultural imagery. In contrast to the polysemic free-play of fashion fantasy by which readers produce lesbian pleasure in the consumption of mainstream magazines, responses to the fashion content in the lesbian magazine *Diva* suggest that in a subcultural context readers deploy a realist mode of reading that demands a monosemic positive images iconography. The article uses the concept of subcultural competency to consider the different ways lesbians read mainstream and subcultural print media and suggests that the conflict over *Diva*'s fashion spreads may be linked to changing patterns of identification and the use of dress for recognizability.

Keywords

lesbian; fashion; gaze; consumption; lifestyle

Introduction

One of the results of the growth and recognition of the pink economy in the late 1980s was the establishment of a number of lesbian and gay 'lifestyle' magazines in the UK and North America in the early 1990s (this would include in the UK *Diva*, *Attitude*, *Phase*, and in the USA and Canada, *Out*, *Girlfriends*, *Curve*, formally *Deneuve*). Although they often had some overtly political content (from articles on lesbian mothers to coverage of Pride) these journals did not see lesbian and gay or queer identities only in political terms. In contrast to previous campaigning journals, the new titles mixed politics and consumption in a move that was in keeping with the new recognition of the pink pound (whose advertising revenue was crucial to them). More and more mainstream and gay-run businesses realized the potential of extending 1980s niche marketing techniques to include gay and, to a lesser extent, lesbian consumers (Clark 1993). As Frank Mort has demonstrated, this increase in consumer possibilities meant that lesbian and gay individuals grew increasingly familiar with the idea that consumption itself marked out ways of participating in a gay life (Mort 1996). The emphasis on lifestyle in these magazines was part of this formation.

I am interested here in how readers consume the magazines, particularly in the ways in which lesbians consume the fashion coverage in *Diva* (with some comparison to other journal and to gay male readers). Looking at fashion allows me to think about the specificity of a lesbian visual pleasure and forms of identification in an area of cultural consumption traditionally aimed at women. Previously with Katrina Rolley, I had analysed how lesbians could extract visual pleasures from mainstream fashion magazines such as *Vogue* and *Elle* (Lewis and Rolley 1996). In this article I want to extend that discussion to consider what happens when fashion, with all its expected pleasures, moves to a venue where same-sex pleasure is the overt rather than covert remit of the publication.

For lesbian magazines, which often inherited a feminist perspective, the inclusion of fashion was a conspicuous departure from previous feminist publications, whose opposition to the fashion industry is legendary. But it was not only a greater adherence to feminist politics that separated out lesbian and gay magazines: the economic base that supported the new commercialized lifestyles and identities was unequal too. As Mort points out, the power of the pink pound was mainly seen as male – with far fewer services aimed at lesbians – and the mode of metropolitan gay life inscribed in the pink and style press relied on (and created opportunities for), shops and bars that mainly catered for male markets. Lesbians, who as women often, but not always, have less (disposable) income, were inevitably seen as a bad financial bet. So the opportunities for advertising, commercial tie-ins, etc. in *Diva* were far less. The new identification-as-consumption model of the pink pound was not embraced by all and to some extent the feminist politics of *Diva* produced an ambivalent attitude to the pink pound's valorization of shopping.

The different consumer habits assumed in lesbians and gay men (which also determine the magazine's access to clothes for fashion editorial) as well as their reading of the fashion images can be related to their different historical relationships to fashion. Whilst lesbians have in recent decades invested heavily in an anti-fashion and anti-consumerism politics and aesthetics – now under review with the advent of the lipstick lesbian – gay men have historically marked out their identity through sartorial savvy, ritualized consumption, and investment in a discourse of taste. Whatever the vogue for 'real' men or dressing down, gay men's magazines do not have to overcome an antipathy to the very idea of fashion in the way that a lesbian and particularly a feminist lesbian publication does. But, whatever the attitude to fashion, dress as a marker of identity is hugely significant in the everyday lives of lesbians and gay men: clothes function as a marker of recognizability to other gays or as a method of passing (which may itself be gay-coded for those in the know, whilst safely enough secured as heterosexual for those to whom one cannot risk being known). Moreover, as consumers of each other's appearance, there is a pleasure to be had in recognizing and being recognized. For these reasons, clothes have an importance in the lives of lesbians and gays – whether or not they consider themselves fashionable – that is rarely experienced by heterosexuals, however much they may affiliate to alternative networks of style and subcultural identities (on the related passings of sexual and racialized identifications see Walker 1993).

But, new departure as their fashion pages may have been, the lesbian lifestyle magazines were not starting with a blank slate. Although fashion was rarely seen on the pages of *Spare Rib*, many lesbians had been reading mainstream fashion magazines for years, without forgetting their lesbian selves as they turned the page. As Katrina and I argued, fashion editorial in mainstream magazines regularly used visual codes that foregrounded the possibility of a lesbian visual pleasure (see also Clark 1993). These codes typically broke down into four sections: images which reference era/locales known to have lesbian historical significance (Brassai's Paris or Vita Sackville West-style English country homes); gendered coupling of female models where they take on a male/female dynamic; or cross-dressing where female models take on male codes; and twinning or mirroring. This reading is based on a recognition that the fundamental contradiction of female magazine consumption – in which women are tutored in looking at, admiring and identifying with other women's bodies – is a potentially eroticized experience for all women readers, not just lesbians. The fashion magazine is widely understood to be a world without men, yet one that is animated by them. Men's conspicuous absence from fashion imagery is in direct relation to their presumed central role in the lives of the female addressee of the magazine: it is for 'his' eyes that the magazines' consumers study the arts of beauty and dress.

It was part of my argument in that piece that the lesbian viewer is engaged in a mode of narcissistic identification with the beautiful woman in the image which – relying on the implicit awareness of other lesbian viewers who, like her, gaze at the beautiful woman – produces a desire both to be and to have the displayed woman. As I gaze at the model, I may simultaneiously at a fantasy level desire to be like her, and desire to have her and, moreover, desire to be, as she is, the recipient of another woman's desiring gaze. Further, in the 'all female' world of the fashion magazine, the logic of a female desiring gaze produces what I call a paradigmatically lesbian viewing position for any woman, whether or not she is consciously lesbian identified. The tradition of an overtly heterosexual rationale in the magazine world plus the commonplace trivialization of fashion (see Evans and Thornton 1989) recoups this subversive position to the point where it is quite clearly not an uncomfortable experience for a heterosexual viewer to gaze at female flesh in this way. She can, after all, imagine that she is looking at them in order to learn how to make herself that desirable for her man. (For a different reading of mainstream magazines' invocation and disavowal of a lesbian reading position, see Fuss 1992.) But it does not police against lesbian pleasure.

It is clear that one of the elements that animated this analysis was the idea of imagined interpretive communities of other lesbians. We were thinking of reception in social terms, in which the psychic mechanisms of fantasy activated by the viewing experience are also socially structured. In this instance, the experience of pleasure seemed to rest on recognizable lesbian visual codes and on the activity of a transgressive, and often narrativized, reading. But what happens when that reading is not transgressive, when a same-sex narrative is the denoted, not the connoted, of the text?

Theorizing the reader of lesbian and gay lifestyle journalism

Now that we had overtly 'lesbian' fashion pages, how much did the putative lesbian 'we' like what we saw? The 'we' who looks is very important. Meaning does not reside in the image itself, but is generated in the interaction between viewer and text in which the codes of the text will be more or less decipherable to different viewers, depending on their historical and cultural moment. In this case, I need to be clear that there is no such thing as 'the' lesbian gaze, singular; since all lesbians are differentiated by class and racializing terms. But we can recognize the impact of such larger formations as subcultural groupings within which the individual lesbian subject may sometimes identify.

Caroline Evans and Lorraine Gamman also make a case for the importance of what they call subcultural competencies (Evans and Gamman 1995). These are what make the lesbian viewer able, for example, to recognize the lesbian subcultural referents and cross-gendered lesbian erotics connoted by a 'Napoleon and Josephine' narrative in *Vogue Italia* (where two women maintain an eroticized butch/femme dynamic sumptuously styled as the historical pair in a suitably lush and imperial setting). Evans and Gamman emphasize that the pleasure apparently produced by the code under discussion does not reside *in* the representation, but in the activity of decoding it. In other words, it is the act of interpretation itself that is eroticized, driven in part by the thrill of detecting a lesbian pleasure in the mainstream location. This means that there is no such thing as a preordained lesbian gaze, so much as a gaze that is able to decode lesbian subcultural referents, variable and shifting as they are: it is the exercise of a subcultural competency that produces lesbian pleasure, a pleasure that would be available to anyone able to exercise a similar competency whether lesbian or not (Evans and Gamman 1995: 35).

This for them can apply equally to the reading of dominant or subcultural texts. I am concerned with the specificities of each: in the case of a 'dominant' text like *Vogue*, I absolutely agree that the eroticization comes via the exercise of a subcultural competency. But this pleasure is heightened into a thrill by the sense of transgression that comes from constructing an alternative narrative. In the case of lesbian magazines, where the same subculturally recognizable codes are the denoted rather than the connoted of the text, they read differently and sometimes, I think, produce less visual pleasure. Context is all.

This may be in part due to production values (money on the page) which in the case of smaller lesbian and gay magazines struggling to get advertising are generally much lower than the mainstream glossies. The high cost luxury mise-en-scène that is part of the visual pleasure of mainstream fashion coverage is absent from most lesbian and gay products such as *Diva* or free papers, *Boyz*, or the *Pink*. One exception to this is the British gay magazine *Attitude*, which is notable for its glossy and gorgeous fashion editorial and is generally more visual-led (in keeping with previous staff experience on the now-defunct gay journal *Square Peg*, which was known for its visuals). At this point, I should also report that of the cluster of titles available in the UK in 1994 (*Shebang*, *Phase*, *Diva*, *Attitude*) only half have survived, and they have only been running for two years. So I want to signal both the newness of the field (magazines are still trying things out and establishing a sense of their readership) and the methodological implications of trying to make deductions from such a small field. This places a terrible burden of representation on my sample, especially when compared to our earlier sample from the mainstream media where we were able to analyse five titles over ten years. So this piece is necessarily rather more exploratory in nature: my comparisons of British and American, and lesbian and gay and mixed magazines, can only be suggestive at this stage.

Although I am primarily talking about lesbian visual pleasure, the comparison with mixed and gay magazines can be illuminating. It has been much documented that in recent years the male body has been objectified in popular culture in ways that were previously thought to be associated with the female body alone. As Mark Simpson discusses, all of this illustrates an increasing willingness on the part of mainstream popular culture to flirt with homoerotic pleasures (Simpson 1994). Gay lifestyle magazines do it in reverse: in seeking to sell homosexuality as lifestyle they overtly celebrate their readers' participation in mainstream culture (as consumers if nothing else), rather than speaking to them in a cocoon of fantasized gay separation.

This means that essential advertising revenue is possible; especially as more and more mainstream advertising campaigns look increasingly at home in a gay venue. I always thought that the advert for vodka (bottom right, Figure 41.1) was homoerotically charged, but once seen in *Attitude*, it looks just perfect for the gay bedroom wall. So, when we look at the editorial fashion coverage in gay lifestyle magazines we are viewing in the context of the increased queering of popular culture (Simpson 1994) plus the crossover of queer-inflected representations into the queer space of the magazine itself. This raises questions about preferred and alternative meanings. During the single reading experience of flicking through a lesbian or gay magazine, viewers are engaged in reading dominant representational codes which may be more or less overtly open to same-sex pleasures (whether it is a vodka advert or a publicity shot of kd lang on the cover of *Diva*) and in reading editorial images that have an overtly gay 'meaning'. To consume a lesbian or gay lifestyle magazine is thus an experience of reading simultaneously with and against the grain, and of re-reading previously consumed images which, like the vodka advert in *Attitude*, are now overlaid with overtly homoerotic connotations in their new gay context. But one of the things that marks out *Diva* as different from *Attitude* is that it gets far less mainstream advertising and hence revenue. In keeping

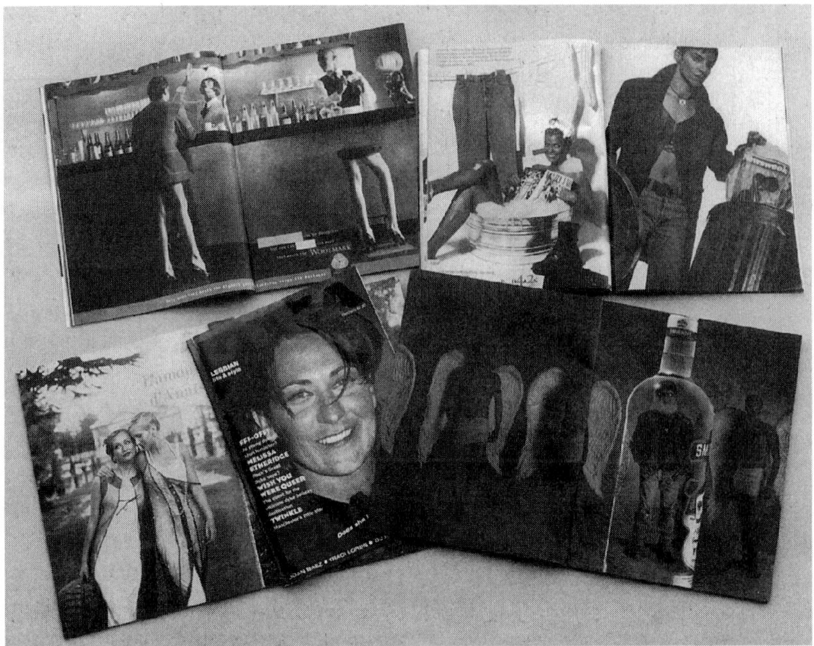

Figure 41.1 Crossover images
(Photographer: Simon Pattle)

with the prevalent assumption that lesbians never have any money to spend, very few mainstream advertising campaigns use *Diva*. Mainstream advertising only comes *Diva*'s way when a specifically lesbian audience is sought (for example, adverts for the pop group the Buffalo Girls and for the film *Carrington*). But not always even then: the lesbian market for kd lang's 1995 album was so obviously secure that the record company decided no wooing was necessary and refused *Diva* an advert or an interview.

Diva does of course carry a mix of advertising and editorial content. But the relationship of the fashion editorial to this mix of copy seems different from the image of a complex and highly sophisticated reading practice, revelling in contradiction in a properly queer and, at times, postmodern way that the other gay magazines construct and/or welcome. *Phase*'s first spread included a tongue-in-cheek homage to lesbian chic (top right, Figure 41.1), reproduced from *Out* magazine, USA. This not only highlights the role of consumption as a gay activity, but also invites the *Phase* reader to identify themself [*sic*] as one who will recognize the iconic nature of the popular cultural examples of lesbian chic on display. In contract, *Diva* got a mixed response to its fashion coverage.

Founded in 1994, *Diva* initially included fashion spreads but has dropped them temporarily from its contents. Editor Frances Williams anticipated that her audience would to some extent apply a realist mode of consumption, so her decision to use ethnically diverse models and 'real' people was not motivated by her own preferences alone. This was coupled with an intent to introduce a greater diversity of lesbian images into what she thought had become a rather stale iconography.

Although some readers responded positively to the fashion pages, I was surprised at the level of complaints they generated: in nearly every case this was based on a realist mode of reception. Criticism centred on the non-representativeness of the models; the problems of objectification; the apparent unsuitability of the clothes featured for accepted/stereotypical/easily recognizable lesbian styles; and the cost of the clothes. Yet, presumably, some of the readers of *Diva* also read *Vogue* and are used to a non-literal consumption of fashion spreads. A feature on lesbian club promoters and bar staff reveals not only their own style choices but also their overview of the increasing fashion literacy and range of options on the lesbian scene (albeit in London only). Their comments suggest that for some lesbians the move away from a style orthodoxy is potentially liberating and some readers did indeed welcome the inclusion of fashion. But the level of negative feedback did leave me wondering what happens to the critical faculties of readers when faced with a lesbian *mise-en-scène*, considering that they must also read some sort of mainstream imagery against the grain, even if not specifically fashion imagery?

My suspicion that readers have different expectations of gay-produced imagery is borne out by Murray Healy's observation that the gay free papers *Pink* and *Boyz* got complaints when the men they pictured were not standard 'real man' beef-cake. As Healy observes, if you want challenging, alternative images of masculinity go to *L'Uomo Vogue* not to the gay press.[1] Again, a positive images iconography is demanded. It seems that some lesbian and gay readers demand unambiguous politically or aesthetically 'safe' images in the gay press whereas they revel in transgressive, contradictory and subversive pleasures in the mainstream. If the exercise of subcultural competencies in the reading of the dominant is eroticized through a relationship of power and knowledge (I know something 'they' don't), why is this pleasure sacrificed in the consumption of gay/subcultural texts? And in what ways is this situation different for lesbian and gay readers? Where the lesbian demand for positive images, though in itself a fantasy of respresentability and wholeness, is based on the possibility of literal identification, the 'real' man demanded in *Boyz* is implicitly understood as a central fantasy of subcultural iconography. So whilst both lesbian readers of *Diva* and gay readers of *Boyz* are demanding an impossible monovalency of the image, they do it in quite distinct ways.

This anxiety about the polysemic nature of imagery in the consumption of the subcultural is at odds with a homoerotic reading of the dominant which relies on the multivalency of the image for the possibility of a queer pleasure. Is the readers' desire for closure in *Diva* something that is anchored in the codes of *Diva*'s imagery, or is it brought to the images by the readers, i.e. in opposition to the magazine's preferred reading? Why, when the advent of *Diva* coincides with a dramatic change in lesbian style, do its fashion pages get a hard time, in contrast to the evidently thriving fashion content at *Attitude*, whose reception is quite different again from that of *Boyz*?

Style counsel: fashion, reading and identification in *Diva*

One of the first spreads in *Diva* was entitled 'Naughty but nice' (Figure 41.2). Here the 'naughty' overtly refers to the devilish horns worn by the models. But it also suggests that the revealing clothes may themselves be naughty. Yet, when we turn the page to discover the 'nice' we find a far less demure picture: maintaining sexualized body contact at all times the two models are now in a rougher, dykier, street-style, posing with an in-your-face knowingness for the camera. On one level this suggests a carnivalesque reversal, in which the grotesque of the lesbian body is inverted as 'nice', whilst something approximating 'proper' femininity is demonized as 'naughty'. This might be called the magazine's preferred reading, in which an audience assumed to have lesbian subcultural competencies would decode the visual pun of the title. But the spread offers another reading that, rather than problematizing the very idea of a binary divide by ridiculing its constituent terms, re-naturalizes the dichotomy by presenting a lesbian binarism in which the more masculine, dyke-referential style of the 'nice' is normatized, whilst the femmier, mainstream fashion of the 'naughty' is presented as subculturally transgressive. Although all the clothes are from a London designer shop, the styling of the 'nice' is quite easily recognizable as a lesbianized version of what was a current club look. The jeans, the leather trousers and big leather belts cut against the cutesy T-shirts and the baby blue satin of the jacket, securing a lesbian-coding for those in the know. But both images are presented as potentially desirable for the reader.

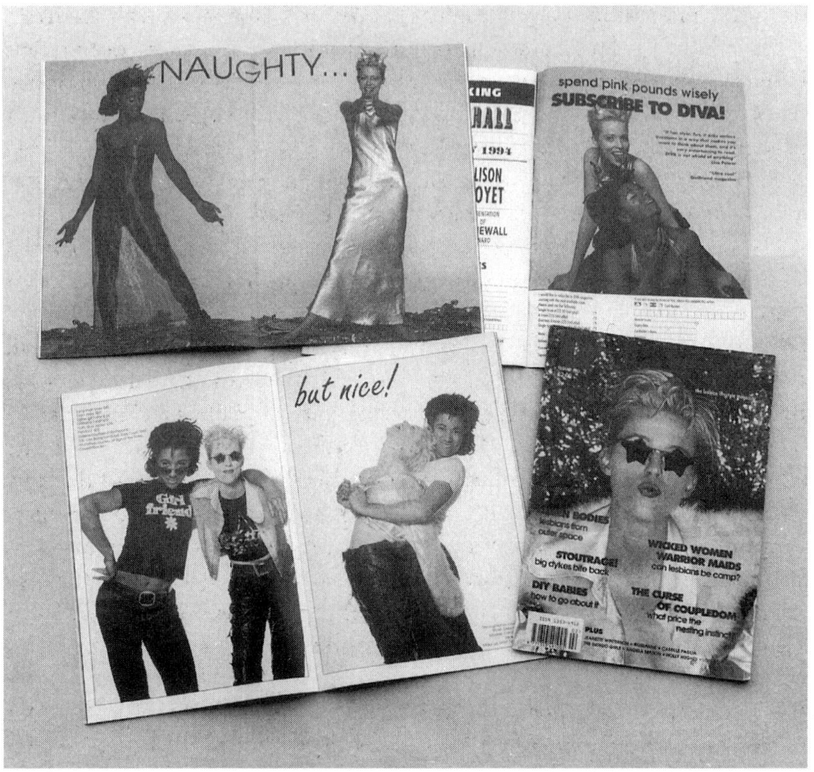

Figure 41.2 Naughty but Nice
(Photographer: Simon Pattle)

In the following edition we see a composite of the naughty/nice narrative ('Subscribe', Figure 41.2). This provides a recognizable lesbian coding alongside a signification of up-to-the-minute style and awareness about lesbian dress debates, as well as a parodic but still effectively eroticized assertion of active lesbian desire. The top figure's gaze out at the viewer (a look that is echoed in the main spread) invites identification and participation. The luscious cleavage at the bottom of the frame is de-objectified (in the pejorative sense) through the model's ownership of her self-display, signified by the parodic performance of ecstasy and re-affirmed by the playful surround of the other horned figure. It is precisely the multiplicity of referents in this image (satyrs, cherubs, dykes, postmodern self-referential butch-femme) that makes it so potentially pleasurable *and* that helps it to overcome the anticipated qualms of those sections of *Diva*'s readership assumed to be concerned about the objectification of the female body. In this, it is clear that the visual language of the fashion spreads is determined to a significant extent by the editor, stylist and photographer's sense of the attitudes of their readers. Some of this may be informed by direct feedback on *Diva* (letters, questionnaires), or based on indirect (word of mouth) reader-response, or come tangentially through hearing responses to images outside the pages of the magazine. In all these ways is their sense of the imaginary boundaries in which they operate constructed.

My sense of *Diva*'s readers is based on conversations with the editor, with women I know who read it, and on the response of non-magazine readers to whom I have shown the photographs. The differing attitudes I saw and heard to dress, desire and the role of reading in the formation of identity suggest two distinct but potentially overlapping modes of reception. One regards lesbianism as an authentic identity based on lived experience outside the magazine, which readers expect *Diva* to properly reflect and represent. This identity is often predicated on the separation from and resistance to dominant models of heterosexual femininity, frequently signified by a refusal of mainstream women's fashion. The other constructs identity *through* reading and *then* seeks social spaces in which that identity can be lived out and recognized, often through the appropriation of mainstream women's fashion.

For this second group, the sense of community engendered by the magazine is paramount. The selective use of mainstream fashion fosters an identity that is initially shared with an imagined interpretive community of readers and then developed experientially in social spaces (like clubs) with others who can decode it. Although the potential to be decoded by others is obviously key, it seems that this type of reader is able to deal both with the swift changes of style and fragmented identifications associated with postmodernity and with the fact that they may not be recognizable. It is no coincidence that these dress codes and senses of identity are predominantly associated with younger women, whose sense of self has been formed in a different and less oppositional relationship to the media than previous generations.

Diva obviously needs to appeal to both sets of readers. In the 'Gotta Lotta Socca' spread (top right, Figure 41.3) the play with imagery has gone: recognizability is key. So, in this spread the subcultural referents are dominant. This, along with the 'real' looking models, produces something almost ethnographic in its documentation of an enshrined (British) lesbian icon: the footballing dyke. In magazine terms, the 'Socca' spread – with its awkward models and patent lack of artifice – is more akin to a lesbian version of teen magazines' 'readers in shopping malls' or to low-brow women's magazines like *Bella* than to high fashion fantasy. Although 'Socca' offers a significant consumer opportunity (buying football strips/sportswear is never cheap) it is clearly not exhorting its readers to enter fancy boutiques in the way that even the 'nice' was earlier. Rather, the football spread facilitates the living out of a more traditionally subcultural lesbian identity through the experience of buying men's clothes in the mainly male domain of the football sports emporium. This potential for resistance is not so simply available in the environs of a trendy fashion shop where almost anything will go.

Although the footballers might be great role models, their anti-erotic becomes even more pronounced in contrast to the presentation of the athlete's impressive physique (centre left, Figure 41.3). This is not because footballers are not eroticized as objects of lesbian desire: indeed they are. But the imputation of an eroticized relationship between them becomes impossible once they must symbolize a resisting subcultural position that is founded on a refusal to join in the 'patriarchal' objectification of women's bodies. In other words, they have simultaneously to be beyond recuperation by a male voyeuristic gaze and to be objects of desire for a lesbian reader. But this must be coded in a classed and masculinized style of androgyny that has typically been resistant to an overtly eroticized objectification (not least because this is seen as implicitly femininizing) in ways that may not apply to femmier personae (which may often be more overtly presented for erotic

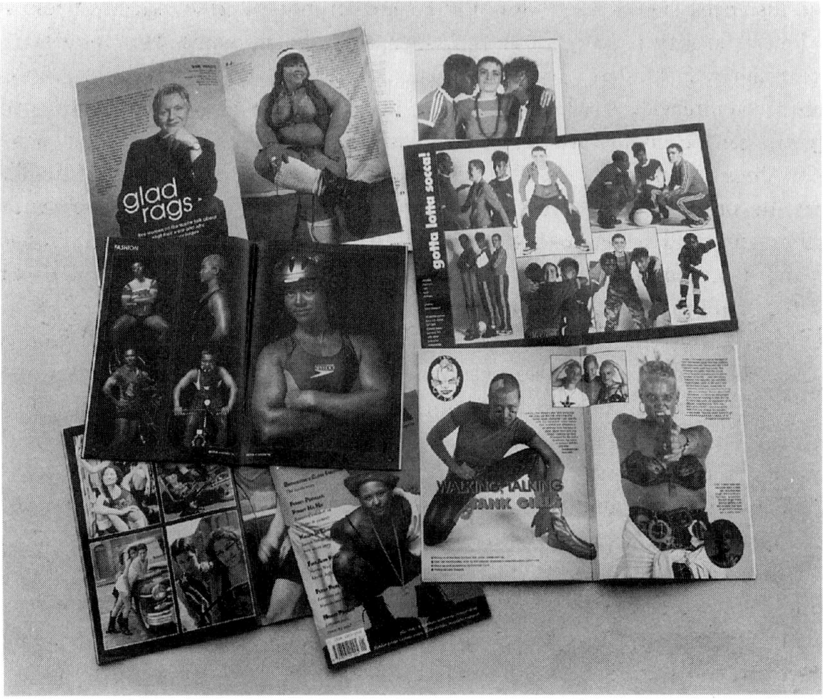

Figure 41.3 Real Lesbians?
(Photographer: Simon Pattle)

contemplation). The awkwardness with which the 'Socca' models respond to their physical proximity looks authentic, not staged, and seems to be borne out in the difficulty of the quandary. But it may also speak to a butch occupation of space, the visual pleasures of which are beyond my recuperation, since one of my 'respondents' did find the 'Socca' spread sexy. So, what different sorts of reader pleasure and/or identification do these different spreads produce? Is the blokey mateyness of the footballers conducive to a butch identification and pleasure where the parodic glamour of 'naughty but nice' is not?

I think that one of the pleasures of *Diva* is the assumed authenticity of the models. They are always identified by name, and in some cases are constructed as the authentic owners of the style they model. The 'Tank Girl' models (bottom right, Figure 41.3) are thanked as fans, further emphasizing the documentary nature of the feature. It is the magazine's policy to use only lesbian models and photographers, driven in part by a feminist desire to provide work for women and lesbians, but also by the pragmatic analysis that it is harder to get 'straight' models to snuggle up realistically for the camera. This brings me back to the subcultural competencies that were in operation in the consumption of *Vogue*. If *Diva* does not identify the models as lesbian, how is the reader expected to know? In part it can be explained by the bodies, which are not stereotypically perfect, and the determined representation of a variety of ethnicities, which draws attention to a politicized affirmative action aesthetic (even as it may activate codes that eroticize the 'exoticism' of ethnic difference). Mainstream magazines do periodically use 'real' women or non-stereotypically beautiful models, but the exceptional nature of these instances signals their deviation from the normal rule. The out lesbian model Jenny Shimizu is an interesting case in point here: her visible ethnicity (in a world where white does not register as ethnic) and intertextually decodable lesbianism, via interviews and features, make her an exotically different visual spectacle which can be effectively contrasted with other model bodies and personae. It also signifies an up-to-the-minute association with fashionable lesbian chic. The fact that she presents as a butch dyke and not a glamour femme only reinforces her authenticity and heightens the transgressive appeal of using a lesbian model who deviates not only from the norm but also from the overexposed media creature of the (femme) lipstick lesbian of lesbian chic (see also O'Sullivan 1994).

But the details of dress, hair and the relations between the pictured women in magazines such as *Diva* are also important, as is the quality of the gaze directed out of the frame towards the reader. I may not get as much pleasure from these as I do from *Vogue*, but I am never in any doubt about their lesbian address. They position me as a lesbian addressee, producing a position of empathy and also of desire. Whilst, for a generation of women reared on the icon of the unobtainable supermodel, the very approachability of these models may be their downfall, as the magazine's lesbian addressee, it is their reality-effect that draws me in. Would this be legible to a reader without the appropriate subcultural competencies?

I feel in many ways that the *Diva* spreads grapple with the same problem as do my friends and I; how to look fashionable and move with the changing trends, whilst still signifying as lesbian? At one time it was relatively easy: you wore whatever you wanted and combined it with big shoes or boots. But then everyone started wearing Doc. Martens and footwear's lesbian coding was undermined. Now it is harder, plus there is a whole generation of lesbians who do not have the same agenda about recognizability and who share a dress aesthetic that owes more to mainstream than to feminist stylistics. The outrage caused by *Diva*'s foray into disparate styles may attest to a struggle over meaning that is lived out through representation and the consumption of material culture.

'We're here, we're queer and we're not going shopping'?: Representing queerness in other lifestyle magazines

In contrast to *Diva*, *Attitude* can play with a male relationship to fashion that is clearly eroticized and fantastic and can, presumably, draw on what Mort identifies as the homosocial spaces and reading habits previously constructed by the men's style press of the 1980s (Mort 1996). There is little recourse to authenticity or documentary in these examples from *Attitude* (Figure 41.4). The splendour of the dressed male figure is more closely akin to the unobtainable glamour of the supermodel, whilst the eroticization of the model is made abundantly clear in the regular inclusion of fashion editorial for perfume 'Heaven Scent' (centre left, Figure 41.4). In this instance, the erotic takes precedence. As Simpson observes, it is perfume/aftershave adverts in the mainstream media that have produced the most overt and narcissitic objectification of the naked male torso. But where homoeroticized perfume adverts in the mainstream produce a troublingly queer ambivalence in which the homoerotic desire for the male body must be to some extent disavowed (Simpson 1994), their presence as editorial in *Attitude* produces the erotic as the dominant meaning: an unproblematic source of pleasure.

We can no longer simply talk about preferred and alternative meanings when the makers of mainstream aftershave adverts clearly know they are producing polysemic and queer imagery – the problem becomes one of relationships *between* meanings, in which the viewer's decoding activities may operate from a variety of positions each of which utilizes a different set of competencies that may be addressed by the text. It is hard to imagine a naked perfume promotion in *Diva*, although the American magazine *Girlfriends* regularly contains a centrefold and a variety of overtly eroticized images. But *Girlfriends* is also more adventurous in its fashion coverage, with spreads that seem to me to be more eroticized than those in *Diva*.

This greater ease, or willingness to play, with fashion may be because of the different attitudes to consumption in American feminism, where feminists have been more likely to organize campaigns around women's power as consumers than in the UK. Or it may simply be that *Diva* is not aiming for the erotic and *Girlfriends*, which features much pro-sex content and is associated with the *On Our Backs* crowd, is. But it is also to do with the more developed narratives of the *Girlfriends*' spreads. This investment in narrative produces similar possibilities for visual pleasure as those Katrina and I detected in mainstream magazines. The range of lesbian positionalities signified within each narrative affords a variety of points of access, identification and objectification.

In some magazines, fashion replaces or has a similar status to erotica, which was previously the place where style and visual transgression were housed. What,

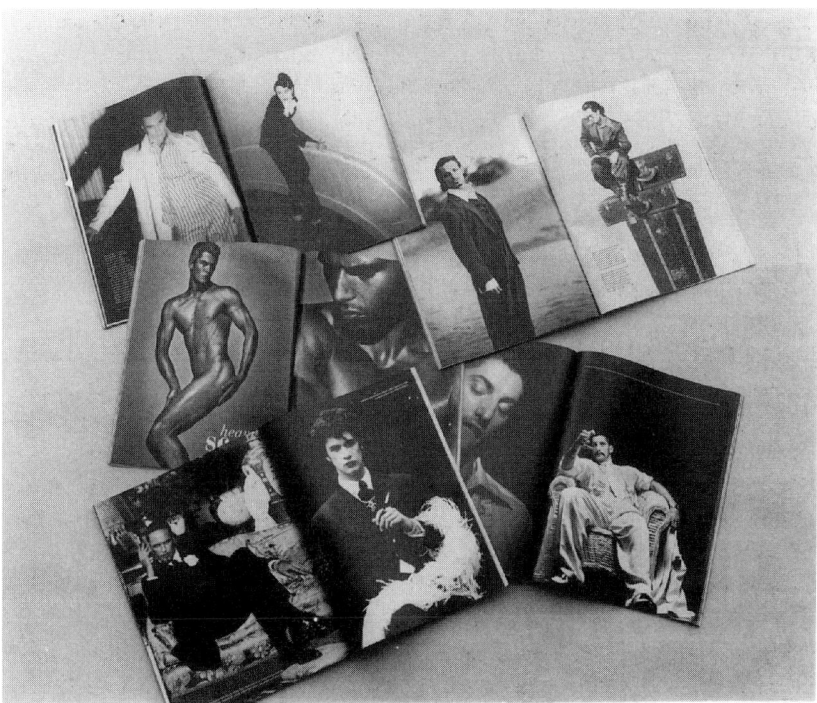

Figure 41.4 Glamour Boys
(Photographer: Simon Pattle)

one might wonder, is the relationship between visuals in *Girlfriend* that are coded as fashion, those identified as erotic, and others, that are labelled as 'portfolio' (artists' photographs which are also style-driven in content)?

The ambivalence that seems to be possible in *Attitude* but not in *Diva* may also be linked to the ownership of the look at the point of production: where *Diva* uses only lesbian photographers, *Attitude* and *Girlfriends* feature photographers of both genders and unspecified sexual orientation. Kobena Mercer, in his analysis of the homosexual pleasures available to him in Mapplethorpe's difficult and ambiguous images of black men, argues that it matters very much who is looking (Mercer 1994). He insists that it is Mapplethorpe's insertion of himself into the subcultural scene he represents (via the self-portraits) that allows him to construct himself and hence the viewer as both owner and object of the homoerotic gaze, leading to a 'participatory observation' and 'ironic ethnography' (Mercer 1994: 195). But in *Attitude* we do not know if the photographer is gay, although they are certainly gay-literate. In *Diva* we do know that the photograph's point of origin is female and can assume from the politics of the magazine that this is lesbian. In *Girlfriends* we know that sometimes the photographer is male. But here, another set of subcultural competencies associated with a lesbian sadomasochism and a pro-sex discourse can intervene to assert a cross-gender, cross-sexuality community of interest that protects a male-produced image from charges of invalidity. In terms of the specific subcultural competencies that are mobilized by *Girlfriends* (its adverts, editorial and features), the inclusion of male photographers' erotic lesbian images becomes an assertion of a lesbian identity that transgresses a subcultural orthodoxy coded variously as vanilla, lesbian and feminist.

If fashion is an arena noted for the transience and instability of its meaning and values, what is its relationship to a field of cultural production driven in part by a desire for certainty (there must be a mass of subjects who identify as lesbian or gay in order to provide a market for the product), where some readers welcome ambivalence in the dominant but are inclined to be anxious about it when encountered in the subcultural? Mercer argues that ambivalence signals the presence of an ideological struggle over meaning. In relation to dominant definitions, this has the potential to be politically progressive: for him, the indecipherability of Mapplethorpe's pictures of black men reveals the ambivalence of the racial fetishization (in which black men are both feared and adored) against which stereotype the very foundations of whiteness as an identity rest. But, in the case of lesbian and gay lifestyle magazines, the destabilization produced by the ambivalent fashion image is not of a dominant norm, but of a subcultural identity that often sees itself as already counter-hegemonic. So what does the recognition of ambivalence give us in this instance? Well, it suggests that lesbian and gay modes of reading are varied and operate differently in different contexts. But it also suggests that this contingency does not just depend on the object consumed but also on the stability of the consumer's sense of self. Without the surety of a dominant heterosexual stereotype to transgress, lesbianism becomes worryingly hard to detect.

Conclusion: dress, recognizability and transgression

It seems that in the case of fashion spreads, lesbian visual pleasure disappears when it is with the grain. Fashion, perhaps, has an easier potential to provide pleasure for gay men, for whom an interest in fashion is often still coded as transgressive, than for lesbians, many of whom experienced fashion as a route to heterosexual conformity. Of course, other forms of lesbian culture, such as film and literature, do manage to produce lesbian pleasures with the grain. So what is specific about fashion? If it is the exercise of a subcultural competency in the act of interpretation that produces pleasure, rather than only the image itself, then maybe fashion with all its potential for visual splendour also needs to evoke narrative? It may be the potential to construct fantasy through narrativized readings that ensures the eroticized lesbian pleasures in the consumption of fashion imagery. Certainly, some narratives can more easily be made to bear same-sex investments than others, but it is probably the absence of narrative in many *Diva* spreads that accounts for their lukewarm reception. Of course, effectively constructing the sort of rich and evocative narrative structures that are so pleasurable in mainstream fashion spreads also tends to cost money, so access to higher production values as well as editorial choice would have an impact here. But it does seem that the more suggestive a spread was, the more my totally unrepresentative group of viewers liked them. But an investment in narrative need not necessarily have to be against the grain, although the reception of gay magazines suggests that lesbian and gay consumers do prefer to read oppositionally. This may be a learned habit, shared with other groups marginalized from or 'misrepresented' in dominant forms of culture (hooks

1992), but it does not explain why many heterosexuals, who might be seen as not very marginal, also prefer the connoted to the denoted. If there is a specifically subcultural investment in oppositional reading practices, how does this transfer to artifacts with subcultural conditions of production?

In this light, the mixed response to the introduction of fashion into new lesbian and gay lifestyle magazines needs to be situated in relation to other visuals in gay-produced culture, to dominant images of lesbians and gays and to changing dominant images of femininity and masculinity, as well as to the increasingly problematic relationship of style to identity for lesbian subcultures. When identity can no longer be decoded from appearance, fashion is both a newly available playground and a danger zone of irrecognizability.

Note

1 Murray Healy, conference presentation at Postmodern Times, City University, July 1995.

References

Clark, Danae (1993) 'Commodity Lesbianism' in Abelove, Barale and Halperin (eds), *The Lesbian and Gay Studies Reader*, London: Routledge.

Evans, Caroline, and Gamman, Lorraine (1995) 'The Gaze Revisited, or Reviewing Queer Viewing' in Burston and Richardson (eds), *A Queer Romance: Lesbians, Gay Men and Popular Culture*, London: Routledge.

—— and Thornton, Minna (1989) *Women and Fashion: A New Look*, London: Quartet.

Fuss, Diane (1992) 'Fashion and the Homospectatorial look', *Critical Inquiry* vol. 18, Summer, pp. 713–37.

hooks, bell (1992) *Black Looks: Race and Representation*, London: Turnaround.

Lewis, Reina, and Rolley, Katrina (1996) '(A)dressing the Dyke: Lesbian Looks and Lesbians Looking' in Horne and Lewis (eds), *Outlooks: Lesbian and Gay Sexualities and Visual Culture*, London: Routledge.

Mercer, Kobena (1994) *Welcome to the Jungle: New Positions in Black Cultural Studies*, London: Routledge.

Mort, Frank (1996) *Cultures of Consumption: Masculinities and Social Space in Late Twentieth-Century Britain*, London: Routledge.

O'Sullivan, Sue (1994) 'Girls Who Kiss Girls and Who Cares?' in Hamer and Budge (eds), *The Good, the Bad and the Gorgeous: Popular Culture's Romance with Lesbianism*, London: Pandora.

Simpson, Mark (1994) *Male Impersonators*, London: Cassell.

Walker, Lisa M. (1993) 'How to Recognize a Lesbian: the Cultural Politics of Looking Like What You Are', *Signs: Journal of Women in culture and Society*, vol. 18, no. 4.

PART SIX

Pornography

Introduction to part six

■ Nicholas Mirzoeff

ONE OF THE MORE striking features of modern visual culture has been that no sooner has a new visual medium been invented than it has been used for pornographic representation, from lithographs and photography to the Internet. Pornography cannot, then, be politely separated from other uses of visual culture. Here I am using pornography to refer to visual material whose primary purpose is to elicit a sexual response in the viewer. By not attaching a more condemnatory description to porn, I inevitably take a position in what has become one of the most contested areas of contemporary life. For while some academics have suggested that the invention of pornography is in itself one of the signs of modernity, it has more notoriously attracted vigorous opposition from some feminists, religious groups and right-wing organizations. I have decided not to include a selection from one of the anti-pornography writers in this volume because I am concerned not with pornography's right to exist but what its actual existence can tell us about visual culture. For most anti-pornography writers, male sexual response is the same to images as to people, as Catherine Mackinnon argues: 'men *have sex* with their *image* of a woman.' There is then no need to pay attention to the imagery and its visual conventions for these are simply means to an end. Accepting this position would negate the entire purpose of this volume to investigate the meanings of contemporary visual culture. Further, by restricting pornography to heterosexual men, this critique ignores the widespread use of pornography by heterosexual women, bisexuals, lesbians, gay men, teenagers exploring their sexual identity and so on. The essays in this final part of the book therefore explore the visuality of pornography and its appeal to groups beyond the traditional straight, white male porn consumer. These two areas are connected because writers exploring sexual subcultures have long been interested in understanding how such groups locate themselves within the standard tropes of (hetero)sexualized looking.

One of the obvious difficulties in policing pornography is to define it in such a way that it does not implicate art and other forms of cultural expression. In the extract from her important book *The Female Nude: Art, Obscenity and Sexuality*, Lynda Nead shows that 'the question of whether or not pornographic images have harmful effects on their viewers, which has dominated twentieth-century views on pornography, is part of a much larger and older debate on the power of representations in general' (Nead 1992). It has become conventional in such discussions to oppose the physical pleasures of pornography with the transcendent, disinterested value of art. In this system, 'art and pornography are caught in a cycle of reciprocal definition, in which each depends on the other for its meaning, significance and status'. Since the invention of mass-produced imagery, this definition has become a legal, rather than aesthetic, question. From the point of view of elite culture, pornography is always a question of mass reproduction as opposed to the singularity of art. Thus D.H. Lawrence's novel *Lady Chatterley's Lover* only became a problem when Penguin proposed to issue a paperback edition in 1961 which, as the trial judge remarked, might be read by 'your wife or servants'. The condescending tone of such remarks accounts for the difficulty in obtaining convictions for obscenity. Nor is pornography what it used to be: erotica produced by women, gays and lesbians intended for their own communities changes the issue. As Nead concludes: 'Rather than ask whom the law should protect from what, the question we should now be putting is, who has the right of access, within the law, to the representation of their sexual desire and pleasure?'

Australian cultural critic Sandra Buckley offers a case study of Nead's question in her essay ' "Penguin in Bondage" ', examining different uses of erotic imagery in Japanese society, a practice she traces to eighteenth-century pornographic woodblock prints (Buckley 1991). The audience for these prints and their descendants in twentieth-century comic books was almost exclusively male until women comic book artists initiated a genre of comics-for-girls around 1970. The extract reprinted here concentrates on these *bishonen* comics which offered their young women readers male protagonists, dramatic story lines and sexually explicit imagery. Surprisingly, the sex scenes were rarely of conventional heterosexual couples. Instead, the 'bed scenes', as they are known, often depict young male homosexual couples, with cross-dressing and gender confusion as added complications. As Buckley put it, such stories 'play endlessly with gendered identity and the relationship between that identity and sexuality, disrupting the myth of biology as destiny'. By 1990, these comics had an audience ranging from teenage girls to male university students and gay men, featuring gay, lesbian and heterosexual storylines. Highlighting the continued strength of gender stereotypes in Japan, Buckley argues that such comics provide an outlet for transgressive desires:

> However idealized or romanticized these love stories may be, they offer a rare respite from the dominant cultural production of sameness (where difference – male/female – exists only as the guarantee of the continued privileging of a phallocentric construct of normative heterosexuality).

> The objective of the *bishonen* narratives is not the transformation or naturalization of difference but the valorization of the imagined potentialities of alternative differentiations.

However, this potential was quickly counterbalanced by the explosion of hard-core 'adult' comics aimed at the (heterosexual) male consumer and differentiated according to taste like any other consumer product. The case of Japanese comics suggests that sexually explicit imagery is neither absolutely oppressive nor absolutely liberating but needs to be analysed case by case according to the circumstances in which it is produced.

One important example of pornography often ignored by its opponents is the role of pornography in gay culture, especially in Europe and the United States. Richard Dyer analyses gay pornography videos using the techniques developed by film criticism, of which he is a well-known practitioner (Dyer 1994). He argues that porn is exciting because of what it offers 'in terms of seeing what we normally do not' and finds that porn films often pay close attention to the narrative techniques of classic Hollywood cinema in which the observer is unobserved: 'the rules of classical cinema are used . . . with exactly the degree of flexibility that characterizes their use in Hollywood.' Yet, as Linda Williams observed in her study of hard-core, pornography is motivated by a desire to make visible as much as possible of the experience of sex, especially those things that are not normally seen by someone engaged in having sex (Williams 1989). For Dyer, such visualizing seems to 'push the classical conventions much further than is normal in Hollywood, perhaps to breaking point'. There is even a pornographic subgenre which he calls 'self-reflexive', calling attention to its own artificiality and acknowledging the presence of the spectator. Looking at the work of porn star Ryan Idol in video and still format, Dyer emphasizes that it is common for the actor to 'draw attention to the porn viewing situation', something that classical film theory suggests should not happen if the illusion is to be sustained. He concludes that gay culture is especially aware of the performative nature of sexuality:

> Owning to one's gay identity – itself so fragile a construct – is perilous: seeing sexuality as performance rather than being is appealing, since it does not implicate that compelling notion, the self . . . [T]he importance of doing this in the age of AIDS could not be greater.

From the gay perspective, porn is not about violence but in a very real sense about survival. Its necessary mixture of the real (sex) and the fictive (narrative) allows it to fulfil such a role, an imperfect vehicle in a dangerous and imperfect world.

References and further reading

Buckley, Sandra (1991) ' "Penguin in Bondage": A Graphic Tale of Japanese Comic Books', in Constance Penley and Andrew Ross (eds), *Technoculture*, Minneapolis: Minnesota University Press.

Dworkin, Andrea (1981) *Pornography: Men Possessing Women,* New York: Putnam.

Dyer, Richard (1994) 'Idol Thoughts: Orgasm and Self-Reflexivity in Gay Pornography', *Critical Quarterly* 36, Spring: 49–62.

Foster, Thomas (ed.) (1997) *Sex Positives? The Cultural Politics of Dissident Sexualities,* New York: New York University Press.

Hunt, Lynn (ed.) (1993) *The Invention of Pornography: Obscenity and the Margins of Modernity,* New York: Zone.

Nead, Lynda (1992) *The Female Nude: Art, Obscenity and Sexuality,* London: Routledge.

Williams, Linda (1989) *Hard Core: Power, Pleasure and the Frenzy of the Visible,* Berkeley: University of California Press.

Chapter 42

Lynda Nead

FROM *THE FEMALE NUDE: ART, OBSCENITY AND SEXUALITY*

Pure and motivated pleasure

CULTURAL DISTINCTIONS ARE made through the production of norms of behaviour and expectations concerning the nature of an encounter with a work of art. In this context, illicit culture may be understood in terms of its deviation from these norms of cultural appropriation. Historically, the association of high art with a repudiation of the physical and sensory world emerges within the context of Enlightenment aesthetics. But in earlier periods too, the frontier between publicly acceptable and unacceptable forms of cultural consumption was established in relation to historically specific sexual and moral criteria. It is probably more accurate, therefore, to speak of the internalization of these cultural norms during the Enlightenment, such that the elevated, 'pure' gaze of the public domain was extended to individual responses to high art in private situations as well as in public.

There are a number of myths, which are frequently recirculated, concerning the stimulating effects on male viewers of nude female statues and paintings. In his *Natural History* Pliny describes an assault on Praxiteles' statue of Aphrodite of Cnidos. It seems that a young man had become so infatuated with the statue that he hid himself one night in the shrine and masturbated on the statue, leaving a stain on its thigh – a testimony to the figure's lifelike qualities and the cue for this particular fantasy of male arousal. Of course, the physical dimensions of the free-standing statue might be seen to enhance the potential for sexual arousal. The statue cannot only be touched, but it can also, in fantasy at least, be held and embraced. The inevitable extension of this kinetic experience is the myth of Pygmalion, in which the female statue is not only embraced but also responds to that embrace. In another permutation of this fantasy of male arousal there is the case from sixteenth-century Italy, of Aretino, who so admired the exceptional realism of a painted nude Venus by Sansorino that he claimed 'it will fill the thoughts of all who look at it with lust'. Over two centuries later, there is the example of the bibliophile Henry George Quin, who crept into the Uffizi in Florence when no one was there, in order to admire the Medici Venus and who confessed to having 'fervently kissed several parts of her divine body'. All three of these instances deserve to be fully examined in the light of their specific historical circumstances; but in the context of this discussion of the formation of cultural distinctions, some different kinds of observations can be made. Although all these examples seem to present a view of artistic appreciation that is open to male sexual arousal, this possibility arises, in all three cases, through exceptional circumstances. For Aretino, the realism of the image seems to draw the viewer directly into a speculation on the female sexual body, rather than towards a meditation on the body in and as art. In the stories from Pliny and Quin in particular, the arousal involves covert behaviour, with the male viewer creeping secretly into the special sanctuary of the statue (the shrine and the gallery), in order to be able to respond sexually to the object, unseen by other viewers. Sexual arousal (and, more precisely, sexual gratification) may be a possible response to an art object, but it is an inappropriate one. The excitement is produced, partly at least, by the transgression of and deviation from norms of public viewing and by the relocation of the work of art within the realm of the forbidden. The viewer's gaze, in all three cases, lacks the elevated intent demanded by high culture and the image is responded to in terms of its content, rather than its formal qualities.

In spite of historical variations, the basic division between respectable, public art and a pure pleasure, and forbidden, private culture and a sensual pleasure is a useful one. Cultural distinctions are, to a certain extent, a matter of defining and controlling the effect of the image or object on the viewer, of drawing the line between the pure gaze of the connoisseur and the motivated gaze of the cultural vandal. The power of representations to *move* their viewers has been the subject of concern within Western culture from the outset. For Plato, all representations are debased since they draw attention away from the real world which is itself only a shadow of the ideal. For Aristotle, the viewer's encounter with a representation is a self-contained, cathartic experience. The audience of a tragedy may be moved to pity and fear but these emotions are exhausted within the duration of the drama and do not extend beyond the period of the play. So, the question of whether or not pornographic images have harmful effects on their viewers, which has dominated twentieth-century views on pornography, is part of a much larger and older debate on the power of representations in general. The potential of representations to move is not intrinsically harmful; after all, works of art are sometimes also believed to be moral exemplars and to guide and improve those who come within their domain. The problem arises in relation to the nature of the influence of the image and the kind of action to which the viewer is inclined. For some writers on the subject, the sole aim of the pornographic representation is to bring about a sexual catharsis in the viewer and it is the singularity of this purpose that sets pornography apart from all other kinds of representations. In his study of Victorian pornography entitled *The Other Victorians* Steven Marcus draws some conclusions about pornography generally:

> Literature possesses . . . a multitude of intentions, but pornography possesses only one . . . [Pornography's] success is physical, measurable, quantifiable; in it the common pursuit of true judgement comes to a dead halt. On this side then, pornography falls into the same category as much simpler forms of literary utterance as propaganda and advertising. Its aim is to move us in the direction of action. Pornography is obsessed with the idea of pleasure, of infinite pleasure, the idea of gratification.[1]

For Marcus, pornography's distinctiveness lies, at once, in measurement and immeasurability. Since its purpose is to move the male viewer towards sexual gratification, this physical response may be easily quantified. But its true character also lies in excess, in offering pleasure and desire beyond boundaries. Marcus's influential study was first published in 1966; six years later, Lord Longford used the same extract to endorse his own view of the damaging effects of pornography. But for Longford, the 'harm' of pornography lies not only in its promiscuous and undifferentiated sexual motivation, but also in the fact that its effects last beyond the duration of exposure to the image. The legacy of pornography, for Longford, is an undiscriminating and sexually motivated society.

It is significant that Marcus draws an analogy between the motivating force of pornography and that of advertising. The analogy draws out the connection between economic and sexual metaphor. Both forms of cultural production are intent on selling and persuading to 'spend'. Both forms might also be said to be promiscuous in their address, in their desire to attract and excite with their images as wide a public as possible. If the pleasures of pornography are defined in terms of motivation, promiscuity and commodification, then the pleasures of art are seen to lie in their opposing values, in contemplation, discrimination and transcendent value. These distinctions have been embodied in legal definitions of obscenity since the nineteenth century. In the debates leading up to the passing of Lord Campbell's Obscene Publications Act in 1857, there was concern that paintings of a sexually explicit nature, held in private collections, might fall within the scope of the proposed Act. Campbell reassured Parliament that this was not the case.

> The pictures in such collections were not intended for sale, but were kept for the owner's contemplation . . . It was not against the masterpieces of Correggio that the Bill was levelled but against the mass of impure publications, which was poured forth on London, to the great injury of the youth of the country.[2]

Art and pornography are being defined here in terms of quality, ownership and access. Art is not on sale; it is reserved for the contemplative viewing of its sole owner. Pornography, on the other hand, is seen as an undifferentiated mass of impurity, bought and sold and wreaking havoc in the public domain. In his attempt to distinguish art and pornography, Campbell's language begins to reinvoke the boundaries of the body. Art is based on a model of continence; it is kept, held within the body, unlike pornography which pours out beyond the body and into the city streets.

Within the British legal system, pornography itself is not against the law; it is the presence of obscenity that constitutes the legal offence. The first legal definition of obscenity was given by Lord Chief Justice, Sir Alexander Cockburn, in an 1868 case *R.* v. *Hicklin*, in which the term was defined as 'the tendency to deprave and corrupt'. But . . . the etymological roots of 'obscene' also convey the sense of matter that is beyond representation, that cannot be shown. Obscenity therefore signifies that which motivates harmful sexual behaviour and that which is beyond the accepted codes of public visibility.

This structural distinction between the harmful effectiveness of obscenity and the intrinsic value of art was enshrined in the Obscene Publications Act of 1959, which introduced the defence of 'artistic merit' in obscenity trials. The physical, moral or spiritual harm believed to be caused by obscenity was now to be weighed against the perceived artistic merit of the work. Artistic value was defined as a justification or amelioration of obscene material. By introducing this defence, the law effectively gave punitive force to the polarization of art and pornography. 'Absolute' obscenity became synonymous with absolute cultural worthlessness; obscenity was defined as much in terms of its absence of artistic value as in terms of its actual potential to pervert, debase or defile.

The attribution to pornography of the power to affect behaviour has cultural implications that go beyond the particularities of the obscene and bear upon our understanding of the significance of cultural representations in general. These implications are nowhere better demonstrated than in the American Congressional report of the Commission on Obscenity and Pornography, which released its findings on 30 September 1970. The report rejected any clear correlation between pornography and acts of sexual violence and advocated a liberalizing of sex education, in order to foster 'healthy' sexual development. The report resulted in a split between members of the Commission and was rejected by the Senate and President. On 25 October 1970, President Nixon's repudiation of the report was published in the *New York Times*:

> The Commission contends that the proliferation of filthy books and plays has no lasting harmful effect on a man's character. If that be true, it must also be true that great books, great paintings and great plays have no ennobling effect on a man's conduct. Centuries of civilization and ten minutes of common sense tell us otherwise.[3]

What Nixon's statement inadvertently reveals is that the supposedly harmful effects of pornography are inseparable from the supposedly beneficial effects of art. Deny the motivating force of pornography and you implicitly deny the fundamental values traditionally ascribed to Western civilization. Art and pornography are caught in a cycle of reciprocal definition, in which each depends on the other for its meaning, significance and status. Momentarily, in the statement in the *New York Times*, this system of cultural distinction breaks down; but it is only momentary and Nixon marshals the combined authority of civilization and common sense to shore up the framing cultural opposition of moral guidance and corruption, of pure and motivated pleasure.

Policing the boundaries

The 1961 trial of Penguin Books, who were planning to issue *Lady Chatterley's Lover* in paperback, has become one of the key moments in the regulation of obscenity. During his summary of the case, the judge, Mr Mervyn Griffith-Jones, expressed his concern that:

> once a book goes into circulation it does not spend its time in the rarefied atmosphere of some academic institution . . . it finds its way into the bookshops and on to bookstalls at 3s 6d a time, into the public libraries where it is available to all and sundry.

The concern in 1961 was that the book would fall into the *wrong* hands, a possibility that was exacerbated by cheap printing methods and lending libraries. Public libraries, which had been established in the mid-nineteenth century for the provision of education for the artisan classes, are here transformed, by the spectre of paperback pornography, into disseminators of vice and immorality. What had been intended for the edification of the working classes could, it seemed, turn into a conduit for their degradation. The concern in 1961 was not so much about the content of the novel, as about the constituency of its audience. Later in the trial, the judge told the jury that the question that they should ask themselves was:

> Would you approve of your young sons, young daughters – because girls can read as well as boys – reading this book? Is it a book you would have lying around in your own house? Is it a book that you would even wish your wife or your servants to read?

The successful defence of the publication of the novel was achieved through the expert witnesses who attested to its literary merit. Nevertheless, the advice given to the jury reveals how the policing of boundaries of cultural distinction involves not so much, or not simply, a policing of obscenity in texts, as a regulation of viewers and viewing situations. Put very simply (and this is typified in the judge's advice given at the *Lady Chatterley* trial), obscenity is that which, at any given moment, a particular dominant group does not wish to see in the hands of another, less dominant, group. This section will therefore examine some of the legislative moves, enacted since the middle of the nineteenth century, to regulate access to the obscene.

In *The Secret Museum* Walter Kendrick traces the emergence of the modern category of pornography and argues that the only possible definition of pornography is in terms of its identity as the illicit or forbidden sphere of culture. Although the later part of his book adopts a strongly anti-feminist stance, as a whole it does present some useful insights into the historical relationships of pornography, censorship and modernity. Kendrick holds that the history of pornography is a relatively recent phenomenon that is inseparable from the history of censorship and the developments of modern mass culture. Rejecting the idea that there are any common formal characteristics among pornographic texts, he cites as evidence the range of objects and publications that were regarded as objectionable and potentially harmful during the nineteenth century – from sexually explicit statuettes unearthed at Pompeii, to Victorian sensation novels and investigative studies of prostitution. According to Kendrick, the history of pornography in the twentieth century takes the form of increased specialization and specification of the obscene. As the legal definition of the non-obscene is widened to include technical, medical, educational and artistic representations, so the category of obscenity is narrowed and increasingly takes on the particular label of 'pornography' – the explicit and illicit representation of sex and sexual bodies for the sole purpose of arousal.

Pompeii provides the model for Kendrick's conceptualization of pornography. The Romans had displayed sexually explicit artefacts on street corners and in public buildings. Only in the eighteenth century were 'gentlemen' archaeologists faced with the paradox of the valuable rarity of the objects, alongside the perception of their immorality. The question was how to enable the dissemination of knowledge, whilst restricting access to the corruption of the obscene:

> What was required was a new taxonomy: if Pompeii's priceless obscenities were to be properly managed, they would have to be systematically named and placed. The name chosen for them was 'pornography', and they were housed in the Secret Museum.[4]

It was in this moment of segregation, in the separation of 'dangerous' works from the rest of ordinary culture, that the objects took on their full 'pornographic' meaning. The Secret Museum was perceived as a safeguard, taken to protect certain, vulnerable sections of the public from corruption and arousal. As one official guide to the Naples collection, published in the 1870s, stated:

> We have endeavoured to make its reading inaccessible, so to speak, to poorly educated persons, as well as to those whose sex and age forbid any exception to the laws of decency and modesty. With this end in mind, we have done our best to regard each of the objects we have had to describe from an exclusively archaeological and scientific point of view. It has been our intention to remain calm and serious throughout. In the exercise of his holy office, the man of science must neither blush nor smile. We have looked upon our statues as an anatomist contemplates his cadavers.

The guide to the Secret Museum is one of repeated attempts, during the nineteenth century, to secure the Pompeiian artefacts for art and science and to repudiate utterly the debased responses associated with obscenity. So the author insists – over-insists perhaps – on the seriousness and objectivity of the enterprise. It is a sacred project rather than a profane one, and in his search for analogies to reassure himself and his readers, he hits upon the anatomist examining a corpse. The pleasure-seeking eye of the voluptuary is dispatched in favour of the dissecting gaze of the scientist. Dead flesh, to be sure, but more animate, nevertheless, than the marble and clay of the statuettes.

In its insistent claims to scientific status, the presentation of the Secret Museum may be compared to nineteenth-century writings on prostitution and public hygiene. The etymology of 'pornography' is the 'writings of harlots' but, as Kendrick points out, this was extended to the precarious status of investigations of prostitution by authors such as Parent-Duchâtelet in France and William Acton in England, in the middle decades of the nineteenth century. Here again, the boundaries between a serious, scientific and moral enterprise and a text of frivolity, arousal and innuendo had to be assiduously maintained. The charts of statistics and tables, the repeated claims to sobriety and objectivity, were attempts to differentiate the social investigation of immorality from the immoral behaviour itself. But in their constant reiteration of social utility and self-control, the texts also served to remind the readers of the possibility of other, more frivolous and forbidden responses to the material. During the nineteenth century, the modern concept of pornography was established by the annexation of texts and objects that seemed to embody 'dangerous' knowledge. At the same time the creation of a legal category of the obscene in the 1857 Obscene Publications Act enabled the pornographic to be constructed as a bounded domain, classified through its identification with the forbidden and the illicit. Pornography in the modern period describes a zone of disorder and irregularity within the standards and rules of moral society.

The drawbacks of Kendrick's analysis have already been alluded to. By conjoining the history of pornography and the history of censorship, Kendrick creates a continuum of social attitudes to the forbidden that makes no attempt to differentiate the various views of censorship held by different historical groups. For Kendrick, there is little to distinguish the middle-class gentlemen legislators of the nineteenth century from the recent, pro-censorship feminist campaigns against pornography. Whilst it may be true that these groups occupy common ground within a broad history of censorship, it is also essential to examine the particularities of and differences between their political aims and strategies. In addition, by restricting his definition of pornography to that which is defined as forbidden within the dominant culture, Kendrick fails to examine or raise the question of the formal and generic characteristics of pornographic representation at given historical periods. Pornography has also to be understood in terms of the production of particular expectations concerning the formal elements of the representation, such as the deployment of narrative devices, of written and pictorial language, and the accessibility and visibility of the body.

What is most convincing about Kendrick's argument, however, is the connection that he makes between pornography, censorship and modern mass culture. If the boundaries of obscenity are policed through the regulation of audiences, then it follows that the greatest threat will be posed by forms with the greatest potential circulation. Following on from Steven Marcus, Kendrick dates the emergence of pornography to the early nineteenth century and the changing concept of a 'public'. Cheaper printing methods and rising literacy rates, along with the concentration of populations in urban centres, made it less and less certain into whose hands a picture or book might fall. The fear was, increasingly, that dangerous material would fall into the hands of 'vulnerable' groups such as women, children and the poor, those with a predisposition to depravity or without the self-discipline to resist it.

If pornography is identified as a problem of mass culture, then, viewed from another perspective, one of the few stable, legal definitions of art is its uniqueness and authenticity. Legislation in Britain affecting the arts has been enacted in a number of areas, including income tax, copyright laws, customs and excise duties, and museums and galleries. In all these cases there has to be a working definition of the category of art, and frequently the boundary of the aesthetic is drawn in relation to the number of copies of the work and the means of production of the copy. For example, under Customs and Excise regulations, hand-produced copies of paintings, pastels and drawings are granted value-added-tax exemption; whilst mass-produced copies are not. Artistic status is thus awarded in relation to the work's distinction from mass culture. If pornography is popularly held to represent sex devoid of human feeling, then equally it is seen to be produced by means that are mechanical and dehumanized. We might expect, therefore, that the difficult or borderline cases will be those that blur the distinguishing characteristics of art and pornography, those that confuse the media, locations and audiences associated with these cultural categories. A memorandum from 1970 to the Obscene Publications Squad lists a number of instances where there might be some difficulty in categorizing material, including 'displays in recognized galleries and books expensively published'. In other words, in its legal and criminal classification, pornography tends to be defined in terms of being mass-produced, cheap and new. This understanding could only be formulated against a conception of art as unique, valuable (priceless) and marked with the aura of age.

To a large extent, the policing of the boundaries of art and obscenity is a question of the projection of imagined viewers and audiences and the invocation of norms of moral and sexual values. This has been built into the law through references to the 'public good' and 'community standards'. In the United States, the Supreme Court case of *Miller* v. *California* in 1973 set out three criteria that need to be met for a work to be found obscene. The first of these criteria is that 'the average person, applying contemporary community standards, would find that the work, taken as a whole, appeals to prurient interest'. In the same year, English juries at obscenity trials were enjoined to 'keep in mind the current standards of ordinary decent people'. These criteria are obviously extremely vague and, possibly as a result, it has proved difficult to win an obscenity conviction within these terms. Nevertheless, the prioritizing of community standards and the assumption of moral consensus has encouraged a normalizing of certain sexualities and an outlawing of those sexual identities and desires that are seen to deviate from the accepted norms. The legacy of these assumptions concerning community standards is seen in recent legislation in Britain and the United States. Although this legislation is not a direct revision of existing obscene publications law, it seeks to extend the regulation of obscenity to publicly funded cultural production. What is more alarming is that obscenity, understood in terms of the promotion of harm and the intention to corrupt, is now being targeted specifically in relation to homosexuality. In Britain the passing into law of Section 28 of the Local Government Act (1987–88) prohibits local authority funding of activities that are deemed to 'promote homosexuality'. In 1989, in the United States, Senator Jesse Helms spearheaded a campaign to prohibit the use of public funds from the National Endowment for the Arts, for work that might be deemed to be 'obscene'. During his campaign, Helms chose as one of his main targets an exhibition by the photographer Robert Mapplethorpe, denouncing his photographs of homosexual erotica as pornographic and obscene. In both contexts, the policing of the boundaries of cultural acceptability is, quite blatantly, a policing of the boundaries of sexual acceptability. Within this legislation, homosexuality and the homosexual body [are] obscene; [they are] beyond representation and must be rendered invisible. In both cases, the strategy adopted is similar, taking the form of pre-emptive measures that anticipate the regulation of the images themselves by promoting self-regulation and self-censorship, prior to the production of the object or funding of the project. Within these recent developments, the traditional role of obscenity legislation to regulate access to 'dangerous' material has become focused on the representation of homosexuality. Now, however, the aim is not simply to restrict but to ensure that it is never made visible at all.

In the extracts from the trial of *Lady Chatterley's Lover* given at the beginning of this section, what is most striking is the certainty on the part of the judge concerning which categories of the community are in need of protection from obscene material. The unspoken norm here is the middle-class gentleman, who is the addressee of the judge's comments and who may also be trusted to come into contact with obscenity without coming to harm. In the 1990s these assumptions regarding the probable audiences of pornography and the function of legislation appear outmoded and irrelevant. It is no longer accurate to assume a male audience for 'straight', heterosexual pornography. Recent studies of video pornography have shown that female viewers are the largest potential growth-market for pornographic films and that women are beginning to play a more powerful role within the industry itself, as producers and directors, as well as stars. It has been argued that predominantly female companies such as Femme Productions are producing new kinds of pornography, aimed at an audience of women and couples in the home. In her book *Hard Core*, Linda Williams has argued that the pornography being produced by Femme offers a new exploration of female sexual desire, as well as different narratives and better production values. She writes:

> If the new pornography for couples and women exemplified by Femme Productions seems safe, almost too legitimate for some masculine eyes, it could be this legitimacy is needed to enable women to create for themselves the safe space in which they can engage in sex without guilt or fear . . . This much is clear: it is no longer for men alone to decide what is, or is not, exciting in pornography.[5]

Whether or not Williams is right in her characterization of the new pornography for women, she is surely correct in her concluding statement. The middle-class gentleman can no longer maintain exclusive control over the production and consumption of sexual imagery. Rather than ask whom should the law protect from what, the question we should not be putting is, who has the right of access, within the law, to the representation of their sexual desire and pleasure?

Notes

1 Steven Marcus (1966) *The Other Victorians: A Study of Sexuality and Pornography in Mid-Nineteenth Century England*, London: Weidenfeld & Nicholson, p. 278.

2 *Hansard Parliamentary Debates*, 3rd series, vol. 146, 25 June 1857: col. 329.

3 *New York Times*, 25 October 1970: 71.

4 Walter Kendrick (1987) *The Secret Museum: Pornography in Modern Culture*, New York: Viking, p. 11.

5 Linda Williams (1990) *Hard Core: Power, Pleasure and the 'Frenzy of the Visible'*, London, Sydney, Wellington: Pandora, p. 264.

Chapter 43

Sandra Buckley

'PENGUIN IN BONDAGE'

A graphic tale of Japanese comic books

[T]HE JAPANESE WORD for the comic books is *manga*. It is said to have been first coined by the Edo woodblock artist Hokusai Katsushika (1760–1849) to describe the comic woodblock images that were so popular at that time. Even the better known and more successful woodblock artists such as Hokusai were not above producing pornographic *manga* prints for a rapidly expanding market. This was a quick and easy way to make money. The introduction and rapid refinement of woodblock printing during the Edo period arguably provided the most significant catalyst in the circulation of pornographic images at that time. The commercialization of pornography developed hand in hand with the technology of reproduction. The *shunga* are today generally referred to as Japanese erotic art, and yet they too date back to this same period and were printed as a form of poster art available for purchase by the Yoshiwara patrons. The *shunga* prints represented the whole range of sexual options available to the patron of the quarters – heterosexual, gay, lesbian, and masturbatory images show a vast repertoire of sexual practices for sale or fantasy. The patron who could not afford the 'real thing' – the price tag on a high-ranking or popular prostitute was well beyond the pocket of the average patron – could always buy a poster and take it home. The most popular images went through multiple editions. Lautrec brought poster art to France, and today we have the pinup. Marilyn Monroe stands, legs splayed, skirt flying, over the same street vent on a million walls. Whether the *shunga* are erotic art or pornography is largely a question of context (context of production, consumption, and viewing); this is an issue we will come back to.

The developments in printing were not the only technological dimension of the Edo pornography industry. Both the *manga* and *shunga* specialized in representations of exotic and unlikely sexual practices involving remarkable acts of contortion and prowess between every imaginable combination of life forms. Variation and originality were important in an increasingly competitive market.

The prints frequently involved any number of an assortment of popular sex aids of the day. The lists of items available for purchase by prostitutes and patrons at any of the local 'knickknack' stores in the Edo brothel quarters (the largest quarter was the Yoshiwara district) would put even the most specialized of today's 'adult accessory stores' to shame.

The consumer audience of the Edo *manga* was predominantly male, and the humor is constructed around the phallocentric fantasy and desire of the male patron. More playfully put, these are phallacies. The same can be said of the woodblock prints, certain genres of popular fiction (which included various styles of illustrated narratives considered by some to be the precursors of the modern Japanese comic book), and even, perhaps I should say especially, the sex aids. Prints of lesbian or male homosexual sex or of prostitutes (male or female) masturbating were extremely popular. Woodblock depictions of lesbian sex almost always involved some form of phallus substitute, most often a dildo strapped to the body of one of the lovers. Images of a woman masturbating with a dildo – covered in animal skin or intricate carvings – strapped to her foot, while acknowledging the active sexual desire of the female, ultimately reinscribe the phallus into the autoerotic moment, and draw attention to the cultural insistence that even if it doesn't take two to tango it does take one plus a phallus.

This phallo-technology was an integral component of the commodification and commercialization of sex in the Edo period. That there was a degree of cooperation and entrepreneurship involved between the suppliers of the sex aids and the woodblock print shops is not documented, but is a reasonable assumption given the highly commercialized environment of the brothel districts. The same association is easily documented today in the pornographic comic books, where page after page of advertisements for increasingly technologized sex aids blur into the image-texts of the surrounding stories, where the 'goods' are contextualized into the sexual practice and fantasy represented there. While the complexity of technology and design has shifted dramatically, the basic concept and function of the manual sex aids on the market in Edo and contemporary Japan have altered very little. Pleasure remains intricately bound to penetration, whether it be anal or vaginal, heterosexual , homosexual, or masturbatory. Today, the silk kimono and wooden dildo of Edo are transformed into leather and steel, with a complimentary rechargeable battery included with each order over 10,000 yen.

It was the Meiji period and the reopening of contact with the West that witnessed the first major crackdown on pornography in Japan. It was the desire to meet with the perceived moral standards of the West that would finally result in the introduction and enforcement of strict censorship codes to regulate the publication of both images and written texts. While there were laws restricting pornography during the Edo period, they had little impact on production and circulation. Throughout the Meiji and Taisho periods there was extensive experimentation with Western-style comic strips and cartoons, but there was a very low tolerance of any explicitly sexual references. It was during the Second World War that the next examples of what might be called pornographic comics appeared. These were produced by the Japanese as propaganda to be dropped on the Allied troops in the Pacific. They showed scenes of G.I. Joe's wife 'having a good time' back home while he fought the good fight on the front, or suffering as a widow at the hands of some lusty, ugly character. Comics dropped on Australian and New Zealand troops depicted their wives being raped by larger-than-life G.I.s stalking the cities on R&R. The Occupation forces did nothing to stifle the rash of political comic strips that flourished in the climate of change immediately after the war. However, the Allied Command was not tolerant of anything that was considering disruptive to social morale, and this included any image that was deemed pornographic. While comics for children and political satire were extremely popular throughout the 1950s, it was not until the late 1960s that the first 'erotic' images would find their way back into the comic repertoire.

[. . .]

By the late 1960s women began to break into the ranks of the comic artists. As teenage girls who had grown up as devotees of the *manga* began to seek a place for themselves within the industry, the narrative structures of the comics-for-girls became far more complex and moved beyond the normative boundaries perpetuated by the male predecessors of this new generation of female comic artists. The first major shift came with *Seventeen*'s serialization of Mizuno Hideko's 'Fire' from 1969 to 1971. The hero is an American rock star by the name of Aaron. It was this story that depicted the first sexually explicit scenes in the postwar comic books. Aaron pursues a life of sex, music, drugs, and violence. His career as a rock star is ended when his hand is badly injured in a violent encounter with the Hell's Angels. It has been argued that the story was in fact a quite conservative morality tale, with Aaron meeting an appropriately sad ending in a ward of a mental institution. This reading, however, ignores the fact that for two years the readers of 'Fire' anxiously awaited the next installment of Aaron's wild life. There are stories of queues of teenage girls waiting for the next issue to hit the shelves of the bookstores.

The serialization of 'Fire' marked several significant shifts in the comics-for-girls. The most obvious shift was to a male protagonist. The object of longing of the female protagonists of the earlier comics was usually male, but the female remained the central focus of the narrative. What is more, the male characters were consistently above reproach, unlike Aaron. Mizuno created a male protagonist who was neither the boy next door nor a shining prince. Aaron was given all the physical characteristics of the princely role, but it was his non-conventional, rebellious behavior that Mizuno developed to attract and hold her readership. The anticipation of sexually explicit images and references was also clearly an important motivation for the teenage female readership.

The shift to male protagonists took a further turn with Ikeda Riyoko's 'Rose of Versailles' (*Margaret*, 1972–74). In this work, heterosexual love was replaced by male homosexual love, complete with 'bed scenes,' as they came to be known in Japanese (*beedo sheenu*), depicting young homosexual couples. It is somewhat problematic to describe the 'bed scene' in 'Rose of Versailles' as homosexual. The protagonist, Oscar, is a girl who has been raised as a boy by her/his military family. Oscar eventually ends up becoming a member of Marie Antoinette's personal guard and falls in love with a nobleman called Von Ferson. In a complicated and playful scene of gender confusion, Oscar dresses her/himself up in splendid evening dress and spends a romantic evening in public with Von Ferson, never disclosing that the boy cross-dressed as a girl is really female after all. Unfortunately for Oscar, Von Ferson eventually declares his real love to be Marie Antoinette.

Another homosexual relationship develops between Oscar and André, the son of Oscar's childhood nursemaid. Oscar wins André's lifelong devotion and love when she/he saves his life. When Oscar finally reveals her/himself to be female, the story takes still another turn. André's love for Oscar is based on his homoerotic desire for the person he perceives to be a beautiful young man. Oscar's declaration that she/he is female is presented as a narrative escape from the 'dilemma' of the homosexual relationship – the normative transformation of homosexual love to heterosexual – the solution is a false one, however, for there is an even greater barrier to Oscar and André's future together, and that is class. The female Oscar cannot marry someone as lowly as André. The story ends with the death of both – André at the barricades and Oscar at the Bastille.

'Rose of Versailles' plays endlessly with gendered identity and the relationship between that identity and sexuality, disrupting the myth of biology as destiny. Gender is mobile, not fixed, in this story. In 1971 Moto Hagio published a short story titled 'The November Gymnasium,' which explored the love–hate relationship of two beautiful young boys, Eric and Thoma. The narrative tension is sustained at the level of suppressed homoerotic desire of the two boys. They are like two sides of a coin; where Eric is strong willed and violent, Thoma is gentle and loving. It is eventually revealed that they are indeed twins. At the end of the story, Thoma dies. The only moment of physical contact Moto allows the two is a brief embrace. However, in 1974 Moto reworked the story of Eric into a much longer serialized comic titled *The Heart of Thoma*. In the later work Moto developed the theme of homoerotic love more openly, as she continued the story of Eric and his relationship of love and rivalry with three other youths after the death of Thoma. Ikeda's story opened the way for a whole new genre of *bishonen* (beautiful young boy) comic stories of homosexual love. These stories of homosexual lovers pursuing one another across an exotic and fantastic landscape of mountains, forests, chalets, and palaces are a far cry from the comic books read by American teenage girls in the 1960s.

It was the *bishonen* comics that first broke the public taboo on the representation of sex in the *manga* in the late 1960s and the 1970s. This trend saw the emergence of the magazine *June*, which specializes in *bishonen* stories. In 1990 the target readership of *June* remains teenage girls, but there is little doubt that it now has an extensive crossover readership that includes a significant gay male following. For a period in the 1970s the comics-for-girls were a major testing ground for the censorship laws. In addition to the homoerotic *bishonen* stories, the popular and influential comic artists branched out into stories of lesbian love and increasingly explicit representations of heterosexual sex. What made it possible for the comics-for-girls to go as far as they did was the so-called bed scene. As long as the characters did not roll over or come out from under the covers completely, there was no technical breach of the law, which specifically concerned itself only with the display of public hair and penis. The bed sheets crept further and further off the body, and occasionally an artist would risk a standing embrace or full-body profile. Buttocks survived the scrutiny of the censors and became a permanent feature by the early 1970s.

The *bishonen* genre continues to be extremely popular among the comics-for-girls on the market today. Sales of popular biweekly and monthly titles remain in the millions. *June* continues to be one of the major selling comics-for-girls as the industry moves into the 1990s. Its sales figures are undoubtedly boosted by the number of gay and crossover readers. The *June* layout is now standardized and relatively predictable. Each month's edition includes a mixture of serialized comic stories, still shots from recent movies with either a homosexual storyline or a popular androgynous actor (the July 1989 issue included stills of Rupert Everett in *Another Country*, Jeremy Irons in *Dead Ringers*, assorted stills of Hugh Grant, and Prince's *Batman* video), reproductions of advertisements featuring male bodies (the same issue included Hugh Grant for *L'Uomo*, a French anti-AIDS campaign poster, and a French advertisement for Nike running shoes showing a group of male marathon runners standing exhausted in the rain), reviews of new record and video releases, listings of popular back issues (under the title '*June*, the Discrimination-Free Comic Magazine'), advice columns (including letters from teenage girls about their own heterosexual problems and inquiring about homosexual love, and also letters from gay males seeking advice on issues from safe sex to new gay clubs), advertisements for gay and transvestite clubs, and the regular feature of a sealed comic story. The sealed story is billed as the 'Secret Series' and presented as the 'hottest' of the stories in each issue.

The 'Secret Series' is sealed on the outer edge and bound into the spine of the comic so that it cannot be read unless one purchases the comic and tears it out. This is an innovative technique on the part of the publishers to deal with the problem known as *tachi-yomi* (literally standing and reading – browsing). Bookstores are always filled with browsers flipping through the pages of the new releases in the comic book section. The images in the 'Secret Series' are actually only marginally 'hotter' than those in the rest of the magazine. The 'Secret Series' does tend to have more violent images than is true for the rest of *June*, and some scenes represent sexual contact in a more sinister or threatening way than the usually highly stylized romanticism of homosexual love that has become the magazine's standard fare. The July 1989 issue's 'Secret Series' includes the threat of cannibalism and the suggestion of fellatio, but neither is shown explicitly, only hinted at. The most 'shocking' image of this image/text is that of two men kissing mouth to mouth. In the *bishonen* comics androgynous figures appear wrapped in each other's arms, naked in bed, passionately making love, gazing longingly into each other's eyes, and kissing each other on the cheek. However, images of the young lovers mouth kissing are rare within the *bishonen* genre to the present. A scene of a man kissing another man's lips is treated as being far more sensuous than any bed scene. The scene in the July 1989 'Secret Series' in which the mouth kiss occurs is clearly demarcated from the rest of the surrounding text by a shift from the usual white background of the frame to a solid purple background. There is no doubt that this is the one scene in this particular text that earns it the 'secret' classification. The visual and narrative tension that develops around the homosexual mouth kiss is not unique to the *manga*. In representations of homosexual love in the Edo *shunga* there was a similar tension. The mouth kiss was associated with the most intimate or intense moments of sexual contact. This was true of both homosexual and heterosexual love, but by the 1960s and 1970s the influence of

Hollywood movies had more than likely diluted the erotic value of the heterosexual mouth kiss, which now abounds in the *manga*, television dramas, and cinema. However, the tension surrounding this scene remained intact in the case of homosexual lovers.

The representation of sexual scenes in the *bishonen manga* has continued to rely upon innuendo and anticipation rather than explicit representations of sexual contact that would fall into any of the established categories of pornographic image, such as the money shot and the meat shot. These 'shots' would be contrary to the spirit of the *bishonen* genre and the expectations of its readers. The androgynous (usually) male characters explore relationships of equality that are free of domination and exploitation. There is often an exaggeratedly demonic 'bad guy' character who acts as a dramatic point of contrast for the gentleness and equality of the relationship of the homosexual lovers. It is not unusual for a narrative to follow a male character in his discovery of the possibilities of homosexual love as he gradually transfers his affections from a woman to a man.

The word *jiyu* (freedom) occurs again and again across the pages of the *bishonen* comics. The feature story of the July 1989 *June* is called 'All My Life' and follows the gradual shift of the older male protagonist's love from his girlfriend to a beautiful young boy. The story abounds in metaphors of freedom created around the older man's dream of opening an animal park. His desire to let the animals roam free, outside of cages and beyond bars, is a barely disguised reference to his own desire to live openly and outside the constraints of dominant social values. His young lover jokes that this would lead to chaos with all the different species living together, to which he replies, 'Yes, but they'd all be free.' The standard narrative progressions of the *bishonen* comics trace the trajectory of sexual fantasies that go beyond the normative boundaries of gender and sexuality. However idealized or romanticized these love stories may be, they offer a rare respite from the dominant cultural production of sameness (where difference – male/female – exists only as the guarantee of the continued privileging of a phallocentric construct of normative heterosexuality). The objective of the *bishonen* narratives is not the transformation or naturalization of difference but the valorization of the imagined potentialities of alternative differentiations.

By the 1980s the market for the *bishonen* comics had expanded far beyond the original readership of pubescent schoolgirls to include gays, heterosexual male university students, and young women, in particular young *okusan* (housewives – literally, 'the person at the back of the house'). One Japanese commentator writing on the *bishonen* comics has suggested that the reason for their popularity among teenage girls can be traced to the unwillingness of Japanese schoolgirls to deal with a growing awareness of their own sexuality. In other words, the *bishonen* comics amount to a denial of sexuality among teenage girls. Such a reading of these *manga* would itself appear to be a denial of the sexual awareness and curiosity of the millions of teenage girls who devour these comics the minute they hit the stands. If anything is being denied or rejected by the readership of the *bishonen* comics, it is the stringent construction of gender and sexual practice in postwar Japanese society.

Some Japanese feminists have suggested that the more affluent Japanese society has become, the more entrenched, but subtle, have become the mechanisms of gender organization operating across the society, from the law to education and

from advertising to domestic architecture. For a brief moment in the *bishonen* comics of the 1960s and 1970s, a new generation of female comic artists and their readership teased out the possibilities of new identifications and tested the boundaries of differentiation. It is probably not a coincidence that the readership of the *bishonen* is constituted of groups within Japanese society that could be described as transitional. The schoolgirl's passage through puberty is a heavily monitored and controlled journey from girlhood to womanhood. Within that society there are two states of womanhood – married and unmarried. The former marks a successful transition and the latter a failed transition. In the 1990s, the teenage schoolgirl continues to be educated for her role as 'good wife wise mother,' despite a national rhetoric of equal opportunity. A popular educational best-seller for mothers asserts that 'having only one science textbook . . . ignores the logical minds of boys and the daily-life orientation of girls.' It goes on to suggest that textbooks for girls include practical daily-life examples of 'how the wash gets whiter when you use bleach and how milk curdles when you add orange juice.' The same male educator suggests that young girls should always wash their own underwear (which should always be white) by hand; in this way a girl can build

> pride and awareness connected with her sex, such as the fact that her body has the capacity to create new life, that she must carefully preserve that function until the day of her marriage . . . how clear it makes a girl's heart to always keep her underwear clean.

The fact that a recent Japanese study showed that 45 per cent of the mothers surveyed want their sons to go on to four-year universities while only 18 per cent answered so for their daughters, is an indication that the level of gender discrimination represented in the above quotations is not limited to male educators. The education system, the family, the media, the entire fabric of society shroud the female pubescent body, and her body is marked with the traces of the encounter. The individuated body is inscribed as the motherbody, as an organ of the body politic. In this context, is it strange that schoolgirls are so attracted to a fantasy world of nonreproductive bodies, as remarkably non-Japanese as they are nongendered, moving across a backdrop of a nonspecific landscape that is nowhere or, more specifically, that is anywhere that is not Japan? These same schoolgirls often continue reading the *bishonen* comics long after they leave school and girlhood for marriage and womanhood. As an *okusan* the young woman occupies the motherly space. She is defined as nurturer to both husband and children. Her sexuality is circumscribed by the boundaries of the motherbody. Little wonder she seeks out the imaginary space of the *bishonen* comics in moments of disengagement.

There are some who go so far as to suggest that Japanese men are never required to pass through that process of separation that has been described as the most traumatic transition for the male – separation from the motherbody. The *nauui* (from the English *now* meaning trendy or vogue) Japanese word for this imperfectly oedipalized male condition is *mazaa-kon* – mother complex. Through his school life the young Japanese male continues to receive the love (always emotional, sometimes physical) and nurturance of the mother. Only when he has left high school is he expected and encouraged to develop a 'healthy' interest in the other sex and marry.

The male then enters into a relationship with the motherbody of the *okusan*. In Japan the majority of male high school graduates enter university, and the ensuing four years constitute a transitional stage in which a relationship of desire and dependence is transferred from the maternal motherbody to the matrimonial motherbody.

The popularity of *manga* reading groups that specialize in collecting and exchanging *bishonen* comics has to be placed in the context of this process of transition. The *bishonen* comics offer a young adult male readership a fantastical space for the exploration of sexual desire outside the closed circuit of the oedipal theater of the family but on the familiar territory of the homosocial formations of their youth. The extent to which the motherbody dominates the male experience of puberty arguably augments the structures of male bonding that are such an overt aspect of male teenage experience in Japan. When the space that might be the site for the exploration of sexual desire of bodies other than the motherbody is foreclosed, male bonding within the traditionally accepted homosocial formations becomes the dominant alternative structure for the formation of intimate relations. These homosocial formations continue to structure the social relationships of the Japanese male throughout his life – the mythology of the 'comrade samurai' transposed onto the contemporary workplace.

The images and stories of androgynous and homosexual lovers might be read as an alternative site of sexual fantasy, where no-body is the motherbody, a brief respite from 'healthy' interests. It is significant that in interviews with fans of the *bishonen* genre, the majority of the male students insisted that they did not consider the characters in these *manga* to be homosexual, arguing that this was a different kind of love from either heterosexual or homosexual love. At about the same time the young male university student graduates to take up his position as a company man, he is also expected to trade in his *bishonen* comics for images of heterosexual pornography. That the initial attraction of the *bishonen* comics was rooted primarily in their homosocial, and not their homoerotic, dimension makes the transfer from these comics to heterosexual, sometimes homophobic, pornography a simple progression.

It would be wrong, however, to suggest that all male readers of the *bishonen* comics are not attracted by the homoerotic dimension of these image-texts. This genre of comic books is a rare example of the depiction of homosexuality in contemporary Japanese popular culture. *June* has acknowledged the significance of this gay readership with a gradual increase of information and visual coverage of gay culture both in Japan and overseas. The gay readership is in some sense the group with the least complicated relationship to these image-texts. In a cultural landscape that remains otherwise generally hostile to overt representation or expression of the homoerotic, these texts offer gay readers a rare site for the possibility of a direct and positive identification without denial or modification. Increasingly, through the late 1970s and the 1980s, *June* has played a role in the construction of a collective gay identity in a society where older traditions of homosexual and bisexual practice have been lost to a puritanism modeled on the most repressive dimensions of Western law and morality. Comics and magazines for a specifically gay market have followed, but *June* continues to cater to a diverse readership.

Although the various categories of readers – female teenagers, adult women, male university students, gay men – are located within quite disparate relations of pleasure to these image-texts, it is not difficult to see how for each group these narratives offer a desirable fantasy space. The *bishonen* stories do not contain desire (male or female) within normative 'phallacies' of gendered subjectivity, but allow the imagination to take flight beyond the territory of homophobic phallogocentrism. The stories themselves and the fluid, often unframed images that are so characteristic of the genre open up a fantasy landscape onto which each reader is free to map his or her own topography of pleasure.

[. . .]

Chapter 44

Richard Dyer

IDOL THOUGHTS

Orgasm and self-reflexivity in gay pornography

WHAT MAKES (GAY) pornography exciting is the fact that it is pornography. I do not mean this in the sense that it is exciting because it is taboo. The excitement of porn as forbidden fruit may be construed in terms of seeing what we normally do not (people having sex), what is morally and legally iffy (gay sex) or what is both the latter and, in Britain, not that obtainable (pornography itself). All of these may constitute porn's thrill for many users, but they are not what I have in mind here.

Nor do I mean that the category 'pornography' makes pornography exciting because it defines the terms of its own consumption and is moreover a major player in the business of constructing sexual excitement. Pornography does indeed set up the expectation of sexual excitement: the point of porn is to assist the user in coming to orgasm. However, it is also the case that no other genre can be at once so devastatingly unsatisfactory when it fails to deliver (nothing is more boring than porn that doesn't turn you on) and so entirely true to its highly focused promise when it succeeds. In this pragmatic sense, porn cannot make users find exciting that which they do not find so. Yet in a wider sense, pornography does help to define the forms of the exciting and desirable available in a given society at a given time. The history of pornography – the very fact that it has a history, rather than simply being an unvarying constant of human existence – shows that excitement and desire are mutable, constructed, cultural. There can be no doubt at all that porn plays a significant role in this, that it participates in the cultural construction of desire. However, this too is not what directly concerns me here.

When I say that it is the fact that it is porn that makes porn exciting, I mean, for instance, that what makes watching a porn video exciting is the fact that you are watching some people making a porn video, some performers doing it in front of cameras, and you. In this perception, *Powertool* (1986) is not about a character meeting other characters in a prison cell and having sex; it is about well-known professional sex performers (notably, Jeff Stryker) on a set with cameras and crew around them; it's the thought and evidence (the video) of this that is exciting. Now I readily concede that this is not how everyone finds porn exciting. For many it is the willing suspension of disbelief, the happy entering into the fantasy that *Powertool* is all happening in a prison cell. I shall discuss first how a video can facilitate such a way of relating to what's on screen, and it may indeed be the most usual way. Yet I do not believe that I am alone or even especially unusual in being more turned on by the thought of the cameras, crew and me in attendance. I shall look at this phenomenon in the rest of the article, focusing especially on the videos of the current gay porn star, Ryan Idol. I shall end by considering the apparent paradox of such self-reflexive porn – that it is able to indicate that it is 'only' porn and yet still achieve its orgasmic aim.

Gay porn videos do not necessarily draw attention to their own making. By way of illustration, let me consider one of the more celebrated scenes in gay porn, the subway sequence which forms the last part of *Inch by Inch* (1985).

A subway draws up at a station; a man (Jeff Quinn) enters a carriage of which the only other occupant is another man (Jim Pulver); after some eye contact, they have sex, that is, in the matchlessly rigorous description of *Al's Male Video Guide* (1986), 'suck, fuck, rim, titplay'; at the next station, another man (Tom Brock) enters the carriage but the video ends, with a title informing us that 'the non-stop excitement continues . . . in the next Matt Sterling film, coming February 1986'.

This sequence unfolds before us as an event happening somewhere of which we are unobserved observers. In other words, it mobilises the conventions of realism and 'classical cinema'.[1] The first term indicates that what we see we are to treat as something happening in the real world. The second refers to the ways in which a film or video places us in relation to events such that we have access to them from a range of vantage points (the many different shots and the mobile camera that compose a single sequence in such cinema), while not experiencing this range as disruptive or (as it is) impossible; a special feature of this cinema is the way it enables the viewer to take up the position of a character within the events, most obviously through the use of point-of-view shots and the shot/reverse shot pattern. Videos do not really give us unmediated access to reality, nor do viewers think that they do. What I am describing are particular (if commonplace) ways of organising narrative space and time in film and video (between which I make no distinction for the purposes of this discussion).

The realism of the *Inch by Inch* sequence is achieved most securely by the use of location shots taken in a subway. These open the sequence and punctuate the action five times, reminding us of a real life setting that had really to exist in order to be filmable. The interior of the subway carriage could be a set – it looks very clean and the graffiti are too legible and too appropriate ('SUCK', 'REBELS', 'BAD BOYS') to be true – but the accuracy of the seating and fittings, the harsh quality of the lighting and the fact that all four sides of the carriage are seen, suggest either an unusually expensive set or an actual carriage rented for the occasion. The lack of camera or set shake suggests that the lights passing outside are indeed passing rather than being passed, but the care with which this is done is itself naturalistic. The high degree of realism in the setting is complemented by filmic elements associated with realism, such as hand-held camera and rough cutting on action. Further, the sound gives the appearance of having been recorded synchronously with the action, so that the grunts, heavy breathing, gagging, blowing and 'dialogue' ('Suck that cock', 'That feels good' etc.) don't sound like they've been added later, as is more usual with porn videos.

The performances too suggest a realism of genuine excitement. Both performers have erections most of the time (by no means the rule in porn) and their ejaculations, partly through the skill of the editing but also in some longer takes, seem to arise directly from their encounter. This compares favourably with the worked-for quality betrayed in much porn by the sudden cut to an ejaculation evidently uninspired by what the performer was doing in the immediately preceding shot. To such technical realism we may add a quality of performance, a feeling of abandonment and sexual hunger (especially on the part of Jim Pulver), unsmiling but without the grimly skilled air of many porn performances.

The quality of abandon relates to the idea of the real that all the above help to construct. This is a notion that anonymous sex, spontaneous, uncontrolled sex, sex that is 'just' sex, is more real than sex caught up in the sentiments that knowing one's partner mobilises or sex which deploys the arts of sexuality. As John Rowberry (1995) puts it, 'The sensibility of wantonness, already considered anti-social behaviour when this video was released, has never been more eloquently presented' (*The Adam Film World Guide*).

The rules of classical cinema are used in the sequence with exactly the degree of flexibility that characterises their use in Hollywood. The first, establishing interior shot of the carriage shows both Jeff and Jim and thus their position in relation to one another. Both sit on the same side of the carriage and the camera is positioned behind Jim's seat pointing along the carriage towards Jeff. The first cut is to a medium close-up of Jeff, with the camera at pretty much the same angle towards him as in the establishing shot – thus the spatial dislocation is only one of relative closeness and not one of position; it may be said to resemble the activity of the human eye in choosing to focus on one element out of all those before it; in short, we don't notice the cut but go along with its intensification of the situation, allowing us to see the lust in Jeff's eyes.

The next cut is to Jim. The direction of Jeff's gaze in the previous shot, as well as the continuing effect of the first, establishing shot, do not make this sudden change of angle disturbing. Moreover, although the camera is at 45 degrees to Jim, just as it was to Jeff, and although Jim is looking to his right off-screen and not at the camera, just as if Jeff was looking to his left off-screen, none the less we treat the shot of Jim as if it is a shot of what Jeff sees, as a point-of-view shot. I think this is true despite one further discrepancy, namely that, although Jeff's gaze is clearly directed at Jim's face (and still is in the next shot of him), none the less this shot of Jim is a medium shot from a lowish angle, which has the effect of emphasising his torso (exposed beneath an open waistcoat), the undone top button on his jeans and his crotch; in other words, Jeff, in the shot on either side of this, is signalled as looking at Jim's face (even, it appears, into his eyes), yet this shot, if taken as a point-of-view shot, has him clearly looking at Jim's body. Yet such literal inaccuracy goes unnoticed, because of the shot's libidinal accuracy – it's not Jim's eyes but his chest and crotch that Jeff wants.

These few shots show how very much the sequence is constructed along the lines of classical cinematic norms, how very flexible these norms are, and in particular how they can be used to convey psychological as much as literal spatial relations. Such handling characterises the whole sequence, which it would be too laborious to describe further. However, the sequence, like much porn, does also push the classical conventions much further than is normal in Hollywood, perhaps to a breaking point.

Linda Williams, in her study of (heterosexual) film/video pornography, *Hard Core: Power, Pleasure and the 'Frenzy of the Visible'*, discusses the way that the genre has been propelled by the urgent desire to see as much as possible of sexuality, by what she calls 'the principle of maximum visibility' (Williams 1989: 48). Two aspects of this are particularly relevant here.

One is the lengths to which porn goes to show sexual organs and actions. Williams lists some of the ways that this has operated:

> to privilege close-ups of body parts over other shots; to overlight easily obscured genitals; to select sexual positions that show the most of bodies and organs . . . to create generic conventions, such as the variety of sexual 'numbers' or the externally ejaculating penis
>
> (Ibid.: 49)

These are what a friend of mine calls 'the plumbing shots' and are presumably what made John Waters remark that porn always looks to him 'like open-heart surgery'. The camera is down on the floor between the legs of one man fucking another, looking up into dangling balls and the penis moving back and forth into the arsehole; or it is somehow hovering overhead as a man moves his mouth back and forth over another's penis; and so on. Such spatial lability goes much further than classical norms, where the camera/viewer may, in effect, jump about the scene but will not see what cannot be seen in normal circumstances (even in actual sex one does not normally see the above because one is doing them). Very often the editing of these sequences betrays gaps in spatial and temporal continuity, ignored, and caused, by the 'frenzied' (to use Williams's suggestive term) will to see. The moment of coming is sometimes shot simultaneously from three different camera positions, which are then edited together, sometimes one or more in slow motion. Such temporal manipulation through editing again breaks the coherence of classicism. Devices like this may work because – as in the 'incorrect' shot of Jim described above – they are in tune with the libidinal drive of the video. But they may also draw attention to the process of video making itself, so that what the viewer is most aware of is the cameraperson down on the floor, the performer's climax shot from several cameras, or the editor poring over the sequence, things that may spoil or may, for some, enhance the excitement of the sequence.

The other aspect of the 'principle of maximum visibility' of interest here, and central to Williams's book, is showing what is not, and possibly cannot be, seen in actual sexual intercourse, most famously the ejaculating penis. Here the difference between straight and gay porn is especially significant. As Williams discusses, much of the 'frenzy' of heterosexual porn is the desire to show and see what cannot be shown and seen, female sexual pleasure, something of no concern to gay (as opposed, of course, to lesbian) porn. Equally, the oddness of showing the man ejaculating outside his partner's body is less striking in gay porn; withdrawal to display (especially when involving removing a condom, or ignoring the fact that in the fucking shots he is using one) is odd, but much (probably most) actual gay sex in fact involves external ejaculation (and did so even before AIDS).

Yet the insistence on seeing the performer's orgasm is an interesting feature of gay porn too. As in straight porn, it brings the linear narrative drive that structures porn to a clear climax and end (cf. Dyer 1992) as well as relating to the importance of the visible in male sexuality. Within gay sex, seeing another's orgasm is delightful because it is a sign that the other is excited by one and is even a sort of gift, a giving of a part of oneself. Such feelings are at play in come shots in gay porn. Additionally, one may see come shots as a further dimension of a video's realism. Come shots are rarely, if ever, faked; we really are seeing someone come. This is happening in the story and fictional world of the video, but it's also happening on a set. Its conventionality, its oddness when involving withdrawal, the often disruptive cut that precedes it, all draw attention to it as a performance for camera. This breaks classical norms, but it is the foundation of the excitement of pornography that I want to discuss in the next section.

If gay porn, like straight, runs the risk of disrupting its own illusionism, some of it has been happy to capitalise on this. Most gay porn is like the subway sequence in *Inch by Inch* (though less accomplished in its deployment of codes of realism and classicism), but a significant amount is not. In its history (not much shorter, according to Waugh (1995), than that of the straight stuff), gay film/video porn has consistently been marked by self-reflexivity, by texts that have wanted to draw attention to themselves as porn, that is, as constructed presentations of sex.

This may be at the level of narrative: films about making porn films (*Giants*, 1983; *Screenplay*, 1984; *Busted*, 1991; *Loaded*, 1992); about taking porn photographs (*Flashback*, 1980; *Juice*, 1984; *Bicoastal*, 1985; *Make It Hard*, 1985; *Rap'n about 'ricans*, 1992); about auditioning for porn films (*The Interview*, 1981; *Abuse Thyself*, 1985; *Screen Test*, 1985); about being a live show performer (*Le beau mec*, 1978; *Performance*, 1981; *Times Square Strip*, 1982; *The Main Attraction*, 1989); about having sex in porn cinemas – just like the patrons (*The Back Row*, 1973; *Passing Strangers*, 1977; *The Dirty Picture Show*, 1979). It may be at the level of cinematic pastiche or intertextual reference (*The Light from the Second Storey Window*, 1973; *Adam and Yves*, 1974; *The Devil and Mr Jones*, 1974; *Five Hard Pieces*, 1977; *Cruisin' 57*, 1979; *Gayracula*, 1983; *Early Erections*, 1989).[2] It may be a display of a star, someone known for being in porn (*Best of the Superstars*, 1981; the *Frank Vickers Trilogy*, 1986–89; *Deep Inside Jon Vincent*, 1990; *Inside Vladimir Correa*, 1991); or more specifically a film about being a porn star, showing him on the job (*Inside Eric Ryan*, 1983; *That Boy*, 1985). There are even successful films that are histories of gay porn (*Good Hot Stuff*, 1975; *Eroticus*, 1983). Where the film does not refer to film porn as such, it may well refer explicitly to the psychic elements necessary for the production of porn: narcissism (e.g. a man making love to his own mirror image (*Le beau mec*, 1978; *Pumping Oil*, 1983)); exhibitionism (e.g. a bodybuilder fantasising posing nude (*Private Party*, 1984)); voyeurism (*Le voyeur*, 1982; *On the Lookout*, 1992); and dreaming and fantasising themselves, two of the commonest motifs in gay porn films, resulting in elaborate narrative structures of flashbacks, inserts, intercutting and stories within stories. All of these elements of content can be supplemented by the form of the film itself. The *Interview* films (1989–) for instance have the subject talking to the off-screen but heard director while stripping, working out and masturbating. *Roger* (1979) cuts back and forth between long shots and close-ups of the action (Roger masturbating), using different shades of red filter, the rhythmic precision of the cutting drawing attention to itself and hence to the film's construction of a celebration of its eponymous subject.

I am far from claiming that this tradition of self-reflexivity is characteristic of most gay porn. If the list I have given (itself very far from complete) is impressive, it constitutes but a drop in the ocean of the massive gay film/video porn business. Yet the tradition is there and encompasses many of the most successful titles. The self-reflexive mode would not be so consistently returned to, did it not sell – and it would not sell if it did not turn people on. Moreover, it is not unreasonable to assume that some people (like me) take pleasure in non-self-reflexive porn by imagining the rehearsals, the camera and crew, by focusing on the performers as performers rather than as characters.

I want to examine gay porno self-reflexivity by focusing on the work of one highly successful contemporary porn star. Ryan Idol is a young man who must have blessed his parents and perhaps God that he was born with so appropriate and serviceable a name. Few stars can have got their own name so often into the title of their videos (*Idol Eyes*, 1990; *Idol Worship*, 1992; *Idol Thoughts*, 1993) or had it used as the basis for so many puns in magazine feature spreads ('Ryan Idol, Yours To Worship' (cover, *Advocate Men*, July 1990); 'Idol Worship' and 'Pinnacle' (cover and feature title, *Advocate Men*, March 1993); 'Richard Gere Was My Idol – So to Speak', *The Advocate Classifieds* , 18 May 1993)). Ryan seems to have no existence, no image, other than that of being the subject of sexual adulation. What is exciting about him is that he is a porn star.

There is with all movie stars a potential instability in the relationship between their being a star and the characters they play. When the fit is perfect – Joan Crawford as Mildred Peirce, Sylvester Stallone as Rocky Balboa – we do not, except in a camp appreciation, sit there thinking that we are seeing a movie star baking pies by the score or becoming World Heavyweight Champion; in so far as the discrepancy worries us at all, we resolve it by seeing the role as expressive of personality qualities in the star – in the case of Joan and Sly, for instance, variations on notions of working-class advancement. There is, in other words, a set of cultural categories to which both role and star image refer, beyond that of simply being a very famous performer in movies. Porn stars – like, to some extent, musical stars – cannot mobilise such reference so easily; they are famous for having sex in videos.

There can be an element of wider social reference in porn stars' images. The extremely successful Catalina company has created an image of the California golden boy, with no existence other than working and making out. This is an image that seems to offer itself as stripped of social specificity, a sort of pornographic utopia uncontaminated by class, gender or race, although it is of course highly specifically white, young, US and well fed. Residually, gay porn stars are still generally given social traits. Jeff Stryker, for instance, perhaps the biggest contemporary star, is repeatedly associated with working-class iconography, through roles (a mercenary in *Stryker Force*, 1987, a garage mechanic in *The Look*, 1988, a farm boy in *The Switch Is On*, 1987) or accessories in pin-ups (spanners, greasy jeans). This is often reinforced by the idea of him as an innocent who, willingly but almost passively, gets into sexual encounters (as in his gaol videos, *Powertool*, 1986 and *Powerful II*, 1989, or the farm boy in the city narrative of *The Switch Is On*). It would however be hard to say anything even as broadly definite as this with Ryan Idol, even though he has played a lifeguard (*Idol Eyes*, 1990), college quarterback (*Score Ten*, 1991) and naval officer (*Idol Worship*, 1992). Even these roles in fact play upon the one clear role that he has, being a porn star.

The sense of his not offering anything but himself as body is suggested by his readiness to play with different body images in his many porn magazine spreads. In *Advocate Men* in July 1990, he has almost bouffant hair with a still boyish face and body. This look is capitalised on in the spread in the November 1991 issue of the short-lived *Dream*, which seemed to be addressing itself to men and women, straight and gay simultaneously; unusually for an Idol spread, there are no shots with erections, he is posed on black satin sheets and his expression is one of practised but unsullied yearning. Before that (at least in terms of publication, if not actual shoot), in *Mandate*, June 1990, the hair is cut much shorter at the sides, the top more obviously held stiffly in place with spray, he uses a leather jacket as prop, and poses more angularly, which, together with harder directional lighting, makes him look both more muscly and more directly sexual. Something similar is achieved in *Jock*, December 1991, though with more tousled hair and the fullest sense of social reference (a locker-room and football gear, part of the publicity for *Score Ten*). By 1993, however, there was a more radical alteration of the image, and in two, almost simultaneous forms. His hair is long and Keanu Reeves-ishly floppy now and his body less defined. In *Advocate Men*, March 1993, he poses by a pool, more in the 'art' style of a gay photographer like Roy Dean than this magazine's usual house style. In *Mandate*, June 1993, he is sweaty, with grease marks on his body, a much raunchier look, which is picked up in his pictures in *The Advocate Classifieds* for 18 May 1993, which have some residual boxing iconography.

There are continuities in this imagery, but these serve to emphasise him qua porn star. The thong tanline is unchanging, a tanline associated with exotic dancers, that is, sex performers. More significantly, he consistently poses in ways that relate very directly to the viewer. He holds his body open to view, his arms framing rather than concealing it, his posture, especially from the hips, often subtly thrust towards the camera (especially notable in shots lying on his side in *Dream* or seated in *Torso*, December 1991). This sense of very consciously offering the body is reinforced by the fact that he almost invariably looks directly, smilingly, seemingly frankly, into the camera, and has an erection. The only variation in the latter is that it is more often free standing or lightly held in the early photos, more often gripped and pointed in the later ones. There is absolutely no sense here of someone being observed (as if voyeuristically) as they go about their business nor of someone posing reluctantly, embarrassedly, just for the money. That impression is reinforced by interview material: 'I'll do maybe one or two adult films, mostly as an outlet for my exhibitionism' (*Advocate Men*, July 1990, p. 48), 'Ryan reveals that he likes showing off his big body. "I like doing it and I like watching it," he says' (*Prowl*, June 1991). In *Ryan Idol: A Very Special View*, 1990, scripted by Ryan himself, he talks at length about the pleasures of posing for photographs and of being an exotic dancer.

His magazine spreads, a vital component of any porn star's image, construct him as nothing other than a porn star, and this is echoed by the information on his life. Porn stars are seldom given an elaborate biography, but there is usually an implication of something in their lives other than pornography. Though Ryan has not made so many videos, he has done very many photo spreads and personal appearances. Interviews with him give the impression that that is what his life consists of, the more so since the establishment of the Ryan Idol International Fan Club (which includes a 'hot-line', a co-star search, a 'Win a Date with Ryan Contest', and a sales catalogue, including posters, T-shirts, pictures, 'paraphernalia' and cologne; in short, 'We're offering [the fans] many, many ways to get closer to Ryan Idol' (*The Advocate Classifieds*, 18 May 1993, p. 51). *A Very Special View* offers a day in the life of a porn star, but unlike other such videos featuring, for instance, Vladimir Correa or Jon Vincent, Ryan's day does not consist of sexual encounters but a photo shoot, a strip show and doing solos for us. His career even has its own narrative dynamic, to do with the gradual extension of what he does on camera. In all his videos he does solos and in most he is sucked off; in *Idol Eyes*, the penis in the close-ups of him fucking Joey Stefano is in fact David Ashfield's, as subsequent coverage revealed; but in *Score Ten* he did his own stunt work and, with a fanfare of publicity in *Idol Thoughts* he sucks someone else off. This trajectory, itself following the pattern of many porn narratives, is part tease, keeping something in reserve for later in the career, but also part play with the question of sexual identity – Ryan makes straight porn videos, was 'open' in early interviews ('I share my lovemaking equally with women and men', *Dream*), though much less equivocally gay more recently (' "Do you enjoy sucking dick?" "What do you think? I think it's a turn-on. And I think that question is pretty much answered in *Idol Thoughts*" ', *Advocate Classifieds*). Such fascination with the 'real' sexual identity of porn stars in gay videos is a major component of the discourse that surrounds them, but it also contributes to the sense that with Ryan sex is performance rather than identity.

His videos further emphasise his existence as porn star. Only two are actually about him being a porn star (*A Very Special View* and the footage in *Troy Saxon Gallery II*, 1991) but the rest all play with the idea of his having his being in the pleasures of looking. In *Idol Eyes* he spies on others having sex but is first really turned on by looking at himself in the mirror, getting into different outfits in front of it and masturbating at his own image. His voice-over talks about his learning to get off on men through getting off on himself (a casebook statement of one of the Freudian aetiologies of homosexuality). Similarly in *A Very Personal View* he jacks off looking at himself in the bathroom mirror, saying in voice-over: 'Nothing wrong with that – I do enjoy being with myself – sometimes it's much more exciting – especially when someone . . . might be watching' (a rider I'll return to). In *Score Ten* he masturbates in front of a fellow student (as payment for the latter's having written a paper for him), posed on the bonnet of a car with the student inside, so that he, Ryan, is framed and kept distant by the windscreen. *Idol Worship* has him strip off and masturbate in the control room of the ship he commands, all the while telling the crew not to look, to keep their eyes on their instruments, orders which they obey. *Trade Off* (1992) is about Ryan and Alex Garret as neighbours spying on each other through their windows. Thus we have voyeurism (*Idol Eyes*, *Trade Off*), narcissism/self-looking (*Idol Eyes*, *A Very Special View*), display (*Score Ten*), denial of looking (*Idol Worship*), a series of entertaining plays on what is at the heart of porn: looking, showing, being looked at.

The most sustained exploration of this is *A Very Special View*, especially in the opening and closing solo sequences. In the first, Ryan is discovered by the camera when he wakes up and masturbates; this is accompanied by a voice-over in which he says he does this every morning and how he enjoys it. The treatment is for the most part classical; we are invited to imagine that Ryan doesn't know we are there and has added the commentary later. Yet even here Ryan teases us with the knowledge that he does know we are, as it were, there.

The sequence is in two parts, the first on the bed, the second in the bathroom. At the end of the first, Ryan is pumping his penis hard and glances at the camera momentarily and then again on a dissolve to the bathroom sequence. It is in the latter that Ryan makes the remark in voice-over quoted above, that it can be more enjoyable to make love to oneself, 'especially if someone might be watching'. Earlier in the sequence he has evoked the possibility of another person being present:

> There is no better way to start the day than to stroke my cock and bring myself to a very satisfying orgasm. Come to think about it, there is one better way and that would be to have someone working on my hard cock as I awake and slowly, slowly getting me off.

This comment runs the risk of reminding the viewer of what is not the case, that he is not in bed with Ryan sucking him off. The later comment alludes to what is the case, that someone is watching him – the camera/us. This immediately precedes his orgasm, so that what is in play as he comes is the fact of looking and being looked at.

When we first see him in the bathroom, he is looking at himself in the mirror, and several other mirrors duplicate his image. He masturbates in the shower, but a close-up towards the end makes it clear that he is still appraising himself in the mirror. When he comes, he looks straight ahead, head on to the camera. But is he looking at the mirror or the camera, at himself or us? Either or both, for our pleasure in him is his pleasure in himself.

The last sequence plays much more strongly on the presence of the camera and Ryan as image. He goes into a friend's bedroom to have a rest. He strips to his briefs and gets on the bed, then turns to the camera, saying 'Do you want to see?', a rhetorical question in a porn video, and takes off his briefs. The sense of him as a performer is emphasised by the mirrors in the room. Not only do they connote display, narcissism and exhibitionism, they are also the means by which we see the cameraman from time to time. Perhaps this is an accident – 'bad' video-making – but with a star like Ryan it is entirely appropriate. What is he but someone being filmed? At two points we see an image of him which the camera draws back to reveal has been a mirror image; any distinction between the real Ryan and the image of Ryan is confounded.

Most remarkable though is Ryan's constant address to the camera. Once he runs the risk of reminding us of other, unavailable possibilities – 'Imagine it anyway you want', he says, but of course should we wish to imagine having sex with him, we have to imagine something other than what we are seeing. But for the rest he talks entirely about the situation we are watching. He speaks of his control over his penis ('I make it do what I want'), an obvious asset in a porn star. He draws attention to the narrative structure of the sequence, its progress towards orgasm, by saying that he is about to come, but won't do it just yet, how he likes to hold off for as long as possible. He even draws attention to the porn viewing situation, by saying twice that he wants the viewer to come with him, something porn viewers generally wish to do. The shouts that accompany his orgasm are punctuated by glances to the camera, still conscious of our intended presence, still reminding us that he is putting on a show for our benefit.

In emphasising self-reflexive gay porn, I not only don't want to give the impression that it is the more common form, but also don't want to suggest that it is superior to less or un-self-reflexive examples. Intellectuals tend to be drawn to the meta-discursive in art; since what they themselves do is a meta-activity, they take special comfort from other things that are meta, like self-reflexive art. Yet it interests me that so viscerally demanding a form as pornography (it must make us come) can be, and so often is, self-reflexive.

According to much twentieth-century critical theory, this ought not to be so. It has long been held that work that draws attention to itself – cultural constructs that make apparent their own constructedness – will have the effect of distancing an audience. A film that draws our attention to its processes of turning us on ought not to turn us on; you shouldn't be able to come to what are merely terms. As Linda Williams (1989: 147) puts it, pornography has a problem: 'sex as spontaneous *event* enacted for its own sake stands in perpetual opposition [in porn films] to sex as an elaborately engineered and choreographed *show* enacted by professional performers for a camera.' Yet, as I have tried to show, in much gay porn, at any rate, the show is the event.

This is of a piece with much gay culture. Being meta is rather everyday for queers. Modes like camp, irony, derision, theatricality and flamboyance hold together an awareness of something's style with a readiness to be moved by it – *La Traviata*, *Now Voyager* and 'Could It be Magic' (in Barry Manilow's or Take That's version) are no less emotionally compelling for our revelling in their facticity. The elements of parody and pastiche and the deliberate foregrounding of artifice in much gay porn are within this tradition. Episodic films like *Like a Horse* (1984) and *Inch by Inch* move from one obviously constructed fantasy to another – from a jungle encounter to a no-place, abstracted leather sequence to an Arab tent, from a studio rooftop to a studio beach to a studio street – without for a moment undermining their erotic charge. This is characteristic of the way we inhabit discourse. We are constantly aware of the instability of even our own discourses, their hold on the world still so tenuous, so little shored up by a network of reinforcing and affirming discourses, and yet our stake in them is still so momentous.

We see their deliberation but still need their power to move and excite; it's thus so easy for us to see porn as both put-on and turn-on.

This, though, is not mainly what is at play in the Idol oeuvre. For here there is no sense of putting on a fantasy, no sense of performing anything other than performance. The idea of sex as performance is generally associated with male heterosexuality, and the element of working hard to achieve a spectacular orgasm is certainly present in much gay porn. Yet performance in the Ryan Idol case means much more display, presentation, artistry, the commitment to entertainment – literally a good show. It is a construction of sexuality as performance, as something you enact rather than express.

Gay men are as romantic and raunchy, as expressive and essentialist, as anyone else. Yet much facilitates a perception of (gay) sex as performance. Owning to one's gay identity – itself so fragile a construct – is perilous: seeing sexuality as performance rather than being is appealing, since it does not implicate that compelling notion, the self. At the same time, dominant culture does little to naturalise our sexuality, making it harder to see gay sex acts as a product of pure need. We are less likely to think of gay sex in terms of biology than of aesthetics.

Paradoxically, there is a kind of realism in pornographic performance that declares its own performativity. What a porn film really is is a record of people actually having sex; it is only ever the narrative circumstances of porn, the apparent pretext for the sex, that is fictional. A video like *A Very Special View* foregrounds itself as a record of a performance, which heightens its realism. It really is what it appears to be.

This realism in turn has the effect of validating the video, and the genre to which it belongs. By stressing that what we are enjoying is not a fantasy, but porn, it validates porn itself. As Simon Watney has argued, the importance of doing this in the age of AIDS could not be greater. And by specifically celebrating masturbation, videos like Ryan's also validate the very response that porn must elicit to survive, that is, masturbation. The most exciting thing of all about porn is that it affirms the delights of that most common, most unadmitted, at once most vanilla and most politically incorrect of sexual acts, masturbation.

Notes

1 For a brief account of 'classical cinema', see the entry in Kuhn and Radstone. For a more exhaustive account, see Bordwell, Staiger and Thompson.

2 These films refer respectively to *A Star is Born*, Garbo, Cocteau and Brando movies, *The Devil and Miss Jones*, 1950s stag movies (and *Five Easy Pieces* of course), *American Graffiti*, *Dracula*, and educational television documentaries.

Bibliography

Al's Male Video Guide (New York: Midway Publications, 1986).

Bordwell, David, Janet Staiger, and Kristin Thompson, *The Classical Hollywood Cinema* (New York: Columbia University Press, 1985).

Dyer, Richard, 'Coming to Terms', in *Only Entertainment* (London: Routledge, 1992).
Kuhn, Annette, and Susannah Radstone (eds), *The Women's International Companion to Film* (London: Virago, 1989).
Rowberry, John (ed.), *The Adam Film World Guide*, vol. 14, no. 11 (Los Angeles: Knight Publishing Corporation, 1993).
Watney, Simon, *Policing Desire: Pornography, AIDS and the Media* (London: Methuen/Comedia, 1987).
Waugh, Tom, *Hard to Imagine: Gay Male Eroticism in Photography and Film, from its Origins to Stonewall* (New York: Columbia University Press, 1995).
Williams, Linda, *Hard Core: Power, Pleasure and the 'Frenzy of the Visible'* (Berkeley/Los Angeles: University of California Press, 1989).

Notes on contributors

Malek Alloula is the author of *The Colonial Harem* (1986).

Oriana Baddeley teaches art history at Camberwell College of Arts. She is the co-author of *Drawing the Line: Art and Cultural Identity in Contemporary Latin America* (1989), with Valerie Fraser.

Anne Balsamo teaches at the Georgia Institute of Technology. She is the author of *Technologies of the Gendered Body: Reading Cyborg Women* (1996).

Roland Barthes was the author of such key texts as *Mythologies* and *Image–Music–Text*.

Geoffrey Batchen teaches in the Department of Art and Art History at the University of New Mexico, Albuquerque, and publishes widely on issues in photography, cyberculture and visual theory.

Suzanne Preston Blier teaches art history at Harvard University. She is the author of *African Vodun: Art, Psychology and Power* (1995).

Susan Bordo is Otis A. Singletary Chair in the Humanities, Professor of Philosophy at the University of Kentucky and the author of *Unbearable Weight* (1993).

Sandra Buckley is Senior Research Fellow in the Center for East Asian Studies and Comparative Literature at McGill University. She is the author of *Broken Silence: Voices of Japanese Feminism* (1997).

Judith Butler teaches in the Department of Rhetoric and Comparative Literature at the University of California, Berkeley. She is the author of *Gender Trouble* (1990), *Bodies That Matter* (1993) and *Excitable Speech* (1997).

Anthea Callen is Professor of Art History at De Montfort University.

Néstor García Canclini publishes widely on issues concerning postmodernism and Latin American art and culture, including *Hybrid Culture: Strategies for Entering and Leaving Modernity* (1995).

Lisa Cartwright teaches English and visual culture at the University of Rochester. She is the author of *Screening the Body: Tracing Medicine's Visual Culture* (1995).

James Clifford is Professor in the History of Consciousness Board at the University of California, Santa Cruz. He is the author of *The Predicament of Culture* (1988) and *Routes: Travel and Translation in the Late Twentieth Century* (1997).

Jonathan Crary teaches art history at Columbia University. He is the author of *Techniques of the Observer* (1990).

Michel de Certeau was the author of *The Practice of Everyday Life* (1984).

René Descartes' *Discourse on the Method* (1637) is regarded as the founding text of modern Western philosophy.

Carol Duncan teaches art history at Ramapo College, New Jersey. Her most recent book is *Civilizing Rituals: Inside Public Art Museums* (1995).

Richard Dyer teaches film studies at the University of Warwick. His many publications include *Stars* (1982) and *Now You See It: Studies on Lesbian and Gay Film* (1990).

John Fiske teaches in the Communications Department at the University of Wisconsin. His publications include *Understanding Popular Culture* (1989) and *Media Matters* (1996).

Michel Foucault was the author of *Discipline and Punish: The Birth of the Prison* (1977).

Anne Friedberg teaches film studies at the University of California, Irvine. She is the author of *Window Shopping: Cinema and the Postmodern* (1993).

Coco Fusco is a New York-based interdisciplinary artist and writer. She explores intercultural and interracial dynamics through a variety of experimental media, performance and journalism. She is the author of *English Is Broken Here: Notes on Cultural Fusion in the Americas* (1995). Her videos include *Pochnovela, The Couple in the Cage* and *Havana Postmodern*. She is an Assistant Professor at the Tyler School of Art of Temple University.

Tamar Garb teaches art history at University College London. She is the author of *Sisters of the Brush: Women's Artistic Culture in Late Nineteenth-Century Paris* (1994).

Paul Gilroy is Professor of Sociology and Cultural Studies at Goldsmiths College, University of London. He has also been associated with the program in African and African-American Studies at Yale University.

Donna Haraway is Professor in the History of Consciousness Board at the University of California, Santa Cruz. Her most recent book is *Modest Witness@Second Millennium FemaleMan meets Oncomouse* (1997).

bell hooks is Distinguished Professor of English at City College in New York. Her many publications include *Reel to Real: Race, Sex and Class at the Movies* (1996).

Martin Jay teaches history at the University of California, Berkeley. He is the author of *Downcast Eyes: The Denigration of Vision in Twentieth-Century French Thought* (1993).

Reina Lewis teaches in the Department of Cultural Studies at the University of East London. She is the author of *Gendering Orientalism: Race, Femininity and Representation* (1996).

Anne McClintock is Associate Professor of English and Women's Studies at Columbia University. She is the author of *Imperial Leather: Race, Gender and Sexuality in the Colonial Contest* (1995).

Marshall McLuhan, author and cultural critic, was the originator of the slogans 'the medium is the message' and 'the global village'.

Nicholas Mirzoeff teaches history and theory of visual culture at the State University of New York, Stony Brook. He is the author of *Bodyscape: Art, Modernity and the Ideal Figure* (1995).

Timothy Mitchell is Associate Professor of Politics and Director of the Hagop Kevorkian Center for Near Eastern Studies at New York University. He is the author of *Colonizing Egypt* (1988) and *Questions of Modernity* (1998).

Lynda Nead teaches art history at Birkbeck College, University of London, and is the author of *The Female Nude: Art, Obscenity and Sexuality* (1992).

Adrian Piper teaches philosophy at Wellesley College, Wellesley, Massachusetts, and is a widely exhibited artist. Her collected essays, *Out of Order, Out of Sight*, were published in 1996.

Griselda Pollock is Professor of Art History and Cultural Studies at the University of Leeds. She is the author of *Vision and Difference: Femininity, Feminism and the Histories of Art* (1988).

Mary-Louise Pratt is the author of *Imperial Eyes: Travel-Writing and Transculturation* (1992).

Ann Reynolds teaches art history at the University of Texas, Austin, and has recently completed a book on Robert Smithson.

Irit Rogoff teaches at Goldsmiths College, University of London.

Andrew Ross is Professor and Director of the American Studies Program at New York University. His books include *No Respect* (1989), *Strange Weather* (1991), *The Chicago Gangster Theory of Life* (1994), and the forthcoming *Real Love: Essays for Cultural Justice* (1998).

Ella Shohat is Professor of Cultural Studies and Women's Studies at the City University of New York Graduate Center. She is co-editor of *Dangerous Liaisons: Gender, Nation and Postcolonial Reflections* (1997).

Robert Stam is Professor of Cinema Studies at New York University and Acting Director of the Center for the Study of Culture, Media and History. His *Tropical Multiculturalism: A Comparative History of Race in Brazilian Cinema and Culture* is forthcoming from Duke University Press.

Marita Sturken is Assistant Profesor at the Annenberg School for Communication at the University of Southern California. She is the author of *Tangled Memories: The Vietnam War, the AIDS Epidemic, and the Politics of Remembering* (1997).

Paul Virilio is the author of *The Vision Machine* (1994).

Thomas Waugh teaches film studies at Concordia University, Montreal. His *Hard to Imagine: Gay Male Eroticism in Photography and Film from their Beginnings to Stonewall* was published in 1996.

Index